Treating Depression

Treating Depression

MCT, CBT, and Third-Wave Therapies

Edited by

Adrian Wells, PhD and Peter L. Fisher, PhD

WILEY Blackwell

This edition first published 2016

Registered Office
John Wiley & Sons Ltd, The Atrium, Southern Gate, Chichester, West Sussex, PO19 8SQ, UK

Editorial Offices
350 Main Street, Malden, MA 02148-5020, USA
9600 Garsington Road, Oxford, OX4 2DQ, UK
The Atrium, Southern Gate, Chichester, West Sussex, PO19 8SQ, UK

For details of our global editorial offices, for customer services, and for information about how to apply for permission to reuse the copyright material in this book please see our website at www.wiley.com/wiley-blackwell.

Library of Congress Cataloging-in-Publication Data

Treating depression : MCT, CBT, and third wave therapies / edited by Adrian Wells and Peter L. Fisher.
pages cm
Includes bibliographical references and index.
ISBN 978-0-470-75905-9 (cloth) – ISBN 978-0-470-75904-2 (pbk.) 1. Depression, Mental–Treatment. 2. Metacognitive therapy. 3. Cognitive therapy. I. Wells, Adrian. II. Fisher, Peter L.

RC537.T735 2016
616.85′27–dc23

2015017696

A catalogue record for this book is available from the British Library.

Cover image: Human Brain Engraving © CraigNeilMcCausland / iStockphoto

Set in 10.5/13pt MinionPro by Aptara Inc., New Delhi, India
Printed and bound in Malaysia by Vivar Printing Sdn Bhd

1 2016

Contents

List of Contributors vii

Preface ix

Section 1 Assessment, Prevalence, and Treatment Outcomes

1 **The Nature of Depression** 3
Martin Connor, Adrian Wells, and Peter L. Fisher

2 **The Assessment of Depression** 24
Arthur M. Nezu, Kelly S. McClure, and Christine M. Nezu

3 **The Efficacy of Cognitive Behaviour Therapy for Depression** 52
Robin B. Jarrett and Jeffrey R. Vittengl

4 **Psychobiological Processes and Therapies in Depression** 81
Pilar Cristancho and Michael E. Thase

Section 2 Psychological Models of Depression

5 **Schema Theory in Depression** 117
David A. Clark and Brendan D. Guyitt

6 **Metacognitive Therapy: Theoretical Background and Model of Depression** 144
Adrian Wells and Peter L. Fisher

7 **Acceptance and Commitment Theory of Depression** 169
Robert D. Zettle

8 **The Theory Underlying Mindfulness-Based Cognitive Therapy as a Relapse Prevention Approach to Depression** 194
Mark A. Lau

9 **Behavioural Activation Theory** 221
Roselinde H. Kaiser, Samuel Hubley, and Sona Dimidjian

10 **A Critique of Theoretical Models of Depression: Commonalties and Distinctive Features** 242
John R. Keefe and Robert J. DeRubeis

Section 3 Treatments for Depression

Introduction to Section 3: Case Study 265

11 **Cognitive Behaviour Therapy for Depression** 269
Yvonne Tieu and Keith S. Dobson

12 **Metacognitive Therapy for Depression** 295
Peter L. Fisher and Adrian Wells

13 **Acceptance and Commitment Therapy: Application to the Treatment of Clinical Depression** 319
Kirk D. Strosahl and Patricia J. Robinson

14 **Treating Acute Depression with Mindfulness-Based Cognitive Therapy** 344
Ruth A. Baer and Erin Walsh

15 **Behavioural Activation Treatment for Depression** 369
Samuel Hubley, Roselinde Kaiser, and Sona Dimidjian

16 **A Critique of Therapeutic Approaches to Depression: Commonalties and Distinctive Features** 393
Robert L. Leahy

Epilogue 414

Index 417

List of Contributors

Ruth A. Baer	University of Kentucky, USA
David A. Clark	University of New Brunswick, Canada
Martin Connor	University of Liverpool, UK
Pilar Cristancho	Washington University in St Louis, USA
Robert J. DeRubeis	University of Pennsylvania, USA
Sona Dimidjian	University of Colorado, USA
Keith S. Dobson	University of Calgary, USA
Peter L. Fisher	University of Liverpool, UK
Brendan D. Guyitt	University of New Brunswick, Canada
Samuel Hubley	University of Colorado, USA
Robin B. Jarrett	University of Texas Southwestern Medical Center, USA
Roselinde H. Kaiser	University of Colorado, USA
John R. Keefe	University of Pennsylvania, USA
Mark A. Lau	Vancouver CBT Centre and University of British Columbia, Canada
Robert L. Leahy	American Institute of Cognitive Therapy
Kelly S. McClure	LaSalle University, USA
Arthur M. Nezu	Drexel University, USA
Christine M. Nezu	Drexel University, USA
Patricia J. Robinson	Mountainview Consulting Group, Washington, USA
Kirk D. Strosahl	University of Washington, USA
Yvonne Tieu	University of Calgary, USA
Michael E. Thase	University of Pennsylvania, USA
Jeffrey R. Vittengl	Truman State University, USA
Erin Walsh	University of Kentucky, USA
Adrian Wells	University of Manchester, UK
Robert D. Zettle	Wichita State University, USA

Preface

Depression is a very common psychological disorder, which affects over 120 million people worldwide. Approximately 10–15% of the population will be affected by depression during their lifetime. The personal, social, and economic burden of depression is profound, and depression is estimated to be the leading cause of disability worldwide. Fortunately there are effective psychological therapies for depression. One of the most studied interventions is cognitive behavioural therapy (CBT), which consists of cognitive and behavioural strategies. These two components of CBT, namely cognitive therapy (CT) and behavioural activation (BA), are equally effective. The high volume of empirical support for these approaches has led to their recommendation in healthcare guidelines as a first-line psychological treatment for depression. The pursuance of newer and alternative treatments has emerged in the last twenty years as a result of an increasing recognition of the limitations of CBT. Approximately half of the patients treated with CBT and behavioural methods recover from depression; this leaves the other half – a significant number of patients – with a partial response or with none at all. Furthermore, amongst those that do recover, there is a substantial rate of relapse that cannot be ignored. Only one third of the patients remain depression-free one year after the completion of psychological interventions.

It is evident that we need to add to the armoury of treatment approaches, with a view to providing a larger choice for both clinicians and patients. Moreover, we must find treatments that are more effective in the immediate term, and especially in the longer term. Fortunately the area has moved forward thanks to an influx of ideas and new techniques from a range of backgrounds. This progress has led to the development of metacognitive therapy (MCT), mindfulness-based cognitive therapy (MBCT), and acceptance and commitment therapy (ACT). These approaches are based on different theoretical models of the causes and maintenance of depression. But we do not yet know whether these newer additions can be more effective than CBT or BA, and we are in danger of not being able to find out, because there is ambiguity concerning the distinctive features of these approaches.

Unfortunately the boundaries and integrity of these newer approaches are not always maintained. In clinical settings, we find that therapists have a tendency to draw on techniques and principles from any combination of CBT and these other approaches, often violating some of the basic principles of any one of the models. Why should this be of concern? Two reasons predominate: first, techniques drawn from different approaches are not always compatible and, when used together, may cancel each other out, annul the desired effects on causal mechanisms, and lead to reduced rather than improved efficacy. Second, when techniques are combined, we move away from the well-controlled evaluation of established, *bona fide* approaches that can be found in treatment manuals, which prevents the assessment of the absolute and relative efficacy of the newer therapies.

If psychological treatments for depression are to be delivered competently and with a high level of treatment fidelity, it is necessary for practitioners to recognize and understand the fundamental differences between, and distinctive features of, each approach. However, the difficulty of acquiring this level of knowledge is often underestimated, as some of the constructs contained in the therapeutic approaches sound similar but vary in the degree of conceptual refinement and specificity.

The present volume was conceived with the aim of addressing these above issues. First, we wanted to bring together in one place evidence-based, effective, and emerging approaches to treating depression. This would serve as a reference treatment manual for therapists and researchers. Second, we aimed to provide a vehicle for showcasing the important conceptual and practical differences that exist between these treatments. Third, we devised a format for the contributions that would allow scrutiny of the goodness of fit between psychological theory and the implementation of the different approaches.

Consequently the volume is divided into three sections. Section 1 comprises four chapters, which provide an overview of the nature of major depressive disorder, the clinical assessment of depression, a review of the effectiveness of CBT, and an account of the psychobiological processes and therapies of depression. Section 2 presents the theoretical foundations of the five psychological interventions and concludes with a critique of the five theories that highlights the similarities and differences between the models on which treatment is based. For Section 3, we have provided the proponents of each approach with a hypothetical case study (which constitutes the Introduction to this section). In response, they have produced a brief treatment manual to illustrate each stage of treatment – assessment, case formulation, and treatment methods – with reference to this same case study. The section concludes with a critique of the distinctive components of each treatment.

Treating Depression has been made possible by its distinguished participants, and we express our gratitude to them for sharing their knowledge and skills. Without their significant contributions we would not be standing on the edge of the next chapter, heralding our quest to resolve this state of significant human suffering.

Adrian Wells, PhD
Peter L. Fisher, PhD

Section 1

Assessment, Prevalence, and Treatment Outcomes

1

The Nature of Depression

Martin Connor, Adrian Wells, and Peter L. Fisher

Introduction

Sadness and despair are common experiences for many people, historically based descriptions reflecting the cultural context. Historical accounts indicate that the cause of severe mood disturbance was attributable to a physical illness for which the sufferer bore no responsibility. Symptoms of severe mood disturbance or melancholia included extreme sadness, an inability to function, and the frequent presence of delusions (Daly, 2007). Melancholia was thought to be caused by an imbalance of the 'bodily humours' (Daly, 2007; Akiskal & Akiskal, 2007). Conversely, accounts of less severe mood problems implied that the sufferer was ultimately responsible. In early Christian monastic settings a constellation of undesirable feelings and behaviours that interfered with devotional duties was known as the 'sin' of acedia (Jackson, 1981). This state was attributed to laziness or a 'lack of care' and was characterized by apathy, loss of hope, drowsiness, and a desire to flee the monastery (LaMothe, 2007). However, acedia was not considered equivalent to normal sadness, since the fourth-century monk John Cassian described it as a 'dangerous foe' that was 'akin to sadness' (Daly, 2007, p. 34). These historical descriptions of the 'symptoms' of melancholia and acedia loosely correspond to those of major depression as defined in modern diagnostic systems, which will be discussed in the next section.

Treating Depression: MCT, CBT and Third Wave Therapies, First Edition.
Edited by Adrian Wells and Peter L. Fisher.

Diagnosing Major Depressive Disorder

Major depression is a common but clinically heterogeneous disorder that is frequently comorbid with others. Current diagnostic methods rely on identifying constellations of psychological and behavioural symptoms through structured clinical interviews (see chapter 2 for a detailed account of assessment measures and processes). Major depressive disorder (MDD) is diagnosed according to either the current (fifth) edition of the American Psychiatric Association's *Diagnostic and Statistical Manual of Mental Disorders* (DSM-V; APA, 2013) or the World Health Organization's International Classification of Diseases (ICD-10; WHO, 1993). Because major depression is a highly recurrent disorder (Boland & Keller, 2008), both systems operationalize it in terms of the occurrence of a single 'depressive episode' (WHO, 1992), also known as a 'major depressive episode' (MDE) (APA, 2013). The diagnostic criteria for a depressive episode are similar in both systems. Both DSM-V and ICD-10 define recurrent depression as the occurrence of two or more episodes that are separated by at least two months during which the criteria for a depressive episode are not met (APA, 2013; WHO, 1993). In DSM-V the term 'major depressive disorder' (MDD) is used to denote the occurrence of one or more major depressive episodes.

Major depression is a clinically heterogeneous disorder (Rush, 2007). The diagnostic criteria are designed to account for such heterogeneity, which means that depressed individuals with markedly divergent symptoms are assigned to the same diagnostic category (APA, 2013; Krueger, Watson, & Barlow, 2005). For example, two individuals diagnosed with a major depressive episode may both experience depressed mood and concentration difficulties. However, one of them may have the accompanying symptoms of significant weight loss and insomnia, while the other may experience significant weight gain and hypersomnia. These differences may be important for the selection of appropriate treatment, and prognosis (APA, 2013; WHO, 1992; Rush, 2007), and therefore DSM-V enables the specification of depressive subtypes and of episode severity (APA, 2013).

Diagnostic Criteria for Major Depressive Disorder

The diagnosis of a major depressive episode requires that at least five of the symptoms listed in Table 1.1 are met for a period of at least two weeks. Importantly, one of the symptoms must be either a depressed mood or a loss

Table 1.1 Summary of DSM-V criteria for an episode of major depression.

1	depressed mood most of the time
2	loss of interest/pleasure in everyday activities
3	weight loss or weight gain, often accompanied by a reduced or increased appetite
4	sleep difficulties: sleeping too much or minimally
5	psychomotor agitation or retardation
6	tiredness, feeling fatigued, lacking energy
7	feelings of worthlessness or guilt
8	poor concentration, difficulty in making decisions
9	frequent thoughts of death, including thoughts and plans of suicide or suicide attempts

of pleasure/interest in everyday activities. It is also necessary that the symptoms reach clinically significant levels, which typically compromise occupational and social functioning.

A closer inspection of the nine main symptoms of depression in Table 1.1 shows that individuals meeting diagnostic criteria for a depressive episode may have minimal overlapping symptoms. Nevertheless, researchers and clinicians have observed what appears to be relatively consistent constellations of depressive symptoms that may respond differently to treatment (Rush, 2007). Consequently, successive revisions of the DSM since version III have included specifiers that enable potentially important clinical characteristics of episodes to be recorded (APA, 2013). These episode specifiers relate to symptom severity, remission status, chronicity, and symptomatic features that may denote depressive subtypes.

The Epidemiology of Major Depression

Surveys of the prevalence of psychiatric disorders have been undertaken since the Second World War. However, estimates of prevalence varied widely, due to differences in methodology. Early estimates of the prevalence of MDD were derived from screening instruments that were not fit for purpose (Kessler et al., 2007). There were two main problems; (1) the screening instruments were prone to poor specificity or sensitivity (or both), which undermined confidence in the resultant prevalence estimates; and (2) the use of different instruments between surveys hindered the interpretation of results. This has become less of an issue since the World Health Organization commissioned the Composite International Diagnostic Interview (CIDI) in the 1980s (Kessler & Ustun, 2004) in order to compare psychiatric prevalence rates between countries according to standardized criteria (Kessler et al., 2007). The CIDI was based on the Diagnostic Interview Schedule (Robins, Helzer, Croughan, & Ratcliff, 1981) and was designed to be administered by lay interviewers. It was also designed to support psychiatric diagnoses according to both ICD and DSM criteria. However, the original version of the CIDI was not designed to capture detailed demographic and clinical data. This meant that countries could only be broadly compared, in terms of overall prevalence rates (Kessler & Ustun, 2004).

The CIDI (version 3) was designed for the World Mental Health Survey Initiative (WMHS) (Kessler, 1999) for the purpose of facilitating the acquisition and comparison of psychiatric epidemiological data within the participating countries (Kessler & Ustun, 2004). In addition to enabling the quantification of lifetime and 12-month diagnoses according to both DSM-IV and ICD-10 criteria, the CIDI-3 also includes items that assess severity, demographic, quality-of-life, and disability data (Kessler & Ustun, 2004). Unlike previous versions, the CIDI-3 included interview probe questions that increase the reliability of autobiographical recall. The methodological rigour used to produce different translations of the CIDI-3 has led to its being described as 'state of the art' for comparing epidemiological findings across participating WMHS countries (Alonso & Lepine, 2007). Two large-scale surveys within the WMHS framework have specifically examined the epidemiology of MDD. These are the European Study of the Epidemiology of Mental Disorders (ESEMeD) (Alonso et al., 2002) and the American National Comorbidity Survey Replication Study (NCS-R) (Kessler et al., 2003).

Overall prevalence rates

The NCS-R and ESEMeD surveys estimated that the 12-month prevalence of MDD according to DSM-IV criteria is 6.6 per cent in American adults and 4.1 per cent in European adults (Alonso et al., 2004; Kessler et al., 2003). In absolute terms, these results indicate that at least 13.1 million US adults experienced a major depressive episode in the preceding year (Kessler et al., 2003). In terms of lifetime rates, 16.2 per cent of Americans and 13.4 per cent of Europeans will experience at least one depressive episode.

In terms of DSM-IV symptomatology, the NCS-R results estimated that 10 per cent of the people identified within the 12-month prevalence time frame were mild, 39 per cent moderate, 38 per cent severe, and 13 per cent very severe according to the Quick Inventory of Depressive Symptomatology Self-Report (QIDS-SR) (Rush et al., 2003; Kessler et al., 2003). Thus, 51 per cent of people were classified as having severe or very severe clinical symptoms in the NCS-R sample, underscoring the significance of major depression as a major public health issue.

Prevalence rates by age and country

The ESEMeD study found that the 12-month prevalence for any psychiatric disorder is highest in the 18- to 24-year age group and lowest for individuals over 65 (Alonso & Lepine, 2007). Comparable results for the prevalence of MDE were found in the NCS-R, where 12-month and lifetime rates in the youngest cohort (18 to 29 years) were significantly higher than in those over 60 years (Kessler et al., 2003). However, the differences between age cohorts may be a function of hierarchical exclusion rules, which typically prohibit a diagnosis of MDE when there is physical comorbidity. The lower 12-month prevalence rate for older cohorts in the NCS-R may be artefactual, as higher levels of physical comorbidity in older adults may have precluded the diagnosis of a depressive episode (Kessler et al., 2010). To investigate this possibility, Kessler et al. (2010) re-analysed the WMHS data by omitting the hierarchical and organic exclusion rules that allowed depression comorbid with a physical disorder to be included. The results indicated that higher rates of physical comorbidity were not responsible for the lower rates of depression typically observed in older cohorts in developed countries (Kessler et al., 2010). An analysis across all the developed countries within the WMHS showed that the 12-month MDE prevalence was significantly lower for the oldest cohort than for the youngest cohort (Kessler et al., 2010). However, episode duration may increase with age. In developed countries, the mean episode in the youngest cohort lasted 25 weeks, by comparison to 31 weeks in the oldest cohort (Kessler et al., 2010).

Gender and prevalence of MDD

One of the most consistent epidemiological findings concerning MDD is that female prevalence rates are typically twice those registered in males

(Boughton & Street, 2007). Both the ESEMeD and the NCS-R study found that 12-month and lifetime MDD prevalence rates for females were approximately twice those for males. Higher female prevalence is known to emerge in adolescence and to continue into adulthood (Boughton & Street, 2007), although no significant gender differences have been found in terms of recurrence or chronicity (Kessler, Mcgonagle, Swartz, Blazer, & Nelson, 1993). However, the results of the United Kingdom's National Survey of Psychiatric Morbidity (NSPB) (Bebbington et al., 2003) have shown that the preponderance of female depression disappears after the age of 55, when there is a reduction in the prevalence of female depression. Boughton and Street (2007) reviewed numerous non-biological theories that have been proposed to explain the higher rates of depression seen in females. Some theories venture that higher levels of neuroticism or dependency in females increase the risk for depression, while others attribute differences to social restrictions imposed by the female role. Alternatively, the construct of major depression may itself be biased towards identifying disorder in females (Boughton & Street, 2007).

Many factors are likely to contribute to gender differences in the prevalence of depression, and there is increasing evidence that gender differences concerning emotional regulation are a key factor (Nolen-Hoeksema, 2012). Emotional regulation refers to activities that enable the individual to modify the nature of an emotional response (e.g. distraction: Nolen-Hoeksema, 2012). However, while females have been shown to employ a wider range of emotional regulatory behaviours than men (Tamres, Janicki, & Helgeson, 2002), it has been proposed that their greater tendency to ruminate on the causes and meaning of negative emotions places a higher proportion of them at risk of developing depression (Nolen-Hoeksema, 2012). Evidence that greater rumination in females may explain their higher risk for MDD has been provided in studies that show rumination to be predictive of higher depression scores (Nolen-Hoeksema, 2000; Nolen-Hoeksema & Aldao, 2011; Nolen-Hoeksema, Mcbride, & Larson, 1997).

Comorbidity

Major depressive disorder is highly comorbid with psychological (Rush et al., 2005) and somatic disorders (Schmitz, Wang, Malla, & Lesage, 2007). In the NCS-R study, 64 per cent of the 12-month MDD cases also met diagnostic criteria for another DSM-IV 12-month disorder (Kessler et al., 2003). However, while MDD was highly comorbid with other psychological disorders, it only preceded other 12-month disorders in 12.6 per cent of cases (Kessler et al., 2003). MDD is often comorbid with physical disorders ranging from 5 per cent to 10 per cent in primary-care settings, and from 8 per cent to 15 per cent in medical inpatient settings (Schmitz et al., 2007). Comorbid depression is associated with greater levels of disability and poorer prognosis for both psychological and physical disorders (Rush et al., 2005; Schmitz et al., 2007).

Where depression is comorbid with a physical disorder, the greatest impairments are found in those who experience chronic physical problems. The Canadian Community & Health Survey (Schmitz et al., 2007) revealed that the prevalence of functional disability in the two weeks prior to interview was significantly higher in respondents with chronic physical disorders and comorbid MDD (46 per cent) than in those with only chronic physical disorders (21 per cent) or only MDD (27.8 per cent). One of the most striking findings about the effect of comorbid depression and physical illness concerns cardiac mortality. In patients hospitalized for myocardial infarction, Lesperance, Frasure-Smith, Talajic, and Bourassa (2002) found a direct dose–response relationship between depressive symptomatology on the Beck Depression Inventory (BDI) (Beck, Steer, & Brown, 1996) and the risk of cardiac mortality during a 5-year follow-up. Notably, the mortality rate in patients who scored 19 or more on the BDI was significantly higher than in those who scored less than 19 on the BDI – after controlling for cardiac disease severity (Lesperance et al., 2002). These results suggest that comorbid depression is associated with increased mortality during recovery from myocardial infarction.

Where another psychological disorder is comorbid with MDD, episodes of illness are typically more severe and last longer (Rush et al., 2005). As described earlier, there is evidence that comorbid dysthymia increases the duration of depressive episodes (Spijker et al., 2002). However, results from the naturalistic CDS study also indicated that comorbid panic (Coryell et al., 1988) or alcohol abuse (Mueller et al., 1994) reduce the likelihood of recovery from an MDE. Coryell et al. (1988) found that comorbid panic and MDD predicted significantly lower levels of recovery than non-comorbid cases (75 per cent versus 86 per cent respectively) over two years, while Mueller et al. (1994) found that comorbid alcoholism reduced the likelihood of recovery by 50 per cent over an observation period of ten years. However, neither of these two studies controlled for treatment differences in their analyses; but they provide evidence that comorbidity serves to increase episode duration and suggests that treatment efficacy will be lower in patients with comorbid conditions.

The moderating effect of comorbidity on treatment outcome has received relatively little attention (Carter et al., 2012; Hamilton & Dobson, 2002). However, there is consistent evidence that elevated anxiety symptomatology during an episode predicts poorer response to medication (Carter et al., 2012) and a lower probability of successful outcome following psychotherapy (Hamilton & Dobson, 2002). Given that anxiety disorders are highly comorbid with MDD – for example, 57 per cent of the 12-month MDD cases met diagnostic criteria for at least one comorbid DSM-IV anxiety disorder (Kessler et al., 2003) – they are likely to be an important moderator of treatment outcome in MDD.

Finally, many previously remitted Axis 1 disorders have not been identified as a risk factor for the development of a major depressive episode with the exception of early-onset simple phobia and panic (Kessler & Wang, 2008). However, generalized anxiety disorder (GAD) has been identified as presenting the highest risk for the development of subsequent comorbid depression (Kessler & Wang, 2008). The high levels of comorbidity between depression and anxiety disorders have been argued to be an artefact of changes in the diagnostic criteria for successive versions of the DSM, which have allowed an increasing number of diagnoses to be made for the same individual (Kessler & Wang, 2008). There have been suggestions that cases of comorbid anxiety and depression may stem from a common pathological process, and that the separation of the disorders from DSM–III onwards has produced an artificial distinction for these patients (Frances et al., 1992). However, future research on the validity of differentiating between the two disorders is still required (Kessler & Wang, 2008).

Course

Depression, once thought to be an acute and self-limiting disorder, is frequently a recurrent and chronic condition. For ethical reasons, few naturalistic studies of the duration of untreated major depressive episodes have been conducted. However, prospective data suggest that the majority of cases remit within one year and that the duration of episodes is longer in more severe cases. Prospective population-based estimates for the duration of depressive episodes obtained in the Netherlands Mental Health Survey and Incidence Study (NEMESIS) (Spijker et al., 2002) are intriguing. Among 250 respondents who experienced a new episode defined according to DSM-III-R criteria, the proportions recovered were 50 per cent at three months, 76 per cent at 12 months, and 80 per cent at 21 months. Spijker et al. (2002) reported that higher severity or comorbid dysthymia predicted longer episodes, while recurrent depression predicted shorter episodes. Posternak et al. (2006) found similar results for a sample of 130 non-chronically depressed patients who experienced a new episode over 15 years within the National Institute of Mental Health's Collaborative Program on the Psychobiology of Depression study (CDS) (Katz, Secunda, Hirschfeld, & Koslow, 1979). Among 84 individuals who did not receive any form of pharmacological treatment for a new MDE diagnosed according to the research diagnostic criteria (RDC) (Spitzer, Endicott, & Robins, 1978), the proportions recovered, defined as no or minimal symptoms over eight consecutive weeks, were 38 per cent at three months, 70 per cent at 12 months, and 75 per cent at two years (Posternak et al., 2006).

The NEMESIS results presented above do not account for treatment status. However, Spijker et al. (2002) found no significant difference in mean episode duration between those who did (67 per cent) and those who did not receive treatment (33 per cent). To explain this finding, Spijker et al. (2002) suggested that treatment seekers were more likely to be severely depressed and would thus have experienced longer episodes, had they not received treatment. The results of both the CDS and the NCS-R study appear to support this explanation. First, non-treatment seekers in the CDS achieved remission more rapidly than the sample as a whole, which implies that they had a better prognosis (Posternak et al., 2006). Secondly, higher severity in the NCS-R was predictive of longer episode duration (mild duration = 13.8 weeks; very severe duration = 23.1 weeks: Kessler et al., 2003). While it is possible that more severely depressed individuals were more likely to seek treatment and thus biased the results of the studies presented here, the overall results suggest that between 30 per cent and 50 per cent of cases will remit after three months and that even more cases will further remit by 12 months.

Recurrence of depressive episodes

The onset of a first major depressive episode often follows distressing life events, but the onset of subsequent episodes is less likely to be preceded by an obvious stressor (APA, 2000). The prospective CDS study (Katz et al., 1979) has provided important information concerning the naturalistic course of depression over two decades. The results indicate that recurrence is very common in patients who seek treatment for MDD, and that the interval between episodes typically decreases with the increasing number of episodes. An important factor that may serve to both reduce the time to recurrence and increase the frequency of episodes is the persistence of residual depressive symptomatology during recovery. The experience of three or more major depressive episodes significantly increases the risk of recurrence.

The CDS results (Katz et al., 1979) showed that 22 per cent in a sample of 141 non-dysthymic patients experienced recurrence within the first year following recovery (Keller, Lavori, Lewis, & Klerman, 1983). The risk of recurrence was highest immediately after the establishment of recovery, but diminished consistently during follow-up (Keller et al., 1983). Over the longer term, recurrence rates at five, ten, fifteen, and twenty years in the CDS were 60 per cent, 75 per cent, 87 per cent, and 91 per cent respectively (Boland & Keller, 2008). An important finding was that the occurrence of three or more previous episodes predicted a significantly increased risk of recurrence, which was estimated to go up by 16 per cent after each episode (Solomon et al., 2000). In addition, while individuals did not demonstrate consistent time patterns between episodes, the overall results showed that the time between episodes decreased as the number of episodes increased. For example, the median time to recurrence following a first episode was 150 weeks, whereas it was 57 weeks following a fifth episode (Solomon et al., 2000). A consistent finding was that the rate and timing of new episodes were associated with the level of residual symptoms in recovered patients. Full recovery led to fewer recurrent episodes; this situation was less frequent than recovery with residual symptoms. For example, recurrence rates in asymptomatic and symptomatic but recovered patients were 66 per cent and 87 per cent respectively; the mean time to recurrence for these groups were 180 and 33 weeks respectively (Boland & Keller, 2008).

The burden of major depressive disorder

One of the most distressing aspects of mood disorders is the strong association with suicidal behaviour. Beautrais et al. (1996) reported that, while 90 per cent of the patients hospitalized for attempted suicide had a psychiatric disorder, mood disorders accounted for 80 per cent of the attributable risk for serious suicide attempts – which themselves strongly predict completed suicide (Yoshimasu, Kiyohara, & Miyashita, 2008). While it has been recommended that suicide prevention strategies should not focus solely on depression (Fleischmann, Bertolote, Belfer, & Beautrais, 2005), MDD itself is likely to be a major predictor of suicide, as it accounted for approximately 28 per cent of the attributable risk for suicide within the ESEMeD study (Bernal et al., 2007). It is estimated that up to 15 per cent of severe MDD cases will die by suicide (APA, 2000). In addition to suicide, MDD is known to increase the risk of physical morbidity. For example, MDD has been shown to predict higher pain and mortality in medical inpatients (Herrmann et al., 1998) and an increased likelihood of both admission to, and mortality in, nursing homes (Onder et al., 2007). In addition to poorer prognoses for cardiac patients with comorbid depression, MDD is itself a risk factor for the development of cardiac problems (Frasure-Smith & Lesperance, 2005).

MDD is also a risk factor for a range of maladaptive behaviours. NCS-R data revealed that 45 per cent of American respondents meeting DSM-IV diagnostic criteria for substance use disorders in the previous 12 months also reported antecedent symptoms meeting criteria for a MDE (Kessler et al., 2003). This implies that depressive symptoms led to substance abuse in such cases. However, it cannot be ruled out that common factors lead to both disorders, as the association between depression and substance abuse is complicated by the interaction between multiple factors (Swendsen & Merikangas, 2000). When the onset of MDD occurs in adolescence, it is associated with an increased risk of poor educational attainment, teenage pregnancy, and impaired future marital relationships (Kessler & Wang, 2008). Within marital relationships, MDD is significantly associated with an increased risk of divorce due to impaired problem solving and communication (Davila, Stroud, & Starr, 2008). Moreover, where one partner has recovered from a depressive episode, the marital relationship may remain at risk, as spousal negativity towards MDD has been shown to predict future episodes (Davila et al., 2008).

MDD is costly to the wider economy. Major depression impairs work performance to a greater degree than arthritis, asthma, migraine, irritable bowel syndrome, and hypertension (Kessler et al., 2008). Unsurprisingly, the economic impact of depression increases with increasing severity, which leads to poorer work performance, increased risk of unemployment, and greater need for treatment (Birnbaum et al., 2010). The cost of treating MDD within the United Kingdom's National Health Service in 1991 was estimated at £417 million. However, the overall economic cost due to absence from work and premature mortality was far higher, of nearly

£3 billion (Churchill et al., 2001). The importance of depression as a personal and economic burden is reflected in the World Health Organization's projection that its contribution to the global burden of disease will rise, moving depression from fourth place in 2001 to second place by 2020; only ischemic heart disease will rank above it. In developed countries depression is projected to be the major burden of disease by 2020 (WHO, 2001). Thus the identification and effective treatment of MDD is an increasingly pressing public health concern (WHO, 2001; WHO, 2008).

Treatment seeking

Despite the high personal and economic costs associated with MDD, depressed individuals frequently delay seeking treatment and, when they do, the recognition of depression is limited. The NCS-R provided data concerning the proportion of individuals with lifetime MDD who sought professional treatment (Wang et al., 2005). Treatment was defined in the NCS-R as any form of professional healing contact – which meant that psychologists, counsellors, spiritual advisors, and herbalists were included along with conventional medical professionals (Wang et al., 2005). The NCS-R results showed that the vast majority (88 per cent) of those with lifetime MDD sought some form of treatment for depressive symptoms. Several factors consistently predicted the probability of initial treatment contact. Females and younger cohorts were more likely to seek treatment than males and older cohorts respectively. However, those of younger age at first onset were less likely to seek treatment than those of older age at first onset. While 37 per cent reported seeking initial treatment in the year following their first depressive episode, treatment seeking was typically delayed, as the median delay was eight years (Wang et al., 2005). Older cohort age and younger age at first onset predicted the longest delays in seeking initial treatment contact. Wang and Kessler (2005) suggested that the delays and the lower treatment-seeking rates associated with early age of first onset cases may have been due to poorer recognition of MDD symptoms in minors.

The results reported by Wang et al. (2005) were limited in that their analyses were unable to identify the proportions of those who actually received treatment. The World Health Organization's Collaborative Study on Psychological Problems in General Health Care (CSPP) (Sartorius et al., 1993) was specifically designed to investigate the detection and treatment of psychological disorders in primary-care settings. The longitudinal CSPP study employed ICD-10 criteria to diagnose psychiatric disorders in a total sample of 26,422 adult patients across 15 sites worldwide. The CSPP results suggest that the identification of MDD is typically low in primary-care settings, as only 15 per cent of those meeting ICD-10 criteria for major depression were correctly diagnosed. Of the remaining depressed individuals, 54 per cent were identified as being psychiatric cases, while 31 per cent received no diagnosis (Lecrubier, 2007). The CSPP results also showed that patients in the youngest cohort were significantly less likely to be diagnosed with major depression than those in older cohorts. For example, only 43 per cent of 18- to 24-year-olds were correctly diagnosed with MDD, by comparison to 59 per cent of 25- to 44-year-olds ($p < .05$; Lecrubier, 2007). The lower rate for the youngest cohort may have arisen because physicians are sometimes unwilling to diagnose a chronic mental disorder such as MDD in younger patients (Lecrubier, 2007). Finally, the CSPP results suggested that, even where correctly diagnosed, patients typically received inadequate treatment for depression from primary-care physicians. However, treatment adequacy in the CSPP was assessed only in terms of whether patients received psychotropic medication (Lecrubier, 2007).

Data from the NCS-R (Kessler et al., 2003) enabled an assessment of the adequacy of both pharmacological and psychological treatments for MDD. Minimal treatment adequacy for MDD in the NCS-R was defined as consisting of either (1) four or more outpatient visits with a physician for pharmacological treatment over 30 days or more; or (2) eight or more outpatient visits with any specialist provider of psychotherapy, each lasting for 30 minutes or more (Kessler et al., 2003). The NCS-R results showed that 57 per cent of the 12-month MDD cases sought help for emotional problems in the 12 months prior to interview. Of these, 90 per cent were treated in healthcare settings and 55 per cent of this sample were treated in specialist mental health settings (Kessler et al., 2003). The highest rate of minimally adequate treatment (64 per cent) was found in specialist mental health settings, where interventions were provided by psychiatrists, psychologists, counsellors, or social workers (Kessler et al., 2003). The rate of minimally adequate treatment in general medical settings was 41 per cent where treatments were provided by primary-care physicians, other medical specialists, or non-specialist nurses (Kessler et al., 2003). Increasing severity according to the QIDS-SR (Rush et al., 2003) and an increasing number of comorbid DSM-IV disorders both significantly predicted treatment seeking and treatment adequacy (Kessler et al., 2003). Finally, the NCS-R results revealed that, of the entire sample that met DSM-IV diagnostic criteria for MDD, only 21.7 per cent received adequate treatment (Kessler et al., 2003).

Conclusion

Major depressive disorder is a highly comorbid and recurrent disorder that affects twice as many females as males. Approximately 5 per cent of adults in developed countries will meet diagnostic criteria for major depression each year, and at least 10 per cent will experience at least one episode in their lifetime. MDD is a major risk factor for suicide and for a range of physical and behavioural sequelae that place a great burden on individuals and on the wider economy. The burden associated with MDD appears to be increasing in developed countries, as younger cohorts demonstrate both the highest 12-month prevalence rates and most severe episodes. The effective treatment of MDD is a pressing public health concern, as highlighted by the World Health Organization's prediction that it will become the major disease burden in developed countries by 2020. The heavy personal, social, and economic burdens associated with major depression demand that effective treatments be available.

References

Akiskal, H. S., & Akiskal, K. K. (2007). In search of Aristotle: Temperament, human nature, melancholia, creativity and eminence. *Journal of Affective Disorders, 100*, 1–6.

Alonso, J., & Lepine, J. P. (2007). Overview of key data from the European Study of the Epidemiology of Mental Disorders (ESEMeD). *Journal of Clinical Psychiatry, 68*, 3–9.

Alonso, J., Angermeyer, M. C., Bernert, S., Bruffaerts, R., Brugha, T. S., Bryson, H. … Vilagut, G. (2004). Prevalence of mental disorders in Europe: Results from the European Study of the Epidemiology of Mental Disorders (ESEMeD) project. *Acta Psychiatrica Scandinavica, 109*, 21–27.

Alonso, J., Ferrer, M., Romera, B., Vilagut, G., Angermeyer, M., Bernert, S. … Bruffaerts, R. (2002). The European Study of the Epidemiology of Mental Disorders (ESEMeD/MHEDEA 2000) project: Rationale and methods. *International Journal of Methods in Psychiatric Research, 11*, 55–67.

APA. (2000). *Diagnostic and statistical manual of mental disorders: DSM-IV-TR*. Washington, DC: American Psychiatric Association.

APA. (2013). *Diagnostic and statistical manual of mental disorders: DSM-V*. Washington, DC: American Psychiatric Association.

Beautrais, A. L., Joyce, P. R., Mulder, R. T., Fergusson, D. M., Deavoll, B. J., & Nightingale, S. K. (1996). Prevalence and comorbidity of mental disorders in persons making serious suicide attempts: A case-control study. *American Journal of Psychiatry, 153*, 1009–1014.

Bebbington, P., Dunn, G., Jenkins, R., Lewis, G., Brugha, T., Farrell, M., & Meltzer, H. (2003). The influence of age and sex on the prevalence of depressive conditions: Report from the National Survey of Psychiatric Morbidity. *International Review of Psychiatry, 15*, 74–83.

Beck, A. T., Steer, R. A., & Brown, G. K. (1996). *Manual for the Beck Depression Inventory* (2nd edn). San Antonio, TX: Psychological Corporation.

Bernal, M., Haro, J. M., Bernert, S., Brugha, T., De Graaf, R., Bruffaerts, R. ... Alonso, J. (2007). Risk factors for suicidality in Europe: Results from the ESEMED study. *Journal of Affective Disorders, 101*, 27–34.

Birnbaum, H. G., Kessler, R. C., Kelley, D., Ben-Hamadi, R., Joish, V. N., & Greenberg, P. E. (2010). Employer burden of mild, moderate, and severe major depressive disorder: Mental health services utilization and costs, and work performance. *Depression and Anxiety, 27*, 78–89.

Boland, R. J., & Keller, M. B. (2008). Course and outcome of depression. In I. H. Gotlib & C. L. Hammen (Eds), *Handbook of depression* (2nd edn, pp. 23–43). New York: Guilford.

Boughton, S. & Street, H. (2007). Integrated review of the social and psychological gender differences in depression. *Australian Psychologist, 42*, 187–197.

Carter, G. C., Cantrell, R. A., Zarotsky, V., Haynes, V. S., Phillips, G., Alatorre, C. I. ... Marangell, L. B. (2012). Comprehensive review of factors implicated in the heterogeneity of response in depression. *Depression and Anxiety, 29*, 340–354.

Churchill, R., Hunot, V., Corney, R., Knapp, M., Mcguire, H., Tylee, A., & Wessely, S. (2001). A systematic review of controlled trials of the effectiveness and cost-effectiveness of brief psychological treatments for depression. *Health Technology Assessment, 5*, 1–173.

Coryell, W., Endicott, J., Andreasen, N. C., Keller, M. B., Clayton, P. J., Hirschfeld, R. M. A., Scheftner, W. A., & Winokur, G. (1988). Depression and panic attacks: The significance of overlap as reflected in follow-up and family study data. *American Journal of Psychiatry, 145*, 293–300.

Daly, R. W. (2007). Before depression: the medieval vice of acedia. *Psychiatry, 70*, 30–51.

Davila, J., Stroud, C. B., & Starr, L. R. (2008). Depression in couples and families. In I. H. Gotlib & C. L. Hammen (Eds.), *Handbook of depression* (2nd edn, pp. 467–491). New York: Guilford.

Fleischmann, A., Bertolote, J. M., Belfer, M., & Beautrais, A. (2005). Completed suicide and psychiatric diagnoses in young people: A critical examination of the evidence. *American Journal of Orthopsychiatry, 75*, 676–683.

Frances, A., Manning, D., Marin, D., Kocsis, J., Mckinney, K., Hall, W., & Kline, M. (1992). Relationship of anxiety and depression. *Psychopharmacology, 106*, S82–S86.

Frasure-Smith, N., & Lesperance, F. (2005). Reflections on depression as a cardiac risk factor. *Psychosomatic Medicine, 67*, S19–S25.

Hamilton, K. E., & Dobson, K. S. (2002). Cognitive therapy of depression: Pretreatment patient predictors of outcome. *Clinical Psychology Review, 22*, 875–893.

Herrmann, C., Brand-Driehorst, S., Kaminsky, B., Leibing, E., Staats, H., & Ruger, U. (1998). Diagnostic groups and depressed mood as predictors of 22-month mortality in medical inpatients. *Psychosomatic Medicine, 60*, 570–577.

Jackson, S. W. (1981). Acedia the sin and its relationship to sorrow and melancholia in medieval times. *Bulletin of the History of Medicine, 55*, 172–181.

Katz, M. M., Secunda, S. K., Hirschfeld, R. M. A., & Koslow, S. H. (1979). Nimh clinical research branch collaborative program on the psychobiology of depression. *Archives of General Psychiatry, 36*, 765–771.

Keller, M. B., Lavori, P. W., Lewis, C. E., & Klerman, G. L. (1983). Predictors of relapse in major depressive disorder. *Journal of the American Medical Association, 250*, 3299–3304.

Kessler, R. C. (1999). The World Health Organization International Consortium in Psychiatric Epidemiology (ICPE): Initial work and future directions: The NAPE lecture 1998. *Acta Psychiatrica Scandinavica, 99*, 2–9.

Kessler, R. C., & Ustun, T. B. (2004). The World Mental Health (WMH) Survey Initiative version of the World Health Organization (WHO) Composite International Diagnostic Interview (CIDI). *International Journal of Methods in Psychiatric Research, 13*, 93–121.

Kessler, R. C., & Wang, P. S. (2008). Epidemiology of Depression. In I. H. Gotlib & C. L. Hammen (Eds), *Handbook of depression* (2nd edn, pp. 5–22). New York: Guilford.

Kessler, R. C., Mcgonagle, K. A., Swartz, M., Blazer, D. G., & Nelson, C. B. (1993). Sex and depression in the National Comorbidity Survey I: Lifetime prevalence, chronicity and recurrence. *Journal of Affective Disorders, 29*, 85–96.

Kessler, R. C., White, L. A., Birnbaum, H., Qiu, Y., Kidolezi, Y., Mallett, D., & Swindle, R. (2008). Comparative and interactive effects of depression relative to other health problems on work performance in the workforce of a large employer. *Journal of Occupational and Environmental Medicine, 50*, 809–816.

Kessler, R. C., Angermeyer, M., Anthony, J. C., De Graaf, R., Demyttenaere, K., Gasquet, I. … Ustun, T. B. (2007). Lifetime prevalence and age-of-onset distributions of mental disorders in the world health organization's world mental health survey initiative. *World Psychiatry, 6*, 168–176.

Kessler, R. C., Berglund, P., Demler, O., Jin, R., Koretz, D., Merikangas, K. R. ... Wang, P. S. (2003). The epidemiology of major depressive disorder: Results from the National Comorbidity Survey Replication (NCS-R). *Journal of the American Medical Association, 289*, 3095–3105.

Kessler, R. C., Birnbaum, H. G., Shahly, V., Bromet, E., Hwang, I., Mclaughlin, K. A. ... Stein, D. J. (2010). Age differences in the prevalence and co-morbidity of DSM-IV major depressive episodes: Results from the WHO world mental health survey initiative. *Depression and Anxiety, 27*, 351–364.

Krueger, R. F., Watson, D., & Barlow, D. H. (2005). Introduction to the special section: Toward a dimensionally based taxonomy of psychopathology. *Journal of Abnormal Psychology, 114*, 491–493.

LaMothe, R. (2007). An analysis of acedia. *Pastoral Psychology, 56*(1), 15–30.

Lecrubier, Y. (2007). Widespread underrecognition and undertreatment of anxiety and mood disorders: Results from 3 European studies. *Journal of Clinical Psychiatry, 68*, 36–41.

Lesperance, F., Frasure-Smith, N., Talajic, M., & Bourassa, M. G. (2002). Five-year risk of cardiac mortality in relation to initial severity and one-year changes in depression symptoms after myocardial infarction. *Circulation, 105*, 1049–1053.

Mueller, T. I., Lavori, P. W., Keller, M. B., Swartz, A., Warshaw, M., Hasin, D. ... Akiskal, H. (1994). Prognostic effect of the variable course of alcoholism on the 10-year course of depression. *American Journal of Psychiatry, 151*, 701–706.

Nolen-Hoeksema, S. (2000). The role of rumination in depressive disorders and mixed anxiety/depressive symptoms. *Journal of Abnormal Psychology, 109*, 504–511.

Nolen-Hoeksema, S. (2012). Emotion regulation and psychopathology: The role of gender. *Annual Review of Clinical Psychology, 8*, 161–187.

Nolen-Hoeksema, S., & Aldao, A. (2011). Gender and age differences in emotion regulation strategies and their relationship to depressive symptoms. *Personality and Individual Differences, 51*, 704–708.

Nolen-Hoeksema, S., Mcbride, A., & Larson, J. (1997). Rumination and psychological distress among bereaved partners. *Journal of Personality and Social Psychology, 72*, 855–862.

Onder, G., Liperoti, R., Soldato, M., Cipriani, M. C., Bernabei, R., & Landi, F. (2007). Depression and risk of nursing home admission among older adults in home care in Europe: Results from the Aged in Home Care (AdHOC) study. *Journal of Clinical Psychiatry, 68*, 1392–1398.

Posternak, M. A., Solomon, D. A., Leon, A. C., Mueller, T. I., Shea, M. T., Endicott, J., & Keller, M. B. (2006). The naturalistic course of unipolar major depression in the absence of somatic therapy. *Journal of Nervous and Mental Disease, 194*, 324–329.

Robins, L. N., Helzer, J. E., Croughan, J., & Ratcliff, K. S. (1981). National Institute of Mental Health Diagnostic Interview Schedule: Its history, characteristics, and validity. *Archives of General Psychiatry, 38*, 381–389.

Rush, A. J. (2007). The varied clinical presentations of major depressive disorder. *Journal of Clinical Psychiatry, 68*, 4–10.

Rush, A. J., Trivedi, M. H., Ibrahim, H. M., Carmody, T. J., Arnow, B., Klein, D. N. … Keller, M. B. (2003). The 16-item Quick Inventory of Depressive Symptomatology (QIDS), clinician rating (QIDS-C), and self-report (QIDS-SR): A psychometric evaluation in patients with chronic major depression. *Biological Psychiatry, 54*, 573–583.

Rush, A. J., Zimmerman, M., Wisniewski, S. R., Fava, M., Hollon, S. D., Warden, D. … Trivedi, M. H. (2005). Comorbid psychiatric disorders in depressed outpatients: Demographic and clinical features. *Journal of Affective Disorders, 87*, 43–55.

Sartorius, N., Ustun, T. B., Costa, J. a. S., Goldberg, D., Lecrubier, Y., Ormel, J., Von Korff, M., & Wittchen, H. U. (1993). An international study of psychological problems in primary care: Preliminary report from the World Health Organization Collaborative project on 'psychological problems in general health care'. *Archives of General Psychiatry, 50*, 819–824.

Schmitz, N., Wang, J., Malla, A., & Lesage, A. (2007). Joint effect of depression and chronic conditions on disability: Results from a population-based study. *Psychosomatic Medicine, 69*, 332–338.

Solomon, D. A., Keller, M. B., Leon, A. C., Mueller, T. I., Lavori, P. W., Shea, M. T. … Endicott, J. (2000). Multiple recurrences of major depressive disorder. *American Journal of Psychiatry, 157*, 229–233.

Spijker, J., De Graaf, R., Bijl, R. V., Beekman, A. T. F., Ormel, J., & Nolen, W. A. (2002). Duration of major depressive episodes in the general population: Results from the Netherlands Mental Health Survey and Incidence Study (NEMESIS). *British Journal of Psychiatry, 181*, 208–213.

Spitzer, R. L., Endicott, J., & Robins, E. (1978). Research diagnostic criteria: Rationale and reliability. *Archives of General Psychiatry, 35*, 773–782.

Swendsen, J. D., & Merikangas, K. R. (2000). The comorbidity of depression and substance use disorders. *Clinical Psychology Review, 20*, 173–189.

Tamres, L. K., Janicki, D., & Helgeson, V. S. (2002). Sex differences in coping behavior: A meta-analytic review and an examination of relative coping. *Personality and Social Psychology Review, 6*, 2–30.

Wang, P. S., Berglund, P., Olfson, M., Pincus, H. A., Wells, K. B., & Kessler, R. C. (2005). Failure and delay in initial treatment contact after first onset of mental disorders in the National Comorbidity Survey Replication. *Archives of General Psychiatry, 62*, 603–613.

WHO. (1992). *The ICD-10 classification of mental and behavioural disorders: Clinical descriptions and diagnostic guidelines*. Geneva: World Health Organisation.

WHO. (1993). *ICD-10, the ICD-10 classification of mental and behavioural disorders: diagnostic criteria for research*. Geneva: World Health Organization.

WHO. (2001). *The World Health Report 2001. Mental health: New understanding, new hope*. Geneva: World Health Organisation.

WHO. (2008). *Integrating mental health into primary care: A global perspective*. Geneva: World Health Organisation.

Yoshimasu, K., Kiyohara, C., & Miyashita, K. (2008). Suicidal risk factors and completed suicide: Meta-analyses based on psychological autopsy studies. *Environmental Health and Preventive Medicine, 13*, 243–256.

Further Reading

Angst, J., Gamma, A., Benazzi, F., Ajdacic, V., & Rössler, W. (2007). Melancholia and atypical depression in the Zurich study: Epidemiology, clinical characteristics, course, comorbidity and personality. *Acta Psychiatrica Scandinavica, 115*, 72–84.

APA. (1980). *Diagnostic and statistical manual of mental disorders: DSM-III*. Washington, DC: American Psychiatric Association.

Bernert, S., Matschinger, H., Alonso, J., Haro, J. M., Brugha, T. S., & Angermeyer, M. C. (2009). Is it always the same? Variability of depressive symptoms across six European countries. *Psychiatry Research, 168*, 137–144.

Cristancho, M. A., O'reardon, J. P., & Thase, M. E. (2011). Atypical depression in the 21st century: Diagnostic and treatment issues. Psychiatric Times, *28*, 42–46.

Decker, H. S. (2007). *How Kraepelinian was Kraepelin? How Kraepelinian are the neo-Kraepelinians? From Emil Kraepelin to DSM-III*. History of Psychiatry, *18*, 337–360.

Fink, M., Bolwig, T. G., Parker, G., & Shorter, E. (2007). Melancholia: Restoration in psychiatric classification recommended. *Acta Psychiatrica Scandinavica, 115*, 89–92.

Frank, E., Prien, R. F., Jarrett, R. B., Keller, M. B., Kupfer, D. J., Lavori, P. W., Rush, A. J., & Weissman, M. M. (1991). Conceptualization and rationale for consensus definitions of terms in major depressive disorder: Remission, recovery, relapse and recurrence. *Archives of General Psychiatry, 48*, 851–855.

Frank, E., Cassano, G. B., Rucci, P., Thompson, W. K., Kraemer, H. C., Fagiolini, A. … Forgione, R. N. (2011). Predictors and moderators of time to remission of major depression with interpersonal psychotherapy and SSRI pharmacotherapy. *Psychological Medicine, 41*, 151–162.

Jarrett, R. B., Eaves, G. G., Grannemann, B. D., & Rush, A. J. (1991). Clinical, cognitive, and demographic predictors of response to cognitive therapy for depression: A preliminary report. *Psychiatry Research, 37*, 245–260.

Keller, M. B. (2003). Past, present, and future directions for defining optimal treatment outcome in depression: Remission and beyond. *Journal of the American Medical Association, 289,* 3152–3160.

Kessler, R. C. (2007). The global burden of anxiety and mood disorders: Putting the European Study of the Epidemiology of Mental Disorders (ESEMeD) findings into perspective. *Journal of Clinical Psychiatry, 68,* 10–19.

Lamothe, R. (2007). An analysis of acedia. *Pastoral Psychology, 56,* 15–30.

Lux, V., Aggen, S. H., & Kendler, K. S. (2010). The DSM-IV definition of severity of major depression: inter-relationship and validity. *Psychological Medicine, 40,* 1691–1701.

Melartin, T., Leskelä, U., Rystälä, H., Sokero, P., Lestelä-Mielonen, P., & Isometsä, E. (2004). Co-morbidity and stability of melancholic features in DSM-IV major depressive disorder. *Psychological Medicine, 34,* 1443–1452.

Morrow, J., & Nolen-Hoeksema, S. (1990). Effects of responses to depression on the remediation of depressive affect. *Journal of Personality and Social Psychology, 58,* 519–527.

Nolen-Hoeksema, S. (1987). Sex differences in unipolar depression: Evidence and theory. *Psychological Bulletin, 101,* 259–282.

Nolen-Hoeksema, S., Morrow, J., & Fredrickson, B. L. (1993). Response Styles and the Duration of Episodes of Depressed Mood. *Journal of Abnormal Psychology, 102,* 20–28.

Rachman, S. (1971). Obsessional ruminations. *Behaviour Research and Therapy, 9,* 229–235.

Romera, I., Pérez, V., Menchón, J. M., Polavieja, P., & Gilaberte, I. (2011). Optimal cutoff point of the Hamilton Rating Scale for Depression according to normal levels of social and occupational functioning. *Psychiatry Research, 186,* 133–137.

Rush, A. J., Kraemer, H. C., Sackeim, H. A., Fava, M., Trivedi, M. H., Frank, E. … Schatzberg, A. F. (2006). Report by the ACNP task force on response and remission in major depressive disorder. *Neuropsychopharmacology, 31,* 1841–1853.

Salokangas, R. K. R., Vaahtera, K., Pacriev, S., Sohlman, B., & Lehtinen, V. (2002). Gender differences in depressive symptoms: An artefact caused by measurement instruments? *Journal of Affective Disorders, 68,* 215–220.

Schatzberg, A. F., & Kraemer, H. C. (2000). Use of placebo control groups in evaluating efficacy of treatment of unipolar major depression. *Biological Psychiatry, 47,* 736–744.

Shapiro, D. A., Barkham, M., Rees, A., Hardy, G. E., Reynolds, S., & Startup, M. (1994). Effects of treatment duration and severity of depression on the effectiveness of cognitive-behavioral and psychodynamic interpersonal psychotherapy. *Journal of Consulting and Clinical Psychology, 62,* 522–534.

Sigmon, S. T., Pells, J. J., Boulard, N. E., Whitcomb-Smith, S., Edenfield, T. M., Hermann, B. A. … Kubik, E. (2005). Gender differences in self-reports of depression: The response bias hypothesis revisited. *Sex Roles*, *53*, 401–411.

Simon, G. E., & Vonkorff, M. (1992). Reevaluation of Secular Trends in Depression Rates. *American Journal of Epidemiology*, *135*, 1411–1422.

Solomon, D. A., Keller, M. B., Leon, A. C., Mueller, T. I., Shea, M. T., Warshaw, M. … Endicott, J. (1997). Recovery from major depression: A 10-year prospective follow-up across multiple episodes. *Archives of General Psychiatry*, *54*, 1001–1006.

Spitzer, R. L., & Wakefield, J. C. (1999). DSM-IV diagnostic criterion for clinical significance: Does it help solve the false positives problem? *American Journal of Psychiatry*, *156*, 1856–1864.

Stewart, J. W., Mcgrath, P. J., Quitkin, F. M., & Klein, D. F. (2009). DSM-IV depression with atypical features: Is it valid? *Neuropsychopharmacology*, *34*, 2625–2632.

Taylor, M. A., & Fink, M. (2008). Restoring melancholia in the classification of mood disorders. *Journal of Affective Disorders*, *105*, 1–14.

Thase, M. E. (2009). Atypical depression: Useful concept, but it's time to revise the DSM-IV criteria. *Neuropsychopharmacology*, *34*, 2633–2641.

Wells, J. E., & Horwood, L. J. (2004). How accurate is recall of key symptoms of depression? A comparison of recall and longitudinal reports. *Psychological Medicine*, *34*, 1001–1011.

2

The Assessment of Depression

Arthur M. Nezu, Kelly S. McClure, and Christine M. Nezu

Introduction

Accurate assessment is critical for the effective treatment of depression (A. M. Nezu, Nezu, Lee, & Stern, 2014). Fortunately, given that over 280 measures of depression have been developed in the past century (Santor, Gregus, & Welch, 2006), practitioners have a plethora of tools at their disposal. This large choice, however, necessitates a careful approach to selecting the best assessment procedure for the task at hand (C. M. Nezu, Nezu, & Foster, 2000). Awareness of the purpose of an assessment, the array of measures available through the literature, and the strengths and weakness of the various instruments for differing purposes can assist therapists in providing the highest quality of treatment.

Depression assessment can begin even earlier, at the public health level, before the need for treatment has become manifest. Screening for depression in communities, primary medical care settings, and crisis intervention centres such as psychiatric and medical emergency departments helps alert individuals to the potential presence of depressive disorders and to the possible need for treatment.

Once depressive symptoms are identified and psychological intervention is sought, the purpose shifts from screening to accurate differential diagnosis, understanding symptom severity, and identifying co-occurring psychological (e.g., personality disorder) or medical (e.g., heart disease) disorders that may influence treatment. In addition, depression-related constructs (i.e., theory-driven mechanisms of action) can be assessed to

Treating Depression: MCT, CBT and Third Wave Therapies, First Edition.
Edited by Adrian Wells and Peter L. Fisher.

inform the process of case formulation and treatment planning (A. M. Nezu, Nezu, & Cos, 2007; A. M. Nezu, Nezu, & Lombardo, 2004). Also, practitioners may want to further evaluate critical items or measures of depression-related constructs such as suicidal ideation in order to identify specific risks to client safety.

The assessment process does not cease, however, with the initiation of treatment. At that point, the purpose can shift to monitoring treatment progress and measuring treatment outcome. The practitioner may want to know any or all of the following: (1) whether the symptoms have decreased in severity, (2) whether or when the disorder has been eliminated, (3) the process by which the symptoms improved, (4) the mechanism of change, and (5) whether safety risk factors, such as suicidal ideation, remain present. Brief instruments that do not take time away from treatment become especially important in this phase. At the same time, the balance between sensitivity and specificity remains as important as it was during the initial assessment.

Clinicians must remain aware that accurate depression assessment is ultimately the product of the information conveyed by the client, the synthesis of that information by the clinician, and the relationship between client and clinician. The assessment procedure and measures are simply tools. The client and the therapist also influence how information is shared and received. Keep in mind that clients with depression are often fatigued, distracted, and have difficulty concentrating; all this can affect many parts of the interview, including attendance and the ability to report past events. Clinicians are therefore encouraged to both observe these behaviours and solve problems with clients in order to facilitate participation in the assessment process even when treatment-interfering symptoms may be present.

Regarding clinician influences, all clinicians, simply by virtue of being human, are vulnerable to normal confirmation biases (A. M. Nezu & Nezu, 1993). Self-awareness about the tendency to elicit information that confirms one's own hypotheses and a comprehensive scientific approach to differential diagnosis that fosters the consideration of multiple explanations for the symptoms and systematically rules out alternative hypotheses can help manage these biases. C. M. Nezu et al. (2000) offer the following ten steps to assist clinicians in this process: (1) determine the goal; (2) adopt a systems approach; (3) individualize assessment and identify obstacles; (4) adapt assessment to overcome obstacles; (5) for each clinical focal area, generate a variety of assessment strategies; (6) for each strategy, generate multiple ideas; (7) conduct a cost–benefit analysis; (8) on the basis of a comparison of these criteria ratings, choose the one(s) with the highest 'utility'; (9) implement assessment procedures; (10) monitor the effects.

This chapter provides an overview of more than 20 measures that may be used in the assessment and treatment of depression for adults. The measures are listed in alphabetical order and separated into two categories: clinician ratings and self-report inventories. We describe each instrument's format, psychometric properties, and utility for various purposes (e.g., screening, diagnosis, treatment monitoring). We selected the measures on the basis of their applicability to the widest breadth of treatment settings. The majority of depression instruments discussed in this chapter measure diagnostic criteria or symptom severity. Unfortunately, there is little room to describe also depression measures designed for child, adolescent, and geriatric populations. Similarly, we could not include measures of depression-related constructs. For a comprehensive review of over 90 measures of depression across the lifespan, 42 measures of depression-related constructs, and 24 reprinted measures that can immediately be used in practice, see Nezu, Ronan, Meadows, and McClure (2000). After describing the measures, we provide a case example and discuss future directions in depression assessment.

Clinician Ratings

The Hamilton Rating Scale for Depression

Originally designed to evaluate the severity of depressive symptoms among patients previously diagnosed with a depressive disorder, the Hamilton Rating Scale for Depression (HAMD) (Hamilton, 1960) is, historically, the most widely used clinician rating of depression, particularly in clinical trials. It is completed by a trained assessor after conducting a semi-structured interview and consists of 21 items, the first 17 items contributing to the typically reported total score, while the remaining four items provide additional qualitative information about one's depression. The HAMD takes about ten minutes to complete and produces a score that reflects the severity of depressive symptoms. For a guide on how to conduct a clinical interview for the valid completion of the HAMD, see Williams (1988).

Although many practitioners view the HAMD as the 'gold standard' of clinician rating scales for depression, recent evaluations have taken a more critical look at its reliability and validity. For example, Bagby, Ryder,

Schuller, and Marshall (2004) examined three major psychometric properties of the HAMD: (1) reliability (internal, interrater, test–retest); (2) item response; and (3) validity (content, convergent, discriminant, factorial, and predictive). On the positive side, these researchers found that internal, interrater, and test-retest reliabilities at the *scale* level were found to be acceptable. In addition, convergent and discriminant validity coefficients for the scale were identified as adequate. On the negative side, however, interrater and retest reliabilities were inconsistent and questionable at the *item* level. In addition, correlations between the HAMD and the Structured Clinical Interview for DSM-IV Axis 1 Diseases (SCID) (First, Spitzer, Gibbon, & Williams, 1997) were low. Further, some important features of the definition of depression as delineated in the fourth edition of the *Diagnostic and Statistical Manual of Mental Disorders* (DSM-IV = APA, 1994) were not fully captured by the HAMD; other symptoms were not assessed at all.

In addition, the multidimensional nature of the HAMD can lead to difficulties in interpreting the meaning of the total score because certain items contribute more to that score than do others. Particularly striking is the contrast between items that address similar constructs, for example, psychomotor retardation versus agitation. Specifically, whereas the most severe form of the first symptom contributes four points to the total HAMD score, an equally severe manifestation of the second symptom contributes only two points. This happens in the absence of any evidence to support such differential item weightings. On a final note, Bagby et al. (2004) argued that, because the HAMD was developed several decades ago, many symptoms of depression now thought to be important are not contained in the instrument.

As would be expected, others disagree with the concerns voiced by Bagby et al. (2004). For example, Corruble and Hardy (2005) argued that, because the HAMD was originally designed to measure depression severity and clinical changes in patients already diagnosed with depression, Bagby et al. (2004) incorrectly extended the original aim of the scale so as to include studies that were carried out with both depressed and non-depressed patients. Corruble and Hardy (2005) also suggest that the HAMD should not be compared to DSM-IV criteria, as the two measures have different objectives. In other words, they suggest that the HAMD assesses depression severity in depressed patients, whereas the DSM-IV criteria define depression or present the conditions for its diagnosis.

A complete copy of the HAMD is available to download from the University of Massachusetts Psychiatry Scales website (http://healthnet.umassmed.edu/mhealth/HAMD.pdf.).

The HAMD-7 This shorter version of the HAMD is based on a unidimensional core group of depression symptoms; thus it eliminates the potential problem related to the multidimensionality of the original HAMD. The specific items included in this measure are depressed mood, guilt, suicide, work and interests, psychic anxiety, somatic anxiety, and general somatic items. The reliability and validity of this instrument in samples of mental health patients appear comparable to the psychometric properties of the full 17-item HAMD (McIntyre, Kennedy, Bagby, & Bakish, 2002). Furthermore, the HAMD-7 demonstrated high rates of sensitivity (.95), specificity (.84), positive predictive power (.94), and negative predictive power (.86). A HAMD-7 cutoff score of ≤ 3 represents full remission and was found to be comparable to the cut-off score of ≤ 7 representing the same construct in the HAMD-17. The HAMD-7 measure is contained in McIntyre et al. (2005).

The GRID-HAMD In 2002 the Depression Rating Scale Standardization Team (DRSST) published the GRID-HAMD (Kalali et al., 2002). Sponsored by the International Society for Central Nervous System (CNS) Drug Development, the DRSST was composed of researchers from academia, the pharmaceutical industry, clinical practice, and relevant government agencies. One of their goals was to improve the limitations of standardization, administration, and scoring present in the HAMD. This group presented its recommendations at the 2001 NIMH-sponsored New Clinical Drug Evaluation Unit (NCDEU) conference, where a new approach to administering and scoring the HAMD was advocated. The DSSRT made the following additions to the HAMD: (1) a grid-like structure that operationalized the intensity and frequency of each item while allowing for these items to be rated simultaneously; (2) structured interview prompts; and (3) scoring guidelines. The DRSST suggested that standardizing the administration and scoring of the HAMD would improve the current scale and would lay the groundwork for developing a new measure as well as future validation studies. The GRID-HAMD is currently available on the web at www.iscdd.org.

The Depression Interview and Structured Hamilton (DISH) The DISH (Freedland et al., 2002) was adapted from the HAMD, but it is intended to serve multiple purposes in the assessment of depression in medical patients.

According to its developers, the DISH can be a screener, a diagnostic instrument for major depressive disorder (MDD) and dysthymia, or a measure of symptom severity. This instrument was developed originally for a multicentre clinical trial that evaluated the treatment of depression or low social support for patients who recently suffered a myocardial infarction – namely the Enhancing Recovery in Coronary Heart Disease study (ENRICHD) (see ENRICHD Investigators, 2000).

An initial validity study found that a SCID diagnosis made by either a clinical social worker or a clinical psychologist agreed with a DISH diagnosis made by a trained nurse or a lay interviewer in 88 per cent of the interviews. In the actual ENRICHD trial, clinicians agreed with 93 per cent of research nurses' DISH diagnoses. On the basis of these initial findings, a National Heart, Lung, and Blood Institute Working Group regarding the assessment and treatment of patients with cardiovascular disease recommended the use of the DISH for 'diagnostic ascertainment' with regard to clinical trials (Davidson et al., 2006).

Readers should consult the Freedland et al. (2002) article for information on how to obtain the DISH.

The Schedule for Affective Disorders and Schizophrenia

The Schedule for Affective Disorders and Schizophrenia (SADS) (Endicott & Spitzer, 1978) is a 90- to 120-minute structured interview protocol administered by trained mental health professionals that measures 24 major psychiatric disorders and specific subtypes (e.g., recurrent MDD). SADS was originally designed to assess the presence of current and lifetime depressive diagnoses in accordance with research diagnostic criteria (RDC) (see Spitzer, Endicott, & Robins, 1978); but the various versions that have evolved over the past three decades also measure change in psychiatric status, a lifetime diagnosis, and specific syndromes like bipolar mood disorders.

A review of 21 studies that investigate the reliability of the SADS indicated it to be a reliable measure (Rogers, 2001). Most studies produced high interrater reliability estimates (most median kappa values were greater than .85) and moderate to high test–retest reliability (intraclass coefficients were generally greater than .70). With regard to the reliability of diagnoses made through SADS interviews, Spitzer, Endicott, and Robins (1978) reported a kappa value of .90 regarding the diagnosis of MDD and one of .81 for a minor depressive disorder diagnosis.

Practitioners will typically come across the SADS as consumers of the literature, because this method has frequently been used to validate other psychological measures. Regarding its clinical utility, however, there are both strengths and drawbacks to consider. The SADS can be used for the full spectrum of adult development, from young adulthood to older adulthood. The protocol has also been translated into several languages. Unfortunately, however, the SADS is not very compatible with more recent versions of the DSM; thus it produces accurate diagnoses for older versions of the DSM, but not necessarily for the DSM-IV-TR version (APA, 2000). In addition, the requisite 1–2 hours for completion may be prohibitive in many treatment settings.

The SADS is available by contacting the Department of Research Assessment and Training at the New York State Psychiatric Institute in New York.

The Structured Clinical Interview for DSM-IV Axis 1 Disorders: Clinician Version

The SCID (First et al., 1997) is a standardized diagnostic clinical interview administered by trained clinicians to assess for DSM-IV disorders in the following six categories: mood episodes, psychotic symptoms, psychotic disorders, mood disorders, substance use disorders, and anxiety and other disorders. This measure provides the clinician with categories of questions and scoring criteria for the items under investigation. The structure of the SCID is also flexible in that it allows clinicians to probe, restate questions, challenge respondents, and ask for clarification. The interview takes 45 to 90 minutes to complete.

The SCID is typically administered through a face-to-face interview but can also be administered over the telephone. However, scores for the lifetime diagnosis of MDD may be inflated with telephone administration (Cacciola, Alterman, Rutherford, McKay, & May, 1999). The SCID can also be used to diagnose depression in medically ill populations, including individuals with chronic pulmonary disease (Koenig, 2006) and primary-care patients (Vuorilehto, Melartin, & Isometsa, 2006).

The SCID was first published in 1983 and has evolved along with the revisions of the DSM-III, DSM-III-R, DSM-IV, and DSM-IV-TR. The psychometric properties of the most current version of the SCID have not yet been published and are commonly estimated on the basis of the previous version. The validity of this instrument can be evaluated in terms of how well it reflects the DSM-IV (APA, 1994) diagnostic criteria and how well it measures the constructs it purports to represent. Segal, Hersen, and Van Hasselt (1994) provided a review of the studies reported until 1994, suggesting that the SCID demonstrates adequate reliability.

The clinician's version of the SCID is available from the American Psychiatric Press, Inc. (www.appi.org).

The Screening Assessment of Depression: Polarity

The Screening Assessment of Depression: Polarity (SAD-P) measure is a 3-item clinician-administered rating scale that provides an evidence-based approach to the differential diagnosis of MDD versus bipolar disorder for patients currently experiencing a major depressive episode (Hirschfeld, Lewis, & Vornik, 2003). The first item pertains to the number of prior episodes of major depression (where 0 = no prior episodes and 1 = one or more prior episodes), whereas the second focuses on family (i.e., first-degree relative) history of depression or mania (where 0 = negative history and 1 = positive history). The third and final item addresses the presence of delusions (e.g., persecutory, grandiose) during the current depressive episode (where 0 = no delusions and 1 = one or more delusions present). A total score of 2 or a higher total score indicates that the practitioner should conduct a more in-depth assessment for bipolar disorder.

The SAD-P (Solomon et al., 2006) was developed within the NIMH Collaborative Program on the Psychobiology of Depression longitudinal study, which followed individuals with a variety of mood disorders for a median length of 16 years. Data from this programme indicated that the SAD-P has adequate psychometric properties for distinguishing unipolar from bipolar disorder. Specifically, overall sensitivity in accurately identifying patients with bipolar disorder was found to be .82, .72 in the bipolar I cross-validation sample, and .58 in the bipolar II cross-validation sample. This measure appears to be applicable mostly during pre-treatment phases such as screening and diagnosis.

Self-Report Measures

The Beck Depression Inventory

The Beck Depression Inventory (BDI) (Beck, Ward, Mendelson, Mock, & Erbaugh, 1961) is perhaps the most widely used self-report measure of depression. It consists of 21 items that measure the severity of the depressive symptoms an individual has experienced during the past two weeks. The symptom categories reflect DSM diagnostic criteria, and the successive versions of the BDI reflect updates in the successive editions of the DSM. The newest version, the BDI-II (Beck, Steer, & Brown, 1996), represents the diagnostic criteria contained in DSM-IV (APA, 1994). The BDI-II measures four symptoms that were not measured in the original BDI: agitation, worthlessness, concentration difficulty, and loss of energy. In addition, the BDI-II inquires about sleep and appetite *increases* – not just about decreases in these functions, as measured in the original BDI.

The strong psychometric properties of the BDI and of the BDI-II have been supported by numerous studies over several decades. As an example, the BDI-II yielded high internal consistency coefficients (alpha = .92 and .93 respectively) and high test–retest reliability ($r = .93$; Beck et al., 1996) in several samples, including individuals with psychiatric diagnoses and college students. Researchers have identified a two-factor structure within the overall measure. One factor has been labelled "cognitive symptoms" (e.g., pessimism, guilt, suicidal thoughts); the other, "somatic–affective symptoms" (e.g., sadness, loss of pleasure, crying, agitation). The BDI-II appears to have a more robust factor structure than the original BDI (Dozois, Ahnberg, & Dobson, 1998). Research utilizing the BDI-II has been conducted in a variety of settings and across several cultures. For example, this instrument was validated in a primary-care setting (Arnau, Meagher, Norris, & Bramson, 2001) and in a sample of southern rural African American women (Gary & Yarandi, 2004). In addition, several variations of the BDI have also been developed for specific settings or populations, as described next.

The Beck Depression Inventory for Primary Care (BDI-PC) The BDI-PC (Beck, Guth, Steer, & Ball, 1997) is a 7-item measure geared towards serving as a screening device in primary-care settings. Theoretical and statistical decision-making rules were used to select the seven items from the BDI-II that were retained for this instrument. First, the somatic and behavioural symptoms of depression were eliminated, in order to avoid confounding between the symptoms of a medical condition that may be due to biological, medical, or substance abuse disorders. The remaining items, which measured psychological–cognitive symptoms (e.g., sadness, pessimism, past failure, loss of pleasure, self-dislike, self-criticism, and suicidal thoughts or wishes), were then only retained if they loaded saliently ($\geq .35$) on the cognitive dimension of BDI-II scores. The resulting questionnaire therefore minimizes the likelihood of a 'false positive' diagnosis of depression.

The Beck Depression Inventory: Fast Screen (BDI-FS) The BDI-FS (Beck, Steer, & Brown, 2000) is the most recent version of the BDI-PC and is an abbreviated self-report inventory that was designed to rapidly screen medical patients for depression using criteria from the DSM-IV (APA, 1994). This measure is primarily composed of the cognitive items of depression (e.g., statements that assess pessimism, self-dislike, previous failure, self-criticism), which are included because they are considered to reflect the archetypal mood of the state of depression independently of features of the medical illness. Items assessing sadness and loss of interest or pleasure in activities are also included. The last item on the BDI-FS inventory assesses suicidal thoughts, which are regarded as an indicator of suicidal risk (Beck et al., 2000). The BDI-FS has been found to be a psychometrically sound depression-screening measure in a variety of medical populations, including patients with sickle cell disease (Jenerette, Funk, & Murdaugh, 2005) and individuals diagnosed with multiple sclerosis (Benedict, Fishman, McClellan, Bakshi, & Weinstock-Guttman, 2003).

The original 21 BDI items are contained in the Beck et al. (1961) article. Both the BDI-II and the BDI-FS are commercially available from Pearson (www.pearsonassess.com).

The Cardiac Depression Scale

The Cardiac Depression Scale (CDS) is a 26-item self-report questionnaire measuring depressive symptoms in cardiac patients. Originally developed in Australia (Hare & Davis, 1996), this instrument was specifically validated on cardiac patients. It allows practitioners the ability to detect the type of depression specific to cardiac patients, which is often characterized as subclinical or 'reactive' (Di Benedetto, Lindner, Hare, & Kent, 2005). This is becoming increasingly important as research continues to document and appreciate the high prevalence and incidence of MDD among various cardiac patient populations (A. M. Nezu, Nezu, & Jain, 2005). A brief visual analogue version of the scale was also recently developed for rapid or repeated assessments (Di Benedetto et al., 2005). High internal consistency (alpha = .90) and test–retest reliability ($r = .86$) estimates have been reported for both versions. An initial factor analysis revealed the following seven factors: sleep, anhedonia, uncertainty, mood, cognition, hopelessness, and inactivity.

Regarding the relative clinical utility of CDS by comparison to other measures of depression, the authors of the CDS posit that this instrument has psychometric advantages over the BDI. Compared with the BDI, which typically produces a positively skewed distribution, the CDS gives scores that have a normal distribution, and this enables the CDS to differentiate the scores in the lower range (Hare & Davis, 1996). The authors also posit that the CDS has some advantages over the Hospital Anxiety and Depression Scale (HADS) (Zigmond & Snaith, 1983), another scale commonly used for medical populations. The CDS includes items of somatic symptoms relevant for cardiac patients, whereas the HADS omits all somatic symptoms of depression and focuses on anhedonia. Future research using the CDS can help researchers better understand how somatic symptoms such as fatigue and reduced concentration may be related to emotional distress (i.e., depression) even more than the cardiac symptoms themselves (Lespérance & Frasure-Smith, 2000).

The CDS is contained in the original Hare and Davis (1996) paper.

The Center for Epidemiological Studies Depression Scale Revised

The Center for Epidemiological Studies Depression Scale (CES-D) (Radloff, 1977) is one of the few self-report paper-and-pencil measures of depression that were originally designed to determine a diagnosis of depressive disorders, and not symptom severity. Therefore its best clinical use is for diagnosis during the screening and assessment phases of treatment. It can also be a useful treatment outcome measure in determining whether the disorder was eliminated.

A principal components analysis of the original CES-D, conducted with data from general population samples, identified four major factors underlying the CES-D. These have been labelled depressed affect, positive affect, somatic and retarded activity, and interpersonal (Radloff, 1977). The CES-D has also demonstrated good reliability and validity in medical settings with individuals diagnosed with cancer (Hann, Winter, & Jacobsen, 1999), as well as with multiple sclerosis (Verdier-Talilefer, Gourlet, Fuhrer, & Alperovitch, 2001).

One particular strength of the CES-D is that it has been studied in many different countries and cultures. In addition, it has been adapted for computer-assisted and telephone interviews, thus creating the potential for practitioners to overcome some language barriers and perhaps provide more evidence-based services to persons with disabilities and to other underserved populations (Muñoz, McQuaid, Gonzalez, Dimas, & Rosales, 1999). Studies have indicated that the psychometric properties of the computerized version were equivalent to those of the paper-and-pencil format (Ogles, France, Lunnen, Bell, & Goldfarb, 1998).

A 10-item version of the CES-D was developed so that this measure may more closely correspond with the DSM-IV criteria for depression and may accommodate the needs of elderly respondents – who may find the original response format confusing, the questions emotionally stressful, and the time taken to complete it burdensome (Irwin, Artin, & Oxman, 1999). Another stated purpose for this revision was to retain the advantageous qualities of a measure that has been valuable to community-based researchers, while increasing its generalizability to current psychiatric understanding. The reliability and validity of this briefer version were found to be similar to those of the original CES-D. Moreover, when using a cut-off score of ≥ 4, the revised version was found to have strong specificity (81–93 per cent) and sensitivity (79–100 per cent) properties (Irwin et al., 1999).

The CES-D is available to download from http://patienteducation.stanford.edu/research/cesd.pdf. The items contained in the 10-item version can be found in the Irwin et al. (1999) paper.

The Depression in the Medically Ill 18 and Depression in the Medically Ill 10 Scales

Whereas some depression measures for medical patients focus on specific illnesses (e.g., the CDS), others were developed to be applicable across medical settings. The Depression in the Medically Ill 18 (DMI-18) and Depression in the Medically Ill 10 (DMI-10) scales (Parker, Hilton, Bains, & Hadzi-Pavlovic, 2002) represent such an approach. Both were specifically designed to measure depression in medical patients where confounding symptoms of medical illness can artificially inflate the estimates of depression severity or cause 'false positive' diagnoses. These scales are comprised solely of cognitive-based items and exclude somatic items such as sleep and appetite disturbance. Nor do these scales contain items regarding suicidal ideation or intent. The scales' developers view the assessment of suicide as appropriate only in the context of face-to-face interaction and not as part of a paper-and-pencil questionnaire.

With regard to their psychometric properties, both versions of the DMI possess strong internal consistency (.93 and .89, respectively; Parker et al., 2002). They also have good concurrent validity, as demonstrated by strong correlations with the BDI-PC and the HADS. Using a cut-off score of ≥ 9 for the DMI-10 yielded sensitivity estimates ranging between 93.5 per cent and 100 per cent. Specificity estimates ranged between 65.7 per cent and 69.8 per cent. A DMI-18 cut-off point of ≥ 20 yielded sensitivity estimates ranging from 91.7 per cent to 95 per cent and specificity estimates between 68.1 per cent and 72.4 per cent. The sound psychometric properties of these scales have also been confirmed in a variety of patient populations, including medically ill patients who visit general practitioners (Parker, Hilton, Hadzi-Pavlovic, & Irvine, 2003), psychiatric outpatients (Parker & Gladstone, 2004), and cardiac patients (Hilton et al., 2006).

Items for both versions are contained in the Parker et al. (2002) article.

The Harvard Department of Psychiatry/National Depression Screening Day Inventory

The Harvard Department of Psychiatry/National Depression Screening Day (HANDS) inventory is 10-item self-report questionnaire that measures symptoms of depression in the general population. Originally developed for the National Depression Screening Day in the United States (Baer et al., 2000), the HANDS is brief and easy to score and provides guidelines that mental health screeners can use in referring individuals for mental health services. Over the years, practitioners have expanded the use of the HANDS beyond public health screening. For example, Fava et al. (2006) used the HANDS to define depression treatment response and remission rates (i.e., scores < 9) and to assess the severity of residual depressive symptoms among patients who had been diagnosed with MDD according to DSM-IV criteria. Theirs was a research application that examined the prevalence of cognitive and physical side effects of antidepressant medication. In addition, Wexler et al. (2006) employed the HANDS to measure depression severity in patients with type 2 diabetes in order to investigate factors that affect the quality of life of primary-care patients.

The HANDS developers used item response theory to select the questionnaire items from other psychometrically sound depression inventories, including the BDI and the Zung Self-Rating Depression Scale (SDS) (Zung, 1965). This measure is also characterized by strong reliability properties (e.g., its internal consistency is .87).

Scores on the HANDS are best interpreted by using a cut-off score of 9, or a higher one (in the range of 0 to 30), to indicate MDD. Research using a sample of individuals who would likely match individuals attending a free depression-screening event in the United States yielded a sensitivity of 95 per cent regarding individuals whose symptoms also met DSM-IV diagnostic criteria for MDD after structured clinical interviews.

The HANDS is contained in the Baer et al. (2000) article.

The Hospital Anxiety and Depression Scale

The Hospital Anxiety and Depression Scale (HADS) was one of the first self-report questionnaires developed to measure depression and anxiety among medical, non-psychiatric patients (Zigmond & Snaith, 1983). It can be used for screening, assessment, and treatment outcome measurement. The 14 items comprising this measure are distributed equally, so as to assess depression and anxiety without using items that reflect physiological symptoms that could also be accounted for by a non-psychiatric illness or its treatment (e.g., dizziness, headaches, insomnia, fatigue). Patients rate each item on a scale of 0 to 3, producing a range of 0 to 21 for each scale.

The HADS has been used heavily since its development. A review study published in 1997 identified over 200 studies that used it (Herrmann, 1997). In 2002, 747 more studies were identified and reviewed by Bjelland, Dahl, Haug, and Neckelmann (2002). Hermann concluded that the HADS is a clinically meaningful screening tool, which is sensitive to changes related to the natural course of depression as well as to responses due to both psychological and pharmacological interventions. Bjelland and colleagues concluded that factor-analytic studies of the HADS generally supported two underlying factors, namely anxiety and depression; that the Cronbach's alpha for the depression scale ranged between .67 and .90 (mean = .82); and that a score of 8 and above on the depression scale yielded a sensitivity and a specificity of .80. Overall, these authors concluded that the HADS performed effectively in identifying depression caseness across somatic, psychiatric, primary-care, and non-patient populations.

This measure can be particularly useful in primary and tertiary medical care settings for patients with diverse medical disorders. It can also be used in more homogeneous medical settings (e.g., an oncology centre). The HADS is also of benefit to those wishing to screen for depression and anxiety simultaneously.

The HADS can be purchased from GL Assessment (www.gl-assessment.co.uk).

The Inventory of Depressive Symptomatology

The Inventory of Depressive Symptomatology (IDS) (Rush et al., 1986; Rush, Gullion, Basco, Jarrett, & Trivedi, 1996) is a 30-item questionnaire that measures depressive symptom severity utilizing items that correspond to the DSM-IV criteria for diagnosing MDD, including atypical symptom features. There is a patient self-report version and a matching clinician rating. Regarding its format, this measure provides equivalent weightings for each symptom item and delineates clearly stated anchors. Cronbach's alpha was found to range between .92 and .94 in a sample of depressed outpatients (Rush et al., 1996). It was also found to correlate highly with the HAMD and to be sensitive to changes in symptom severity as a function of antidepressant medication. Most research on the IDS has supported its use for measuring change in symptom severity as a function of treatment. However, practitioners can use this measure for depression screening and assessment as well.

The Quick Inventory of Depressive Symptomatology (QIDS) A shorter, 16-item version of the IDS, named QIDS, is also available (Rush, Carmody, & Reimitz, 2000). This measure is geared more to diagnostic applications, as it only includes items from the IDS that specifically address DSM-IV criteria for diagnostic symptoms. This self-report questionnaire addresses the following nine domains: sad mood, concentration, self-criticism, suicidal ideation, interest, fatigue, sleep disturbance, appetite problems, and psychomotor agitation/retardation. An evaluation of the psychometric properties of the QIDS as demonstrated on a sample of patients with chronic depression yielded estimates of high internal consistency (alpha = .86) and strong associations with the HAMD (Rush et al., 2003). Additional evaluations among patients in the Sequenced Treatment Alternatives to Relieve Depression (STAR*D) trial (Rush et al., 2006) and among outpatients diagnosed with either MDD or bipolar disorder (Trivedi et al., 2004), further support the clinical utility and sensitivity of both the IDS and the QIDS.

Both versions are available in multiple languages and can be downloaded from a website that provides further information about their psychometric properties (www.ids-qids.org).

The Mood Disorder Questionnaire

The Mood Disorder Questionnaire (MDQ) (Hirschfeld et al., 2000) is a 13-item self-report inventory that measures manic and hypomanic symptoms and behaviours such as elevated energy and increased interest in sex. Each question begins with a yes/no item and is followed by 4-point scale for measuring the severity of the symptom. Miller, Klugman, Berv, Rosenquist, and Ghaemi (2004) recently evaluated the sensitivity and specificity of the MDQ in a group of 37 patients with bipolar spectrum disorder and 36 patients with unipolar depression. Results indicated that the overall sensitivity was .58, but higher in bipolar I disorder (.69) than in bipolar II disorder patients (.30). A recent factor analysis of the MDQ identified a two-factor structure: an elevated mood overactivity factor and an irritable behaviour factor (Mangelli, Benazzi, & Fava, 2005). More extensive psychometric evaluations are needed and will likely be published in the future. At this point in time, the MDQ can assist practitioners in identifying bipolar disorder in the screening phase and in diagnosing bipolar disorder in the assessment phase. However, it should be used in conjunction with a thorough clinical interview or with additional measures (or both) and after more research that supports its psychometric properties.

The MDQ is contained in the Hirschfeld et al. (2000) article.

The Patient Health Questionnaire Depression Scale

The Patient Health Questionnaire Depression Scale (PHQ-9) is a 9-item self-report questionnaire that assesses the nine signs and symptoms of major depression delineated in DSM-IV (Spitzer, Kroenke, & Williams, 1999). It was developed for use in busy primary-care medical settings to assist physicians and other medical care providers in detecting the presence of depression among primary-care patients. Typically in less than ten minutes, patients select the frequency of depressive symptoms that they experienced in the past two weeks and then turn over the form to their medical provider for scoring and interpretation. Major depression is diagnosed if five or more of these nine symptoms have been present in at least 'more than half the days during the past two weeks' and if one of the symptoms is depressed mood or anhedonia. One of the nine symptoms (*thoughts that you would be better off dead, or thoughts of hurting yourself in some way*), if present at all, counts regardless of its duration. PHQ-9 scores range from 0 to 27, and practitioners can also use the cut-off points of 5, 10, 15, and 20 to represent the thresholds for mild, moderate, moderately severe, and severe depression respectively. For a single-screening cut-off point, a PHQ-9 score of 10 (or a higher one) has been recommended (Kroenke, Spitzer, & Williams, 2001).

Evaluation indicates that the PHQ-9 has sound psychometric properties. Regarding its reliability, internal consistency as measured by Cronbach's alpha ranges from .86 to .89, and test–retest reliability (intraclass correlations) ranges from .81 to .96 (Kroenke et al., 2001). In addition, the PHQ has been validly applied to various medical populations, for instance individuals suffering from traumatic brain injury (Fann et al., 2005).

The PHQ-9 may be particularly useful in culturally diverse settings. It has been translated and validated in many languages, including Spanish (Diez-Quevedo, Rangil, Sanchez-Planell, Kroenke, & Spitzer, 2001), German (Löwe, Gräfe, Zipfel, Witte, Loerch, & Herzog, 2004; Löwe, Spitzer, et al., 2004), and Nigerian (Adewuya, Ola, & Afolabi, 2006). It can also measure a common construct of depression across various diverse population samples (i.e., African American, Chinese American, Latino, non-Hispanic white patient groups; see Huang, Chung, Kroenke, Delucchi, & Spitzer, 2005).

Although the PHQ-9 was developed for use in primary-care settings, it can also be used for diagnosis and screening in other settings. There are also two additional versions of this measure. The PRIME-MD (Spitzer et al., 1994) is the clinician-administered counterpart from which the PHQ-9 was originally derived. The PRIME-MD measures the presence of five common psychiatric disorders, whereas the PHQ-9 measures only one of the five disorders. An even shorter self-report version is also available, the PHQ-2 (Kroenke, Spitzer, & Williams, 2003), which inquires only about depressed mood and anhedonia. Kroenke et al. (2003) evaluated the criterion validity of the PHQ-2 with reference to the structured interview conducted by independent mental health professionals. They reported that the PHQ-2 was able to detect MDD with a sensitivity of 83 per cent and a specificity of 92 per cent using an optimal cut-off score of 3.

The PHQ-9 can be downloaded from the website of the MacArthur Initiative on Depression and Primary Care (www.depression-primarycare.org).

The Zung Self-Rating Depression Scale

The Zung Self-Rating Depression Scale (SDS) (Zung, 1965) is a 20-item self-report questionnaire measuring the cognitive, behavioural, and affective symptoms of depression. It is one of the most widely used self-report depression questionnaires, translated into and examined within many cultures including Dutch, Finnish, and Japanese populations. It is fairly quick to complete (it takes approximately ten minutes) and has sound psychometric properties. For example, a study of 85 depressed and 28 non-depressed patients in a Dutch day clinic (de Jonghe & Baneke, 1989) found the internal consistency to be .82 and the split-half reliability to be .79.

It appears that the SDS has three underlying factors. However, different researchers have interpreted these factors differently, possibly due to culturally related variables, although the explanation for these differences has not been specifically assessed. For example, Sakamoto, Kijima, Tomoda, and Kambara (1998) assigned the labels 'cognitive symptoms', 'affective symptoms', and 'somatic symptoms' to the factors that emerged from a principal components analysis conducted with 2,187 Japanese college students. The goodness-of-fit index (GFI) was estimated to be .94. The authors' interpretation was further supported by a confirmatory factor analysis in a sample of 597 Japanese undergraduates (GFI = .92). On the other hand, Kivelae and Pahkala (1987) labelled the three factors that emerged from their principal components analysis on a sample of 290 depressed Finnish adults aged 60 and older as 'depressed mood', 'loss of self-esteem', and 'irritability and agitation'.

The Zung SDS is available to download from the University of Massachusetts Psychiatry Scales website (http://healthnet.umassmed.edu/mhealth/mhscales.cfm).

Case Example

To illustrate how the previous measures can be used in treatment, consider the example of June, a 42-year-old woman who attended outpatient treatment for help with relationship problems. June and her boyfriend in a five-year relationship had been having more arguments since her mother passed away the year before. After this loss, June was increasingly reluctant to be socially active. She felt criticized by her boyfriend, even though she believed he was 'simply trying to help'. June believed that these problems were contributing to their relationship difficulties. At the point of initial assessment, one depression symptom (decreased interest), one risk factor (loss of a loved one), and two symptoms that co-occur with depression (relationship conflict and tendency to feel overly criticized) had been reported.

Therefore the clinician should definitely determine whether a diagnosis of major depressive disorder would be appropriate or should be ruled out.

At this early stage the therapist should proceed to conduct a semi-structured clinical interview that allows for flexible questioning, at a pace that helps June feel supported while discussing each symptom of a major depressive episode. During the interview, the clinician should include a careful suicide assessment and discuss any safety measures needed to prevent June from hurting herself. As a thorough discussion of how to conduct a suicide assessment is beyond the scope of this chapter, readers are referred to Dexter-Mazza and Korslund (2007).

After the interview, the clinician can complete a clinician rating scale such as the GRID HAM-D, while June herself completes a self-report questionnaire (e.g., BDI-II, PHQ-9, or QIDS). The clinician should then quickly score the measure in order to compare June's written self-report to their previous conversation and to be sure that her written report does not suggest any increased risk for self-harm. If no additional suicide risk is reported, June and the clinician can agree to meet again for continued assessment.

After the initial assessments, the clinician should develop a preliminary case conceptualization that includes developmental risk factors (e.g., early childhood trauma), depression-related triggers (e.g., recent stressors), and an explanation of how the symptoms are maintained (e.g., mechanisms of action) (see A. M. Nezu et al., 2004, for a comprehensive cognitive behavioural case conceptualization model with a specific example of its application to depression). The follow-up assessment, especially the evaluation of any factors that serve as 'mechanisms of action', is likely to rely heavily upon the case conceptualization. For example, if the clinician initially identifies various problem-solving deficits, she or he may find it helpful to administer specific problem-solving measures in order to be able to determine whether these deficits become reduced over time as the depression symptoms decrease. On the other hand, a clinician using a mindfulness conceptualization may be better assisted by measures of acceptance and quality of life and may find a frequent documentation of the depressive symptoms less informative.

Regardless of the explanatory mechanism(s), the clinician and June should continue to discuss on a regular basis how June is feeling, whether she thinks about harming herself, and how satisfied she is with her life and her relationship with her boyfriend.

Future Directions

In general, the most recent generation of depression instruments offers improvements in three areas. First, many older measures have been updated to correspond to DSM-IV diagnostic criteria for depression. Second, certain newer measures assess depression with better specificity, particularly for individuals with co-occurring medical illnesses or in specific clinical contexts, such as primary-care settings. Third, researchers have attempted to understand the validity and reliability of current depression measures across many cultures and ethnicities, although much more research is needed in this area.

The future of the assessment of depression may largely be influenced by the new editions of the DSM-V and ICD-11. Although it is too early to predict exactly what impact these will specifically have for the assessment of depression, there are a few general approaches to the development of the new diagnostic systems that will impact the assessment of all disorders.

First, the DSM-V and the ICD-11 are a collaborative effort among several international groups, including the American Psychiatric Institute for Research and Education, three National Institute of Health (NIH) institutes in the United States, and the World Health Organization. This international approach increases the likelihood that any revisions to the diagnostic criteria for depression will be informed by cross-cultural research. Similarly, all contributors to the new editions are asked to consider whether the current diagnostic criteria assess the correct symptoms, threshold levels, and typification of course and characteristics across cultures (Kupfer et al., 2002). Therefore it is likely that revision of the diagnostic criteria for depression will necessitate updates to the current diagnostic instruments. In addition, improved cultural validity of the diagnostic criteria for depression may improve the cultural validity of the diagnostic instruments that correspond to the new criteria.

The developers of the DSM-V and ICD-11 have considered employing a dimensional rather than a category-based approach to diagnosis. It is unlikely that a dimensional approach will be taken for all the disorders, as the developers also aspire to produce a revision that can be adopted as seamlessly as possible. We can anticipate an increased interest in research on the dimensional descriptions and understanding of depression and a corresponding demand for instruments that can be used in these studies.

In addition to changes in depression assessment that may be instigated by updates to the diagnostic systems, there are three issues regarding depression research that may also influence the future of assessment. The first issue involves evidence-based practice. More practitioners entering the field are being trained to incorporate research within their practices (Levant, 2004). These therapists will be looking for low-cost instruments that they can administer, score, interpret, and record in a database frequently and easily. Critical items that assess suicidal ideation and behaviours are also particularly helpful in this context. Surprisingly few instruments meet all such criteria. For example, some are quick and easy and assess critical items; however, weekly administration may become costly. Others are cost-free, but do not provide enough specificity on the critical items. More attention needs to be paid to depression assessment in this context in order for instruments to both meet the needs of evidence-based practice and encourage continued research within practice settings. Similarly, additional research should be conducted on the reliability and validity of depression instruments in this context.

The second issue involves randomized clinical trials. Now that several treatments for depression have been established as efficacious, randomized clinical trials are beginning to also examine the *process* of depression treatment. In their review of the methods for capturing the process of change in therapy, Hayes and colleagues (2008) posit that randomized clinical trials are beginning to move beyond the simple question of whether treatments are effective and more towards the question of *how* treatments are effective and *for whom*. These studies will examine moderators, mediators, predictors, and the shape of change. Some treatments may provide smooth, linear improvements. Others may provide more rapid improvement, characterized by a quadratic shape, whereas others may facilitate concentrated improvements at the end of treatment that appear in a cubic trajectory when displayed graphically. Accurate assessment will be critical for a precise understanding of the psychotherapy process, so future studies on the reliability and validity of depression assessment instruments in this context will also be needed.

The third context involves comparisons among cognitive behavioural therapy, metacognitive therapy, and third-wave therapies. Future studies will likely include such questions as: Is symptom improvement necessary in order for us to obtain benefits from treatment? Can effective depression treatment improve the quality of life without significant symptom reduction? Is symptom reduction a cause or a consequence of improved quality of life? Again, understanding the validity and reliability of depression assessment in this context will be critical.

References

Adewuya, A. O., Ola, B. A., & Afolabi, O. O. (2006). Validity of the Patient Health Questionnaire (PHQ-9) as a screening tool for depression amongst Nigerian university students. *Journal of Affective Disorders, 96*, 89–93.

APA. (1994). *Diagnostic and statistical manual of mental disorders: DSM-IV*. Washington, DC: American Psychiatric Association.

APA. (2000). *Diagnostic and statistical manual of mental disorders: DSM-IV-TR*. Washington, DC: American Psychiatric Association.

Arnau, R. C., Meagher, M. W., Norris, M. P., & Bramson, R. (2001). Psychometric evaluation of the Beck Depression Inventory-II with primary care medical patients. *Health Psychology, 20*, 112–119.

Bagby, R. M., Ryder, A. G., Schuller, D. R., & Marshall, M. B. (2004). The Hamilton Depression Rating Scale: Has the gold standard become a lead weight? *American Journal of Psychiatry, 161*, 2163–2177.

Baer, L., Blais, M., Cukor, P., Fava, M., Jacobs, D. G., Kessler, R. … O'Laughlen, J. (2000). Development of a brief screening instrument: The HANDS. *Psychotherapy and Psychosomatics, 69*, 35–41.

Beck, A. T., Steer, R. A., & Brown, G. K. (1996). *Manual for the BDI-II*. San Antonio, TX: Psychological Corporation.

Beck, A. T., Steer, R. A., & Brown, G. K. (2000). *Manual for the Beck Depression Inventory–Fast Screen for medical patients*. San Antonio, TX: Psychological Corporation.

Beck, A. T., Guth, D., Steer, R. A., & Ball, R. A. (1997). Screening for major depression disorders in medical inpatients with the Beck Depression Inventory for Primary Care. *Behaviour Research, and Therapy, 35*, 785–791.

Beck, A. T., Ward, C. H., Mendelson, M., Mock, J., & Erbaugh, J. (1961). An inventory for measuring depression. *Archives of General Psychiatry, 4*, 561–571.

Benedict, R. H. B., Fishman, I., McClellan, M. M., Bakshi, R., & Weinstock-Guttman, B. (2003). Validity of the Beck Depression Inventory–Fast Screen in multiple sclerosis. *Multiple Sclerosis, 9*, 393–396.

Bjelland, I., Dahl, A. A., Haug, T. T., & Neckelmann, D. (2002). The validity of the Hospital Anxiety and Depression Scale: An updated review. *Journal of Psychosomatic Research, 52*, 69–77.

Cacciola, J. S., Alterman, A. I., Rutherford, M. J., McKay, J. R., & May, D. J. (1999). Comparability of telephone and in-person structured clinical interview for DSM-III-R (SCID) diagnoses. *Assessment, 6*, 235–242.

Corruble, E., & Hardy, P. (2005). Why the Hamilton Depression Rating Scale endures. *American Journal of Psychiatry, 162*, 2394.

Davidson, K. W., Kupfer, D. J., Bigger, J. T., Califf, R. M., Carney, R. M., Coyne, J. C. … Suls, J. M. (2006). Assessment and treatment of depression in patients with cardiovascular disease: National Heart, Lung, and Blood Institute Working Group Report. *Annals of Behavioural Medicine, 32*, 121–126.

de Jonghe, J. F., & Baneke, J. J. (1989). The Zung Self-Rating Depression Scale: A replication study on reliability, validity and prediction. *Psychological Reports, 64*, 833–834.

Dexter-Mazza, E. T., & Korslund, K. E. (2007). Suicide risk assessment. In M. Hersen & J. C. Thomas (Eds), *Handbook of clinical interviewing with adults* (pp. 95–113). Thousand Oaks, CA: Sage.

Di Benedetto, M., Lindner, H., Hare, D. L., & Kent, S. (2005). A Cardiac Depression Visual Analogue Scale for the brief and rapid assessment of depression following acute coronary syndromes. *Journal of Psychosomatic Research, 59*, 223–229.

Diez-Quevedo, C., Rangil, T., Sanchez-Planell, L., Kroenke, K., & Spitzer, R. L. (2001). Validation and utility of the Patient Health Questionnaire in diagnosing mental disorders in 1003 general hospital Spanish inpatients. *Psychosomatic Medicine, 63*, 679–686.

Dozois, D. J. A., Ahnberg, J. L., & Dobson, K. S. (1998). A psychometric evaluation of the Beck Depression Inventory-II. *Psychological Assessment, 10*, 83–89.

Endicott, J., & Spitzer, R. L. (1978). A diagnostic interview: The Schedule for Affective Disorders and Schizophrenia. *Archives of General Psychiatry, 35*, 837–844.

ENRICHD Investigators. (2000). Enhancing Recovery in Coronary Heart Disease patients (ENRICHD): Study design and methods. *American Heart Journal, 139*, 1–9.

Fann, J. R., Bombardier, C. H., Dikmen, S., Esselman, P., Warms, C., A., Pelzer, E. … Temkin, N. (2005). Validity of the Patient Health Questionnaire-9 in assessing depression following traumatic brain injury. *Journal of Head Trauma Rehabilitation, 20*, 501–511.

Fava, M., Graves, L. M., Benazzi, F., Scalia, M. J., Iosifescu, D. V., Alpert, J. E. … Papakostas, G. I. (2006). A cross-sectional study of the prevalence of cognitive and physical symptoms during long-term antidepressant treatment. *Journal of Clinical Psychiatry, 67*, 1754–1759.

First, M. B., Spitzer, R. L., Gibbon, M., & Williams, J. B. (1997). *User's guide for the Structured Clinical Interview for DSM-IV Axis I disorders*. Washington, DC: American Psychiatric Press.

Freedland, K. E., Skala, J. A., Carney, R. M., Raczynski, J. M., Taylor, C. B., Mendes de Leon … Veith, R. C. for the ENRICHD Investigators. (2002). The

Depression Interview and Structured Hamilton (DISH): Rationale, development, characteristics, and clinical validity. *Psychosomatic Medicine, 64*, 897–905.

Gary, F. A., & Yarandi, H. N. (2004). Depression among southern rural African American women: A factor analysis of the Beck Depression Inventory-II. *Nursing Research, 53*, 251–259.

Hamilton, M. (1960). Development of a rating scale for depression. *Journal of Neurology, Neurosurgery and Psychiatry, 23*, 56–62.

Hann, D., Winter, K., & Jacobsen, P. (1999). Measurement of depressive symptoms in cancer patients: Evaluation of the Center for Epidemiological Studies–Depression Studies Depression Scale (CES-D). *Journal of Psychosomatic Research, 46*, 437–443.

Hare, D. L., & Davis, C. R. (1996). Cardiac Depression Scale: Validation of a new depression scale for cardiac patients. *Journal of Psychosomatic Research, 40*, 379–386.

Hayes, A. M., Laurenceau, J., & Cardaciotto, L (2008). Methods for capturing the process of change. In A. M. Nezu & C. M. Nezu (Eds), *Evidence-based outcome research: A practical guide to conducting randomized controlled trials for psychosocial interventions* (pp. 335–358). New York: Oxford University Press.

Herrmann, C. (1997). International experiences with the Hospital Anxiety and Depression Scale: A review of validation data and clinical results. *Journal of Psychosomatic Research, 42*, 17–41.

Hilton, T. M., Parker, G., McDonald, S., Heruc, G. A., Olley, A., Brotchie, H., Friend, C., Walsh, W. F. (2006). A validation study of two brief measures of depression in the cardiac population: The DMI-10 and DMI-18. *Psychosomatics, 47*, 129–135.

Hirschfeld, R. M. A., Lewis, L., & Vornik, L. A. (2003). Perceptions and impact of bipolar disorder: How far have we really come? Results of the National Depressive and Manic–Depressive Association 2000 survey of individuals with bipolar disorder. *Journal of Clinical Psychiatry, 64*, 161–174.

Hirschfeld, R. M. A., Williams, J. B. W., Spitzer, R. L., Calabrese, J. R., Flynn, L., Keck, P. E. Jr., … Walsh, W. F. (2000). Development and validation of a screening instrument for bipolar spectrum disorder: The Mood Disorder Questionnaire. *American Journal of Psychiatry, 157*, 1873–1875.

Huang, F. Y., Chung, H., Kroenke, K., Delucchi, K. L., & Spitzer, R. L. (2006). Using the Patient Health Questionnaire-9 to measure depression among racially and ethnically diverse primary care patients. *Journal of General Internal Medicine, 21*, 547–552.

Irwin, M., Artin, K., & Oxman, M. N. (1999). Screening for depression in the older adult. *Archives of Internal Medicine, 159*, 1701–1704.

Jenerette, C., Funk, M., & Murdaugh, C. (2005). Sickle cell disease: A stigmatizing condition that may lead to depression. *Issues in Mental Health Nursing, 26,* 1081–1101.

Kalali, A., Bech, P., Williams, J., Kobak, K., Lipsitz, J., Engelhardt, N. … Rothman, M. (2002). The New GRID-HAM-D: Results from field trials. *European Neuropsychopharmacology, 12*(S3), 239.

Kivelae, S., & Pahkala, K. (1987). Factor structure of the Zung Self-Rating Depression Scale among a depressed elderly population. *International Journal of Psychology, 22,* 289–300.

Koenig, H. G. (2006). Predictors of depression outcomes in medical inpatients with chronic pulmonary disease. *American Journal of Geriatric Psychiatry, 14,* 939–948.

Kroenke, K., Spitzer, R. L., & Williams, J. B. (2001). The PHQ-9: Validity of a brief depression severity measure. *Journal of General Internal Medicine, 16,* 606–613.

Kroenke, K., Spitzer, R. L., & Williams, J. B. (2003). The Patient Health Questionnaire-2: Validity of a two-item depression screener. *Medical Care, 41,* 1284–1292.

Kupfer, D. J., First, M. B., & Regier, D. A. (2002). *A research agenda for DSM-V.* Washington, DC: American Psychiatric Association.

Lespérance, F., & Frasure-Smith, N. (2000). Depression in patients with cardiac disease: A practical review. *Journal of Psychosomatic Research, 48,* 379–391.

Levant, R. F. (2004). The empirically validated treatments movement: A practitioner/educator perspective. *Clinical Psychology: Science and Practice, 11,* 219–224.

Löwe, B., Gräfe, K., Zipfel, S., Witte, S., Loerch, B., & Herzog, W. (2004). Diagnosing ICD 10 depressive episodes: Superior criterion validity of the Patient Health Questionnaire. *Psychotherapy and Psychosomatics, 73,* 386–390.

Löwe, B., Spitzer, R. L., Gräfe, K., Kroenke, K., Quenter, A., Zipfel, S., … Herzog, W. (2004). Comparative validity of three screening questionnaires for DSM-IV depressive disorders and physicians' diagnoses. *Journal of Affective Disorders, 78,* 131–140.

Mangelli, L., Benazzi, F., & Fava, G. A. (2005). Assessing the community prevalence of bipolar spectrum symptoms by the Mood Disorder Questionnaire. *Psychotherapy and Psychosomatics, 74,* 120–122.

McIntyre, R. S., Kennedy, S., Bagby, R. M., & Bakish, D. (2002). Assessing full remission. *Journal of Psychiatry & Neuroscience, 27,* 235–239.

McIntyre, R. S., Konarski, J. Z., Mancini, D. A., Fulton, K. A., Parikh, S. V., Grigoriadis, S. … Kennedy, S. H. (2005). Measuring the severity of depression and remission in primary care: Validation of the HAMD-7 scale. *Canadian Medical Association Journal, 173,* 1327–1334.

Miller, C. J., Klugman, J., Berv, D. A., Rosenquist, K. J., & Ghaemi, S. N. (2004). Sensitivity and specificity of the Mood Disorder Questionnaire for detecting bipolar disorder. *Journal of Affective Disorders, 81*, 167–171.

Muñoz, R. F., McQuaid, J. R., Gonzalez, G. M., Dimas, J., & Rosales, V. A. (1999). Depression screening in a women's clinic using automated Spanish and English language voice recognition. *Journal of Consulting and Clinical Psychology, 67*, 502–510.

Nezu, A. M., & Nezu, C. M. (1993). Identifying and selecting target problems for clinical interventions: A problem-solving model. *Psychological Assessment, 5*, 254–263.

Nezu, A. M., Nezu, C. M., & Cos, T. A. (2007). Case formulation for the behavioural and cognitive therapies: A problem-solving perspective. In T. D. Eells (Ed.), *Handbook of psychotherapy case formulation* (2nd ed., pp. 349–378). New York: Guilford.

Nezu, C. M., Nezu, A. M., & Foster, S. L. (2000). A 10-step guide to selecting assessment measures in clinical and research settings. In A. M. Nezu, G. F. Ronan, E. A. Meadows, & K. S. McClure (Eds), *Practitioner's guide to empirically based measures of depression* (pp. 17–24). New York: Kluwer Academic/Plenum Publishers.

Nezu, A. M., Nezu, C. M., & Jain, D. (2005). *The emotional wellness way to cardiac health: How letting go of depression, anxiety, and anger can heal your heart.* Oakland, CA: New Harbinger.

Nezu, A. M., Nezu, C. M., & Lombardo, E. R. (2004). *Cognitive-behavioural case formulation and treatment design: A problem-solving approach.* New York: Springer.

Nezu, A. M., Nezu, C. M., Friedman, J., & Lee, M. (forthcoming). Assessment of depression. In I. H. Gotlib & C. L. Hammen (Eds), *Handbook of depression and its treatment* (2nd edn). New York: Guilford.

Nezu, A. M., Nezu, C. M., Lee, M., & Stern, J. B. (2014). Assessment of depression. In I. H. Gotlib & C. L. Hammen (Eds.), *Handbook of depression* (3rd edn, pp. 25–44). New York: Guilford.

Nezu, A. M., Ronan, G. F., Meadows, E. A., & McClure, K. S. (2000). *Practitioner's guide to empirically based measures of depression.* New York: Kluwer Academic/Plenum Publishers.

Ogles, B. M., France, C. R., Lunnen, K. M., Bell, M. T., & Goldfarb, M. (1998). Computerized depression screening and awareness. *Community Mental Health Journal, 34*, 27–38.

Parker G., & Gladstone G. (2004). Capacity of the DMI-10 depression in the medically ill screening measure to detect depression 'caseness' in psychiatric outpatients. *Psychiatry Research, 127*, 283–287.

Parker, G., Hilton, T., Bains, J., & Hadzi-Pavlovic, D. (2002). Cognitive-based measures screening for depression in the medically ill: The DMI-10 and DMI-18. *Acta Psychiatrica Scandinavia, 105*, 419–426.

Parker, G., Hilton, T., Hadzi-Pavlovic, & Irvine, P. (2003). Clinical and personality correlates of a new measure of depression: A general practice study. *Australian and New Zealand Journal of Psychiatry, 37*, 104–109.

Radloff, L. S. (1977). The CES-D Scale: A self-report depression scale for research in the general population. *Applied Psychological Measurement, 1*, 385–401.

Rogers, R. (2001). Schedule of Affective Disorders and Schizophrenia (SADS). In R. Rogers (Ed.), *Handbook of diagnostic and structured interviewing* (pp. 84–102). New York: Guilford.

Rush, A. J., Carmody, T., & Reimitz, P. E. (2000). The Inventory of Depressive Symptomatology (IDS): Clinician (IDS-C) and self-report (IDS-SR) ratings of depressive symptoms. *International Journal of Methods in Psychiatric Research, 9*, 45–59.

Rush, A. J., Gullion, C. M., Basco, M. R., Jarrett, R. B., & Trivedi, M. H. (1996). The Inventory of Depressive Symptomatology (IDS): Psychometric properties. *Psychological Medicine, 26*, 477–486.

Rush, A. J., Giles, D. E., Schlesser, M. A., Fulton, C. L., Weissenburger, & Burns, C. (1986). The Inventory for Depressive Symptomatology (IDS): Preliminary findings. *Psychiatry Research, 18*, 65–87.

Rush, A. J., Bernstein, I. H., Trivedi, M. H., Carmody, T. J., Wisniewski, S., Mundt, J. C. … Fava, M. (2006). An evaluation of the Quick Inventory of Depressive Symptomatology and the Hamilton Rating Scale for Depression: A Sequenced Treatment Alternatives to Relieve Depression trial report. *Biological Psychiatry, 59*, 493–501.

Rush, A. J., Trivedi, M. H., Ibrahim, H. M., Carmody, T. J., Arnow, B., Klein, D. N. … Keller, M. B. (2003). The 16-item Quick Inventory of Depressive Symptomatology (QIDS), clinician rating (QIDS-C), and self-report (QIDS-SR): A psychometric evaluation in patients with chronic major depression. *Biological Psychiatry, 54*, 573–583.

Sakamoto, S., Kijima, N., Tomoda, A., & Kambara, M. (1998). Factor structures of the Zung Self-Rating Depression Scale (SDS) for undergraduates. *Journal of Clinical Psychology, 54*, 477–487.

Santor, D. A., Gregus, M., & Welch, A. (2006). Eight decades of measurement in depression. *Measurement, 4*, 135–155.

Segal, D. L., Hersen, M., & Van Hasselt, V. B. (1994). Reliability of the Structured Clinical Interview for DSM-III-R: Evaluative Review. *Comprehensive Psychiatry, 35*, 316–327.

Solomon, D. A., Leon, A. C., Maser, J. D., Truman, C. J., Coryell, W., Endicott, J. … Keller, M. B. (2006). Distinguishing bipolar major depression from unipolar major depression with the Screening Assessment of Depression–Polarity (SAD-P). *Journal of Clinical Psychiatry, 67*, 434–442.

Spitzer, R. L., Endicott, J., & Robins, E. (1978). Research diagnostic criteria. *Archives of General Psychiatry, 35*, 773–782.

Spitzer, R. L., Kroenke, K., & Williams, J. B. (1999). Patient Health Questionnaire Study Group: Validity and utility of a self-report version of PRIME-MD: The PHQ Primary Care Study. *Journal of the American Medical Association, 282*, 1737–1744.

Spitzer, R. L., Williams, J. B., Kroenke, K., Linzer, M., deGruy, F. V., Hahn, S. R., Brody, D., & Johnson, J. G. (1994). Utility of a new procedure for diagnosing mental disorders in primary care: The PRIME-MD 1000 study. *Journal of the American Medical Association, 272*, 1749–1756.

Trivedi, M. H., Rush, A. J., Ibrahim, H. M., Carmody, T. J., Biggs, M. M., Suppes, T. … Johnson, J. G. (2004). The Inventory of Depressive Symptomatology, clinician rating (IDS-C) and self-report (IDS-SR), and the Quick Inventory of Depressive Symptomatology, clinician rating (QIDS-C), and self-report (QIDS-SR) in public sector patients with mood disorders: A psychometric evaluation. *Psychological Medicine, 34*, 73–82.

Verdier-Talilefer, M. H., Gourlet, V., Fuhrer, R., & Alperovitch, A. (2001). Psychometric properties of the Center for Epidemiologic Studies–Depression Scale in multiple sclerosis. *Neuroepidemiology, 20*, 262–267.

Vuorilehto, M., Melartin, T., & Isometsa, E. (2006). Depressive disorders in primary care: Recurrent, chronic, and co-morbid. *Psychological Medicine, 35*, 673–682.

Wexler, D. J., Grant, R. W., Wittenberg, E., Bosch, J. L., Cagliero, E., & Delahanty, L. (2006). Correlates of health-related quality of life in type 2 diabetes. *Diabetologia, 49*, 1489–1497.

Williams, J. B. W. (1988). A structured interview guide for the Hamilton Depression Rating Scale. *Archives of General Psychiatry, 45*, 742–747.

Zigmond, A. S., & Snaith, R. P. (1983). The Hospital Anxiety and Depression Scale. *Acta Psychiatrica Scandinavica, 67*, 361–370.

Zung, W. W. K. (1965). A self-rating depression scale. *Archives of General Psychiatry, 12*, 63–70.

Further Reading

First, M. B., Gibbon, M., Spitzer, R. L., & Williams, J. B. (1996). *Structured Clinical Interview for DSM-IV Axis 1 disorders (non-patient edition) (SCID-I/NP, Version 2.0)*. New York: Biometrics Research Department, New York State Psychiatric Institute.

Nezu, A. M., Nezu, C. M., Trunzo, J. J., & McClure, K. S. (1998). Treatment maintenance for unipolar depression: Relevant issues, literature review, and recommendations for research and clinical practice. *Clinical Psychology: Science & Practice, 5*, 496–512.

3

The Efficacy of Cognitive Behavioural Therapy for Depression

Robin B. Jarrett and Jeffrey R. Vittengl

Cognitive behavioural therapy (CBT) is a leading, scientifically evaluated treatment for major depressive disorder (MDD), other psychiatric disorders, and psychological problems. Here we use the terms 'cognitive therapy' (CT) and 'cognitive behavioural therapy' interchangeably, to refer to interventions that grew out of (1) learning theory and functional analysis (Ferster, 1973) and social learning theory (Bandura, 1977) and (2) phenomenological or perceptual models of human behaviour (Kelly, 1955; Beck, 2005). We think of CBT as an umbrella term, comprehensive enough to cover its early, 'traditional' referents (e.g., Beck, Rush, Shaw, & Emery, 1979; Rehm, 1981) as well as later, 'developing' interventions that some call 'the third wave' (Öst, 2008) – while they differ as to which formulations within CBT comprise each of the three 'waves'. These developing interventions include mindfulness-based cognitive therapy, metacognitive therapy, and acceptance and commitment therapy, which are described in this volume. In spite of our broad application of terminology, we are aware of the spirited theoretical differences that proponents articulate (as discussed in chapter 10). We hope that these theoretical distinctions will promote testable hypotheses that can advance our understanding of the role of psychosocial variables and of language (including psychotherapy) on the course of mood disorders (and related ones). Nevertheless, it remains to be seen to what extent the language used by the proponents of each wave of CBT will result in noticeable distinctions in application and will produce measurable and meaningful differences in depressed patients' lives.

Treating Depression: MCT, CBT and Third Wave Therapies, First Edition.
Edited by Adrian Wells and Peter L. Fisher.

In this chapter we highlight the significant contributions that CBT has made to increasing the array of effective treatment options for patients with MDD (e.g., Beck, 2005). In our empirical summary of the efficacy of CBT for depressed adults, we aim to ask critical questions in order to 'raise the bar' for what clinicians and patients may expect from future research on psychosocial treatments for mood disorders. The challenges and standards that we highlight for CBT apply at least to the same degree to other interventions – both already established (e.g., interpersonal psychotherapy, pharmacotherapy) and developing ones (e.g., mindfulness-based cognitive therapy, on which see chapters 8 and 14; metacognitive therapy, on which see chapters 6 and 12; and acceptance and commitment therapy, on which see chapter 13). We aim to raise the standards in conceptualizing and operationalizing outcomes. Here we focus on outcomes such as psychosocial functioning and symptoms; however, additional dependent variables are also important. For example, an important developing literature suggests that CBT for mood disorders is financially cost-effective (Myhr & Payne, 2006; Layard, 2006a, 2006b). Other aspects of rigorous evaluation are also important but are omitted here due to space (see Öst, 2008 for well-applied standards and established methods for evaluating clinical research – e.g., the psychotherapy outcome study methodology rating form).

MDD is a common illness, typically chronic or recurrent, with prominent personal, relational, and public health consequences. The lifetime prevalence of MDD is about 16 per cent (Kessler, Berglund, Demler, Jin, & Walters, 2005), and most people with MDD experience multiple major depressive episodes (Judd, 1997; Mueller et al., 1999), each episode increasing the risk of another relapse or recurrence (Solomon et al., 2000; Mueller et al., 1999). Life interference (e.g., lost work productivity, poorer functioning in social relationships, mortality, lower quality of life) due to acute depressive episodes and subthreshold symptoms before and after episodes is at least comparable to life interference in other chronic illnesses – even cancer, diabetes, and heart disease (Simon, 2003; Murray & Lopez, 1996). This underscores the need to develop the most effective (in terms of outcomes and financial costs) and accessible interventions for the public's benefit (Layard 2006a, 2006b).

We focus the present critical review of the outcomes of CBT for MDD on the time-limited treatments that developed around Beck and colleagues' (1979) manual *Cognitive Therapy of Depression*, because these treatments have been the primary focus of efficacy research on CBT for depression (see chapters 5 and 11 for descriptions of, and initial data relevant to, developing strategies within CBT for depression).

Acute-phase CBT contains behavioural components that may activate patients, in spite of their negative affect and pessimistic predictions, to seek and receive reinforcement from their natural environments, as reinforcement is often reduced when patients are depressed. CBT is also designed to reduce depressive symptoms by helping patients to identify thoughts associated with negative affect and by teaching them to test the validity of these thoughts through logical and empirical methods. In so doing, patients learn to generate more realistic alternatives when negative thoughts are not supported by the available information and to initiate and complete problem solving when they are. We acknowledge that the necessity and order of, and the distinctions between, so-called behavioural (radical or otherwise) and cognitive (including content and processing) components of CBT continue to be debated among us.

Current understanding of the causes and the pathology of MDD is incomplete (see, e.g., chapter 4), and all existing treatments produce suboptimal outcomes for many patients. Historically researchers have focused on the short-term reduction of depressive symptoms, but now they are beginning to examine longer range outcomes and measure psychosocial functioning in ways that capture results important to patients and clinicians. Existing interventions vary in side effects, cost, availability, and endurance of positive effects. By asking hard questions and by raising the standard of what constitutes treatment success, we hope to encourage those who work in our field to build on the successes of CBT and advance treatment improvement and innovation in the next generation.

We assert that the goal for our field is to articulate how mood disorders can be prevented and cured. We assert that current and future research can be evaluated on the basis of the extent to which it advances this goal. Affordable treatments that are effective and can be made available to improve public health internationally would be major innovations in the field. It is with this optimism and enthusiasm for the future that we ask questions below about what we really know concerning the effectiveness of CBT for depression in adults.

First we consider the literature on the efficacy of the acute-phase CBT offered to adults with depression. We then consider studies of continuation-phase CT treatment (C-CT) after patients achieve a response (i.e., when depressive symptoms are substantially reduced or eliminated) following an acute-phase intervention. For the joint purpose of providing evidence that may guide current practice in CBT and of raising questions for future research, we review the strengths as well as the current limits of CBT in producing and maintaining health. We will assert that (1) research on and practice of CBT must move beyond short-term symptom reduction to achieve long-term health, and (2) the field of basic and applied research needs to focus on the goal of *preventing and curing* mood disorders rather than settling for transient symptom reduction and omitting assessment of other crucial aspects of human functioning.

As a heuristic, we use changes in the course of depressive illness to help us organize the existing literature. Depressed patients' symptom levels and diagnostic status at different points during and after treatment may be described using the terms 'response', 'remission', 'recovery', 'relapse', and 'recurrence'. Throughout this chapter we follow definitions of these terms established by the MacArthur Foundation (Frank et al., 1991) and reinforced by the American College of Neuropsychopharmacology (Rush et al., 2006). In particular, acute-phase treatment (e.g., CBT) is applied with the goal of first producing a response defined as a clinically important reduction in depressive symptoms (e.g., 50 per cent reduction in Hamilton Rating Scale for Depression [HRSD] scores: see Rush et al., 2006). Remission follows response when the diagnostic criteria for a major depressive episode are no longer met and reduced symptom levels are maintained for several weeks (the specific interval varies across investigations and can range from days to months). Remission may be 'full' when patients have very low or no remaining depressive symptoms or only 'partial' when residual symptoms continue. Acute-phase treatments often are discontinued after remission but may be followed by continuation-phase treatments (e.g., C-CT) with the goals of reducing relapse and recurrence and of producing recovery. Recovery follows remission when diagnostic criteria for a major depressive episode are not met and lowered symptoms levels are maintained for several months, although, like the preceding course-of-illness markers, sub-syndromal symptoms may persist. Persistent recovery is the goal of maintenance-phase treatments. Unfortunately, too many patients relapse when they meet the criteria for a major depressive episode after remission but before recovery. After recovery, patients will have a recurrence when they meet the criteria for a major depressive episode. We note that, although recommendations to standardize the field's use of these changes points is more than two decades old, one investigator's 'recovery' is still another investigator's 'remission'.

How Much does Acute-Phase CBT Reduce Depressive Symptoms?

Acute-phase CBT typically consists of 16–20 sessions spread over 3–4 months. These sessions have the purpose of teaching people compensatory skills and different ways thinking to reduce the symptoms of and their own vulnerability to MDD (e.g., Beck et al., 1979). Acute-phase CBT has been evaluated in a number of clinical studies of adults, including several major randomized clinical trials (RCTs) that compared acute-phase CBT to active (e.g., pharmacotherapy, behaviour therapy) or nonactive (e.g., placebo, waitlist) control conditions. Patients with MDD who complete acute-phase CBT on average experience a large reduction – usually 1–3 standard deviations (*SD*s) – in depressive symptoms (e.g., Craighead, Sheets, Brosse, & Ilardi, 2007; Vittengl, Clark, Kraft, & Jarrett, 2005), as measured by instruments such as the Hamilton Rating Scale for Depression (HRSD) clinical interview (Hamilton, 1960) and the Beck Depression Inventory (BDI) self-report questionnaire (Beck, Ward, Mendelson, Mock, & Erbaugh, 1961). Similarly, about 50–70 per cent of patients who complete acute-phase CBT no longer meet the criteria for a major depressive episode (e.g., Cuijpers, Karyotaki, et al., 2014; Craighead et al., 2007).

Because improvement due to environmental and biological changes unrelated to protocol treatment may account for some patients' gains during any treatment for depression, comparisons of acute-phase CBT with non-active and other active treatments provide better estimates of acute-phase CBT's effects than simple pre- to post-treatment changes. One way to quantify differences between treatment groups involves computing effect size d, the difference between treatment groups' symptom measure means in standard deviation (*SD*) units (Cohen, 1988). For example, if at the end of a clinical trial the average BDI score in the treatment group is 8, the average BDI in the control group is 15, and the *SD* for the BDI is 10 in both groups, then $d = .70$ is in favour of the treatment group. Here d is computed as $(15–8)/10 = .70$. Effect size d from many studies can be combined through meta-analysis to yield an overall estimate of a treatment's effectiveness.

In their summary of meta-analyses, Butler, Chapman, Forman, and Beck (2006) found – on the basis of Gloaguen, Cottraux, Cucherat, and Blackburn (1998) – that acute-phase CBT compared favourably to wait list/placebo ($d = .82$, a large effect), pharmacotherapy ($d = .38$, a small effect), and behaviour therapy ($d = .05$, a trivial effect). As a point of comparison, a meta-analysis of clinical trials submitted to the US Food and Drug

Administration suggested that antidepressant pharmacotherapy yields an effect size of .32 by comparison to pill placebo (Kirsch et al., 2008). Butler et al. (2006) noted, however, that the advantage of acute-phase CBT over pharmacotherapy may be overestimated due to the fact that early studies provided suboptimal pharmacotherapy. Similarly, other reviews (e.g., Hollon et al., 2005; Cuijpers, Weitz, et al., 2014) and subsequent RCTs (e.g., DeRubeis, et al., 2005; Segal et al., 2006) suggest that acute-phase pharmacotherapy and acute-phase CBT do not differ significantly in reducing depressive symptoms.

A third RCT comparing acute-phase CBT, behaviour therapy, and pharmacotherapy (Dimidjian et al., 2006) revealed no significant differences among treatments for less severely depressed patients, but an advantage of behaviour therapy and of pharmacotherapy over acute-phase CBT in more severely depressed patients (scores $\geq$ 20 on HRSD). The latter finding recalls the somewhat poorer performance of acute-phase CBT by comparison to pharmacotherapy and to interpersonal psychotherapy for more severely depressed patients in the National Institute of Mental Health Treatment of Depression Collaborative Research Program (Elkin et al., 1989). DeRubeis et al. (2005) have shown, however, that more severely depressed patients (HRSD $\geq$ 20) can be treated with acute-phase CBT safely and effectively by comparison to pharmacotherapy (e.g., 58 per cent response rate in both conditions; 46 per cent remission rate for pharmacotherapy and 40 per cent for CBT; 16 per cent attrition from pharmacotherapy and 15 per cent from CBT). One possibility in the negative studies is that therapists need more extensive training or greater consultation in order to produce positive outcomes in patients with more severe depression (Hollon et al., 2005). As we discuss below, if this hypothesis receives support, it will be important to identify CBT's 'active' ingredients and to develop practical, accessible educational programmes that teach therapists and patients these critical processes in order to increase CBT's impact on public health.

Continuous effect sizes, such as *d*, are very useful in quantifying average treatment effects in a research context. Arguably, *d* is less useful in clinical contexts when considerations for individual patients are discrete (e.g., making the prescriptive decision: Should this patient be treated with acute-phase CBT? What are the chances of a positive response to treatment?). Cohen (1988) offered the U_3 statistic, which is useful in making clinical decisions. This statistic may be interpreted as the proportion of people in a treatment group (e.g., acute-phase CBT) with better outcomes (e.g., lower symptom scores) than the average person in the comparison group (e.g., placebo,

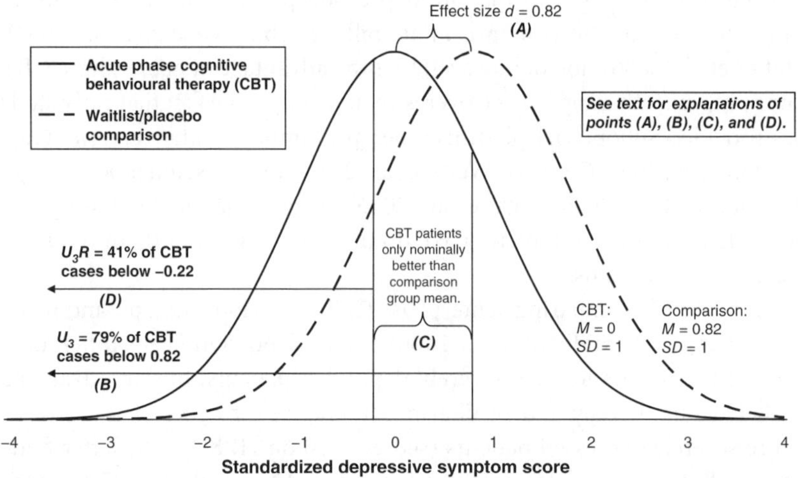

Figure 3.1 Proportion of acute-phase CBT patients with symptom scores nominally (U_3) and reliably (U_3R) better than the average patient in waitlist/placebo. Copyright ©: J. R. Vittengl, Truman State University, and R. B. Jarrett, the University of Texas Southwestern Medical Center at Dallas. Reprinted with permission from the authors.

waitlist, or other depression-specific treatment). U_3 can be estimated easily by locating *d* (the difference between means [*M*s] in standard deviation [*SD*] units) in the standard normal curve and identifying the proportion of observations below this threshold (e.g., consult the *z* table at the back of a statistics textbook). For example, for treatments that do not differ ($d = .00$), half of the patients have scores at least nominally lower than the average of the comparison group (i.e., $U_3 = 50$ per cent, because 50 per cent of scores in the standard normal distribution are below zero).

Butler et al. (2006) computed U_3 for acute-phase CBT using Gloaguen et al.'s (1998) effect sizes. They reported that 79 per cent of patients treated with CBT have lower BDI scores than the average patient in the waitlist or placebo group (see Figure 3.1), 65 per cent have lower BDI scores than expected from pharmacotherapy, and 52 per cent have lower BDI scores than expected from behaviour therapy. The remaining patients treated with acute-phase CBT have the same BDI scores as (or higher than) those expected from placebo/waitlist (21 per cent), pharmacotherapy (35 per cent), and behaviour therapy (48 per cent). These numbers, again, support the efficacy of acute-phase CBT, especially by comparison to the waitlist and placebo groups.

An important limitation of U_3 is that the statistic counts any score in the acute-phase CBT distribution that is nominally better than the comparison group mean. For example, U_3 includes trivial differences, such as CBT patients who score only 1 point lower on the BDI than the average patient in the waitlist or placebo group. Neil Jacobson and colleagues (e.g., Jacobson & Truax, 1991; Jacobson, Roberts, Berns, & McGlinchey, 1999) challenged researchers and clinicians to consider the psychometric properties of symptom measures in deciding whether individual patients' scores differ reliably (e.g., before vs after test, or in comparison to a benchmark). If symptom measures like the BDI and the HRSD were perfectly reliable ($r = 1.0$), then U_3 would directly signal the proportion of patients who are reliably (not just nominally) better than the average score in the comparison group. In reality depressive symptom measures such as the BDI and the HRSD usually offer acceptable but always imperfect reliability (e.g., r is often in the range .7–.9). Consequently, we suggest that U_3 should be corrected to reflect the proportion of acute-phase CBT patients who are reliably ($p < .05$) better than the average patient in the comparison group. We named this reliable-difference statistic U_3R (i.e., U_3 corrected for reliable differences in scores).

We computed U_3R by subtracting patients from U_3 who are only nominally (not reliably) better than the average patient in the comparison group. First we considered the magnitude of difference in individual scores (e.g., between a patient in acute-phase CBT and the average patient in the control group) necessary to be reliable. Following Jacobson and Truax's (1991) formula for the standard error of difference, two scores on the same measure are reliably different at $p < .05$, two-tailed, when they are at least $1.96\sqrt{2 - 2r}\ SD$ apart – where 1.96 reflects the threshold in the standard normal distribution for $p < .05$, two-tailed, and r is the reliability of the symptom measure (e.g., the HRSD or BDI). For instance, on measures with reliabilities of .7, .8, and .9, acute-phase CBT patients' scores must differ at least 1.52, 1.24, and .88 SD from the comparison group mean if they are to be reliably different. We then considered that effect size d represents an overall shift in the distribution of scores from which these thresholds can be subtracted to correct U_3 and compute U_3R. If a measure with reliability $r = .70$ generates an effect size $d = 1.00$ in meta-analysis, then $U_3 = 84$ per cent of patients are nominally better than the average person in the control group, but $U_3R = 30$ per cent of patients are reliably better than the average person in the control group, for example. Here U_3 is derived as 84 per cent of scores below 1.00 in the standard normal curve, and U_3R is derived as 30 per cent of scores below −.52 (computed 1.00 – 1.52 = −.52).

We applied Seggar, Lambert, and Hansen's (2002) estimate of the BDI's reliability (.86) to Gloaguen et al.'s (1998) effect size for acute-phase CBT versus waitlist or placebo (.82) to compute U_3R. As shown in Figure 3.1, the effect size $d = .82$ can be represented as the difference between the standardized depressive symptom mean of .82 in the waitlist or placebo comparison group and the mean of .00 in the CBT group (see point *A* in Figure 3.1). That is, the CBT group has a mean symptom score .82 *SD* lower than the comparison group at the end of acute-phase treatment. In the distribution of CBT scores, 79 per cent of cases are at least nominally below the comparison group mean of .82. This 79 per cent is the U_3 statistic (see point *B* in Figure 3.1). However, because the BDI is not perfectly reliable, some of the CBT cases below .82 are not reliably lower than .82 (see point *C* in Figure 3.1). Given a reliability coefficient of .86 for the BDI, only CBT cases that are at least 1.04 *SD* below .82 are reliably better ($p < .05$) than the average patient in the comparison group. Here 1.04 is computed as $1.96\sqrt{2 - 2(.86)}$. We subtracted 1.04 from the mean of the comparison group (.82), and this yielded a position of −.22 in the standard normal curve. About 41 per cent of CBT observations fall below −.22 (see point *D* in Figure 3.1). This 41 per cent is the U_3R statistic. Consequently, when including this correction for 'imperfect measurement', we estimated that patients who receive CBT have a 41 per cent chance of a reliably lower BDI score than the average patient in the placebo or waitlist control groups.

It is interesting to note that our 41 per cent estimate for acute-phase CBT is comparable to the estimate (derived by different methods) that only 40 per cent of depressed patients who respond to pharmacotherapy improve due to specific biological effects of the medication instead of placebo effects (Hollon, Thase, & Markowitz, 2002). Future researchers may want to refine our 41 per cent estimate if better estimates for effect size *d* or for the reliability of BDI become available. The purpose of U_3R here is to emphasize the finding that too many patients (roughly 59 per cent) leave acute-phase CBT *without* reliably greater improvement than expected from controls in the waitlist or placebo group. Clinically, we call this outcome a 'non-response' and, empirically, we have very little data guiding us how to best treat acute-phase CBT non-responders. For example, we do not know whether they are best treated by switching to pharmacotherapy or by some other psychosocial intervention. This is a major gap; and it affects patients' lives. Similarly, it is unknown whether either of these treatments might be efficaciously combined with acute-phase CBT to reduce depressive symptoms and to begin to improve psychosocial functioning. Research on the moderators and mechanisms for acute-phase CBT non-response is an area ripe for both applied and basic research. The field will benefit from methodological standards and illustrations of how to best design studies and analyze data that are focused on addressing these gaps.

How Many Patients Are Well at Exit from Acute-Phase CBT?

Previous reviews suggest that about 50 per cent of the patients who begin acute-phase CBT will respond to this treatment (e.g., Hollon et al., 2005), and more recent RCTs are similar (e.g., 58 per cent in Dimidjian et al., 2006; 58 per cent in DeRubeis et al., 2005; 72 per cent CBT *completers* in Segal et al., 2006; 56 per cent in Jarrett, Minhajuddin, Gershenfeld, Friedman, & Thase, 2013). The concept of response involves (1) the assumption that the patient changes due to acute-phase CBT; and (2) the observation that the patient's depressive symptoms decrease by some relative (e.g., ≥ 50 per cent reduction in BDI) or some absolute (e.g., HRSD ≤ 10 and no MDD), a priori criterion by which 'response' is defined (e.g., Rush et al., 2006). Our estimate that 41 per cent of patients treated with acute-phase CBT have reliably lower scores than those expected from the waitlist and placebo groups is quite conservative, but not dramatically lower than a 50 per cent response rate based on observed symptom scores. Thus the assumption, in the concept of response, that patients change due to acute-phase CBT may usually be satisfied by the symptom thresholds selected for response (e.g., defining the response as a reduction of at least 50 per cent in symptoms may filter out most patients who improve only by smaller amounts, due to extra treatment changes in biology or in the environment).

On the other hand, traditional symptom thresholds that define response are not rigorous enough to capture 'wellness', in part because they can involve simple reductions in scores. For example, persons whose symptoms do not meet DSM-IV and DSM-V criteria for MDD often report significant impairment in major social roles (e.g., at work and in relationships with family and friends). These persons include depressed patients who respond to treatment but often do not fully 'remit' (e.g., they have 'subthreshold' symptoms; Zimmerman, Posternak, & Chelminski, 2007) and persons with dysthymic disorder (e.g., Leader & Klein, 1996). Moreover, residual symptoms after response to acute-phase treatment are a powerful predictor of relapse and recurrence (Jarrett et al., 2001; Fava, Fabbri, & Sonino, 2002). In short, patients with depressive symptoms below the threshold for a diagnosis of MDD frequently are not normalized in their psychosocial functioning, with significant consequences for public health (e.g. Judd, Schettler, & Akiskal, 2002). Consequently we suggest that the goal of an adequate trial of CBT (e.g., acute-phase CBT, followed by C-CT, if needed) is to produce *sustained remission that develops into full recovery* (i.e., to achieve an asymptomatic status that lasts).

To illustrate one approach to identifying asymptomatic status, we selected cut-offs on the BDI and HRSD on the basis of two types of data. First, Grundy, Lambert, and Grundy (1996) and Seggar et al. (2002) identified cut-off scores on the 17-item HRSD (3.97) and on the BDI (4.09) respectively: individuals below these scores are more likely to belong to the asymptomatic population than to the general population – considering its relatively high prevalence of MDD and other depressive disorders. Second, scores of HRSD ≥ 4 (on the 17-item scale) and of BDI ≥ 5 mark the point on the continuum of residual symptomatology at which C-CT begins to reduce relapse or recurrence significantly by comparison to discontinued acute-phase CBT (Jarrett, Vittengl, & Clark, 2008). Consequently we selected scores of HRSD ≤ 3 and BDI ≤ 4 as representing asymptomatic outcomes after acute-phase CBT. Other thresholds for asymptomatic status are of course possible (e.g., Zimmerman et al., 2007, suggested HRSD ≤ 2), and some authors advocate the addition of positive markers of well-being (e.g., autonomy, mastery, self-acceptance) to low symptom levels in defining recovery (Fava, Ruini, & Belaise, 2007).

We compared HRSD ≤ 3 and BDI ≤ 4 cut-offs to data from the major clinical trials summarized for acute-phase CBT (Craighead et al., 2007) in the influential text *A Guide to Treatments that Work* (Nathan & Gorman, 2007). As shown in Table 3.1, we gathered summary statistics (*N*, *M*, and *SD*, or *SE* used to estimate *SD*) available in the published reports (with the exception of O'Leary & Beach, 1990, from which insufficient data were available) and added two recent RCTs from which sufficient data were available (Dimidjian et al., 2006, and Segal et al., 2006; insufficient data were available in DeRubeis et al., 2005). Craighead et al. (2007) counted Keller et al.'s (2000) Cognitive Behavioral Analysis System of Psychotherapy (CBASP) trial (McCullough, 2000) as a behaviour therapy, although some may view CBASP as a variant of acute-phase CBT, albeit with additional theories and unique interventions. Consequently, we computed estimates with and

Table 3.1 Examples of depressive symptom levels at exit from acute phase cognitive therapy for depression.

	Hamilton Rating Scale for Depression (HRSD)			*Beck Depression Inventory (BDI)*		
Source	*N*	*M*	*SD*	*N*	*M*	*SD*
Blackburn et al. (1997)	24	10.70	7.60	24	19.00	12.50
Dimidjian et al. (2006)	34	8.85	6.22	35	13.71	12.53
Elkin et al. (1989)	37	7.60	5.80	37	10.20	8.70
Hollon et al. (1992)	16	8.80	7.80	16	7.90	9.50
Jacobson et al. (1991)	20	4.49	2.78	20	6.49	6.57
Jacobson et al. (1996)	44	6.80	5.70	44	9.70	9.20
Jarrett et al. (1999)	36	10.25[a]	8.10[a]	36	11.72	9.72
Keller et al. (2000)	216	15.10[b]	10.14[b]	—	—	—
Murphy et al. (1984)	19	6.42	6.16	19	9.53	8.21
Rush et al. (1977)	15	5.80	3.67	18	5.94	5.33
Segal et al. (2006)	88	5.84	4.67	88	10.29	10.19

[a]21-item HRSD.
[b]24-item HRSD.
Clinical trials include those summarized for acute phase CBT (Craighead et al., 2007) in the influential text *A Guide to Treatments that Work* (Nathan & Gorman, 2007), plus additional recent major studies. All HRSD values are based on the 17-item version of the instrument except as noted.

without Keller et al.'s (2000) large RCT. In addition, most trials used the 17-item version of the HRSD, but Jarrett et al. (1999) and Keller et al. (2000) reported results from the 21- and 24-item HRSD respectively. We also computed our estimates with and without Jarrett et al.'s and Keller et al.'s HRSD data.

As shown in Table 3.1, *all* of the studies' symptom means at exit from acute-phase CBT exceeded the very rigorous cut-offs for asymptomatic status (HRSD ≤ 3; BDI ≤ 4). Pooling across the samples in Table 3.1, the overall mean HRSD scores (ranging from $M = 7.04$, $SD = 5.60$ – without Keller et al., 2000 or Jarrett et al., 1999 – to $M = 10.42$, $SD = 7.88$, with both Keller et al., 2000 and Jarrett et al., 1999) and BDI ($M = 10.72$, $SD = 9.82$; Keller et al., 2000 did not report BDI data) are in the mildly depressed range. Assuming a normal distribution, the pooled *M* and *SD* indicate that only about 17–24 per cent of patients are asymptomatic on the HRSD (scores 0–3), and 25 per cent of patients are asymptomatic on the BDI (scores 0–4), at exit from acute-phase CBT. Although more precise estimates might be obtained through meta-analysis of all acute-phase CBT trials – or, better, through a 'mega-analysis' of the pooled raw data that does not assume a normal distribution and uses a consistent set of HRSD items – we believe that our substantive point is robust: most patients exit acute-phase CBT with at least residual symptoms.

Some may object that the preceding standards and analysis are too stringent. We assert, however, that even 'efficacious' interventions for depressed adults need improvement; and hypothesized improvements require rigorous evaluation. We view most of the acute-phase research on CBT for depressed adults as showing that CBT is *beginning* to reduce symptoms and to restore functioning for about half of the patients who begin this treatment. Whereas the reason for the lack of remission, sustained or otherwise, complete or partial, is undoubtedly multi-determined, one of the simplest reasons why acute-phase CBT may not produce remission and recovery in responders is that 16–20 sessions are simply an 'inadequate dose'. By this we mean that the patient received too few sessions, or the duration of treatment was too short for people who suffer from a chronic or a recurrent mood disorder. The research on preventing relapse and recurrence through CBT (described below) begins to evaluate this hypothesis.

How Many Responders to Acute-Phase CBT Relapse or Experience Recurrence?

The potential for CBT to produce enduring effects is one of its most promising features (Hollon, Steward, & Strunk, 2006). We analyzed the world's literature published through July 2006 to examine relapse (i.e., a return of the index episode) and recurrence (i.e., the development of a new episode of MDD) rates after response to CBT in adults who manifested MDD (Vittengl, Clark, Dunn, & Jarrett, 2007). A meta-analysis showed that, after acute-phase CBT is discontinued, approximately 29 per cent of responders will relapse or experience a recurrence in the first year and that this rate will grow to about 54 per cent within two years. In general, a mean proportion of 39 per cent of responders relapsed or had a recurrence over a mean of 74 weeks, on the basis of the 13 studies examined (see Table 3.2 from Vittengl et al., 2007).

There was significant variation in relapse and recurrence rates across the studies, and these rates appeared to be moderated by differences in research

Table 3.2 Comparisons of relapse/recurrence rates among acute phase treatment responders: Meta-analytic findings summarized.

Focus Treatment	*Comparison Treatment*	*Data Sources*	*Effect Size AUC (CI_{95})*	*Clinical Implication*
Acute Phase Treatments				
Acute CBT Discontinued	Acute pharmacotherapy discontinued	7 studies with data 52–104 weeks after the end of acute phase treatment.	.61 (.54– .67)	Acute CBT reduces the risk of relapse/recurrence by 22%.
Acute CBT Plus Pharmacotherapy Discontinued	Pharmacotherapy discontinued	6 studies with data 52–104 weeks after the end of acute phase treatment.	.61 (.54– .68)	Acute CBT reduces the risk of relapse/recurrence by 23%.
Acute CBT Discontinued	Acute CBT plus pharmacotherapy discontinued	3 studies with data 52–104 weeks after the end of acute phase treatment.	.51 (.42– .61)	No significant difference between treatments.
Acute CBT Discontinued	Other depression-specific psychotherapies discontinued	4 studies with data 52–104 weeks after the end of acute phase treatment.	.50 (.42– .58)	No significant difference between treatments.
Continuation Phase Treatments				
Continuation CBT	Non-Active Control	4 studies with data at the end of 35–52 weeks of continuation phase treatment.	.61 (.53-.68)	Continuation CBT reduces the risk of relapse/recurrence by 21%.
Continuation CBT	Non-active control	4 studies with data 69–312 weeks after the end of continuation phase treatment.	.64 (.57– .72)	Continuation CBT reduces the risk of relapse/recurrence by 29%.
Continuation CBT	Active control	5 studies with data at the end of 20–52 weeks of continuation phase treatment.	.56 (.50– .62)	Continuation CBT reduces the risk of relapse/recurrence by 12%.
Continuation CBT	Active control	8 studies with data 10–255 weeks after the end of continuation phase treatment.	.57 (.52– .61)	Continuation CBT reduces the risk of relapse/recurrence by 14%.

CBT = cognitive behavioral therapy; AUC = area under the curve; AUC > .50 indicates that the focus treatment produces less relapse than the comparison treatment; CI_{95} = 95% confidence interval; acute = acute phase; continuation = continuation phase.
The citations for the studies referenced above and the quantitative methods underpinning the meta-analysis can be found in Vittengl, et al., 2007.

designs (Vittengl et al., 2007). Specifically, higher relapse and recurrence rates occurred in studies that (1) had longer follow-up periods, (2) estimated relapse and recurrence by using survival analysis rather than simple proportions, (3) assessed therapist *competence* in CBT, and (4) used a diagnosis of 'major depressive episode' (MDE) to define relapse and recurrence. Lower relapse and lower recurrence were found in studies that (1) measured therapist *adherence* to CBT, (2) used cross-sectional measurement during follow-up, and (3) specified a criterion score on an instrument to define relapse and recurrence. It is important to realize that most of these seven moderators were inter-correlated and that the number of studies evaluating long-term effects after acute-phase CBT remains small. Nonetheless, this list of moderators is useful for interpreting the data available and for planning future, rigorous studies.

How Do Relapse and Recurrence Rates after Acute-Phase CBT Compare to Those of Alternative Treatments?

The meta-analysis showed that these relapse and recurrence rates were significantly lower after discontinuing acute-phase CBT than after discontinuing pharmacotherapy (Vittengl et al., 2007). This suggests that CBT has a prophylactic effect of some duration yet to be specified (see Kashner, Henley, Golden, Rush, & Jarrett, 2007, for an estimate). Effects after acute-phase CBT did not differ significantly from outcomes after other 'depression-specific psychotherapies' (e.g., behaviour therapy). Below we highlight the evidence for these conclusions.

When acute-phase treatments were discontinued, acute-phase CBT reduced relapse and recurrence significantly more than pharmacotherapy across seven studies (see Table 3.2). In fact, on the basis of the mean area under the curve (AUC), there is a 61 per cent chance that patients will have a superior outcome (they will not suffer relapse or recurrence) in acute-phase CT by comparison to pharmacotherapy alone. Six studies (see Table 3.2) showed that this finding was replicated when acute-phase pharmacotherapy was added to CBT. There was no difference when acute-phase CBT plus pharmacotherapy was compared to acute-phase CBT alone, or again when treatments were discontinued during follow-up (three studies; Table 3.2); and this suggests that acute-phase CBT is a key component in attempts to reduce relapse.

When relapse and recurrence rates after acute-phase CBT was discontinued were compared to relapse and recurrence rates after other depression-specific psychotherapies, there were no significant differences (four studies; Table 3.2). It is important to note that comparisons with other psychosocial interventions not aimed at reducing depression are yet to be completed; hence conclusions are not warranted.

Does C-CT Reduce Relapse and Recurrence among Responders to Acute-Phase Treatments?

Continuation-phase CT appears to reduce relapse further for acute-phase CBT responders, on the basis of meta-analytic reviews (Vittengl et al., 2007; Biesheuvel-Leliefeld et al., 2015; Clarke, Mayo-Wilson, Kenny, & Pilling, 2015). There have been a number of different designs used in evaluating continuation formulations of CBT, each formulation having the primary aims of reducing relapse and sustaining remission. For example, continuation-phase treatments may 'match' the acute-phase modality (first acute-phase CBT, then C-CT, as illustrated by Blackburn & Moore, 1997 and by Jarrett et al., 2001; Jarrett et al., 2013) or may employ contrasting modalities (first acute-phase pharmacotherapy, then C-CT, as illustrated by Fava et al., 2004, and by Paykel et al., 2005).

Four early studies (see Table 3.2) suggest that C-CT can reduce relapse and recurrence by comparison to non-active control conditions (e.g., assessment only, with no further protocol based treatment). In this comparison, there is a 61 per cent chance that patients treated with C-CT will have a superior outcome (not relapse or experience recurrence) when compared to non-active controls. Within these studies, the Klein et al. (2004) trial actually tested a form of maintenance-phase CBT, in that the aim was to prevent a 'recurrence': the authors had excluded the patients who had already relapsed. When C-CT was discontinued, meta-analysis suggested that patients had a 64 per cent chance of not experiencing a relapse or recurrence by comparison to controls, who did not receive an active form of continuation-phase treatment. These studies further extend the evidence that cognitive therapy has the potential to prevent or delay episodes of MDD.

Since we completed our meta-analysis, new studies have been published that are important for CBT and relapse prevention. For example, Dobson et al. (2008) compared the rates of relapse and recurrence among adults who had been diagnosed with MDD, responded to an acute-phase treatment (CT, behavioural activation, or pharmacotherapy), and were followed for two years. CT responders and behavioural activation responders discontinued the treatment, and pharmacotherapy responders were assigned randomly to one year of pill placebo or to one year of continuation-phase pharmacotherapy and then withdrawn in the second year. During the first year of follow-up, prior CT patients (39 per cent) relapsed significantly less than pharmacotherapy responders who received pill placebo (59 per cent). Relapse rates over one year for prior behavioural activation (50 per cent) and continued pharmacotherapy (53 per cent) were intermediate. In the second year of follow-up among the smaller sample of patients who had not relapsed during the first year, there was a trend for the psychotherapies to reduce recurrence by comparison to prior continuation-phase pharmacotherapy (i.e., 24 per cent for prior CT; 26 per cent for prior BA; 52 per cent for prior continuation-phase pharmacotherapy). These results support the hypothesis that both cognitive therapy and behavioural activation have enduring effects and reduce relapse more than pharmacotherapy. Importantly, additional results suggest that these forms of CBT cost less than pharmacotherapy (Dobson et al., 2008; Myhr & Payne, 2006).

It is also important to note that there are several different formulations in which cognitive behavioural interventions have been used to reduce relapse and perhaps recurrence. The preventive effects of these variations of cognitive therapy using a continuation phase form of CBT are reviewed and described by Bockting, Hollon, Jarrett, Kuyken, and Dobson (2015).

How Clinically Significant Is the Change after Exposure to CBT?

As discussed above, most of the research on CBT has focused on reducing depressive symptoms, including in the form of relapse and recurrence. We assert that, in addition to low depressive symptoms, complete evaluations of 'wellness' or health include assessments of psychosocial functioning that are ideally longitudinal (e.g., assessment of the level of, and of change in the quality of, interpersonal problems or functioning at work and in social relationships). That is, the clinical significance of CBT's effects involves the depth of improvement in relation to depressive symptoms, the breath of improvement or how well it encompasses patients' functioning in their many social roles and environments, and the durability of symptom and functioning improvements over periods that are sufficient to offset the treatment's costs in time, effort, and money.

Parallel to findings about depressive symptoms, research suggests that CBT improves psychosocial functioning substantially but does not normalize psychosocial functioning for many patients. For example, we found that many acute-phase CBT patients move from impaired social functioning to levels of functioning similar to those expected in non-patient, community samples (Vittengl, Clark, & Jarrett, 2014). The proportions of patients scoring in the 'healthy' ranges increased from 46 per cent to 60 per cent for dyadic (e.g., marital) adjustment, from 27 per cent to 63 per cent for interpersonal problems, and from 11 per cent to 65 per cent for social adjustment from entering to exiting acute-phase CBT; and gains were maintained among responders across two years of follow-up. Improvements in depressive symptoms occurred earlier, during acute-phase CBT, and accounted for nearly all of the improvement in psychosocial functioning. Unfortunately, a number of patients (35–40 per cent) exited acute-phase CBT with significant remaining psychosocial impairment (Vittengl et al., 2004). Similar conclusions have been found regarding the effect of acute phase CT on quality of life (Jha, Minhajuddin, Thase, & Jarrett, 2014).

Hirschfeld et al. (2002) reached similar conclusions in their evaluation of CBASP, pharmacotherapy, and the combination of CBASP and pharmacotherapy. Patients with chronic MDD began acute-phase treatment with significant psychosocial impairment but improved substantially (e.g., pre–post effect size of about 1.0 for improvement in social adjustment in CBASP, 1.0 in pharmacotherapy, and 1.5 in combined treatment). Nonetheless, significant psychosocial impairment remained (e.g., mean social adjustment was about 1.5, 1.6, and 1.0 *SD* poorer than community norms for CBASP, pharmacotherapy, and combined treatment, respectively). In the acute phase, depressive symptoms improved earlier and more than psychosocial adjustment (effect sizes were about twice as large), and the change in depressive symptoms accounted for about one half to two thirds of the improvement in psychosocial functioning in the CBASP group, for somewhat more of it in the combined-treatment group, and for nearly all psychosocial improvement in the pharmacotherapy group.

Although psychosocial functioning improves during acute-phase CBT, persistent psychosocial dysfunction predicts relapse or recurrence (Vittengl, Clark, Thase, & Jarrett, 2015). For example, among persons who experienced a major depressive episode followed by eight consecutive weeks of minimal or no depressive symptoms, those with moderate psychosocial impairment when euthymic were three times more likely to meet the criteria for a major depressive episode during the next 6–12 months of naturalistic follow-up than were those with very good psychosocial functioning when euthymic (Solomon et al., 2004). Further, we found that, during two years after response to acute-phase CBT, poor psychosocial functioning predicted depressive relapse or recurrence beyond the prediction from residual depressive symptoms (Vittengl, Jarrett, & Clark, 2009). We also found that psychosocial functioning often decreased in the month immediately before depressive relapse or recurrence. Consequently, deteriorations in psychosocial functioning provide targets for monitoring and change during treatments that are focused on preventing relapse or recurrence (or both).

When defined rigorously, remission and recovery from major depressive episodes are clinically significant outcomes, because they reflect the depth and durability of wellness. For example, we defined remission and recovery as a state of minimal or no depressive symptoms, maintained continuously for at least six weeks and, respectively, eight months (35 weeks) after the end of acute-phase CBT (Vittengl, Clark, & Jarrett, 2009). We showed that remission and recovery are more than simply the absence of relapse or recurrence. Although the definition of absence of relapse and recurrence can allow for moderate depressive symptoms (e.g., at the level found in dysthymic disorder), after response to acute-phase CBT we found no patients in our sample who remained 'less depressed' – either they either remitted and recovered or they relapsed or recurred. After response to acute-phase CBT, C-CT increased remission slightly (88 per cent vs 97 per cent) and recovery significantly (62 per cent vs 84 per cent) by comparison to assessment control. Similarly high rates of remission and recovery were found in a subsequent trial of C-CT (Vittengl, Clark, Thase, & Jarrett, 2014). Thus responders to acute-phase CBT often sustain 'health' over clinically significant intervals of time, and continuation CT can increase patients' chances of these enduring, positive outcomes.

Research to Do or Watch: Collaboration with Neuroscience and Basic Psychology to Develop the Paradigm

The field of CBT can advance by integrating new and existing data (e.g., López-León et al., 2008), by revising models (e.g., Robinson & Sahakian,

2008), and by taking advantage of or inventing technologies. For example, Beck (2008) traces the history of how the cognitive model developed and revises the model so as to incorporate important new data from behavioural genetics and cognitive neuroscience, as well as personality and social psychology. Specifically, Beck asserted that early trauma influences the development of dysfunctional beliefs and cognitive vulnerability. Daily stressors activate attentional biases and mild symptoms of depression (i.e., cognitive reactivity), which, through repetition, can produce a 'mode', which becomes hypersalient and takes charge of processing information. Beck points out that the risk for depression increases in the presence of a hypersensitive amygdala and genetic polymorphism (e.g., short variant of the 5-HTTLPR or serotonin transporter gene), which are also associated with reduced cognitive appraisal or heightened cognitive bias. He hypothesized that such cognitive distortion may mediate the association between genetic polymorphisms and an overreaction to stress that is conducive to developing depression. Beck has continuously nurtured change. He forecasts further evolution of the cognitive paradigm through collaboration with neuroscience, cognitive science, personality and social psychology – all of these fields resulting in a closer integration of results from biology and basic and applied psychology (Beck, 2008).

How Generalizable Are the Findings from Randomized Trials on CBT for Depression?

In the past decade the distinction between 'efficacy' research (which is often based in academic research clinics) and 'effectiveness' research (which is based in 'field' or practice settings) has drawn attention to the problem that the generalizability of findings from CBT efficacy studies was largely untested. Most of the clinical trials we cited above are from samples of middle-aged, Caucasian women. An evaluation of CBT for depression with diverse and specialized samples (e.g., Miranda et al., 2006; Roy-Byrne et al., 2006; Schraufhagel, Wagner, Miranda, Roy-Byrne, 2006) allows the field opportunities to find moderators of effects and will identify populations for which CBT for depression does or does not require adaption and innovation. While this review has focused on CBT for unipolar adults, important and promising findings have been reported with adult bipolar patients (Lam et al., 2005) and with vulnerable youth (Horowitz & Garber, 2006; Kennard, Stewart, Hughes, Jarrett, & Emslie, 2008, Kennard et al., 2008).

Where Are the Mechanisms of Effect and What Do We Teach and Disseminate?

The call for identifying the mechanisms, both psychological and biological, underlying the effects of CBT for depression has been frequent and, to date, largely unanswered. If research can identify which psychological components or processes of CBT produce positive outcomes in the course of depressive illness, then we will know what to emphasize in teaching CBT to providers, patients, and, perhaps, people vulnerable to depression. Although CBT for depression can improve the course of illness for some depressed patients, cognitive behavioural therapists are still relatively few in number (Layard, 2006a, 2006b), and it is difficult to quantify their adherence and competence. Even when researchers in efficacy studies succeed in demonstrating 'treatment integrity' by measuring adherence to and competency within the corresponding model, we still have not demonstrated which processes within the treatment delivery or utilization produce the positive outcomes. When the field identifies these processes, we will be in the position to take advantage of developing technologies in information processing, tracking of behaviors, and delivery so as to increase the public health impact of CBT for depression not just in academic medical centres, or not even in outlying counties of the United States, but also in every country where the means to receive, process, and transmit information can be imported and the risk for depression remains.

What Do We Measure? A Key to Advancing Understanding

We are concerned that, if our field lacks a basic consensus on 'core' measurement in patient-oriented depression research, then disagreement as to which key constructs to measure may slow advances in understanding. We support a 'common metric' designed to facilitate communication among us and with people outside who are affected by our field. Because clinicians and their depressed patients live in a world where access to treatment is influenced, in part, by the type of diagnosis rendered, we recommend that researchers interested in mood continue to measure symptoms and syndromal states. Supplementing this 'common metric' with an assessment of additional important and interesting constructs such as 'psychosocial functioning' (see above) or 'psychological flexibility' as well as constructs within from biology and neuroscience will contribute to understanding how these variables function in the course of depressive illness. We acknowledge that what we measure reflects not only our underlying theories or conceptualization, but also our value systems. Retaining a common core of measurement, supported by better technologies, will allow findings to be compared and replication to succeed or fail, and will help to identify gaps in understanding. The impact of research will increase as a result of measuring constructs that are easily understood by makers of public policy and can be used to improve public health. At the same time, we look forward to unique measurement (and constructs) outside of the core of symptoms and syndromes, which will allow us to unravel the role of yet to be identified and perhaps promising variables that could hold the key to significant discoveries in mood disorders and psychosocial treatment.

Summary

Here we have summarized the findings that support the efficacy of CBT for depressed adults. We highlight many areas ripe for future research and provide a few guiding principles. We conclude that CBT reduces the symptoms of MDD for about half of the adults who begin it. For patients who respond to CBT, the risk of relapse, and perhaps recurrence, can decrease by comparison to the corresponding risk for patients who did not have CBT or discontinued pharmacotherapy. While this progress in interventions research is helpful when one considers the starting point, we assert that the needs of our patients require our field to raise the standards for assessing the efficacy of interventions for depressed people. Specifically, *the goal for our field is to articulate how mood disorders can be prevented and cured*. We document that too many adults leave CBT with residual symptoms of MDD, suboptimal psychosocial functioning, and high risk for relapse or recurrence. Note that many introductions to research reports on MDD (including ours) mention that the consequences of suffering from depression are comparable to those of other chronic illnesses such as cancer, diabetes, and heart disease. (We note that what is less often mentioned is the comorbity of these disorders, or even their potential temporal relationships). Researchers of other chronic diseases have not set the bar at reducing symptoms and producing 'a little less' cancer, diabetes, or heart disease; instead they are focused on prevention and cure. We welcome collaboration with basic science (e.g., biology, neuroscience) and new technology. We look forward to rigorous research on methods of disseminating and innovating evidence-based practice, which is centred squarely on nothing short of recovery, cure, and prevention of mood disorders. (Manuscript submitted August 8, 2008, and revised November 25, 2008. References updated May 13, 2015.)

Acknowledgements

This work was supported in part by a National Institute of Mental Health (NIMH) MH-01571 to Robin B. Jarrett. The NIMH had no further role in the collection, analysis, or interpretation of data, in the writing of the chapter, or in the decision to submit it for publication.

We are grateful to Abu Minhajuddin, PhD, for his review and critique of the U_3R statistic and to Todd Dunn, MS, for his comments on an earlier draft. We thank the patients, students, clinicians, and associates at the Psychosocial Research and Depression Clinic in the Department of Psychiatry at the University of Texas Southwestern Medical Center for their dedication to the goals described here.

References

Bandura, A. (1977). *Social learning theory*. Englewood Cliffs: Prentice Hall.

Beck, A. T. (2005). The current state of cognitive therapy: A 40-year retrospective. *Archives of General Psychiatry, 62*, 953–959.

Beck, A. T. (2008). The evolution of the cognitive model of depression and its neurobiological correlates. *American Journal of Psychiatry, 165*, 969–977.

Beck, A. T., Rush, A. J., Shaw, B. F., & Emery, G. (1979). *Cognitive therapy of depression*. New York: Guilford.

Beck, A. T., Ward, C. H., Mendelson, M., Mock, J., & Erbaugh, J. (1961). An inventory for measuring depression. *Archives of General Psychiatry, 4*, 561–571.

Biesheuvel-Leliefeld, K. M., Kok, G. D., Bockting, C. H., Cuijpers, P., Hollon, S. D., van Marwijk, H. J., & Smit, F. (2015). Effectiveness of psychological interventions in preventing recurrence of depressive disorder: Meta-analysis and meta-regression. *Journal of Affective Disorders, 174*, 400–410.

Blackburn, I. M., & Moore, R. G. (1997). Controlled acute and follow-up trial of cognitive therapy and pharmacotherapy in outpatients with recurrent depression. *British Journal of Psychiatry, 171*, 328–334.

Bockting, C., Hollon, S. D., Jarrett, R. B., Kuyken, W., & Dobson, K. (2015). A lifetime approach to major depressive disorder: The contributions of psychological interventions in preventing relapse and recurrence. *Clinical Psychology Review*, doi:10.1016/j.cpr.2015.02.003.

Clarke, K., Mayo-Wilson, E., Kenny, J., & Pilling, S. (2015). Can non-pharmacological interventions prevent relapse in adults who have recovered from depression? A systematic review and meta-analysis of randomised controlled trials. *Clinical Psychology Review*, *39*, 58–70.

Butler, A. C., Chapman, J. E., Forman, E. M., & Beck, A. T. (2006). The empirical status of cognitive behavioural therapy: A review of meta-analyses. *Clinical Psychology Review*, *26*, 17–31.

Cohen, J. (1988). *Statistical power analysis for the behavioural sciences* (2nd edn). Hillsdale, NJ: Erlbaum.

Craighead, W. E., Sheets, E. S., Brosse, A. L., & Ilardi, S. S. (2007). Psychosocial treatments for major depressive disorder. In P. E. Nathan & J. M. Gorman (Eds), *A guide to treatments that work* (3rd edn, pp. 289–307). New York: Oxford.

Cuijpers, P., Karyotaki, E., Weitz, E., Andersson, G., Hollon, S. D., & van Straten, A. (2014). The effects of psychotherapies for major depression in adults on remission, recovery and improvement: A meta-analysis. *Journal of Affective Disorders*, *159*, 118–126.

Cuijpers, P., Weitz, E., Twisk, J., Kuehner, C., Cristea, I., David, D. … Hollon, S. D. (2014). Gender as predictor and moderator of outcome in cognitive behavior therapy and pharmacotherapy for adult depression: An "individual patient data" meta-analysis. *Depression and Anxiety*, *31*, 941–951.

DeRubeis, R. J., Hollon, S. D., Amsterdam, J. D., Shelton, R. C., Young, P. R., Salomon, R. M. … Gallop, R. (2005). Cognitive therapy vs medications in the treatment of moderate to severe depression. *Archives of General Psychiatry*, *62*(4), 409–416.

Dimidjian, S., Hollon, S. D., Dobson, K. S., Schmaling, K. B., Kohlenberg, R. J., Addis, M. E. … Jacobson, N. S. (2006). Randomized trial of behavioural activation, cognitive therapy, and antidepressant medication in the acute treatment of adults with major depression. *Journal of Consulting and Clinical Psychology*, *74*, 658–670.

Dobson, K. S., Hollon, S. D., Dimidjian, S., Schmaling, K. B., Kohlenberg, R. J., Gallop, R. J. … Jacobson, N. S. (2008). Randomized trial of behavioural activation, cognitive therapy, and antidepressant medication in the prevention of relapse and recurrence in major depression. *Journal of Consulting and Clinical Psychology*, *76*, 468–477.

Elkin, I., Shea, M., Watkins, J. T., Imber, S. D., Sotsky, S. M., Collins, J. F. … Parloff, M. B. (1989). National Institute of Mental Health Treatment of Depression Collaborative Research Program: General effectiveness of treatments. *Archives of General Psychiatry*, *46*, 971–982.

Fava, G. A., Fabbri, S., & Sonino, N. (2002). Residual symptoms in depression: An emerging therapeutic target. *Progress in Neuro-Psychopharmacology & Biological Psychiatry, 26*, 1019–1027.

Fava, G. A., Ruini, C., & Belaise, C. (2007). The concept of recovery in major depression. *Psychological Medicine, 37*, 307–317.

Fava, G. A., Ruini, C., Rafanelli, C., Finos, L., Conti, S., & Grandli, S. (2004). Six-year outcome of cognitive behavior therapy for prevention of recurrent depression. *American Journal of Psychiatry, 161*, 1872–1876.

Ferster, C. B. (1973). A functional analysis of depression. *American Psychologist, 10*, 857–870.

Frank, E., Prien, R. F., Jarrett, R. B., Keller, M. B., Kupfer, D. J., Lavori, P. W. … Weissman, M. M. (1991). Conceptualization and rationale for consensus definitions of terms in major depressive disorder: Remission, recovery, relapse, and recurrence. *Archives of General Psychiatry, 48*, 851–855.

Gloaguen, V., Cottraux, J., Cucherat, M., & Blackburn, I. M. (1998). A meta-analysis of the effects of cognitive therapy in depressed patients. *Journal of Affective Disorders, 49*, 59–72.

Grundy, C. T., Lambert, M. J., & Grundy, E. M. (1996). Assessing clinical significance: Application to the Hamilton Rating Scale for Depression. *Journal of Mental Health, 5*, 25–33.

Hamilton, M. (1960). A rating scale for depression. *Journal of Neurology, Neurosurgery and Psychiatry, 23*, 56–61.

Hirschfeld, R. M. A., Dunner, D. L., Keitner, G., Klein, D. N., Koran, L. M., Kornstein, S. G. … Keller, M. B. (2002). Does psychosocial functioning improve independent of depressive symptoms? A comparison of nefazodone, psychotherapy, and their combination. *Biological Psychiatry, 51*, 123–133.

Hollon, S. D., Steward, M. O., & Strunk, D. (2006). Enduring effects for cognitive behavior therapy in the treatment of depression and anxiety. *Annual Review of Psychology, 57*, 285–315.

Hollon, S. D., Thase, M. E., & Markowitz. J. C. (2002). Treatment and prevention of depression. *Psychological Science in the Public Interest, 3*, 39–77.

Hollon, S. D., Jarrett, R. B., Nierenberg, A. A., Thase, M. E., Trivedi, M., & Rush, A. J. (2005). Psychotherapy and medication in the treatment of adult and geriatric depression: Which monotherapy or combined treatment? *Journal of Clinical Psychiatry, 66*, 455–468.

Horowitz, J. L., & Garber, J. (2006). The prevention of depressive symptoms in children and adolescents: A meta-analytic review. *Journal of Consulting and Clinical Psychology, 74*(3), 401–415.

Jacobson, N. S., & Truax, P. (1991). Clinical significance: A statistical approach to defining meaningful change in psychotherapy research. *Journal of Consulting and Clinical Psychology, 59*, 12–19.

Jacobson, N. S., Roberts, L. J., Berns, S. B., & McGlinchey, J. B. (1999). Methods for defining and determining the clinical significance of treatment effects: Description, application, and alternatives. *Journal of Consulting and Clinical Psychology, 67*, 300–307.

Jarrett, R. B., Vittengl, J. R., & Clark, L. A. (2008). How much cognitive therapy, for which patients, will prevent depressive relapse? *Journal of Affective Disorders, 111*, 185–192.

Jarrett, R. B., Kraft, D., Doyle, J., Foster, B. M., Eaves, G., & Silver, P. (2001). Preventing recurrent depression using cognitive therapy with and without a continuation phase: A randomized clinical trial. *Archives of General Psychiatry, 58*, 381–388.

Jarrett, R. B., Minhajuddin, A., Gershenfeld, H., Friedman, E. S., & Thase, M. E. (2013). Preventing depressive relapse and recurrence in higher-risk cognitive therapy responders: A randomized trial of continuation phase cognitive therapy, fluoxetine, or matched pill placebo. *JAMA Psychiatry, 70*, 1152–1160.

Jarrett, R. B., Schaffer, M., McIntire, D., Witt-Browder, A., Kraft, D., & Risser, R. C. (1999). Treatment of atypical depression with cognitive therapy or phenelzine: A double-blind placebo controlled trial. *Archives of General Psychiatry, 56*, 431–437.

Jha, M. K., Minhajuddin, A., Thase, M. E., & Jarrett, R. B. (2014). Improvement in self-reported quality of life with cognitive therapy for recurrent major depressive disorder. *Journal of Affective Disorders, 167*, 37–43.

Judd, L. L. (1997). The clinical course of unipolar major depressive disorders. *Archives of General Psychiatry, 54*, 989–991.

Judd, L. L., Schettler, P. J., & Akiskal, H. S. (2002). The prevalence, clinical relevance, and public health significance of subthreshold depressions. *Psychiatric Clinics of North America, 25*, 685–698.

Kashner, M. T., Henley, S. S., Golden, R. M., Rush, J. A. & Jarrett, R. B. (2007). Assessing the preventive effects of cognitive therapy following relief of depression: A methodological innovation. *Journal of Affective Disorders, 104*, 251–261.

Keller, M. B., McCullough, J. P., Klein, D. P., Arnow, B., Dunner, D. L., Gelenberg, A. J. … Zajecka, J. (2000). A comparison of nefazodone, the cognitive behavioral analysis system for psychotherapy, and their combination for the treatment of chronic depression. *The New England Journal of Medicine, 342*, 1462–1470.

Kelly, G. (1955). *The psychology of personal constructs*. New York: Norton.

Kennard, B., Stewart, S. M., Hughes, J. L., Jarrett, R. B., & Emslie, G. J. (2008). Developing cognitive–behavioural therapy to prevent depressive relapse in youth. *Cognitive and Behavioural Practice 15*, 387–399.

Kennard, B. D., Emslie, G. J., Mayes, T. L., Nightingale-Teresi, J., Nakonezny, P., Hughes, J. L. … Jarrett, R. B. (2008). Cognitive behavioral therapy to prevent relapse in pediatric responders to pharmacotherapy for major depressive disorder. *Journal of the American Academy of Child and Adolescent Psychiatry 47*, 1395–1404.

Kessler, R. C., Berglund, P., Demler, O., Jin, R., & Walters, E. E. (2005). Lifetime prevalence and age-of-onset distributions of DSM-IV disorders in the National Comorbidity Survey Replication. *Archives of General Psychiatry, 62*, 593–602.

Kirsch, I., Deacon, B. J., Huedo-Medina, T. B., Scoboria, A., Moore, T. J., & Johnson, B. T. (2008). Initial severity and antidepressant benefits: A meta-analysis of data submitted to the food and drug administration. *PLoS Medicine, 5*, 260–268.

Klein, D. N., Santiago, N. J., Vivian, D., Blalock, J. A., Kocsis, J. H., Markowitz, J. C. … Keller, M. B. (2004). Cognitive–behavioral analysis system of psychotherapy as a maintenance treatment for chronic depression. *Journal of Consulting and Clinical Psychology, 72*, 681–688.

Lam, D., Hayward, P., Watkins, E. R., Bright, J., Wright, K., & Sham, P. (2005). Relapse prevention in patients with bipolar disorder: Cognitive therapy outcomes after 2 years. *American Journal Of Psychiatry, 162*, 324–329.

Layard, R. (2006a). The case for psychological treatment centres. *British Medical Journal, 332*, 1030–1032.

Layard, R. (Ed.). (2006b). *The depression report: A new deal for depression and anxiety disorders* (Centre for Economic Performance's Mental Health Policy Group Report). London: London School of Economics.

Leader, J. B., & Klein, D. N. (1996). Social adjustment in dysthymia, double depression and episodic major depression. *Journal of Affective Disorders, 37*, 91–101.

López-León, S. Janssen, A. C., Gonzalez-Zuloeta, A. M., Del-Favero, S. J., Claes, B. A., Oostral, B. A. … van Duijn, C. M. (2008). Meta-analyses of genetic studies on major depressive disorder. *Molecular Psychiatry, 13*, 772–785.

McCullough, J. P. (2000). *Treatment for chronic depression: Cognitive Behavioral Analysis System of Psychotherapy*. New York: Guilford.

Miranda, J., Green, B. L. Krupnick, J. L., Chung, J., Siddique, J., Belin, T. … Revicki, D. (2006). One-year outcomes of a randomized clinical trial treating depression in low-income minority women. *Journal of Consulting and Clinical Psychology, 74*, 99–111.

Mueller, T. I., Leon, A. C., Keller, M. B., Solomon, D. A., Endicott, J., Coryell, W. … Maser, J. D. (1999). Recurrence after recovery from major depressive disorder during 15 years of observational follow-up. *American Journal of Psychiatry, 156*, 1000–1006.

Murray, C. J. L., & Lopez, A. D. (Eds). (1996). *The global burden of disease: A comprehensive assessment of mortality and disability from diseases, injuries, and risk factors in 1990 and projected to 2020*. Cambridge, MA: Harvard School of Public Health.

Myhr, G., & Payne, K. (2006). Cost-effectiveness of cognitive behavioural therapy for mental disorders: Implications for public health cared funding policy in Canada. *Canadian Journal of Psychiatry, 51*, 662–670.

Nathan, P. E., & Gorman, J. S. (2007). *A guide to treatments that work* (3rd edn). New York: Oxford.

O'Leary, K. D., & Beach, S. R. (1990). Marital therapy: A viable treatment for depression and marital discord. *American Journal of Psychiatry, 147*, 183–186.

Öst, L.-G. (2008). Efficacy of the third wave of behavioral therapies. A systematic review and meta-analysis. *Behaviour Research and Therapy, 48*, 296–321.

Paykel, E. S., Scott, J., Cornwall, P. L., Abbott, R., Crane, C., Pope, M., & Johnson, A. L. (2005). Duration of relapse prevention after cognitive therapy in residual depression: Follow-up of controlled trial.[see comment]. *Psychological Medicine, 35*, 59–68.

Rehm, L. P. (Ed.). (1981). *Behaviour therapy for depression*. New York: Academic Press.

Robinson, O. J. & Sahakian, B. J. (2008). Recurrence in major depressive disorder: A neurocognitive perspective. *Psychological Medicine, 38*, 315–318.

Roy-Byrne, P., Sherbourne, C., Miranda, J. Stein, M., Craske, M., Golinelli, D., & Sullivan, G. (2006). Poverty and response to treatment among panic disorder patients in primary care. *American Journal of Psychiatry, 163*, 1419–1425.

Rush, A. J., Kraemer, H. C., Sackeim, Fava, M., Trivedi, M. H., Frank, E. … Schatzberg, A. F (2006). Report by the ACNP task force on response and remission in major depressive disorder. *Neuropsychopharmacology, 31*, 1841–1853.

Schraufhagel, T. J., Wagner, A. W., Miranda, J., & Roy-Byrne, P. P. (2006). Treating minority patients with depression and anxiety: What does the evidence tell us? *General Hospital Psychiatry, 28*, 27–36.

Segal, Z. V., Kennedy, S., Gemar, M., Hood, K., Pedersen, R., & Buis, T. (2006). Cognitive reactivity to sad mood provocation and the prediction of depressive relapse. *Archives of General Psychiatry, 63*, 749–755.

Seggar, L. B., Lambert, M. J., & Hansen, N. B. (2002). Assessing clinical significance: Application to the Beck Depression Inventory. *Behaviour Therapy, 33*, 253–269.

Simon, G. E. (2003). Social and economic burden of mood disorders. *Biological Psychiatry, 54*, 208–215.

Solomon, D. A., Keller, M. B., Leon, A. C., Mueller, T. I., Lavori, P. W., Shea, M. T. … Endicott, J. (2000). Multiple recurrences of major depressive disorder. *American Journal of Psychiatry, 157*, 229–233.

Solomon, D. A., Leon, A. C., Endicott, J., Mueller, T. I., Coryell, W., Shea, M. T. … Keller, M. B. (2004). Psychosocial impairment and recurrence in major depression. *Comprehensive Psychiatry, 45*, 423–430.

Vittengl, J. R., Clark, L. A., & Jarrett, R. B. (2004). Improvement in social–interpersonal functioning after cognitive therapy for recurrent depression. *Psychological Medicine, 34*, 643–658.

Vittengl, J. R., Clark, L. A., & Jarrett, R. B. (2009). Continuation-phase cognitive therapy's effects on remission and recovery from depression. *Journal of Consulting and Clinical Psychology, 77*, 367–371.

Vittengl, J. R., Jarrett, R. B., & Clark, L. A. (2009). Deterioration in psychosocial functioning predicts relapse/recurrence after cognitive therapy for depression. *Journal of Affective Disorders, 112*, 135–143.

Vittengl, J. R., Clark, L. A., Dunn, T. W. & Jarrett, R. B. (2007). Reducing relapse and recurrence in unipolar depression: A comparative meta-analysis of cognitive therapy's effects. *Journal of Consulting and Clinical Psychology, 75*, 475–488.

Vittengl, J. R., Clark, L. A., Kraft, D., & Jarrett, R. B. (2005). Multiple measures, methods, and moments: A factor-analytic investigation of change in depressive symptoms during acute phase cognitive therapy. *Psychological Medicine, 35*, 693–704.

Vittengl, J. R., Clark, L. A., Thase, M. E., & Jarrett, R. B. (2014). Stable remission and recovery after acute-phase cognitive therapy for recurrent major depressive disorder. *Journal of Consulting and Clinical Psychology, 82*, 1049–1059.

Vittengl, J. R., Clark, L. A., Thase, M. E., & Jarrett, R. B. (2015). Predictors of longitudinal outcomes after unstable response to acute phase cognitive therapy for major depressive disorder. *Psychotherapy*, 52, 268–277.

Zimmerman, M., Posternak, M. A., & Chelminski, I. (2007). Heterogeneity among depressed outpatients considered to be in remission. *Comprehensive Psychiatry, 48*, 113–117.

4

Psychobiological Processes and Therapies in Depression

Pilar Cristancho and Michael E. Thase

Introduction

Understanding the nature of depression – as well as the best ways to treat it – is a challenge that is nearly as old as civilization. Although much progress has been made, it is also true that, at the end of the first decade of the twenty-first century, we still struggle to understand both the nature and treatment of this challenging, complex, and fundamentally human disorder. In this chapter we will briefly review the leading neurobiological theories of depression and the major classes of antidepressant therapies.

Monoamine Hypotheses

The first modern theories of the neurobiology of depression focused on deficits in monoamines such as norepinephrine (NE) (Schildkraut, 1965), serotonin (5-hydroxytryptamine, 5-HT) and dopamine (DA). These theories were partially based on clinical observations made during the early years of psychopharmacology. For example, the serendipitous discovery that a medication used to treat tuberculosis – iproniazid – had antidepressant effects (Delay, Laine, & Buisson, 1952) led to the recognition that drugs that inhibit the enzyme monoamine oxidase (MAOIs) may initiate their antidepressant effects by increasing synaptic levels of NE, 5-HT, and DA. The antidepressant properties of a second drug, imipramine, were likewise recognized during the search for safer antipsychotic medications (Kuhn, 1958).

Treating Depression: MCT, CBT and Third Wave Therapies, First Edition.
Edited by Adrian Wells and Peter L. Fisher.

Imipramine and related tricyclic antidepressants (TCAs) were subsequently found to inhibit the uptake of NE and, to a lesser extent, that of 5-HT into neurons, thereby increasing the concentration of monoamines at the synaptic cleft. Conversely, the relevance of a third drug, known to cause depression as a side effect – the antihypertensive reserpine – was heightened by the recognition that this drug depleted neuronal stores of monoamines (Goodwin & Bunney, 1971). These observations fostered a generation of research that measured the concentrations of monoamine neurotransmitters and their metabolites in bodily fluids such as urine, plasma, and cerebrospinal fluid (CSF). Several important weaknesses in the monoamine hypotheses were uncovered, including:

1) Whereas antidepressants increase synaptic neurotransmitter levels in hours or days, it takes weeks or longer for clinical improvement to be fully evident (Stahl, 2005).
2) Cocaine and other stimulant drugs rapidly enhance noradrenergic and dopaminergic neurotransmission, yet they do not have sustained antidepressant effects.
3) Dietary depletion of tryptophan, the essential amino acid needed for synthesis of serotonin, does not provoke depression in healthy individuals, nor does it worsen untreated depressive episodes (Delgado et al., 1999).

Nevertheless, it was also clear that all known antidepressant medications initiated their effects through monoaminergic neurons and that some depressed patients had low urinary levels of the NE metabolite 3-methoxy-4-hydroxypheylglycol (MHPG) (Ressler & Nemeroff, 2000) or low CSF levels of the serotonin metabolite 5-hydroxyindoleacetic acid (5-HIAA) (Maes & Meltzer, 1995), the latter finding being also linked to completed suicide, violent suicidal attempts, and other violent behaviours (Maes & Meltzer, 1995). Evidently, alterations in the function of monoaminergic systems were an important piece in the complex neurobiological nature of depression.

Subsequent research focused on the intraneuronal or 'downstream' aspects of monoamine neurotransmission, the possible role of other neurotransmitters and neuromodulators, and, most recently, functional interactions of groups of neurons or neurocircuits (Thase, 2008a).

Intracellular Effects

The effects of antidepressants that increase monoamine levels at neuronal synapses are subsequently transduced via pathways or cascades of intracellular reactions that follow the binding of the neurotransmitter to post-synaptic receptors; these processes ultimately may activate or de-activate specific genes (Thase, 2008a). For example, both 5-HT and NE bind to receptors that are linked to guanine nucleotide triphosphate-binding proteins, which are also known as G proteins. G proteins induce membrane-bound enzymes such as phospholipase C, protein kinase C, and adenyl cyclase to catalyze the formation of the so-called second messengers cyclic monophosphate (cAMP) and diacylglycerol (DAG). In the next step of the cascade, cAMP activates the intracellular enzyme protein kinase A (PKA), whereas DAG activates the protein kinase C (PKC). These enzymes in turn induce phosphorylation of the cAMP response element-binding protein (CREB) – a gene transcription factor. Phosphorylation of CREB is a crucial step in this process, because it facilitates the expression of a number of relevant genes, including those that code for synthesis of the corticotrophin-releasing hormone (CRH), the glucocorticoid receptors (GR), the brain-derived neurotrophic factor (BDNF), and the intracellular receptor for BDNF, TRK-B. These proteins, which are involved in the brain's response to stress, have also been implicated in the pathogenesis of depression (Duman, Schlesinger, Kodama, Russell, & Duman, 2007; Shelton, 2007).

Serotonin Systems

The cell bodies for most 5-HT neurons in the brain are located in the dorsal raphe nuclei of the pons, which have axons projecting to all regions relevant to the regulation and expression of emotion, motivation, and neurovegetative function. Serotonin neurons have a number of specific receptors, which are classified into seven different families (5-HT1 to 5-HT7). Among them, the post-synaptic 5-HT1A receptor is consistently decreased in depression and implicated in suicide (Pitchot et al., 2005). Using positron emission tomography (PET) scanning and *in vivo* receptor imaging techniques, Drevets et al. (2007) found reduced receptor-binding capacity in the mesotemporal cortex and raphe nuclei in depressed individuals.

It has long been suspected that the familial and heritable aspects of depressive vulnerability were linked to one or more genes relevant to 5-HT neurotransmission. Considerable attention has been devoted to the gene that codes for the serotonin transporter (5-HTT), which both is the target of selective serotonin reuptake inhibitors (SSRIs) and has a functional polymorphism in the promoter region. Two major alleles have been identified: a functional or long (*l*) form and a less functional short (*s*) form; a third, less prevalent allele – which codes for a less functional variant of *l* – also has been identified. The presence of at least one copy of the *s* allele reduces the synthesis of 5-HTT, resulting in decreased serotonin uptake by comparison with the fully functional *l* allele (Greenberger et al., 1999). Approximately 15 per cent to 20 per cent of the population is homozygous for the short allele (*ss*), and about 40 per cent to 50 per cent of the population is heterozygous (*sl*). The proposed link between the 5-HTT polymorphism and depression may be mediated by individual differences in emotional reactivity, such that individuals with the *s* allele show an increased or prolonged activation of brain responses to threatening stimuli (Brown & Hariri, 2006), which may in turn confer increased risk of depression following exposure to adverse life events (Caspi et al., 2003). Although not all studies have confirmed a relationship between this gene and stress-related depression, other investigators have identified relationships with other relevant correlates of vulnerability, such as higher rates of neuroticism, increased levels of dysfunctional attitudes, and less capable use of coping strategies (Brown & Hariri, 2006).

Noradrenergic Systems

The TCAs and newer medications – noradrenergic reuptake inhibitors – primarily initiate effects by inhibiting the neuronal uptake of norepinephrine; this is the secondary target of serotonin norepinephrine reuptake inhibitors (SNRIs). Most noradrenergic neurotransmission in the brain originates from cell bodies in the locus coeruleus, located in the dorsal wall of the rostral pons region of the brain stem, and projects 'upward', in tracts that are co-localized with 5-HT tracts. Whereas 5-HT tracts often have tonic or inhibitory effects on neuronal circuits, NE neurotransmission typically has more phasic, stress-responsive activity (Thase, 2008a). The major subtypes of norepinephrine receptors are classified as α and β. Studies of NE receptor dynamics have suggested that receptor abnormalities occur in depression, where evidence of hypersensitivity of $\alpha 2$ autoreceptors and heteroreceptors (located on 5-HT neurons) indicates that there is low activity in the prefrontal cortex. Animal studies suggest that these changes can be reversed by chronic antidepressant treatment, which desensitizes these receptors and increases the release of NE in prefrontal cortex (Elhwuegi, 2004). Other changes observed in some – but not all – studies include a decrease of NE metabolites in the CSF, reduced neuronal activity in the locus coeruleus (LC), upregulation of β receptors, and decreased activity of the synthetic enzyme tyrosine hydroxylase (Ressler & Nemeroff, 2000).

Dopaminergic Systems

Although DA is not a primary target of most antidepressants, disturbances of DA are implicated in several classical symptoms of severe depression (psychomotor retardation and anhedonia), DA systems are down-regulated by chronic mild stress, there are important interactions between DA and 5-HT systems in the regulation of reward-related behaviours (Thase, 2008a), and there is evidence that D2 receptors in the nucleus accumbens are implicated in the therapeutic effects of diverse interventions (Gershon, Vishne, & Grunhaus, 2007). In addition to the prototypic dopaminergic antidepressant nomifensine, which was withdrawn from use in the 1980s because of safety concerns, the alerting medication modafinil and several D2 receptor agonists, ropinirole and pramipexole, have shown antidepressant activity (Goldberg, Burdick, & Endick, 2004; Zarate et al., 2004; Frye et al., 2007). Given the therapeutic limitations of the SSRIs and SNRIs, ongoing efforts from pharmaceutical companies have focused on the development of safe and well-tolerated 'triple' reuptake inhibitors to capitalize on the hypothesis that the addition of DA agonism will improve treatment efficacy.

Other Neurotransmitter Systems

Several other neurotransmitter systems have been implicated in the pathogenesis of depression and some of their most salient aspects are summarized below.

Acetylcholine (ACh) Observations from some early studies suggested that an excess of Ach can cause depressive symptoms (see, for example, Janowsky, el-Yousef, & Davis, 1974). More recent studies have indicated that altered function of type-2 muscarinic (M2) receptors may be involved in bipolar depression (Cannon et al., 2006), and a polymorphism in the gene encoding for this receptor has been linked to depression (Wang et al., 2004). Most recently, IV administration of the M2 antagonist scopolamine has shown promising results in studies of depressed patients (Furey & Drevets, 2006).

γ-Amino-Butyric acid (GABA) GABA is the main inhibitory neurotransmitter in the brain; and alcohol, sedative–hypnotic medications, and some antiepileptics bind to GABA-A receptors (Sanacora & Saricicek, 2007). Gabaergic neurons have been implicated in the neuronal circuitry that mediates the development of learned helplessness (Berton et al., 2007), and low inhibitory gabaergic activity has been proposed to play a role in the pathophysiology of depression (Thase, 2008a). However, gabaergic medications that have been studied in depression to date, including alprazolam (a benzodiazepine) and valproate, have not been found to have strong antidepressant effects on core depressive symptoms (Sanacora & Saricicek, 2007).

Glutamate Glutamate, which is widely distributed in the brain as the main excitatory neurotransmitter (Pittenger, Sanacora, & Krystal, 2007), has two kinds of receptors: *α*-amino-3-hydroxy-5methylisoxazole-4-propionic-acid (AMPA) and N-methyl-D-aspartate (NMDA). AMPA receptors appear to be important in neuroplasticity. NMDA receptors regulate the influx of sodium and calcium to the neurons, and excessive glutamatergic activity via these receptors can damage neurons through a process called excitotoxicity. The anaesthetic ketamine and the recreational drug of abuse phencyclidine (PCP) bind to NMDA receptors (Pittenger et al., 2007). Recently there has been great interest in determining whether glutamatergic dysfunction is implicated in the pathophysiology of depression and, in one study, the administration of an intravenous ketamine compound showed a large and rapid antidepressant effect (Zarate et al., 2006). Although psychotomimetic effects preclude the routine therapeutic use of ketamine, further exploration of the glutamatergic systems may lead to the discovery of a new class of antidepressant medications.

HPA Axis Dysregulation in Depression and the Role of Stress It has long been known that many episodes of depression occur in close temporal association with life stress; and elevated levels of the stress hormone cortisol was one of the first widely replicated biological correlates of depression (Burke, Davis, Otte, & Mohr, 2005). The possible role of abnormalities of the hypothalamic–pituitary adrenal axis (HPA) in the pathogenesis of depression has therefore been extensively investigated. The HPA axis is the main endocrine system involved in dynamic responses to stress. This response is driven by the release of corticotrophin-releasing factor (CRF) in both cortical neurons and the hypothalamus. CRF acts on the pituitary gland to release the adrenocorticotropic hormone (ACTH), which in turn triggers the release of cortisol from the adrenal glands. Cortisol exerts a wide range of metabolic and immunomodulatory effects on the body.

In addition to hypercortisolemia, depressed patients have been found to exhibit higher levels of CRH in CSF (Nemeroff et al., 1984) and, in post-mortem tissues, increased concentrations of CRH and CRH messenger ribonucleic acid (RNA) in the hypothalamic periventricular nucleus (Raadsheer, Hoogendijk, Stam, Tilders, & Swaab, 1994). Neuroendocrine function tests that asses the integrity of the HPA axis are abnormal in about 50 per cent of severely depressed patients, although lower rates of test abnormality are typically observed in less severely depressed outpatients (Thase, 2008a). Studies using pre- and post-test results to monitor HPA axis abnormalities longitudinally have found that failure to normalize test results is associated with poorer outcomes (Kunugi et al., 2006).

Although hypercortisolism is best thought of as a state-dependent abnormality, the integrity of the HPA axis can be adversely affected by stress early in life (Coplan et al., 2001). Animal studies have revealed that even short periods of separation from a mother can result in persistent abnormalities in stress responses (Coplan et al., 2006). In humans, a growing body of evidence suggests that exposure to traumatic experiences during childhood results in dysregulation of the HPA axis and an associated increase in the risk of depression and anxiety disorders in adulthood (Heim & Nemeroff, 2001). More recent research has suggested that polymorphisms of the CRH type 1 receptor (CRHR1) gene may be a possible moderator of the effects of child abuse on the subsequent development of depression in adulthood (Bradley et al., 2008).

Disturbances of Sleep and Its Regulation

Sleep disturbances such as insomnia and hypersomnia are characteristic features of major depression (Thase, 2006a), and insomnia is a risk factor for the development of depression (e.g., Johnson, Roth, & Breslau, 2006).

In addition to the processes that regulate the circadian rhythm, the normal sleep–wake cycle is controlled in part by monoaminergic systems and, for several decades before the introduction of modern neuroimaging methods, polysomnography (PSG) provided a window through which the neurobiology of depression could be studied (Thase, Jindal, & Howland, 2002). Studies utilizing PSG in depression have documented the characteristic difficulties that depressed people have with falling asleep and staying asleep, as well as three other correlates: decreased slow-wave sleep (SWS), an increase in the amount and intensity of rapid eye movement (REM) sleep, and reduced latency to the onset of the first REM sleep period (Thase et al., 2002). These disturbances were found to have some predictive value for differential response to psychotherapy and pharmacotherapy (Thase, 2006a). Although no longer widely studied, it is fair to conclude that the PSG correlates of depression have direct pathophysiologic relevance, though not of sufficient specificity for use in diagnosis or treatment planning.

Neuroplasticity and Neurogenesis

A more recent hypothesis about the nature of depression has been constructed on the basis of the ground-breaking findings pertaining to neurogenesis (i.e., the differentiation of new neurons from precursor or stem cells). Long thought not to occur in the adult brain, studies have confirmed that neurogenesis occurs primarily in the dentate region gyrus of the hippocampus (Eriksson et al., 1998; Ming & Song, 2005). BDNF and other neurotrophic factors not only help to promote neurogenesis but also are involved in learning and memory processes; various types of laboratory stress have been shown to inhibit neurogenesis and to suppress BDNF synthesis (Chambers, Potenza, Hoffman, & Miranker, 2004; Pittenger & Duman, 2008). Other studies have linked these effects to stress-related elevations in glucocorticoids and glutamate (Pittenger & Duman, 2008). In animal studies, the administration of antidepressants can both prevent and reverse these stress-related changes (Warner-Schmidt & Duman, 2006).

The principal site of neurogenesis, the hippocampus, is an important limbic structure with three other relevant links to the pathophysiology of depression:

1) The hippocampus is rich in glucocorticoid receptors and a principal site of inhibitory regulation of HPA responses to stress.

2) Sustained high levels of corticosteroids can result in the death of hippocampal neurons and can decrease the integrity of HPA feedback inhibition (Sapolsky, 2003).
3) The hippocampus plays a critical role in storage and retrieval of memories and has widespread connections to other brain areas implicated in mood regulation – such as the prefrontal cortex, the anterior thalamic nuclei, the amygdala, the basal ganglia, and the hypothalamus (Drevets, 2000).

Decreased hippocampal volume has been found in patients with depression (e.g., Sheline, Sanghavi, Mintun, & Gado, 1999; Frodl et al., 2002). A post-mortem study confirmed these findings, showing reduction in volumes of the hippocampus as well as of the amygdala (Bielau et al., 2005). In one study hippocampal volume loss was negatively correlated with the cumulative lifetime duration of untreated depression, which might suggest progressive damage associated with the repeated stress from recurrent episodes (Sheline et al., 1999). However, there is also evidence that decreased hippocampal volume can be found in patients experiencing their first major depressive episode (Frodl et al., 2002).

Although these findings are no doubt relevant to the pathophysiology of depression, some aspects deserve further investigation. For instance, the role of new neurons in the dentate gyrus of the hippocampus is still not well defined. It is not known whether the changes in hippocampal size noted in depressed patients precede or occur as a consequence of depressive episodes. Finally, experimental administration of BDNF does not have universally beneficial effects and can actual cause neuronal damage in some brain regions. For instance, when its precursor (pro-BDNF) binds to the p75 receptor, it causes reduction in dendritic spines and cell death (Lu, Pang, & Wo, 2005), and BDNF exerts a depression-like effect when administered to the nucleus accumbens (Eisch et al., 2003). Intact BDNF function in the mesolimbic dopamine pathway was likewise necessary for the development of depression-like behaviour following social defeat in another animal experiment (Berton et al., 2006). These caveats should be considered in future studies designed to advance our understanding of the role of neurogenesis in the nature of depression.

Neuroimaging Studies in Depression

The most widely replicated neuroimaging finding in depression has been reduced activity in the dorsolateral prefrontal cortex (DLPFC), particularly in the regions classified as Brodman areas 9 and 46 (e.g., Harvey et al., 2005). Normalization of DLPFC activity has been reported after successful antidepressant treatment (e.g., Nitschke & Mackiewicz, 2005; Mayberg et al., 2004). This abnormality is far from universal and a significant proportion of depressed individuals have normal DLPFC activity (Fitzgerald et al., 2006).

Neuroimaging studies could predict response to treatment. A PET scan study of depressed subjects who responded to six weeks of antidepressant medications showed hypermetabolism in the rostral anterior cingulate by comparison to controls, whereas depressed subjects who did not respond had hypometabolism of the same area (Mayberg et al., 1997).

Other brain areas also show abnormal findings. The hippocampus' volume is reduced in depressed patients (Frodl et al., 2002). The amygdala, which has important connections with the ventrolateral and lateral prefrontal cortex and with the medial orbital cortex, has shown decrease in blood flow and metabolism (Abercromie et al., 1998; Drevets et al., 1992). Two basal ganglia structures, the caudate and the putamen, which have widespread connections with the cerebral cortex (Alexander, DeLong, & Strick, 1986), show some functional and structural abnormalities in depressed patients. The caudate exhibits decreased brain metabolism and decreased volume (Krishnan et al., 1990), and the putamen's volume is smaller in depressed patients than in normal controls (Husain et al., 1990). In addition, asymptomatic but genetically at risk subjects show hypometabolism of the caudate and the putamen.

Neural Network Models of Depression

On the basis of their neuroimaging findings, Mayberg and colleagues proposed a network model of abnormal connections between paralimbic structures and cortical structures as a possible pathophysiological mechanism of depression. Their findings include:

1) Similar patterns of brain metabolism consistent with hypoperfusion of paralimbic cortical structures and the temporal cortex are observed in

both patients with endogenous depression and depressed patients with underlying neurological disease such as Parkinson's, Huntington's disease and basal ganglia stroke (Mayberg, Lewis, Regenold, & Wagner, Jr, 1994).

2) A reciprocal relationship in brain metabolism is observed in the induction of sadness in normal individuals, with an *increase* in metabolism in limbic and paralimbic structures, including the sugenual cingulate (Brodman area 25) and the ventral, mid-, and posterior insula, and a *decrease* in blood flow to cortical regions such as the right DLPFC, the inferior parietal, the dorsal anterior cingulate, and the posterior cingulate.
3) A reversed pattern of that observed in sadness is seen with successful treatment of depression: Blood flow is i*ncreased* to those cortical regions and *decreased* to those limbic and paralimbic structures. (Mayberg et al., 2005).

Treatment

Overview The so-called somatic therapies include several generations of antidepressant medications and a growing family of nonpharmacologic strategies, now grouped together as neuromodulation strategies. Clinical experience led to the widespread acceptance of the TCAs as the standard for first-line treatment of depressive disorders by the end of the 1960s; the TCAs held this position for approximately twenty years, until supplanted by the SSRIs. Although the rapid marketplace success of the SSRIs was no doubt catalysed by vigorous commercial promotion, by the end of the 1990s it was clear that this class of medication also offered substantial advantages over the TCAs in terms of tolerability and safety in overdose. Moreover, it is now nearly twenty years since the SSRIs became the standard of antidepressant therapy – and there is no indication of an heir apparent. Thus it is possible that relatively inexpensive, generically available SSRIs will remain the first-choice antidepressant for at least another decade or more, until neuroscience developments make it possible to more precisely match individual patients with specific antidepressants.

Acute-phase pharmacotherapy The acute phase of antidepressant therapy describes the period between the initiation of treatment and a successful outcome (APA, 2000, 2000b). After an initial evaluation, visits for clinical management during pharmacotherapy usually are 15 to 30 minutes long and, in addition to the prescription of medication, should include symptom assessment, psychoeducation, and supportive clinical management (APA, 2000a, 2000b). Few physicians used standardized symptom measures such as the HAM-D in clinical practice, though there is a growing emphasis on the use of self-report scales for the purpose of helping to objectively document and monitor progress. Commonly used self-report scales include the Beck Depression Inventory (BDI) and the depression subscale of the Patient Health Questionnaire (PHQ9). During the acute phase of treatment patients may be seen weekly, every other week, or – if severity or suicidality are not clinical concerns – monthly. Selection of the specific medication is usually based on factors such as the patient's past treatment history, cost, safety, and tolerability (APA, 2000a, 2000b). However, there is only about a 50 per cent chance that the first choice of treatment will work; and additional treatment trials may be necessary. In the Sequenced Alternatives to Relieve Depression (STAR*D) study, perhaps the largest systematic study of depression treatment ever undertaken, about 20 per cent remained depressed after four treatments.

First-generation antidepressants Until the introduction of fluoxetine in late 1987, there were essentially two types of antidepressant medications: the TCAs and the MAOIs. As reviewed earlier, these medications initiate antidepressant effects by potentiating monoamine neurotransmission. With the exception of one medication, clomipramine, the TCAs primarily exert this effect by inhibiting norepinephrine uptake. The MAOIs inhibit the enzymatic degradation of norepinephrine, serotonin, and dopamine. Both types of antidepressants are now generally relegated to use as third- or fourth-line strategies, though they continue to be uniquely valuable medications for some depressed people who have responded to therapy with newer antidepressants. However, even though the value of the MAOIs for patients with features of atypical depression was appreciated long before these meta-analyses were completed, most physicians preferred the TCAs for first-line therapy, because the MAOIs were associated with risks for drug–drug interactions and for a particular type of dietary interaction, the so-called 'cheese effect' (i.e., a rapid rise in blood pressure following ingestion of foodstuffs rich in the amino acid tyramine). Attempts to develop safer MAOIs have been only partially successful, as evidenced by minimal contemporary use of the two 'newer' members of this class of drugs: a transdermally delivered formulation of seligiline, which is only available in the United States, and moclobemide, which is a reversible inhibitor of the MAO A isoenzyme that is not available for use in the United States (Thase & Denko, 2008).

Second-generation antidepressants Most of the antidepressants that have been introduced over the past two decades belong to two classes: the selective serotonin reuptake inhibitors (SSRIs) and the serotonin-norepinephrine reuptake inhibitors (SNRIs) – the SSRIs being more widely considered to be the first line of pharmacotherapy. Clinical experience, expert opinion, and meta-analyses of comparative studies generally conclude that the SSRIs, while no more effective than the TCAs and the MAOIs, are easier to prescribe (i.e., they can often be started at therapeutic doses, with less subsequent need for titration), have more favourable tolerability profiles, and are significantly less dangerous in overdose (APA, 2000b; Thase & Denko, 2008). As was the case when the TCAs were compared with the MAOIs, a meta-analysis of inpatient studies found that the SSRIs were less effective than TCAs such as imipramine, amitriptyline, and clomipramine (Anderson, 1998).

SSRIs are drugs that selectively and potently inhibit of the 5-HT uptake transporter. The selectivity of action largely explained the tolerability advantage of the SSRIs by comparison to the TCAs, which frequently cause the side effects mediated by blockade of cholinergic (e.g., dry mouth or constipation), histaminergic (sedation), and adrenergic receptors (orthostatic hypotension) (Edwards & Anderson, 1999). Nor do the SSRIs share the TCAs' strong effects on cardiac conduction, which accounts for the lower fatality risk after overdose (Buckley & McManus, 2002). There are six members of the SSRI class: fluoxetine, fluvoxamine, sertraline, paroxetine, citalopram, and escitalopram. Common side effects include gastrointestinal symptoms such as nausea and diarrhea, insomnia, and sexual dysfunctions such as diminished libido and delay to orgasm. Various members of the SSRI class also have an established efficacy for anxiety disorders including panic, obsessive compulsive and generalized social anxiety, and post-traumatic stress disorders. Meta-analyses and qualitative reviews suggest that no one SSRI is inherently superior to the others (Edwards & Anderson, 1999; Thase & Denko, 2008), though escitalopram appears to have a modest efficacy advantage compared to its 'parent' compound, citalopram (Kennedy, Andersen, & Lam, 2006). As only escitalopram is still patent-protected, most pharmacy benefits plans follow 'stepped care' protocols that favour prescription of the less expensive, generically available drugs. Comparability is not the same thing as interchangeability, however, and there are both pharmacokinetic and pharmacodynamic differences between the various drugs that can have important clinical implications for particular patients. These differences include the incidence of certain side effects, the risk of drug–drug interactions, and the likelihood of discontinuation, emergent symptoms following the abrupt cessation of therapy (Edwards & Anderson, 1999; Thase & Denko, 2008).

The SNRIs – venlafaxine, desvenlafaxine, duloxetine, and milnacipran – are now the second most widely prescribed class of antidepressants. Of these drugs, only the relatively little used immediate release form of venlafaxine is currently widely available, as a generic and milnacipran has not received approval for the treatment of depression in the United States. Introduced after the SSRIs, the SNRIs are often ranked as second-line therapies, in part because they are somewhat less well tolerated than the SSRIs and in part because the most widely used members of this class are not yet available in generic formulations (Thase & Denko, 2008). It was hoped that the SNRIs would have the safety and tolerability advantages of the SSRIs but, on the basis of the second mechanism of action, would also have the efficacy advantage of the most potent TCAs for severe depression. The data from RCTs have only partly supported this prediction, however, and across studies the SNRIs have only a small (i.e., 5 per cent to 7 per cent) efficacy advantage by comparison to SSRIs (Papakostas, Thase, Fava, Nelson, & Shelton, 2007; Thase et al., 2007; Thase, 2008b). The SNRIs have all of the common side effects of the SSRIs as well as some additional side effects attributable to noradrenergic effects – such as constipation, dry mouth, and increases in pulse and blood pressure.

Bupropion, the only antidepressant referred to as a norepinephrine and dopamine reuptake inhibitor (NDRI), is the only widely used drug that does not directly affect serotonin neurotransmission (Thase & Denko, 2008). A number of head-to-head RCTs have been conducted comparing bupropion and various SSRIs, and meta-analyses indicated almost exact parity with the SSRIs (Thase et al., 2005; Papakostas et al., 2006). Unlike the SSRIs and SNRIs, bupropion does not have an established efficacy for the treatment of any anxiety disorders, and some clinicians have been reluctant to use this medication to treat patients with prominent anxiety. The major rationale for selecting bupropion instead of an SSRI or an SNRI is that it has a much lower incidence of treatment-emergent sexual side effects (Thase et al., 2005; Thase et al., 2006). Bupropion is also widely used as an adjunct to SSRIs, which can be thought of as an ersatz 'triple reuptake inhibitor' combination therapy.

Two other second-generation antidepressants – nefazodone and mirtazapine – do not have clinically significant effects on monoamine uptake and are sometimes referred to as 'norepinephrine and serotonin receptor modulators'. Like bupropion, these drugs are not associated with high rates of sexual side effects, but – unlike bupropion and the SSRIs and SNRIs – they convey some additional advantages for the treatment of insomnia. Clinical use of nefazodone has diminished substantially since it was shown to have a higher risk of liver problems than other antidepressants (Thase & Denko, 2008). Wider scale use of mirtazapine has been limited by a higher incidence of weight gain and sedation than the SSRIs, SNRIs, and bupropion (Thase & Denko, 2008).

The high rate of nonresponse to standard medications has led to the adjunctive use of other medications that do not have primary antidepressant effects to augment or enhance patient outcomes. These include several older medications such as lithium salts and thyroid hormone, and newer options such as the second-generation antipsychotic (SGA) medications (Thase, 2004). Among the SGAs, aripiprazole, quetiapine, and olanzapine specifically combined with the antidepressant fluoxetine have been approved in the United States; regulatory review is ongoing in other countries. There is little question about the efficacy of the SGAs as a class, though important questions persist about the relative efficacy, cost effectiveness, and safety of these medications when compared to older augmentation options. Beyond the potential for these medications to cause metabolic side effects such as weight gain, dyslipidemia, and glucose intolerance (Newcomer, 2007), there is also uncertainty about the magnitude of the risk for tardive dyskinesia, which must be faced during longer term therapy.

Antidepressants, suicidality, and treatment of depressed teenagers

Although reports suggesting a possible association between the second-generation antidepressants and treatment-emergent suicidality began to surface shortly after the introduction of fluoxetine (Teicher, Glod, & Cole, 1990), this topic only gained widespread attention a few years ago, in conjunction with more far-reaching concerns about the increasing use of antidepressants in children and adolescents (see, for example, Bridge et al., 2007; Mann et al., 2006). The FDA reviewed the data from 24 double-blind, placebo-controlled RCTs of antidepressants administered to youth and found a two-fold increase in the risk of suicidal behaviour (i.e.,

4 per cent versus 2 per cent) during the first few weeks after initiation of therapy. Importantly, there were no completed suicides in these studies. The FDA subsequently reviewed age-related trends in a larger number of RCTs in adults and reached the same conclusion for 18- to 24-year-olds. As a result, all antidepressants now carry a 'black box warning' that summarizes the risk of treatment-emergent suicidality. In the two years that followed the FDA's action, there was a significant decrease in the prescription of antidepressants to youth (Kurian, Arbogast, Ray, Fuchs, & Cooper, 2006; Nemeroff et al., 2007) and, for the first time in two decades, an increase in the rate of completed suicide in this segment of the population (Gibbons, Hur, Bhaumik, & Mann, 2006). The decision as to whether to prescribe or not an antidepressant for a depressed teenager or young adult must obviously take into account the known risks and the uncertain benefits, as well as the potential utility of psychotherapy. In any event, the treatment plan should include close follow-up and instructions about the availability of after-hours or emergency services.

Longer term antidepressant therapy

Depression frequently runs an episodic or recurrent course and, for patients who respond to antidepressant medications, longer courses of therapy are recommended in order to reduce the risks of relapse or recurrence. The acute phase of therapy is thus followed by a second or continuation phase of therapy, which may last from 4 to 12 months (APA, 2000a, 2000b). A meta-analysis of RCTs of continuation-phase therapy found that patients who received active antidepressants had about half the risk of relapse across a 6- to 9-month interval as compared to patients switched to placebo (Geddes et al., 2003). All medications with established antidepressant efficacy appear to be effective for relapse prevention, although there are differences in the incidence of side effects such as sexual dysfunction and weight gain (Thase & Denko, 2008). In addition to preventing relapse, continuation-phase pharmacotherapy is also intended to help ensure a stable and complete symptomatic remission and restoration of social functioning (APA, 2000a, 2000b). As the continuation phase progresses, patients are seen less frequently, the norm typically being monthly sessions during the final months of the continuation phase.

Even longer courses of maintenance-phase pharmacotherapy are indicated for individuals who have experienced three or more depressive episodes (APA, 2000a, 2000b). A number of placebo-controlled studies have demonstrated the efficacy of maintenance-phase pharmacotherapy across 12, 18, or 24 months (see, for example, Geddes et al., 2003 or Thase, 2006b). During the maintenance-phase pharmacotherapy patients are typically seen monthly or quarterly, although some extremely stable patients are seen on an annual basis.

Maintenance-phase pharmacotherapy is sometimes discussed as if it may be a life-long requirement, akin to the role of insulin therapy for someone with diabetes. This view reflects fact that there is a high risk of relapse during the first 6 to 12 months after the withdrawal of antidepressant treatment, regardless of the duration of remission during continuation or maintenance therapy (Thase, 2006b). The notion of lifelong treatment also does not take into account the possibility that new forms of treatment with more enduring, even curative benefits may be introduced in the future (Thase, 2006b). Nevertheless, maintenance-phase pharmacotherapy usually does not begin with a particular endpoint in mind, and an assessment of the benefits and risks of ongoing treatment should be collaboratively performed at each follow-up visit.

Neuromodulation strategies Advances in biomedical engineering and neuroimaging have played a key role in the development of a new therapeutic field in psychiatry called neuromodulation. These strategies use device-based interventions that primarily target the neural circuitry of mood instead of selected neuronal synapses. In addition to electro-convulsive therapy (ECT) – the oldest device used in psychiatry – the neuromodulation strategies include vagus nerve stimulation (VNS), transcranial magnetic stimulation (TMS), and deep brain stimulation (DBS). In this chapter we will review only the newer interventions.

VNS is an implantable device initially developed to treat epilepsy. Observations of mood improvement independent of seizure control in patients with epilepsy led to further studies in depression. In 2005 the Food and Drug Administration (FDA) approved VNS for the treatment of resistant depression. VNS requires the surgical implantation of both a small generator on the chest wall and an electrode that is wrapped around the left vagus nerve in the neck. Electrical impulses are transmitted from the generator to the afferent fibres of the vagus nerve, which carries impulses to the nucleus tractus solitarius in the brain stem. This nucleus connects to other brain regions – including limbic structures, the locus ceruleus, and the raphe nuclei. It is postulated that VNS antidepressant effects are due to actions on these brainstem monoamine centres as well as on limbic structures involved in mood regulation – such as the amygdala, the hippocampus, and the cingulated gyrus – as evidenced by PET imaging studies (Nemeroff et al., 2006; George et al., 2000).

The one-year clinical trial that led to FDA's approval of VNS compared treatment as usual (TAU) to VNS added to TAU (n = 205). Response rate – defined as 50 per cent reduction in depressive symptoms – was 27 per cent for the VNS plus TAU group versus 13 per cent for the TAU group. The majority of patients (70 per cent) who received VNS had severe and chronic depressions and had not benefitted from at least four antidepressant trials (George et al., 2005). In clinical practice antidepressant effects appear similar. For example, our group recently reported on the one-year outcomes of 15 severely depressed and highly treatment-resistant outpatients. Response and remission rates were 29 per cent and 7 per cent respectively, according to the Beck Depression Inventory (Conolly, Cristancho, Cristancho, O'Reardon, & Baltuch, 2008). VNS is well tolerated and has generally mild side effects, including hoarseness, dyspnea, and cough. However, this surgical intervention is usually reserved for patients with severe and treatment-resistant depression.

TMS is a neuromodulation intervention based on the principle of electromagnetic induction discovered by Faraday in 1931. According to this principle, a changing magnetic field induces a current in a nearby conductor. The TMS device consists of an insulated coil of wire that is placed on the patient's scalp and a console that delivers an electrical current to the coil. The flow of current to the coil generates a pulsed and strong magnetic field (1.5–3.0 Tesla, similar to an MRI machine) that passes through the cranium with minimal impedance. This rapidly changing magnetic field induces an electrical current in the underlying cerebral cortex and is believed to cause neuronal depolarization.

Initially, TMS was used as a tool to investigate brain function, including cortical plasticity and cognition (Fitzgerald, Brown, & Daskalakis, 2002). In 1995 George and colleagues demonstrated that repetitive TMS over the left DLPC relieved depression in several patients (George et al., 1995). They targeted this area on the basis of previous neroimaging studies that suggested that that hypofunction the DLPFC is involved in the pathophysiology of depression (George et al., 1995). Numerous controlled trials have subsequently demonstrated the antidepressant effects of TMS (George et al., 1997; Avery et al., 2006, Fizgerald et al., 2003), meta-analyses showing superior antidepressant effects over sham stimulation (MacNamara, Ray, Arthurs, & Boniface, 2001; Kozel & George, 2002; Gross, Nakamura,

Pascual Leone, & Fregni, 2007). In the United States TMS was approved in 2008 for the treatment of unipolar non-psychotic depression, after a large randomized controlled trial (n = 301). After four weeks TMS over the left DLPC proved superior to sham stimulation, showing significant reduction of scores in the Montgomery Asberg Depression Rating Scale (MADRS) (p =.038) (O'Reardon et al., 2007).

Although clearly less effective than ECT, TMS is an attractive alternative because it is an office-based procedure and patients undergoing stimulation are awake, require no sedation or anaesthesia, and do not experience cognitive side effects. Common side effects include mild headaches and scalp discomfort. Patients should wear earplugs due to the loud clicking sound from the stimulation. The only serious potential side effect is the inadvertent induction of a seizure, which is an extremely rare event, only 12 cases of seizure being reported in the TMS literature (Loo, McFarquhar, & Mitchell, 2008).

DBS is a novel intervention that involves the neurosurgical implant of two small electrodes (implanted bilaterally) in subcortical brain areas implicated in the pathogenesis of depression. DBS is different from other neurosurgical procedures such as cingulotomy or limbic leucotomy; it does not destroy brain tissue and is potentially reversible. DBS electrodes are connected, via extension wires tunnelled through the skin, to two generators implanted bilaterally in the chest. Operated by the generator, the electrode delivers continuous high-frequency electrical stimulation to targeted areas. Surgical complications such as symptomatic hemorrhage, infection, and seizure occur in about 1–4 per cent of cases (Higgins & George, 2009).

Although DBS is now widely used as treatment for movement disorders, its use in depression is investigative and reserved for patients with severe, chronic, and treatment-resistant depression who have failed to respond to psychotherapy, medications, and ECT. DBS targets specific nodes within interconnected brain circuits that involve cortical, subcortical, and limbic brain regions that ultimately modulate mood (Shah, Ebmeier, Glabus, & Goodwin, 2008). Mayberg and colleagues implanted DBS electrodes in the subgenual cingulated white matter (Brodmann area 25), on the basis of neuroimaging, and demonstrated hyperactive brain metabolism in this area in six depressed patients. In this study four patients responded at six months (Mayberg et al., 2005). Bewernick et al. (2010) targeted the nucleus accumbens – a key structure of the brain reward system. They reported response in 5 out of 10 patients after 12 months. Malone and colleagues chose to target the ventral anterior internal capsule/ventral striatum based on previous evidence of improvement in comorbid depressive symptoms in patients treated with DBS for OCD and from experience derived from ablative procedures in the same area showing improvement in depressive symptoms. In this group of 15 patients, response rates were 47 per cent at 3 months, 40 per cent at six months and 53 per cent at last follow up (Malone et al., 2009). Even though an invasive intervention, DBS thus shows promise for relieving depression in patients with the most severe forms and for whom many other alternatives have failed.

Conclusions

Depression is an extremely heterogeneous clinical condition, associated with a number of psychobiological disturbances. Some of these, such as hypercortisolism, are largely state-dependent and are more likely to be observed among individuals with more severe symptoms; this association underpins the classical subtype of endogenous depression or melancholia. Other disturbances are more trait-like and are associated with an early age of onset and greater heritability. As possibly exemplified by limbic reactivity, such vulnerability 'markers' may predispose to heightened responses to stress, influencing symptom expression early in life and potentially altering developmental trajectories. Although some psychopathologists have found it heuristically useful to view these psychobiological processes from a dichotomous perspective, in reality the processes are closely interwoven across lifetime. Indeed both the predominant symptoms of depression and the response to particular types of treatment can change over time. From a psychobiologically informed developmental perspective, the first lifetime depressive episode is characteristically provoked by some type of stress or adversity, and those at higher genetic risk are the most likely to develop a clinically significant depressive episode (Caspi et al., 2003). The association between life events and onset of depression is much less pronounced over time, however, and many individuals at midlife experience recurrent depressive episodes almost 'out of the blue'. A for those who live into their seventh or eighth decade without experiencing depression – a true test of hardiness in the twenty-first century – the psychobiological effects of cerebrovascular disease and Alzheimer's disease can cause depression even in those with minimal heritable risk.

Despite nearly 50 years of research, the psychobiological nature of depression is still not well understood. Nevertheless, there has been great progress, particularly in terms of understanding neural circuitry, genetic risk factors, and the intracellular processes involved with both the illness and some of its treatments. For example, it is now possible to use radionucleotide-labelled messenger RNA to monitor the activity of specific gene activity, both in response to changes in clinical state and in response to specific treatments. Neuroimaging studies have documented changes in several regions of the brain, both in resting studies and in response to various challenge paradigms, which reveal both commonalities and differences between depression and 'normal sadness' in healthy individuals. The growth of research that followed the recognition of a link between limbic activation in response to threat or stress and the less functional *s* allele of the serotonin transporter underscores the field's current capacity to implement and test new paradigms. We are also on the threshold of a new generation of research that addresses heritable resilience factors – namely genes that may be associated with a lower risk of illness. As more fine-grained knowledge about the psychobiological nature of depression continues to accumulate, it will hopefully become possible to move beyond the current generation of antidepressant medications, which are tied to monoamine systems, and identify novel medications and noninvasive neuromodulation strategies that may be more effective, better tolerated, or useful for people who are not helped by the current standards.

References

Abercromie, H. C., Schaefer, S. M., Larson, C. L., Oakes, T. R., Lindgren, K. A., Holden, J. E., … Davidson, R. J. (1998). Metabolic rate in the right amygdala predicts negative affect in depressed patients. *Neuroreport*, *9*, 3301–3307.

Alexander, G. E., DeLong, M. R., & Strick, P. R. (1986). Parallel organization of functionally segregated circuits linking basal ganglia and cortex. *Annual Review of Neuroscience*, *9*, 357–381.

APA. (2000a). *Diagnostic and statistical manual of mental disorders: DSM-IV-TR*. Washington, DC: American Psychiatric Association.

APA. (2000b). Practice guideline for the treatment of patients with major depressive disorder. *American Journal of Psychiatry*, *157*(Suppl. 4), 1–45.

Anderson, I. M. (1998). SSRIS versus tricyclic antidepressants in depressed inpatients: A meta-analysis of efficacy and tolerability. *Depression and Anxiety*, *7*(Suppl 1), 11–17.

Avery, D. H., Holtzheimer, P. E., 3rd, Fawaz, W., Russo, J., Neumaier, J., Dunner, D. L. … Roy-Byrne, P. (2006). A controlled study of transcranial magnetic stimulation in medication-resistant major depression. *Biological Psychiatry, 59*(2), 187–194.

Berton, O., McClung, C. A., Dileone, R. J., Krishnan, V., Renthal, W., Russo, S. J. … Nestler, E. J. (2006). Essential role of BDNF in the mesolimbic dopamine pathway in social defeat stress. *Science, 311*(5762), 864–868.

Bewernick, B. H., Hurlemann, R., Matusch, A., Kayser, S., Grubert, C., Hadrysiewicz, B. … Schlaepfer, T. E. (2010). Nucleus accumbens deep brain stimulation decreases ratings of depression and anxiety in treatment-resistant depression. *Biological Psychiatry, 67*, 110–116.

Bielau, H., Trübner, K., Krell, D., Agelink, M. W., Bernstein, H. G., Stauch, R. … Baumann, B. (2005). Volume deficits of subcortical nuclei in mood disorders: A postmortem study. *European Archives of Psychiatry and Clinical Neuroscience, 255*, 401–412.

Bradley, R. G., Binder, E. B., Epstein, M. P., Tang, Y., Nair, H. P., Liu W. … Ressler, K. J. (2008). Influence of child abuse on adult depression: Moderation by the corticotropin-releasing hormone receptor gene. *Archives of General Psychiatry, 65*, 190–200.

Bridge, J. A., Iyengar, S., Salary, C. B., Barbe, R. P., Birmaher, B., Pincus, H. A., Ren, L., & Brent, D. A. (2007). Clinical response and risk for reported suicidal ideation and suicide attempts in pediatric antidepressant treatment: A meta-analysis of randomized controlled trials. *Journal of the American Medical Association, 297*(15), 1683–1696.

Brown, S. M., & Hariri, A. R. (2006). Neuroimaging studies of serotonin gene polymorphisms: Exploring the interplay of genes, brain, and behavior. *Cognitive, Affective, & Behavioral Neuroscience, 6*, 44–52.

Buckley, N. A., & McManus, P. R. (2002). Fatal toxicity of serotoninergic and other antidepressant drugs: Analysis of United Kingdom mortality data. *BMJ, 325*, 1332–1333.

Burke, H. M., Davis, M. C., Otte, C., & Mohr, D. C. (2005). Depression and cortisol responses to psychological stress: A meta-analysis. *Psychoneuroendocrinology, 30*, 846–856.

Cannon, D. M., Carson, R. E., Nugent, A. C., Eckelman, W. C., Kiesewetter, D. O., Williams, J. … & Drevets, W. C. (2006). Reduced muscarinic type 2 receptor binding in subjects with bipolar disorder. *Archives of General Psychiatry, 63*(7), 741–747.

Caspi, A., Sugden, K., Moffitt, T. E., Taylor, A., Craig, I. W., Harrington, H. … Poulton, R. (2003). Influence of life stress on depression: Moderation by a polymorphism in the 5-HTT gene. *Science, 301*, 386–389.

Chambers, R. A., Potenza, M. N., Hoffman, R. E., & Miranker, W. (2004). Simulated apoptosis/neurogenesis regulates learning and memory capabilities of adaptive neural networks. *Neuropsychopharmacology*, *29*(4), 747–758.

Conolly, P., Cristancho, P., Cristancho, M., O'Reardon, J. P., & Baltuch, G. (2008). Abstract presented at the meeting of the American Association of Neurological Surgeons, Vancouver, June 1–4.

Coplan, J. D., Smith, E. L., Altemus, M., Mathew, S. J., Perera, T., Kral, J. G. ... Rosenblum, L. A. (2006). Maternal–infant response to variable foraging demand in nonhuman primates: Effects of timing of stressor on cerebrospinal fluid corticotropin-releasing factor and circulating glucocorticoid concentrations. *Annals of the New York Academy of Sciences*, *1071*, 525–533.

Coplan, J. D., Smith, E. L., Altemus, M., Scharf, B. A., Owens, M. J., Nemeroff, C. B., Gorman, J. M., & Rosenblum, L. A. (2001). Variable foraging demand rearing: Sustained elevations in cisternal cerebrospinal fluid corticotropin-releasing factor concentrations in adult primates. *Biological Psychiatry*, *50*, 200–204.

Delay, J., Laine, B., & Buisson, J. F. (1952). Note concernant l'action de l'isonicotinylhydrazide dans le traitement des états dépressifs. *Annales Médico-psychologiques*, *110*, 689–692.

Delgado, P. L., Miller, H. L., Salomon, R. M., Licinio, J., Krystal, J. H., Moreno, F. A. ... Charney, D. S. (1999). Tryptophan-depletion challenge in depressed patients treated with desipramine or fluoxetine: Implications for the role of serotonin in the mechanism of antidepressant action. *Biological Psychiatry*, *46*, 212–220.

Drevets, W. C. (2000). Functional anatomical abnormalities in limbic and prefrontal cortical structures in major depression. *Progress in Brain Research*, *126*, 413–431.

Drevets, W. C., Thase, M. E., Moses-olko, E. L., Price, J., Frank, E., Kupfer, D. J., & Mathis, C. (2007). Serotonin-1A receptor imaging in recurrent depression: Replication and literature review. *Nuclear Medicine and Biology*, *34*, 865–877.

Drevets, W. C., Videen, T. O., Price, J. L., Preskorn, S. H., Carmichael, S. T., & Raichle, M. E. (1992). A functional anatomical study of unipolar depression. *Journal of Neuroscience*, *12*, 3628–3641.

Duman, C. H., Schlesinger, L., Kodama, M., Russell, D. S., & Duman, R. S. (2007). A role for MAP kinase signaling in behavioral models of depression and antidepressant treatment. *Biological Psychiatry*, *61*, 661–670.

Edwards, J. G., & Anderson, I. (1999). Systematic review and guide to selection of selective serotonin reuptake inhibitors. *Drugs*, *57*(4), 507–533.

Eisch, A. J., Bolaños, C. A., de Wit, J., Simonak, R. D., Pudiak, C. M., Barrot, M., Verhaagen, J., & Nestler, E. J. (2003). Brain-derived neurotrophic factor in the ventral midbrain–nucleus accumbens pathway: A role in depression. *Biological Psychiatry*, *54*(10), 994–1005.

Elhwuegi, A. S. (2004). Central monoamines and their role in major depression. *Progress in Neuropsychopharmacology and Biological Psychiatry*, *28*, 435–451.

Eriksson, P. S., Perfilieva, E., Björk-Eriksson, T., Alborn, A. M., Nordborg, C., Peterson, D. A., & Gage, F. H. (1998). Neurogenesis in the adult human hippocampus. *Nature Medicine*, *4*(11), 1313–1317.

Fitzgerald, P. B., Brown, T. L., & Daskalakis, Z. J. (2002). The application of transcranial magnetic stimulation in psychiatry and neurosciences research. *Acta Psychiatrica Scandinavica*, 2002, *105*, 324–340.

Fitzgerald, P. B., Brown, T. L., Marston, N. A., Daskalakis, J., De Castella, A., & Kulkarni, J. (2003). Transcranial magnetic stimulation in the treatment of depression: A double blind, placebo-controlled trial. *Archives of General Psychiatry*, *60*(10), 1002–1008.

Fitzgerald, P. B., Oxley, T. J., Laird, A. R., Kulkarni, J., Egan, G. F., & Daskalakis, Z. J. (2006). An analysis of functional neuroimaging studies of dorsolateral prefrontal cortical activity in depression. *Psychiatry Research*, *148*(1), 33–45.

Frodl, T., Meisenzahl, E. M., Zetzsche, T., Born, C., Groll, C., Jäger, M. … Möller, H. J. (2002). Hippocampal changes in patients with a first episode of major depression. *American Journal of Psychiatry*, *159*(7), 1112–1118.

Frye, M. A., Grunze, H., Suppes, T., McElroy, S. L., Keck, P. E. Jr, Walden, J. … Post, R. M. (2007). A placebo-controlled evaluation of adjunctive modafinil in the treatment of bipolar depression. *American Journal of Psychiatry*, *164*(8), 1242–1249.

Furey, M. L., & Drevets, W. C. (2006). Antidepressant efficacy of the antimuscarinic drug scopolamine: A randomized, placebo-controlled clinical trial. *Archives of General Psychiatry*, *63*, 1121–1129.

Geddes, J. R., Carney, S. M., Davies, C., Furukawa, T. A., Kupfer, D. J., Frank, E., & Goodwin, G. M. (2003). Relapse prevention with antidepressant drug treatment in depressive disorders: A systematic review. *Lancet*, *361*, 653–661.

George, M. S., Rush, A. J., Marangell, L. B., Sackeim, H. A., Brannan, S., Davis, S. M. … Goodnick, P. (2005). A one-year comparison of vagus nerve stimulation with treatment as usual for treatment-resistant depression. *Biological Psychiatry*, *58*, 364–373.

George, M. S., Sackeim, H. A., Rush, A. J., Marangell, L. B., Nahas, Z., Husain, M. M. … Ballenger, J. C. (2000). Vagus nerve stimulation: A new tool for brain research and therapy. *Biological Psychiatry*, *47*(4), 287–295.

George, M. S., Wassermann, E., Kimbrell, T. A., Little, J. T., Williams, W. E., Danielson, A. L. … Hallett, M. (1997). Mood improvement following daily prefrontal transcranial magnetic stimulation in patients with depression: A placebo controlled crossover trial. *American Journal of Psychiatry*, *154*, 1752–1756.

George, M. S., Wasserman, E. M., Williams, W. A., Callahan, A., Ketter, T. A., Baser, P. … Post, R. M. (1995). Daily repetitive transcranial magnetic stimulation (rTMS) improves mood in depression. *Neuroreport*, *6*(14), 1853–1856.

Gershon, A., Vishne, T., & Grunhaus, L. (2007). Dopamine D2-like receptors and the antidepressant response. *Biological Psychiatry*, *61*, 145–153.

Gibbons, R. D., Hur, K., Bhaumik, D. K., & Mann, J. J. (2006). The relationship between antidepressant prescription rates and rate of early adolescent suicide. *American Journal of Psychiatry*, *163*(11), 1898–1904.

Goldberg, J. F., Burdick, K. E., & Endick, C. J. (2004). Preliminary randomized, double-blind, placebo-controlled trial of pramipexole added to mood stabilizers for treatment-resistant bipolar depression. *American Journal of Psychiatry*, *161*(3), 564–566.

Goodwin, F. K., & Bunney, W. E., Jr (1971). Depression following reserpine: A re-evaluation. *Seminars in Psychiatry*, *3*, 435–448.

Greenberger, B. D., Tolliver, T. J., Huang, S. J., Li O, Bengel, D. … Murphy, D. L. (1999). Genetic variation in the serotonin transporter promoter region affects serotonin uptake in human blood platelets. *American Journal of Medical Genetics*, *88*, 83–87.

Gross, M., Nakamura, L., Pascual Leone, A., & Fregni, F. (2007). Has repetitive transcranial magnetic stimulation (rTMS) treatment for depression improved? A systematic review and meta-analysis comparing the recent vs the earlier rTMS studies. *Acta Psychiatrica Scandinavica*, *116*, 165–173.

Harvey, P. O., Fossati, P., Pochon, J. B., Levy, R., Lebastard, G., Lehéricy, S. … Dubois, B. (2005). Cognitive control and brain resources in major depression: An fMRI study using the n-back task. *Neuroimage*, *26*(3), 860–869.

Heim, C., & Nemeroff, C. B. (2001). The role of childhood trauma in the neurobiology of mood and anxiety disorders: Preclinical and clinical studies. *Biological Psychiatry*, *49*(12), 1023–1039.

Higgins, E., & George, M. S. (2009). Deep brain stimulation and cortical stimulation. In E. Higgins & M. S. George (Eds), *Brain stimulation therapies for clinicians* (pp. 121–145). Arlington, TX: American Psychiatric Publishing.

Husain, M. M., McDonald, W. M., Doraiswamy, P. M., Figiel, G. S., Na C., & Escalona, P. R. (1990). A magnetic resonance imaging study of putamen nuclei in major depression. *Psychiatry Research: Neuroimaging*, *40*, 95–99.

Janowsky, D. S., el-Yousef, M. K., & Davis, J. M. (1974). Acetylcholine and depression. *Psychosomatic Medicine*, *36*(3), 248–257.

Johnson, E. O., Roth, T., & Breslau, N. (2006). The association of insomnia with anxiety disorders and depression: Exploration of the direction of risk. *Journal of Psychiatric Research*, *40*, 700–708.

Kennedy, S. H., Andersen, H. F., & Lam, R. W. (2006). Efficacy of escitalopram in the treatment of major depressive disorder compared with conventional selective serotonin reuptake inhibitors and venlafaxine XR: A meta-analysis. *Journal of Psychiatry & Neuroscience, 31*(2), 122–131.

Kozel, A., & George, M. (2002). Meta-analysis of left prefrontal repetitive transcranial magnetic stimulation (rTMS) to treat depression. *Journal of Psychiatric Practice, 8*, 270–275.

Krishnan, K. R., Husain, M. M., McDonald, W. M., Doraiswamy, P. M., Figiel, G. S., Boyko, O. B., Ellinwood, E. H., & Nemeroff, C. B. (1990). In vivo stereological assessment of caudate volume in man: Effect of normal aging. *Life Sciences, 47*(15), 1325–1329.

Kuhn, R. (1958). The treatment of depressive states with G22355 (imipramine hydrochloride). *American Journal of Psychiatry, 115*, 459–464.

Kunugi, H., Ida, I., Owashi, T., Kimura, M., Inoue, & Nakagawa, S. (2006). Assessment of the dexamethasone/CRH test as a state dependent marker for hypothalamic–pituitary adrenal axis (HPA) axis abnormalities in major depressive episode: A multicenter study. *Neuropsychopharmachology, 31*(1), 212–220.

Kurian, B. T., Arbogast, P. G., Ray, W. A., Fuchs, D. C., & Cooper, W. O. (2006). Effect of government regulatory changes on SSRI prescriptions in children. *Pharmacoepidemiology and Drug Safety, 15*: S16.

Loo, C. K., McFarquhar, T. F., & Mitchell, P. B. (2008). A review of the safety of transcranial magnetic stimulation as a clinical treatment for depression. *International Journal of Neuropsychopharmacology, 11*, 131–147.

Lu, B, Pang, P. T., & Woo, N. H. (2005). The yin and yang of neurotrophin action. *Nature Review Neuroscience, 6*, 603–614.

MacNamara, B., Ray, J. L., Arthurs, O. J., & Boniface, S. (2001). Transcranial magnetic stimulation for depression and other psychiatric disorders. *Psychological Medicine, 31*(7), 1141–1146.

Maes, M., & Meltzer, H. Y. (1995). The serotonin hypothesis of major depression. In F. E. Bloom & D. J. Kupfer (Eds), *Psychopharmacology: The fourth generation of progress* (pp. 933–944). New York: Raven.

Malone, D. A., Dougherty, D. D, Rezai, A., Carpenter, L., Friehs, G., Eskandar, E. N. … Greenberg, B. D. (2009). Deep brain stimulation of the ventral capsule/ventral striatum for treatment-resistant depression. *Biological Psychiatry, 65*(4), 267–275.

Mann, J. J., Emslie, G., Baldessarini, R. J., Beardslee, W., Fawcett, J. A., Goodwin, F. K. … Wagner, K. D. (2006). ACNP task force report on SSRIs and suicidal behavior in youth. *Neuropsychopharmacology, 31*(3), 473–492.

Mayberg, H. S., Keightley, M., Mahurin, R. K., & Brannan, S. K. (2004). Neuropsychiatric aspects of mood and affective disorders. In S. C. Yudofsky & R. E. Hales (Eds), *Essentials of neuropsychiatry and clinical neurosciences* (pp. 503–504). Washington: American Psychiatric Publishing.

Mayberg, H. S., Lewis, P. J., Regenold, W., & Wagner, H. N., Jr (1994). Paralimbic hypoperfusion in unipolar depression. *Journal of Nuclear Medicine, 35*(6), 929–934.

Mayberg, H. S., Brannan S. K., Mahurin, R. K., Jerabek, P. A., Brickman, J. S, Tekell, J. L. ... Fox, P. T. (1997). Cingulate function in depression: A potential predictor of treatment response. *Neuroreport, 8*(4), 1057–1061.

Mayberg, H. S., Lozano, A. M., Voon, V., McNeely, H. E., Seminowicz, D., Hamani, C., Schwalb, J. M., & Kennedy, S. H. (2005). Deep brain stimulation for treatment-resistant depression. *Neuron, 45*, 651–660.

Ming, G. L., & Song, H. (2005). Adult neurogenesis in the mammalian central nervous system. *Annual Review of Neuroscience, 28*, 223–250.

Nemeroff, C. B., Kalali, A., Keller, M. B., Charney, D. S., Lenderts, S. E., Cascade, E. F., Stephenson, H., & Schatzberg, A. F. (2007). Impact of publicity concerning pediatric suicidality data on physician practice patterns in the United States. *Archives of General Psychiatry, 64*(4), 466–472.

Nemeroff, C. B., Mayberg, H. S., Krahl, S. E., McNamara, J., Frazer, A., Henry, T. R. ... Brannan, S. K. (2006). VNS therapy in treatment resistant depression: Clinical evidence and putative neurobiological mechanism. *Neuropsychopharmacology, 31*, 134–155.

Nemeroff, C. B., Widerlov, E., Bissette, G., Walleus, H., Karlsson, I., Eklund, K. ... Vale, W. (1984). Elvated concentrations of CSF corticotrophin-releasing factor-like inmmunoreactivity in depressed patients. *Science, 226*, 1342–1344.

Newcomer, J. W. (2007). Metabolic considerations in the use of antipsychotic medications: A review of recent evidence. *Journal of Clinical Psychiatry, 68*, 20–27.

Nitschke, J. B., & Mackiewicz, K. L. (2005). Prefrontal and anterior cingulate contributions to volition in depression. *International Review of Neurobiology, 67*, 73–94.

O'Reardon, J. P., Solvason, H. B., Janicak, P. G., Sampsom, S., Isenberg, K. E., Nahas, Z. ... Sackeim, H. A. (2007). Efficacy and safety of transcranial magnetic stimulation in the acute treatment of major depression: A multisite randomized controlled trial. *Biological Psychiatry, 62*, 1208–1216.

Papakostas, G. I., Thase, M. E., Fava, M., Nelson, J. C., & Shelton, R. C. (2007). Are antidepressant drugs that combine serotonergic and noradrenergic mechanisms of action more effective than the selective serotonin reuptake inhibitors in treating major depressive disorder? A meta-analysis of studies of newer agents. *Biological Psychiatry, 62*(11), 1217–1227.

Papakostas, G. I., Nutt, D. J., Hallett, L. A., Tucker, V. L., Krishen, A., & Fava, M. (2006). Resolution of sleepiness and fatigue in major depressive disorder: A comparison of bupropion and the selective serotonin reuptake inhibitors. *Biological Psychiatry, 60*(12), 1350–1355.

Pitchot, W., Hansenne, M., Pinto, E., Reggers, J., Fuchs, S., & Ansseau, M. (2005). 5-hydroxytryptamine 1A receptors, major depression, and suicidal behavior. *Biological Psychiatry, 58*, 854–858.

Pittenger, C., & Duman, R. S. (2008). Stress, depression, and neuroplasticity: A convergence of mechanisms. *Neuropsychopharmacology, 33*, 88–109.

Pittenger, C., Sanacora, G., & Krystal, J. H. (2007). The NMDA receptor as a therapeutic target in major depressive disorder. *CNS & Neurological Disorders: Drug Targets, 6*(2), 101–115.

Raadsheer, F. C., Hoogendijk, W. J. G, Stam, F. C., Tilders, F. H. J., & Swaab, D. F. (1994). Increased numbers of corticotrophin-releasing hormone expressing neurons in the hypothalamic paraventricular nucleous of depressed patients. *Neuroendocrinology, 60*, 433–436.

Ressler, K. L., & Nemeroff, C. B. (2000). Role of serotoninergic and noradrenergic systems in the pathophysiology of depression and anxiety disorder. *Depression and Anxiety, 12*(1), 2–19.

Sanacora, G., & Saricicek, A. (2007). GABAergic contributions to the pathophysiology of depression and the mechanism of antidepressant action. *CNS & Neurological Disorders: Drug Targets, 6*(2), 127–140.

Sapolsky, R. M. (2003). Stress and plasticity in the limbic system. *Neurochemical Research, 28*(11), 1735–1742.

Schildkraut, J. J. (1965). The catecholamine hypothesis of affective disorders: A review of supporting evidence. *American Journal of Psychiatry, 22*(122), 509–522.

Shah, P. J., Ebmeier, K. P., Glabus, M. F., & Goodwin, G. M. (1998). Cortical grey matter reductions associated with treatment-resistant chronic unipolar depression. Controlled magnetic resonance imaging study. *British Journal of Psychiatry, 172*, 527–532.

Sheline, Y. I., Sanghavi, M., Mintun, M. A., & Gado, M. H. (1999). Depression duration but not age predicts hippocampal volume loss in medically healthy women with recurrent major depression. *Journal of Neuroscience, 19*(12), 5034–5043.

Shelton, R. C. (2007). The molecular neurobiology of depression. *Psychiatric Clinics of North America, 30*, 1–11.

Stahl, S. M. (2005). Depression and bipolar disorders. In S. M. Stahl (Ed.), *Esssential psychopharmacology: Neuroscientific bases and practical applications* (pp. 135–197). New York: Cambridge University Press.

Teicher, M. T., Glod, C., & Cole, J. O. (1990). Emergence of intense suicidal preoccupation during fluoxetine treatment. *American Journal of Psychiatry, 147*(2), 207–210.

Thase, M. E. (2004). Therapeutic alternatives for difficult-to-treat depression: A narrative review of the state of the evidence. *CNS Spectrums, 9*(11), 808–16, 818–21.

Thase, M. E. (2006a). Depression and sleep: Pathophysiology and treatment. *Dialogues in Clinical Neuroscience, 8*, 217–226.

Thase, M. E. (2006b). Preventing relapse and recurrence of depression: A brief review of therapeutic options. *CNS Spectrums, 11*(12) (Suppl. 15), 12–21.

Thase, M. E. (2008a). Neurobiological aspects of depression. In I. H. Gotlib & C. L. Hammen (Eds), *Handbook of depression* (pp. 187–217). New York: Guilford.

Thase, M. E. (2008b). Are SNRIs More Effective than SSRIs? A review of the current state of the controversy. *Psychopharmacology Bulletin, 41*(2), 58–85.

Thase, M. E., & Denko, T. (2008). Pharmacotherapy of mood disorders. *Annual Review of Clinical Psychology, 4*, 53–91.

Thase, M. E., Jindal, R., & Howland, R. H. (2002). Biological aspects of depression. In I. H. Gotlib & C. H. Hammen (Eds), *Handbook of depression* (pp. 192–218). New York: Guilford.

Thase, M. E., Clayton, A. H., Haight, B. R., Thompson, A. H., Modell, J. G., & Johnston, J. A. (2006). A double-blind comparison between bupropion XL and venlafaxine XR: Sexual functioning, antidepressant efficacy, and tolerability. *Journal of Clinical Psychopharmacology, 26*(5), 482–488.

Thase, M. E., Pritchett, Y. L., Ossanna, M. J., Swindle, R. W., Xu J., & Detke, M. J. (2007). Efficacy of duloxetine and selective serotonin reuptake inhibitors: Comparisons as assessed by remission rates in patients with major depressive disorder. *Journal of Clinical Psychopharmacology, 27*(6), 672–676.

Thase, M. E., Haight, B. R., Richard, N., Rockett, C. B., Mitton, M., Modell, J. G. … Wang, Y. (2005). Remission rates following antidepressant therapy with bupropion or selective serotonin reuptake inhibitors: A meta-analysis of original data from 7 randomized controlled trials. *Journal of Clinical Psychiatry, 66*(8), 974–981.

Wang, J. C., Hinrichs, A. L., Stock, H., Budde, J., Allen, R., Bertelsen, S., … Bierut, L. J. (2004). Evidence of common and specific genetic effects: Association of the muscarinic acetylcholine receptor M2 (CHRM2) gene with alcohol dependence and major depressive syndrome. *Human Molecular Genetics, 13*(17), 1903–1911.

Warner-Schmidt, J. L., & Duman, R. S. (2006). Hippocampal neurogenesis: Opposing effects of stress and antidepressant treatment. *Hippocampus, 16*(3), 239–249.

Zarate, C. A., Jr, Payne, J. L., Singh, J., Quiroz, J. A., Luckenbaugh, D. A., Denicoff, K. D., Charney, D. S., & Manji, H. K. (2004). Pramipexole for bipolar II depression: A placebo-controlled proof of concept study. *Biological Psychiatry, 56*(1), 54–60.

Zarate, C. A., Jr, Singh, J. B., Carlson, P. J., Brutsche, N. E., Ameli, R., Luckenbaugh, D. A., Charney, D. S., & Manji, H. K. (2006). A randomized trial of an N-methyl-D-aspartate antagonist in treatment-resistant major depression. *Archives of General Psychiatry, 63*(8), 856–864.

Further Reading

Alonso, R., Griebel, G., Pavone, G., Stemmelin, J., Le Fur, & G., Soubie, P. (2004). Blockade of CRF (1) or V (1b) receptors reverses stress-induced suppression of neurogenesis in a mouse model of depression. *Molecular Psychiatry, 9*, 278–286.

Altar, C. A., Whitehead, R. E., Chen, R., Wortwein, G., & Madsen, M. M. (2003). Effects of electroconvulsive seizures and antidepressant drugs on brain-derived neurotrophic factor protein in rat brain. *Biological Psychiatry, 54*(7), 703–709.

Altar, C. A., Cai, N, Bliven, T. T., Juhasz, M., Connor, J. R., Acheson, A. L. … Wiegand, S. J. (1997). Anterograde transport of brain-derived neurotrophic factor and its role in the brain. *Nature, 389*, 856–860.

Aydemir, C., Yalcin, E. S., Aksaray, S., Kisa, C., Yildirim, S. G., Uzbay, T., & Goka, E. (2006). Brain-derived neurotrophic factor (BDNF) changes in the serum of depressed women. *Progress in Neuropsychopharmacology and Biological Psychiatry, 30*, 1256–1260.

Bench, C. J., Friston, K. J., Brown, R. G., Frackowiak, R. S., & Dolan, R. J. (1993). Regional cerebral blood flow in depression measured by positron emission tomography: The relationship with clinical dimensions. *Psychological Medicine, 23*, 579 590.

Chen, B, Dowlastshahi, D., McQueen, G., Wang, J. F., & Young, T. (2001). Increased hippocampal BDNF immunoreactivity in subjects treated with antidepressant medication. *Biological Psychiatry, 50*, 260–265.

Davison, R. J. (2000). Affective style psychopathology and resilience: Brain mechanisms an plasticity. *American Psychology, 55*, 1196–1214.

De Bellis, M. D., Geracioti, T. D., Jr, Altemus, M., & Kling, M. A. (1993). Cerebrospinal fluid monoamine metabolites in fluoxetine-treated patients with major depression and in healthy volunteers. *Biological Psychiatry, 33*, 636–641.

Dougherty, D. D., Weiss, A. P., Cosgrove, G. R., Alpert, N. M., Cassem, E. H., Nierenberg, A. A. … Rauch, S. L. (2003). Cerebral metabolic correlates as potential predictors of response to anterior cingulotomy for treatment of major depression. *Journal of Neurosurgery, 99*(6), 1010–1017.

Drevets, W. C. (1999). Prefrontal cortical amygdalar metabolism in major depression. *Annals of the New York Academy of Sciences, 877*, 614–637.

Drevets, W. C., Price, J. L., Simpson, J. R., Todd, R. D., Reich, T., Vannier, M., & Raichle, M. E. (1997). Subgenual prefrontal abnormalities in mood disorders. *Nature, 386*, 824–827.

Duric, V., & McCarson, K. E. (2005). Hippocampal neurokinin-1 receptor and brain-derived neurotrophic factor gene expression is decreased in rat models of pain and stress. *Neuroscience, 133*(4), 999–1006.

George, M. S., Lisanby, S. H., & Sackeim, H. A. (1999). Transcranial magnetic stimulation: Applications in neuropsychiatry. *Archives of General Psychiatry*, *56*(4), 300–311.

Gonul, A. S., Akdeniz, F., Taneli, F., Donat, O., & Eker, C. (2005). Effect of treatment on serum brain-derived neurotrophic factor levels in depressed patients. *European Archives of Psychiatry and Clinical Neuroscience*, *255*, 267–268.

Gould, E., Cameron, H. A., Daniels, D. C., Woolley, C. S., & McEwen, B. S. (1992). Adrenal hormones suppress cell division in the adult rat dentate gyrus. *Journal of Neuroscience*, *12*(9), 3642–3650.

Hajszan, T., MacLusky, N. J., & Leranth, C. (2005). Short-term treatment with the antidepressant fluoxetine triggers pyramidal denditric spine synapse formation in rat hippocampus. *European Journal of Neuroscience*, *21*, 1299–1303.

Hastings, R. S., Parsey, R. V., Oquendo, M. A., Arango, V., & Mann, J. J. (2004). Volumetric analysis of the prefrontal cortex, amygdala, and hippocampus in major depression. *Neuropsychopharmacology*, *29*(5), 952–959.

Heldt, S. A., Stanek, L., Chhatwal, J. P., & Ressler, K. J. (2007). Hippocampus-specific deletion of BDNF in adult mice impairs spatial memory and extinction of aversive memories. *Molecular Psychiatry*, *12*, 656–670.

Kandel, E. R., Schwartz, J. H., & Jessell, T. M. (1991). *Principles of neural science* (3rd edn). New York: Appleton & Lange.

Karege, F., Vaudan, G., Schwald, M., Peroud, N., & La Harpe, R. (2005). Neurotrophin levels in postmortem brains of suicide victims and the effect of antemortem diagnosis and psychotropic drugs. *Brain Research: Molecular Brain Research*, *136*, 29–37.

Lee, H. J., Kim, J. W., Yim, S. V., Kim, M. J., Kim, S. A., Kim, Y. J. … Chung, J. H. (2001). Fluoxetine enhances cell proliferation and prevents apoptosis in dentate gyrus of maternally separated rats. *Molecular Psychiatry*, *6*(6), 610, 725–728.

Madsen, T. M., Treschow, A., Bengzon, J., Bolwig, T. G., Lindvall, O., & Tingström, A. (2000). Increased neurogenesis in a model of electroconvulsive therapy. *Biological Psychiatry*, *47*(12), 1043–1049.

Malberg, J., & Duman, R. S. (2003). Cell proliferation in adult hippocampus is decreased by inescapable stress: Reversal by fluoxetine treatment. *Neuropsychopharmacology*, *28*, 1562–1571.

Maletic, V., Robinson, M., Oakes, T., Lyengar, S., Ball, G., & Russell, J. (2007). Neurobiology of depression: An integrated view of key findings. *International Journal of Clinical Practice*, *61*(12), 2030–2040.

Mann, J. J., Brent, D. A., & Arango, V. (2001). The neurobiology and genetics of suicide and attempted suicide: A focus on the serotonergic system. *Neurospychopharmacology*, *24*, 467–477.

Melia, K. R., Rasmussen, K., Terwilliger, R. Z., Haycock, J. W., Nestler, E. J., & Duman, R. S. (1992). Coordinate regulation of the cyclic AMP system with firing rate and expression of tyrosine hydroxylase in the rat locus coeruleus: Effects of chronic stress and drug treatments. *Journal of Neurochemistry*, *58*(2), 494–502.

Mongeau, R., Blier, P., & de Montigny, C. The serotonergic and noradrenergic systems of the hippocampus: Their interactions and the effects of antidepressant treatments. *Brain Research: Brain Research Reviews*, *23*(3), 145–195.

Naranjo, C. A., Tremblay, & L. K., Busto, U. E. (2001). The role of the brain reward system in depression. *Biological Psychiatry*, *25*(4), 781–823.

Nestler, E. J., Alreja, M., & Aghajanian, G. K. (1999). Molecular control of locus coeruleus neurotransmission. *Biological Psychiatry*, *46*(9), 1131–1139.

Nestler, E. J., McMahon, A., Sabban, E. L., Tallman, J. F., & Duman, R. S. (1990). Chronic antidepressant administration decreases the expression of tyrosine hydroxylase in the rat locus coeruleus. *Proceedings of the National Academy of Sciences*, *87*(19), 7522–7526.

Nibuya, M., Takahashi, M., Russell, D. S., & Duman, R. S. (1999). Repeated stress increases catalytic TrkB mRNA in rat hippocampus. *Neuroscience Letters*, *267*(2), 81–84.

O'Reardon, J. P., Cristancho, P., & Peshek, A. D. (2006). Vagus nerve stimulation (VNS) and treatment of depression: To the brainstem and beyond. *Psychiatry*, *3*(5), 54–63.

O'Reardon, J. P., Peshek, A. D., Romero, R., & Cristancho, P. (2006). Neuromodulation and transcranial magnetic stimulation (TMS): A 21st century paradigm for therapeutics in psychiatry. *Psychiatry*, *3*, 30–40.

Oppedal, R., Khan, D., & Brown, E. (2007). Hypothyroidism in patients with asthma and major depressive disorder. *The Primary Care Companion to the Journal of Clinical Psychiatry*, *9*(6), 466–468.

Plotsky, P. M., Owens, M. J., & Nemeroff, C. B. (1995). Neuropeptide alterations in mood disorders. In F. E. Bloom & D. J. Kupfer (Eds), *Psychopharmacology: The fourth generation of progress* (pp. 971–981). New York: Raven.

Rickels, K., Chung, H. R., Csanalosi, I. B., Hurowitz, A. M., London, J., Wiseman, K., Kaplan, M., & Amsterdam, J. D. (1987). Alprazolam, diazepam, imipramine, and placebo in outpatients with major depression. *Archives of General Psychiatry*, *44*(10), 862–866.

Smith, M. A., Makino, S., Kvetnansky, R., & Post, R. M. (1995). Stress and glucocorticoids affect the expression of brain-derived neurotrophic factor and neurotrophin-3 mRNAs in the hippocampus. *Journal of Neuroscience*, *15*, 1768–1777.

Vollmayr, B., Simonis, C., Weber, S., Gass, P., & Henn, F. (2003). Reduced cell proliferation in the dentate gyrus is not correlated with the development of learned helplessness. *Biological Psychiatry*, *54*(10), 1035–1040.

Wilhelm, K., Siegel, J., Finch, A., Hadzi-Pavlovic, D., Mitchell, P. B., Parker, G., & Schofield, P. R. (2007). The long and the short of it: Associations between 5-HTT genotypes and coping with stress. *Psychosomatic Medicine*, *69*, 614–620.

Wooley, C. S., Gould, E., & McEwen, B. S. (1990). Exposure to excess glucocorticoids alters dendritic morphology of adult hippocampal pyramidal neurons. *Brain Research*, *29*(1–2), 225–231.

Section 2

Psychological Models of Depression

5

Schema Theory in Depression

David A. Clark and Brendan D. Guyitt

Introduction

There are two indisputable characteristics concerning the aetiology of depression that have been recognized since the advent of modern psychiatry. The first is the strong link between depression and human experience. On the basis of clinical observation, Freud (1917) theorized in *Mourning and Melancholia* that the basis of depression or melancholia was the internalization or the symbolic representation of a significant object loss. Contemporary psychological research has repeatedly demonstrated an aetiological role for negative life events in the pathogenesis of depression, especially for those events that involve perceived or actual loss of valued resources (Mazure, 1998; Monroe & Hadjiyannakis, 2002). Depression, then, is a maladaptive response to life experience that remains endemic to humanity despite difficulty in reconciling how it could be adaptive for the survival of the species (Beck, 1995).

The second indisputable fact about the genesis of depression is the large variability in its pathoplasticity. There are substantial individual differences in susceptibility to depression, even in the face of significant negative life events. In fact less than half of the variance in depression is accounted for by life events (see Paykel & Cooper, 1992) and it is well known that the majority of individuals who experience a difficult and stressful life event do not develop a depressive episode (Brown & Harris, 1978; Coyne & Whiffen, 1995; Mazure, 1998). These findings have led to considerable research into

Treating Depression: MCT, CBT and Third Wave Therapies, First Edition.
Edited by Adrian Wells and Peter L. Fisher.

the genetic, biological, and psychological determinants of vulnerability to depression.

The cognitive perspective is perhaps the dominant contemporary psychological approach to conceptualizing vulnerability to depression. A basic postulate is that differences in the predisposition to depression are evident in how individuals understand or meaningfully interpret their experiences. Depression occurs when individuals interpret adverse experiences in a personally negative and enduring fashion. They perceive themselves as helpless about effecting positive change, and the future as bleak and hopeless (i.e., Abramson, Metalsky, & Alloy, 1989; Beck, 1987, 2008; Ingram, 2003). This cognitive perspective on depression adopts a diathesis–stress framework, in which preexisting cognitive vulnerability remains dormant until activated by a congruent negative life event, whereupon maladaptive cognitive structures dominate the information-processing system, producing the manifest symptoms of depression (Clark, Beck, & Alford, 1999). Gladstone and Parker (2001) referred to this model as the 'lock and key hypothesis'. Early adverse life circumstances establish a 'vulnerability lock' or cognitive structure (i.e., a schema) that is later primed by a matching life experience (i.e., a 'key'). A principal feature of these cognitive diathesis–stress accounts of depression onset is the idea that some form of enduring mental representation or memory of human experience is an integral factor in depression vulnerability.

Indeed it is important to recognize that most psychological theories of depression posit a critical role for the mental representation of human experience. By mental representation we mean the human ability to operate largely on the basis of stored information about, or internal models of, the environment – as opposed to having simple reactions to immediate sensory experience (O'Brien & Opie, 2004). This ability is evident in our capacity to represent, learn, and remember 'external objects, relations and states of affairs' (Obrien & Opie, 2004, pp. 1–2). Early psychoanalytic theory, for example, viewed depression in terms of an internalized object loss and a set of standards and values for judging oneself that can lead to self-directed hostility (Freud, 1917, 1930; see Brenner, 1991; Haddid et al., 2008). Later psychoanalytic formulations viewed depression in terms of a distorted intrapsychic representation or a set of unconscious cognitive structures (beliefs) about the self and our relationship with others that originates in adverse child–parent experiences (e.g., Arieti & Bemporad, 1980). Bowlby's attachment theory characterized depression as internalized mental representations of dysfunctional mother–child attachments (Bowlby, 1969).

Blatt's theory viewed depression in terms of internalized representations of self and object that can be classified very broadly as anaclitic (i.e., dependent) or introjective (i.e., self-defining) personality configurations (Blatt, 1974; Blatt & Maroudas, 1992). What all of these theories have in common is the recognition that some form of enduring, idiosyncratic internalized representation of human experience is necessary to explain the origins of depression.

In cognitive theories of depression the concept of schema has been the most widely accepted construct for conceptualizing the internal representation of loss, failure, and deprivation that predominates in major depression. A schema is 'a stored body of knowledge that interacts with incoming information to influence selective attention and memory search' (Ingram, Miranda, & Segal, 1998, p. 24). In hopelessness theory, an enduring depressogenic inferential style involving a tendency to generate negative inferences about the causes, consequences, and self-implications of stressful life events is a distal contributory cause of depression by virtue of increasing the likelihood that the person would develop hopelessness (Abramson et al., 1989). Although not explicitly mentioned by the authors, the notion of maladaptive inferential style is compatible with schema theory. For Gotlib and Hammen's cognitive–interpersonal conceptualization of depression, negative interpersonal and selfhood schemas play an important role in the aetiology and maintenance of depression (Gotlib & Hammen, 1992). Alternatively, Wells' self-regulatory executive function (SREF) model proposes that the cognitive–attentional processes that predispose to emotional distress are driven in part by procedures for dealing with stressful situations that are metacognitive in nature and are stored as networks or plans in long-term memory (Wells & Matthews, 1994).

The concept of schema is widely utilized in cognitive theories of depression, but its conceptualization is not unitary. Even though other perspectives on mental representation have been offered (e.g., Teasdale & Barnard, 1993), an evaluation of the schema concept is warranted in view of its continuing importance to most cognitive theories of depression.

In this chapter we begin with a review and critical evaluation of Beck's use of the term 'schema' in his cognitive theory of depression. Beck's cognitive theory has contributed much to popularizing the notion of schema as the optimal conceptualization of the negative mental representation in depression. We trace the development of Beck's concept of 'schema', review its empirical basis, and contrast it with Young's schema-focused therapy – another variant of cognitive therapy that capitalizes on the schema concept and has gained considerable traction among practising clinicians. A direct comparison is made between Beck's and Young's differing perspectives on schema. This is followed by an evaluation of schema theory in light of current advances in the cognitive science of memory. The chapter concludes by considering whether the schema concept has any future in psychological theories of depression.

Beck's Schema Theory of Depression

The early version

The concept of schema is central to Beck's cognitive theory of depression. In the earliest days of its formulation, Beck (1964, 1967) proposed that cognitive structures or schemas are responsible for the cross-situational consistency of human behaviour and, hence, account for the enduring aspects of emotional disorders like depression. Schema became the central concept in his cognitive explanation of vulnerability to depression and the lynchpin of the faulty information-processing system that characterizes depression. The symptoms of depression follow from a faulty information-processing system, which exhibits a negative self-referential bias because of the domination of dysfunctional schemas (i.e., attitudes and beliefs) about the self, the world, and the future (Beck, 1967, 1987, 2008). The schema concept is such a key pillar in Beck's cognitive formulation that evidence invalidating this concept would throw the entire theoretical account into question.

Beck (1967) stated that the schema concept was selected for the mental representation of emotional experience because of its familiarity and its ability to represent single, discrete ideas (e.g., what a shoe is) as well as more complex, global knowledge such as self-concept. He adopted the following definition of schema:

> A complex pattern, inferred as having been imprinted in the organismic structure by experience, that combines with the properties of the presented stimulus object or of the presented idea to determine how the object or idea is to be perceived and conceptualized. (Beck, 1967, p. 282)

As enduring cognitive structures, schemas not only screen, organize, and evaluate input from the internal and external world to the information-processing system but can engage in a self-reflective, self-generative process – such as when a depressed person engages in rumination (Papageorgiou & Wells, 2004) or in private self-evaluation (Beck, 1967). Schemas are the meaning-making structures of the cognitive organization and are responsible for the cognitions that occupy the stream of consciousness (Beck, 1964). Human cognition is the product of both top-down, schema-driven processes and bottom-up processes that involve stimulus input and raw sensory experience. Moreover, schemas have an executive function in the cognitive model, directing attentional resources so that information that is schema-congruent has priority over schema-incongruent information.

In the cognitive model the negative schemas of depression are distinguished by their content, structure, and function. The content or propositional elements of depressive schemas (Ingram & Kendall, 1986) consist of negative idiosyncratic generalized attitudes, beliefs, and assumptions about the self, one's personal world, the future, and interpersonal relations (Beck, 1967; Beck, Rush, Shaw, & Emery, 1979). Examples of depressive schema content are 'I'm a total loser', 'No one really likes me', 'I'm a burden on my family', 'I have no future', 'I will never succeed at anything in this life', 'I've been abandoned by everyone', 'I am incapable of ever feeling happy again', and the like. Because schema content consists of mental representations of the self, the future, and other people, cognitive theory considers this content to be central to the aetiology and persistence of, and to recovery from, a depressive episode (Beck, 1964, 1967; Beck et al., 1979). Two characteristics of schema content, accessibility (i.e., the ease with which schemas are used in information processing) and availability (i.e., whether the schema exists or not), determine the dominance of schematic content within information processing (Ingram et al., 1998; Segal, 1988). In depression, the negative schematic content is available (i.e., exists) as a result of early adverse developmental experiences (Ingram, 2003) and becomes highly accessible (i.e., attains a low threshold value) as a result of repeated activation. In consequence, once the negative schemas are activated in the depression-prone individual by a negative life experience, they will dominate the selection, encoding, retrieval, and interpretation of self-referential information.

Beck (1967) argued that depressogenic schemas are distinguished not only by their negative self-referent content, but also by certain structural characteristics, which also define their dysfunctional nature. The negative schemas of depression tend to be inflexible, closed, impermeable, and concrete. As a result, the negative cognitions associated with depressive schemas are highly plausible to the depressed patient and hence are difficult to modify, even when challenged by incongruent information. Furthermore, because of these structural abnormalities, depressogenic schemas will dominate the information-processing system once they are activated by a matching life event (Beck, 1987). The very nature of depressogenic schemas means that their individual elements or constructs are organized with a high degree of interrelatedness (Segal, 1988). According to Beck's cognitive model, the dysfunctional nature of negative schematic structure, organization, and content constitutes the central mechanism for creating affective disturbance. It determines how depressed individuals understand the significant experiences of their daily life (Beck, 1967). The function of these memory representations or schemas, then, is to guide our interpretation of experiences, which in turn determines our emotional response.

Figure 5.1 illustrates the cognitive model of depression. A consequence of negative self-referent schema activation by a precipitating negative life event is the development of a self-perpetuating negativity bias in the information-processing system. This is evident in the selective encoding, interpretation, and recall of negative self-referent information. In this regard Beck (1963) proposed six errors of inference or reasoning that characterize the processing bias in depression: arbitrary inference, selective abstraction, overgeneralization, dichotomous thinking, personalization, and magnification/minimization. In addition, depressogenic schema activation leads to the production of negative automatic thoughts that are specific, involuntary, and somewhat transient negative thoughts about oneself ('I know I failed the job interview because I have no ability'), one's personal world ('No one ever invites me out'), and one's future ('Depression will ruin my life') and seem highly plausible to the depressed individual (Beck, 1963, 1976). Later Beck (1987) also identified various classes of depressogenic schemas such as *intermediary beliefs* (i.e., rules that we use to evaluate ourselves, other people, and our experience), *conditional rules* (i.e., if/then inferences such as 'If I am criticized, then it means I have failed'), and *core beliefs* (i.e., absolute value-statements predicated on the self, such as 'I am a total failure, loser'). The cognitive model recognizes that the interaction between underlying cognitive processes and depressive symptoms is bidirectional, symptom occurrence feeding back to ensure continued activation of depressogenic schemas.

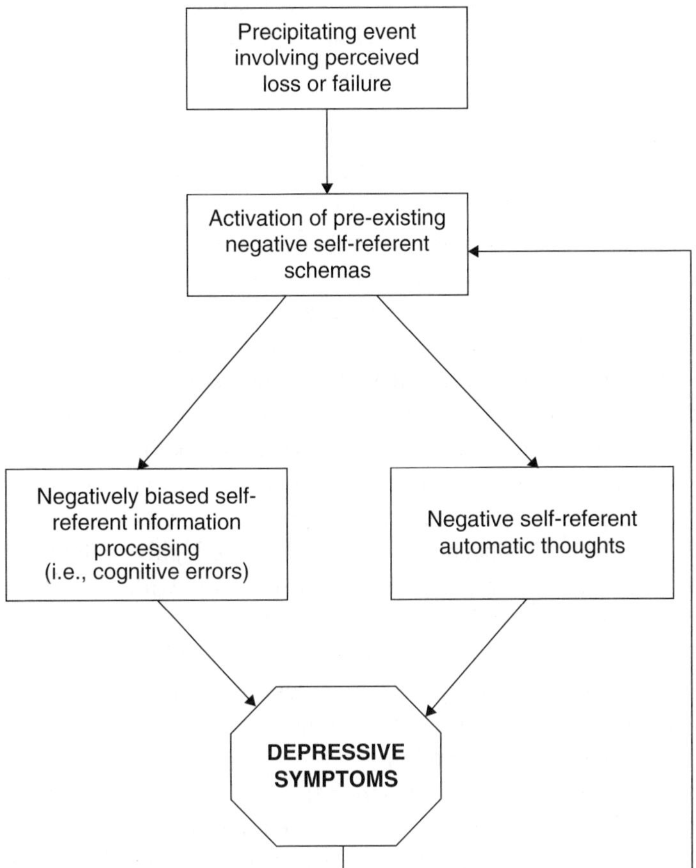

Figure 5.1 Beck's cognitive model of depression.

The reformulated cognitive model

Several notable revisions have been made to Beck's schema concept since it was first introduced 45 years ago (see Beck, 1987, 1996, 2008; Clark et al., 1999). The first is an increased emphasis on early developmental adversity – for example parental loss, neglect, childhood physical and sexual abuse, and severe criticism or rejection – as the point of origin of depressogenic schemas. According to schema models, these early adverse events lead to the development of negative attitudes to oneself and others, thereby creating heightened stress sensitivity and a cognitive vulnerability for depression (Gladstone & Parker, 2001; Harkness, 2008; Ingram, 2003). For example, experiencing parental loss during childhood could prompt a belief such as: 'If I lose an important person, then I am helpless' (Beck, 2008).

A second revision was the elaboration of a congruency hypothesis in which the prepotent negative self-schemas remain latent until they are activated by a negative life experience that matches the individual's negative schematic content. Beck (1983) described two cognitive personality orientations that capture the main concerns that define depressogenic schemas. Sociotropy describes an orientation towards interpersonal relationships in which self-worth is based on receiving love and acceptance from others, whereas in autonomy one is oriented towards mastery and independence and derives self-worth from productivity, achievement, and control. Examples of depressogenic sociotropic schemas would be 'I am unlovable' or 'I must please others to gain their acceptance', whereas the schemas of a depressed autonomous individual might be 'I am helpless' or 'I have achieved nothing significant in my life'. Thus the highly sociotropic individual is more susceptible to depression when faced with a negative interpersonal event – such as loss of a valued relationship or withdrawal of love and acceptance – and the highly autonomous individual is more likely to become depressed when experiencing a loss of independence or achievement caused, say, by the onset of a serious medical illness or by the failure to receive a valued job promotion.

A third development was an elaboration and clarification of the varied functions of schemas. Beck (1996) proposed that there are different types of schemas that account for the biopsychosocial nature of the organism (see also Clark et al., 1999). *Cognitive–conceptual schemas* are responsible for the selection, retrieval, and interpretation of information; *affective schemas* represent the perception of feeling states; *physiological schemas* represent somatic functions and processes; *behavioural schemas* encode response dispositions and readiness-for-action programmes; and *motivational schemas* are related to the behavioural domain and represent goal-directedness. Beck (1996) also introduced the concept of *mode*, which is 'a specific cluster of interrelated cognitive-conceptual, affective, physiological, behavioural and motivational schemas organized to deal with particular demands placed on the organism' (Clark et al., 1999, p. 88). He argued that the various psychiatric disorders can be conceptualized in terms of primal modes that are critical for survival. Depression, then, involves activation of a *primal loss mode* in which there is a perceived loss of vital resources (cognitive–conceptual schemas), a subjective state of sadness (affective schemas), perceived fatigue or physiological deactivation (physiological schemas), lack of goal-directedness or pleasurable engagement (motivational schemas), and withdrawal and inactivity (behavioural schemas) (Clark et al., 1999). Later on Beck (2008) argued that, through repeated activation, the negative schemas become organized into a depressive mode that becomes hypersalient, so that negative appraisals and interpretations strengthen and the ability to reappraise them becomes more limited. The end result is the development of clinical depression and maladaptive information-processing patterns, which become more routinized and resistant to change so that little or no external triggers are needed for the onset of depression.

Empirical support

Over the last two decades a prodigious empirical literature has developed around Beck's schema theory. Most of the research has focused on negative schematic content and its influence on the aetiology, course, and treatment of depression. Schema research has been particularly interested in testing various aspects of cognitive vulnerability both at the onset of depressive episodes and in the prediction of relapse and recurrence in formerly depressed individuals. The majority of studies have relied on self-report measures of schema content, especially the Dysfunctional Attitudes Scale (DAS) (Weissman & Beck, 1978), and early studies adopted weaker retrospective and cross-sectional research designs that compared the DAS scores of the depressed with those of non-clinical controls. The 40-item DAS captures the two main types of depressogenic schema content: social approval ('I cannot be happy unless most people I know admire me') and performance evaluation ('It is difficult to be happy unless one is good looking, intelligent, rich, and creative'). In later years more powerful prospective and information-processing experiments have appeared in the published literature, which thus provides a better test of the causal role of negative schemas in depression. It is beyond the scope of this chapter to review this extensive research, but the reader is referred to various published reviews that offer a critical evaluation of Beck's schema concept (e.g., Clark et al., 1999; Dozois & Beck, 2008; Haaga, Dyck, & Ernst, 1991; Ingram et al., 1998; Jacobs, Reinecke, Gollan, & Kane, 2008; Scher, Ingram, & Segal, 2005). What follows is a brief overview of key aspects of schema theory that have been investigated in cognitive studies of depression.

One of the most basic findings in early studies was that episodic major depression is characterized by negative self-referential beliefs, as indicated by high DAS scores that drop down to non-clinical range once the depression remits (e.g., Blackburn & Smyth, 1985; Hollon, Kendall, & Lumry, 1986). Later studies revealed that recovered depressives who are at high risk for future depressive episodes have enduring negative self-referential schemas, as predicted by the cognitive model; but these schemas must be primed by some activating stimulus, such as a negative mood or a distressing life experience (e.g., Miranda, Gross, Persons, & Hahn, 1998; Miranda & Persons, 1988). More recently, priming has evolved into cognitive reactivity studies, which examine whether schematically vulnerable individuals are more emotionally reactive to stressful experiences (e.g., negative mood stimuli, life experiences, etc.) and whether this heightened reactivity predicts onset, relapse, and recurrence of depression (Scher et al., 2005). For example, depressed patients treated with pharmacotherapy demonstrated greater cognitive reactivity (greater increases in DAS scores) to a sad mood induction than patients treated with cognitive therapy, and this increased reactivity predicted depressive relapse (Segal, Gemar, & Williams, 1999; Segal et al., 2006; see also Fresco, Segal, Buis, & Kennedy, 2007). Furthermore, a positive relationship may exist between cognitive reactivity and a marker of biological vulnerability (i.e., response to acute tryptophan depletion) in remitted depression (Booij & van der Does, 2007). Although these findings are consistent with a vulnerability perspective on negative schematic content, mood-priming studies cannot rule out the possibility that elevated DAS scores are a consequence of depressed mood.

The most convincing evidence for negative schema vulnerability comes from behavioural high-risk research designs. In a seminal study conducted at the University of Wisconsin and at Temple University, non-depressed undergraduates with high cognitive vulnerability (i.e., high DAS and high Cognitive Style Questionnaire scores) had a significantly higher rate of major and minor depressive episodes over a 2.5-year follow-up than students with low cognitive vulnerability (Alloy et al., 2006; Iacoviello, Alloy, Abramson, Whitehouse, & Hogan, 2006).

A central feature of Beck's schema theory is the notion of cognitive diathesis–stress. It is predicted that vulnerable individuals will be more susceptible to depressive episodes when they experience a significant negative life event that activates negative schematic content. In support of this prediction, a number of studies have found a positive interaction between dysfunctional attitudes and negative life events – an interaction that predicts an increase in subsequent depressive symptoms or the onset of a depressive episode (e.g., Hankin, Abramson, Miller, & Haeffel, 2004; Hankin, Fraley, & Abela, 2005; Lewinsohn, Joiner, & Rohde, 2001), although elevated DAS scores, even in the presence of life stressors, did not predict subsequent depressive episodes when controlling for a past history of depression (Otto et al., 2007). Evidence of a specific association between type of life event and negative schematic content has been less consistent, the strongest evidence pointing to a congruence between negative social schemas and interpersonal events, but not between autonomy and negative achievement events (e.g., Husky, Mazure, Maciejewski, & Swendsen, 2007; Robins, 1990; Segal, Shaw, Vella, & Katz, 1992; see Iacoviello, Grant, Alloy, & Abramson, forthcoming; Mazure, Bruce, Maciejewski, & Jacobs, 2000 for contrary results). Overall, there is evidence that negative schematic content does interact with negative life events in predicting depressive mood, symptoms, and episodes, although negative findings have also been reported. Moreover, support for a stronger version of the model – one that links specific types of life experiences with specific belief content – appears to be even more equivocal.

Although negative self-referent schematic content is significantly reduced through cognitive therapy, the strength of negative schemas predicts response to cognitive therapy. Various studies have found that higher pre-treatment negative schema content, as indicated by DAS scores, is associated with poorer outcome for a cognitive therapy of depression and a greater risk for relapse (see Hamilton & Dobson, 2002 for review). For example, in the NIMH Treatment of Depression Collaborative Research Program, high pre-treatment DAS scores predicted a poorer response to cognitive behaviour therapy and imipramine with clinical management (Sotsky et al., 1991). More recently, Beevers, Wells, and Miller (2007) found that pre-treatment negative cognition (which included the DAS) predicted slower response to outpatient treatment. In addition Jarrett, Vittengl, Doyle, and Clark (2007) reported that cognitive therapy significantly reduced dysfunctional attitudes, that most of this change occurred relatively early in therapy, and that reduction in depressive symptoms predicted a concurrent change in dysfunctional attitudes rather than the reverse. Contrary to expectation, the interaction of high pre-treatment DAS and absence of severe negative life events predicted poor treatment outcome (Simons, Gordon, Monroe, & Thase, 1995). Overall, these studies indicate that a strong presence of negative schematic content is associated with poorer treatment response, although the exact relationship with change in depressive symptoms and with the impact of negative life events remains to be determined.

One important issue that remains unresolved in research on negative schemas is whether self-report measures like the DAS are the best way to assess schematic content or whether behavioural responses to information-processing tasks may be a more sensitive indicator. There is evidence that certain laboratory-based cognitive tasks may be more sensitive to negative schema content than questionnaire responses (Hedlund & Rude, 1995; Rude, Covich, Jarrold, Hedlund, & Zenter, 2001), although measures of implicit self-esteem (i.e., less direct, more automatic measures of negative schema content) have not consistently shown the characteristic negativity bias that would be expected in depression (e.g., Franck, De Raedt, & De Houwer, 2008). A second unresolved issue is whether schematic content or structure is more indicative of cognitive vulnerability to depression (Dozois & Beck, 2008). For example, depressed individuals display a greater degree of interconnectedness among the negative elements of their self-schema, especially of the relational self-schema, and reduced interconnectedness among the positive elements; and this cognitive organization appears to be more stable than the negative schematic content (Dozois, 2002, 2007 Dozois & Dobson, 2001, 2003). Even though progress has been made in providing empirical evidence that the structure or organization of negative self-schemas as well as their content might be a marker of vulnerability to depression, more fine-grained prospective and laboratory-based research is needed before the causal status of negative schemas can become an established finding.

Young's Schema-Focused Therapy

In the late 1980s Jeffery Young developed schema-focused therapy (SFT) (Young, 1990, 1999; Young, Klosko, & Weishaar, 2003) as a refinement, elaboration, and extension of Beck's cognitive therapy to individuals with personality disorders or chronic, longstanding Axis I disorders. The central feature of Young's therapeutic approach was an enhanced concept of schema that was thought to provide a better conceptualization and therapeutic heuristic for the pervasive, absolutistic, and enduring core dysfunctional beliefs about self and others as well as for the chronic interpersonal difficulties that characterize personality disorders (Young, 1999; Young et al., 2003).

As a therapeutic approach, SFT takes a broader, more eclectic approach than standard cognitive therapy, drawing on intervention strategies from diverse therapeutic perspectives – namely cognitive behavioural, interpersonal, attachment, gestalt, object relations, constructivist, and psychoanalytic. What is clearly distinctive about SFT, however, is its concept of schema – the focal point of the therapy. SFT hypothesizes 18 specific early maladaptive schemas (EMSs), which are defined as broad, stable, and enduring 'self-defeating emotional and cognitive patterns that begin early in our development and repeat throughout life' (Young et al., 2003, p. 7). While each EMS differs in content, SFT does not propose schema-disorder specificity; that is, it does not propose that certain EMSs are uniquely linked to specific psychological conditions. For example, any of the 18 EMSs may be associated with depression, although schemas that fall under the *disconnection and rejection* domain may be the most prominent (Young & Mattila, 2002). This domain involves the schemas of abandonment/instability, mistrust/abuse, emotional deprivation, defectiveness/shame, and social isolation/alienation.

One of the central propositions of SFT is that EMSs are 'understandable conclusion[s] based on painful realities' experienced during childhood (Young & Mattila, 2002, p. 292). Because of their strong developmental origins, EMSs are considered more fundamental to personality and human functioning than the dysfunctional schemas targeted in standard cognitive therapy. For example, schemas within the disconnection and rejection domains are thought to develop from the child's experience of a 'cold, rejecting, withholding, lonely, explosive, unpredictable, or abusive' family environment (Young et al., 2003, p. 14). Most EMSs are unconditional mental representations of adverse, unavoidable childhood experiences (e.g., 'People in my life are unreliable'). Others, however, are conditional beliefs that are similar to Beck's concept of conditional assumptions (Beck et al., 1979). Conditional EMSs are activated when an individual seeks to avoid feared consequences. For example, an individual may 'subjugate, self-sacrifice, seek approval, inhibit emotions, or strive to meet higher standards' in order feel better (Young et al., 2003, p. 22). Often conditional schemas develop from attempts to avoid the domination of unconditional schemas (e.g., 'I will self-sacrifice so my partner will not abandon me').

Standard versus schema-focused cognitive therapy

Table 5.1 summarizes differences between Beck and Young in their views on the maladaptive schemas that characterize psychopathological states. One of the main differences between Beck's concept of schema and Young's

Table 5.1 Distinguishing features of schema in standard cognitive therapy versus schema-focused therapy.

Beck's Schema Concept	*Young's Schema Concept*
• Origins in a variety of adverse developmental experiences, with minimal childhood-schema specificity	• Strong emphasis on developmental origins, with greater childhood-schema specificity
• Greater specificity of schema content to type of psychopathology (i.e., cognitive content specificity)	• Less specificity of types of EMS to psychopathology
• Content and structural biases characterize maladaptive schemas	• Emphasizes the verbal content of EMSs
• Both self-report and information-processing paradigms are employed in schema research	• Exclusive reliance on self-report for EMS research
• Undifferentiated classification of schematic content	• More detailed delineation of schematic content
• Recognizes both automatic and elaborative schematic processing	• EMSs are considered highly accessible, hence emphasis on retrospective self-report
• Posits a specific match between schema activation and triggering life event	• Broad range of stimuli may activate EMSs
• Includes behavioural elements in the schema concept	• Behaviour is viewed as maladaptive coping responses to EMS activation
• Introduced concept of 'mode' to emphasize schema interconnectedness and the representation of high-order emotional states	• Little emphasis on schema interconnectedness or higher order levels of mental representation
• Maladaptive schemas are intensified through repeated activation and schema-congruent processing	• EMSs are intensified through reliance on maladaptive coping responses

concept of EMSs is the importance placed on schematic organization and structure. In standard cognitive therapy, depressogenic schemas possess faulty structural characteristics, a biased organizational system, and negative self-referent verbal content. Young (1999), on the other hand, defines EMSs in terms of verbal content alone. They are considered highly accessible structures that can be reliably detected through self-report measures (Riso & McBride, 2007). Given the more structural view of schemas in Beck's cognitive model, its advocates consider behavioural performance on information-processing tasks to be the best measure of schema activation, whereas practically all research on EMSs relies on retrospective self-report measures such as the Young Schema Questionnaire (Young, 1990, 1998).

The two approaches to the concept of schema also differ in their focus on specificity. Whereas Beck's content specificity hypothesis focuses on the relation between specific schematic content and certain types of psychopathological states (Beck, 1987; Clark et al., 1999), Young et al. (2003) do not argue for schema disorder specificity but rather posit that specific types of adverse developmental and childhood experiences are the origins of EMSs. Although Beck (1967, 2008) also considers adverse childhood experiences and disrupted parent–child relations critical to the development of maladaptive schemas, SFT provides a more detailed account of how certain unmet emotional needs in childhood contribute to each EMS. If a child's need for an appropriate level of security, autonomy, freedom of expression, spontaneity, and self-control are not met because the child receives either too much or to little, EMSs are more likely to develop. In relation to Beck, this delineation reflects a greater emphasis on disturbances in developmental processes as being crucial for EMS development. Greater importance is also placed on a how a child's inborn emotional temperament may interact with life circumstances to either facilitate or hinder the development of EMS (Young et al., 2003). Shy children, for example, may be less able to cope with abandonment from significant attachment figures because they are less able to make other social connections. Although there is considerable evidence that childhood adversity and disrupted parent–child relations are linked to vulnerability to depression (see Ingram, 2003), evidence that specific types of negative childhood experiences lead to specific types of schematic vulnerability is weak (e.g., Gladstone & Parker, 2001).

SFT, with its description of the 18 EMSs, provides a more complex classification of maladaptive schematic content than the standard cognitive model. Beck (1967) suggested that the general themes of 'personal deficiency, of self-blame, and of negative expectations' (p. 285) characterize depressive schemas; and later he introduced the cognitive personality constructs of sociotropy and autonomy (Beck, 1983, 1987) as a further refinement of the notion of cognitive vulnerability to depression. In contrast, SFT argues that the schematic themes of individuals with characterological or chronic difficulties can be more finely classified (Oei & Baranoff, 2007).

SFT and standard cognitive therapy also take a different view on the role of behaviour in disorders like depression. Beck (1996) includes behaviour within the schema construct, while Young et al. (2003) consider behaviour a coping response to EMS activation. Beck's behavioural schemas include learned and automatic survival behaviour, which, in the case of depression, tends to be dominated by withdrawal and inactivity (Clark et al., 1999). In contrast, SFT considers withdrawal and inactivity maladaptive coping responses to EMS activation, which otherwise consists of memories, emotions, cognitions, and bodily sensations. Individuals often use different coping responses following activation of the same schema; therefore behaviour is not 'intrinsic to the schema' (Young et al., 2003, p. 33). This conceptualization reflects the strong emphasis in SFT on coping responses as an EMS maintenance factor. Although maladaptive coping responses such as avoidance may be adaptive initially, the responses eventually perpetuate the EMS long after the external conditions have changed.

Finally, Beck and Young differ in their usage of the term 'mode'. Beck (1996) defined mode as a cluster of interrelated schemas that describe a broader, more complex level of mental representation, which is needed in order to account for the emotional states seen in psychopsychological conditions (Clark et al., 1999). Young et al. (2003), however, view 'mode' as the set of EMSs and corresponding coping responses that characterize the predominant state of an individual at any given moment. Young et al. (2003) propose ten different modes, which are labelled for different types of overarching client presentation (e.g., 'vulnerable child'). Thus in SFT modes represent another means by which to classify individuals – and not a higher level of information representation, as in Beck's theory.

Empirical evidence for early maladaptive schema

As previously discussed, there are substantial differences between the standard cognitive model and SFT in their perspectives on schemas. Hence an evaluation of the empirical status for EMSs is critical in light of these conceptual differences. Although Young et al. (2003, p. 24) conclude that a 'considerable amount of research' has established the validity of the EMS construct, a review of the literature revealed a scarcity of empirical studies. The relevant research has been dominated by factor analyses of the long form of the Young Schema Questionnaire (YSQ-LF; Young, 1990). Based as it is on clinical observation, the YSQ-LF is the original 205-item questionnaire developed to assess 16 EMSs. Early studies using principal component analysis with varimax rotation were able to extract only 11 of the 16 EMS dimensions on a consistent basis (Schmidt, Joiner, Young, & Telch, 1995; Lee, Taylor, & Dunn, 1999). Later studies have continued to report variability in the measure's factor structure (see Oei & Baranoff, 2007 for a review), and replication is needed in both clinical and community samples. Ironically, the YSQ-LF has yet to be studied on a sample of individuals who all exhibit chronic characterological difficulties – which is the population hypothesized to exhibit EMSs. To date, the temporal stability of the YSQ-LF has not been adequately investigated, and evidence for its construct validity, cited by Young et al. (2003), comes mainly from unpublished dissertation research. A shorter 75-item version of the YSQ-LF (YSQ-SF) (Young, 1998) has also demonstrated reliability and validity problems. Ball (2007) discussed structural difficulties with the YSQ-SF that may contribute to these weaknesses. Improvements were evident when factor analysis of a corrected research version of the YSQ-SF produced 14 EMSs, 11 of which had adequate reliability (Cecero, Nelson, & Gillie, 2004).

Oei and Baranoff (2007) provide an excellent review of the validity of the YSQ-LF and the YSQ-SF in predicting self-reported depressive symptoms. Across two YSQ-LF studies (Harris & Curtin, 2002; Schmidt et al., 1995) and three YSQ-SF studies (Baranoff, Oei, Kwon, & Cho, 2006; Glaser, Campbell, Calhoun, Bates, & Petrocelli, 2002; Welburn, Coristine, Dagg, Pontefract, & Jordon, 2002), different EMS combinations emerged as significant predictors of depressive symptoms. Although no clear pattern emerged, the defectiveness and abandonment EMSs were most prominent. This finding is consistent with the prediction that the disconnection and rejection domain is most closely related to depression (Young & Mattila, 2002).

In summary, the empirical case for Young's EMSs is far from complete and, while the existing evidence is encouraging, more research is clearly needed (Oei & Baranoff, 2007). The YSQ-SF and the YSQ-LF lack a reliable factor structure and neither one assesses all the 18 EMS proposed by Young et al. (2003), although this may reflect psychometric weaknesses in the instruments rather than the validity of the model. The relationship between the EMSs and depression also needs clarification. Indeed Ball (2007, p. 124) states that 'very little is known about the existence or relevance of early maladaptive schemas in different clinical groups'. Until these psychometric and conceptual issues are resolved, it remains unknown whether SFT provides a better conceptualization of maladaptive schemas than the standard cognitive model.

Schema Theory and Cognitive Science

The schema construct has gained widespread heuristic value among cognitive–clinical psychologists in their cognitive models of vulnerability, persistence, and treatment of psychopathological states such as depression. However, the schema construct is not as widely accepted within contemporary cognitive science and other conceptualizations have been proposed to account for the mental representation of human experience.

Beck (1967) offered a pragmatic definition of schema that lacks the conceptual sophistication found in cognitive science models of mental representation. As a result, the term 'schema' has come to designate a heuristic that refers to higher levels of knowledge representation – levels that direct other processes within the information-processing system. This is an entirely reasonable use of the term, since it has been clearly shown that the selection, abstraction, interpretation, and integration of new information is influenced, at least in part, by preexisting knowledge and memory (Alba & Hasher, 1983). In reality, though, the schema construct is just one of several ways to account for the brain's representation and storage of information. The critical question for schema theory is whether this construct is the best way to describe the architecture of mental representation within the brain. Several criticisms of schema theories have been raised, which point for instance to (1) a lack of specificity in how knowledge is represented, (2) an inadequate account of emotion, (3) an overreliance on propositional representation, (4) an inability to fully represent the details of complex events, and (5) an unsatisfactory account of schema change (e.g., Alba & Hasher, 1983; Dalgleish, 2004; Power & Champion, 1986; Teasdale & Barnard, 1993). We briefly consider each of these criticisms below.

Although Beck's definition of schema may lack specificity (e.g., Power & Champion, 1986; Teasdale & Barnard, 1993), other cognitive theorists have provided some additional details (e.g., Mandler, 1984). Schemas are distinct cognitive structures, each schema representing a class of events or a type of object that an individual often encounters. For example, most individuals will have a schema for dogs that involves patterns of cognition, emotion, physiological response, and behaviour associated with dogs. The different elements of a schema are connected, so that activation of one part of a schema (e.g., seeing a dog) will spread through the entire schema. If a person had prior negative experiences with a dog, schema activation would include fear and a watchful or avoidant response. The activation occurs in an all-or-nothing fashion and schema content is stored in the form of sentence-like, propositional structures that cognitive scientists believed to be the fundamental building blocks of knowledge representation (Sternberg, 1996). Thus later accounts of schemas, such as Beck's (1996) reformulation of different schema types, have proposed 'subschema' elements or 'schema subsystems', which acknowledge that a more complex representational structure is needed if one is to account for the complexities of human experience.

Despite increased conceptual elaboration of schema theory in its clinical variants, cognitive science has proposed alternative modes of mental representation because of perceived inadequacies in a schema account of memory for complex events (Alba & Hasher, 1983). One of the first alternatives to schema theory was the concept of associative networks, such as defined in the semantic network model (Collins & Loftus, 1975). In this model each concept (e.g., 'dog') is represented by a node and human semantic structure; and processing is replicated by spreading the activation between concepts. Later on Bower (1981) extended the semantic network model so as to include emotion nodes, in response to research showing that memory was often mood- or state-dependent. Although emotional network theory was influential throughout the 1980s, problems became apparent when it had difficulty accounting for some basic findings in mood research. Critics also argued that semantic networks provided an unsatisfactory account of higher order levels of meaning, emotion, organization, and knowledge representation, because they represented knowledge in a single and uniform format (Teasdale & Barnard, 1993).

Teasdale and Barnard (1993) proposed an alternative to schema and network theories that involves the representation of cognition and affect at multiple levels of conceptualization. In their interacting cognitive subsystems (ICS) model (Barnard & Teasdale, 1991; Teasdale, Segal, & Williams, 1995), information on a topic at one level of representation feeds into the creation of information related to that topic at other levels of representation. Referring to schema in a more heuristic sense, Teasdale and Barnard (1993) contend that mental representation at an implicational level more fully accounts for complex emotional states like depression. ICS implicational code represents a more universal or holistic level of meaning, which involves regularities and patterns of information (Teasdale et al., 1995). More recently, Dalgleish (2004) proposed a multilevel or multiformat model of emotions that involves representation at schematic, propositional, analogical, and associative levels. Known as SPAARS, this model combines elements of schematic and associative networks to give a more complete account of the cognitive representation and processes involved in emotional experience.

The Future of Schema Theory in Depression

Popularized by Beck's cognitive theory of depression, schemas continue to be a dominant construct in cognitive theories of vulnerability and in the treatment of depression. Earlier conceptualizations have given way to more complex formulations, which emphasize the diverse nature of schematic elements, their interconnectedness, and their organization into macrostructures that provide a more elaborate account of the mental representation of complex human emotional experience. As noted in our review of the empirical research for Beck's schema theory, there is considerable, though not always consistent, support for the model. In this respect schema theory has been a valuable heuristic, which has taught us much about vulnerability, resilience, and recovery from depression. Naturally, many issues remain for further investigation – for instance, the role of adverse developmental experiences in the origins of maladaptive schemas, the biological correlates of schema vulnerability (see Beck, 2008 for a discussion), and the schematic organization involved in recovery or recurrence of depressive episodes. Whether other clinical versions of schema theory, such as schema-focused therapy, offer greater predictive value in treatment and in the prevention of more chronic and characterological forms of depression has yet to be confirmed.

The considerable empirical evidence surrounding schema theory in depression has not dampened criticisms of the schema approach. Cognitive–clinical researchers have responded by offering more detailed accounts of schema content, organization, and structure that may yield a better explanation for complex emotional states. However, some of the basic criticisms of schema theory remain, and alternative models of mental representation derived more directly from cognitive science may provide a richer conceptual basis for psychopathological states like depression. Whether multilevel representation will give new insights into the cognitive basis of depression must await for empirical research to catch up with the theoretical developments. In the meantime, schema theory will continue to provide a very useful heuristic for understanding the nature and influence of biased information-processing in depression.

References

Abramson, L. Y., Metalsky, G. I, & Alloy, L. B. (1989). Hopelessness depression; A theory-based subtype of depression. *Psychological Review*, *96*, 358–372.

Alba, J. W., & Hasher, L. (1983). Is memory schematic? *Psychological Bulletin*, *93*(2), 203–231.

Alloy, L. B., Abramson, L. Y., Whitehouse, W. G., Hogan, M. E., Panzarella, C., & Rose, D. T. (2006). Prospective incidence of first onsets and recurrences of depression in individuals at high and low cognitive risk for depression. *Journal of Abnormal Psychology*, *115*(1), 145–156.

Arieti, S., & Bemporad, J. R. (1980). The psychological organization of depression. *American Journal of Psychiatry*, *137*, 1360–1365.

Ball, S. A. (2007). Cognitive–behavioural and schema-based models for the treatment of substance use disorders. In L. P. Riso, P. L. du Toit, D. J. Stein, & J. E. Young (Eds), *Cognitive schemas and core beliefs in psychological problems: A scientist-practitioner guide* (pp. 111–138). Washington, DC: American Psychological Association.

Baranoff, J., Oei, T. P. S., Kwon, S. M., & Cho, S. (2006). Factor structure and internal consistency of the Young Schema Questionnaire (short form). *Journal of Affective Disorders*, *93*, 133–140.

Barnard, P. J., & Teasdale, J. D. (1991). Interacting cognitive subsystems: A systematic approach to cognitive–affective interaction and change. *Cognition and Emotion*, *5*, 1–39

Beck, A. T. (1963). Thinking and depression. I: Idiosyncratic content and cognitive distortions. *Archives of General Psychiatry*, *9*, 324–333.

Beck, A. T. (1964). Thinking and depression. II. Theory and therapy. *Archives of General Psychiatry*, *10*, 561–571.

Beck, A. T. (1967). *Depression: Causes and treatment*. Philadelphia: University of Pennsylvania Press.

Beck, A. T. (1976). *Cognitive therapy of the emotional disorders*. New York: New American Library.

Beck, A. T. (1983). Cognitive therapy of depression: New perspectives. In P. J. Clayton & J. E. Barrett (Eds), *Treatment of depression: Old controversies and new approaches* (pp. 265–290). New York: Raven Press.

Beck, A. T. (1987). Cognitive models of depression. *Journal of Cognitive Psychotherapy: An International Quarterly, 1*, 5–37.

Beck, A. T. (1995). The descent of man: An evolutionary perspective on major depression. *Newsletter of the Society for Research in Psychopathology, 3*, 3–6.

Beck. A. T. (1996). Beyond belief: A theory of modes, personality, and psychopathology. In P. M. Salkovskis (Ed.), *Frontiers of cognitive therapy* (pp. 1–25). New York: Guilford.

Beck, A. T. (2008). The evolution of the cognitive model of depression and its neurobiological correlates. *American Journal of Psychiatry 165*, 969–977.

Beck, A. T., Rush, A. J., Shaw, B. F., & Emery, G. (1979). *Cognitive therapy of depression*. New York: Guilford.

Beevers, C. G., Wells, T. T., & Miller, I. W. (2007). Predicting response to depression treatment: The role of negative cognition. *Journal of Consulting and Clinical Psychology, 75*, 422–431.

Blackburn, I. M., & Smyth, P. (1985). A test of cognitive vulnerability in individuals prone to depression. *British Journal of Clinical Psychology, 24*, 61–62.

Blatt, S. J. (1974). Levels of object representation in anaclitic and introjective depression. *Psychoanalytic Study of the Child, 29*, 107–157.

Blatt, S. J., & Maroudas, C. (1992). Convergences among psychoanalytic and cognitive–behavioral theories of depression. *Psychoanalytic Psychology, 9*, 157–190.

Booij, L., & Van der Does, A. J. W. (2007). Cognitive and serotonergic vulnerability to depression: Convergent findings. *Journal of Abnormal Psychology, 116*, 86–94.

Bower, G. H. (1981). Mood and memory. *American Psychologist, 36*(2), 129–148.

Bowlby, J. (1969). *Attachment and loss: Volume 1. Attachment*. London: Hogarth Press.

Brenner, C. (1991). A psychoanalytic perspective on depression. *Journal of the American Psychoanalytic Association, 39*, 25–43.

Brown, G. W., & Harris, T. (1978). *Social origins of depression: A study of psychiatric disorder in women*. London, England: Tavistock Publications.

Cecero, J., Nelson, J., & Gillie, J. (2004). Tools and tenets of schema therapy: Toward the construct validity of the Early Maladaptive Schema Questionnaire–Research Version (EMSQ-R). *Clinical Psychology & Psychotherapy, 11*, 344–357.

Clark, D. A., & Beck, A. T., with Alford, B. (1999). *Scientific foundations of cognitive theory and therapy of depression*. New York: Wiley.

Collins, A. M., & Loftus, E. F. (1975). A spreading-activation theory of semantic processing. *Psychological Review, 82*(6), 407–428.

Coyne, J. C., & Whiffen, V. E. (1995). Issues in personality as diathesis for depression: The case of sociotropy–dependency and autonomy–self-criticism. *Psychological Bulletin, 118*, 358–378.

Dalgleish, T. (2004). Cognitive approaches to posttraumatic stress disorder: The evolution of multirepresentational theorizing. *Psychological Bulletin, 130*, 228–260.

Dozois, D. J. A. (2002). Cognitive organization of self-schematic content in nondysphoric, mildly dysphoric, and moderately–severely dysphoric individuals. *Cognitive Therapy and Research, 26*, 417–429.

Dozois, D. J. A. (2007). Stability of negative self-structures: A longitudinal comparison of depressed, remitted, and nonpsychiatric controls. *Journal of Clinical Psychology, 63*, 319–338.

Dozois, D. J. A., & Beck, A. T. (2008). Cognitive schemas, beliefs and assumptions. In K. S. Dobson & D. J. A. Dozois (Eds), *Risk factors for depression* (pp. 121–143). Oxford: Elsevier.

Dozois, D. J. A., & Dobson, K. S. (2001). A longitudinal investigation of information processing and cognitive organization in clinical depression: Stability of schematic interconnectedness. *Journal of Consulting and Clinical Psychology, 69*, 914–925.

Dozois, D. J. A., & Dobson, K. S. (2003). The structure of the self-schema in clinical depression: Differences related to episode recurrence. *Cognition and Emotion, 17*, 933–941.

Franck, E., De Raedt, R., & De Houwer, J. (2008). Activation of latent self-schemas as a cognitive vulnerability factor for depression: The potential role of implicit self-esteem. *Cognition and Emotion, 22*, 1588–1599.

Fresco, D. M., Segal, Z. V., Buis, T., & Kennedy, S. (2007). Relationship of posttreatment decentering and cognitive reactivity to relapse in major depression. *Journal of Consulting and Clinical Psychology, 75*, 447–455.

Freud, S. (1917). *Mourning and melancholia. In The standard edition of the complete psychological works of Sigmund Freud (Vol. 14*, pp. 239–258). London: Hogarth Press.

Freud, S. (1930). *Civilization and its discontents. In The standard edition of the complete psychological works of Sigmund Freud (Vol. 21*, pp. 64–145). London: Hogarth Press.

Gladstone, G., & Parker, G. (2001). Depressogenic cognitive schemas: enduring beliefs or mood state artefacts? *Australian and New Zealand Journal of Psychiatry, 35*, 210–216.

Glaser, B., Campbell, L. F., Calhoun, G. B., Bates, J. M., & Petrocelli, J. V. (2002). The Early Maladaptive Schema Questionnaire–Short Form: A construct validity study. *Measurement and Evaluation in Counseling and Development, 35*, 2–13.

Gotlib, I. H., & Hammen, C. L. (1992). *Psychological aspects of depression: Toward a cognitive-interpersonal integration*. Chichester, England: John Wiley & Sons, Ltd.

Haaga, D. A. F., Dyck, M. J., & Ernst, D. (1991). Empirical status of cognitive theory of depression. *Psychological Bulletin, 110*, 215–236.

Haddid, S. K., Reiss, D., Spotts, E. L., Ganiban, J., Lichtenstein, P., & Neiderhiser, J. M. (2008). Depression and internally directed aggression: Genetic and environmental contributions. *Journal of the American Psychoanalytic Association, 56*, 515–550.

Hamilton, K. E., & Dobson, K. S. (2002). Cognitive therapy of depression: Pretreatment patient predictors of outcome. *Clinical Psychology Review, 22*, 875–893.

Hankin, B. L., Fraley, R. C., & Abela, J. R. Z. (2005). Daily depression and cognitions about stress: Evidence for a traitlike depressogenic cognitive style and the prediction of depressive symptoms in a prospective daily diary study. *Journal of Personality and Social Psychology, 88*(4), 673–685.

Hankin, B. L., Abramson, L. Y., Miller, N., & Haeffel, G. J. (2004). Cognitive vulnerability–stress theories of depression: Examining affective specificity in the prediction of depression versus anxiety in three prospective studies. *Cognitive Therapy and Research, 28*(3), 309–345.

Harkness, K. L. (2008). Life events and hassles. In K. S. Dobson & D. J. A. Dozois (Eds), *Risk factors for depression* (pp. 317–341). Oxford: Elsevier.

Harris, A. E., & Curtin, L. (2002). Parental perceptions, early maladaptive schemas, and depressive symptoms in young adults. *Cognitive Therapy and Research, 26*, 405–416.

Hedlund, S., & Rude, S. E. (1995). Evidence of latent depressive schemas in formerly depressed individuals. *Journal of Abnormal Psychology, 104*, 517–525.

Hollon, S. D., Kendall, P. C., & Lumry, A. (1986). Specificity of depressotypic cognitions in clinical depression. *Journal of Abnormal Psychology, 95*, 52–59.

Husky, M. M., Mazure, C. M., Maciejewski, P. K., & Swendsen, J. D. (2007). A daily life comparison of sociotropy–autonomy and hopelessness theories of depression. *Cognitive Therapy and Research, 31*, 659–676.

Iacoviello, B. M., Grant, D. A., Alloy, L. B., & Abramson, L. Y. (forthcoming). Cognitive personality characteristics impact the course of depression: A prospective test of sociotropy, autonomy and domain-specific life events. Cognitive Therapy and Research.

Iacoviello, B. M., Alloy, L. B., Abramson, L. Y., Whitehouse, W. G., & Hogan, M. E. (2006). The course of depression in individuals at high and low cognitive risk for depression: A prospective study. *Journal of Affective Disorders, 93*, 61–69.

Ingram, R. E. (2003). Origins of cognitive vulnerability to depression. *Cognitive Therapy and Research, 27*, 77–88.

Ingram, R. E., & Kendall, P. C. (1986). Cognitive clinical psychology: Implications of an information processing perspective. In R. E. Ingram (Ed.), *Information processing approaches to clinical psychology* (pp. 3–21). Orlando, FL: Academic Press.

Ingram, R. E., Miranda, J., & Segal, Z. V. (1998). Cognitive vulnerability to depression. New York: Guilford.

Jacobs, R. H., Reinecke, M. A., Gollan, J. K., & Kane, P. (2008). Empirical evidence of cognitive vulnerability for depression among children and adolescents: A cognitive science and developmental perspective. *Clinical Psychology Review, 28*, 759–782.

Jarrett, R. B., Vittengl, J. R., Doyle, K., & Clark, L. A. (2007). Changes in cognitive content during and following cognitive therapy for recurrent depression: Substantial and enduring, but not predictive of change in depressive symptoms. *Journal of Consulting and Clinical Psychology, 75*, 432–446.

Lee, C. W., Taylor, G., & Dunn, J. (1999). Factor structure of the Schema Questionnaire in a large clinical sample. *Cognitive Therapy and Research, 23*, 441–451.

Lewinsohn, P. M., Joiner, T. E., & Rohde, P. (2001). Evaluation of cognitive diathesis–stress models in predicting major depressive disorder in adolescents. *Journal of Abnormal Psychology, 110*(2), 203–215.

Mandler, G. (1984). *Mind and body: Psychology of emotion and stress*. New York: Plenum.

Mazure, C. M. (1998). Life stressors as risk factors in depression. *Clinical Psychology, Science and Practice, 5*, 291–313.

Mazure, C. M., Bruce, M. L., Maciejewski, P. K., & Jacobs, S. C. (2000). Adverse life events and cognitive-personality characteristics in the prediction of major depression and antidepressant response. *American Journal of Psychiatry, 157*(6), 896–903.

Miranda, J., & Persons, J. B. (1988). Dysfunctional attitudes are mood–state dependent. *Journal of Abnormal Psychology, 97*, 76–79.

Miranda, J., Gross, J. J., Persons, J. B., & Hahn, J. (1998). Mood matters: Negative mood induction activates dysfunctional attitudes in women vulnerable to depression. *Cognitive Therapy and Research, 22*, 363–376.

Monroe, S. M., & Hadjiyannakis, K. (2002). The social environment and depression: Focusing on severe life stress. In Gotlib, I. H., & Hammen, C. L. (Eds), *Handbook of depression* (pp. 314–340). New York: Guilford.

O'Brien, G., & Opie, J. (2004). Notes toward a structuralist theory of mental representation. In H. Clapin, P. Staines, & P. Slezak (Eds), *Representation in mind: New approaches to mental representation* (pp. 1–20). Oxford: Elsevier.

Oei, T. P. S., & Baranoff, J. (2007). Young Schema Questionnaire: Review of psychometric and measurement issues. *Australian Journal of Psychology, 59*(2), 78–86.

Otto, M. W., Teachman, B. A., Cohen, L. S., Soares, C. N., Vitonis, A. F., & Harlow, B. L. (2007). Dysfunctional attitudes and episodes of major depression: Predictive validity and temporal stability in never-depressed, depressed, and recovered women. *Journal of Abnormal Psychology, 116*, 475–483.

Papageorgiou, C., & Wells, A. (2004). Nature, functions, and beliefs about depressive rumination. In Papageorgiou, C., & Wells, A. (Eds), *Depressive rumination: Nature, theory and treatment* (pp. 3–20). Chichester, England: John Wiley & Son, Ltd.

Paykel, E. S., & Cooper, Z. (1992). Life events and social stress. In E. S. Paykel (Ed.), *Handbook of affective disorders* (2nd edn, pp. 149–170). New York: Guilford.

Power, M. J., & Champion, L. A. (1986). Cognitive approaches to depression: A theoretical critique. *British Journal of Clinical Psychology, 25*, 201–212.

Riso, L. P., & McBride, C. (2007). Introduction: A return to a focus on cognitive schemas. In L. P. Riso, P. L. du Toit, D. J. Stein, & J. E. Young (Eds), *Cognitive schemas and core beliefs in psychological problems: A scientist-practitioner guide* (pp. 3–9). Washington, DC: American Psychological Association.

Robins, C. J. (1990). Congruence of personality and life events in depression. *Journal of Abnormal Psychology, 99*(4), 393–397.

Rude, S. S., Covich, J., Jarrold, W., Hedlund, S., & Zenter, M. (2001). Detecting depressive schemata in vulnerable individuals: Questionnaires versus laboratory tasks. *Cognitive Therapy and Research, 25*, 103–116.

Scher, C. D., Ingram, R. E., & Segal, Z. V. (2005). Cognitive reactivity and vulnerability: Empirical evaluation of construct activation and cognitive diatheses in unipolar depression. *Clinical Psychology Review, 25*, 487–510.

Schmidt, N. B., Joiner, T. E., Young, J. E., & Telch, M. J. (1995). The Schema Questionnaire: Investigation of psychometric properties and the hierarchical structure of maladaptive schemas. *Cognitive Therapy and Research, 19*, 295–321.

Segal, Z. V. (1988). Appraisal of the self-schema construct in cognitive models of depression. *Psychological Bulletin, 103*(2), 147–162.

Segal, Z. V., Gemar, M., & Williams, S. (1999). Differential cognitive response to a mood challenge following successful cognitive therapy or pharmacotherapy for unipolar depression. *Journal of Abnormal Psychology, 108*, 3–10.

Segal, Z. V., Shaw, B. F., Vella, D. D., Katz, R. (1992). Cognitive and life stress predictors of relapse in remitted unipolar depressed patients: Test of the congruency hypothesis. *Journal of Abnormal Psychology, 101*(1), 26–36.

Segal, Z. V., Kennedy, S., Gemar, M., Hood, K., Pedersen, R., & Buis, T. (2006). Cognitive reactivity to sad mood provocation and the prediction of depressive relapse. *Archives of General Psychiatry, 63*, 749–755.

Simons, A. D., Gordon, J. S., Monroe, S. M., & Thase, M. E. (1995). Toward an integration of psychological, social, and biological factors in depression: Effects on outcome and course of cognitive therapy. *Journal of Consulting and Clinical Psychology*, *63*, 369–377.

Sotsky, S. M., Glass, D. R., Shea, M. T., Pilkonis, P. A., Collins, J. F., Elkin, I. … Oliveri, M. E. (1991). Patient predictors of response to psychotherapy and pharmacotherapy: Findings in the NIMH Treatment of Depression Collaborative Research Program. *American Journal of Psychiatry*, *148*, 997–1008.

Sternberg, R. J. (1996). *Cognitive psychology*. New York: Harcourt Brace.

Teasdale, J. D., & Barnard, P. J. (1993). *Affect, cognition and change: Re-modelling depressive thought*. Hove, England: Lawrence Erlbaum.

Teasdale, J. D., Segal, Z., & Williams, J. M. G. (1995). How does cognitive therapy prevent depressive relapse and why should attentional control (mindfulness) training help? *Behaviour Research and Therapy*, *33*(1), 25–39.

Weissman, M. M., & Beck, A. T. (1978). Development and validation of the Dysfunctional Attitudes Scale. Paper presented at the annual meeting of the Association for the Advancement of Behavior Therapy, Chicago.

Welburn, K. R., Coristine, M., Dagg, P., Pontefract, A., & Jordon, S. (2002). The Schema Questionnaire–Short Form: Factor analysis and relationship between schemas and symptoms. *Cognitive Therapy and Research*, *26*, 519–530.

Wells, A., & Matthews, G. (1994). *Attention and emotion: A clinical perspective*. Hove, England: Lawrence Erlbaum.

Young, J. E. (1990). *Cognitive therapy for personality disorders: A schema-focused approach*. Sarasota, FL: Professional Resource.

Young, J. E. (1998). *The Young Schema Questionnaire Short Form*. New York: Cognitive Therapy Centre.

Young, J. E. (1999). *Cognitive therapy for personality disorders: A schema-focused approach* (3rd edn). Sarasota, FL: Professional Resource.

Young, J. E., & Mattila, D. E. (2002). Schema-focused therapy for depression. In M. A. Reinecke & M. R. Davison (Eds), *Comparative treatments of depression* (pp. 291–316). New York: Springer.

Young, J. E., & Klosko, J. S., & Weishaar, M. E. (2003). *Schema therapy: A practitioner's guide*. New York: Guilford.

6

Metacognitive Therapy: Theoretical Background and Model of Depression

Adrian Wells and Peter L. Fisher

Metacognitive therapy (MCT) (Wells, 1999) is based on an information-processing model of self-regulation called the self-regulatory executive function (S-REF) model (Wells & Matthews, 1994, 1996). The model developed from an analysis of experimental work on emotion and attention combined with clinical observation. Research on attention and emotion was chosen as a rigorous basis for developing a model of emotional disorder because many of the symptoms of disorder appear to be associated with abnormalities in the selection of thought content and the topic of attention concerns the psychology of selection of subjective experience and of sustained or focused processing.

According to Wells and Matthews (1994), symptoms of emotional disorder appear to be associated with abnormalities or biases in the selection or maintenance of some thoughts over others. For example, in depression attention is allocated predominantly to the cognitive activity of rumination, which involves thoughts about the causes of depressive symptoms, while in generalized anxiety attention is allocated to worry about how to deal with possible danger in the future.

The S-REF model proposes that psychological disorder is the result of the activation and execution of a specific style of thinking in response to negative thoughts. This style leads to an extension of negative internal experiences of thoughts, beliefs, and emotions. A central clinical implication, in its simplest form, is that removal of this style of thinking will allow the individual to exit the cycles of sustained and recurrent processing that maintain disorder.

Treating Depression: MCT, CBT and Third Wave Therapies, First Edition.
Edited by Adrian Wells and Peter L. Fisher.

In MCT the therapist is not concerned with the content of the negative thoughts and general beliefs about self and world. Instead, therapists focus on the manner in which the patient reacts to negative thoughts, beliefs, and emotions; and they do so with the aim of reducing extended thinking and fixation of attention. In the metacognitive model cognition is controlled by a separate level of cognition rather than by the 'schemas' or ordinary beliefs that are held as central in CBT. This separate level is the metacognitive level.

Metacognition means 'cognition applied to cognition'. It is that aspect of information processing that monitors, controls, appraises, and organizes cognition (Flavell, 1979). The idea that cognition can be monitored and controlled by another dimension of cognition implies the existence of two levels of cognition (Nelson & Narens, 1990; Wells, 2009). MCT directs the treatment to working in the metacognitive system or at the metacognitive level rather than trying to modify the non-metacognitive level – which we may call the 'ordinary cognitive content' level.

Theoretical Background

A general and universal pattern of thinking and cognitive processing that occurs in psychological disorder was identified by Wells and Matthews (1994), who called it the cognitive attentional syndrome (CAS). The CAS consists of thinking in the form of worry and rumination, focusing attention on sources of threat (a process called threat monitoring), and developing coping behaviours that are unhelpful because they interfere with effective self-regulation or impair change in knowledge. Many of the coping strategies are metacognitive in nature in that they are intended, implicitly or explicitly, to alter the status of cognition. For example, the depressed patient often reduces his or her activity levels so as to spend more time analysing the reasons underlying personal failure and sadness.

Worry and rumination are prolonged chains of thinking that are largely verbal. They are aimed at anticipating and planning ways of avoiding, or coping with, potential danger (worry) or at analysing and understanding the meaning of emotions and past events (rumination). In the model, these are seen as predominantly verbal (appraisal-based) coping strategies; but they are problematic for self-regulation, the long-term control of distressing emotions, and the abandonment of distressing ideas.

Another feature of the CAS, threat monitoring, involves focusing and maintaining attention on potential sources of threat. These threats are often internal and involve thoughts, sensations, and emotions. Thus the anxious or the depressed person monitors for certain 'bad' thoughts or feelings that may signal danger. For example, a depressed patient described monitoring for an increase in energy levels as a means of determining whether she might be starting to recover, and later in therapy reported checking her concentration each morning, in order to try and work out whether her illness was returning. By monitoring for symptoms of depression she had many false alarms and a sustained sense of impending doom and threat.

While the above responses are ways of coping that involve specific thinking styles, other coping behaviours are also identified as problematic in the theory. In particular, behaviours leading to the avoidance of a nonexistent threat are a problem because they interfere with accurately updating erroneous knowledge.

In the metacognitive model, what and how an individual thinks is controlled and modified by metacognition; hence, if an individual dwells on his/her own sense of inadequacy, this is because metacognition leads to sustained analysis of the self on this dimension. Most people have negative thoughts and emotions that might occur frequently, but for most these experiences are transitory and do not constitute a psychological problem. However, metacognition can lead to processing styles that cause an extension of negative ideas of this kind. According to the theory, psychological disorder is a direct function of the extent to which negative thoughts and feelings are recycled and extended rather than let go. The principal factor leading to extended and sustained negative (threat-related) experiences is the CAS; therefore metacognition that drives the CAS is of central importance in MCT.

MCT delineates two broad subtypes of metacognitive content at the belief level: positive beliefs and negative beliefs. Positive beliefs concern the advantages of the CAS and include beliefs about the usefulness of worry, threat monitoring, and thought control. For example, a person believed: 'Worrying about my health will help me detect problems before it is too late.' This led to repeated catastrophizing about symptoms of fatigue and loss of energy, with concomitant negative affect and a perpetuation of symptoms.

Aside from positive beliefs, negative metacognitive beliefs are of more direct importance in psychological disorder and can be viewed as the 'turbocharger' behind distress. Negative beliefs concern themes related to the uncontrollability of mental processes and the threat imparted by thoughts. Most patients believe that their worrying, ruminating, and conceptual processing is uncontrollable and a symptom of their illness rather than a strategy that remains under voluntary control. Some systems of therapy reinforce this unhelpful model of psychological functioning by presenting the idea that depression or anxiety is a consequence of chemical imbalance in the brain or the result of automatic or unconscious psychological processes.

In the metacognitive approach, processes of worry and rumination and the features of the CAS remain under voluntary control, as they are part of the individual's strategy for coping. However, believing that these processes are uncontrollable leads to failure in the attempt to control them, with the subsequent effect that the negative processing is extended. In some instances, belief in their uncontrollability supports counterproductive means of control, such as using alcohol and seeking reassurance from others. Reassurance seeking effectively transfers control over one's thinking to another person, while using alcohol transfers control to a substance; both methods prevent the individual from discovering that s/he has self-control. Furthermore, alcohol can have a direct effect on thinking and behaviour, causing episodes of diminished self-control.

In addition to uncontrollability, other important negative beliefs concern the threatening nature of thoughts and feelings. For example, individuals with depression believe that worry or stress can lead to psychological breakdown, and therefore they worry about worry. This extension of negative thinking prolongs the sense of danger and threat and makes it escalate.

The Metacognitive Model of Depression

The S-REF model of psychological dysfunction has provided the framework for the development of disorder-specific models aimed at capturing the most salient metacognitive beliefs and the most distinct features of the CAS. The metacognitive model of depression is now described.

Negative thoughts and a lowering of mood and motivation are normal features of everyday life. For most people, they are transitory experiences, lasting minutes, hours, or days. However, the person with depression becomes locked into experiencing repeated and prolonged episodes of this kind. In such cases the person is unable to shift out of analysing causes of sadness and reasons for the failure to achieve personal goals. The fundamental problem is *perseveration* in this kind of thinking. As we have seen earlier, such perseveration occurs as a distinct cognitive attentional syndrome (CAS).

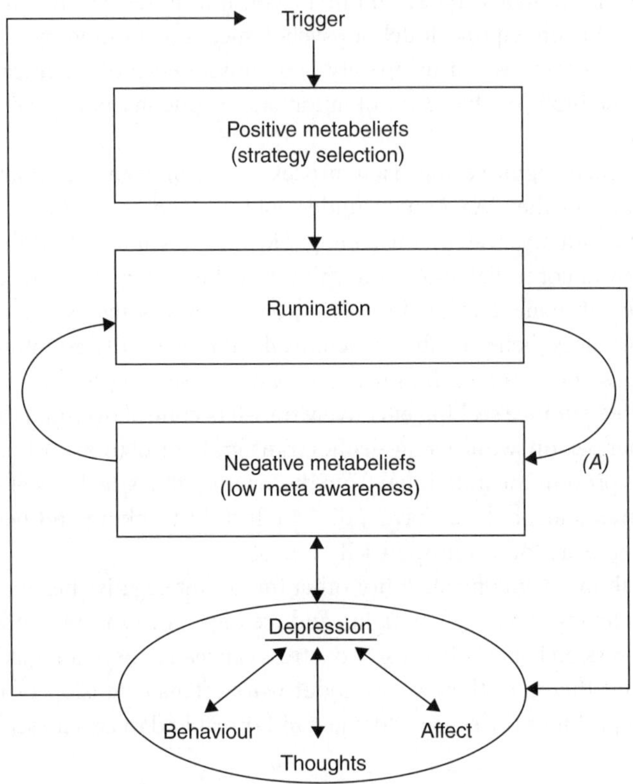

Figure 6.1 The metacognitive model of depression.
Source: A. Wells, 2009. *Metacognitive therapy for anxiety and depression.* New York: Guilford Press, p. 199. Reproduced with permission.

The metacognitive model of depression (Wells, 2009) is presented in Figure 6.1. The model explains the factors that lead to maintenance of the CAS and the mechanisms linking the CAS with symptoms of depression.

In Figure 6.1 there are several key psychological variables involved: (1) positive metacognitive beliefs about the need to ruminate as a means of understanding and overcoming depression and self-deficiencies; (2) negative metacognitive beliefs concerning the uncontrollability of rumination, the psychological vulnerability of the self, and the danger of depressive experiences; (3) diminished meta-awareness of rumination; (4) the CAS (typified by rumination in the central loop of the model, but also including threat monitoring and worry) and unhelpful coping – such as through social withdrawal or use of alcohol – included under behaviours.

Rumination and the other features of the CAS are insidious processes, and their intensity and duration is modulated by metacognition. Typical triggers for more intense rumination episodes are negative thoughts. Specific symptoms such as feeling fatigued, loss of motivation, or feeling sad can give rise to an initial thought of the form: 'Why do I feel this way?' The trigger thought activates beliefs about the need to engage in sustained thinking (rumination) about the meaning and causes of these experiences. Positive metacognitive beliefs also concern the value of monitoring for signs and symptoms of low mood and the value of questioning the reasons for feelings as a means of coping. In some instances there are positive beliefs about sadness as a means of emotional self-regulation. For example, some patients have described how they maintain a level of pessimism because this prevents the more unpleasant emotions associated with being disappointed in life. Examples of positive metacognitive beliefs include the following:

'If I analyse why I have failed I will be able to prevent failure in future.'
'If I work out why I'm depressed I will be able to get better.'
'Checking how sad I feel will help me know when I'm starting to recover.'
'Analysing if I'm to blame will help me work out what to do.'
'Dwelling on how bad I feel will make me feel worse and force me to get better.'

Positive beliefs give rise to sustained brooding or patterns of attention and coping that have the effect of prolonging negative thinking and increasing the awareness of sadness. This direct effect is depicted as the arrow labelled '*A*' in Figure 6.1.

Because rumination has a negative effect on cognition and leads to the persistence of symptoms, and because psychosocial factors (e.g., what the person learns about depression through contact with the medical system) can generate a sense of loss of control, negative metacognitive beliefs are activated and strengthened. In particular, the person believes that rumination and sadness are uncontrollable. In some cases the person believes that rumination and negative feelings are symptomatic of a biological disease. Patients may further interpret these symptoms as a sign of personal weakness or that something is wrong with their mind. These beliefs contribute to failures to disrupt rumination and to control the unhelpful coping patterns whose suspension could ultimately alleviate the depressed mood. Examples of negative metacognitive beliefs include:

'My thinking has changed; I'm no longer in control.'
'There's nothing I can do, I can't think normally.'
'I'm mentally weak for being like this.'
'All I can do is hope it goes away.'
'I've lost control of my mind.'

Figure 6.1 also shows that part of the constellation of negative metacognitions is a reduced awareness of the process of rumination or a lack of knowledge that rumination is a central process in maintaining depression. The depressed person sees rumination as part of the solution; and the process may have occurred for so long that the individual is unaware of its pervasive nature. The sum effect is that meta-awareness of the occurrence of rumination and of its extent and frequency is often low.

Depressive symptoms and behaviours can act as further sources of negative thoughts that activate positive beliefs about sustained thinking and other forms of maladaptive coping, as depicted by the feedback loop from depression to trigger in Figure 6.1. Furthermore, the individual can become fearful of subsequent depressive episodes; this is the source of worry about relapse that can underpin some mixed anxiety–depression presentations.

An example of a case conceptualization using the model is presented in Figure 6.2. In this case, the patient suffered a second episode of depression, which lasted approximately three years. He had responded partially to a combination of antidepressant, antipsychotic, and mood stabilizers but reported sustained depression, lack of motivation, hopelessness, and loss of interest.

When asked about the length of time he spent thinking about his symptoms and his future each day, he initially reported that his mind was 'blank' much of the time, but after careful questioning he reported that his feelings were worse immediately after waking up in the morning. On waking up he would initially feel 'normal' and would then have the thought 'Am I back to normal?' This thought acted as a trigger for his positive metacognitive belief: 'By analysing the way I feel I can know when I am over it.' This would prompt him to focus on and analyse his feelings, which would lead to a spiral of rumination in which he focused on his level of fatigue and sense of dread at starting the day.

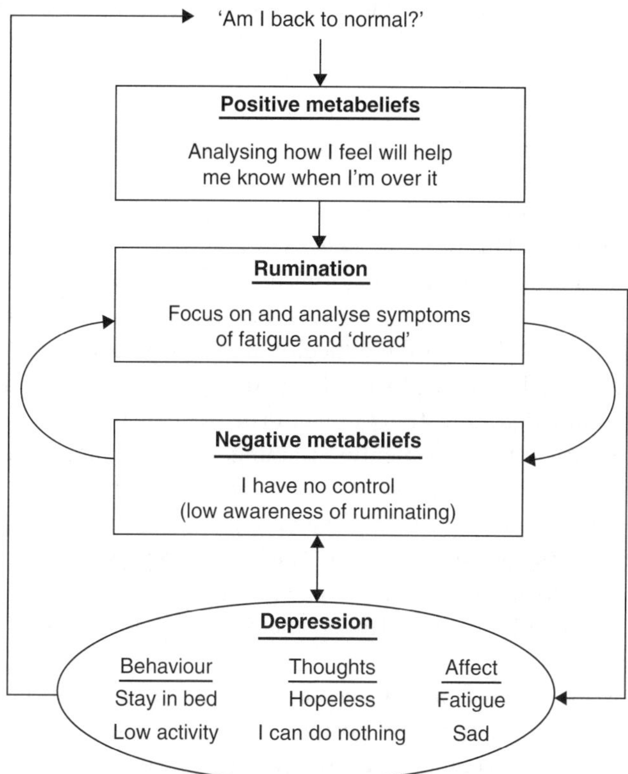

Figure 6.2 Example of a depression case formulation.

He often remained in bed and failed to engage in activities that could help to displace this thinking process. His limited experience of controlling it and of his lack of response to medication – to which he had responded more favourably during the previous episode – led him to believe that there was nothing he could do to aid his recovery. It was apparent from the therapist's assessment that this patient had not really considered that his rumination was part of the problem and was maintaining his depression.

MCT

The metacognitive therapist formulates the maintenance of depression in terms of rumination or worry, threat monitoring, and unhelpful coping behaviours. Central in the therapeutic process is to increase the patient's awareness of the CAS and to introduce greater flexibility in responding to negative thoughts and feelings. This means introducing metacognitive control and alternative responses that counteract it.

After case conceptualization and after having been made aware of the role of rumination, patients practise the technique of attention training (ATT) (Wells, 1990) as a means of strengthening metacognitive flexibility and control over thinking. This procedure also acts as a strategy for counteracting inactivity and provides a focal point for initial sessions and an activity for homework. A rationale for ATT is given, which communicates that depression is maintained through the difficulty of standing back from thoughts and 'taking control' of unhelpful thinking processes that have become dominated by rumination. One strategy that can help to regain awareness of one's control and strengthen it is attention training, which will allow the patient to discover that they can regulate the focus of attention regardless of internal or external stimuli. The therapist emphasizes that this technique is not a distraction strategy. The aim is not to reduce awareness of one's thoughts or to suppress their content, but to simply retain flexible control over the allocation of attention – regardless of whether thoughts, events, or feelings enter consciousness.

Therapy also focuses on reducing and limiting the extent of rumination and worry by using rumination postponement experiments configured so as to challenge metacognitive beliefs about the uncontrollability of these responses. The therapist also uses Socratic dialogue to verbally challenge the belief that depression is an irreversible mental condition. Counterevidence is reviewed – such as daily fluctuations in mood (when this is evidence available), or the effects of engaging in distracting or pleasurable activities, to help the patient discover how mood is affected by a range of factors.

Patients are instructed to respond to negative thoughts with *detached mindfulness* (DM) (Wells & Matthews, 1994; Wells, 2005) and are given in-session practise of a range of techniques that replace their overreliance on thinking as a means of dealing with negative thoughts, doubts, worries, and disappointments. Initially metaphors are used to illustrate the concept of DM. The therapist may use the telephone metaphor: 'Your thoughts are a little like a telephone ringing, you cannot stop it; but let me ask you a question, must you always answer it?' This is followed by a meta-level guided discovery process in which the patient is asked if s/he has ever stepped back from negative thoughts and refrained from 'answering' them. This can lead to the discovery of further examples of the CAS, as some patients confuse the concept of not engaging with thoughts with suppression or other counterproductive strategies. Next the therapist introduces specific experiential exercises designed to enable the patient to directly experience and shape up the correct response of DM. Several techniques have been devised for this purpose; these include the free association task, the tiger task, and the suppression and counter-suppression exercise (Wells, 2005, 2009). For example, the therapist instructs the patient to close his eyes, take a mental step back and passively watch what happens in the mind when a series of words is presented. The goal is to refrain from dealing with any spontaneous thoughts or mental experiences when exposed to a string of neutral words such as 'tree', 'bicycle', 'elephant', 'birthday', 'friends', 'walking', 'seaside', 'chocolate', 'sky', 'holiday'. The therapist then engages in a careful discussion about the patient's subjective experiences during the exercise, taking care to determine whether spontaneous thoughts or memories occurred and how the patient related to them. The goal is to help the patient discover that s/he can let spontaneous mental events go. The therapist typically ends the discussion with the question: 'What happened to the first thought you had by the time we reached the end?' DM is usually practised several times and eventually incorporates 'trigger' words in order to shape the experience of letting go of thoughts. In order to increase compliance with rumination reduction strategies, the therapist challenges the patient's positive beliefs about the need to ruminate by questioning any evidence that rumination has worked and by examining the mechanisms by which it could be useful. Simply by asking the patient to ruminate more as a means of overcoming depression can be a powerful way of illustrating how the strategy is counterproductive. Usually the patient understands the point without having to follow up with actual increased rumination.

Later in the course of treatment, strategies are used for removing residual unhelpful coping behaviours and threat monitoring. Relapse prevention consists of writing out new plans for dealing with negative thoughts and changes in mood in the future. A key strategy for achieving this is the 'new plan summary sheet', which contrasts specific individual features of the CAS with the new style of response developed during treatment.

The components of MCT are set out in the treatment manual (Wells, 2009) and are illustrated in more detail in chapter 12 (on treatment) in this volume.

Empirical Status of the Metacognitive Model

The generic S-REF model of psychological disorder is supported by a large number of studies on clinical and analogue populations. These studies have demonstrated reliable links between the perseverative thinking forms of worry and rumination and measures of cognitive and emotional vulnerability (see Wells, 2009 for a review). The S-REF is also supported by objective laboratory findings on attentional bias in emotional disorder.

An extensive literature demonstrates the deleterious effects of both worry and rumination on well-being and performance. Early work on worry appeared in the area of test anxiety research (Wine 1971; Sarason, 1984), where the cognitive (worry) rather than the emotional (bodily reaction) component of anxiety has been found to disrupt performance. The S-REF model predicts that worry is closely linked to metacognitive beliefs, and it follows from this that metacognition should therefore be relevant to test anxiety. Matthews, Hillyard, and Cambell (1999) demonstrated positive correlations between metacognition and the worry and tension components of test anxiety. Two factors emerged, which could be interpreted as maladaptive and more adaptive coping; and the analysis suggested that the extent to which coping is adaptive partly reflects metacognitive variables.

Worry appears to have a range of negative psychological effects. Brief periods of activity lead to higher anxiety, more depression, and more negative thoughts in high worriers by comparison with low worriers (Borkovec, Robinson, Pruzinsky, & DePree, 1983). In individuals with high levels of social anxiety, worrying or ruminating after a social event was associated with an increased recall of negative self-relevant information, negative bias in self-judgements, and more recall of anxiety sensations on a subsequent occasion of anticipating a social interaction (Mellings & Alden, 2000).

The idea that features of the CAS such as worry and rumination interfere with emotional recovery and repair has been directly tested in the context of stress exposure. Butler, Wells, and Dewick (1995) and Wells and Papageorgiou (1995) asked subjects to watch a stressful film and then to engage in different types of thinking during a brief post-film period. Subjects asked to worry during the thinking period showed the greatest occurrence of intrusive images over a subsequent 3-day period. Such intrusions have been considered to represent failed emotional processing (e.g. Rachman, 1980).

It is now well established from longitudinal predictive studies and from laboratory-based manipulations of the process that rumination has negative psychological consequences. In particular, it prolongs depressed mood after stressful life events (Nolen-Hoeksema, 2000; Nolen-Hoeksema & Morrow, 1991; Nolen-Hoeksema & Larson, 1999). Rumination also biases thinking and affects behaviour (Spasojevic, Alloy, Abramson, Maccoon, & Robinson, 2004).

Attentional monitoring for threat (threat monitoring) is also central to the CAS. Wells and Matthews (1994) argued that bias in attention tasks using emotional or disorder-related stimuli is an index of this effect. In studies using the emotional Stroop task, there is abundant evidence of slow response in naming the colour of words that are congruent with disorder or are high in emotionality (Mathews & Macleod, 1985; Gotlib & Cane, 1985; Kaspi, McNally, & Amir, 1995). Some theorists have argued that attention bias of this kind is automatic and schema-driven processing; however, Wells and Matthews (1994, see also Matthews & Wells, 2000) review several lines of evidence that support the S-REF-based counterproposal that the effect is related to the individual's strategy for processing. For instance, these bias effects appear to be sensitive to priming by self-relevant material in depressed subjects (Segal & Vella, 1990) and by a self-focus manipulation in non-clinical subjects (Richards & French, 1992). Such processes appear to operate in time intervals that are normally equated with voluntary rather than automatic processing. There is also a stronger effect when similar types of Stroop material are presented together rather than different types presented in random order (Richards, French, Johnson, Naparstek, & Williams, 1992). This suggests that expecting certain types of threat stimuli may enhance bias in anxiety-prone subjects. Automatic processes would not be affected by strategy or expectancy, which suggests that these tasks reflect strategic processing. In a connectionist simulation study, Matthews and Harley (1996) explored possible automatic (hard-wired) or strategic simulations of the emotional Stroop effect. Only the strategic simulation of a continuation of monitoring for threat while performing other tasks produced impairment in the naming of colours associated with emotional words.

Metacognitive Control Strategies

The metacognitive model proposes that metacognition is closely linked with the concept of coping and with the individual's choice of a coping strategy. Many strategies in psychological disorder consist of coping through the control of cognition. This occurs in the form of thought suppression or by responding to thoughts with sustained negative thinking (worry or rumination). What is the evidence of thought control strategies having ironic effects and contributing to disorder?

Research on thought suppression has shown that attempts not to think of a target thought – such as the thought of a white bear – can lead to an immediate enhancement of the thought or to a subsequent rebound effect (Purdon, 1999; Wegner, Schneider, Carter, & White, 1987; Wenzlaff & Wegner, 2000). However, suppression studies have produced equivocal results, which call into question the reliability of the immediate or delayed effects observed. The safe conclusion is that trying to suppress thoughts is not consistently effective. Moreover, there appear to be important effects that can be more reliably attributed to individual differences in the choice of a thought control strategy.

The metacognitive model specifies that using the strategies of coping dominated by the CAS should be problematic for emotional well-being and for adaptive outcomes. More specifically, using perseverative forms of thinking such worry as a thought control strategy should be linked to disorder. To begin testing this assertion, Wells and Davies (1994) developed the Thought Control Questionnaire (TCQ). This measure assesses individual differences in five strategies that are used to control distressing thoughts: worry, punishment, reappraisal, social control, and distraction. Worry and punishment are two strategies that constitute the CAS and are therefore hypothesized to be the most consistently problematic.

TCQ worry and punishment have emerged as cross-sectional positive correlates of vulnerability to psychological disorder and stress symptoms (Roussis & Wells, 2006; Wells & Davies, 1994). They distinguish patients with disorders such as depression or generalized anxiety disorder (GAD) from non-patient controls (Wells & Carter, 2009), and motor-vehicle accident victims with acute stress disorder from victims without such disorder (Warda & Bryant, 1998). Patients with obsessive–compulsive disorder also use more worry and punishment (Amir, Cashman, & Foa, 1997; Abramowitz, Whiteside, Kalsky, & Tolin 2003), and these strategies predict lower levels of recovery in patients with depression and/or post-traumatic stress disorder (PTSD) (Reynolds & Wells, 1999). There is evidence from longitudinal studies that TCQ worry levels soon after a trauma predict the development of PTSD later on; this evidence is consistent with a causal role of worrying in such developments (Holeva, Tarrier, & Wells, 2000). Roussis and Wells (2009) showed that TCQ worry was a positive predictor of the development of future PTSD symptoms, and this relationship was independent of worry assessed as a symptom of anxiety or stress.

Metacognitive Beliefs

In order to test the metacognitive model of psychological disorder, it was important to develop a measure of metacognitive beliefs. The Metacognitions Questionnaire was developed for this purpose. There are two versions of this measure: a 65-item version (Cartwright-Hatton and Wells, 1997) and a 30-item version (Wells & Cartwright-Hatton, 2004). Each has an equivalent number of factors and they assess the same constructs.

Positive and negative beliefs about thoughts are correlated positively with trait measures of emotion and worry (Cartwright-Hatton & Wells, 1997; Wells & Papageorgiou, 1998), are elevated in patients with anxiety disorders (Wells & Carter, 2001), are positively correlated with depression (Papageorgiou & Wells, 2001a, 2001b), psychotic symptoms (Morrison, Wells, & Nothard, 2002; Stirling, Barkus, & Lewis, 2007), alcohol abuse (Spada & Wells, 2006), and stress in Parkinson's disease (Allott, Wells, Morrison, & Walker, 2005). These are a few examples of the large number of studies that have demonstrated positive relationships between metacognitive beliefs, psychological vulnerability, and disorder (see Wells, 2009 for a comprehensive review).

The studies reviewed above that have examined worry and rumination as prospective predictors of negative emotional outcomes are consistent with a causal role of these factors. Similarly, the effects of laboratory manipulations of worry (Wells & Papageorgiou, 1995) and the effects observed with experimental increases in rumination (Lyubomirsky & Nolen-Hoeksema, 1995) and suppression (Wenzlaff & Wegner, 2000) are supportive of a causal influence of these variables.

However, of particular relevance in evaluating the metacognitive model of depression is the available evidence on relationships between metacognitive beliefs and depressive symptoms. Some of these data are derived from direct tests of the model and are briefly summarized in the next section.

Tests of the metacognitive model of depression

In a semi-structured interview study, Papageorgiou and Wells (2001a) explored metacognitive beliefs about rumination among patients with

DSM-IV recurrent major depressive disorder. All patients reported both positive and negative beliefs about rumination. The positive beliefs centred on the theme that rumination was a useful coping strategy, while the negative beliefs focused on rumination being uncontrollable and harmful.

Subsequently tests of the metacognitive model of depression have relied on two measures of metacognition: the Positive Beliefs about Rumination Scale (PBRS) (Papageorgiou & Wells, 2009) and the Negative Beliefs about Rumination Scale (NBRS) (Papageorgiou & Wells, 2003). Both scales are positively correlated with rumination and with depression in non-clinical and clinically depressed patients. These beliefs also distinguish patients with recurrent major depression from patients with panic disorder, agoraphobia, or social phobia (Papageorgiou & Wells, 2001b).

An important question concerns the causal status of metacognitive beliefs in the development of depression symptoms. Yilmaz, Grencoz, and Wells (2011) examined the individual contribution of these factors in a sample of individuals over a period of six months. Higher levels of negative beliefs about uncontrollability and the danger of worrying predicted an increase in depression symptoms scores.

Several studies have used path analysis and structural equation modelling to test the depression model and the mediated and direct relationships between the factors specified. The model proposes that the relationship between positive metacognitive beliefs and depression should be partially or fully mediated by rumination (the CAS). Papageorgiou and Wells (2001b) demonstrated the existence of mediation for both state and trait measures of depression in non-patients.

A more complete model, which incorporates both positive and negative metacognitive beliefs, was tested in a subsequent study of depressed and non-depressed individuals (Papageorgiou & Wells, 2003). The model tested was one in which positive metacognitive beliefs lead to rumination, and rumination leads to negative metacognition and to depression. In depressed participants the model was a good fit to the data; but in the non-depressed group it was a poor fit. Tests suggested that the fit of the model could be improved in the non-clinical sample by including both direct and indirect paths between rumination and depression. These results suggest that direct and indirect effects of rumination on depression might depend on whether or not the individual is currently depressed. Overall, these data supported indirect and direct effects of rumination on depression. They also supported indirect effects of positive metacognitive beliefs and direct effects of negative metacognitive beliefs, which is consistent with the model (see Figure 6.1).

Roleofs and colleagues (2007) tested the structural model in undergraduate students and added to the model a link that represented self-discrepancies, implicated as a factor activating positive metacognitive beliefs in the original S-REF model. They found evidence that positive metacognitive beliefs partially mediated the relationship between self-discrepancies and rumination. They also demonstrated direct and indirect links between rumination and depression, negative metacognitions acting as a mediator.

Overall, these findings are consistent with a role of metacognitive beliefs in depression and depression-related thinking processes, as specified in the model. It is important to note, however, that many of these data are cross-sectional in origin and that data on the causal role of such beliefs are less abundant at the present time.

Summary of evidence

As the previous section shows, there is a large and consistent body of data that can be seen as supporting the metacognitive approach to psychological disorder and, specifically, the metacognitive model of depression. There is strong support for a relationship between features of the CAS – namely worry, rumination, biased attention, and metacognitive-directed coping strategies – and psychological disorder. Rumination leads to a persistence of depression, and unhelpful thought control strategies of worry and punishment distinguish depressed patients from non-patients. Both positive and negative metacognitive beliefs are correlated with depression and rumination, and the pattern of relationships among these variables is consistent with the pattern predicted by the model. There is some initial indication that metacognition is related to depression when traditional schemas are statistically partialled out. The causal role of the CAS is supported by data that have manipulated worry and rumination, and also by the longitudinal studies of metacognition and rumination/worry that show that these factors predict future negative affect and stress outcomes.

The Effectiveness of MCT and Techniques in Depression

MCT has been evaluated in the form of a full treatment package. The individual component of attention training has also been examined as a stand-alone technique providing some partial dismantling of the treatment.

Wells and colleagues (2009) used an A–B multiple-baseline design to evaluate the effects associated with 6–8 sessions of full MCT. Four patients with chronic and recurrent major depressive disorder were treated weekly after individual baseline periods and were followed up for six months after treatment. Large improvements were observed in depression, anxiety, and metacognition. The mean pre-treatment score on the Beck Depression Inventory was 24.4 and the mean post-treatment score decreased to 6.5. At post-treatment and at a three-month follow-up, all patients met the standardized criteria for recovery on this measure. At a six-month follow-up, one patient had lost the recovery status but continued to meet the criteria of reliable improvement, while the rest retained their recovery status.

This study of brief MCT was followed by an uncontrolled trial (N = 12) of patients with treatment-resistant major depressive disorder (Wells et al., 2012). Patients received up to eight sessions of MCT and were assessed at post-treatment, then at a six- and a 12-month follow-up. There was no significant change in symptoms during baseline, but significant improvements occurred in all measures at post-treatment and were maintained across a 12-month follow-up. Using objective criteria for recovery on the Beck Depression Inventory showed that 70 per cent of completers were recovered at post-treatment, and the percentage remained 60 at both a six- and a 12-month follow-up.

Two studies have examined the effects of attention-training technique (ATT), which normally forms a component of MCT for depression. Papageorgiou and Wells (2000) tested these effects across four consecutive patients suffering from recurrent major depression. In these cases the duration of the current depressive episode ranged from four to eleven months and the number of previous episodes ranged from two to four. After a three– to five-week no-treatment baseline period patients received five to eight sessions of ATT. In each case marked improvements in depression and anxiety could be observed, and treatment gains were maintained across the 12-month follow-up period. The treatment was associated with reductions not only in depression but also in rumination, self-focus, and metacognitions. At a 12-month follow-up, none of the patients met diagnostic criteria for major depressive disorder.

Attention training was used as part of a 'cognitive control' training package by Siegle, Ghinassi, and Thase (2007). Depressed patients were randomly allocated either to the attention treatment plus treatment as usual or simply to treatment as usual. Those patients who received two weeks of the attention-augmented treatment showed significantly greater improvement in depression and rumination than those who received treatment as usual. Improvements after two weeks of the attention treatment was greater than the average change associated with the usual six-week treatment programme in depression. Preliminary data from a subset of the attention treatment patients revealed neuropsychological changes showing increases in right amygdala activity in response to positive words and a decreased response to negative or neutral words.

Nordahl (2009) conducted a study of MCT in an outpatient setting. Treatment-resistant patients with mixed depression–anxiety disorders were randomized to receive either treatment as usual – which was cognitive behaviour therapy – or the new MCT. Most participants had a depressive disorder. The results showed that, overall, MCT led to greater improvements in symptoms than CBT. Statistically, MCT was superior to CBT in reducing anxiety and worry and equivalent to it in reducing depressive symptoms. However, follow-up data in this study could not be collected due to design constraints.

MCT has been evaluated as a group treatment for depression. Papageorgiou and Wells (2015) treated ten patients who had failed to respond to antidepressant medication and CBT. All patients completed the treatment, which suggests that the intervention was acceptable; 70 per cent of patients recovered, while a further 20 per cent improved both at post-treatment and at a six-month follow-up. In a Norwegian evaluation of MCT presented as a group intervention, Dammen, Papageorgiou and Wells (2015) also demonstrated high rates of recovery from depression at post-treatment and at follow-up, significant improvements being also made in comorbid diagnoses.

MCT has been evaluated in the treatment of other emotional disorders and has produced significant improvements in depressive comorbid symptoms. This effect has been demonstrated in trials of post-traumatic stress disorder (Wells & Sembi, 2004; Wells et al., 2008) and in generalized anxiety disorder (Wells & King, 2006; Wells et al., 2010). A meta-analysis by Normann, van Emmerik, and Morina (2014) confirmed that MCT is effective in treating anxiety and depression. There were large effect sizes across controlled trials, significantly more effective than in waitlist control groups ($g = 1.81$), and the treatment was more effective than cognitive behaviour therapy ($g = 0.97$).

The few studies conducted to date suggest that MCT and individual components such as ATT can be effective in the treatment of depression. However, the available data are limited and the design of some of these studies necessitate caution in attributing the effects to MCT treatment components. However, the results do seem to suggest that the changes observed occurred in a short period of time and the effects were large. The data on the effects of MCT on depressive symptoms within the context of other disorders – for example GAD, PTSD, and mixed anxiety–depression – suggest that MCT may be particularly useful as a transdiagnostic treatment. In each case, the treatment appears to have a positive impact on depressive symptoms.

Conclusions

The metacognitive model of depression is a model of how individuals regulate cognition in response to negative thoughts about loss and feelings such as sadness or low interest. It identifies a pattern of thinking – labelled 'the cognitive attentional syndrome' – as central to the persistence and strengthening of negative affect and negative ideas. Disorder is equated with the perpetuation of negative ideas and emotion that should normally be transitory internal experiences. These experiences become prolonged through cycles of extended thinking and fixation on a threat. Rumination (and often worry) is a central feature of the CAS in depression, along with monitoring or checking for depression symptoms and signs (or their absence). This pattern of responses emerges from the individual's metacognition, which consists principally of positive beliefs about rumination as a means of dealing with sadness and self-discrepancies, and of negative beliefs about the uncontrollability and meaning of negative thinking and depression.

There is often a lack of awareness that rumination is pervasive and problematic; this is referred to as 'low meta-awareness' in the model (Figure 6.1), which at least partially reflects the effects of the patient's metacognitive beliefs. In these beliefs rumination is seen as a solution rather than a problem in overcoming depression.

The MCT approach directs the therapist towards conceptualizing depression in terms of cognitive processes and mental control rather than in terms of content of schemas or negative automatic thoughts. These latter events are seen as the triggers or outputs of the CAS rather than as events that should be evaluated against reality and replaced. Instead, the metacognitive therapist helps the patient see that there are alternative responses to negative thoughts and feelings that do not involve sustained negative processing and reasoning. In this way the individual discovers that emotions and negative ideas are transitory experiences, unrelated to the broader self. In consequence, they are less likely to become more elaborated and fixed concepts and experiences.

The MCT therapist does not focus on the content of beliefs, except those at the metacognitive level. These include challenging the patient's positive beliefs about rumination and monitoring and challenging the patent's erroneous negative beliefs about the uncontrollability of rumination and the intransient nature of a depressed mood.

Learning to respond to negative thoughts through DM and rumination postponement helps to build the necessary metacognitive monitoring and control skills for detecting and stopping ruminative thinking styles. Techniques such as attention training help the client to disconnect the control of cognition from the experience of internal and external events and thereby to develop a new relationship with thoughts that is characterized by greater flexibility and a sense of choice over subjective experience. These factors create the foundation for healthier forms of metacognitive knowledge and mental control.

Although support for the metacognitive model has accumulated, further research is necessary in particular areas, especially those relating to the causal role of positive and negative metacognitive beliefs. An area of research that is currently lacking concerns the causal role of threat monitoring in depression and the reciprocal effects that depression may have on fundamental processes of metacognitive monitoring and control. An interesting question concerns the effect that rumination may have on metacognitive functioning and whether rumination, mood, or both impact on the quality of functioning. Depression presents motivational and energetic characteristics that appear to differentiate it from the effects seen in anxiety, and such effects may be dependent on or moderated by metacognition.

The results of treatment studies have so far proven to be encouraging, given the rapid effects associated with MCT and ATT, and especially the effects in treatment-resistant cases. The treatment effect sizes have been large; but many of these effects are uncontrolled, which has a tendency to engender overestimation. However, the results imply that MCT offers an alternative treatment for depression that might repay continued evaluation with the improved levels of efficacy that are much needed in this disorder.

References

Abramowitz, J. S., Whiteside, S., Kalsky, S. A., & Tolin, D. A. (2003). Thought control strategies in obsessive-compulsive disorder: A replication and extension. *Behaviour Research and Therapy*, *41*, 529–554.

Allott, R., Wells, A., Morrison, A. P., & Walker R. (2005). Distress in Parkinson's disease: Contributions of disease factors and metacognitive style. *British Journal of Psychiatry*, *187*, 182–183.

Amir, N., Cashman, L., & Foa, E. B. (1997). Strategies of thought control in obsessive–compulsive disorder. *Behaviour Research and Therapy*, *35*, 775–777.

Borkovec, T. D., Robinson, E., Pruzinsky, T., & DePree, J. A. (1983). Preliminary exploration of worry: Some characteristics and processes. *Behaviour Research and Therapy*, *21*, 9–16.

Butler, G., Wells, A., & Dewick, H. (1995). Differential effects of worry and imagery after exposure to a stressful stimulus. *Behavioural and Cognitive Psychotherapy*, *23*, 45–56.

Cartwright-Hatton, S., & Wells, A. (1997). Beliefs about worry and intrusions: The Meta-Cognitions Questionnaire and its correlates. *Journal of Anxiety Disorders*, *11*, 279–296.

Dammen, T., Papageorgiou, C., & Wells, A. (2015). An open trial of group metacognitive therapy for depression in Norway. *Nordic Journal of Psychiatry*, *69*, 126–131.

Flavell, J. H. (1979). Metacognition and metacognitive monitoring; A new area of cognitive–developmental inquiry. *American Psychologist*, *34*, 906–911.

Gotlib, I. H., & Cane, D. B. (1985). Construct accessibility and clinical depression: A longitudinal investigation. *Journal of Abnormal Psychology*, *96*, 199–204.

Holeva, V., Tarrier, N., & Wells, A. (2000). Prevalence and predictors of acute stress disorder and PTSD following road traffic accidents: Thought control strategies and social support. *Behavior Therapy*, *32*, 65–83.

Kaspi, S. P., McNally, R. J., & Amir, N. (1995). Cognitive processing of emotional information in posttraumatic stress disorder. *Cognitive Therapy and Research*, *19*, 433–444.

Lyubomirsky, S., & Nolen-Hoeksema, S. (1995). Effects of self-focused rumination on negative thinking and interpersonal problem solving. *Journal of Personality and Social Psychology*, *69*, 176–190.

Mathews, A., & Macleod, C. (1985). Selective processing of threat cues in anxiety states. *Behaviour Research and Therapy*, *23*, 563–569.

Matthews, G., & Harley, T. A. (1996). Connectionist models of emotional distress and attentional bias. *Cognition and Emotion*, *10*, 561–600.

Matthews, G., & Wells, A. (2000). Attention, automaticity and affective disorder. *Behavior Modification*, *24*, 69–93.

Matthews, G., Hillyard, E. J., & Cambell, S. E. (1999). Metacognition and maladaptive coping as components of test anxiety. *Clinical Psychology and Psychotherapy*, *6*, 111–125.

Mellings, T. M. B., & Alden, L. E. (2000). Cognitive processes in social anxiety: The effects of self-focus, rumination and anticipatory processing. *Behaviour Research and Therapy*, *38*, 243–257.

Morrison, A. P., Wells, A., & Nothard, S. (2002). Cognitive and emotional predictors of predisposition to hallucinations in non-patients. *British Journal of Clinical Psychology*, *41*, 259–270.

Nelson, T. O., & Narens, L. (1990). Metamemory: A theoretical framework and some new findings. In G. H. Bower (Ed.), *The psychology of learning and motivation* (pp. 125–173). New York: Academic Press.

Nolen-Hoeksema, S. (2000). The role of rumination in depressive disorders and mixed anxiety/depressive symptoms. *Journal of Abnormal Psychology*, *109*, 504–511.

Nolen-Hoeksema, S., & Larson, J. (1999). *Coping with loss*. Mahwah, NJ: Lawrence Erlbaum.

Nolen-Hoeksema, S., & Morrow, J. (1991). A prospective study of depression and posttraumatic stress symptoms after a natural disaster: The 1980 Loma Prieta earthquake. *Journal of Personality and Social Psychology*, *61*, 115–121.

Nordahl, H. M. (2009). Effectiveness of brief metacognitive therapy versus cognitive–behavioral therapy in a general outpatient setting. *International Journal of Cognitive Therapy*, *2*, 152–159.

Normann, N., van Emmerik, A. A. P., & Morina, N. (2014). The efficacy of metacognitive therapy for anxiety and depression: A meta-analytic review. *Depression and Anxiety*, *31*, 402–411.

Papageorgiou, C., & Wells, A. (2000). Treatment of recurrent major depression with attention training. *Cognitive and Behavioral Practice*, *7*, 407–413.

Papageorgiou, C., & Wells, A. (2001a). Metacognitive beliefs about rumination in recurrent major depression. *Cognitive and Behavioral Practice*, *8*, 160–164.

Papageorgiou, C., & Wells, A. (2001b). Positive beliefs about depressive rumination: Development and preliminary validation of a self-report scale. *Behavior Therapy*, *32*, 13–26.

Papageorgiou, C., & Wells, A. (2003). An empirical test of a clinical metacognitive model of rumination and depression. *Cognitive Therapy and Research*, *27*, 261–273.

Papageorgiou, C., & Wells, A. (2009). A prospective test of the clinical metacognitive model of rumination and depression. *International Journal of Cognitive Therapy*, *2*, 123–131.

Papageorgiou, C., & Wells, A. (2015). Group metacognitive therapy for severe antidepressant and CBT resistant depression: A baseline-controlled trial. *Cognitive Therapy and Research*, *39*, 14–22.

Purdon, C. (1999). Thought suppression and psychopathology. *Behaviour Research and Therapy, 37*, 1029–1054.

Rachman, S. (1980). Emotional processing. *Behaviour Research and Therapy, 18*, 51–60.

Reynolds, M., & Wells, A. (1999). The Thought Control Questionnaire: Psychometric properties in a clinical sample and relationships with PTSD and depression. *Psychological Medicine, 29*, 1089–1099.

Richards, A., & French, C. C. (1992). An anxiety-related bias in semantic activation when processing threat/neutral homographs. *Quarterly Journal of Experimental Psychology, 40*, 503–528.

Richards, A., French, C. C., Johnson, W., Naparstek. J., & Williams, J. (1992). Effects of mood manipulation and anxiety on performance of an emotional Stroop task. *British Journal of Psychology, 8*, 479–491.

Roleofs, J., Papageorgiou, C., Gerber, R. D., Huibers, M., Peeters, F., & Arntz, A. (2007). On the links between self-discrepancies, rumination, metacognitions and symptoms of depression in undergraduates. *Behaviour Research and Therapy, 45*, 1295–1305.

Roussis, P., & Wells, A. (2006). Post-traumatic stress symptoms: Tests of relationships with thought control strategies and beliefs as predicted by the metacognitive model. *Personality and Individual Differences, 40*, 111–122.

Roussis, P., & Wells, A. (2009). Psychological factors predicting stress symptoms: Metacognition, thought control strategies and varieties of worry. *Anxiety, Stress and Coping, 21*, 213–225.

Sarason, I. G. (1984). Test anxiety, stress and cognitive interference: Reactions to tests. *Journal of Personality and Social Psychology, 46*, 929–938.

Segal, Z. V., & Vella, D. D. (1990). Self-schema in major depression: Replication and extension of a priming methodology. *Cognitive Therapy and Research, 14*, 161–176.

Siegle, G. J., Ghinassi, F., & Thase, M. E. (2007). Neurobehavioral therapies in the 21st century: Summary of an emerging field and an extended example of cognitive control training for depression. *Cognitive Therapy and Research, 31*, 235–262.

Spada, M., & Wells, A. (2006). Metacognitions about alcohol use in problem drinkers. *Clinical Psychology and Psychotherapy, 13*, 138–143.

Spasojevic, J., Alloy, L. B., Abramson, L. Y., Maccoon, D., & Robinson, M. S. (2004). Reactive rumination: Outcomes, mechanisms and developmental antecedents. In C. Papageorgiou & A. Wells (Eds), *Depressive rumination: Nature, theory and treatment* (pp. 43–58). Chichester, England: John Wiley & Sons, Ltd.

Stirling, J., Barkus, E., & Lewis, S. (2007). Hallucination proneness, schizotypy and metacognition. *Behaviour Research and Therapy, 45*, 1401–1408.

Warda, G., & Bryant, R. A. (1998). Thought control strategies in acute stress disorder. *Behaviour Research and Therapy, 36*, 1171–1175.

Wegner, D. M., Schneider, D. J., Carter, S. R., & White, T. L. (1987). Paradoxical effects of thought suppression. *Journal of Personality and Social Psychology, 53*, 5–13.

Wells, A. (1990). Panic disorder in association with relaxation induced anxiety: An attentional training approach to treatment. *Behavior Therapy, 21*, 273–280.

Wells, A. (1999). A metacognitive model and therapy for generalized anxiety disorder. *Clinical Psychology and Psychotherapy, 6*, 86–95.

Wells, A. (2005). Detached mindfulness in cognitive therapy: A metacognitive analysis and ten techniques. *Journal of Rational–Emotive and Cognitive Behavior Therapy, 23*, 337–355.

Wells, A. (2009). *Metacognitive therapy for anxiety and depression*. New York: Guilford.

Wells, A., & Carter, K. (2001). Further tests of a cognitive model of generalized anxiety disorder: Metacognitions and worry in GAD, panic disorder, social phobia, depression and nonpatients. *Behavior Therapy, 32*, 85–102.

Wells, A., & Carter, K. (2009). Maladaptive thought control strategies in generalized anxiety disorder, major depressive disorder and non-patient groups and relationships with trait-anxiety. *International Journal of Cognitive Therapy, 2*, 224–234.

Wells, A., & Cartwright-Hatton, S. (2004). A short form of the Metacognitions Questionnaire: Properties of the MCQ 30. *Behaviour Research and Therapy, 42*, 385–396.

Wells, A., & Davies, M. (1994). The Thought Control Questionnaire: A measure of individual differences in the control of unwanted thought. *Behaviour Research and Therapy, 32*, 871–878.

Wells, A., & King, P. (2006). Metacognitive therapy for generalized anxiety disorder: An open trial. *Journal of Behavior Therapy and Experimental Psychiatry, 37*, 206–212.

Wells, A., & Matthews, G. (1994). *Attention and emotion: A clinical perspective*. Hove, England: Lawrence Erlbaum.

Wells, A., & Matthews, G. (1996). Modelling cognition in emotional disorder: The S-REF model. *Behaviour Research and Therapy, 34*, 881–888.

Wells, A., & Papageorgiou, C. (1995). Worry and the incubation of intrusive images following stress. *Behaviour Research and Therapy, 33*, 579–583.

Wells, A., & Papageorgiou, C. (1998). Relationships between worry, obsessive–compulsive symptoms and meta-cognitive beliefs. *Behaviour Research and Therapy, 36*, 899–913.

Wells, A., & Sembi, S. (2004). Metacognitive therapy for PTSD: A preliminary investigation of a new brief treatment. *Journal of Behavior Therapy and Experimental Psychiatry, 35*, 307–318.

Wells, A., Fisher, P. L., Myers, S., Wheatley, J., Patel, T., & Brewin, C. (2009). Metacognitive therapy in recurrent and persistent depression: A multiple baseline study of a new treatment. *Cognitive Therapy and Research*, *33*, 291–300.

Wells, A., Fisher, P. L., Myers, S., Wheatley, J., Patel, T., & Brewin, C. (2012). Metacognitive therapy in treatment-resistant depression: A platform trial. *Behaviour Research and Therapy*, *50*, 367–373.

Wells, A., Welford, M., King, P., Papageorgiou, C., Wisely, J., & Mendel, E. (2010). A pilot randomized trial of metacognitive therapy vs applied relaxation in the treatment of adults with generalized anxiety disorder. *Behaviour Research and Therapy*, *48*, 429–434.

Wells, A., Welford, M., Fraser, J., King, P., Mendel, E., Wisely, J., Knight, A., & Rees, D. (2008). Chronic PTSD treated with metacognitive therapy: An open trial. *Cognitive and Behavioral Practice*, *15*, 85–92.

Wenzlaff, R. M., & Wegner, D. M. (2000). Thought suppression. *Annual Review of Psychology*, *51*, 59–91.

Wine, J. D. (1971). Test anxiety and the direction of attention. *Psychological Bulletin*, *76*, 92–104.

Yilmaz, E. A., Grencoz, T., & Wells, A. (2011). The temporal precedence of metacognition in the development of anxiety and depression symptoms in the context of life-stress: A prospective study. *Journal of Anxiety Disorders*, *25*, 389–396.

Further Reading

Beck, A. T., Rush, A. J., Shaw, B. F., & Emery, G. (1979). *Cognitive therapy of depression*. New York: Guilford.

Wells, A. (1995). Metacognition and worry: A cognitive model of generalized anxiety disorder. *Behavioural and Cognitive Psychotherapy*, *23*, 301–320.

Westen, D., & Morrison, K. (2001). A multidimensional meta-analysis of treatments for depression, panic, and generalized anxiety disorder: An empirical examination of the status of empirically supported therapies. *Journal of Consulting and Clinical Psychology*, *69*, 875–899.

7

Acceptance and Commitment Theory of Depression

Robert D. Zettle

This chapter presents a theoretical overview of depression from an acceptance and commitment perspective. While the earliest randomized clinical trials of what is now known as acceptance and commitment therapy (ACT) (Hayes, Strosahl, & Wilson, 1999, 2012) evaluated its relative efficacy in addressing depression (Zettle & Hayes, 1986; Zettle & Rains, 1989), ACT was not explicitly or exclusively created for the treatment of mood disorders. From its inception, ACT was developed as a transdiagnostic approach, more focused on targeting pathogenic processes common to diverse forms of human suffering, including depression, than on seeking disorder-specific symptomatic relief (Hayes, 1987). Accordingly, although ACT has been adapted and applied to treating depression (Zettle, 2004, 2007; Zettle & Hayes, 2002), there is essentially no corresponding theory that is unique to depression. As a result, what I will present here is an overview of the philosophical–theoretical foundations upon which the acceptance and commitment approach is based, and particularly how an associated conceptual, albeit generic, model of psychological inflexibility and psychopathology can be specifically extended to depression.

ACT is informed by relational frame theory (RFT) (Hayes, Barnes-Holmes, & Roche, 2001) as a contextualistic–behavioural account of human language and cognition. The original impetus for RFT was twofold in nature. One side of it was the philosophical recognition that existing approaches to human language and related phenomena were primarily mentalistic rather than contextualistic. Secondly, behaviour-analytic accounts of verbal behaviour (Skinner, 1957), by focusing more on

Treating Depression: MCT, CBT and Third Wave Therapies, First Edition.
Edited by Adrian Wells and Peter L. Fisher.

speaking than on listening, were also found to be inadequate, especially when self-talk was involved. The roots of ACT and RFT are clearly located within the behaviour-analytic wing of the cognitive behavioural therapy movement; and this was the second component of RFT's original impetus (Hayes, 2004). However, both ACT and RFT acknowledge the challenges posed by human cognition to behaviour analysis and the possibility that additional behavioural processes may emerge from language (Zettle, 2005).

An overview of functional contextualism as the philosophical foundation for RFT will be provided before coverage of RFT. This chapter concludes with a conceptual model of depression that, in turn, is derived from how language contributes to psychological rigidity and related human suffering according to RFT (Wilson, Hayes, Gregg, & Zettle, 2001).

Overview of Functional Contextualism

Contextualism constitutes one of the four philosophical systems or 'world hypotheses' identified by Pepper (1942) as applicable to psychology (Hayes, Hayes, & Reese, 1988). Of the greatest relevance for our purposes are the distinctions that can be drawn between contextualism and the worldview of mechanism (Hayes & Brownstein, 1986). An acceptance and commitment approach to depression appears unique in that it explicitly articulates its philosophical grounding in functional contextualism. By contrast, alternative cognitive behavioural theories appear to at least implicitly endorse mechanism. Critical distinctions between functional contextualism and mechanism can be clarified by summarizing the two positions on the following philosophical issues: (a) the nature of 'truth', and (b) the view of behaviour and its causes.

Nature of 'truth'

According to Pepper (1942), mechanism adopts a 'correspondence-based' truth criterion, whereas contextualism subscribes to 'successful working'. Mechanists ultimately evaluate the 'goodness' or quality of any theory of depression by the degree to which it accurately maps onto what is already known, or, even better, corresponds to what is eventually 'discovered' about how depression is put together. In short, the 'best' theory of depression is the one that best predicts how its constituent parts are related to one another to create the disorder. Being able to efficaciously treat depression is certainly not unimportant, but it is regarded as secondary to being able to first adequately understand it from a structural perspective. Unfortunately, the variables that are often implicated in understanding depression are ones that cannot be directly impacted. Consequently, the relative emphasis is on prediction alone, rather than upon both prediction and influence (Hayes & Brownstein, 1986).

In contrast to mechanism, functional contextualism is more explicitly pragmatic in adopting the ability to both predict *and* influence behaviour (Hayes, 1993) with adequate scope, precision, and depth (Biglan & Hayes, 1996; Hayes, Follette, & Follette, 1995; Hayes & Hayes, 1992) – as its truth criterion. 'Successful working', however, cannot be specified in the abstract, but only in conjunction with clearly articulated goals, lest it becomes dogmatic (Hayes, 1993). These goals are themselves, in turn, contextually determined and vary, for example, according to whether the focus is primarily scientific or therapeutic.

From the perspective of functional contextualism, an acceptance and commitment account of depression is 'true' to the extent that it eventually results in more useful ways of assisting those who struggle with it. Scientifically, the ultimate test of ACT is if it can be shown to be a better way of alleviating human suffering in general and depression in particular, with adequate scope, precision, and depth. The therapeutic goals against which the truth criterion of 'successful working' is evaluated are guided by client valuing. Individually articulated client values become the reference point within ACT against which specific client behaviours and related goals (e.g., 'Has trying to figure out why you're depressed moved you closer to or further away from what you say is most important to you in life?') are evaluated.

The view of behaviour and its causes

The fundamental explanatory model of mechanism is that of the machine, while that of contextualism is the 'act in context' (Pepper, 1942). To the mechanist, behaviour is spoken of as a noun (e.g., 'language' vs 'languaging') and commonly regarded as a thing, much like a car engine, which can be adequately explained by specifying the parts that comprise its structure and how they relate to each other (Hayes & Brownstein, 1986). A 'good' mechanistic theory of depression is one that can account for how the various signs and symptoms that purportedly distinguish it from other syndromally classified forms of psychopathology (APA, 1994) originate and are maintained. Because the correspondence-based truth criterion of mechanism can be approached by prediction alone, it is perfectly legitimate to maintain that one part of the psychological system (e.g., ways of thinking: Beck, 1967) assumes priority or even causal status in accounting for other components within it (e.g., changes in overt behaviour and mood) (Hayes & Brownstein, 1986).

Functional contextualism regards behaviour not as a thing whose psychological structure is to be predicted by increasingly sophisticated hypothetico-deductive theories, but as the activity of the whole and integrated organism, which interacts in and with historical and situational contexts (Hayes, 1993). The 'acts in context' that typify depression constitute both behavioural deficits (e.g., social withdrawal, discontinuation of previously pleasurable activities, etc.) and behavioural excesses (e.g., hypersomnia, thinking about suicide, etc.). The ability of one behaviour, such as ignoring the positive, to serve a controlling function over another is not precluded, although such behaviour–behaviour relationships are themselves conceptualized as under contextual control (Hayes & Brownstein, 1986; Zettle, 1990).

To satisfy the truth criterion of successful working, the causes of behaviour more generally and of depression in particular are limited to contextual variables that, when manipulated, can be shown not only to predict behaviour, but to influence it as well. The historical contexts of which depression is a function, such as previous learning experiences and life events, obviously cannot be directly altered, not because such variables were fundamentally non-manipulable in principle at the time of their occurrence, but because they are not presently accessible. However, the stimulus functions of such events, as will be seen, may be transformed by helping clients retell the stories they have constructed about their histories. Current situational influences upon depression are more directly addressed by alterations in therapist behaviour in the session and indirectly by supporting clients in making changes within their physical and social environments.

Summary

While a certain degree of technical eclecticism may be possible when differing treatment approaches to depression incorporate particular therapeutic techniques developed by others, eclecticism is not possible at the philosophical level because of conflicting truth criteria. In effect, mechanism and contextualism not only have divergent ways of looking at the world of depression, but also use differing benchmarks or standards by which to evaluate their work within this domain.

Overview of Relational Frame Theory

The presentation of RFT here is of necessity abbreviated and the interested reader is encouraged to consult Hayes et al. (2001) for a more expansive account of it. The term 'relational frame' (or the more technically correct gerund form 'relational framing') refers to behaviour. Most importantly and in line with functional contextualism, framing events relationally, speaking, and listening are all viewed as verbal acts in context that are acquired, shaped, and maintained through operant conditioning.

Nature of relational framing

Most simply and broadly stated, relational framing refers to a kind of relational activity (Hayes & Hayes, 1989), or to responding to one event or stimulus on the basis of its relationship to one or more others, which is arbitrarily applicable and not dependent on the physical properties of the stimuli involved. Naming, comparing contrasting, and evaluating are some common forms of relational framing. In depression, for example, clients may negatively appraise their current life circumstances by comparison to a preferred past and a dreaded future. No matter how satisfying the here-and-now is, it is always possible to create misery by contrasting it to some imagined time and/or place we would rather be.

Properties of relational framing

Relational framing displays three properties that distinguish it from the type of limited relational responding exhibited by organisms that lack language: mutual entailment, combinatorial entailment, and transformation of stimulus functions.

Mutual entailment The arbitrary relationship established between stimuli that are framed relationally is bidirectional. A child who learns that a dime is more valuable than a nickel also simultaneously learns that a nickel is less valuable than a dime even when this relationship is not directly taught. A common type of bidirectionality that occurs in depression involves frames of coordination between the self and negative evaluations (e.g., 'I *am* stupid') that establish a functional identity or fusion between the two relata (i.e., 'I' = 'stupid' and 'stupid' = 'I').

Combinatorial entailment Once a given stimulus, such as a nickel, has been separately related to other stimuli, such as both a dime and penny, new arbitrary relationships can be derived among the array of relata without being explicitly trained or taught. For example, a child who is separately taught that a nickel is less than a dime and that a nickel is greater than a penny will infer that a dime is greater than a penny and that a penny is less than a dime. Combinatorial entailment in depression may further the verbal construction of an inferior self- concept through interpersonal comparisons (Zettle, 2007). If 'Jack has his life together better than I do' and 'Jill has her life together better than Jack', then 'I also don't have my life together as well as Jill does'.

Transformation of stimulus functions Through mutual and combinatorial entailment, discriminative, eliciting, establishing, and reinforcing functions that either already exist or are arbitrarily established for a given stimulus can be transformed and transferred to other stimuli within the same relational network (Hayes, Luoma, Bond, Masuda, & Lillis, 2006). For example, participants were first taught to select the middle-sized member (B) within an array of abstract visual stimuli (Dougher, Hamilton, Fink, & Harrington, 2007) that was then paired with mild shock. Subsequently, participants were presented with the smaller (A) or the larger (C) stimuli used in the initial training. According to classical conditioning principles, equivalent – but, by comparison to B, diminished – skin conductance changes should have been obtained for both A and C. Instead, in line with RFT, participants exhibited a conditioned response to C that exceeded that of B. The transformational property of relational framing may in part explain how the hopelessness that clients often express about their future is established. If 'today is bad' and tomorrow will be even worse, a future (i.e., 'there/then') is verbally constructed via temporal framing that is even more aversive than whatever circumstances are currently present (i.e., 'here/now').

Development of relational framing

Developmentally, the first type of relational framing that is acquired is naming. Through what in effect constitutes naturalistic discrete trials training with multiple exemplars, children initially acquire a frame of coordination between objects and their names. Over enough trials and through a process that parallels the acquisition of generalized imitative responding (Gewirtz & Stengle, 1968), a frame of coordination or naming is established as an operant response class that quickly expands. Other functional classes of relational operants, such as opposition and comparison, are thought to be shaped and acquired in a similar manner.

Another repertoire of derived relational responding normally established early on in life that is of particular clinical relevance involves deictic framing (Hayes et al., 2001, pp. 38–39). In deictic framing, relations are consistently specified and, accordingly, differentially reinforced from the perspective of a speaker. Young children asked to tell what they are doing right now will likely be chided and corrected if they state what another child is doing at the moment, or what they did yesterday. In line with multiple-exemplar training, each time children are asked questions of this type, the context of what they, as well as others who are present, may be doing or have just done will be different. The only constants over such interchanges are the relational properties of 'I' versus 'you', 'here' versus 'there', and 'now' versus 'then'. What emerges is perspective taking (McHugh & Stewart, 2012), which provides a basis both for the experience of spirituality (Hayes, 1984) and for a 'theory of mind' (Carruthers & Smith, 1996). As will be seen, a weakened sense of self as context and the resulting loss of perspective taking are thought to contribute to various forms of psychopathology, including depression. Particularly during emotional reasoning, depressed clients who are unable to contact a sense of themselves that stands apart from negative self-referential thoughts and emotions lack a vantage point from which they might mindfully respond to such psychological events.

Summary

RFT represents neither the first nor certainly the only attempt to provide a comprehensive and systematic account of human language, cognition, and problem solving (see Chomsky, 1965; Gibson & Ingold, 1993). However, it is the first to do so from a functional contextualistic perspective in which the ability of humans to derive arbitrary stimulus relations and language are viewed as emerging from the same behavioural processes. From this vantage point, the more critical issue is not whether arbitrarily applicable relational responding serves as the basis for languaging or vice versa, but whether being able to identify and impact the psychological processes common to both enhances our ability to predict and influence both clinical and subclinical forms of human suffering. Unlike other theories of language and cognition, RFT points rather directly to an array of pathogenic processes that are presumably supported by language and relational framing. Perhaps the most widely recognized language-driven process that appears to contribute specifically to depression is rumination (Zettle, 2007). This is especially so when clients rigidly insist that understanding and figuring out their depression is necessary before they can get on with their lives.

An Acceptance and Commitment Model of Depression

From an acceptance and commitment perspective, a primary basis of suffering is psychological inflexibility, or an inability to make the adjustments necessary to sustain value-directed behaviour (Hayes et al., 2006, p. 5). The phenomenon just mentioned – putting valued living on hold until the mystery of why one is depressed is resolved – is but one example of this. Because psychological rigidity is defined functionally, sometimes it takes the form of persisting in the same futile behaviour, while in other contexts it can involve impulsively shifting to and fro in an array of ineffective actions. Under both sets of circumstances, a long-term course of valued action is precluded and clients are left with a sense of life as something to be endured rather than as a vital and meaningful process to be engaged in.

An acceptance and commitment model of psychopathology has identified six core pathogenic processes that contribute to psychological inflexibility (Hayes et al., 2006): fusion, experiential avoidance, attachment to a conceptualized self, living in the past or future, excessive rule following, and lack of valued action. The degree to which each process functions independently of the others and which one(s) may be dominant with a given client can only be determined on a case-by-case basis. In agreement with functional contextualism, the six processes are viewed as a way of guiding case conceptualization within ACT more generally (Bach & Moran, 2008), and in working with depressed clients in particular (Zettle, 2007). In contrast to a mechanistic perspective, the model is not seen as revealing something essential about the structure of psychopathology. In what follows, for ease of discussion, the specific roles of each of the dysfunctional processes within depression will be considered one by one. How language and relational framing may in turn contribute to each process will be further explicated and, when available, supportive research will be discussed and summarized.

Fusion

Fusion refers to how certain stimulus functions that are transformed and derived through language can dominate over behavioural regulation that comes from contact with direct contingencies and other derived stimulus functions (Strosahl, Hayes, Wilson, & Gifford, 2004). In effect, during fusion, what we say and think about the world influences behaviour to a greater extent than does direct, experiential contact with that world. Fusion per se is not always pathogenic. For instance, it is not when we are able to find meaning and value in circumstances that are impoverished and degrading (e.g., Frankl, 1965). Fusion contributes, however, to depression when direct experiences that would otherwise support valued living are relationally framed in certain ways. For example, the attainment of a goal, such as finishing a project at work, may be dismissed as 'not being good enough' when framed as disconnected from the value of being a responsible employee. More particularly, fusion appears to contribute to depression through relational framing at multiple levels – evaluating, reason giving, and storytelling.

Evaluating At the simplest level of languaging, fusion occurs when evaluations of referents are responded to as if they were descriptions of them. Negative self-statements that foster attachment to a self conceptualized as damaged (e.g., 'I *am* worthless') provide perhaps the most common instance of fusion within depression and will be considered in greater detail shortly. As a ubiquitous type of relational framing, however, evaluating is hardly restricted to how we talk about ourselves and extends to the ongoing stream of our other thoughts, feelings, and related psychological experiences.

During language development, most verbal–social communities teach children the appropriate use of certain descriptive terms, such as 'bad', 'awful', 'terrible', and so on, in talking about negative life events like the loss of a loved one or physical injury. Doing so establishes a frame of coordination or equivalence and bidirectionality between the words used in talking about the events and the events themselves (e.g., death = 'bad' / 'bad' = death). Additionally, through the transfer of stimulus functions, the word 'bad' itself now assumes some of the same psychological properties of losing a loved one. Through combinatorial entailment, any new event, such as losing a job, which is now also evaluated as 'bad' may exert an emotional impact similar to the death of a family member (job loss = 'bad', 'bad' = death, job loss = death). If and when this occurs, the stimulus functions derived from how the event is framed relationally – 'Being fired *is as bad as* someone's dying' – dominate or prevail over those directly related to the event itself and its description (e.g., 'I received written notice of my termination'). Empirical support for the process of fusion at this level of relational framing is provided by research on dysphoric mood induction procedures such as the Velten (1968), which attest to the emotional impact of responding literally to simple mood-related statements (Finegan & Seligman, 1995).

Reason giving Formulating accounts of why depression is present to begin with or explanations of how and why it precludes value-directed behaviour provides an intermittent level of relational framing that may additionally contribute to psychological inflexibility (Zettle & Hayes, 1986). With both types of reason giving, clients may 'buy into' verbal constructions that point to reasons that cannot be altered for the initiation and continuation of depression. Sometimes reason giving may cite previous life events – such as a divorce or a job loss – as 'causes' of depression that are simply inaccessible and thus currently non-manipulable. The greater problem with this way of thinking about depression lies not so much in fusion with reasons as causes, but in the additional fusion with how the relationship between the purported causes of depression and its treatment is framed (e.g., 'My depression can't be effectively treated until what caused it in the first place is identified and corrected') (Zettle, 2007).

More commonly cited as reasons for depression than external circumstances are private events such as negative, unwanted thoughts and related feelings of guilt, sadness, regret, and so on (Bloor, 1983; Rippere, 1977). Private events are commonly cited as reasons for a range of undesirable behaviours and are regarded as 'good', valid explanations (Hayes, 1987). While thoughts and feelings are certainly potentially more accessible than previous life events, acceptance and commitment theory holds that attempting to alter them is often just as futile and may contribute further to psychological inflexibility and the continuation of depression. Dismantling research within cognitive therapy that has called into question the contribution of cognitive restructuring components lends some related empirical support to this perspective (Jacobson et al., 1996).

Several lines of research provide support for this purported relationship between fused reason giving and psychological rigidity within depression. Those who offer more reasons for depression, as assessed by the Reasons for Depression Questionnaire (RFD) (Addis, Truax, & Jacobson, 1995; Thwaites, Dagnan, Huey, & Addis, 2004), ruminate more in response to depressed mood (Addis & Carpenter, 1999) and report higher levels of both depression and psychological inflexibility, as measured by the Acceptance and Action Questionnaire (AAQ) (Hayes et al., 2004). A regression analysis indicated that both the RFD and the AAQ significantly and independently accounted for variability in depression levels – findings supportive of viewing reason giving as a process that contributes to psychological inflexibility but is not synonymous with it (Garst & Zettle, 2006). Of greater practical importance is that depressed clients who score high on the RFD are more treatment-resistant and display higher levels of post-treatment depression, even when controlling for its levels at pre-treatment (Addis & Jacobson, 1996).

Storytelling In storytelling clients relate multiple explanations of depression to one another as well as to autobiographical facts, to produce a coherent and meaningful narrative account of their lives and experiences with depression. Storytelling can be viewed as a network of relational frames that essentially constructs reasons for reasons (Zettle, 2007). Similar to fusion at the level of individual thoughts and reason giving, fusion that occurs with the life story is not in and of itself pathogenic, as long as psychological flexibility is not compromised.

All too often, however, this rarely appears to be the case, especially with clients who have struggled with chronic, clinical depression. Such clients may assume a 'victim role' and somewhat self-righteously insist that depression is an inevitable outcome, given how they were traumatized and mistreated – either by life itself or at the hands of others ('With what I've gone through, I have every right to be depressed'). At this level of fusion, the life story is responded to as a set of immutable and indisputable 'facts' rather than as something that can in principle be retold and reconstructed with a different outcome. Within this context, depression itself may be regarded and wielded as a constant reminder, evidence, and validation of the mistreatment the client has suffered. When this occurs, 'getting better' becomes incompatible with 'being right' about the life story. In effect, 'being right', 'getting even', and not letting transgressors 'off the hook' trump 'getting better' (Zettle, 2007).

From an acceptance and commitment perspective, depressed clients who respond favourably to therapy would be expected to show reductions in the rigidity with which the pre-treatment life story is held. A literature search revealed no research by proponents of ACT that has addressed this issue, but one recent dissertation from a narrative therapy perspective (White &

Epston, 1990) that has. Depressed clients successfully treated with either client-centered (Rogers, 1951) or process-experiential therapy (Greenberg, Rice, & Elliott, 1993) showed greater changes in their life stories than their non-recovered counterparts (Hardtke, 2008).

Experiential avoidance

Experiential avoidance is conceptualized as intentional efforts to alter the frequency or form of selective private events – such as negative thoughts, guilt, sadness, regret, and other unwanted emotions – or the contexts in which they occur (Hayes et al., 2006). In large measure, fusion sets the stage for experiential avoidance. It is perhaps easiest to see how these two processes work together to produce psychological rigidity at the level of specific thoughts. Not all negative thoughts (e.g., 'I am responsible for the economy failing') are targeted for experiential avoidance, but only those with which clients are fused (e.g., 'I am responsible for my marriage failing').

According to RFT, we are doomed to be haunted by our own self-awareness. Through the bidirectional transformation of stimulus functions, merely thinking about and recalling an unpleasant life event can have a psychological impact similar to that experienced when the event first occurred. Because experiential avoidance is defined functionally, efforts to avoid or escape from fused, depressing thoughts and memories can take varied forms, ranging from distraction to suicidality (Zettle, 2007). Two of the most common forms of experiential avoidance appear to be thought suppression (Wenzlaff, 1993) and rumination (Nolen-Hoeksema, 1990). Only the former is discussed here; a consideration of the role that rumination plays in depression will be offered a bit later.

The thought suppression literature consistently shows that efforts to suppress unwanted thoughts backfire in that those thoughts rebound with increased strength (Wegner, 1994). In the case of depression, other negative thoughts are often focused upon in order to divert attention away from a targeted thought. Not surprisingly, such a strategy is less effective than using neutral thoughts as distractors (Wenzlaff, Wegner, & Roper, 1988), reinduces the dysphoric mood present when the initial suppression occurred (Wenzlaff, Wegner, & Klein, 1991), and apparently contributes to rumination and increased depression (Wenzlaff & Luxton, 2003). The futility of experiential avoidance and how it can exacerbate depression are features further underscored by the finding that the recurrence of a dysphoric mood can reinstate thought suppression (Wenzlaff et al., 1991), thereby creating a downward, spiralling relationship between these two private events and allowing depression to lead a life of its own.

Deliberate efforts to control unwanted affective states appear to be similarly counterproductive and no more successful than those directed towards thinking. From an acceptance and commitment perspective, dysphoria and sadness are not pathological but rather healthy, adaptive emotions in reaction to loss and blocked goal attainment (Klinger, 1975; Neese, 2000). To the extent that emotional suffering is linked to valuing, appreciating the sources of our clients' sorrow may even help illuminate what matters most to them as a focal point within ACT (Zettle, 2007). Dysphoria and sadness only become problematic to the extent that failed efforts to experientially control them can escalate into clinical depression. Proponents of an acceptance and commitment approach are in agreement with others who have argued that depression is most usefully regarded as a 'secondary emotion', as constituting a reaction to another emotional reaction, such as dysphoria or guilt (Leventhal & Martell, 2006). Support for this formulation is provided by finding that participants who report high levels of experiential avoidance were significantly more disturbed then their low avoidant counterparts in response to equivalent levels of induced dysphoric mood (Gird & Zettle, 2009). What is referred to within ACT as 'clean pain' (e.g., dysphoria and sadness), which is an inevitable consequence of leading a full, engaged life, becomes exacerbated into the 'dirty pain' of clinical depression through the process of experiential avoidance (Hayes et al., 1999; Zettle, 2007), thereby leaving clients feeling depressed about feeling depressed (cf. Fennell & Campbell, 1984; Fennell & Teasdale, 1987).

Attachment to a conceptualized self

One of the hallmarks of depression and a part of the 'negative cognitive triad' (Beck, 1967) is disparaging thoughts about the self. The potential problem, according to an acceptance and commitment model of depression, is not negative self-thoughts per se, but *fused* negative thoughts about the self that participate via relational framing in the construction of a negative self concept. Not surprisingly, discomfort in and believability of self-relevant negative thoughts appear to be closely linked and to covary as a function of the level of associated attachment or fusion with them (Masuda, Hayes, Sackett, & Twohig, 2004). Critical self-referential thoughts take the generic form of 'I *am* … stupid, incompetent, unlovable, no good', and so on and, along with demographic details such as ones involving gender, age, marital status, and the like, help form the conceptualized self. In the early stages of depression, clients are likely to engage in suppression, rumination, or other forms of experiential avoidance in order to control unwanted thoughts about the self. Doing so is more likely to make the problem of depression bigger rather than smaller, and the time and energy invested in experiential avoidance is diverted away from value-directed behaviour.

As depression itself becomes exacerbated through the process of experiential control, fused self-identification with the disorder (e.g., 'I *am* depressed' vs 'I am a middle-aged, married male who is experiencing depression') may come to dominate and rule over other ways in which clients think about themselves. In effect, through the bidirectional transformation of stimulus functions, clients become their depression. If and when this occurs, depression itself is maintained and potentially heightened for at least two reasons. For one, with such a fused self-identity, efforts to remove the depression are psychologically tantamount to an assault on a fundamental sense of who the client is, and can accordingly be expected to be resisted. Secondly, depressed clients can become so fused with a verbal construction of themselves as damaged that their ability to view their own negative self-talk and related depressive experiences non-judgementally, from the self as perspective established via deictic framing, is severely compromised. As suggested by RFT, another behaviour commonly engaged in by clients who struggle with depression – a behaviour that further contributes to psychological rigidity and also appears to be incompatible with being mindfully present – is rumination.

Living in the past or in the future

Thinking about the causes, implications, and possible solutions to depression has the appearance of problem solving. However, from an acceptance and commitment perspective, ruminating can be viewed as relational framing that serves an experiential avoidant function.

Although rumination, by comparison to worrying, appears to be more focused on the past than on the future (Papageorgiou & Wells, 2003; Watkins, Moulds, & Mackintosh, 2005), the status of thoughts about the future within the negative cognitive triad of depression (Beck, 1967) and the high rates of comorbidity between depression and anxiety disorders, especially generalized anxiety disorder (Mineka, Watson, & Clark, 1998), suggest that depressed clients are often likely to be preoccupied with the future as well. Either way, clients who struggle with depression display fusion with a verbally constructed past or future (or both) that limits their ability to respond in a psychologically flexible manner to what appears in the here and now (Davis & Nolen-Hoeksema, 2000). Living in the past or in the future further locks depression in place by being at odds with living a valued life in the moment and with responding mindfully (Kabat-Zinn, 1994) to psychological events.

From an RFT perspective, mindfulness can be viewed as nominally framing private events in the here and now (e.g., 'There's a thought'). As such, it functionally undermines both temporal (e.g., 'How much longer am I going to feel this way?') and evaluative (e.g., 'Why do I feel this way?') relational framing (Fletcher & Hayes, 2005). Research documenting an incompatibility between ruminating and mindfulness (Ramel, 2007; Ramel, Goldin, Carmona, & McQuaid, 2004) and the role of the former in the initiation, maintenance, and recurrence of depression is by now fairly extensive and will only be briefly summarized here. Whether construed as a coping style (Nolen-Hoeksema, 1990) or as an analytical and evaluative response set (Watkins & Teasdale, 2001), rumination has been implicated in depression in both correlational–prospective (e.g., Nolen-Hoeksema, Parker, & Larson, 1994) and experimental research (e.g., Lyubomirsky, Tucker, Caldwell, & Berg, 1999) with non-depressed (e.g., Nolen-Hoeksema & Morrow, 1991), dysphoric (e.g, Lyubomirsky & Nolen-Hoeksema, 1993), and depressed (Rimes & Watkins, 2005) participants. Also, in line with an acceptance and commitment model of depression, ruminative 'problem solving' appears to contribute to psychological inflexibility by producing both a more restricted range of possible solutions and an unwillingness to commit to them (Lyuobmirsky & Nolen-Hoeksema, 1993; Ward, Lyubomirsky, Sousa, & Nolen-Hoeksema, 2003).

Excessive rule following

According to RFT, rules are viewed as frames of coordination between two relational networks that control behaviour (Barnes-Holmes et al., 2001). Instructions, advice, commands, and requests – whether issued by others or formulated by oneself – are common types of rules that may come to exert functional control over behaviour (Zettle, 1990). As with languaging and relational framing more broadly, the degree to which rule following may contribute to depression is contingent upon the extent to which it limits valued living. At least two functional units of rule-governed behaviour, tracking and pliance (Zettle &

Hayes, 1982), are thought to more broadly contribute to psychological inflexibility.

Tracking is rule following under the control of an apparent correspondence between the rule (e.g., 'The quickest way to get to Kansas City from Wichita is by the turnpike') and external contingencies, independently of the delivery of the rule (Barnes-Holmes et al., 2001; Zettle & Hayes, 1982). The critical external contingencies that participate in tracking can either be appetitive or aversive in nature. Although tracking under appetitive control is typically repertoire-expanding, tracking controlled by aversive contingencies is often rigid and inflexible (Wilson & Murrell, 2004). The type of value-directed actions that ACT seeks to support is one example of appetitive tracking (e.g., ways of being a loving parent), while pursuing a fearful and overly cautious approach to life exemplifies avoidant tracking. The operative rule or 'track' (Zettle & Hayes, 1982) in the former may be something like 'There is an infinite number of things I can do to be a "good parent" to my children', while the one that controls avoidant behaviour may be 'If I don't take risks, I won't make mistakes'.

Pliance is rule-governed behaviour, under the control of apparent, socially mediated consequences, for maintaining a correspondence between the rule itself and the behaviour specified by the rule. Following advice and suggestions has been learned as operant behaviour by virtue of the consequences of doing or not doing so. Because punishment for non-compliance tends to be more widely used than positive reinforcement in consequating rule following, pliance is also typically under aversive control. Loosely speaking, depressed clients may adopt a risk-averse approach to living, not so much to avoid mistakes as to spare themselves the criticism and scorn of others, who have offered advice on what to do to avoid certain errors. Similarly, clients may pursue certain courses of action not because they are congruent with personal values, but because doing so is what they are 'supposed' or 'expected' to do. What may appear on the surface to be valued action is functionally avoidant behaviour.

Support, especially for the impact of pliance in generally limiting psychological flexibility and in creating an insensitivity to external contingencies of reinforcement, has come from laboratory investigations of rule governance and human operant responding (see, for example, Hayes, Zettle, & Rosenfarb, 1989). However, later research that examined the behaviour of dysphoric or depressed participants by using similar preparations has produced inconsistent findings (Baruch, Kanter, Busch, Richardson, & Barnes-Holmes, 2007; McAuliffe, 2004; Rosenfarb, Burker, Morris, & Cush, 1993), suggesting the need for a more extensive experimental analysis of rule following and for a better understanding of the roles that avoidant tracking and pliance may play in depression.

Lack of valued action

Reductions in both pleasurable and task-oriented activities often occur in depression (Beck, Rush, Shaw, & Emery, 1979, pp. 197–203). From an acceptance and commitment perspective, what is most critical is not the change in activity levels itself, but the extent to which such a change constitutes a reduction in valued living. Within ACT, values are defined as 'verbally construed global life consequences' (Hayes et al., 1999, p. 206); and value-congruent behaviour is viewed as naturally reinforcing. Values such as 'being a good parent' are not themselves verbally constructed, but they can be accessed and contacted via language. Accessing them may be useful therapeutically because it serves an augmenting function.

Augmenting is a third unit of rule-governed behaviour due to relational networks that serve an establishing function (Michael, 2000) by altering the capacity of certain events to function as reinforcers and punishers (Barnes-Holmes et al., 2001; Zettle & Hayes, 1982). For example, certain parenting behaviours – such as changing diapers and toilet training – can be seen as 'burdens' or, alternatively, can be reframed as actions that are consistent with the value of 'being a good parent'. The naturally reinforcing consequences of such actions may be increased when the actions are placed within a frame of coordination with valuing. Moreover, the mere reaffirmation and clarification of values, even without engagement in overt actions consistent with them, may help attenuate reactions of physiological and psychological stress (Creswell et al., 2005).

The potential contribution of a lack of valued action to psychological inflexibility and depression is underscored by the finding that those who are less successful at living their most important values report higher levels of experiential avoidance, depression, and fusion with negative thoughts (Plumb, Hayes, Hildebrandt, & Martin, 2007). Additionally, in agreement with the purported roles (discussed in the previous section) that avoidant tracking and pliance may play in depression, individuals who, according to a values questionnaire (Blackledge & Ciarrochi, 2005), based their selection of 'values' upon feeling 'ashamed guilty or anxious if I didn't' (avoidant tracking) or chose them 'because somebody else wants me to' (pliance) also reported higher levels of depression, experiential avoidance, and fusion with negative thoughts.

Summary

From an RFT perspective, the conceptual model just presented, which highlights how relational framing may contribute to core processes that, in turn, support depression, can be regarded as essentially yet another verbal construction. While I believe that the model of depression offered is consistent with a broader acceptance and commitment conceptualization of psychological inflexibility and human suffering, it should be acknowledged that it is not the only one that could be presented. What has been presented is not *the* ACT model of depression, and others familiar with ACT might offer somewhat different versions. Fusion with the current model is also discouraged for another reason. Holding it lightly may increase the likelihood that 'new and improved' models will subsequently be developed. The present model is undoubtedly 'wrong' in some respects; but, right now, exactly how it is wrong remains unknown and unclear. For example, in accordance with functional contextualism, it may prove more useful in the future to speak of fewer (see Hayes et al., 2012, p. 67) or more than the six core processes incorporated in the current model.

Conclusion

This chapter began with a discussion of some of the fundamental differences between the philosophical systems of functional contextualism and mechanism. That also seems to be an appropriate place at which to end it. Without an appreciation of the philosophical distinctions between mechanism and functional contextualism (see Hofmann & Asmundson, 2008), disagreements across differing cognitive behavioural theories and conceptualizations of depression may appear to be of a capricious, trivial, or arbitrary nature. Moreover, an understanding of differing philosophical positions is especially pertinent in clarifying why proponents of ACT regard the critical differences between it and approaches representative of the second wave in cognitive behaviour therapy, such as cognitive therapy (Beck et al., 1979), as fundamentally paradigmatic in nature, inextricably linked to discrepant values, and therefore likely ultimately unresolvable (Zettle, 1990). This is not to suggest that functional contextualism is 'better than' mechanism in any meaningful sense of the term. Indeed, a comparative evaluation of them could only be made against some truth criterion, which itself cannot be justified on grounds that transcend a philosophical level of analysis (Hayes, 1993). For the functional contextualist, the bottom line clinically is being able to better assist clients who suffer from and struggle with depression. The most valued therapeutic approach, whether that is ACT or some alternative, is the one that best attains this goal.

References

Addis, M. E., & Carpenter, K. M. (1999). Why, why, why? Reason-giving and rumination as predictors of response to activation- and insight-oriented treatment rationales. *Journal of Clinical Psychology, 55*, 881–894.

Addis, M. E., & Jacobson, N. S. (1996). Reasons for depression and the process and outcome of cognitive–behavioral psychotherapies. *Journal of Consulting and Clinical Psychology, 64*, 1417–1424.

Addis, M. E., Truax, P., & Jacobson, N. S. (1995). Why do people think they are depressed? The reasons for depression questionnaire. *Psychotherapy, 32*, 476–483.

APA. (1994). *Diagnostic and statistical manual of mental disorders: DSM-IV*. Washington, DC: American Psychiatric Association.

Bach, P. A., & Moran, D. J. (2008). *ACT in practice: Case conceptualization in acceptance and commitment therapy*. Oakland, CA: New Harbinger.

Barnes-Holmes, D., O'Hora, D., Roche, B., Hayes, S. C., Bissett, R. T., & Lyddy. F. (2001). Understanding and verbal regulation. In S. C. Hayes, D. Barnes-Holmes, & B. Roche (Eds), *Relational frame theory: A post-Skinnerian account of language and cognition* (pp. 103–117). New York: Plenum.

Baruch, D. E., Kanter, J. W., Busch, A. M., Richardson, J. V., & Barnes-Holmes, D. (2007). The differential effect of instructions on dysphoric and nondysphoric persons. *The Psychological Record, 57*, 543–554.

Beck, A. T. (1967). *Depression: Clinical, experimental, and theoretical aspects*. New York: Harper & Row.

Beck, A. T., Rush, A. J., Shaw, B. F., & Emery, G. (1979). *Cognitive therapy of depression*. New York: Guilford.

Biglan, A., & Hayes, S. C. (1996). Should the behavioral sciences become more pragmatic? The case for functional contextualism in research on human behavior. *Applied and Preventive Psychology: Current Scientific Perspectives, 5*, 47–57.

Blackledge, J. T., & Ciarrochi, J. (2005). Initial validation of the Personal Values Questionnaire. Unpublished manuscript, University of Wollongong, Wollongong, New South Wales, Australia.

Bloor, R. (1983). 'What do you mean by depression?' A study of the relationship between antidepressive activity and personal concepts of depression. *Behaviour Research and Therapy, 21*, 43–50.

Carruthers, P., & Smith, P. K. (1996). *Theories of theories of mind*. Cambridge: Cambridge University Press.

Chomsky, N. (1965). *Aspects of the theory of syntax*. Cambridge, MA: MIT Press.

Creswell, J. D., Welch, W. T., Taylor, S. E., Sherman, D. K., Gruenewald, T. L., & Mann, T. (2005). Affirmation of personal values buffers neuroendocrine and psychological stress responses. *Psychological Science, 16*, 846–851.

Davis, R. N., & Nolen-Hoeksema, S. (2000). Cognitive inflexibility among ruminators and nonruminators. *Cognitive Therapy and Research, 24*, 699–711.

Dougher, M. J., Hamilton, D. A., Fink, B. C., & Harrington, J. (2007). Transformation of the discriminative and eliciting functions of generalized relational stimuli. *Journal of the Experimental Analysis of Behavior, 88*, 179–197.

Fennell, M. J. V., & Campbell, E. A. (1984). The Cognitions Questionnaire: Specific thinking errors in depression. *British Journal of Clinical Psychology, 23*, 81–92.

Fennell, M. J. V., & Teasdale, J. D. (1987). Cognitive therapy for depression: Individual differences and the process of change. *Cognitive Therapy and Research, 11*, 253–271.

Finegan, J. E., & Seligman, C. (1995). In defense of the Velten Mood Induction Procedure. *Canadian Journal of Behavioural Science, 27*, 405–419.

Fletcher, L., & Hayes, S. C. (2005). Relational frame theory, acceptance and commitment therapy, and a functional analytic definition of mindfulness. *Journal of Rational Emotive and Cognitive Behavior Therapy, 23*, 315–336.

Frankl, V. E. (1965). *Man's search for meaning: An introduction to logotherapy*. Boston: Beacon Press.

Garst, M. L., & Zettle, R. D. (2006). The relationship among reason-giving, experiential avoidance, and levels of depression. Unpublished manuscript, Wichita State University, Kansas.

Gewirtz, J. L., & Stengle, K. G. (1968). Learning of generalized imitation as the basis for identification. *Psychological Review, 5*, 374–397.

Gibson, K. R., & Ingold, T. (1993). *Tools, language and cognition in human evolution*. Cambridge: Cambridge University Press.

Gird, S., & Zettle, R. D. (2009). Differential response to a mood induction procedure as a function of level of experiential avoidance. *The Psychological Record, 59*, 537–550.

Greenberg, L. S., Rice, L. N., & Elliott, R. (1993). *Facilitating emotional change: The moment-by-moment process*. New York: Guilford.

Hardtke, K. K. (2008). The story-teller, the story and change: A narrative exploration of outcome in brief experiential treatments for depression. *Dissertation Abstracts International, 68* (7), 4826B.

Hayes, S. C. (1984). Making sense of spirituality. *Behaviorism, 12*, 99–110.

Hayes, S. C. (1987). A contextual approach to therapeutic change. In N. S. Jacobson (Ed.), *Psychotherapists in clinical practice: Cognitive and behavioral perspectives* (pp. 327–387). New York: Guilford.

Hayes, S. C. (1993). Analytic goals and varieties of scientific contextualism. In S. C. Hayes, L. J. Hayes, H. W. Reese, & T. R. Sarbin (Eds), *Varieties of scientific contextualism* (pp. 109–118). Reno, NV: Context Press.

Hayes, S. C. (2004). Acceptance and commitment therapy, relational frame theory, and the third wave of behavior therapy. *Behavior Therapy, 35*, 639–665.

Hayes, S. C., & Brownstein, A. J. (1986). Mentalism, behavior–behavior relations, and a behavior analytic view of the purposes of science. *The Behavior Analyst, 9*, 175–190.

Hayes, S. C., & Hayes, L. J. (1989). The verbal action of the listener as a basis for rule-governance. In S. C. Hayes (Ed.), *Rule-governed behaviour: Cognition, contingencies, and instructional control* (pp. 153–190). New York: Plenum.

Hayes, S. C., & Hayes, L. J. (1992). Some clinical implications of contextualistic behaviorism: The example of cognition. *Behavior Therapy, 23*, 225–249.

Hayes, S. C., Barnes-Holmes, D., & Roche, B. (Eds). (2001). *Relational frame theory: A post-Skinnerian account of human language and cognition*. New York: Plenum.

Hayes, S. C., Follette, W. C., & Follette, V. (1995). Behavior therapy: A contextual approach. In A. S. German & B. Messer (Eds), *Essential psychotherapies: Theory and practice* (pp. 128–181). New York: Guilford.

Hayes, S. C., Hayes, L. J., & Reese, H. W. (1988). Finding the philosophical core: A review of Stephen C. Pepper's *World hypotheses*. *Journal of the Experimental Analysis of Behaviour, 50*, 97–111.

Hayes, S. C., Strosahl, K. D., & Wilson, K. G. (1999). *Acceptance and commitment therapy: An experiential approach to behavior change*. New York: Guilford.

Hayes, S. C., Strosahl, K. D., & Wilson, K. G. (2012). *Acceptance and commitment therapy: The process and practice of mindful change* (2nd edn). New York: Guilford.

Hayes, S. C., Zettle, R. D., & Rosenfarb, I. (1989). Rule following. In S. C. Hayes (Ed.), *Rule-governed behavior: Cognition, contingencies, and instructional control* (pp. 191–220). New York: Plenum.

Hayes, S. C., Luoma, J. B., Bond, F. W., Masuda, A., & Lillis, J. (2006). Acceptance and commitment therapy: Model, processes and outcomes. *Behaviour Research and Therapy, 44*, 1–25.

Hayes, S. C., Strosahl, K. D., Wilson, K. G., Bissett, R. T., Pistorello, J., Tomarino, D. … McCurry, S. M. (2004). Measuring experiential avoidance: A preliminary test of a working model. *The Psychological Record, 54*, 553–578.

Hofmann, S. G., & Asmundson, G. J. G. (2008). Acceptance and mindfulness-based therapy: New wave or old hat? *Clinical Psychology Review, 28*, 1–16.

Jacobson, N. S., Dobson, K. S., Truax, P. A., Addis, M. E., Koerner, K., Gollan, J. K., Gortner, E., & Prince, S. E. (1996). A component analysis of cognitive-behavioral treatment for depression. *Journal of Consulting and Clinical Psychology, 64*, 295–304.

Kabat-Zinn, J. (1994). *Wherever you go, there you are: Mindfulness meditation in everyday life*. New York: Hyperion.

Klinger, E. (1975). Consequences of commitment to disengagement from incentives. *Psychological Review, 82*, 1–25.

Leventhal, A. M., & Martell, C. R. (2006). *The myth of depression as disease: Limitations and alternatives to drug treatment. Westport, CT*: Praeger.

Lyubomirsky, S., & Nolen-Hoeksema, S. (1993). Self-perpetuating properties of dysphoric rumination. *Journal of Personality and Social Psychology, 65*, 339–349.

Lyuobmirsky, S., Tucker, K. L., Caldwell, N. D., & Berg, K. (1999). Why ruminators are poor problem solvers: Clues from the phenomenology of dysphoric rumination. *Journal of Personality and Social Psychology, 77*, 1041–1060.

Masuda, A., Hayes, S. C., Sackett, C. F., & Twohig, M. P. (2004). Cognitive defusion and self-relevant negative thoughts: Examining the impact of a ninety-year-old technique. *Behaviour Research and Therapy, 42*, 477–485.

McAuliffe, D. (2004). *Rule-following and depressive symptomology in an adolescent population*. Unpublished doctoral dissertation, National University of Ireland-Maynooth, Co., Kildare.

McHugh, L., & Stewart, I. (2012). *The self and perspective taking: Contributions and applications from modern behavioural science*. Oakland, CA: Context Press.

Michael, J. (2000). Implications and refinements of the establishing operation concept. *Journal of Applied Behaviour Analysis, 33*, 401–410.

Mineka, W. R., Watson, D., & Clark, L. A. (1998). Comorbidity of anxiety and unipolar mood disorders. *Annual Review of Psychology, 49*, 377–412.

Neese, R. M. (2000). Is depression an adaptation? *Archives of General Psychiatry, 57*, 14–20.

Nolen-Hoeksema, S. (1990). *Sex differences in depression*. Stanford, CA: Stanford University Press.

Nolen-Hoeksema, S., & Morrow, J. (1991). A prospective study of depression and post-traumatic stress symptoms after a natural disaster: The 1989 Loma Prieta earthquake. *Journal of Personality and Social Psychology, 61*, 115–121.

Nolen-Hoeksema, S., Parker, L. E., & Larson, J. (1994). Ruminative coping with depressed mood following loss. *Journal of Personality and Social Psychology, 67*, 92–104.

Papageorgiou, C., & Wells, A. (2003). An empirical test of a metacognitive model of rumination and depression. *Cognitive Therapy and Research, 27*, 261–273.

Pepper, S. C. (1942). *World hypotheses: A study in evidence*. Berkeley, CA: University of California Press.

Plumb, J. C., Hayes, S. C., Hildebrandt, M. J., & Martin, L. M. (2007). Values and valued action as key processes in clinical intervention. Paper presented at the symposium 'Engaging in life: Values and valued action as catalysts for change' (J. C. Plumb, Chair). Meeting of the Association for Behavior Analysis, San Diego, May.

Ramel. W. (2007). *Mindfulness, depression, and cognitive processes*. Paper presented at the ACT Summer Institute III, Houston, Texas, July.

Ramel, W., Goldin, P. R., Carmona, P. E., & McQuaid, J. R. (2004). The effects of mindfulness meditation on cognitive processes in patients with past depression. *Cognitive Therapy and Research, 28*, 433–455.

Rimes, K. A., & Watkins, E. (2005). The effects of self-focused rumination on global negative self-judgments in depression. *Behaviour Research and Therapy, 43*, 1673–1681.

Rippere, V. (1977). Common-sense beliefs about depression and antidepressive behaviour: A study of social consensus. *Behaviour Research and Therapy, 15*, 465–473.

Rogers, C. (1951). *Client-centered therapy: Its current practice, implications and theory*. Boston: Houghton Mifflin.

Rosenfarb, I. S., Burker, E. J., Morris, S. A., & Cush, D. T. (1993). Effects of changing contingencies on the behavior of depressed and nondepressed individuals. *Journal of Abnormal Psychology, 102*, 642–646.

Skinner, B. F. (1957). *Verbal behavior*. New York: Appleton-Century-Crofts.

Strosahl, K. D., Hayes, S. C., Wilson, K. G., & Gifford, E. V. (2004). An ACT primer: Core therapy processes, intervention strategies, and therapist competencies. In S. C. Hayes & K. D. Strosahl (Eds), *A practical guide to acceptance and commitment therapy* (pp. 31–58). New York: Springer.

Thwaites, R., Dagnan, D., Huey, D., & Addis, M. E. (2004). The Reasons for Depression Questionnaire (RFD): UK standardization for clinical and non-clinical populations. *Psychology and Psychotherapy: Theory, Research and Practice, 77*, 363–374.

Velten, E. (1968). A laboratory task for the induction of mood states. *Behaviour Research and Therapy, 6*, 473–482.

Ward, A., Lyubomirsky, S., Sousa, L., & Nolen-Hoeksema, S. (2003). Can't quite commit: Rumination and uncertainty. *Personality and Social Psychology Bulletin, 29*, 96–107.

Watkins, E., Moulds, M., & Mackintosh, B. (2005). Comparisons between rumination and worry in a non-clinical population. *Behaviour Research and Therapy, 43*, 1577–1585.

Watkins, E., & Teasdale, J. D. (2001). Rumination and overgeneral memory in depression: Effects of self-focus and analytic thinking. *Journal of Abnormal Psychology, 110*, 353–357.

Wegner, D. M. (1994). *White bears and other unwanted thoughts: Suppression, obsession, and the psychology of mental control.* New York: Guilford.

Wenzlaff, R. M. (1993). The mental control of depression: Psychological obstacles to emotional well-being. In D. M. Wegner & J. W. Pennebaker (Eds), *Handbook of mental control* (pp. 238–257). Englewood Cliffs, NJ: Prentice Hall.

Wenzlaff, R. M., & Luxton, D. D. (2003). The role of thought suppression in depressive rumination. *Cognitive Therapy and Research, 27*, 293–308.

Wenzlaff, R. M., Wegner, D. M., & Klein, S. B. (1991). The role of thought suppression in the bonding of thought and mood. *Journal of Personality and Social Psychology, 60*, 500–508.

Wenzlaff, R. M., Wegner, D. M., & Roper, D. W. (1988). Depression and mental control: The resurgence of unwanted thoughts. *Journal of Personality and Social Psychology, 55*, 882–892.

White, M., & Epston, D. (1990). *Narrative means to therapeutic ends.* New York: W. W. Norton.

Wilson, K. G., & Murrell, A. R. (2004). Values work in acceptance and commitment therapy: Setting a course for behavioural treatment. In S. C. Hayes, V. M. Follette, & M. M. Linehan (Eds), *Mindfulness and acceptance: Expanding the cognitive-behavioral tradition* (pp. 120–151). New York: Guilford.

Wilson, K. G., Hayes, S. C., Gregg, J., & Zettle, R. D. (2001). Psychopathology and psychotherapy. In S. C. Hayes, D. Barnes-Holmes, & B. Roche (Eds), *Relational frame theory: A post-Skinnerian account of human language and cognition* (pp. 211–237). New York: Plenum.

Zettle, R. D. (1990). Rule-governed behavior: A radical behavioral answer to the cognitive challenge. *The Psychological Record, 40*, 41–49.

Zettle, R. D. (2004). ACT with affective disorders. In S. C. Hayes & K. D. Strosahl (Eds), *A practical guide to acceptance and commitment therapy* (pp. 77–102). New York: Springer.

Zettle, R. D. (2005). The evolution of a contextual approach to therapy: From comprehensive distancing to ACT. *International Journal of Behavioural Consultation and Therapy, 1*, 77–89.

Zettle, R. D. (2007). *ACT for depression: A clinician's guide to using acceptance and commitment therapy in treating depression.* Oakland, CA: New Harbinger.

Zettle, R. D., & Hayes, S. C. (1982). Rule-governed behavior: A potential theoretical framework for cognitive–behavioral therapy. In P. C. Kendall (Ed.), *Advances in cognitive–behavioral research and therapy* (pp. 73–118). New York: Academic Press.

Zettle, R. D., & Hayes, S. C. (1986). Dysfunctional control by client verbal behavior: The context of reason-giving. *The Analysis of Verbal Behavior*, 4, 30–38.

Zettle, R. D., & Hayes, S. C. (2002). Brief ACT treatment of depression. In F. W. Bond & W. Dryden (Eds), *Handbook of brief cognitive behaviour therapy* (pp. 35–54). Chichester, England: John Wiley & Sons, Ltd.

Zettle, R. D., & Rains, J. C. (1989). Group cognitive and contextual therapies in treatment of depression. *Journal of Clinical Psychology*, 45, 438–445.

8

The Theory Underlying Mindfulness-Based Cognitive Therapy as a Relapse Prevention Approach to Depression

Mark A. Lau

Despite the success of both pharmacological and psychosocial interventions – including those described elsewhere in this book – in treating active episodes of major depressive disorder (MDD), MDD remains a lifelong illness with a high risk for relapse and recurrence (Berti Ceroni, Neri, & Pezzoli, 1984; Judd, 1997; Keller, Lavori, Lewis, & Klerman, 1983). What is more, relatively little attention has been paid to the development of interventions specific for reducing this risk after recovery. In an effort to redress this shortage, John Teasdale, Zindel Segal, and Mark Williams (1995) elaborated a mindfulness-based cognitive vulnerability model of depressive relapse. This model provided the rationale for the development of mindfulness-based cognitive therapy (MBCT), a novel, group-based, psychosocial intervention integrating mindfulness training with cognitive therapy techniques, specifically crafted to reduce relapse in recurrent major depression.

This chapter begins with a summary of the historical background that provided the impetus for the development of a mindfulness-based cognitive theory of depression and of MBCT itself. Mindfulness-based cognitive theory, how this theoretical model links to the design of MBCT, and MBCT itself are then described. The subsequent section reviews the empirical support for this model and its specific assumptions; this includes a review of the efficacy of MBCT in reducing depressive relapse risk and depressive symptoms themselves. The chapter concludes with suggestions for further work based on this integrative approach.

Treating Depression: MCT, CBT and Third Wave Therapies, First Edition.
Edited by Adrian Wells and Peter L. Fisher.

Historical Background

The importance of developing novel approaches to managing MDD is in large part created by the tremendous burden that depression imposes on its sufferers and on society. Lifetime prevalence rates for MDD are estimated to be between 3 and 13 per 100 individuals, and lifetime risk is estimated at 17–19 per cent (Kessler et al., 1994). Alarmingly, the burden of ill health associated with MDD is expected to increase, both absolutely and relatively, such that, by 2020, depression will move from its current position of the fourth greatest burden of disease to become the second, immediately after ischaemic heart disease (Murray & Lopez, 1997). This increase is due in part to the high rate of relapse and recurrence for this disorder (Berti Ceroni et al., 1984; Judd, 1997; Keller et al., 1983). To illustrate, individuals who recover from an initial episode of depression exhibit a 50 per cent chance of developing a second episode, and, for those with a history of two or more episodes, the risk of relapse or recurrence (or both) increases to 70–80 per cent. These data point to the necessity of preventing depressive relapse and recurrence as an important adjunct in the effective management of this disorder.

Currently, the most validated and widely used approach to preventing depressive relapse and recurrence is maintenance pharmacotherapy (e.g., Kupfer et al., 1992). In this approach, patients are maintained on their antidepressant medication (ADM) for months or years after they have recovered from the episode for which they were originally treated. However, some individuals cannot take ADMs (e.g., pregnant women); and many of those who do experience side effects or low adherence rates – or both (Cooper et al., 2007). In the late 1980s, the clear need for alternatives to ADMs led to the consideration of psychotherapy as a potential approach to prevent depressive relapse. This notion was based on the demonstration that negative life events often precede the onset of depression, in particular the onset of the first or second depressive episode (e.g., Lewinsohn, Allen, Seeley, & Gotlib, 1999; Ma & Teasdale, 2004). Moreover, these negative life events, such as a loss or a rejection, often have interpersonal consequences. This psychosocial view of depression provided the rationale behind evaluating a maintenance version of interpersonal psychotherapy, designed to prevent depressive relapse and recurrence. In turn, this evaluating led to the first demonstration that a maintenance version of psychotherapy could prevent depressive relapse (Frank et al., 1990).

These encouraging results fuelled further curiosity about whether a maintenance version of cognitive therapy might also be effective in protecting patients from depressive relapse. This curiosity led David Kupfer of the John D. and Catherine T. MacArthur Foundation to ask Zindel Segal to develop a maintenance version of cognitive therapy with the goal of reducing depressive relapse. Segal subsequently invited John Teasdale and Mark Williams to collaborate on this project. The trio initially set out with the intention to simply make minor adaptations to cognitive therapy in order to create a maintenance version of this acute treatment. However, as you will see later, a careful theoretical analysis of the processes underlying depressive relapse and recurrence led them to explore some new possibilities, which ultimately led to the development of MBCT.

As mentioned above, the starting point of the project to develop a new psychotherapy for the prevention of depressive relapse was cognitive therapy. Cognitive therapy was first developed as a structured symptom-focused approach to treating depression (Beck, Rush, Shaw, & Emery, 1979). This therapy is guided by an ongoing cognitive conceptualization of the patient's difficulties on the basis of Beck's cognitive model of depression (Beck, 1967; Beck et al., 1979). The cognitive model posits that one's emotional and behavioural reactions to a given situation are mediated through one's thoughts about, interpretations of, or meanings attributed to that situation. In depression, the content of these thoughts is predominantly negative regarding the self, the world, and the future. These thoughts ultimately derive from negative or depressogenic self-schemas, formed as a result of previous experiences, typically from childhood, which serve to negatively bias the processing of self-relevant information (J. M. G. Williams, Watts, MacLeod, & Mathews, 1997).

At the time when Segal, Teasdale, and Williams were meeting, cognitive therapy had already become a significant alternative to pharmacotherapy for the treatment of acute depression. Furthermore, cognitive therapy as an acute depression treatment had been shown to reduce depressive relapse rates to the range of 20–36 per cent from a range of 50–78 per cent for discontinuation pharmacotherapy (Blackburn, Eunson, & Bishop, 1986; Evans et al., 1992; Shea et al., 1992; Simons, Murphy, Levine, & Wetzel, 1986). This finding had two important implications with respect to developing a maintenance version of cognitive therapy. First, given the demonstration that cognitive therapy reduced relapse rates to the range of 20–36 per cent, a maintenance version would have little room to improve upon this. On the more encouraging side, these results suggested that something about cognitive therapy provided long-term protection from depressive relapse. This led Segal and his colleagues to modify their approach from simply adapting cognitive therapy so as to create a maintenance version to answering two central questions designed to guide their development of a standalone relapse prevention treatment: (1) What are the psychological mechanisms underlying cognitive vulnerability to relapse? And (2) how might cognitive therapy reduce depressive relapse and recurrence?

Mindfulness-Based Cognitive Vulnerability Model of Depressive Relapse

This model was developed in an effort to explain the finding that there is an increased risk of depressive relapse or recurrence in proportion to the increasing number of prior depressive episodes. Segal, Williams, & Teasdale (2002) proposed three key mechanisms underlying cognitive vulnerability to depressive relapse: (1) mood-activated depressogenic attitudes and beliefs; (2) a ruminative response style; and (3) a decreased activation threshold of relapse pathways over time.

Mood-activated depressogenic attitudes and beliefs

A core feature of the cognitive model is that depressogenic self-schemas represent a diathesis that can increase risk for major depression. According to this model, these schemas are typically latent until activated by a life event that is severe and schema-congruent (Beck et al., 1979; Monroe & Simons, 1991). Initial efforts to validate this hypothesis relied primarily on a questionnaire measure of dysfunctional schemas, the Dysfunctional Attitudes Scale (DAS) (Weissman & Beck, 1979). However, the majority of studies using this measure failed to demonstrate differences in DAS scores between recovered depressed subjects (i.e., subjects at increased risk for depression) and controls (e.g., Hamilton & Abramson, 1983; Silverman, Silverman, & Eardley, 1984; Simons, Garfield, & Murphy, 1984) and therefore failed to provide support for this aspect of the cognitive model of depression.

Instead, Teasdale's (1988) consideration of a distinct but related model of cognitive vulnerability to depressive relapse, the differential activation hypothesis, could account for the results of these studies. Teasdale built on Beck's cognitive model by proposing that,

> in addition to any differences in cognitive organization that may be apparent in the non-depressed state, and in addition to any idiosyncratic cognitive schemas that may be activated by a limited class of environmental situations, vulnerability to severe and persistent depression is powerfully related to differences in patterns of thinking that are activated *in the depressed state*. (Teasdale, 1988, p. 251)

Thus, if the activation of negative thinking patterns is minimal, an individual might experience only a temporary lowering of mood in response to a sad event. Conversely, if a depressive state induces a significant activation of negative thinking patterns, this can precipitate further negatively biased self-referential information processing, which maintains or worsens the depressed mood. Furthermore, the extent to which a depressed mood activates negative thinking depends on the strength of their association. The differential activation hypothesis assumes that this association is established during early episodes of depression and strengthened with each subsequent episode (Teasdale & Barnard, 1993; Segal, Williams, Teasdale, & Gemar, 1996).

Ruminative response style

In addition to differences in the content of thoughts activated in vulnerable individuals when experiencing sad or mildly dysphoric mood states, these individuals also demonstrate important differences in the way they deal with these moods. While some people respond to low mood by distracting themselves from this experience in a variety of ways, others focus their attention on their depressive experience, analyzing it in an effort to solve the problem of their depressed mood. This second way of responding, referred to as a 'ruminative response style', is associated with the prolongation of depressed feelings, whereas the tendency to respond with distraction is associated with short-lived depressed feelings (Lyubomirsky & Nolen-Hoeksema, 1995; Nolen-Hoeksema, 1991; Nolen-Hoeksema & Morrow, 1991).

Decreased activation threshold of relapse pathways over time

There is good evidence that the relationship between psychological stress and depressive relapse changes over time (Lewinsohn et al., 1999; Post, 1992). The likelihood that major life events precede the onset of a depressive episode decreases from the first to subsequent episodes. Rather, Post (1992) suggested that each new episode of depression contributes to small reductions in the neurobiological threshold that triggers depression. As time increases, this threshold lowers to the point where episodes may occur autonomously, that is, in the absence of a major life event.

In sum, when an individual who is at risk for depression experiences a lowering of mood, habitual depressive thinking patterns result as depressogenic schemas are automatically activated. Not only does this thinking style repeat itself; it further intensifies the depressed mood, which results in the production of additional depressive thoughts. In this way mild and transient mood states can escalate into more severe and disabling depressed states (Teasdale et al., 1995).

How Cognitive Therapy Prevents Depressive Relapse

With respect to designing a prophylactic psychological intervention for depression, it was important for Segal, Teasdale, and Williams to understand how using cognitive therapy for the acute treatment of depression reduced the risk of subsequent relapse or recurrence. As described above, a core feature of the cognitive model is that vulnerability to depression is related to the persistence of underlying dysfunctional attitudes. On the basis of this feature, it was reasonable to assume that cognitive therapy reduced depressive relapse risk by modifying those dysfunctional attitudes; however, this view was not empirically supported (Barber & DeRubeis, 1989). For example, in the above-mentioned studies, cognitive therapy and pharmacotherapy typically did not differ with respect to post-treatment measures of dysfunctional attitudes. Rather, Barber and DeRubeis (1989) concluded that cognitive therapy taught the individual specific skills that would help him/her stay well.

At the time Segal and colleagues were addressing this question, it was generally assumed that cognitive therapy was effective because it taught the patient skills that would help him/her change the content of his/her depressive thoughts. However, these researchers' more detailed theoretical analysis suggested the possibility that cognitive therapy led to changes in one's relationship to depressive thoughts and feelings (Teasdale et al., 1995). Briefly, a consequence of repeatedly identifying automatic thoughts and evaluating their content, typically on a thought-record form, was that the cognitive therapy patient developed a broader perspective on, or some distance from, his/her thoughts and feelings. As a result, instead of seeing these thoughts and feelings as necessarily true or as a reflection of themselves, patients would come to view them simply as passing events in the mind that were not necessarily true representations of the self. In line with this view, Ingram and Hollon (1986) proposed that cognitive therapy facilitates an individual's ability to switch to a metacognitive mode of processing that focuses on depressive thoughts, which is typically referred to as 'distancing' or 'decentring'. Although the concept of 'decentring' had been previously recognized as one of the elements of cognitive therapy (e.g., Beck et al., 1979), it was typically viewed simply as a means to an end – namely the end of thought-content change. On the contrary, Teasdale et al. (1995) suggested, on the basis of both their theoretical analysis and their clinical experience, that 'decentring' was the central mechanism of action in cognitive therapy. Following from this, the ability to see one's thoughts simply as 'thoughts' instead of necessarily true reflections of reality was viewed as the fundamental skill by which cognitive therapy protected people against future depression.

The mechanism of 'decentring' is very similar to those associated with the concepts of detached mindfulness (Wells & Matthews, 1994, 1996) and re-perceiving (Shapiro, Carlson, Astin, & Freedman, 2006). The concept of detached mindfulness emerged from the self-regulatory executive function (S-REF) (Wells & Matthews, 1994; 1996) theory of psychological disorder. In this context, detached mindfulness refers to bringing an objective awareness to thoughts as events, not as facts, and thereby choosing not to engage with them – for example by analyzing them – and not to influence them by trying to push them away (Wells, 2006). Re-perceiving refers to a shift in one's perspective whereby one disidentifies or dissociates from one's thoughts and views one's moment-by-moment experience with greater clarity and objectivity (Shapiro et al., 2006).

In summary, if one is to decrease relapse risk, the answers to the two questions described above suggested the development of an intervention that would (1) increase one's awareness of negative thinking at times of potential relapse and (2) facilitate one's ability to uncouple or disengage from the reactivated negative thought streams. In this way the intervention would help to normalize thinking patterns in states of mild sadness, so that these moods would remain mild and not escalate to more severe affective states (Segal et al., 2002).

The shift in focus from teaching patients skills designed to change their thought content to teaching them how to decentre from their thoughts and feelings led Segal and colleagues to consider alternative approaches to cognitive therapy that could prevent depressive relapse. One such approach was mindfulness meditation – as suggested by Marsha Linehan, who had developed dialectical behaviour therapy. This was a treatment for suicidal behaviours that included the teaching of skills in mindfulness meditation. This suggestion led Segal and his colleagues to consider mindfulness training as taught in the mindfulness-based stress reduction (MBSR) programme developed by Jon Kabat-Zinn and his colleagues at the University of Massachusetts Medical Center (Kabat-Zinn, 1990). MBSR was originally designed to improve the quality of life for individuals who suffered from intractable chronic pain by teaching them mindfulness skills with the intention of helping them to develop a decentred relationship to their own thoughts and feelings.

Mindfulness has been defined as a non-judgemental, present-centered awareness in which each thought, feeling, or sensation that arises in the attentional field is acknowledged and accepted as it is (Kabat-Zinn, 1990; Shapiro & Schwartz, 2000; Segal et al., 2002). It involves directly observing one's thoughts and emotions with a non-judgemental attitude, as they arise in the stream of consciousness, rather than engaging in ruminative, elaborative thinking about one's experience and its origins, implications, and associations. In consequence, mindfulness is viewed as a metacognitive state involving non-elaborative attention to one's internal subjective experience of bodily sensations, thoughts, and emotions (Bishop et al., 2004; Grabovac, Lau, & Willett, 2011). Furthermore, it is seen as a self-regulation strategy for disengaging from information-processing modes that heighten stress and emotional distress or perpetuate psychopathology (Bishop et al., 2004; Segal et al., 2002; Teasdale et al., 1995).

Bishop (2002), however, has argued that the lack of precision and specificity of the definition of mindfulness presented above has impeded investigations into the mediating role and the mechanisms of action of mindfulness. In an attempt to overcome this obstacle, Bishop et al. (2004) developed a more precise and specific two-component operational definition of mindfulness. The first component of this definition describes a self-regulation of attention in order to maintain a focus on present-moment experience. The second component refers to a specific quality of this attention turned to present-moment experience: a quality that is characterized by curiosity, openness, and acceptance. These two components have been represented in several discussions of mindfulness and psychotherapy (e.g., Brown & Ryan, 2003; Germer 2005; Hayes & Feldman, 2004).

Mindfulness also refers to the practice of cultivating mindfulness, typically through various meditation techniques originating from Buddhist spiritual traditions (Germer, 2005; Hanh, 1976). In the past twenty years there has been a surge in the clinical use of mindfulness, in an effort to accomplish essentially two goals. First, mindfulness can increase one's insight into how automatic, habitual patterns of reactivity to physical sensations, thoughts, and emotions increase stress and emotional distress. Second, mindfulness can reduce one's vulnerability to these reactions, thereby producing lasting improvements in emotional well-being (Linehan, 1993; Teasdale, 1999).

This understanding of the benefits of mindfulness training led Teasdale et al. (1995) to propose that mindfulness training would lead to increased mindfulness, which would facilitate decentring skills and disengagement from dysphoria-activated depressive thinking and rumination. In order to accomplish this goal, Segal et al. (2002) developed a treatment that integrates mindfulness meditation training derived from the MBSR programme with elements of cognitive therapy that are thought to reduce the risk of relapse. Specifically, their goal was to offer individuals at risk for depression a series of mindfulness and cognitive therapy exercises that would help them to develop mindfulness – that is, a non-judgemental awareness of their present-moment experience – in order to facilitate their own detection of depression-related thinking patterns and their acquisition of more flexible, deliberate responses at times of potential relapse. In this way an at-risk individual experiencing a dysphoric mood would avoid a potential relapse because s/he would be less likely to be influenced by the mood-activated depressive thinking that had previously contributed to a downward spiral of depression. The MBCT programme and how the combination of mindfulness and cognitive therapy approaches work together to accomplish these goals will now be briefly described.

MBCT

The MBCT programme, as originally developed and evaluated, consisted of eight weekly two-hour group sessions and four follow-up group sessions for one year after the end of the eight weekly sessions; the size of these groups went up to 12 patients. MBCT combines traditional MBSR meditation practices such as the body scan, mindful stretching, and mindfulness of breath, body, sounds, and thoughts with traditional cognitive therapy techniques such as psycho-education about depression symptoms and automatic thoughts, exercises designed to demonstrate how the nature of one's thoughts changes with one's mood, and the creation of a relapse prevention plan. In addition, Segal et al. (2002) introduced a new meditation called 'the three-minute breathing space' in order to facilitate present-moment awareness in everyday upsetting situations. Finally, participants in MBCT are invited to engage in approximately one hour of formal and informal daily meditation practice and exercises directed at integrating the application of awareness skills to everyday life.

The first four MBCT sessions are devoted in large part to developing participants' non-judgemental awareness of their moment-by-moment experience. This is accomplished mostly via formal meditation practices (body scan; mindfulness of breath, body, sounds, thoughts), which help participants to deconstruct their experience into the component elements of physical sensations and accompanying thoughts and emotions. This training is complemented by a cognitive therapy exercise designed to teach the cognitive model, as described above. Specific awareness of a depression-related experience is facilitated through psycho-education about the nature of depressive symptoms and negative automatic thoughts. Such awareness increases one's ability to detect experiences that might lead to potential relapse.

The second half of the programme is directed towards developing more flexible, deliberate responses at times of potential relapse. Session 5 makes explicit the use of acceptance as a skilful first step towards preventing relapse. Before this, participants practised acceptance implicitly during their meditations, by bringing an open and non-judgemental awareness to their experience. The theme of session 6 is to make explicit the notion that 'thoughts are not facts', in order to help participants to decentre from their thinking – that is, to change their relationship with thoughts so that they may relate *to* their thoughts, seeing them simply as discrete mental events, rather than relating *from* their thoughts. Specifically, MBCT participants are instructed to take a breathing space as a first step towards increasing their chance of becoming aware of their present-moment experience, including that of thinking and having thoughts. This is often accompanied by a sense of having a choice in how they respond to their thoughts. They are then offered response options such as simply watching their thoughts come and go, viewing thoughts as mental events rather than as facts, or writing thoughts down on paper (Segal et al., 2002). In this way MBCT differs from traditional cognitive therapy in that it does not emphasize reality testing or disputing the individual's thoughts. In session 7 participants develop specific action plans that can be utilized at the time of potential relapse. The final session is focused on preparing participants to maintain the momentum and discipline developed during the programme.

Empirical Support

Over the past two decades, a handful of systematic reviews and meta-analyses based on several randomized controlled trials have demonstrated the efficacy of MBCT for the prevention of depressive relapse (e.g., Bondolfi et al., 2010; Coelho, Canter, & Ernst, 2007; Godfrin & van Heeringen, 2010; Kuyken et al., 2008; Ma & Teasdale, 2004; Meadows et al., 2014; Ree & Craigie, 2007; Teasdale et al., 2000; Williams et al., 2014). In the first two MBCT trials (Ma & Teasdale, 2004; Teasdale et al., 2000), individuals who had recovered from at least two episodes of depression, were symptom-free, and were off medication for at least three months before the study were randomized either to receive MBCT or to continue with treatment as usual (TAU). In both trials, the samples were stratified according to the number of previous episodes (two vs three or more) and the recency of the last episode of depression (0–12 months vs 13–24 months). There was a significant interaction between the number of previous episodes and treatment condition in both studies on the primary outcome measure – occurrence of relapse or recurrence. For the participants with only two previous depressive episodes (who were slightly fewer than one quarter of the samples in both studies), the relapse rates between the MBCT and the TAU groups were not statistically different, 56 per cent and 50 per cent of MBCT participants versus 31 per cent and 20 per cent of TAU participants relapsing in the two studies. For participants with a history of three or more depressive episodes, who comprised over 75 per cent of the samples, MBCT (as compared to TAU) reduced the risk of relapse approximately by half over a one-year follow-up. Specifically, for the intent-to-treat analyses in the first multicentre trial, significantly fewer participants relapsed in the MBCT (40 per cent) than in the TAU (66 per cent) group; this yielded an *h* value of.53, considered a medium effect size (Cohen, 1988). Similar results were reported in Ma & Teasdale (2004), where fewer participants relapsed in the MBCT (36 per cent) than in the TAU (78 per cent) group; this yielded an *h* value of .88, indicating a large effect size (Cohen, 1988). The benefits of MBCT for individuals with a history of three or more episodes could not be accounted for by a greater use of antidepressant medication, as those in the MBCT group actually used less medication than those in the TAU group. In summary, based in large part on the results of these two studies, MBCT was seen to have an additive benefit to usual care for individuals with three or more previous depressive episodes (Coelho et al., 2007).

More recent studies continue to support the benefits of MBCT in recurrent depression (Bondolfi et al., 2010; Meadows et al., 2014; Williams et al., 2014). In one of these studies, although there was a significantly longer time to relapse for MBCT plus TAU versus TAU alone (Bondolfi et al., 2010), there was no difference in relapse rates between MBCT and TAU due to a lower rate of relapse in the TAU group as compared to previous studies (Ma & Teasdale, 2004; Teasdale et al., 2000).

MBCT was also compared to maintenance antidepressant treatment in preventing relapse among remitted depressed patients in two randomized controlled trials (Kuyken et al., 2008; Segal et al., 2010). Kuyken et al. (2008) randomized individuals who had recovered from depression, were taking antidepressant medication, and had a history of three or more depressive episodes to either MBCT or maintenance antidepressant medication (M-ADM). There was no significant difference in relapse rates between MBCT (47 per cent) and M-ADM (60 per cent) participants over a 15-month follow-up period, 75 per cent of the MBCT participants withdrawing from their ADM during the follow-up period. Furthermore, the MBCT group reported significantly fewer residual depressive symptoms than the antidepressant treatment group on the Hamilton Rating Scale for Depression (HRSD) (Hamilton, 1960) – 7.05 (vs 8.69) – and on the Beck Depression Inventory-II – 12.61 (vs 17.02) and improved quality of life, with no difference of cost between these two treatments.

In a second study, Segal et al. (2010) randomized patients with a history of recurrent MDD, and who had been treated to remission through pharmacotherapy, to one of the three conditions: MBCT plus discontinuation of their medication; M-ADM; or placebo. Patients were followed for 18 months. In this study there was a significant interaction between the stability of remission and relapse of depression. Remission was categorized as stable versus unstable. For formerly depressed patients who were categorized as unstable remitters, the two active treatment conditions had lower relapse rates (27 per cent for M-ADM, 28 per cent for MBCT) than the placebo group (71 per cent). Interestingly, among stable remitters, relapse rates were not significantly different across the three conditions (59 per cent for M-ADM, 62 per cent for MBCT and 50 per cent for placebo).

None of the above cited outcome studies was designed in a way that permits attributing the findings to MBCT-specific effects. In line with the recommendations of Coelho et al. (2007), MBCT research should directly investigate potential mechanisms underlying the efficacy of MBCT in order to rule out non-specific factors such as group participation or therapeutic attention and to explicitly evaluate the assumptions underlying the development of MBCT. In response to these comments, J. M. G. Williams et al. (2008) recommended the use of a 'dismantling' paradigm where MBCT is compared to a group-based control treatment that contains just the psycho-educational component of MBCT, but no meditation training.

This type of dismantling study was recently conducted to evaluate the role of mindfulness meditation in preventing depressive relapse (Williams et al., 2014). Formerly depressed participants with a history of at least three episodes of depression were randomly allocated to MBCT and TAU; cognitive psychological education (CPE); or TAU. CPE, an active control condition, consisted of all the elements of, and was matched in time with, the eight-session MBCT programme without the experiential cultivation of mindfulness through meditation practice. Patients were followed for 12 months. There was a significant interaction between the severity of childhood trauma and the treatment group. For individuals categorized as having experienced a childhood trauma of low severity, rates of relapse were 51 per cent, 45 per cent, and 43 per cent for MBCT, CPE, and TAU respectively. However, for individuals categorized as having experienced a childhood trauma of high severity, rates of relapse were 41 per cent, 54 per cent, and 65 per cent for MBCT, CPE, and TAU respectively. As the effect of CPE fell between MBCT and TAU, it is possible that the psycho-education or group support in CPE conferred some protection against relapse. In addition, as there were differences in the amount of regular treatment-related activity outside sessions between MBCT and CPE, it is possible that this, rather than the mindfulness meditation itself, explained the superiority of MBCT over CPE. Future research is necessary to further clarify the specific contributions of MBCT versus non-specific factors.

Overall, the conclusion of a recent meta-analysis of MBCT randomized controlled trials is that MBCT is effective for preventing depressive relapse in individuals with recurrent MDD. This conclusion has been supported by several other reviews and meta-analyses of both controlled and uncontrolled studies (e.g., Coelho et al., 2007). Furthermore, recent studies have demonstrated that the benefits of MBCT appear to be maintained, even long after patients are no longer receiving treatment (e.g., Meadows et al., 2014).

Interestingly, a growing number of researchers have extended the application of the mindfulness-based cognitive vulnerability model of depressive relapse from the prevention of depressive relapse to the treatment of acute depression. Specifically, some have postulated that teaching patients mindfulness skills in order to help them to distance themselves from ruminative, depressive thought patterns may also be effective in reducing depressive symptoms. In agreement with this notion, MBCT has been shown to reduce residual depressive symptoms in several randomized controlled trials (van der Velden et al., 2015) for individuals with residual symptoms (e.g., Kingston, Dooley, Bates, Lawlor, & Malong, 2007; Kuyken et al., 2008) as well as in individuals diagnosed with unipolar depression or bipolar disorder, in remission, and with a history of suicidal ideation or behaviour (J. G. M. Williams et al., 2008). More recently, MBCT was shown to reduce residual depressive symptoms in a randomized controlled trial irrespective of the number of previous episodes of major depression (Geschwind, Peeters, Huibers, van Os, & Wichers, 2012). In addition, MBCT has been shown to be effective in reducing depressive symptoms in individuals with current depression in controlled (e.g., Barnhoffer et al., 2009; Foley, Baillie, Huxter, Price, & Sinclair, 2010; van Aalderen et al., 2012) and uncontrolled studies (e.g., Eisendrath et al., 2008; Finucane & Mercer, 2006; Kenny & Williams, 2007; Ree & Craigie, 2007). Together, these results provide indirect support for the application of the psychological vulnerability model of depressive relapse to the treatment of acute depression.

There are varying degrees of additional support for the assumptions of the psychological vulnerability model of depression, which underlie the development of MBCT. These include (1) evidence that supports the idea that dysphoria-activated increases in negative information processing (a processing known as 'cognitive reactivity': see below) are a potential causal risk factor for depressive relapse; (2) the benefits of decentring for the prevention of depressive relapse; and (3) the assumption that MBCT increases mindfulness, decreases rumination, and disrupts autonomous relapse processes.

Is cognitive reactivity a causal risk factor of depressive relapse?

Given that cognitive reactivity (CR) is an increased activation of depressive or negative thinking patterns whereby a formerly depressed individual experiences dysphoric mood, a critical component of the mindfulness-based cognitive theory of depression is that CR represents a causal risk factor in recurrent depression. Kraemer et al. (1997) have proposed four specific criteria for defining risk-factor status in order to increase the consistency and precision with which this term is used: (1) Is the factor associated with the outcome – in other words, is it a *correlate*? (2) Does the factor precede the outcome – in other words, is it a *risk factor*? (3) Can the factor change or be changed – in other words, is it a *variable* risk factor? And (4) does manipulation of the factor change the outcome – in other words, is it a *causal* risk factor?

Lau, Segal, and Williams (2004) evaluated the extant literature to determine whether CR could be considered a causal risk factor of depressive relapse. Briefly, with respect to the first criterion, a considerable number of cross-sectional studies comparing individuals at risk for depression (i.e., individuals who had recovered from depression) with never-depressed controls, on various cognitive measures (e.g., the DAS), before and during the induction of a sad mood (Ingram, Miranda, & Segal, 1998; Lau et al., 2004; Scher, Ingram, & Segal, 2005), have provided sufficient evidence to establish CR as a *correlate* of vulnerability to depressive relapse.

Mood-priming and longitudinal studies provide a convergent set of results generally supporting the second of Kraemer et al.'s four criteria – that is, the information-processing patterns activated in depressed mood will determine whether this state will escalate to the level of major depression (Lewinsohn et al., 1999; Segal, Gemar, & Williams, 1999; Segal et al., 2006; R. M. Williams, 1988). For example, Segal et al. (1999) and Segal et al. (2006) demonstrated that CR scores (as indexed by increased DAS scores: see Weissman & Beck, 1979) in depressed patients with remission independently predicted depressive relapse risk. These results do provide sufficient support for considering CR as a *risk factor* for depressive relapse.

Until recently, there was only indirect support from two studies (Segal et al., 1999, and Segal et al., 2006) for the third of Kraemer et al.'s four criteria. In these two studies, individuals treated to remission with either pharmacotherapy or cognitive therapy did not differ on pre-sad mood-induction DAS scores. However, recovered pharmacotherapy patients demonstrated a significant increase in their post-sad mood induction DAS scores as compared to recovered cognitive therapy patients, who showed no change in DAS scores at similar levels of sadness. These results are consistent with the notion that cognitive therapy, or psychotherapy in general, somehow mitigated CR in patients treated with cognitive therapy. Such a conclusion is qualified by the fact that the studies did not include a pre-treatment CR assessment. Direct evidence that CR can be modified comes from a recent pilot study of thirty formerly depressed individuals whose CR was assessed before and after MBCT treatment. Participants demonstrated increased CR at baseline, but CR was significantly reduced after MBCT treatment (Lau & Yu, 2008). Thus CR can be considered a *variable* risk factor, as there is evidence that it can be reduced.

Finally, indirect support for CR as a *causal* risk factor comes from the two studies described above (Segal et al., 1999 and Segal et al., 2006), where increased CR as assessed after treatment was shown to be associated with increased relapse risk. Again, because pre-treatment assessment of CR was not conducted in any of these studies, future research where baseline CR is assessed would be required to provide direct support for the fourth criterion (Lau et al., 2004; Scher et al., 2005).

Does the ability to decentre from thoughts and feelings help to prevent depressive relapse?

A second assumption of the model is that the ability to decentre from thoughts and feelings is critical to disengaging from ruminative cognitive–affective processing and to preventing depressive relapse. Specifically, when one identifies personally with negative thoughts and feelings, which are thereby experienced as 'me' or 'reality', these experiences will have a much stronger impact. Conversely, the shift in one's cognitive perspective described so far as 'decentring' or 'disidentification', whereby subjects relate 'to their negative experiences as mental events in a wider context or field of awareness' (Teasdale et al., 2002, p. 276), might mean that negative experiences activated by a dysphoric mood will be less likely to lead to depressive relapse. Support for this assumption comes from four lines of research.

First, Watkins, Teasdale, & Williams (2003) demonstrated that the ability to decenter may reduce the maintenance of a depressed mood. Building on previous research that uses sad-mood inductions, this study investigated whether cognitive manipulations could affect the maintenance of induced sad mood in never depressed participants. In this study, scrambled Velten sentences were used as mood-maintaining primes, which participants were required to unscramble. Contextual questions – that is, questions designed to induce wider awareness of the temporal and personal context of the individual's current mood (e.g., 'How long does any mood last?') – versus control questions, which made no reference to mood (e.g., 'How long does this weather last?'), were embedded in a list of scrambled sentences. Contextual questions lead to a reduction in the length of a sad mood by comparison to control questions. These results are consistent with the notion that increased contextual awareness may reduce the activation of mood-linked negative representations.

Second, Teasdale and colleagues (2002) demonstrated that changes in the ability to decentre from negative thinking – which is also known as 'metacognitive awareness' – were associated with reduced risk of relapse. They conducted two studies to evaluate whether improvements in metacognitive awareness mediated any reduction in the risk of relapse that resulted from either of two psychological treatments – cognitive therapy or MBCT. In these studies metacognitive awareness was measured using the Measure of Awareness and Coping in Autobiographical Memory (MACAM) (Moore, Hayhurst, & Teasdale, 1996). The MACAM involves analyzing the autobiographical memories stimulated by depression-related cues, and it measures the ability to see negative thoughts and feelings as passing mental events rather than as an aspect of self.

The first of the two studies was carried out as part of a clinical trial designed to determine whether cognitive therapy could reduce relapse in depressed individuals who achieved partial remission through pharmacotherapy (Paykel et al., 1999). These patients, who received 20 weeks of pharmacotherapy, were randomized to receive either clinical management alone or clinical management together with cognitive therapy. The analysis of MACAM scores in the cognitive therapy-treated individuals showed that cognitive therapy reduced relapse through its effect of increasing metacognitive awareness. However, this analysis did not rule out the alternative explanation that the changes in metacognitive awareness were correlates of effective belief change. This alternative explanation was specifically addressed by examining MACAM scores in the original MBCT randomized controlled trial (Teasdale et al., 2000). As in the findings of the first study, increased metacognitive awareness was associated with MBCT-related reductions in relapse risk. A limitation of both studies was that neither could perform a full mediational analysis to demonstrate the causal status of metacognitive awareness change in the reduction of relapse risk.

Third, additional indirect evidence comes from the demonstration that decentring moderates the relationship between post-treatment CR and depressive relapse (Fresco, Segal, Buis, & Kennedy, 2007). In this study, decentring was measured using the Experiences Questionnaire (EQ) (Fresco, Moore, et al., 2007). Following up on the original report that low versus high CR was associated with lower relapse rates over an 18-month follow-up period (Segal et al., 2006), individuals with high post-acute treatment decentring scores and low CR had the lowest rates of depressive relapse.

Fourth, Bieling et al. (2012) demonstrated that individuals from the Segal et al. (2010) study who had received MBCT had higher decentring scores when measured with the EQ (Fresco, Moore, et al., 2007) and with the Toronto Mindfulness Scale (TMS) (Lau et al., 2006). Moreover, increased decentring as measured with the EQ-Wider experiences subscale was associated with lower levels of depression at 6-month follow-up.

Does MBCT increase mindfulness?

One of the important assumptions in mindfulness-based cognitive theory is that mindfulness is an important contributor to the prevention of depressive relapse. However, when MBCT was originally developed and evaluated, reliable and valid mindfulness self-report measures were lacking. A number of self-report mindfulness measures have since been developed – for example, the Freiburg Mindfulness Inventory (FMI) (Buchheld, Grossman, & Walach, 2001), the Kentucky Inventory of Mindfulness Skills (KIMS) (Baer, Smith, & Allen, 2004), the Mindful Attention Awareness Scale (MAAS) (Brown & Ryan, 2003) and the TMS (Lau et al., 2006). Early results from three uncontrolled studies demonstrated that MBCT increased self-reported mindfulness on the FMI (Eisendrath et al., 2008), on the MAAS (Ree & Criagie, 2007), and on the TMS (Lau & Yu, 2008). However, these studies could not determine whether these changes were specific to MBCT and whether increased mindfulness mediated the effects of MBCT in preventing relapse and reducing depressive symptoms. More recently, Bieling et al.'s (2012) analysis of the Segal et al. (2010) randomized controlled trial of MBCT versus pharmacotherapy versus placebo demonstrated MBCT-specific increases in self-reported mindfulness on the TMS. Furthermore, increased scores on the curiosity subscale of the TMS were associated with lower depression scores at six-month follow-up. Overall, several randomized controlled trials have demonstrated that self-reported mindfulness either was correlated with post-treatment symptoms of depression or risk of relapse or significantly mediated post-treatment symptoms of depression (van der Velden at al., 2015).

Does MBCT reduce rumination?

Another assumption of the model is that rumination is an important cognitive vulnerability factor for recurrent depression (Nolen-Hoeksema, 1991) and that MBCT would be expected to reduce rumination. Rumination is thought to facilitate the avoidance of emotional and behavioural meaning (Borkovec, Roemer, & Kinyon, 1995). Baer (2003) has proposed that mindfulness training provides exposure to emotions and thoughts, thereby reducing avoidance behaviour. For example, two of the outcome studies cited above contained a self-report measure of rumination, the Ruminative Response Scale (Treynor, Gonzalez, & Nolen-Hoeksema, 2003). Eisendrath et al. (2008) reported that MBCT led to a significant post-treatment reduction in rumination. Kingston et al. (2007) reported that MBCT was associated with a trend towards a reduction in rumination. The lack of significance was likely due to the small number of participants in the study ($n = 19$), as the effect size (Cohen's $d = 1.16$) was large. In addition, several randomized controlled trials have demonstrated that rumination was either associated with, or mediated, post-treatment symptoms of depression or risk of relapse (van der Velden at al., 2015).

Does MBCT disrupt autonomous relapse processes?

A key element of the MBCT model is that MBCT was designed to help individuals disrupt autonomous relapse processes involving dysphoria-activated depressogenic thinking patterns. Support for this notion comes from the demonstration that MBCT was more effective than TAU for individuals with three or more than for individuals with only two previous episodes (Segal et al., 2002). Furthermore, MBCT was more effective than TAU for depression onsets where no antecedent major life stressors were reported; however, when depressive episodes were preceded by a major life stressor, there was no difference between MBCT and TAU in effectiveness at preventing depressive relapse (Ma & Teasdale, 2004). Thus MBCT appears to be more effective at reducing relapse rates in individuals whose depressive relapse is more likely to be due to autonomous processes than to a major life stressor.

Conclusion

In conclusion, mindfulness-based cognitive theory of depression is a direct derivative of experimental psychology, learning theory, and cognitive science (Segal, Teasdale & Williams, 2004). This theory proposes that, when individuals at risk for depression experience a mild dysphoric mood, habitual depressive thinking patterns are automatically activated, thereby contributing to the development of more severe and disabling depressed states (Teasdale, Segal, & Williams, 1995). In order to decrease relapse risk, this theory suggested the development of an intervention that would facilitate the ability of at-risk individuals to decentre from dysphoria-activated negative thinking at times of potential relapse (Segal et al., 2002). This rationale led to the development of an integrative treatment that combines mindfulness meditation with cognitive therapy techniques in order to prevent depressive relapse and, more recently, to treat depressive symptoms themselves. The demonstration of MBCT's benefits in preventing depressive relapse for individuals with three or more previous depressive episodes in three randomized controlled trials conducted by two different research groups (Godfrin & van Heeringen, 2010; Ma & Teasdale, 2004; Teasdale et al., 2000) establishes MBCT as an *efficacious* treatment (Chambless & Hollon, 1998). A recent systematic review of MBCT's mechanisms of change for recurrent depression confirmed that MBCT may work through some of the mechanisms predicted from the mindfulness-based cognitive theory of depression (e.g., mindfulness, rumination, or meta-awareness) but that further rigorous research is required (van der Velden et al., 2015). Finally, elements of the MBCT programme have been combined with relapse prevention therapy (Witkiewitz, Marlatt, & Walker, 2005) to create a version of mindfulness-based relapse prevention that supports clients' recovery from substance use disorders. It remains to be determined whether aspects of mindfulness-based cognitive theory of depression, alone or in combination with other interventions, can be effective in the treatment of other psychological disorders.

References

Baer, R. A. (2003). Mindfulness training as a clinical intervention: A conceptual and empirical review. *Clinical Psychology: Science and Practice*, *10*(2), 125–143.

Baer, R. A., Smith, G. T., & Allen, K. B. (2004). Assessment of mindfulness by self-report: The Kentucky Inventory of Mindfulness Skills. *Assessment*, *11*, 191–206.

Barber, J. P., & DeRubeis, R. J. (1989). On second thought: Where the action is in cognitive therapy for depression. *Cognitive Therapy and Research*, *13*, 441–457.

Barnhoffer, T., Crane, C., Hargus, E., Amarasinghe, M., Winder, R., & Williams, J. M. G. (2009). Mindfulness-based cognitive therapy as a treatment for chronic depression. *Behaviour Research and Therapy*, *47*, 366–373.

Beck, A. T. (1967). *Depression: Causes and treatment*. Philadelphia: University of Pennsylvania Press.

Beck, A. T., Rush, A. J., Shaw, B. F., & Emery, G. (1979). *Cognitive therapy of depression*. New York: Guilford.

Berti Ceroni, G., Neri, C., & Pezzoli, A. (1984). Chronicity in major depression: A naturalistic perspective. *Journal of Affective Disorders*, *7*(2), 123–132.

Bieling, P. J., Hawley, L. L., Bloch, R. T., Corcoran, K. M., Levitan, R. D., Young, L. T., Macqueen, G. M., & Segal, Z. V. (2012). Treatment-specific changes in decentering following mindfulness-based cognitive therapy versus antidepressant medication or placebo for prevention of depressive relapse. *Journal of Consulting and Clinical Psychology*, *80*, 365–372.

Bishop, S. R., Lau, M. A., Shapiro, S., Carlson, L., Anderson, N. D., Carmody, J. … Devins, G. (2004). Mindfulness: A proposed operational definition. *Clinical Psychology: Science and Practice*, *11*, 230–241.

Blackburn, I. M., Eunson, K. M., & Bishop, S. (1986). A two-year naturalistic follow-up of depressed patients treated with cognitive therapy, pharmacotherapy, and a combination of both. *Journal of Affective Disorders*, *10*, 67–75.

Bondolfi, G., Jermann, F., Van der Linden, M. V., Gex-Fabry, M., Bizzini, L., Rouget, B. W. … Bertschy, G. (2010). Depression relapse prophylaxis with mindfulness-based cognitive therapy: Replication and extension in the Swiss health care system. *Journal of Affective Disorders*, *122*, 224–231.

Borkovec, T. D., Roemer, L., & Kinyon, J. (1995). Disclosure and worry: Opposite sides of the emotional processing coin. In J. W. Pennebaker (Ed.), *Emotion, disclosure, and health* (pp. 47–70). Washington, DC: American Psychological Association.

Brown, K. W., & Ryan, R. M. (2003). The benefits of beings present: Mindfulness and its role in psychological well-being. *Journal of Personality and Social Psychology*, *84*, 822–848.

Buchheld, N., Grossman, P., & Walach, H. (2001). Measuring mindfulness in insight meditation (Vipassana) and meditation-based psychotherapy: The development of the Freiburg Mindfulness Inventory (FMI). *Journal for Meditation and Meditation Research*, *1*, 11–34.

Chambless, D. L., & Hollon, S. D. (1998). Defining empirically supported therapies. *Journal of Consulting and Clinical Psychology*, *66*(1), 7–18.

Coelho, H. F., Canter, P. H., & Ernst, E. (2007). Mindfulness-based cognitive therapy: Evaluating current evidence and informing future research. *Journal of Consulting Clinical Psychology*, *75*(6), 1000–1005.

Cohen, J. (1988). *Statistical power analysis for the behavioural science* (2nd ed.). Hilldale, NJ: Lawrence Erlbaum.

Cooper, C., Bebbington, P., King, M., Brugha, T., Meltzer, H., Bhugra, D., & Jenkins, R. (2007). Why people do not take their psychotropic drugs as prescribed: Results of the 2000 National Psychiatric Morbidity Survey. *Acta Psychiatrica Scandinavica, 116*, 47–53.

Eisendrath, S. J., Delucchi, K., Bitner, R., Fenimore, P., Smit, M., & McLane, M. (2008). Mindfulness-based cognitive therapy for treatment resistant depression: A pilot study. *Psychotherapy and Psychosomatics, 77*(5), 319–320.

Evans, J. D., Hollon, S. D., DeRubeis, R. J., Piasecki, J. M., Grove, W. M., Garvey, M. J., & Tuason, V. B. (1992). Differential relapse following cognitive therapy and pharmacotherapy for depression. *Archives of General Psychiatry, 49*, 802–808.

Finucane, A., & Mercer, S. W. (2006). An exploratory mixed-methods study of the acceptability and effectiveness of mindfulness-based cognitive therapy for patients with active depression and anxiety in primary care. *BMC Psychiatry, 6*(1), 14–28.

Foley, E., Baillie, A., Huxter, M., Price, M., & Sinclair, E. (2010). Mindfulness-based cognitive therapy for individuals whose lives have been affected by cancer: A randomized controlled trial. *Journal of Consulting and Clinical Psychology, 78*, 72–79.

Frank, E., Kupfer, J. M., Perel, J. M., Cornes, C., Jarrett, D. B., Mallinger, A. G. … Grochocinski, V. J. (1990). Three-year outcome for maintenance therapies in recurrent depression. *Archives of General Psychiatry, 47*(12), 1093–1099.

Fresco, D. M., Segal, Z. V., Buis, T., & Kennedy, S. (2007). Relationship of posttreatment decentering and cognitive reactivity to relapse in major depression. *Journal of Consulting and Clinical Psychology, 75*(3), 447–455.

Fresco, D. M., Moore, M. T., van Dulmen, M. H. M., Segal, Z. V., Ma, S. H., Teasdale, J. D., Williams, J. M. G. (2007). Initial psychometric properties of the experiences questionnaire: Validation of a self-report measure of decentering. *Behaviour Therapy, 38*(3), 234–246.

Germer, C. K. (2005). Mindfulness: What is it: What does it matter? In C. K. Germer, R. D. Siegel, & P. R. Fulton (Eds), *Mindfulness and psychotherapy* (pp. 3-27. New York: Guilford.

Geschwind, N., Peeters, F., Huibers, M., van Os, J., & Wichers, M. (2012). Efficacy of mindfulness-based cognitive therapy in relation to prior history of depression: Randomised controlled trial. *British Journal of Psychiatry, 201*, 320–325.

Godfrin, K. A., & van Heeringen, C. (2010). The effects of mindfulness-based cognitive therapy on recurrence of depressive episodes, mental health and quality of life: A randomized controlled study. *Behaviour Research and Therapy, 48*, 738–746.

Grabovac, A. D., Lau, M. A., & Willett, B. R. (2011). Mechanisms of mindfulness: A Buddhist psychological model. *Mindfulness, 2*(3), 154–166.

Hamilton M. (1960). Rating scale for depression. *Journal of Neurology, Neurosurgery, and Psychiatry, 23*, 56–62.

Hamilton, E. W., & Abramson, L. Y. (1983). Cognitive patterns and major depressive disorder: A longitudinal study in a hospital setting. *Journal of Abnormal Psychology, 92*(2), 173–184.

Hanh, T. C. (1976). *The miracle of being awake: A manual on meditation for the use of young activists*. Bankok, Thailand: Sathirakoses-Nagapradipa Foundation.

Hayes, A. M., & Feldman, G. (2004). Clarifying the construct of mindfulness in the context of emotion regulation and the process of change in therapy. *Clinical Psychology: Science and Practice, 11*(3), 255–262.

Ingram, R. E., & Hollon, S. D. (1986). Cognitive therapy of depression from an information processing perspective. In R. E. Ingram (Ed.), *Information processing approaches to clinical psychology* (pp. 259–281). San Diego: Academic Press.

Ingram, R. E., Miranda, J., & Segal, Z. V. (1998). *Cognitive vulnerability to depression*. New York: Guilford.

Judd, L. J. (1997). The clinical course of unipolar major depressive disorders. *Archives of General Psychiatry, 54*, 989–991.

Kabat-Zinn, J. (1990). *Full catastrophe living: Using the wisdom of your mind to face stress, pain and illness*. New York: Dell Publishing.

Keller, M. B., Lavori, P. W., Lewis, C. E., & Klerman, G. L. (1983). Predictors of relapse in major depressive disorder. *Journal of the American Medical Association, 250*(24), 3299–3304.

Kenny, M. A., & Williams, J. G. M. (2007). Treatment-resistant depressed patients show a good response to mindfulness-based cognitive therapy. *Behaviour Research and Therapy, 45*(3), 617–625.

Kessler, R. C., McGonagle, K. A., Zhao, S., Nelson, C. B., Hughs, M., Eshleman, S., Wittchen H. U., & Kendler, K. S. (1994). Lifetime and 12-month prevalence of DSM-III-R psychiatric disorders in the United States: Results from the National Comorbidity Survey. *Archives of General Psychiatry, 51*(1), 8–19.

Kingston, T., Dooley, B., Bates, A., Lawlor, E., & Malong, K. (2007). Mindfulness-based cognitive therapy for residual depressive symptoms. *Psychology and Psychotherapy: Theory, Research and Practice, 80*(2), 193–203.

Kraemer, H. C., Kazdin, A. E., Offord, D. R., Kessler, R. C., Jensen, P. S., & Kupfer, D. J. (1997). Coming to terms with the terms of risk. *Archives of General Psychiatry, 54*, 337–343.

Kupfer, D. J., Frank, E., Perel, J. M., Cornes, C., Mallinger, A. G., Thase, M. E., McEachran, A. B., & Grochocinski, V. J. (1992). Five-year outcome for maintenance therapies in recurrent depression. *Archives of General Psychiatry, 49*(10), 769–773.

Kuyken, W., Byford, S., Taylor, R. S., Watkins, E., Holden, E. White, K. … Teasdale, J. D. (2008). Mindfulness-based cognitive therapy to prevent relapse in recurrent depression. *Journal of Consulting and Clinical Psychology*, *76*(6), 966–978.

Lau, M. A., & Yu, A. R. (2008). Using mindfulness-based cognitive therapy to reduce cognitive reactivity: A risk factor of depressive relapse. Paper presented at the ABCT Annual Meeting, Orlando, Florida.

Lau, M. A., Segal, Z. V., & Williams, J. M. G. (2004). Teasdale's differential activation hypothesis: Implications for mechanisms of depressive relapse and suicidal behaviour. *Behaviour Research and Therapy*, *42*, 1001–1017.

Lau, M. A., Bishop, S. R., Segal, Z. V., Buis, T., Anderson, N. D., Carlson, L. … Devins, G. (2006). The Toronto Mindfulness Scale: Development and validation. *Journal of Clinical Psychology*, *62*, 1445–1467.

Lewinsohn, P. M., Allen, N. B., Seeley, J. R., & Gotlib, I. H. (1999). First onset versus recurrence of depression: Differential processes of psychosocial risk. *Journal of Abnormal Psychology*, *108*, 483–489.

Linehan, M. M. (1993). *Cognitive–behavioral treatment of borderline personality disorder*. New York: Guilford.

Lyubomirsky, S., & Nolen-Hoeksema, S. (1995). Effects of self-focused rumination on negative thinking and interpersonal problem solving. *Journal of Personality and Social Psychology*, *69*(1), 176–190.

Ma, S. H., & Teasdale, J. D. (2004). Mindfulness-based cognitive therapy for depression: Replication and exploration of differential relapse prevention effects. *Journal of Consulting and Clinical Psychology*, *72*, 31–40.

Meadows, G. N., Shawyer, F., Enticott, J. C., Graham, A. L., Judd, F., Martin, P. R. … Segal, Z. (2014). *Australian & New Zealand Journal of Psychiatry*, *48*, 743–755.

Monroe, S. M., & Simons, A. D. (1991). Diathesis: Stress theories in the context of life stress research. *Psychological Bulletin*, *110*(3), 406–425.

Moore, R. G., Hayhurst, H., & Teasdale, J. D. (1996). Measure of awareness and coping in autobiographical memory: Instructions for administering and coding. Unpublished manuscript, Department of Psychiatry, University of Cambridge.

Murray, C. J. L., & Lopez, A. D. (1997). Alternative projections of mortality and disability by cause 1990–2020: Global Burden of Disease Study. *Lancet*, *349*, 1498–1504.

Nolen-Hoeksema, S. (1991). Responses to depression and their effects on the duration of depressive episodes. *Journal of Abnormal Psychology*, *100*, 569–582.

Nolen-Hoeksema, S., & Morrow, J. (1991). A prospective study of depression and posttraumatic stress symptoms after a natural disaster: The 1989 Loma Prieta earthquake. *Journal of Personality and Social Psychology*, *61*, 115–121.

Paykel, E. S., Scott, J., Teasdale, J. G. M., Johnson, A. L., Garland, A., Moore, R. … Pope, M. (1999). Prevention of relapse in residual depression by cognitive therapy. *Archives of General Psychiatry*, *56*(9), 829–835.

Post, R. M. (1992). Transduction of psychological stress into the neurobiology of recurrent affective disorder. *American Journal of Psychiatry, 149*, 999–1010.

Ree, M. J., & Craigie, M. A. (2007). Outcomes following mindfulness-based cognitive therpay in a heterogeneous sample of adult outpatients. *Behavioural and Cognitive Psychotherapy, 24*(2), 70–86.

Scher, C. D., Ingram, R. E., & Segal, Z. V. (2005). Cognitive vulnerability: Empirical evaluation of construct activation and cognitive diatheses in unipolar depression. *Clinical Psychology Review, 25*(4), 487–510.

Segal, Z. V., Gemar, M., & Williams, S. (1999). Differential cognitive response to a mood challenge following successful cognitive therapy or pharmacotherapy for unipolar depression. *Journal of Abnormal Psychology, 108*, 3–10.

Segal, Z. V., Teasdale, J. D., & Williams, J. M. G. (2004). Mindfulness-based cognitive therapy. In S. C. Hayes, V. M. Follette, & M. M. Linehan (Eds), *Mindfulness and Acceptance: Expanding the Cognitive-Behavioral Tradition* (pp. 45–65). New York: Guilford.

Segal, Z. V., Williams, J. M. G., & Teasdale, J. D. (2002). *Mindfulness-based cognitive therapy for depression: A new approach for preventing relapse.* New York: Guilford.

Segal, Z. W., Williams, J. M. G., Teasdale, J. D., & Gemer, M. (1996). A cognitive science perspective on kindling and episode sensitization in recurrent affective disorder. *Psychological Medicine, 26*(2), 371–380.

Segal, Z. V., Kennedy, S., Gemar, M., Hood, K., Pedersen, R., & Buis, T. (2006). Cognitive reactivity to sad mood provocation and the prediction of depressive relapse. *Archives of General Psychiatry, 63*, 749–755.

Segal, Z. V., Bieling, P., Young, T., MacQueen, G., Cooke, R., Martin, L. … Levitan, R. D. (2010). Antidepressant monotherapy vs sequential pharmacotherapy and mindfulness-based cognitive therapy, or placebo, for relapse prophylaxis in recurrent depression. *Archives General Psychiatry, 67*, 1256–1264.

Shapiro, S. L., Carlson, L. E., Astin, J. A., & Freedman, B. (2006). Mechanisms of mindfulness. *Journal of Clinical Psychology, 62*(3), 373–386.

Shapiro, S. L., & Schwartz, G. E. (2000). Intentional systemic mindfulness: An integrative model for self-regulation and health. *Advances in Mind–Body Medicine, 15*, 128–134.

Shea, M. T., Elkin, I., Imber, S. D., Sotsky, F. M., Watkins, J. T., Collins, J. F. … Parloff, M. B. (1992). Course of depressive symptoms over follow-up: Findings from the NIMH treatment of depression collaborative research program. *Archives of General Psychiatry, 49*, 782–787.

Silverman, J. S., Silverman, J. A., & Eardley, D. A. (1984). Do maladaptive attitudes cause depression? *Archives of General Psychiatry, 41*(1), 28–30.

Simons, A. D., Garfield, S. L., & Murphy, G. E. (1984). The process of change in cognitive therapy and pharmacotherapy for depression: Changes in mood and cognition. *Archives of General Psychiatry, 41*(1), 45–51.

Simons, A. D., Murphy, G. E., Levine, J. L., & Wetzel, R. D. (1986). Cognitive therapy and pharmacotherapy for depression: Sustained improvement over one year. *Archives of General Psychiatry*, *43*, 43–50.

Teasdale, J. D. (1988). Cognitive vulnerability to persistent depression. *Cognition and Emotion*, *2*, 247–274.

Teasdale, J. D. (1999). Metacognition, mindfulness and the modification of mood disorders. *Clinical Psychology & Psychotherapy*, *6*(2), 146–155.

Teasdale, J. D., & Barnard, P. J. (1993). *Affect, cognition and change: Re-modelling depressive thought*. Hilldale, NJ: Lawrence Erlbaum.

Teasdale, J. D., Segal, Z. V., & Williams, J. M. G. (1995). How does cognitive therapy prevent relapse and why should attentional control (mindfulness) training help? *Behaviour Research and Therapy*, *33*, 25–39.

Teasdale, J. D., Moore, R. G., Hayhurst, H., Pope, M., Williams, S., & Segal, Z. V. (2002). Metacognitive awareness and prevention of relapse in depression: Empirical evidence. *Journal of Consulting and Clinical Psychology*, *70*, 275–287.

Teasdale, J. D., Segal, Z. V., Williams, J. M. G., Ridgeway, V. A., Soulsby, J. M., & Lau, M. A. (2000). Prevention of relapse/recurrence in major depression by mindfulness-based cognitive therapy. *Journal of Consulting and Clinical Psychology*, *68*, 615–623.

Treynor, W., Gonzalez, R., & Nolen-Hoeksema, S. (2003). Rumination reconsidered: A psychometric analysis. *Cognitive Therapy and Research*, *27*, 247–259.

van Aalderen, J. R., Donders, A. R. T., Giommi, F., Spinhoven, P., Barendregt, H. P., & Speckens, A. E. M. (2012). The efficacy of mindfulness-based cognitive therapy in recurrent depressed patients with and without a current depressive episode: A randomized controlled trial. *Psychological Medicine*, *42*, 989–1001.

van der Velden, A.M., Kuyken, W., Wattar, U., Crane, C., Pallesen, K. J., Dahlgaard, J., Fjorback, L. O., & Piet, J. (2015). A systematic review of mechanisms of change in mindfulness-based cognitive therapy in the treatment of recurrent major depressive disorder. *Clinical Psychology Review*, *37*, 26–39.

Watkins, E., Teasdale, J. G. M., & Williams, R. M. (2003). Decentering and distraction reduce overgeneral autobiographical memory in depression. *Psychological Medicine*, *30*(4), 911–920.

Weissman, A. N., & Beck, A. T. (1979). The dysfunctional attitudes scale: A validation study. *Dissertations Abstracts International*, *40*, 1389–1390B (University Microfilm N. 79–19, 533).

Wells, A. (2006). Detached mindfulness in cognitive therapy: A metacognitive analysis and ten techniques. *Journal of Rational–Emotive and Cognitive Behavior Therapy*, *2*, 337–355.

Wells, A., & Matthews, G. (1994). *Attention and emotion: A clinical perspective*. Hove, England: Psychology Press.

Wells, A., & Matthews, G. (1996). Modelling cognition in emotional disorder: The S-Ref model. *Behaviour Research and Therapy*, *34*, 881–888.

Williams, J. M. G., Watts, F. N., MacLeod, C., & Mathews, A. (1997). *Cognitive psychology and emotional disorders* (2nd edn). Chichester: John Wiley & Sons, Ltd.

Williams, J. M. G., Alatiq, Y., Crane, C., Barnhoffer, T., Fennell, M. J. V., Duggan, D. S., Hepburn, S., & Goodwin, G. M. (2008). Mindfulness-based cognitive therapy (MBCT) in bipolar disorder: Preliminary evaluation of immediate effects on between-episode functioning. *Journal of Affective Disorders*, *107*, 275–279.

Williams, J. M. G., Crane, C., Barnhoffer, T., Brennan, K., Duggan, D. S., Fennell, M. J. V. … Russell, I. T. (2014). Mindfulness-based cognitive therapy for preventing relapse in recurrent depression: A randomized dismantling trial. *Journal of Consulting and Clinical Psychology*, *82*, 275–286.

Williams, R. M. (1988). Individual differences in the effects of mood on cognition. Unpublished doctoral dissertation, University of Oxford.

Witkiewitz, K., Marlatt, A. G., & Walker, D. (2005). Mindfulness-based relapse prevention for alcohol and substance use disorders. *Journal of Cognitive Psychotherapy*, *19*(3), 211–228.

9

Behavioural Activation Theory

Roselinde H. Kaiser, Samuel Hubley and Sona Dimidjian

Behavioural approaches to depression are characterized by explicit targeting of behaviour change to alleviate depression and prevent relapse. Such approaches are predicated on the theory that, by altering behaviour, it is possible to alter mood, cognition, and biology. Interest in behavioural treatments has gained momentum in recent years, and both clinical and related basic research is rapidly evolving. Such developments build on a long history of behavioural theory and its application to the problem of depression. The current chapter explores central tenets of the behavioural theory of depression and the ways in which they inform contemporary behavioural activation (BA) approaches to depression.

Behavioural Theory of Depression: Early Models and Core Concepts

Contemporary BA treatments are rooted in behavioural theory influenced by both classical and operant conditioning principles. Wolpe's (1958) emphasis on reciprocal inhibition was the first application of classical principles of conditioning in the clinical realm. These principles specify the ways in which behaviour is a function of learned associations between what we do and particular contexts or stimuli: for example, a person who performed poorly on an important work task may become conditioned to associate the office with a sense of failure and hence may avoid going to work. Wolpe's therapeutic approach was based on the pairing of a problem behaviour with

---

Treating Depression: MCT, CBT and Third Wave Therapies, First Edition.
Edited by Adrian Wells and Peter L. Fisher.

an incompatible adaptive behaviour – a pairing that aimed to suppress the problem behaviour. Wolpe's emphasis on the learned emotional associations with particular contexts and stimuli, and on the clinical value of learning incompatible behavioural responses in such contexts, was an early precursor to many of the strategies of contemporary BA approaches.

While Wolpe focused upon classical conditioning, Thorndike (1911) pioneered the theoretical precursor to operant conditioning in his formulation of the 'law of effect'. Thorndike proposed that actions that result in favourable effects are more likely to be repeated than actions that cause unfavourable effects. Thorndike's seminal research on such 'instrumental learning' provided the foundation upon which later behaviour theory was built – in particular, Skinner's frequently cited operant conditioning model of learning (Skinner, 1953; 1957). The concept of operant conditioning expands upon the law of effect to explain behaviour as a result of reinforcement contingencies, i.e., animals learn to engage in or refrain from behaviours depending on the type of consequence that resulted. For example, in a series of seminal studies, Skinner showed that rats learned to associate pressing a lever with receipt of food, and subsequently increased the frequency of their lever-pressing behaviour (Skinner, 1953). Thus, in Skinner's model of operant conditioning, behaviour is determined by positive reinforcement (the addition of a stimulus that serves to increase the occurrence of a behaviour), negative reinforcement (the removal of a stimulus that serves to increase the occurrence of a behaviour), positive punishment (the addition of a stimulus that serves to decrease the occurrence of a behaviour), and negative punishment (the removal of a stimulus that serves to decrease the occurrence of a behaviour) (Skinner, 1957; 1974). These four categories of contingency were identified as necessary and sufficient factors in explaining the likelihood that an organism would, or would not, repeat a behaviour.

Other key principles articulated by Skinner – and important for later behavioural theories of depression – were extinction, natural versus arbitrary reinforcement, and schedules of reinforcement. In extinction, a behaviour is dropped from the animal's repertoire if that behaviour is no longer reinforced. Natural reinforcers can be defined as stimuli that are inherently reinforcing (e.g., food when one is hungry), whereas arbitrary reinforcers hold reinforcing properties only through repeated pairing with natural reinforcers (e.g., money). Finally, Skinner emphasized the temporal sequence of reinforcement. He suggested that immediate reinforcement or punishment is more powerful than delayed reinforcement or punishment and that the schedule of reinforcement affects the target behaviour's resilience to extinction. A behaviour is more easily learned when it is reinforced continuously; however, a behaviour that is reinforced intermittently is less vulnerable to extinction.

In linking operant conditioning to human psychopathology, Skinner also directly addressed the application of these principles to depression. For example, Skinner suggested that the absence of reinforcement leads to decreased frequency of adaptive behaviour (extinction), which in turn leads to loss of confidence, agency, and ultimately depression. In addition, Skinner proposed that excessive punishment can contribute to depression, either because behaviours are directly punished, or because punishment makes positive reinforcement less likely; in both cases the frequency of adaptive behaviours is decreased (Skinner, 1974).

The basic tenets of Skinner's learning theory were extended by clinical researchers to address more fully the phenomenon of depression. In particular, Ferster (1973) and Lewinsohn (1974) were leaders in developing behavioural models and in generating empirical research paradigms to test core principles and applied treatment strategies. Lewinsohn's basic model contained three central assumptions regarding reinforcement for the depressed individual. These assumptions were: (1) low rates of response-contingent positive reinforcement directly elicit depressed behaviours such as sadness, fatigue, and various physiological experiences; (2) reinforcement is limited due to idiographic factors – such as a restricted relationship with reinforcers (low impact of reinforcement, narrowed range of activities engaged in that are potentially reinforcing), a low availability of reinforcers in the environment, and an inability to elicit such reinforcement; and (3) the low rate of response-contingent positive reinforcement is a sufficient explanation for the impoverished behavioural repertoire of the depressed individual (Lewinsohn, 1974). Each of these key assumptions plays an important role in the onset and maintenance of depression, and each is explored in theoretical and empirical contexts below.

The driving concept in Lewinsohn's behavioural model is described by the first assumption: that the depressed individual receives reduced response-contingent reinforcement for an active and healthy engagement with his or her environment and that, in turn, this low level of reinforcement directly leads to the experience of depression. For example, the depressed person engages in fewer activities over time and enters a reduced reinforcement cycle in which activity is decreased, therefore positive reinforcement is decreased, therefore the person becomes more passive and depressed.

While the first assumption establishes the relationship between reduced positive reinforcement and negative mood, the second offers possible reasons for this reduced reinforcement. The amount of positive reinforcement in a person's daily life is highly variable and is influenced by idiographic factors such as the range and impact of the reinforcement, its availability, and the individual's ability to elicit reinforcement. Decreased reward from interpersonal exchanges may stem from a paucity of reinforcers in one's context (for example, the low availability of interpersonal partners); from a diminished capacity for reward (for example, a reduced enjoyment of social interaction); or from inadequate skills in accessing potentially available reinforcers (for example, poor social skills).

Finally, the third assumption predicts a future reduction of reward-seeking behaviour such that the depressed person fails to engage in activities because the learned association between active behaviour and reinforcement is extinguished. Activities that are not associated with reinforcement are less likely to be repeated and, as the association is weakened, the behaviour is dropped from the individual's repertoire of activities. In examining the changing behavioural repertoire of the depressed person, two important distinctions made by Lewinsohn's model must be noted. First, the reinforcement deprivation is unique both in terms of contingency and in terms of the class of behaviour to which it is linked; reduced reinforcement is specific to response-contingent, non-depressed behaviour. The emphasis on contingency is an important one. Lewinsohn noted, for instance, that 'the degree to which the individual's behavior is maintained by reinforcement is assumed to be the critical antecedent condition for the occurrence of depression, rather than the total amount of reinforcement received' (Lewinsohn, 1974, p. 160). In other words, arbitrary rewards that are not contingent upon activity are not likely to decrease the individual's depression. Second, the reinforcement deprivation is exclusive to non-depressed behaviour, such as active engagement with the environment or social contacts. In contrast, reinforcement for depressed (e.g., non-adaptive, avoidant) behaviour may be comparatively increased, in turn increasing the likelihood that depressed behaviour will occur more frequently in the future. Reinforcement for depressive behaviour may be positive (for example, increased attention or concern on the part of family members or friends) or negative (for example, decreased exposure to social evaluation by peers).

In behaviour theory closely parallel to that of Lewinsohn, Ferster highlighted the importance of increased avoidance and escape activity on the part of the depressed person, describing such behaviour as a function of 'aversive control' (Ferster, 1973; 1974). For example, a depressed individual may find it difficult to leave the house and confront a critical co-worker. If the individual stays home from work and therefore avoids this interpersonal (and likely aversive) context, staying home is reinforced. Ferster suggested that, as depression escalates, the individual is caught in a downward spiral of avoidance maintained by negative reinforcement, in which avoidance behaviours dominate the repertoire. Over time, such behaviours are extended to novel situations at the expense of active non-depressed behaviour. Hence the individual's response repertoire is increasingly restricted and passive, as negative reinforcement contingencies for depressed behaviours reduce more active non-depressed behaviours. The behavioural models of Lewinsohn and Ferster thus emphasize compatible aspects of the depressed person's developing reinforcement schedule; active pursuit of response-contingent positive events is reduced at the same time as avoidance and escape behaviours are increased, which results in withdrawal and passivity along with sad mood.

Finally, Carilyn Fuchs and Lynn Rehm proposed a behavioural model of depression congruent with those of Lewinsohn and Ferster that emphasized self-control. Fuchs and Rehm (1977) highlighted three processes that increase the risk of depression and maintain depression over time. These are deficits in self-monitoring (undue focus on negative events and on immediate vs delayed consequences), self-evaluation (comparison to excessive standards), and self-reinforcement (low rates of positive reinforcement and high rates of punishment). Fuchs and Rehm's emphasis on both self-monitoring and reinforcement represented another early example of a behavioural approach to depression. The deficient control processes they highlighted represent a clarification of a particular type of reinforcement that is lacking in the depressed person's life and contributes to the maintenance of depression.

The Empirical Status of the Theory

Research conducted in the 1970s by Lewinsohn and colleagues provided some initial evidence for the behavioural theory of depression. Researchers investigated the theoretical relationship between response-contingent positive reinforcement and mood in a systematic manner, requiring first that the total amount of such reinforcement received by the depressed person be less than that received by non-depressed persons and, second, that fluctuations in the intensity of depression covary with the rate of reinforcement.

Early research on the behavioural model of depression was pursued using a number of useful monitoring tools, both retrospective and longitudinal. First, the Pleasant Events Schedule (PES) is a 320-item measure that asks respondents to indicate the frequency of pleasurable events over the past month (typically events in which the person must actively participate) and to rate the subjective enjoyment associated with each activity (MacPhillamy & Lewinsohn, 1972, 1974). Second, the Unpleasant Events Schedule (UPES) is a 320-item measure that lists the frequency of negative events as well as the subjective aversiveness of each event (Lewinsohn & Talkington, 1979).

Empirical studies using the PES and the UPES with depressed, psychiatric control, and normal samples revealed that depressed individuals engage in a lower rate of pleasant activities than their non-depressed counterparts (Lewinsohn & Graf, 1973; Lewinsohn & Libet, 1972; MacPhillamy & Lewinsohn, 1974; Lewinsohn & Amenson, 1978). However, another early study suggested that depressed individuals largely encounter unpleasant events with the same frequency as non-depressed persons (Lewinsohn & Talkington, 1979). In more recent research exploring specific behaviours that are reduced in the depressed person's repertoire, a daily diary study suggested that depressed college students engage in a lower rate of social, physical, and academic activities when compared to their non-depressed counterparts (Hopko & Mullane, 2008). This evidence provides intriguing support for the behavioural model, and further longitudinal work may serve to isolate the relationship between the frequency of pleasurable events and changes in depression over time.

Researchers were additionally interested in isolating the functional relationship between response-contingent rewards and changes in mood monitored over time. Lewinsohn and colleagues integrated daily mood-monitoring assessment in several empirical explorations. In this research, a significant association was found between mood and the number of pleasant activities (Lewinsohn & Libet, 1972) as well as a high correlation between the enjoyability of a pleasant event and mood rating (Lewinsohn & Amenson, 1978). Notably, recent research has provided support for the relationship between activation and positive mood. Hopko, Armento, Cantu, Chambers, and Lejuez (2003) conducted mood-monitoring research that supported and extended Lewinsohn and colleagues' exploration, not only by monitoring the relationship between behaviour and reward on a daily basis but also by closely tracking that relationship every two hours. Researchers found not only that depressed participants report less general activity and higher negative affect, but also that there was a contiguous relationship between reward value and each activity (Hopko, Armento, et al., 2003; see also Hopko & Mullane, 2008). Taken as a whole, this research indicates that changes in reinforcement are highly related to mood and to changes in mood over time.

As was noted above, the subjective enjoyability (or aversiveness) of an event is an important determinant of the reinforcement potential of that event; hence Lewinsohn and colleagues made it a point to include such ratings in the PES and the UPES. The point that there are idiographic differences in people's reinforcement potential is inherent in the second major assumption of Lewinsohn's behavioural theory of depression and formed another important research focus. The theory postulates that the depressed person not only engages in a lower rate of response-contingent reinforcing activities, but also has a restricted reinforcement potential due to a lower subjective impact of reinforcement and to a decreased range of activities perceived as reinforcing. This restricted reinforcement potential has been supported by research indicating that depressed persons report a lower level of pleasure and lower perceived potential for being reinforced by activities (MacPhillamy & Lewinsohn, 1974); additionally they report engaging in a restricted range of pleasurable activities (Lewinsohn & Graf, 1973; MacPhillamy & Lewinsohn, 1974). In research by Hopko and colleagues, it was found that depressed individuals report not only a lower degree of pleasure obtained via daily activities but also a decreased expectation of future reward as a result of current behaviour (Hopko, Amento, et al., 2003; Hopko, Lejuez, Ruggiero, & Eifert, 2003; Hopko & Mullane, 2008). Thus depressed persons may not only be characterized by lower subjective enjoyment of reinforcing events, but also be more pessimistic about the possibility of future rewards; this supports the third theoretical point outlined by Lewinsohn's model, which indicates that a weakened association between behaviour and reinforcement essentially puts the depressed person on an extinction schedule, eliminating active behaviours from his or her repertoire over time.

Interestingly, research has also indicated that depressed persons may experience negative events as being more punishing than do their non-depressed counterparts. Although the frequency of unpleasant events appeared to be similar across groups, the aversive impact of the events was rated higher by depressed persons in both retrospective report (Lewinsohn & Talkington, 1979) and daily monitoring (Lewinsohn & Amenson,

1978). In research that conducted the physiological assessment of autonomic response to aversive stimuli (electroshock), depressed individuals showed higher galvanic skin response during shock than non-depressed participants (Lewinsohn, Lobitz, & Wilson, 1973), supported the idea that depressed individuals are more sensitive to punishment. Thus, in comparison to non-depressed individuals, the depressed individual is characterized by a lower rate of activity, has a narrowed behavioural repertoire of possible reinforcing activities, and receives less reinforcement from pleasant events and more punishment from unpleasant events.

In conjunction with a uniquely restricted relationship with reinforcers, the depressed individual is hypothesized in Lewinsohn's model to find the availability of reinforcement restricted and to be less skilful in eliciting reinforcement from the environment. In particular, the depressed individual may have difficulty eliciting interpersonal reinforcement due to poor social skills or anxiety in social contexts. Research in this area found that depressed individuals interacting in small groups showed a lower rate of interpersonal actions, elicited fewer actions from other people, emitted a lower rate of positive reactions, and were slower to respond appropriately to others (Libet & Lewinsohn, 1973).

Taken together, the results of early empirical research on basic conditioning and the results of later research designed to test the behavioural theory of depression yield a significant body of literature supporting the model. Depressed persons appear to be characterized by lower rates of response-contingent rewards in their daily lives, and their experience of pleasurable events covaries with changes in mood. Additionally, depressed persons reportedly engage in a restricted range of activities, obtain less pleasure from these activities than their non-depressed peers, are more sensitive to punishment associated with unpleasant events, and demonstrate a lower ability to elicit reinforcement from their interpersonal environment.

Early Behavioural Treatments for Depression: Key Elements

Given the growing empirical support for the behavioural theory of depression as explicated by Lewinsohn and colleagues, the logical next step was to investigate the potential for changing a depressed individual's reinforcement schedule and thus for changing his or her mood. In other words, the next step was to apply the theory in a clinical context by treating depression through behavioural methods. Among these early therapeutic approaches, the BA approach developed by Lewinsohn and colleagues has been the most influential (Lewinsohn, Sullivan, & Grosscup, 1980). This treatment took the principles of functional assessment of behaviour and reinforcement deprivation, applied them to concrete intervention techniques, and outlined how to use them in clinical practice.

Given the driving hypothesis that depressed individuals are less active in seeking reinforcement and more restricted in their behaviours, activity monitoring was a major emphasis of the Lewinsohn approach to behavioural therapy. In the Lewinsohn approach, clients first complete activity monitoring in the form of the PES and UPES; then an idiographic profile is compiled indicating each client's response to various events and the frequency of those events in her or his daily life. This profile is then summarized in an activity schedule that serves to track the correlation between activity and mood fluctuations over the course of treatment and to identify activation targets for increasing positive reinforcement in the client's environment.

The next treatment component, building upon the activity schedule, consists of increasing the patient's experience of pleasant events – both those that are intrinsically rewarding and those that lead to social reinforcement (Lewinsohn et al., 1980). Intrinsically rewarding activities are those that are enjoyable in and of themselves; this category includes physically pleasurable activities, such as going for a walk or eating a favorite meal. In scheduling these activities, the therapist and the client work together; they begin with easily accomplished and available activities and progress over time to more challenging tasks. Behaviours that lead to social reinforcement are also important targets of treatment; this category includes engaging in conversation with someone new or participating in team-oriented activities with colleagues. Central to obtaining social reinforcement is the development of proactive interpersonal skills. Social reinforcement is a powerful source of reward, but pursuit of this reinforcement requires additional practice and skills training. Thus, in the Lewinsohn model, the client and the therapist work closely together not only in identifying activity targets but also in preparing the client with skills training and role playing, so as to maximize the likelihood of successful reinforcement. As clients are increasingly activated and build a skill set, they tend to become more confident, to exert more control over reinforcement contingencies, and to make important gains.

The treatment structure outlined by Lewinsohn follows a general course: the therapist presents the rationale for behaviour therapy, conducts a functional analysis using the PES and the UPES, establishes a system for future analysis (usually the activity schedule), and works with the client to pinpoint important person–environment interactions that are related to the client's depression (Lewinsohn et al., 1980). Together, the therapist and the client establish therapy activation goals that are to be implemented and monitored in the client's daily context. A unique and critical aspect of behavioural therapy is the emphasis on homework performed outside the therapy session; in session, the therapist and client work together to identify appropriate activation targets and to develop the skills necessary for obtaining reinforcement from the environment. Outside the session, behavioural assignments and experience of reinforcement are accomplished as the client interacts with her or his real-world environment. The long-term gains of behaviour therapy are a result of the client's acquisition of skills and learning that are (1) reinforced between sessions as a result of activation homework and (2) generalizable to future events and novel circumstances (Lewinsohn & Libet, 1972; Lewinsohn et al., 1980).

Early Behavioural Treatments for Depression: Evidence Base

Early behavioural treatments for depression were subject to empirical scrutiny in the 1970s and 1980s. A number of clinical trials were conducted that examined the efficacy of behavioural approaches by comparing behavioural therapies to other forms of psychotherapy and antidepressant medication. This early period of comparative trials highlighted the potential value of behavioural theory and expanded its application to the treatment of depression.

Several key research projects compared behavioural treatments to alternative therapies and a number of intriguing findings emerged from this body of work. For instance, Rehm's self-control model was tested among volunteers who met criteria for depression according to the Minnesota Multiphasic Personality Inventory (MMPI-II). Self-monitoring and self-reinforcement via activity scheduling were compared between a group of clients who received self-control therapy, a non-specific treatment group, and a waitlist control group. Results indicated that self-control participants showed significantly greater reduction in global measures of depression in both self-report and behavioural methodologies (Fuchs & Rehm, 1977).

Wilson (1982) compared the efficacy of two behavioural treatments – task assignment (similar to Lewinsohn's model for activity scheduling) and relaxation training – to a minimal contact control treatment in volunteers with high levels of depressive symptoms as defined by the Beck Depression Inventory (BDI). All three treatments were delivered with either amitriptyline or placebo. Results showed that both task assignment and relaxation training were associated with marked improvement on measures of depressive symptoms as well as with increased rates of reinforcement. The addition of medication appeared to speed the participants' response to treatment, but treatment gains for both interventions and across medication versus placebo conditions were equivalent at follow-up (Wilson, 1982).

A third research study, headed by McLean and Hakstian (1979, 1990), compared the efficacy of non-specific psychotherapy, behaviour therapy, relaxation therapy, and medication, for clinically depressed clients. Analyses demonstrated that behaviour therapy was superior to all other interventions at post-treatment and at follow-up, on measures of both depressive symptoms and social adjustment. It was proposed that behavioural therapy is particularly effective in treating depression on account of its highly structured nature, its focus on activation and social learning, and its ability to foster a sense of mastery in clients (McLean & Hakstian, 1979).

In a comparison of behaviour therapy with cognitive therapy among women of low socioeconomic status, it was found that both treatments demonstrated equivalent benefits on measures of post-treatment depression; however, follow-up assessment revealed that symptoms of depression reported on the Hamilton Mood Rating Scale had decreased for behavioural therapy participants to a greater extent than for cognitive therapy participants (Comas-Diaz, 1981). The author speculated that the advantage of behaviour therapy is that skills taught in session and applied in homework between sessions can be extended or generalized so as to encompass new events after the conclusion of therapy.

Another research paradigm compared two therapies that differed in the type of reinforcement delivered by therapists: one used response-contingent positive reinforcement modeled after Lewinsohn, the other used non-response-contingent positive reinforcement, providedin the form of reflective statements and alliance building. Results revealed that, although treatment benefits were equivalent on most measures of depression, the intensity of depressive symptoms was reduced to a greater extent in the response-contingent treatment group (Padfield, 1976).

Finally, the efficacy of brief cognitive, behavioural, and relational/insight therapies was compared in a sample of elderly depressed individuals. The behavioural treatment closely followed the structure of Lewinsohn's intervention: it emphasized client education about the model and self-efficacy in tracking activity–mood relationships and it incorporated strategies of activation that included social skills, time management, and problem solving. Results showed that, while all three treatments resulted in comparable reductions in depression after treatment, at follow-up these improvements were maintained more effectively by clients in cognitive or behavioural treatments (Gallagher & Thomspon, 1982). Later research by the same group, comparing cognitive, behavioural, and psychodynamic therapies, again showed equivalent gains post-treatment (Thomspon, Gallagher, & Steinmetz Breckenridge, 1987).

In contrast to these findings, in a study with college students, Shaw (1977) compared cognitive, behavioural, and non-directive therapies with a waitlist control condition and found that cognitive group therapy was more effective in reducing depressive symptoms than behaviour modification or non-directive therapy. In addition, all therapy conditions were more effective than the waitlist condition. However, a one-month follow-up assessment showed a slight increase in depressive symptoms in the cognitive therapy group but stable depression scores in the behavioural group, suggesting that behavioural therapy may be more effective than cognitive therapy in preventing relapse.

Finally, several studies have examined the effects of behavioural and activation-oriented treatments on specific behaviours that are targeted by those treatments. For example, research by Hodgson (1981) indicated that behavioural treatment was associated with improved behavioural functioning. However, it is notable that the effects of behavioural treatment may be a general improvement in several domains of functioning rather than an improvement specific to the domain of behaviour that is targeted by therapeutic strategies. A study by Zeiss, Lewinsohn, and Munoz (1979) compared behavioural therapies that either focused on interpersonal skills or on pleasant events scheduling. Interestingly, researchers found that, while patients improved over time on dimensions of social interaction, behaviour that elicits positive reinforcement, and cognitive style, they did not differentially improve depending on treatment modality. Instead patients improved on most dimensions, whether those specific targets were focal points in therapy or not. In addition, some evidence suggests that cognitive therapies may also benefit behavioural functioning. A study by McNamara and Horan (1986) showed that cognitive interventions were associated with improvement in both cognitive style and behaviour, which suggests indirect effects of cognitive therapies on behavioural functioning.

Taken together, these early comparative trials provided the initial building blocks for an evidence base of behavioural and activation-oriented treatments for depressed individuals. Although the methodological rigor of many of these early studies was often lacking, they highlighted the promise of such interventions. The development of this evidence base was, however, stalled, as burgeoning interest in cognitive approaches to depression began to eclipse behavioural approaches during the 1980s and early 1990s. Rapid expansion of cognitive therapy research started to capture the clinical spotlight.

Integration with and Ascendance of Cognitive Therapy

The basic structure of BA, as developed by Lewinsohn and colleagues, strongly influenced future generations of behavioural treatments for depression. Moreover, as the approach of Lewinsohn and colleagues evolved, it was expanded to include a range of cognitive elements as well. The 'coping with depression' course represented a broader treatment approach, which integrated both cognitive and behavioural elements. This shift towards greater reliance on cognitive-change strategies was reflected in other treatments of depression as well, perhaps most notably in the development of cognitive therapy by Beck and colleagues.

The central premise underlying cognitive therapy is that depression results from dysfunctional cognitions (Beck, 1967). Although behavioural theory acknowledged that depressed individuals may be characterized by a negative cognitive style, cognitive change was not a primary target of intervention. In contrast, cognitive theorists assign a causal role to maladaptive cognitive style and isolate cognitions as a primary target of change in the context of therapy. Thus, while each model of depression allows for maladaptive cognitive and behavioural repertoires, the significance of each aspect is weighted differently in each, and therapeutic targets are prioritized according to these underlying theoretical differences. Cognitive therapy integrated behavioural activation strategies, but did so with the express purpose of changing cognition. Behavioural techniques (between-session assignments, activity monitoring and scheduling, and graded task assignment) were strongly emphasized early in cognitive therapy, particularly for more severely depressed patients. Note, however, that the goal of such assignments in the context of cognitive therapy is, typically, to test the validity or usefulness of thoughts associated with behaviours rather than to increase contact with rewards or to change contingencies, as one would attempt to do in behavioural therapy.

Numerous studies conducted in the 1980s and 1990s provided empirical support for the efficacy of cognitive therapy (Hollon & Ponniah, 2010; Hollon, Thase, & Markowitz, 2002). Nevertheless, as research on the efficacy of cognitive therapy accumulated, some researchers began to wonder what distinguished behavioural from cognitive treatment paradigms and what are the active ingredients of modern therapies.

Is Behavioural Activation Necessary and Sufficient?

While comparative research studies strive to find differences in efficacy between treatment packages, dismantling studies represent a more precise and controlled effort to isolate active treatment ingredients of larger treatment packages. Given the hybrid nature of cognitive therapy, which integrates the strategies of behavioural activation with cognitive restructuring tactics, the importance of identifying the necessary and sufficient treatment components became evident. In the mid-1990s Neil Jacobson and colleagues embarked upon a research programme that compared the following therapies: (1) the full cognitive therapy package (CT), with its focus on core dysfunctional schemas, automatic thoughts, and behavioural activation; (2) a version of cognitive therapy that focused on automatic thoughts (AT) and behavioural activation; and (3) a behavioural activation-only component (BA).

Notably, investigators paid special attention to therapists' adherence to each condition, ensuring that treatment protocols were closely followed and that interventions beyond the scope of the assigned therapy were not implemented. The resulting analysis revealed that the three conditions were comparably efficacious in treating acute depression and in preventing relapse over time (Jacobson et al., 1996; Gorter, Gollan, Dobson, & Jacobson, 1998). Jacobson and colleagues concluded that the BA component appeared to be not only a necessary but a sufficient component of cognitive therapy. It was, in their opinion, the active ingredient.

This study revitalized interest in purely behavioural approaches to depression and led Jacobson and colleagues to return to the early behavioural theories and approaches of Ferster (1973) and Lewinsohn (1974). In developing a more comprehensive behavioural approach that was not defined solely as a component of CT, contemporary BA drew upon these early behavioural roots (Jacobson, Martell, & Dimidjian, 2001). This approach was tested in a subsequent study conducted at the University of Washington, in which BA was compared to CT and antidepressant medication (ADM) in a placebo-controlled trial. Results suggested that BA was comparable in efficacy to ADM and superior to CT in the treatment of participants with moderate to severe depression (Dimidjian et al., 2006). Further analysis revealed that a subset of participants with moderate to severe depression, functional impairment, and reduced social support were more likely to respond to BA therapy than to CT (Coffman, Martell, Dimidjian, Gallop, & Hollon, 2007). Depression ratings after treatment revealed that, while 22% of the patients assigned to CT reported scores greater than 30 on the second edition of the Beck Depression Inventory (BDI-2), 0% of the patients assigned to BA reported scores this high (Coffman et al., 2007). A comparison of mean post-treatment BDI-2 scores demonstrates that non-responsive patients with scores above 20 reported significantly higher depression ratings in the CT than in the BA group: $t(68) = -5.73, p < .0001$, $d = 2.82$ (Coffman et al., 2007). Hence this study suggested that, for particularly challenging cases of depression, consistent focus on behavioural strategies may be preferable to a focus on cognitive change. Additionally, for more severely depressed participants, BA retained significantly more participants in treatment than did antidepressant medication (Dimidjian et al., 2006). For less severely depressed participants, all interventions performed comparably in terms of alleviating symptoms and the severity of depression (Dimidjian et al., 2006).

In parallel to the study at the University of Washington, Hopko and colleagues designed a treatment called "brief behavioural activation treatment for depression" (BATD), an intervention that aims to increase the frequency of overt behaviours that bring the client into contact with reinforcing environmental contingencies (Hopko, Lejuez, Ruggiero, et al., 2003). This treatment was specifically designed to be brief and to include a highly structured approach. Early case study and other empirical evidence was promising; BATD was associated with significant decrease in the symptoms of depression for individual clients (Lejuez, Hopko, LePage, Hopko, & McNeil, 2001; Hopko, Lejuez, & Hopko, 2004), psychiatric inpatients (Hopko, Lejuez,

LePage, et al., 2003) and cancer patients in primary care (Hopko, Bell, Armento, Hunt, & Lejuez, 2005). In addition, BATD was successful with clients reporting co-occurring diagnoses, such as anxiety (Hopko, Lejuez, LePage, et al., 2003; Hopko et al., 2004).

Behavioural activation strategies are also an increasing point of focus for the development of interventions for clients with more complex diagnostic profiles. Studies have explored the utility of BA for patients with comorbid depression and post-traumatic stress disorder (PTSD) (Jakupcak et al., 2006; Mulick & Naugle, 2004; Wagner, Zatzick, Ghesquiere, & Jurkovich, 2007). Other investigators have examined the use of BA interventions for patients with substance use disorders and depression (Magidson et al., 2011) or to target personality traits (Magidson, Roberts, Collado-Rodriguez, & Lejuez, 2014). Given the higher complexity of treating co-occurring diagnoses, these results are particularly encouraging.

In sum, the research studies presented above have contributed to constructing an evidence base for behavioural and activation-oriented treatments; they also outline the evolution of such treatments from basic behavioural models to treatment strategies predicated upon the theories of Skinner, Lewinsohn, and Ferster. Such findings suggest that BA and related treatments may be especially promising treatments for depression.

Summary

Behavioural theory suggests, most fundamentally, that humans develop behaviour as a result of interacting with the environment and of contingencies that increase or reduce the likelihood of repeating specific behaviours in the future. When an individual is less responsive to reinforcement or experiences a reduction in reinforcement in his or her environment, that individual is likely to become more passive and withdrawn and less inclined to seek reward. Such propositions form the basis of the behavioural model of depression. They also inform behavioural approaches to treatment by highlighting the central role of activation in alleviating depression. Rooted in early work by Ferster and Lewinsohn in the early 1970s, contemporary behavioural activation theory holds that increasing contact with response-contingent positive reinforcement for non-depressed behaviour plays a causal role in improving mood. Meanwhile, decreasing avoidant responses to life challenges and to negative emotions is also important in breaking the individual's habits of escape and withdrawal. As discussed in chapter 20, therapy techniques drawing on behavioural theory aim to increase activity and decrease avoidance in an idiographic manner, via functional analysis and guided activation (Jacobson et al., 2001; Dimidjian, Martell, Addis, & Herman-Dunn, 2008). These treatments build upon the core elements of behavioural theory and provide an exciting new arena of clinical research and application.

References

Beck, A. T. (1967). *Depression: Clinical, experimental and theoretical aspects.* New York: Harper & Row.

Coffman, S. J., Martell, C. R., Dimidjian, S., Gallop, R., & Hollon, S. D. (2007). Extreme nonresponse in cognitive therapy: Can behavioral activation succeed where cognitive therapy fails? *Journal of Consulting and Clinical Psychology, 75*, 531–541.

Comas-Diaz, L. (1981). Effects of cognitive and behavioral group treatment on the depressive symptomatology of Puerto Rican women. *Journal of Consulting and Clinical Psychology, 49*, 627–632.

Dimidjian, S., Martell, C. R., Addis, M. E., & Herman-Dunn, R. (2008). Behavioral activation for depression. In D. H. Barlow (Ed.), *Clinical handbook of psychological disorders: A step-by-step treatment manual* (4th edn, pp. 328–364). New York: Guilford.

Dimidjian, S., Hollon, S. D., Dobson, K. S., Schmaling, K. B., Kohlenberg, R. J., Addis, M. E. … Jacobson, N. S. (2006). Randomized trial of behavioral activation, cognitive therapy, and antidepressant medication in the acute treatment of adults with major depression. *Journal of Consulting and Clinical Psychology, 74*, 658–670.

Ferster, C. B. (1973). A functional analysis of depression. *American Psychologist*, 857–870.

Ferster, C. B. (1974). Behavioral approaches to depression. In R. J. Friedman & M. M. Katz (Eds), *The psychology of depression: Contemporary theory and research* (pp. 29–45). Oxford: Wiley & Sons.

Fuchs, C. Z., & Rehm, L. P. (1977). A self-control behavior therapy program for depression. *Journal of Consulting and Clinical Psychology, 45*, 206–215.

Gallagher, D. E., & Thompson, L. W. (1982). Treatment of major depressive disorder in older adult outpatients with brief psychotherapies. *Psychotherapy: Theory, Research and Practice, 19*, 482–490.

Gortner, E. T., Gollan, J. K., Dobson, K. S., & Jacobson, N. S. (1998). Cognitive–behavioral treatment for depression: Relapse prevention. *Journal of Consulting and Clinical Psychology, 66*, 377–384.

Hodgson, J. W. (1981). Cognitive versus behavioural–interpersonal approaches to the group treatment of depressed college students. *Journal of Counseling Psychology*, *28*, 243–249.

Hollon, S. D., & Ponniah, K. (2010). A review of empirically supported psychological therapies for mood disorders in adults. *Depression and Anxiety*, *27*(10), 891–932.

Hollon, S. D., Thase, M. E., & Markowitz, J. C. (2002). Treatment and prevention of depression. *Psychological Science*, *3*(9), 39–77.

Hopko, D. R., & Mullane, C. M. (2008). Exploring the relation of depression and overt behavior with daily diaries. *Behaviour Research and Therapy*, *46*, 1085–1089.

Hopko, D. R., Lejuez, C. W., & Hopko, S. D. (2004). Behavioral activation as an intervention for coexistent depressive and anxiety symptoms. *Clinical Case Studies*, *3*, 37–48.

Hopko, D. R., Lejuez, C. W., Ruggiero, K. J., & Eifert, G. H. (2003). Contemporary behavioral activation treatments for depression: Procedures, principles, and progress. *Clinical Psychology Review*, *23*, 699–717.

Hopko, D. R., Armento, M. E. A., Cantu, M. S., Chambers, L. L., & Lejuez, C. W. (2003). The use of daily diaries to assess the relations among mood state, overt behaviour, and reward value of activities. *Behaviour Research and Therapy*, *41*, 1137–1148.

Hopko, D. R., Bell, J. L., Armento, M. E. A., Hunt, M. K., & Lejuez, C. W. (2005). Behavior therapy for depressed cancer patients in primary care. *Psychotherapy: Theory, Research, Practice, Training*, *42*, 236–243.

Hopko, D. R., Lejuez, C. W., LePage, J. P., Hopko, S. D., & McNeil, D. W. (2003). A brief behavioral activation treatment for depression: A randomized pilot trial within an inpatient psychiatric hospital. *Behavior Modification*, *27*, 458–469.

Jacobson, N. S., Martell, C. R., & Dimidjian, S. (2001). Behavioral activation treatment for depression: Returning to contextual roots. *Clinical Psychology: Science and Practice*, *8*, 255–270.

Jacobson, N. S., Dobson, K. S., Truax, P. A., Addis, M. E., Koerner, K., Gollan, J. K., Gortner, E., & Prince, S. E. (1996). A component analysis of cognitive–behavioral treatment for depression. *Journal of Consulting and Clinical Psychology*, *64*, 295–304.

Jakupcak, M., Roberts, L. J., Martell, C., Mulick, P., Michael, S., Reed, R. … McFall, M. (2006). A pilot study of behavioral activation for veterans with posttraumatic stress disorder. *Journal of Traumatic Stress*, *19*, 387–391.

Lejuez, C. W., Hopko, D. R., LePage, J. P., Hopko, S. D., & McNeil, D. W. (2001). A brief behavioral activation treatment for depression. *Cognitive and Behavioral Practice*, *8*, 164–175.

Lewinsohn, P. M. (1974). A behavioral approach to depression. In R. J. Friedman & M. M. Katz (Eds), *The psychology of depression: Contemporary theory and research* (pp. 157–178). Oxford: John Wiley & Sons.

Lewinsohn, P. M., & Amenson, C. S. (1978). Some relations between pleasant and unpleasant mood-related events and depression. *Journal of Abnormal Psychology, 87*, 644–654.

Lewinsohn, P. M., & Graf, M. (1973). Pleasant activities and depression. *Journal of Consulting and Clinical Psychology, 41*, 261–268.

Lewinsohn, P. M., & Libet, J. (1972). Pleasant events, activity schedules, and depressions. *Journal of Abnormal Psychology, 3*, 291–295.

Lewinsohn, P. M., & Talkington, J. (1979). Studies on the measurement of unpleasant events and relations with depression. *Applied Psychological Measurement, 3*, 83–101.

Lewinsohn, P. M., Lobitz, W. C., & Wilson, S. (1973). 'Sensitivity' of depressed individuals to aversive stimuli. *Journal of Abnormal Psychology, 81*, 259–263.

Lewinsohn, P. M., Sullivan, J. M., & Grosscup, S. J. (1980). Changing reinforcing events: An approach to the treatment of depression. *Psychotherapy: Theory, Research and Practice, 17*, 322–334.

Libet, J. M., & Lewinsohn, P. M. (1973). Concept of social skill with special reference to the behavior of depressed persons. *Journal of Consulting and Clinical Psychology, 40*, 304–312.

MacPhillamy, D. J., & Lewinsohn, P. M. (1972). The measurement of reinforcing events. *Proceedings of the 80th Annual Convention of the American Psychological Association, 7*, 399–400.

MacPhillamy, D. J., & Lewinsohn, P. M. (1974). Depression as a function of levels of desired and obtained pleasure. *Journal of Abnormal Psychology, 83*, 651–657.

Magidson, J. F., Roberts, B. W., Collado-Rodriquez, A., & Lejuez, C. W. (2014). Theory-driven interventions for changing personality: Expectancy value theory, behavioural activation, and conscientiousness. *Developmental Psychology, 50*(5), 1442–1450.

Magidson, J. F., Gorka, S. M., MacPherson, L., Hopko, D. R., Blanco, C., Lejuez, C. W., & Daughters, S. B. (2011). Examining the effect of the life enhancement treatment for substance use (LETS ACT) on residential substance abuse treatment retention. *Addictive Behaviors, 36*(6), 615–623.

McLean, P. D., & Hakstian, A. R. (1979). Clinical depression: Comparative efficacy of outpatient treatments. *Journal of Consulting and Clinical Psychology, 47*, 818–836.

McLean, P. D., & Hakstian, A. R. (1990). Relative endurance of unipolar depression treatment effects: Longitudinal follow-up. *Journal of Consulting and Clinical Psychology, 58*, 482–488.

McNamara, K., & Horan, J. J. (1986). Experimental construct validity in the evaluation of cognitive and behavioral treatments for depression. *Journal of Counseling Psychology, 33*, 23–30.

Mulick, P. S., & Naugle, A. E. (2004). Behavioral activation for comorbid PTSD and major depression: A case study. *Cognitive and Behavioural Practice, 11*, 378–387.

Padfield, M. (1976). The comparative effects of two counseling approaches on the intensity of depression among rural women of low socioeconomic status. *Journal of Counseling Psychology, 23*, 209–214.

Shaw, B. F. (1977). Comparison of cognitive therapy and behaviour therapy in the treatment of depression. *Journal of Consulting and Clinical Psychology, 45*, 543–551.

Skinner, B. F. (1953). *Science and human behavior*. New York: Appleton-Century-Crofts.

Skinner, B. F. (1957). The experimental analysis of behaviour. *American Scientist, 45*, 343–371.

Skinner, B. F. (1974). *About Behaviorism*. New York: Alfred A. Knopf.

Thompson, L. W., Gallagher, D., & Steinmetz Breckenridge, J. (1987). Comparative effectiveness of psychotherapies for depressed elders. *Journal of Consulting and Clinical Psychology, 55*, 385–390.

Thorndike, E. L. (1911). *Animal Intelligence*. New York: Macmillan.

Wagner, A. W., Zatzick, D. F., Ghesquiere, A., & Jurkovich, G. J. (2007). Behavioral activation as an early intervention for posttraumatic stress disorder and depression among physically injured trauma survivors. *Cognitive and Behavioral Practice, 14*, 341–349.

Wilson, P. H. (1982). Combined pharmacological and behavioural treatment of depression. *Behavioural Research and Therapy, 20*, 173–184.

Wolpe, J. (1958). *Psychotherapy by Reciprocal Inhibition*. Stanford, CA: Stanford University Press.

Zeiss, A. M., Lewinsohn, P. M., & Munoz, R. F. (1979). Nonspecific improvement effects in depression using interpersonal skills training, pleasant activity schedules, or cognitive training. *Journal of Consulting and Clinical Psychology, 47*, 427–439.

Further Reading

Bandura, A. (1977). Self-efficacy: Toward a unifying theory of behavioral change. *Psychological Review*, 181–215.

Cuijpers, P., Van Straten, A., & Warmerdam, L. (2007). Behavioral activation treatments of depression: A meta-analysis. *Clinical Psychology Review, 27*, 318–326.

Ekers, D., Richards, D., & Gilbody, S. (2008). A meta-analysis of randomized trials of behavioural treatment of depression. *Psychological Medicine*, *38*, 611–623.

Hammen, C. (2005). Stress and depression. *Annual Review of Clinical Psychology*, *1*, 293–319.

Joiner, T. E., Metalsky, G. I., Katz, J., & Beach, S. R. H. (1999). Depression and excessive reassurance-seeking. *Psychological Inquiry*, *10*, 269–278.

Lewinsohn, P. M., & Atwood, G. E. (1969). Depression: A clinical research approach. *Psychotherapy: Theory, Research and Practice*, *6*, 166–171.

Wolf, N. J., & Hopko, D. R. (2007). Psychosocial and pharmacological interventions for depressed adults in primary care: A critical review. *Clinical Psychology Review*, *28*, 131–161.

10

A Critique of Theoretical Models of Depression: Commonalties and Distinctive Features

John R. Keefe and Robert J. DeRubeis

Challenging Beliefs in Depression: Locus, Distraction, or Harm?

A primary departure between schema theory and new-wave cognitive behavioural treatments concerns the role of maladaptive beliefs in depressive change: whether they are the wellspring of depression and whether it is helpful, harmful, or beside the point to try to change them. Classical cognitive therapy proposes that negativistic, dysfunctional thinking leads directly to alterations in mood, behaviour, and physiology. Core flaws in cognitive processing emerge from systems of irrationally negative beliefs (e.g., 'Nothing I do will ever improve my lot in life', 'People are constantly judging me') that prevent the patient from making reality-based assessments of him-/herself self and of his/her place in the world, and they lead to a chronically negative attributional style. These beliefs and their distortions discourage patients from making realistic and useful internal and external reassessments and changes, so as to work through their depression. Cognitive therapy – as represented in this collection by both Beck's and Young's conceptions of schema theory – posits that a gradual challenging of these beliefs and the consequent restructuring of depressogenic schematic content are beneficial – and perhaps necessary – both for diminishing symptoms and for preventing their reemergence. Acceptance and commitment therapy (ACT), mindfulness-based cognitive therapy (MBCT), and metacognitive therapy (MCT) reject the assumption that such restructuring is

Treating Depression: MCT, CBT and Third Wave Therapies, First Edition.
Edited by Adrian Wells and Peter L. Fisher.

necessary – in fact they propose that it is either harmful (ACT) or as harmful as it is helpful (MBCT and MCT). The authors of the chapters on ACT, MBCT, and MCT provide a variety of reasons for their assertions, along with evidence that is consistent with the assertions and corroborates the reasons. What is generally lacking in the descriptions – and this is true in many areas of modern psychology – is strong tests in the form of experiments, the results of which would point clearly to one theoretical view in preference of a competing one.

The authors of the chapters that deal with these three forms of therapy describe how attempts to change beliefs through direct challenges to their content are unlikely to succeed or are even pointless, because the contents of beliefs are not the problem in depression or in other undesirable or pathological states. Working from an ACT perspective, Zettle (chapter 7 in this volume) goes further, stating that such efforts will inevitably, or at least very likely, cause the patient to get further mired in the very process of mentation that is already capturing his/her attention in harmful ways. To different degrees and in different ways, ACT, MBCT, and MCT propose that a core problem in depression is the patients' maladaptive attachment to thoughts as they occur and give these patients an idea of their essence, of who they are. For instance, ACT emphasizes that depressive clients are 'unable to contact a sense of themselves that stands apart from negative self-referential thoughts' (p. 175). MBCT and MCT stress that the core maladaptive belief in depression is that engagement with negative thoughts is important to overcome negative feelings. Adrian Wells and Peter Fisher (chapters 6 and 12 in this volume) state that 'psychological disorder is a direct function of the extent to which negative thoughts are recycled and extended rather than let go' (p. 243). Put another way, these therapies all share a unique focus on the patient's *stance* towards the contents of his/her consciousness rather than on attempting – exclusively, or even at all – to change the contents themselves.

Despite arising from different theoretical foundations (which is especially true of ACT), all these three theoretical–therapeutic models emphasize a chief and uniquely therapeutic function of mindfulness. We broadly define mindfulness as a focus on 'keeping one's consciousness alive to the present reality' and as 'the clear and single-minded awareness of what actually happens to us and in us at the successive moments of perception' (respectively Nyanaponika Thera and Thich Hanh, as quoted in Brown & Ryan, 2003) – in contrast to rumination about the past or engaging in active struggle with moment-to-moment thoughts. Importantly, however, ACT, MBCT, and MCT differ in their specific therapeutic approach to mindfulness, in their clinical theory, both general and related to mindfulness, and in the putative mindfulness mechanisms they trigger in the resolution of depressive symptoms. For example, MCT focuses on suspension of the processing itself rather than on suspension through the lens of Buddhist mindfulness practices, as does MBCT. Generally, though in various ways, mindfulness is thought to introduce depressed patients to a newfound flexibility and freedom of focus and action.

Beck's and Young's schema theories

Schema therapy, of either the Beck or the Young variety, presupposes a core dysfunction of the meaning-making structures (or schemas) that lead all inferential and learning processes. Direct engagement with these schemas is considered necessary both in order to reduce depressive symptoms and in order to protect against relapse, should the patient find him-/herself in schema-activating situations. This raises the interesting theoretical question of whether cognitive – or, broadly, schema-focused – therapies, insofar as they prevent relapse, do so through a permanent (or at least enduring) alteration of schema content or by diminishing the person's access to the maladaptive schema(s) while increasing access to more adaptive and presumably valid ones. If the latter is the case, new questions about the stability of the 'new regime' come into play. For instance, will access to the old schema dominate once again, if the environment provides relevant triggers? The two paths opened by this question are similar to the possibilities allowed in the cognitive memory literature by the question whether aversive memories, seemingly diminished or erased due to reconsolidation, have been changed to be less aversive or whether reconsolidation has pruned the pathways to activation of the still aversive memory content (Tronson & Taylor, 2007).

As discussed by David Clark and Brendan Guyitt in chapter 5 of this volume, schema theory – and indeed cognitive therapy as a whole – must grapple with mixed, contradictory process outcome data concerning the mediating role of belief change in depression. The authors highlight a recent randomized controlled trial (RCT) that tracks the evolution of both cognitive-process variables and symptom change over the course of cognitive behavioural therapy (CBT) (Jarrett, Vittengl, Doyle, & Clark, 2007). Surprisingly, the trial found that, while beliefs substantially and stably changed for those who responded well to treatment (so-called 'responders'), what they describe as early symptom change during therapy predicted later belief change rather than the other way around.

Nevertheless, Jarrett and colleagues (2007) did not measure these cognitive and symptomatic constructs at coherent intervals that matched the assertions made ('early' symptom/belief change occurred during week 5, roughly around the ninth session of therapy); a more frequent assessment may have shown more complex relations between cognitive change and symptom change. Further, by the time of the 'early' symptom assessment in week 5, most patients had made most of their improvement, so that there was very little to predict about depressive change after week 5. As will be discussed in greater detail later in this chapter, it is common for responders in nearly all studied psychotherapies for depression to show the bulk of within-treatment symptom change during early sessions (see Ilardi & Craighead, 1994). In addition, as cognitive change was both more moderate and occurred more gradually across the later course of therapy by comparison to the drop in depression by week 5, it is perhaps unsurprising that controlling for the powerful week 5 change in depression nullified the predictive ability of cognitive change. And, even if we take these analyses at face value, while depression was still predicted to change from pre- to post-therapy, when residualizing for all cognitive changes, the residualized effect size for depression change dropped from d = 1.55 to d = 0.74. This is a large effect size decrease (d = 0.81), and might point towards contributing factors of cognitive change. Additional analyses might also have considered the role of cognitive change in predicting further change (e.g., relapse protection, further improvement) after therapy, above and beyond symptom levels at termination.

It is nevertheless possible that, for many, the initial response in cognitive therapy may be driven by factors other than, or additional to, cognitive changes. It is also conceivable that explicit self-report measures such as the Dysfunctional Attitude Scale do not tap into nascent, developing changes in beliefs that may occur over the course of therapy, but rather into beliefs that have become more firm and consolidated. Put another way: a patient may be changing before s/he is able to access and report those changes. Implicit behavioural measures putatively drawing upon belief or schema content may yield more valid indicators of not-yet-consolidated shifts in schema content during therapy. Nock et al. (2010) provide evidence of the clinical use of implicit measures, showing that implicit cognitions that link death and the self predict later suicidal behaviour in suicide attempters over and above depressive symptom level, psychiatric diagnosis, presence of past suicide attempts, clinician prediction, and – importantly to our discussion here – patient self-prediction.

Psychopathological- and therapeutic-process evidence concerning Jeffrey Young's conception of early maladaptive schemas (EMSs), which forms the core of Young's schema theory, is sparser. There are preliminary data suggesting that EMSs are relatively stable during treatment for depression, changing only minimally over the course of standard CBT, interpersonal therapy, or psychopharmacology (Renner, Lobbestael, Peeters, Arntz, & Huibers, 2012). Conversely, measures of EMSs appear to change as a result of schema therapy for heterogeneous conditions, and those changes have been found to be associated with symptom reduction (Nordahl, Holthe, & Haugum, 2005; van Vreeswijk, Spinhoven, Eurelings-Bontekoe, & Broersen, 2014). It has yet to be shown, however, that EMSs change over the course of schema therapy, specifically for depression. Furthermore, to our knowledge, time series analyses examining the course of change of EMSs at any time during therapy have yet to be performed. These would be especially germane to determining whether EMS change is an epiphenomenon of symptom change and its contributors or a driver of symptom change itself – and perhaps a protection from relapse.

In response to increasing evidence concerning the role of compensatory skills in the treatment of depression, schema theory should better address how changes in coping strategies (e.g., cognitive reframing, distancing) may also help to explain change and resilience, in addition to – or in interaction with – changes in schema (Barber & DeRubeis, 1989). Such an addition would track advances in research on the psychotherapeutic process. Compensatory skills have been shown to predict resistance to relapse after remission following standard cognitive therapy (Strunk, DeRubeis, Chiu, & Alvarez, 2007); they may even be a transtheoretical mediator of change. For example, Connolly Gibbons et al. (2009) found a relation between improved compensatory skills and symptom change through follow-up not only in cognitive behavioural therapies, but in psychodynamic therapies as well. Notably, Strunk et al. (2007) found that both in-session evidence of the patient's usage of cognitive therapy techniques (behavioural activation, automatic thought work, and schema work) and increases in the patient's ability to draw upon compensatory skills independently predicted resistance to relapse, with minimal intercorrelation between measures of the two constructs. This suggests that both classical cognitive therapy constructs (e.g., thought restructuring) and compensatory skills (perhaps including mindfulness) may be additively or synergistically useful in the treatment of depression and in the prevention of relapse.

Therapies with a focus on one's stance towards consciousness rather than on the contents of consciousness (ACT, MCT, MBCT)

For the therapies that utilize the concept of mindfulness, broadly construed, the biggest threat is not the existence of idiosyncratic, catastrophic, or maladaptive beliefs, but rather a persistent focus on otherwise 'normal' negative thoughts and mood that, for others, are transient. These normal negative fluctuations in thought and mood become concretized in different ways, according to the individual theory. MBCT frames mindfulness ('decentring') in terms of reducing the threat of cognitive reactivity – a phenomenon by which negative mood induction activates negative schemas. In this way MBCT is – in agreement with its name – the most similar to schema therapy among the mindfulness therapies. It recognizes the ontology of schemas and their role as depressogenic agents, but it proposes that it is more beneficial to change the role of the schemas than to attempt to change their contents. The threat of cognitive reactivity – or mood-induced activation of negative information processing – helps explain the concern that any focus on negative thoughts and emotions (even thought challenge) might lead to the activation of a persisting negative cognitive mode. However, recently published data indicate that change in cognitive reactivity per se might not explain relapse over and above emotional reactivity and baseline schemas (Jarrett et al., 2012; van Rijsbergen et al., 2013). While it is increasingly convincing that compensatory skills – a construct that includes the application of mindfulness principles – play a role in protecting against depressive relapse (e.g., Strunk et al., 2007), betting on cognitive reactivity to explain the singular benefit of mindfulness over belief challenge seems in turn increasingly unsupported. If cognitive reactivity does not usefully index vulnerability to relapse, the danger of a direct challenging of beliefs in cognitive therapy may be overstated. Another ambiguity in the theory is whether beliefs or schemas are ever thought to change as a result of mindfulness interventions – as would be hoped for in schema-based therapies – or whether the patient merely deactivates the schema in the short term and then learns a very helpful coping skill (i.e., mindfulness) in order to prevent further activation of that schema.

Though in many ways very similar, MCT and MBCT differ substantially in clinical theory on the matter of beliefs. MCT goes beyond MBCT, to emphasize not only a form of mindfulness but the existence of beliefs at the metacognitive level that are crucial to the maintenance of depression. In MBCT (as described in chapter 8), lack of mindfulness is something that arises almost *ex nihilo* – or perhaps from more commonly defined schemas. Unlike MBCT, MCT asserts not only that the focused processing of negative thoughts is detrimental (as in rumination), but that there are particular, definable systems of beliefs – different from 'normal' cognitive beliefs – that cause a ruminative or antimindful attentional–processing style. In doing so, MCT resituates the important beliefs at the metacognitive level of analysis, while deemphasizing schema-level change in (the content of) belief.

MCT's variant of mindfulness practices are thought to model more adaptive and more common[1] metacognitive behaviour. To rehearse the ideas presented in chapter 6 in this volume, its authors propose the existence of both 'positive' metacognitive beliefs (beliefs as to why rumination is 'positive') and 'negative' metacognitive beliefs (beliefs as to why thoughts are uncontrollable and how perilous having these thoughts is). The metacognitive beliefs themselves are examined and challenged, the goal being to reduce the attention directed at negative stimuli and to adopt a more adaptive metacognitive mode (i.e., detached mindfulness). Through this process, the patient 'discovers that emotions and negative ideas are transitory experiences, unrelated to the broader self' (p. 163). The malignancy of the positive beliefs presented by the authors – unlike the pathogenic potential of many of the wildly unrealistic beliefs targeted by traditional cognitive therapy ('I am doomed to failure') – seems to be dependent on the obsessive force of penetration or inflexibility of the belief. For example, one such belief is: 'If I analyse why I have failed I will be able to prevent failure in the future' (p. 149). To suggest that this belief is necessarily pathological seems a stretch; a more adaptively functioning person might be well served by the belief that he or she can learn from failure. Rather there is something about the obsessiveness or pervasiveness of the belief, combined with other factors (e.g., lack of a useful perspective on the problem and lack of internal or external agency to change the features of the world that are identified in the analysis of a failure), that puts it at the core of the pathology.

The MCT authors describe the depressive bias towards negative stimuli as if 'negative' (and, by necessity, 'not negative') were a content-free label that is automatically – perhaps pre-consciously – applied to all stimuli across internal and external environments. This is difficult to imagine, as there are few almost universally negative stimuli (e.g., pain), and what is or is not negative might differ strongly from situation to situation, or even from mood to mood. What is unclear is the nature of the mental structures and representations that do the triage so as to identify the negative in a way that, for depressed people, results in such a powerful pathological fixation on this kind of stimulus. It is interesting that Wells and Fisher reject the prominence of schemas in the MCT model, as something like a schema would describe a mental construct that could determine what, in different situations and states, is 'negative' at a metacognitive or attentional level. Furthermore, why are these metacognitive beliefs presumed to exist at a different level from standard cognitive beliefs or schemas? The experimental evidence provided in chapter 6 does not paint a picture in which 'metacognitive' beliefs are clearly dissociated from other beliefs structurally (e.g., as belonging to a superlevel). It would be helpful to develop ways to distinguish what is structurally a purely 'metacognitive' belief versus a first-order belief and to see whether these 'metacognitive' beliefs meaningfully dissociate from schemas.

We can imagine ACT as an even more extreme version of MBCT/MCT, in that engagement with negative cognitions is not merely less useful than mindfulness, or a waste of time, but a distinctly iatrogenic activity. ACT proposes that being completely mindful all of the time is not only protective of health but, in a philosophical way, almost the goal of being human. In ACT, avoiding negative emotions – when these emotions are 'pure' and not a function of a depressive state (e.g., a ruminating about ruminating) – may in itself be pathogenic and may distance an individual from a sense of authentic self and valued living. In general function – that is, by proposing that avoidance of emotions can lead to pathology – this is a stance not necessarily different from that of therapies as remote from ACT as psychodynamic therapy, which claims that the experience of a disavowed emotion relieves psychodynamic conflict (Busch, Milrod, Singer, & Aronson, 2011), or process-experiential therapy, which claims that one must experience a maladaptive emotion in order to transform it (Greenberg & Watson, 2005). We find this notion within behavioural theory generally, which posits that avoidance of negative stimuli may lead to pathogenic reinforcement schedules. ACT is distinctive in that, while non-CBT therapies (e.g., psychodynamic or process-experiential) engage in the elaboration of the meanings behind, or constituting, these emotions, ACT rejects any explanation, on the grounds that it gets mired in further rumination (a stance that MCT also particularly shares), reification, and unhelpful storytelling. In ACT, a common roadblock to remission is the clients' insistence that 'understanding and figuring out their depression is necessary before they can get on with their lives' (chapter 7, p. 176, in this volume).

However, ACT diverges strongly even from many CBTs in that it extends this rejection of confrontation still further, to cognitions and beliefs. The act of evaluating experience is harmful, except insofar as the evaluation goes towards determining what is a value-driven life for the individual. A healthy individual will be not just mindful of, but *acceptant* of any thoughts s/he has; combative engagement with negative thoughts breaks this mindful acceptance. There is relatively little empirical evidence concerning comparative therapy process between ACT and cognitive therapy in depression that could elucidate to what extent thought challenge is anathema to a successful treatment. A report of a recent RCT comparing ACT to cognitive therapy in a mixed sample of anxiety and depression patients included analyses that suggest that session-to-session patient use of cognitive therapy-typical thought change strategies by comparison to ACT-typical acceptance strategies positively mediates symptom change in cognitive therapy but not in ACT, whereas relative greater use of ACT-typical acceptance strategies mediates symptom change in ACT but not in cognitive therapy (Forman et al., 2012). Thus thought challenge may not itself be iatrogenic, but perhaps only within the context of a treatment that strongly disavows thought challenge as part of its rationale. Given the robust literature of controlled experiments establishing the therapeutic efficacy of CBT for depression, a claim that to challenge thoughts (a core technique of CBTs) is *universally* iatrogenic is difficult to sustain and would require clear empirical confirmation.

Behavioural activation: On its own?

Unlike the other four therapies discussed, behavioural activation theory barely engages in this discourse about the role of beliefs in the generation and maintenance of psychopathology – such a role is neither here nor there. While behavioural activation recognizes that depressive patients are characterized by negativistic cognitive styles, it does not consider beliefs especially relevant to treatment. However, neither does it make any strong predictions as to whether a focus on beliefs would be (1) on average somewhat helpful, but less efficient than addressing behaviour; (2) useless or nearly useless, in addition to taking effort and time away from due focus on behaviour (i.e., an opportunity cost); or (3) iatrogenic. This stance is unsurprising for a unitarily behaviourist account of depression.

However, it may also be relevant to our discussion of beliefs to note that the reemergence of behavioural activation was predicated on a dismantling RCT that suggested a therapeutic benefit of behavioural activation alone equivalent to a complete or partial cognitive therapy package (Jacobson et al., 1996). A standard interpretation of this study is that the lack of direct cognitive challenge and restructuring in the behavioural activation condition suggests that cognitions or beliefs do not mediate change in the cognitive therapy of depression and that behavioural activation is all that is needed (Longmore & Worrell, 2007). There is indeed increasing evidence that behavioural activation alone may produce powerful outcomes in depression, especially for highly depressed patients (e.g., Dimidjian et al., 2006; Dobson et al., 2008). In some ways, in retrospect, this finding is unsurprising: a recent high-quality meta-analysis suggested that dismantling studies tended to show no significant differences between full treatments and the dismantled treatments (Bell, Marcus, & Goodlad, 2013). Notably, this meta-analysis used a sample of predominantly cognitive behavioural therapies that excluded both behavioural and cognitive components from target therapies, suggesting that neither modality supplies 'the' crucial therapeutic ingredient across these trials.

Not mentioned by those authors, however, is the limitation of dismantling studies as aids in drawing inferences about mechanisms, or even about the relative potency of the component parts of an intervention. If the effects of components are independent and additive, and if there are no ceiling effects (i.e., more is simply better), then no difference in efficacy should be observed between therapy A + B (the entire package) and component A versus component B. Other assumptions about the functional relations among components (synergistic vs interfering) and the relation between time spent and benefit (diminishing returns vs linear vs exponential relation between time and benefit) would imply different effects of comparing one component against another. Although the idea is appealing that one can conduct definitive tests of the relative potency of components or of the relative importance of mechanisms of therapeutic approaches, in fact these are difficult issues, as reflected in the statements of most authors in this section that the empirical literature is consistent with, or even supports, their conjectures, but that much is left to be determined by future research.

In addition, some have juxtaposed the fact that behavioural activation took place at the beginning of all three treatments (cognitive therapy, partial cognitive therapy, behavioural activation) and that change was also front-loaded at the beginning of treatment. A popular conjecture is that, because behavioural activation occurred at the change-heavy beginning of each treatment, this is further evidence that behavioural activation predominantly drove change in the sample (Longmore & Worrell, 2007). Nevertheless, this pattern is a bit of a red herring, as symptomatic change tends to occur in earlier versus later phases of nearly any therapy type for most mood and anxiety disorders (Hayes, Laurenceau, Feldman, Strauss, & Cardaciotto, 2007; cf. Ilardi & Craighead, 1994) and may be a feature of treatment responders generally. Thus early change may not reflect the action of any of the presumed change-inducing features of any particular treatment approach. A dismantling trial that aimed to test the hypothesis suggested by Longmore and Worrell (2007) would include a cognitive therapy condition that left out the behavioural activation component.

Furthermore, to draw conclusions about questions of mediation from this study is a category error. As Hofmann (2008) underlines, a component analysis is necessarily unable to address questions of mediation (i.e., what intermediary variables are altered by therapy to produce change), as cognitions are liable to change in response to interventions other than direct cognitive challenge. That is to say: interventions may produce change in surprising, counter-theoretical ways (cf. Lambert & Ogles, 2004). For example, by upregulating the experience of positive reinforcement, behavioural activation could provide evidence to spur a patient to reassess his/her beliefs concerning the futility of ever feeling happy. The Jacobson trial itself reported a finding to this effect. Changes in attributional style early on in treatment predicted change in depressive symptoms in the course of behavioural activation. On the other hand, one could also imagine that cognitive therapy may potentiate the pursuit of positive reinforcement by diminishing pessimistic beliefs, but that the more potent mechanism is the shift towards pursuing environments that can provide positive reinforcement. This possibility is consistent with another finding from the Jacobson trial, one that shows a positive relation between the frequency of pleasant events and symptom change in cognitive therapy.

Ultimately, it is impossible to determine, from Jacobson et al.'s (1996) trial or from any dismantling study, what mediates symptom change in depression – and whether beliefs and schemas are truly irrelevant to behavioural therapy. Broadly, without process research we cannot firmly conclude whether a therapy works as a result of its proposed theoretical mechanism, of counter-theoretical mechanisms, or of some mixture therein. Future research on behavioural activation may need to address the possible mediating role of belief constructs within an ostensibly behavioural treatment. One may even find that current behavioural activation techniques affect cognitive constructs in surprising ways. Just as much, cognitive therapy researchers may wish to consider the role of changes in reinforcement patterns in patient improvement.

Proximate or Distal Causation of Pathology?

Theories of psychopathology can operate in two timeframes of causation: (1) they can explain the development of psychopathology in the immediate present (e.g., what processes immediately led to and/or currently sustain a depression), and (2) they can explain the long-term development of vulnerability, for example why different individuals exposed to similar stressors do or do not develop psychopathology. A comprehensive theory of psychopathology will thus be able to explain not only the mechanism of how depression is instantiated and maintained in the near term (proximate causation), but why certain people do and do not end up in a clinical depression (distal causation). The two poles we perceive on this point would be behavioural activation at one end – where one gives with great precision a behavioural account of how depression begins and is maintained, but has relatively little to say about distal effects – and, again, schema theory at the other end – which constitutes a pole by proposing both proximate and distal causation of pathology.

Schema theories of both varieties hinge on the 'lock-and-key hypothesis', which posits that early-life experiences can establish vulnerabilities in the form of maladaptive cognitive–affective schemas (a 'lock') that are then activated by particular types of (usually adverse) life experiences (a 'key'): a classic stress–diathesis model that delineates a distal cause (development of vulnerabilities) and a proximate cause (stress). MBCT also draws implicitly upon classical Beck schema theory in terms of its pathological model, with the obvious addition of mindfulness into the mix of factors. It does not distinguish itself significantly from schema theory in its etiological scope.

Beck's and Young's theories of schema diverge from each other regarding (1) the types of pathogenic schemas that characterize depression and (2) the developmental focus. Like psychodynamic therapy, Young's schema theory proposes that, if basic emotional needs are not met in childhood, individuals may develop in a conflict-concordant manner maladaptive schemas and rigid modes of coping with lack of fulfilment of their needs (e.g., the surrender of agency, during youth, to overcontrolling parents could lead to development of the subjugation schema, in which one defines oneself as 'less than' in order to avoid the need to retaliate or express anger against frustrating figures). One could imagine that an enhanced focus on complex developmental issues may be particularly useful for depression patients with personality disorders, who have complicated presentations and longstanding disability. Indeed, the impetus for developing a revised schema theory was to better account for the rigid and striking behaviour and phenomenology of patients with personality disorders, in addition to the difficulty of treating such conditions. Unfortunately, the only randomized controlled trial comparing Young's schema therapy to Beck's cognitive therapy for depression showed no difference in efficacy between cognitive therapy and schema therapy, even when moderating the effect through the presence of a personality disorder (Carter et al., 2013). On the other hand, schema-focused therapy has been shown to be particularly efficacious in the treatment of borderline personality disorder (Farrel, Shaw, & Webber, 2009; Giesen-Bloo et al., 2006). Regardless of whether or not Young's schema theory more accurately describes the developmental processes that give rise to more complex cases of depression, these preliminary data suggest that schema therapy is possibly just as efficacious as standard cognitive therapy on a population level.

In Young's model, the sheer number of schemas and related modes may reflect an unnecessary complexity, and in any event calls for empirical tests of the specific claims. To our knowledge, there are only preliminary data suggesting that particular EMSs characterize and thus may represent a vulnerability to depression (abandonment/instability, failure, emotional deprivation, and enmeshment; Renner et al., 2012). As mentioned before, it remains to be seen whether these EMSs change over the course of schema therapy for depression, and whether any such change would bear predictive clinical value. The data from the RCT in Carter et al. (2013), described above, raise the question: even if particular EMSs from Young's theory may describe particular depressive patients more comprehensively than Beck's original formulations, is it possible that the optimal *interventions* for patients with some EMSs are found in other types of therapies? Thus a further advancement in the theory might be to hypothesize a clearer theoretical relation between the presence of different dominant schemas in depression and differential technique use.

Behavioural activation theory's account of the proximate development of depression is convincing and coherent. A schedule (i.e., a characteristic pattern) of response-contingent positive reinforcement (e.g., reward for action) normally maintains its own existence through its own reinforcement. As low rates of response-continent positive reinforcement are thought to directly elicit depressed behaviours, a stable schedule of positive reinforcement protects against non-transient depressive behaviours. When this pattern of positive reinforcement is substantially disrupted, a depressed individual may enter a downward behavioural spiral, where that individual has an extinction of reinforcement-seeking behaviour due the absence of reinforcers and a possible increase in avoidant behaviour designed to reduce exposure to negative stimuli during this vulnerable period. The protective schedule of positive reinforcement thus evaporates.

Conversely, behavioural activation theory does not clearly delineate who will and who will not fall into the behavioural cycle – why some rebound from adversity, maintaining their positive reinforcement schedule, and some collapse. Simple behavioural explanations are not immediately forthcoming: for example, it is suggested that depressed individuals do not experience more negative events on a day-to-day basis than non-depressed individuals. However, there is evidence that proximate and past highly stressful life events do predict conversion to depression, perhaps in a causal manner (Kendler, Karkowski, & Prescott, 1999; Kendler, Hettema, Butera, Gardner, & Prescott et al., 2003; Kessler, 1997). It might be fruitful to see a behaviourist account of why past stress or trauma may sensitize to depressive reactivity (Harkness, Bruce, & Lumley, 2006).

Hubley, Kaiser, and Dimidjian (chapter 15) allude to notions of dispositional variation in explaining individual differences. For instance, some individuals may be predisposed to experiencing positive events in a less behaviourally potent way, such that positive reinforcement is less effective. One could imagine that an individual with less powerful positive reinforcement might be more likely to fall into a depressive cycle after a disruption of positive reinforcement. Remaining reinforcers after disruption may be less likely to maintain their positive reinforcement schedule because they are inherently experienced as less reinforcing. Thus – with less positive reinforcement – the beginning of the negative behavioural cycle described by behavioural activation may be more likely to begin for these individuals. Hubley, Kaiser, and Dimidjian also describe other idiographic factors that might lead to the development of a depression after reinforcement schedule disruption (e.g., lack of reinforcement in the environment itself). It is unclear whether they are suggesting that any person with these behavioural factors (i.e., a perfect storm of disasters in the reinforcing environment) will necessarily fall into depression, whether the proximate cause is all you need to explain. If not, we arrive again at the question of why some patients falter and some persevere. Behavioural activation's distal theory of causation needs clarity and explication.

MCT as presented herein is not much more advanced than behavioural activation in proposing a lifespan theory of psychopathological development. What sorts of stimuli or experiences in the immediate term trigger a shift from a relatively 'normal' metacognitive style to a pathogenic style? Similarly, how do latent errors in metacognition arise – are they constitutional, or do they arise as a result of biopsychosocial developmental processes? Are they there all along in some form (e.g., as a vulnerability) or do they develop more proximately to the onset of depression?

ACT's proposed mechanisms of depression[2] lay depressive causation almost entirely in the 'here and now'. While other theories of development serve to differentiate those likely from those unlikely to suffer from depression, the mental processes underlying ACT's theory (or theories) of depression imply that the capacity for depression is universal and endogenous to humans. Indeed, given Zettle's characterization of the theory, it might seem surprising that most people *are not* clinically depressed. 'We are doomed to be haunted by our own self-awareness', Zettle writes, as 'merely thinking about and recalling an unpleasant life event can have a psychological impact similar to that experienced when the event first occurred' (p. 180 in this volume). Several other qualities of mind in the ACT model further imply a precariousness of mental stability in the here and now (e.g., possibility of quotidian words such as 'bad' attaining semantic significance equivalent to that of death).

In this turn towards universal threat of depression, ACT comes close to rejecting entirely the notion of distal causation of depression as described here, with only a nod towards 'the historical contexts of which depression is a function' (p. 172 in this volume). Moreover, the role of said historical contexts can also be arbitrary, as when Zettle (in the same chapter 7) describes patients who believe that they cannot get better because of unchangeable historical events or until past traumas are resolved. For Zettle, the most important consequence of these beliefs is that patients holding them act *as if* they were true, thus transforming such 'unchangeable' historical context into real roadblocks to naturalistic or treatment-driven remission of their depression. Just as ACT deemphasizes the role of beliefs or schemas as an ontologically 'real' source of a depressogenic way of being, ACT assumes that stories or historical context have no essential content and can or should 'be retold and reconstructed with a different outcome' (p. 179 in this volume) – there is no trace of a 'real' thing to be grappled with, merely something to be reframed for the benefit of the here and now. Whether the 'historical context' of depression in ACT functions in an essential way (i.e., some histories are likely to help in causing a depression), in an arbitrary way, or both is ambiguous. On the one hand, ACT's rejection of distal causation is consistent with the ever present threat of pathogenesis lurking within systems of language and thought – the threat that these mechanisms are very powerful and, by implication, could happen at any time in the here and now. On the other hand, this rejection is unsatisfying in the context of the broader literature on the developmental aetiology of depression, which consistently suggests that some individuals are more likely to develop a depression than others (see Gotlib & Hammen, 2010; Monroe & Harkness, 2005 for reviews). A stronger incorporation of these powerful empirical findings concerning depressive vulnerability may be necessary to bolster the theory's validity.

Note that, whether the theory explains both proximate and distal causation or not, this does not necessarily mean that the theory has or has not explained remission (immediate breaking of depressogenic patterns) and relapse/recurrence prevention (reduction of vulnerability to depression). For example, whereas MCT does not include a strong theory of distal causation, the theory of its therapy contains an explanation of both the immediate resolution of a depressive episode and how vulnerability can be lessened against future episodes – namely through detached mindfulness and metacognitive control of rumination and metabeliefs. In comparison, behavioural activation, while providing a very strong theory of proximate causation that lends itself to explaining remission, does not include elements that would account for how a course of behavioural activation might prevent relapse or recurrence, aside from the development of social skills. Otherwise it is not clear how breaking a behavioural cycle via behavioural activation would prevent the later renewal of the negative behavioural cycle that defines the theory's proximate causation. Relapse and recurrence prevention implies a need for a longlasting change that could influence an individual's reinforcement schedules in the future such that s/he would be less likely to become depressed. Similarly, ACT's proposal that 'value-congruent behaviour' (such as the behaviour that one would pursue at the end of a successful experience in ACT) is 'naturally reinforcing' might be interpreted as a form of relapse or recurrence prevention. Yet the pessimistic theory of causation in ACT – the view that, for many people, the system of language itself necessarily leads to depression – seems to counterbalance the auto-reinforcement of 'value-congruent behaviour' or the use of mindfulness: Is mindfulness, or the increased pursuit of 'value-congruent behaviour,' enough to obviate the threat of depression in ACT?

Overall, the theoretical coherence and coverage of all these theories – but perhaps especially the new-wave therapies – could benefit from a deeper consideration of the developmental antecedents of depressive psychopathology and of how the latter may inform the process and mechanisms of successful depression treatment.

Notes

1. While MBCT proposes that most people do not have mindfulness skills but rather gain them through focused study, MCT seems to imply that most people have some degree of mindfulness normally and that it is in the individuals who have a compromised mindfulness that psychopathology arises.
2. It may be, in the eyes of some, ironic or unacceptable for us to define ACT's proposed routes to depressions as 'mechanisms' in the way in which other cognitive behavioural therapies might treat a mechanism. Zettle describes ACT as operating under the aegis of a holistically defined 'functional contextualism' that 'regards behaviour not as a thing whose psychological structure is to be predicted … but as the activity of the whole and integrated organism, which interacts in and with historical and situational contexts' (p. 172 in this volume). Although Zettle does not write with the same (perhaps mechanical) certainty of cause and effect that one encounters for example in the behavioural activation chapter, he nevertheless goes on to describe a theory of mind with certain features, which allow for and lead to the onset of a clinical depression. In other ways ACT does seem to propose modalities in which these features of mind almost necessarily lead to depressive states (e.g., linguistic fusion of the self and fleeting negative assessments via mutual entailment between the word 'I' and negative words). With the important caveat that Zettle does not mean to claim that relational frame theory provides a precise, mechanical recipe for depression, it seems to us as though treating these roads to depression as theoretical mechanisms is coherent.

References

Barber, J. P., & DeRubeis, R. J. (1989). On second thought: Where the action is in cognitive therapy for depression. *Cognitive Therapy and Research, 13*(5), 441–457.

Bell, E. C., Marcus, D. K., & Goodlad, J. K. (2013). Are the parts as good as the whole? A meta-analysis of component treatment studies. *Journal of Consulting and Clinical Psychology, 81*(4), 722–736. doi: 10.1037/a0033004.

Brown, K. W., & Ryan, R. M. (2003). The benefits of being present: Mindfulness and its role in psychological well-being. *Journal of Personality and Social Psychology, 84*(4), 822–848.

Busch, F. N., Milrod, B. L., Singer, M. B., & Aronson, A. C. (2011). *Manual of panic-focused psychodynamic psychotherapy: eXtended range*. New York: Routledge.

Carter, J. D., McIntosh, V. V., Jordan, J., Porter, R. J., Frampton, C. M., & Joyce, P. R. (2013). Psychotherapy for depression: A randomized clinical trial comparing schema therapy and cognitive behavior therapy. *Journal of Affective Disorder, 151*(2), 500–505. doi: 10.1016/j.jad.2013.06.034.

Connolly Gibbons, M. B., Crits-Christoph, P., Barber, J. P., Stirman, S. W., Gallop, R., Goldstein, L. A.... Ring-Kurtz, S. (2009). Unique and common mechanisms of change across cognitive and dynamic psychotherapies. *Journal of Consulting and Clinical Psychology, 77*(5), 801–813.

Dimidjian, S., Hollon, S. D., Dobson, K. S., Schmaling, K. B., Kohlenberg, R. J., Addis, M. E. ... Jacobson, N. S. (2006). Randomized trial of behavioral activation, cognitive therapy, and antidepressant medication in the acute treatment of adults with major depression. *Journal of Consulting and Clinical Psychology, 74*(4), 658–670.

Dobson, K. S., Hollon, S. D., Dimidijan, S., Schmaling, K. B., Kohlenberg, R. J., Gallop, R. ... Jacobson, N. S. (2008). Randomized trial of behavioral activation, cognitive therapy, and antidepressant medication in the prevention of relapse and recurrence in major depression. *Journal of Consulting and Clinical Psychology, 76*(3), 468–477.

Farrell, J. M., Shaw, I. A., & Webber, M. A. (2009). A schema-focused approach to group psychotherapy for outpatients with borderline personality disorder: A randomized controlled trial. *Journal of Behavior Therapy and Experimental Psychiatry, 40*(2), 317–328.

Forman, E. M., Chapman, J. E., Herbert, J. D., Goetter, E. M., Yuen, E. K., & Moitra, E. (2012). Using session-by-session measurement to compare mechanisms of action for acceptance and commitment therapy and cognitive therapy. *Behavior Therapy, 43*(2), 341–354.

Giesen-Bloo, J., van Dyck, R., Spinhoven, P., van Tilburg, W., Dirksen, C., van Asselt, T. ... Arntz, A. (2006). Outpatient psychotherapy for borderline personality disorder: Randomized trial of schema-focused therapy vs transference-focused therapy. *Archives of General Psychiatry, 63*(6), 649–658.

Gotlib, I. H., & C. L. Hammen (Eds). (2010). Vulnerability, risk, and models of depression. (2010). *Part II of Handbook of depression* (2nd ed., pp. 163–360). New York: Guilford.

Greenberg, L. S., & Watson, J. C. (2005). *Emotion-focused therapy for depression*. Washington, DC: American Psychological Association.

Harkness, K. L., Bruce, A. E., & Lumley, M. N. (2006). The role of childhood abuse and neglect in the sensitization to stressful life events in adolescent depression. *Journal of Abnormal Psychology, 115*(4), 730–741.

Hayes, A. M., Laurenceau, J.-P., Feldman, G., Strauss, J. L., & Cardaciotto, L. (2007). Change is not always linear: The study of nonlinear and discontinuous patterns of change in psychotherapy. *Clinical Psychology Review, 27*(6), 715–723.

Hofmann, S. G. (2008). Common misconceptions about cognitive mediation of treatment change: A commentary to Longmore and Worrell (2007). *Clinical Psychology Review, 28*(1), 67–70.

Ilardi, S. S., & Craighead, W. E. (1994). The role of nonspecific factors in cognitive-behavioral therapy for depression. *Clinical Psychology: Science and Practice, 1*(2), 138–156.

Jacobson, N. S., Dobson, K. S., Truax, P. A., Addis, M. E., Koerner, K., Gollan, J. K. … Prince, S. E. (1996). A component analysis of cognitive–behavioral treatment for depression. *Journal of Consulting and Clinical Psychology, 64*(2), 295–304.

Jarrett, R. B., Vittengl, J. R., Doyle, K., & Clark, L. A. (2007). Changes in cognitive content during and following cognitive therapy for recurrent depression: Substantial and enduring, but not predictive of change in depressive symptoms. *Journal of Consulting and Clinical Psychology, 75*(3), 432–446.

Jarrett, R. B., Minhajuddin, A., Borman, P. D., Dunlap, L., Segal, Z. V., Kidner, C. L. … Thase, M. E. (2012). Cognitive reactivity, dysfunctional attitudes, and depressive relapse and recurrence in cognitive therapy responders. *Behaviour Research and Therapy, 50*(5), 280–286.

Kendler, K. S., Karkowski, L. M., & Prescott, C. A. (1999). Causal relationship between stressful life events and the onset of major depression. *American Journal of Psychiatry, 156*(6), 837–841.

Kendler, K. S., Hettema, J. M., Butera, F., Gardner, C. O., & Prescott, C. A. (2003). Life event dimensions of loss, humiliation, entrapment, and danger in the prediction of onsets of major depression and generalized anxiety. *Archives of General Psychiatry, 60*(8), 789–796.

Kessler, R. C. (1997). The effects of stressful life events on depression. *Annual Review of Psychology, 48*, 191–214.

Lambert, M. J., & Ogles, B. M. (2004). The efficacy and effectiveness of psychotherapy. In M. J. Lambert (Ed.), *Bergin and Garfield's handbook of psychotherapy and behaviour change* (5th ed., pp. 139–193). New York: Wiley.

Longmore, R. J., & Worrell, M. (2007). Do we need to challenge thoughts in cognitive behaviour therapy? *Clinical Psychology Review, 27*(2), 173–187.

Monroe, S. M., & Harkness, K. L. (2005). Life stress, the 'kindling' hypothesis, and the recurrence of depression: Considerations from a life stress perspective. *Psychological Review, 112*(2), 417–445.

Nock, M. K., Park, J. M., Finn, C. T., Deliberto, T. L., Dour, H. J., & Banaji, M. R. (2010). Measuring the suicidal mind: Implicit cognition predicts suicidal behavior. *Psychological Science, 21*(4), 511–517.

Nordahl, H. M., Holthe, H., & Haugum, J. A. (2005). Early maladaptive schemas in patients with or without personality disorders: Does schema modification predict symptomatic relief? *Clinical Psychology and Psychotherapy, 12*(2), 142–149.

Renner, F., Lobbestael, J., Peeters, F., Arntz, A., & Huibers, M. (2012). Early maladaptive schemas in depressed patients: Stability and relation with depressive symptoms over the course of treatment. *Journal of Affective Disorders, 136*(3), 581–590.

Strunk, D. R., DeRubeis, R. J., Chiu, A. W., & Alvarez, J. (2007). Patients' competence in and performing of cognitive therapy skills: Relation to the reduction of relapse following treatment for depression. *Journal of Consulting and Clinical Psychology, 75*(4), 523–530.

Tronson, N. C., & Taylor, J. R. (2007). Molecular mechanisms of memory reconsolidation. *Nature Reviews Neuroscience, 8*(4), 262–275.

van Rijsbergen, G. D., Bockting, C. L. H., Burger, H., Spinhoven, P., Koeter, M. W. J., Ruhé, H. G.… Schene, A. H. (2013). Mood reactivity rather than cognitive reactivity is predictive of depressive relapse: A randomized study with 5.5-year follow-up. *Journal of Consulting and Clinical Psychology, 81*(3), 508–517.

van Vreeswijk, M. F., Spinhoven, P., Eurelings-Bontekoe, E. H., & Broersen, J. (2014). Changes in symptom severity, schemas and modes in heterogeneous psychiatric patient groups following short-term schema cognitive–behavioural group therapy: A naturalistic pre-treatment and post-treatment design in an outpatient clinic. *Clinical Psychology and Psychotherapy, 21*(1), 29–38. doi: 10.1002/cpp.1813.

Further Reading

Keller, M. C., Neale, M. C., & Kendler, K. S. (2007). Association of different adverse life events with distinct patterns of depressive symptoms. *American Journal of Psychiatry, 164* (10), 1521–1529.

Section 3

Treatments for Depression

Introduction to Section 3: Case Study

Implementing effective psychological treatment for depression requires considerable therapeutic skill and knowledge of the therapeutic model that underpins the treatment. The theoretical basis for each of the treatment approaches was described in Section 2. In the present section we have aimed to provide an in-depth understanding of how to deliver each treatment approach. To this end, the contributors were handed the description of a hypothetical patient with depression and were asked to show how they would assess, formulate, and treat this patient. By using the same case material we hope to illuminate the fundamental differences that exist between the five treatments presented in this volume.

Case Presentation

Gail is a 48-year-old Caucasian woman, married, with two teenage daughters who are doing well at school. She works part-time in the healthcare profession and was recently referred to the department of clinical psychology by her general physician, as she has been suffering from persistent depression and mild levels of anxiety. She has been on Paroxetine (30mg a day) for the past eight months, with little noticeable improvement in her mood.

Treating Depression: MCT, CBT and Third Wave Therapies, First Edition.
Edited by Adrian Wells and Peter L. Fisher.

Complaints and History

At the pre-treatment screening interview Gail met the DSM-V diagnostic criteria for recurrent major depressive disorder (APA, 2013). The current episode had persisted for 16 months, prior to which she felt that her mood had been reasonable for approximately six months. Gail had experienced numerous episodes of depression in the past; she thought that the first episode had occurred when she was 19, during her second year at university. She felt that her life had been plagued by depression, approximately twenty of the last thirty years of her life having been affected by significant episodes of low mood. There was a time in her early thirties when she felt genuinely content for three to four continuous years. This was the longest depression-free period in Gail's adult life that she could recall. More typically she would experience episodes of depression for six to nine months, then she would have an improved mood for a period of a few months before returning to the 'misery and despair that depression brings'.

In terms of the symptoms, she described a persistent low mood, with only a few 'reasonable days' in the last month; and by 'reasonable' she meant days when she was not tearful and was able to enjoy the company of her family. She was currently tearful almost every day, with persistent feelings of sadness and emptiness. She had a marked lack of interest in her work and wasn't interested in pursuing any of her previous pastimes either. Indeed, Gail felt that she 'didn't really do anything anymore', and any activities she engaged in were initiated by her husband or by her children. Six months before she had reduced the number of hours of work, as she felt she couldn't cope with the demands of her job. She reported that, although she now only works two days a week, she finds these working days very difficult to manage because she feels tired all the time; she has to put a great deal of effort into concentrating while at work, and she is frequently concerned that she is making mistakes or forgetting to execute vital tasks. Gail also reported being concerned that her colleagues will try to make conversation: she had nothing to say to them, which made her feel embarrassed. After the reduction in work hours, she has found herself sleeping much more, and also during the day. On the other hand she complains of an initial insomnia on most nights: it takes her approximately two hours to fall asleep, as her mind is whirring. Generally, when she falls asleep, she sleeps well, but she experiences early-morning waking up at least once a week. Usually she has difficulty getting out of bed in the morning and tends to lay there thinking about how she feels. She reports being easily tired by almost anything. She has made sure that her daughters do 'more than their fair share of cooking and cleaning', as all that is too much for her. This frequently causes her a great deal of concern, as she thinks that she shouldn't burden her children so much. She also feels guilty about contributing less to the household income and she worries about not being a good mother.

Generally her appetite is reasonable and she has remained at a steady weight over the past six months, although she acknowledged that on some days she tends to comfort eat and then feels guilty about not exercising. She has fleeting thoughts about death and often thinks 'It would be better if I don't wake up'; but she is not currently suicidal. She reported having hoarded a number of tablets in the past, should things have gotten worse; but she never attempted suicide.

A significant degree of hopelessness was expressed during the assessment interview. Gail feels very much that the rest of her life will continue along the same path. She thinks that the best she can hope for is longer periods of a 'normal mood', but she is very concerned that she will have to continue to experience long periods of depression. She is pessimistic about getting help from therapy, because she has had numerous forms of non-directive counselling since her early twenties, with seemingly minimal impact. Over the past thirty years Gail has also been on many different forms of antidepressant medication. She feels that, at times, the medication may have helped; but she is unconvinced of its usefulness for her.

Gail's background is largely unremarkable; she was the youngest of four children – two boys and one other girl. She described currently good relationships with all of her siblings and remembered her childhood fondly. She did reasonably well at school, where she had a few close friends and was very active in a variety of sports. At 18 she went to study English literature at university, and subsequently she trained professionally. Both her parents died over a decade ago; occasionally she feels sad about this, especially as her daughters were able to have only a brief relationship with their grandparents. She feels that she has a supportive family environment but was very conscious that, since her depression returned, her relationships with her husband and two daughters had deteriorated – which, again, she felt was her fault and made her feel very guilty. In addition to the clinical interview, Gail also completed some self-report measures, scoring 37 (severe depression) on the Beck Depression Inventory (BDI-II) (Beck, Steer, & Brown, 1996) and 14 (mild anxiety) on the Beck Anxiety Inventory (Beck, Epstein, Brown, & Steer, 1988).

References

APA. (2013) *Diagnostic and statistical manual of mental disorders: DSM-5*. Washington, DC: American Psychiatric Association.

Beck, A. T., Steer, R. A., & Brown, G. K. (1996). *Manual for the Beck Depression Inventory* (2nd edn). San Antonio, TX: Psychological Corporation.

Beck, A. T., Epstein, N., Brown, G., & Steer, R. A. (1988). An inventory for measuring clinical anxiety: Psychometric properties. *Journal of Consulting and Clinical Psychology*, 56, 893–897.

11

Cognitive Behaviour Therapy for Depression

Yvonne Tieu and Keith S. Dobson

Cognitive behaviour therapy (CBT) is a widely researched and endorsed therapeutic approach for a range of disorders. Its evidence base is strong, and the Task Force on Promotion and Dissemination of Psychological Procedures of the American Psychological Association (APA) considers it be an empirically supported treatment for a number of disorders and age groups (Chambless et al., 1998). Although cited as one of the most commonly used psychotherapeutic techniques with adult clients (Leichensring, Hiller, Weissberg, & Leibing, 2006), CBT represents a diverse spectrum of interventions (see K. S. Dobson, 2009; O'Donohue & Fisher, 2009). Within the spectrum of CBT approaches, that of cognitive therapy (CT) has attracted perhaps the greatest amount of attention (K. S. Dobson, 2008). Even within CT, however, none of the interventions is solely cognitive in nature; they include behavioural elements or involve a focus on emotional responding. This chapter discusses CBT. The discussion will include the theoretical model that underlies CBT and the clinical application of CBT to the treatment of a particular client (Gail). Particular attention will be paid to how to assess, formulate, and treat the presented case from a CBT perspective.

Cognitive Behavioural Theory and Therapy

Interest in the application of CT to cases of depression was piqued by the publication of *Cognitive Therapy of Depression* (A. T. Beck, Rush, Shaw, & Emery, 1979). Aaron Beck's cognitive model discusses the relationship

---

Treating Depression: MCT, CBT and Third Wave Therapies, First Edition.
Edited by Adrian Wells and Peter L. Fisher.

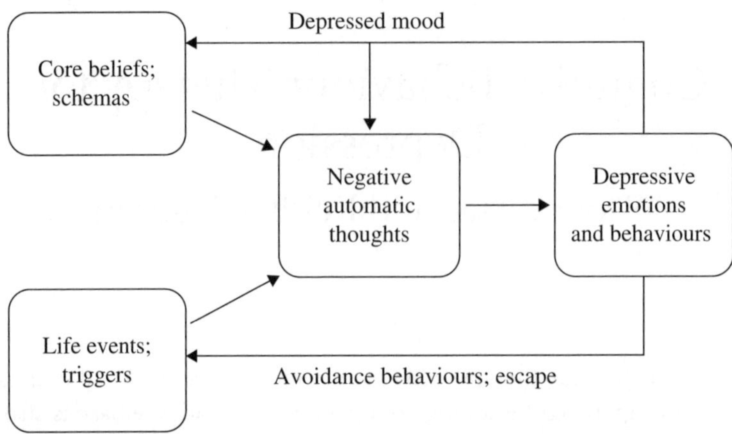

Figure 11.1 The cognitive model of depression (Dobson, 2008).

between depressed mood and negative automatic thoughts, cognitive biases (or thinking errors), and core beliefs or assumptions (now often referred to as 'schemas'). As Figure 11.1 indicates, the negative nature of thoughts and representations is held to increase the risk for depressive feelings and behaviour (K. S. Dobson, 2008).

When applied to depressed individuals, CT focuses on negative thinking patterns and on how the content and process of these thoughts relate to the emotional, behavioural, and situational components and symptoms of depression. CT is a cohesive combination of cognitive and behavioural interventions intended to assess and alter erroneous negative beliefs and change maladaptive information-processing styles (A. T. Beck et al., 1979). As therapy proceeds, clients are taught to conduct behavioural experiments to test their beliefs. In order to design such experiments, cognitive therapists identify a client's negative thoughts and beliefs by using techniques that will be outlined below with the help of Gail's case. However, CBT is a system of treatment and in this capacity it encompasses the formal features typically seen in psychotherapy. The cases usually follow a pattern of assessment, case conceptualization, and behavioural work to engage the client in his/her life and to assess thinking; then automatic thought assessment and change, work on dysfunctional schemas, and a final stage of termination and relapse planning. (Dobson & Dobson, 2009; Wenzel, 2013). These stages are described in turn below, even though it is acknowledged that in real life the process is fairly dynamic and a therapist could, for example, cycle back to assessment at various points in a treatment programme if a new problem emerged, or if there was any need to obtain a different perspective on an already acknowledged problem.

CBT is a system of therapy with its own conceptual model and set of associated interventions. This model of therapy is commonly used in the field of psychotherapy, hence it receives wide training (Norcross, Hedges, & Prochaska, 2002). There are several variants of CBT (K. S. Dobson, 2009), but perhaps the best known is that of CT. These treatments generally emphasize the assessment and modification of unhealthy thoughts and behaviours. The model holds that mental health is associated with good adaptation to the environment; therefore accurate perception of one's environment and optimal adaptive behaviour are treatment goals. The model's emphasis on change is predicated on the general notion that people with mental disorders or emotional disturbances are somewhat out of step with their environment and need to develop skills in order to perceive it accurately, to reflect on their personal goals from within their social world, and to enhance their behavioural repertoire so as to move towards the fulfilment of these goals. At the same time CBT is highly flexible, in that the particular life goals or directions can be driven by the individual client; thus the approach can be applied broadly, to a wide range of clinical disorders and to clients with diverse social and cultural backgrounds.

CBT is distinct from a number of other treatment approaches in several respects. It explicitly focuses on the relationship between thinking processes and behavioural and emotional outcomes, and in consequence views cognitive processes as mediators of other outcomes. Thus, while this perspective shares some commonalities with psychodynamic therapy in terms of focus on 'core work', its own focus is very different from that of the experiential therapies – including mindfulness therapies, which deemphasize the role of cognition and in some cases explicitly shift attention to emotion as a primary area of concern. Another distinction of CBT is that it is a time-limited and relatively structured form of psychotherapy. Various forms of CBT have lent themselves well to written presentation in treatment manuals, and this manualization has in turn been associated with an increased emphasis on the use of CBT in randomized clinical trials by comparison to other treatment models. At the same time CBT therapists also recognize the importance of the therapeutic relationship and of non-specific aspects of psychotherapy (cf. D. J. G. Dobson & Dobson, 2009; Kazantzis, Dattilio, & Dobson, forthcoming) as the crucible in which therapy techniques are employed. Unlike in some other models of therapy, however, the therapeutic relationship is considered to be a necessary but not a sufficient prerequisite for patient change in CBT.

Although all forms of therapy provide a conceptual model for the interventions that are being used, CBT incorporates a relatively specific model for case conceptualization. This conceptualization is predicated on a full understanding of the individual case (Persons, 2008), but it also has common elements with conceptualizations for different patients, who come into therapy with common problems (Nezu, Nezu, & Lombardo, 2004). It has also been argued that the cognitive model provides an integrative framework (Alford & Beck, 1997), which allows for the broad applicability of CBT across diverse disorders and cases. As will be demonstrated through the example of Gail, the development of a case conceptualization is a crucial feature of CBT, as it certainly does determine the nature of preferred or indicated interventions with specific patients.

One of the distinctive characteristics of CBT is its empowerment of the patient. For example, CBT encourages the use of psycho-education, so that patients can understand the interventions that are contemplated and can even participate in the process of making treatment decisions and plans. Many CBT programmes describe the patient as an expert in his/her own life and as a collaborator in the treatment programme. CBT is thus not a treatment done 'to', but rather 'with', the patient. This engagement of the patient is also related to an explicit focus in CBT on planning for termination and on planning to prevent relapse. However, unlike some other treatments, where 'termination' is seen as a final phase of therapy, CBT views the ending of acute treatment as a progression towards maintenance of gains and relapse prevention (Antony, Ledley, & Heimberg, 2005; Dobson & Dobson, 2009). Booster sessions, occasional check-ins, and follow-up appointments are not regarded as evidence of treatment failure in CBT, but rather as the logical consequence of living in a complicated world and as a reflection of the value that the patient places on consultations with a CBT expert.

Assessment

Intake assessment for depression in CT typically involves several elements (Dozois & Dobson, 2009). Many settings require a formal diagnosis and, while a formally structured interview such as the Structured Clinical Interview for the DSM-V (SCID) (First, Williams, Karg, & Spitzer, 2015) would likely be used only in a research setting, most clinicians review symptoms with their clients when they have to determine whether a diagnosis of major depressive disorder is warranted. To assess the severity of depression, common instruments are either a clinician rating system such as the Hamilton Rating Scale for Depression (HRSD) (Hamilton, 1960) or a self-report form such as the Beck Depression Inventory-II (BDI-II) (A. T. Beck, Steer, & Brown, 1996). Ancillary problems such as anxiety, sleep, or other conditions may also be assessed either through questionnaires, sleep diaries, and other daily charts or through direct inquiry with the client. In addition to a questionnaire-based assessment, both a clinical interview and observation often aid in the investigation of the client's current activities and concerns (or problems).

Gail was interviewed clinically and her symptoms were assessed. It was determined that she met the criteria for recurrent major depressive disorder. Other diagnoses were not formally explored, although the therapist suspected that she might also meet the criteria for an anxiety disorder, which may have preceded the onset of her depressive episodes. Due to this initial impression, she was administered a BDI-II and Beck Anxiety Inventory (BAI) (A. T. Beck, Epstein, Brown, & Steer, 1988). In light of Gail's concern about making mistakes at work, her work activities as well as her sleep were inquired about. With the help of a cognitive model outlined by J. Beck (2011), details about Gail's negative automatic thoughts and cognitive schemas were assessed in the interview and across sessions, as more information was gathered. This model was utilized to formulate a cognitive behavioural case conceptualization and to understand how Gail's negative automatic thoughts and cognitive schemas were related to, and affected, her symptoms of depression.

Case conceptualization

There are numerous ways to conceptualize clients' problems to aid treatment as well as establish a working relationship with clients within the CBT framework (see Dobson & Dobson, 2009; J. Beck, 1995, 2011; Persons & Davidson, 2001, 2008). In CBT developing a case conceptualization and writing it down in the therapist's case notes is considered to be a key part of the therapy (Persons, 2008). As the case evolves and becomes more sophisticated, it can be shared with the client. This process of dialogue allows for further refinements in the understanding of problems on both sides – by therapist and by client alike; helps to give the client a sense of predictability about his/her distress; and directs the planning of interventions. The case conceptualization often becomes more elaborate as the treatment progresses. Early on in assessment and treatment planning, for example, the case conceptualization might consist of fairly basic ideas of how specific situations elicit negative thoughts. In the case of Gail, the model presented by K. S. Dobson (2008) was selected to explore her reactions to a specific stressor, while the cognitive behavioural case formulation was based on suggestions provided by J. Beck (2011).

K. S. Dobson's model (2008) was utilized to demonstrate to Gail the cognitive behavioural model of depression on the basis of one of the situations she discussed in therapy. The model was presented to Gail as a visual psycho-educational tool and as 'evidence' for the relevancy of examining her thoughts and behaviours, which were both contributing to and maintaining her depression. Gail had mentioned that she sometimes found it easier to understand concepts if she saw a picture or diagram depicting the concept, thus the therapist presented this model as a visual aid to describing the relationship between Gail's negative automatic thoughts and her depressive mood.

The case formulation included the CBT model as depicted in Figure 11.1, and was further refined by suggestions from J. Beck's (2011) text on CT. The therapist's rationale for including this material in the case formulation was that, while K. S. Dobson's (2008) model effectively presents the cognitive behavioural model of depression, there were numerous elements in Gail's case that required more detailed conceptualization if they were to inform treatment. Although Figure 11.1 was used to succinctly capture specific cognitive behavioural examples of Gail's depression, given the recurrent nature of her symptoms, the therapist thought it best to consult Beck's case formulation suggestions to better understand Gail's core beliefs. Several of Gail's comments provided insight into her existing cognitive schemas and biases. The therapist followed the model and asked Gail about ideas in three domains: her (potentially negative) view of herself, her (negative) interpretation of events, and her view of her future. Together, these domains have been labelled the 'cognitive triad' (A. T. Beck et al., 1979). Gail's self-oriented beliefs were that she wasn't a 'good' mother, wife, employee, and co-worker but that she should be. When questioned further about these beliefs, Gail reported that she was easily overwhelmed by situations and did not know how to handle stress very well. Her schema regarding others indicated a belief that people were demanding: 'They always want more and more from me.' Her beliefs about therapists were particularly negative, based on previous failed treatment, and she openly expressed this idea: 'You can't help me, because nothing has worked before.' Gail's beliefs about the future were pessimistic, summarized by her concern that she was going to continue to experience periods of depression. Her schemas about the world were also negative, as evidenced by statements such as: 'It's dog-eat-dog out there.'

It was critical to understand Gail's schemas and beliefs – that is, to understand how various situations or triggers could activate the schemas presented above and cause her to respond with depressive thoughts and behaviours. Gail also exhibited a faulty information processing, which involved systematic cognitive errors that led her to perceive her immediate experiences in an unrealistic manner. For example, in discussing her most recent employment performance appraisal, which contained some negative comments, Gail was unable to recall any positive comments made about her work performance; she also demonstrated some personalization of her superior's comments when she remarked: 'He said those things because he doesn't like me.' This situation probably activated her negative self-schema and served to confirm the belief that she was not a good employee. It also served as confirmatory evidence for the criticalness of others, and both interpretations reinforced and maintained her depressed mood.

The majority of Gail's comments suggested that she had core beliefs centred around her helplessness, as she emphasized her feelings of incompetence and inability to handle situations (J. Beck, 2011). Gail's belief that she was helpless 'coloured' her perception of situations, triggered negative automatic thoughts, and led to depressive thoughts and behaviours. Although discussions of the origins of Gail's depression are not essential in a CBT conceptualization, her pattern of response presumably began in childhood, with parents who expected a lot of her while she was willing to comply with their hopes and expectations. Gail reported that her childhood was mostly happy and that she had been what her parents called 'an ideal child'. When she went away to university, however, she was far away from her family and quickly became overwhelmed by academic demands. As a means of coping, Gail often withdrew from social situations and preferred to remain in her dorm room. When asked what her thoughts were at that time in her life, Gail responded that she didn't think she was smart enough to be at university and that 'I felt very lonely, but I didn't know what to do about it'. Again, Gail's sense of helplessness was conveyed as she described this time of her life.

To conceptualize Gail's depressive pattern, the recent situation of her performance appraisal was outlined in Figure 11.2. Her negative automatic thought process exacerbated her depressive mood and reinforced her core belief that she was not a good employee. It also increased her avoidance

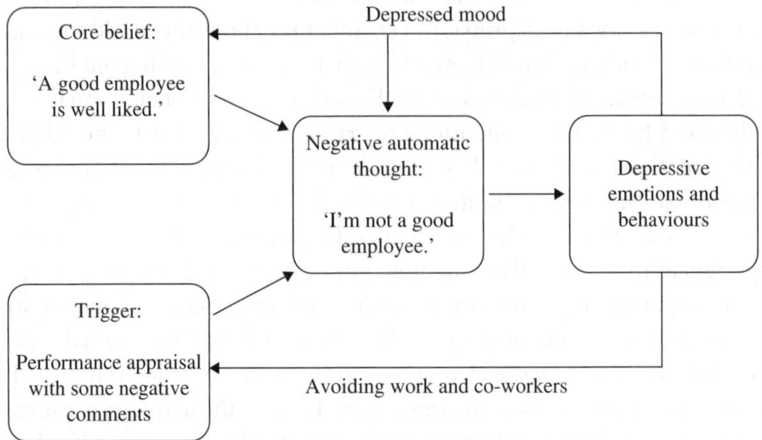

Figure 11.2 The cognitive model of depression as applied to Gail.

behaviour, which, over time, would likely lead to other performance problems and negative appraisals from others. Both figures were presented to Gail as a way to discuss the cognitive behavioural model of depression and demonstrate the application of a CBT model to her performance appraisal. They were utilized as visual psycho-educational tools designed to enhance Gail's understanding of CBT concepts and to make her literally see the relevance of CBT to her depression.

Gail's case conceptualization demonstrates another important aspect of the cognitive model of depression: it involves a vulnerability stress formulation. Both the vulnerability (i.e., the presence of certain schemas) and the stressors or activating events need to be considered if one is to fully understand the genesis of problematic thoughts, emotional reactions, and behavioural patterns. For Gail, the general vulnerability was related to the demands or expectations that she put on herself and felt from others ('oughts', 'shoulds'), and which were signalled by the general sense of disappointment she felt about herself and the pervasive guilt she experienced. The activating events were generally those that interacted with the above core schemas and involved an actual or potential appraisal of failure to meet a behavioural standard or requirement, whether as a mother, a wife, or an employee. It was this interaction between vulnerability and stressors that led to Gail's emotional distress and exacerbated her tendencies to withdraw or act in a depressed manner.

Given the presented symptoms, Gail met the criteria for major depressive disorder, recurrent, with melancholic features, as described in DSM-V (APA, 2014). In addition to the case conceptualization, this diagnosis guided the recommendations for treatment and helped the therapist and Gail to set realistic expectations for treatment outcomes, given the nature of her disorder. Over the course of therapy, as suggested by J. Beck (2011), the case conceptualization was refined as data were collected and hypotheses were confirmed, disconfirmed, or modified.

Treatment

The therapeutic relationship A key feature of cognitive behaviour therapy is the importance placed on the therapeutic relationship, which is based on trust, good rapport, and collaboration (A. T. Beck et al., 1979). Gail was initially quite sceptical of the therapist's abilities to alleviate her mood problems. Rather than argue with this scepticism or cite statistics, the therapist offered to work with Gail, so that they could see together whether or not the therapy was working. The therapist also recognized the absolute importance in a case like this to do regular assessment with the BDI-II, in order to have material (or evidence) to discuss with Gail. As the therapist demonstrated empathy and understanding of Gail's problems, she began to feel more at ease with the therapist even by the end of their first session. The therapist also demonstrated an interest in this issue, but explicitly inquired about Gail's reactions to therapy and to the therapist. It was important to distinguish CBT from other therapies that Gail had received, while showing empathy with her past failures. The therapist was mindful of her pessimism and planned to monitor for hopelessness and suicidality. If necessary, a more detailed suicide assessment would have been conducted, and emergency services offered. Through active collaboration with Gail, the therapist acknowledged Gail's autonomy and offered her an opportunity to begin gaining mastery and control over the course of treatment; the therapist also started to shape her behaviour in a subtle manner, so as to prepare her for an eventual termination of therapy.

Session structure Another feature of cognitive behavioural therapy is the structure of sessions (Dobson & Dobson, 2009; Wenzel, 2013). For the most part, each session is relatively predictable and focused, in order to maximize therapeutic gains within each session and to keep the client and the therapist on task. Each session typically begins with a brief mood check and review of the homework assigned in the previous session. Current problems are reviewed quickly, and a combination of problem targets, homework issues, and new objectives becomes the grist for setting an agenda for the session. In some cases the agenda is formalized, time segments being allocated to different issues so as to ensure that the time is used optimally and that the major problem(s) receive sufficient attention. While early on in treatment therapists typically take more responsibility in suggesting an agenda, there is a shift of responsibility to the client over the course of time, as he or she learns the model and helps the therapist to identify key current concerns.

The bulk of the session is dedicated to the discussion of items on the agenda and to the use of various cognitive and behavioural techniques to challenge a client's cognitions and to promote change. After discussing each part of the agenda, the therapist and the client will often review what has been discussed and will determine whether some appropriate homework can be assigned. At the end of each session a summary of the overall discussion is made, the overall plan for homework is reviewed (and adjusted, if necessary), and client feedback about the session is sought. Minor adjustments may be made to the general structure of sessions as therapy progresses, since the therapist will want to individualize the therapy in order to meet each client's needs.

The first session Part of the first session with Gail was spent discussing formal aspects of the treatment – such as the limits of confidentiality, record keeping, payment, and informed consent. The therapist then inquired about the problems that Gail had; and, when she reported depression-related problems, the therapist inquired about other symptoms of depression, with a view to generating a diagnosis. The therapist dedicated a fair amount of time to probing whether he could understand some of Gail's problems by using the framework of cognitive theory. He provided a description of the general efficacy of this treatment for depression and briefly described how cognitive behavioural therapy would presumably move forward.

THERAPIST: So, Gail, if I understand correctly, a lot of your problems right now center around the concern that other people, like your boss, are pretty critical of you.

GAIL: Yes, it seems like there is a 'bar' that I just can't jump over, but no one will tell me how high the bar is, or even where it is.

THERAPIST: So that puts you in a pretty difficult situation! You must feel pretty helpless, when you aren't even told what you have to do, and then people are watching and judging.

GAIL: Yes, sometimes it feels like I should just give up.

THERAPIST: So, your ideas that the 'bar' is unclear, that no one helps you, but they are sitting there in judgement all seem to be pretty clearly linked to your feeling helpless and you want to give up at times. Is that right?

GAIL: Um, yes, I suppose so. But I don't really see these as 'ideas' – it is just the way things are.

THERAPIST: Yes, I can see that. In this form of therapy, we recognize that these thoughts or ideas are related to how you feel and what you do; it's natural to feel helpless and want to do nothing if you think the situation is stacked against you. But I am also interested in going back and looking at these ideas with you, to understand where they come from, and to see if they can maybe be shifted in some way to be more helpful to you. If we could do that together, to explore these ideas and maybe help you to feel less helpless and more positive, would that be a 'plus' for you?

GAIL: Sure, but it seems hard.

THERAPIST: Yes, it is not always easy, especially if you have thought and felt this way for some time. But I am pretty confident that I have some tools that we can try, which often help people in just your situation. Is that something you would be willing to try?

GAIL: I suppose so. I am pretty low right now, so I am not optimistic, but I am here to learn and to try something different, I guess.

THERAPIST: That's great. All we can ever do is try. And it won't always be easy. Just coming here and talking about problems won't be enough. But with some effort together, and some practical ideas that you can implement between our sessions, I think we can make some headway.

Education about depression was also provided to Gail, in order to normalize her symptoms and to discuss which ones she found most distressing as a means to focus her treatment goals. In terms of treatment goals, the overarching goals of CT for depression are to learn to identify and modify dysfunctional thoughts and behaviours with the potential to recognize and change the underlying cognitive patterns that lead to the dysfunctional thoughts and behaviours (A. T. Beck et al., 1979). An additional goal for therapy would be to prevent relapse and recurrence of depression.

Gail was most interested in making improvements to her mood, which the therapist agreed would be an important first step, as he suspected that such changes would further forge a therapeutic alliance. Gail also mentioned how to she wanted to improve her sleep, and 'do the things I used to do before my depression, like playing card games with my daughters, and going for walks with my husband'. The therapist suggested that Gail's progress could be monitored through self-report measures (e.g., BDI-II, BAI, etc.) as well as through reports from collateral sources, such as her husband and children. Lastly, Gail wanted to feel less guilty but was unable to specify in what context she wanted to reduce her guilt. The therapist hypothesized that Gail's feelings of guilt were probably due to her core beliefs and perfectionistic tendencies. Thus the identification of and change to her negative thinking was hypothesized to address her schemas and to bring about changes in her mood and behaviour. Overall, despite her pessimism about therapy in general, Gail was viewed as a good candidate for CBT.

In view of her scepticism about therapy, Gail was given reassurances about the general efficacy of CBT for depression. She was informed that, in depression, clients typically receive psychotherapy twice a week for an initial period of approximately three weeks. Once her mood improved and stabilized, Gail would be seen once a week for approximately 14 more sessions – about 20 in total – although this figure would be adjusted on the basis of her response to treatment. It was explained to her that the later sessions would perhaps be spread out over a longer period, so that the eighteenth and the nineteenth sessions would take place two weeks after the preceding one, and the final session three or four weeks after the nineteenth. Such 'fading' of the final sessions allows for more practice time between therapeutic contacts and for an assessment of the client's readiness for termination.

Gail's expectations regarding her treatment were elicited – in order for the therapist both to gather her initial feedback and optimism and to ensure that Gail's expectations were realistic. In addition, misconceptions that Gail may have had about therapy in general were discussed and dispelled. For example, she expressed some surprise that the treatment included homework, as her previous therapy never had. She was also concerned that the therapist was going to put pressure on her to perform in some unknown ways. In response, the therapist again stated that any treatment only works if it changes how someone lives his or her real life, outside of therapy. Gail accepted this idea and noted that it was 'funny' how her previous therapist had never said anything like this. Also, in regard to the idea of pressure, the therapist told Gail that in most cases she would assign herself the homework, and that it would only be work that she thought was important and relevant to her feeling better. At the same time the therapist acknowledged that Gail might have reacted to the word 'homework' itself, given her sense of failure in university, and he offered that, if she wanted, they could instead use the word 'assignment' or 'mission', if that felt less oppressive. Gail said she would think about it, and they could come up with a term together.

Session homework Gail was reminded that her depression was attributable to her thoughts and beliefs about herself and the world around her, which reiterated the importance and power of her cognitions on her mood. Thus, while the therapist considered the use of an activity log to record Gail's major activity each hour as her first homework assignment, he reflected on this consideration. He asked a few brief questions, which quickly revealed that Gail often had a fairly active week between work, home. and family duties. If anything, her week was overly busy and failed to leave her time for herself or for her marital relationship – or simply time to relax.

Given these circumstances, homework gave way to the idea of keeping a thought record, which was designed to better identify and monitor Gail's negative automatic thoughts and the situations that triggered such thoughts. Gail was also asked to refine her treatment goals, so that therapy could proceed accordingly and could move towards the achievement of her outlined goals. Following the assigning of homework, the therapist summarized the session.

THERAPIST: Gail, even in this first hour together I have learned quite a bit about your background and your current problems. We spent some time talking about depression in general and what symptoms you experience. We discussed how thoughts are connected to feelings and behaviours and how cognitive behavioural therapy can likely work for you. We've also talked about your goals and the kinds of things we'll be doing in therapy in order to achieve those goals. And, as part of treatment, we also discussed the importance of 'homework', or some other word we will come up with, to translate what we talk about here into real action plans to change your life. Finally, you have agreed to start to monitor your thoughts, so that we can start to get a better handle on what you actually say to yourself. Was there anything else I missed?

GAIL: No, I think that was everything. This seems like a lot. I wonder if I can really do all of this.

THERAPIST: That reaction is pretty normal for someone who feels depressed, and that life is stacked up against you. Does it seem like I am too hopeful for you?

GAIL: Maybe a bit.

THERAPIST: OK, well, let's agree then that we can work together, and see how things go. If you think that I am pushing you too hard, I hope you will be able to tell me, so that we can also look at that thought, and maybe I can learn to adjust my expectations, too!

GAIL: OK, that seems fair.

The second session Gail's second session followed a similar format to her first, in that there was a brief check-in regarding changes in her mood since the last meeting, her homework was briefly reviewed, and then the session proceeded to focus on the development of an agenda. Gail's mood had improved slightly as she was feeling more hopeful about therapy, and, on the basis of some reading she had done, she set an additional, tentative goal of eliminating her use of medication over time. The therapist suggested that her medication dosage should be kept stable for most of the period of therapy (in part, so that she could credit herself rather than the absence of medication and could make internal attributions for any changes that were to take place), but that, in conjunction with the prescribing physician, they would revisit this idea and would work towards reducing her dosage, or even stopping her medication altogether near the end of treatment – if that would still be important to her and would seem a good decision at that point. The therapist asked for Gail's permission to consult with the physician before any final decision about her medication plan.

Gail's initial thought record was reviewed, and the therapist highlighted the relationship between her thoughts, her mood, and her behaviour in order to reiterate the cognitive model and its future impact on Gail's depressed mood. The therapist noted that several of Gail's thoughts were about critical judgements made by others (employer, co-workers, husband); and she endorsed this general pattern. As some aspects of the thought record were somewhat incomplete, the therapist and Gail spent some time fleshing out the record in session, and Gail was given the 'mission' of continuing to monitor her thoughts with the help of the thought record.

One of Gail's major worries was about her sleep. The therapist asked several questions in order to assess problems within this range and recommended a number of sleep hygiene interventions. He had Gail incorporate the following suggestions into her daily routine over time: sleep as much as needed to feel refreshed; get up and go to bed at the same time every day; use the bed only for sleep and sex; begin to engage in some regular exercise (perhaps starting with a limited activity of walking three times a week and gradually progressing to a daily activity of some kind); avoid caffeine and other stimulants in the afternoon, and certainly in the period before bedtime; avoid being too hungry or too full at bedtime; keep the bedroom at a moderate or cool room temperature; and do not watch the clock. Finally, if she could not sleep within 20 minutes or was awake for longer than 20 minutes, Gail was encouraged to get out of bed and do something quiet or boring until sleepy, at which point she could return to bed to sleep (cf. Casola, Goldsmith, & Daiter, 2006). These recommendations were all written down and given to her as a set of 'suggestions' that she could start to implement. Some planning and troubleshooting were completed in order to ensure a successful integration of sleep hygiene techniques and to enhance compliance with the above suggestions. For example, it was discussed that Gail's husband often complained if Gail went to bed before 11:00 p.m. In response, the therapist and Gail agreed that it was fine to adopt 10:30 p.m. as a regular bedtime if that was part of her treatment, and Gail felt comfortable having this discussion with her husband.

Another item on Gail's agenda was her concern about loss of interest in activities she previously enjoyed. However, when asked what activities she typically engaged in, she was unable to provide much detail. Hence the therapist suggested that another mission might be to think about her busy schedule and consider whether there was some pleasurable activity that she could insert into it, even once, to see what effect it had on her mood.

Session homework In addition to the implementation of sleep hygiene techniques and the assignment of a pleasurable activity of her choice, Gail was asked to once again complete a thought record to further assess which situations triggered her negative automatic thoughts. Although such issues did not emerge in this session, the therapist was mindful about any possible difficulty in the completion of homework; had such issues emerged, these foreseeable obstacles would have been discussed with Gail, and her attitude towards homework would have been examined. It may be the case that homework remains incomplete due to a practical problem – such as not fully understanding what the task is; due to a psychological problem – such as negative cognitions regarding the assignment; or due to the therapist's hesitation to investigate why homework is not being completed (J. Beck, 2011). In any of these situations, the therapist should assign appropriate homework in order to encourage the generalization and maintenance of therapeutic gains. The therapist's inattention to homework problems sends the client a strong (negative) signal that homework does not really matter.

Third session and beyond To address Gail's interests, some behavioural activation methods were utilized. The goal of encouraging pleasurable activity led to an assignment in which Gail generated a list of pleasurable and/or important things she wanted to do. Together, she and the therapist developed strategies for increasing both the range and the effectiveness of her activities, and the effect of these actions on her mood and thoughts were evaluated. The therapist was especially mindful of either negative ideas that interfered with the performance of these planned actions or cognitions that negated their positive effects after completion. The therapist and Gail planned and conducted several behavioural experiments, to test out her ideas about 'important' activities. For example, Gail listed 'playing card games with my daughters' as a pleasurable activity. As an experiment, Gail was to engage in this activity after dinner on one evening. However, she was reluctant to do so because she thought that she would be too tired from work, her daughters would be too busy and would not want to spend time with her, or she would have some other task to accomplish. Despite these negative thoughts, Gail was encouraged to complete the task and to record the outcome on her thought record. As it turned out, her daughters responded quite positively to the suggestion of card games and Gail accumulated evidence that contradicted her previously held negative beliefs. Table 11.1 represents her initial thought record for this situation and her modified thought record after she conducted this homework exercise.

Another behavioural experiment that Gail conducted involved asking a fellow co-worker to have lunch with her. Gail had previously mentioned that she was not particularly social when at work and wanted to spend more time getting to know her co-workers. Thus the therapist and Gail decided that Gail should select a co-worker whom she had some interest in getting to know better and ask him/her to lunch one day. The following dialogue demonstrates Gail's automatic negative thoughts regarding the experiment.

THERAPIST: So, how did the lunch date work out?

GAIL: Well, not so great because I had a lot of negative thoughts before asking Karen out to lunch. [Gail hands over thought record to therapist.] I was really worried she would say no and that I wouldn't be able to handle that.

THERAPIST: Because that would mean she didn't like you, right?

GAIL: Yeah. We've never really been friends and I thought that may be because she didn't want to be friends.

Table 11.1 Gail's thought record before and after her behavioural experiment.

Situation	*Automatic Thoughts (Believability: 1–100%)*	*Feelings (Rated strength: 1–100%)*	*Behaviour*	*New Evidence*	*New Automatic Thoughts*	*Feelings*	*Behaviour*
Planned to play cards with my daughters; evening time	I am too tired. (40%) They are too busy. (60%) The last thing they want is to spend time with me. (60%)	Tired (80%) Lonely (70%) Afraid (50%)	Sit watching TV alone				
Planned to play cards with my daughters; evening time; actually asked them this time				They agreed, and seemed interested. We played cards, and they talked about other times we had done so.	They aren't too busy for me. (40%) I feel less tired. (80%) Maybe if I try, things can work out better than if I do not. (30%) I love my daughters. (100%) I hope they are not just humouring me. (20%)	Happy (60%) Less lonely (50%) Enthusiastic (40%)	Played cards for about an hour, until the girls had to go to bed.

THERAPIST: So what did Karen say?

GAIL: She said no, and right away I thought 'I knew it! She doesn't like me. Nobody here likes me.' I felt sad right away, but then she said that she couldn't this week because she was really busy, but we could have lunch next week if I wanted.

THERAPIST: And how did you feel then?

GAIL: Relieved, I guess. I mean, I don't think she said no because she doesn't want to be friends since she offered to have lunch next week. So I guess all that worry about nobody liking me was pretty wrong.

THERAPIST: Right. It sounds like those negative thoughts about Karen not liking may not be entirely true since she is willing to have lunch, just not this week.

Gail's responses to such experiments helped the therapist to continue to develop the case conceptualization and to adjust the course of therapy. The experiments highlighted Gail's negative automatic thoughts, which are a focus of cognitive behavioural therapy for depression.

In order to alter Gail's negative automatic thoughts, the three key questions of CT were posed to Gail: What is the evidence for or against a particular negative thought? What is an alternative realistic thought? What does this thought mean to you or about you? (see D. J. G. Dobson & Dobson, 2009). These questions are used by cognitive therapists to pinpoint patterns of thoughts and triggers for negative automatic thoughts. The therapist then associates these patterns or triggers to a client's core beliefs and, in collaboration with the client, examines the evidence that supports or refutes negative schemas. Where the evidence exists or can be developed through experiments, alternative and more functional thoughts or beliefs are encouraged. These techniques were used to address Gail's guilt and her core beliefs about herself – since guilt is often associated with a belief about a personal demand and with underlying expectations about one's own conduct. As the following dialogue demonstrates, the therapist utilized these questions to examine Gail's automatic negative thought that she was not a 'good' employee (this discussion occurred in the middle part of the session, as the problem had been put on the agenda earlier on in the same session).

THERAPIST: So, if I understand right, your boss criticized you again. Tell me more about this situation.

GAIL: It was in a team meeting, and I made a suggestion, trying to get more involved like you and I talked about, and she said 'Oh, thanks Gail' in a kind of sarcastic, off-handed way. It made me feel like an idiot.

THERAPIST: So, tell me more about the exact situation. What was your meeting about, and what did you say?

GAIL: [Provides more factual information, with clarification from the therapist]

THERAPIST: And when your boss said 'Oh, thanks Gail.' Were those her exact words?

GAIL: Something like that.

THERAPIST: Well, let's be precise. It might be important.

GAIL: I think that's what she said.

THERAPIST: OK, so when she said that, did anyone look shocked? Did anyone else seem to react to this comment?

GAIL: No, I don't think so. I looked down at my papers, so I'm not sure what other people thought.

THERAPIST: And what happened next?

GAIL: Nothing, the meeting just continued. A guy from the Finance Department said something, I think.

THERAPIST: And when your boss said this, what did that mean to you?

GAIL: I thought: 'There she goes again. She thinks that I'm irrelevant.'

THERAPIST: Go with me a minute. What if it was true, and I am not saying it is, but if it was true that she thought you were irrelevant, what would that mean to you?

GAIL: Uh, I guess it means I should quit. That I have no future there.

THERAPIST: And if that was true? That you're irrelevant and have no future at that job.

GAIL: Then I'm basically useless. (Sighs) No wonder I'm depressed.

THERAPIST: OK, well, Gail, what you have just shown me is how critical that thought is that she maybe made a negative and dismissing comment. It is no wonder this strikes you so hard, since it seems that this idea is pretty closely tied to an underlying fear of being 'useless'. I wonder if this underlying fear might actually make you more sensitive to seeing criticism where it might or might not exist? Does that make sense to you?

GAIL: I think you mean kind of like if I look for something, then I will see it. So I'm extra sensitive to people who might be putting me down? And when I see it, then it proves what I expected all along?

THERAPIST: Exactly! [Goes on to discuss the self-reinforcing nature of schemas]

It was crucial for Gail to examine the biases and expectations that she brought to various relationships, and especially those where she felt she might be judged. The discussion was also broadened to examine past relationship stresses and failures and to note her thoughts regarding relationships and social interactions. The therapist's conceptualization suggested that much of Gail's depression emanated from expectations that she had about herself in various relationships.

As the treatment developed, the therapist thought that it was important to assess the developmental experiences associated with the genesis of Gail's interpersonal expectations, as such an historical exercise might reveal how these silent assumptions developed. It was also important to assess whether Gail's pattern of perfectionism was related to these beliefs.

THERAPIST: Gail, I'd like to spend some time thinking about how you've come to develop your sensitivity to judgement from others. Have you ever thought about where these beliefs are coming from?

GAIL: Sort of. I've found it hard to take criticism from anyone for most of my life. And rather than risk being scolded or put down, I just work really hard to give people what they wanted.

THERAPIST: Can you think of a specific example of this pattern?

GAIL: I can think of a time in school where we would have weekly spelling tests, and every week I got 100 per cent and my name was put on this board of perfect spellers. My parents were very proud of this fact. One week, I got 90 per cent on the spelling test and everyone in the class was shocked that I had made a mistake. My mother even said: 'I'm so disappointed Gail. You were so close to getting 100 per cent all year.' I felt so stupid and embarrassed that for the next week I studied even harder for the spelling test.

THERAPIST: It sounds like you worked very hard to do your best, but when you didn't do well it was all the harder to deal with it.

GAIL: Yeah, it's like once you got used to being told 'you're so smart' or 'you're doing a great job' that any little mistake detracted from that and I wasn't seen as a good person anymore.

THERAPIST: So getting consistent approval from others became an important way for you to know that you are a good person.

GAIL: Yeah, I guess I wanted people to acknowledge that I was a good girl.

Through discussion, it became clear that, although Gail's early life was in some senses idyllic, her behaviour was often referenced to her accomplishments and her ability to meet her parents' expectations. Although a 'good girl', Gail learned to look outside of herself for validation. She also learned that validation came through accomplishment. So, having had loving, caring, and evaluating parents was an advantage in her development, but also a liability, as it set up a belief system in which she needed validation from others in order to feel worthwhile.

The ongoing advantages and costs associated with Gail's belief system were discussed with her, and she was encouraged to consider the potential benefits and costs associated with keeping or changing these ideas. To the extent that she wanted to change, some broad-based shifts in her beliefs were encouraged through imagery, imagination, repeated homework, and behavioural assignments, so that she could truly shift her core beliefs. For example, she was encouraged to continue to express her ideas at work.

THERAPIST: Now, Gail, you've mentioned wanting to speak up more at meetings. Would you want to create a behavioural experiment to try this out?

GAIL: Sure, I've been feeling more confident about myself so I think this would be a good time to try it out.

THERAPIST: Well, let's discuss the details. What kind of ideas would you want to bring up at these meetings?

GAIL: Well, we meet once every week and anyone who wants to update everyone else on what's going on in their area can do so at this meeting. I'm the only one in my particular area, but I've only provided updates when people ask for them. I generally don't provide regular updates because I'm worried about what people will think of me.

THERAPIST: How often have people asked for updates?

GAIL: I'd say about once a month. My co-workers aren't too familiar with what I do and they're always surprised to hear how much has changed from month to month.

THERAPIST: So having more recent updates on your work would be beneficial to your co-workers?

GAIL: Probably. I guess if they heard about my work on a weekly basis they would have a better understanding of what I do.

THERAPIST: That sounds like a great experiment for us to try out.

GAIL: Yes, and I'll monitor my thoughts as usual. I think I'll even ask my co-workers what they thought of my update, just to check the accuracy of my thoughts about speaking at the meetings.

With repeated practice and some clearly positive feedback from others (and eventually from her boss, who did turn out to be stingy in her praise), Gail began to trust her own judgement more. She also began to insist on more and more varied social relations with her family, which incorporated some fun activities. While somewhat resistant at first, her husband and daughters eventually accepted this shift in activity; and the shift allowed Gail new ways to relate to members of her family. On one Thanksgiving visit home to see her elderly parents, she even took the risk of talking about how their focus on her accomplishments had affected her development. In response, they were able to remind her of other experiences, which demonstrated other ways in which they had tried to show how they loved her no matter what; and their relationship was broadened and strengthened. This part of the therapy reflected what is sometimes referred to as schema therapy (Leahy, 2015), which has a focus on core beliefs and schemas.

Relapse prevention

Relapse planning for Gail included the suggestion that she diversify her identity, in an attempt to change her own core beliefs still further while also trying to expand her social network. Gail was encouraged to maintain her sleep hygiene techniques and to engage in pleasurable activities, in addition to monitoring and examining her negative beliefs. As therapy progressed, Gail became more responsible for the course of her therapy and was encouraged to become her own therapist, to continue the practice of techniques she had learned, and to maintain the gains she had made in therapy as a means to prepare herself for the termination of treatment. There was a review of the symptoms she had initially displayed, and the same questionnaires were used, in order to demonstrate her improvement. Together, the therapist and Gail reviewed her case conceptualization, which by now was very detailed and complete, in order to trace the onset of her depression and to reinforce her need to continue to develop a sense of self that was not based on the evaluations of others. The 'fading' of sessions was also a means to prevent relapse and to monitor the stabilization and improvement of Gail's mood.

Adjunct therapies

One of the issues that had been identified in Gail's case was that of medications. She had expressed a desired to stop using medications as a possible goal, and the therapist had agreed to revisit this issue later on in treatment.

By the fifteenth session it became clear that Gail was basically non-depressed and that the focus of treatment had shifted to an examination of her history and of the roots of her belief system. The therapist asked Gail about the goal of reducing or eliminating medications. After discussion, Gail was able to articulate her belief that CBT was responsible for the changes she had recently experienced, especially as she had not changed her medication regime at all during this period. At the same time she was nervous about stopping her medications. Given these circumstances, the therapist and Gail agreed that she would continue to take her medications, but that, maybe in six months or so, she could talk with her physician about reducing them. The therapist said that he would be willing to meet with Gail at that time and support her during that period, if that seemed appropriate. The decision as to whether or not to proceed and the timing of the action were left with Gail to decide. The therapist agreed to write a letter to the physician, to indicate that CBT was coming to an end, and to recommend this plan.

The only other item to consider for adjunct treatment in this case was couple therapy. It became clear during the course of treatment that Gail applied her belief about critical others and her need to 'perform' in her relationship with her husband, Robert. Indeed, she expressed that part of her initial attraction to Robert had been that he was a 'strong and determined' man, with a sense of purpose. It was clear, though, that Robert from time to time had expectations of others, including Gail, who sometimes let him down. This pattern led the therapist to check with Gail whether or not a formal course of couple therapy might be indicated. She expressed a desire to continue to work in CBT, and to work on the relationship through her own individual therapy. Hence a compromise was made. At the seventh session, Robert was invited to part of a CBT session, to receive some psycho-education regarding depression as well as information about the likely course of treatment and its potential impact on the couple's relationship. Both Robert and Gail responded well to this session. Gail said that it 'liberated' her to take more chances with Robert; and Robert said that it helped him to understand how some of what he had done had affected Gail negatively, and that this insight would motivate him to modify his patterns.

Other considerations

Suicidality Even though Gail had not expressed suicidal intentions, it was essential to monitor her helplessness and hopelessness throughout treatment. Therapists who work with depressed clients are encouraged to familiarize themselves with local legislation regarding the duty to protect clients and regarding involuntary hospitalization. It is good practice to have a list of available crisis services at hand, if needed, and to advise clients about steps to take if they find themselves in a crisis. Appropriate planning for the therapist's holidays and the establishment of back-up clinical and emergency services are also considered aspects of good practice.

Anxiety Gail's initial responses on the BAI suggested mild to moderate anxiety. It is not uncommon for anxiety to increase over the course of therapy in depressed clients, as they begin to interact more with the world and to confront ongoing issues. Gail's concern about evaluation from others, although not in the form of classical social anxiety disorder, certainly did raise apprehension and worry in her from time to time. Had Gail's anxiety resulted from the same underlying core beliefs that maintained her depression (e.g., perfectionism), it is most likely that her anxiety would also have dissipated through therapy.

Summary

The case of Gail has been used here as an illustration of the principles and practice of cognitive behavioural therapy. In many respects, her case was well suited to the practice of CBT, as it included core beliefs or schemas that were triggered by activating situations. On the basis of the information provided, several targets for intervention were developed and several successful methods were employed, which led to reduced depression and improved functioning. The ongoing evaluation of goals, Gail's responses to treatment and to the therapist, and the therapist's sensitivity to potentially problematical aspects of the client–therapist relationship all worked together to ensure that the treatment plan was focused on important issues for Gail.

The therapist and Gail continued to monitor progress and to anticipate the end of treatment from time to time. The possibility of relapse was explicitly discussed with Gail, and the therapist and Gail planned for an exacerbation of problems around the end of therapy. An action plan was also developed, to test how Gail could react to some mild depressive symptoms after the end of treatment. The therapist scheduled a follow-up session at six months to assess Gail's state and to ensure that she was using the skills learned over the course of therapy. It was noted, though, that Gail could cancel this appointment if it was not needed, could return to therapy earlier if required, or could schedule some booster sessions (for example, if she made the decision to cease taking antidepressant medications), if these were needed to help her maintain her treatment successfully. Treatment was concluded after 18 sessions, with Gail's approval and appreciation.

References

APA. (2014). *Diagnostic and statistical manual of mental disorders: DSM-V*. Washington, DC: American Psychiatric Association.

Alford, B. A., & Beck, A. T. (1997). *The integrative power of cognitive therapy*. New York: Guilford.

Antony, M. M., Ledley, D. R., & Heimberg, R. G. (Eds). (2005). *Improving outcomes and preventing relapse in cognitive-behavioural therapy*. New York: Guilford.

Beck, A. T., Steer, R. A., & Brown, G. K. (1996). *Manual for the BDI-II*. San Antonio, TX: Psychological Corporation.

Beck, A. T., Epstein, N., Brown, G., & Steer, R. A. (1988). An inventory for measuring clinical anxiety: Psychometric properties. *Journal of Consulting and Clinical Psychology*, *56*, 893–897.

Beck, A. T., Rush, A. J., Shaw, B. F., & Emery, G. (1979). *Cognitive therapy of depression*. New York: Guilford.

Beck, J. (2011). *Cognitive behavior therapy: Basics and beyond*. New York: Guilford.

Casola, P. G., Goldsmith, R. J., & Daiter, J. (2006). Assessment and treatment of sleep problems. *Psychiatric Annals*, *36*, 862–868.

Chambless, D. L., Baker, M. J., Baucom, D. H., Beutler, L. E., Calhoun, K. S., Crits-Christoph, P. … Woody, S. R. (1998). Update on empirically validated therapies, II. *The Clinical Psychologist*, *51*, 3–16.

Dobson, D. J. G., & Dobson, K. S. (2009). *Evidence-based practice of cognitive-behaviour therapy*. New York: Guilford.

Dobson, K. S. (2008). Cognitive therapy for depression. In M. A. Whisman (Ed.), *Adapting cognitive therapy for depression: Managing complexity and comorbidity* (pp. 3–35). New York: Guilford.

Dobson, K. S. (Ed.) (2009). *Handbook of cognitive-behavioral therapies* (3rd edn). NY: Guilford.

Dozois, D. J. A., & Dobson, K. S. (2009). Assessment of depression. In M. M. Antony & D. H. Barlow (Eds), *Handbook of assessment, treatment planning, and outcome evaluation: Empirically supported strategies for psychological disorders* (2nd edn). New York: Guilford.

First, M. B., Williams, J. B. W., Karg, R. S, & Spitzer, R. L. (2015). *User's guide for the Structured Clinical Interview for DSM-5Axis I Disorders*. Washington, DC: American Psychiatric Press.

Hamilton, M. A. (1960). A rating scale for depression. *Journal of Neurology, Neurosurgery, and Psychiatry, 23*, 56–61.

Kazantzis, N., Dattilio, F., & Dobson, K. S. (forthcoming). *The therapeutic relationship in cognitive behavior therapy: A clinician's guide to the heart and soul of effective practice*. New York: Guilford.

Leahy, R. L. (2015). *Emotional schema therapy*. New York: Guilford.

Leichensring, F., Hiller, W., Weissberg, M., & Leibing, E. (2006). Cognitive–behavioral therapy and psychodynamic psychotherapy: Techniques, efficacy, and indications. *American Journal of Psychotherapy, 60*, 233–259.

Nezu, A. M., Nezu, C., & Lombardo, E. (2004). *Cognitive–behavioral case formulation and treatment design: A problem-solving approach*. New York: Springer.

Norcross, J. C., Hedges, M., & Prochaska, J. O. (2002). The face of 2010: A Delphi poll on the future of psychotherapy. *Professional Psychology: Research and Practice, 33*, 316–322.

O'Donohue, W., & Fisher, J. E. (Eds). (2009). *General principles and empirically supported techniques of cognitive behavior therapy*. Hoboken, NJ: John Wiley & Sons, Inc.

Persons, J. B. (2008). *The case formulation approach to cognitive–behaviour therapy*. New York: Guilford.

Wenzel, A. (2013). *Strategic decision making in cognitive behavioral therapy*. Washington, DC: APA Books.

12

Metacognitive Therapy for Depression

Peter L. Fisher and Adrian Wells

Introduction

Psychological accounts of depression are predicated on the premise that specific psychological processes maintain or contribute to the development of the disorder (or both). Logically, it follows that the construction of an efficacious treatment requires the identification of the key psychological mechanism(s) that underpin the disorder and the development of treatment components that effectively and efficiently modify these processes. This chapter presents an application of metacognitive therapy (MCT) to depression that is grounded in this two-stage research and development process.

Thus far, this deceptively simple two-stage process of identification and modification has been only moderately successful in producing efficacious psychological treatments for depression. Remission rates at post-treatment and at one-year follow-up are in the region of 45 per cent and 25 per cent respectively (see chapter 2 for a more detailed analysis of the treatment's efficacy). Constraints on current levels of treatment efficacy may reflect that empirical investigations have not identified the core processes, which in turn means that maximal efficacy cannot be achieved as treatments target largely peripheral processes. For example, rumination is closely linked to depression (e.g. Nolen-Hoeksema, 2000), and it is recognized that, when rumination decreases, depressive symptoms do so too. However, a limited understanding of the processes that maintain rumination will limit the treatment's efficacy.

Treating Depression: MCT, CBT and Third Wave Therapies, First Edition.
Edited by Adrian Wells and Peter L. Fisher.

One model that specifies how rumination is maintained is the metacognitive model of depression (Wells, 2009). This conceptualization of depression is derived from a broader theory of psychopathology, which is in turn based on what is known as the self-regulatory executive function (S-REF) model (Wells & Matthews, 1994, 1996). The S-REF model specifies that emotional disorders are the consequence of a particular style of thinking, which consists of perseverative thinking (worry/rumination), counterproductive attentional strategies, and maladaptive coping responses to the occurrence of negative thoughts or emotional states. Collectively, these processes comprise the cognitive attentional syndrome (CAS), which is guided by biased metacognition. A detailed account of the metacognitive theory of depression can be found in chapter 6.

Brief Overview of MCT for Depression

The metacognitive model of depression specifies that, for treatment to be maximally effective, the activation and use of the CAS in response to thoughts and feelings that trigger it must be reduced. This translates into (1) limiting rumination, (2) enabling the abandonment of threat monitoring and of counterproductive coping strategies, and (3) modifying the positive and negative metacognitive beliefs that orchestrate and maintain the CAS.

MCT for depression (Wells, 2009) is a brief psychological intervention designed to be delivered over a course of approximately eight one-hour sessions conducted on a weekly basis; and it is structured in the following way. Treatment begins by developing an idiosyncratic case formulation based on the metacognitive model; this process is followed by socialization to the model. Patients are helped to understand that rumination, excessive self-focused attention to the physical and cognitive components of depression, as well as behavioural inactivity and avoidance serve to maintain and intensify depression and that these processes are driven by positive and negative metacognitive beliefs. The next step in treatment is to enhance awareness of metacognitive control over processing and to increase flexibility of attention, thereby reducing excessive self-focus and activation of the CAS: the Attention Training Technique (ATT) is used to achieve these goals. MCT then proceeds by identifying and modifying negative metacognitive beliefs about the uncontrollability of rumination, while providing patients with alternative, non-conceptually based strategies to be used in response to negative thoughts and feelings. Verbal and behavioural reattribution strategies as well as experiential exercises are employed in order to enable patients to disengage from rumination, threat monitoring, and counterproductive coping strategies. The final sessions focus on developing a relapse prevention plan, on consolidating treatment strategies, and, if necessary, on modifying residual positive and negative metacognitive beliefs.

This chapter illustrates the use of MCT for depression, from assessment through to relapse prevention, using the case example of Gail.

Assessment

Initial clinical assessment

Gail met the diagnostic criteria for major depressive disorder (recurrent). She reported a persistent low mood and derived little pleasure from any activities. In terms of the associated diagnostic criteria, Gail had initial insomnia and described being easily fatigued and having difficulties concentrating. There was a very prominent feeling of guilt, which centred around her perceived inadequate care for her children and her being 'a difficult wife'. No current suicidal ideation was reported: although Gail did feel that it might be better for her family if one morning she didn't wake up, no active plans were reported. Gail scored 37 on the Beck Depression Inventory (BDI-II) (Beck, Steer, & Brown, 1996) and 14 on the Beck Anxiety Inventory (Beck, Epstein, Brown, & Steer, 1988) – results that indicated, respectively, a severe level of depression and a mild level of anxiety.

A somewhat despondent attitude towards psychological treatment was evident; Gail did not believe she would ever be free from depression. At best she expected that she would make a temporary improvement but then would 'plunge' back into depression once more, as had happened in her prior experiences of pharmacological and psychological interventions. She had been on Paroxetine for over eight months, but felt no discernible improvement to her mood. Gail also reasoned that her lack of response to medication and previous psychological therapy (non-directive counselling) meant that her 'brain was wired differently from other people's'. Despite her clear level of despondency and hopelessness, Gail was motivated to engage in treatment, as she viewed even temporary relief as a significant benefit.

Metacognitive assessment

The MCT therapist explored the main metacognitive beliefs and each aspect of the CAS. To aid the assessment, Gail completed a self-report measure: the Major Depressive Disorder Scale (MDD-S; Wells, 2009). The MDD-S assesses positive and negative metacognitive beliefs about rumination, severity of depression, frequency of rumination, and a range of maladaptive coping strategies. Gail's pre-treatment response to each item on the MDD-S is shown in Figure 12.1. Gail completed the MDD-S at the beginning of each session and this process served several important functions – which included socializing the patient to the primary goals of MCT and providing the therapist with clear guidance as to which components of the metacognitive model should receive attention at each stage in the treatment. Each metacognitive belief endorsed on the MDD-S was explored with a view to obtaining an accurate account of each belief. For example, Gail gave a rating of 60 per cent to this item: 'If I analyse why I feel this way, I'll find answers.' Then she explained that, by repeatedly analysing her thoughts and feelings, she would be able to find solutions to her continued depression and also to work out the most effective methods of being a better mother and of improving the quality of her relationship with her husband.

Treatment

Session 1

The first goal of this session was for the therapist to develop a case formulation by conducting a detailed review of Gail's triggering thoughts, of the nature of her rumination, and of her emotions, metacognitive beliefs, and coping strategies during a recent episode of rumination. The construction of Gail's case formulation (see Figure 12.2) began by the therapist's helping her to recognize the triggering thoughts and feelings that led to an extended period of rumination. This is as illustrated in the patient–therapist dialogue below:

THERAPIST: Has there been a time, recently, when you noticed your mood worsen?

GAIL: Yesterday. We were having a meal, I'd asked my daughters to do the washing up and I was overwhelmed by sadness.

THERAPIST: What went through you mind at that point?

MDD-S

Major Depressive Disorder Scale

1. How severe and disabling has your depression been in the last week? (Circle a number below).

0	1	2	3	4	5	6	7	8
Not at all				Moderately				Extremely– The worst it has ever been

(Circled: 6)

2. How much time in the last week have you been thinking about and analyzing your thoughts and feelings and trying to understand why you are like this? (Circle a number below)

0	1	2	3	4	5	6	7	8
None of the time				Half of the time				All of the time

(Circled: 6)

3. How often in the past week have you done the following in order to cope with your depression? (Place a number from the scale below next to each item)

0	1	2	3	4	5	6	7	8
None of the time				Half of the time				All of the time

Item	Rating	Item	Rating	Item	Rating
Tried to rest more	2	Decreased my activities	7	Analyzed why I felt like this	6
Tried to reason things out	7	Tried not to think about things	4	Got angry at myself	6
Used alcohol	0	Punished myself	3	Increased my sleep	2

4. How often in the past week have you avoided the following? (Place a number from the scale below next to each item)

0	1	2	3	4	5	6	7	8
None of the time				Half of the time				All of the time

Item	Rating	Item	Rating	Item	Rating
Interests / hobbies	6	Getting on with work	4	Solving problems	3
Social situations	6	Making decisions	5	Planning ahead	5

5. Below are a number of beliefs that people have about their depressive thinking (called rumination). Indicate how much you believe each one by placing a number from the scale below next to each item.

0	10	20	30	40	50	60	70	80	90	100
I do not believe this at all										I'm completely convinced this is true

Item	Rating	Item	Rating
I cannot control my depressive thoughts (rumination)	8	Ruminating helps me cope	60
My depressive thoughts are a sign I'm losing my mind	3	If I analyze why I feel this way I'll find answers	60
My depressive thoughts control me	7	Ruminating helps me understand my depression	90
I'm defective / abnormal for thinking like this	8	Ruminating helps me solve problems	40

Figure 12.1 Gail's MDD-S self-report form at pre-treatment.
Source: Wells, A. (2009). *Metacognitive Therapy for Anxiety and Depression*. New York: Guilford Press, © 2008.

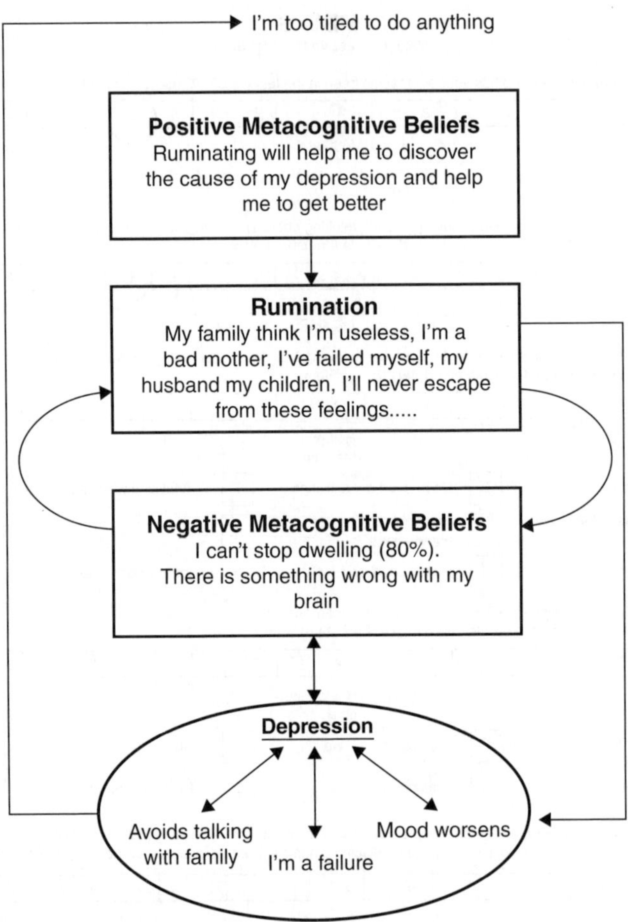

Figure 12.2 Idiosyncratic case formulation.

GAIL: I was too tired to clear up. I thought that my daughters were thinking I was a terrible mother.

THERAPIST: So you noticed the thought 'I'm too tired to clear up', which was quickly followed by negative thoughts about what your daughters thought about you as a mother. Did you go on to think about other things?

GAIL: I guess I just started to question what my family really thinks about me; that my husband was thinking I was useless.

THERAPIST: How long did you think about these issues?

GAIL: Pretty much for the rest of the evening.

At this point the therapist helped Gail to label this extended thinking as rumination and to make a distinction between the initial triggering thought 'I'm too tired' and the rumination response. Then the therapist went on to highlight the negative impact that rumination has on both mood and behavior. The next step was to elicit the negative metacognitive beliefs about the uncontrollability of rumination.

THERAPIST: What happened to your mood when you were thinking about how terrible everything is?

GAIL: I started to feel more useless and depressed; I thought I was going to start crying in front of my children again.

THERAPIST: What did you then do?

GAIL: I slumped on the sofa, pretending to watch TV and not talking to anyone, because I really didn't want to cry. But that just made me feel worse as I was aware that I was not talking to my family and couldn't concentrate on the TV.

THERAPIST: So did thinking in this manner, or ruminating, lead you to feel worse, and have a negative effect on your behaviour?

GAIL: Yes, when you look at it that way, it did at that time.

THERAPIST: Would it help if you could reduce the amount you think like that?

GAIL: I'm not sure. I really wish I could just switch off from time to time, just to get a break from myself. But I can't stop thinking about how bad everything is.

THERAPIST: So it sounds as if you believe that rumination is uncontrollable: How much do you believe that rumination is uncontrollable on scale of 0 to 100?

GAIL: About 80 per cent.

The therapist has elicited the negative metacognitive beliefs about the uncontrollability of rumination and has started to illustrate to Gail that rumination intensifies her levels of sadness and also leads to behaviors that feed back into depressive rumination; in other words the therapist has begun to enhance Gail's level of meta-awareness with a view to modifying metacognitive beliefs and strategies. The final step was to identify positive metacognitive beliefs about the value or function of rumination.

THERAPIST: Are there any benefits to ruminating?

GAIL: I'm not sure; I guess by going over and over the same old ground I might start to think differently about things, that solutions to some of the problems will appear.

THERAPIST: How much to do you believe that rumination will lead you to discover solutions on a scale of 0 to 100 per cent?

GAIL: Well, I think that, if I can understand the causes of my depression, I would be able to overcome it. I really believe that, about 80 per cent.

Socialization Socialization began by reviewing the case formulation with Gail and by increasing her awareness of the role of rumination in exacerbating and maintaining depression. The therapist shared the case formulation with Gail and highlighted that her tendency to dwell on her negative thoughts or ruminate in response to them serves to deepen her low mood and maintain depression. Furthermore, the therapist helped Gail to understand that she also held positive metacognitive beliefs about the usefulness of rumination – specifically, that she thought that rumination would help her to understand the cause of her depression, which in turn would allow her to overcome her low mood. The therapist then pointed out to Gail that her beliefs about the uncontrollable nature of rumination were exacerbating her low mood (contributing to hopelessness) and that they also led to a low level of effort being put into trying to interrupt the ruminative process.

To facilitate socialization into the model, the therapist asked Gail a series of interlinked questions about the effects of rumination, about her metacognitive beliefs, and about her coping responses. Examples of the questions asked are: How long have you spent ruminating? What impact does ruminating have on your mood? Has rumination provided you with answers to the cause of your depression? Has it had the effect of helping you to overcome your depression? Gail acknowledged that she had experienced several long periods of depression and that each depressive episode was accompanied by prolonged periods of rumination; she also recognized that rumination had not allowed her to overcome depression or to understand why she experiences prolonged depressive episodes. To help consolidate the socialization process, the therapist asked Gail: 'Would it help if you spent more time ruminating in response to your negative feelings and thoughts?' Gail replied that, if she did that, it would make her situation worse. Therefore this question served the dual purpose of highlighting the negative impact of rumination and of starting to challenge Gail's positive metacognitive beliefs about rumination.

Attention Training Technique The first session concluded by introducing Attention Training Technique (ATT; Wells, 1990) in order to help Gail develop her awareness and knowledge about her level of metacognitive control over rumination and to reduce self-focused processing. ATT was conducted at the end of every subsequent treatment session and also practised between sessions, at least once per day for the duration of treatment. ATT comprises an externally focused auditory attention task that involves selective attention, attention switching, and divided attention and is conducted sequentially over a 12-minute period. Selective attention is practised for approximately five minutes, which is followed by five minutes of attention switching, then by a final two-minute phase of divided attention. The therapist introduced ATT as a method through which Gail could achieve control over her ruminative thinking style, foster her own awareness of her level of control, and develop flexibility in her response to spontaneously occurring negative thoughts.

Immediately prior to commencing the ATT, the therapist evaluated Gail's current level of self-focus on a simple six-point Likert Scale (which ranges from +3 for completely self-focused to -3 for completely externally focused). Gail reported that she was very self-focused and rated herself at +2 on the six-point scale. The therapist then began the ATT exercise by emphasizing that the task was to practise focusing attention as guided. It was explained to Gail that, if she experienced any negative intrusive thoughts or feelings during the ATT exercise, she should regard these thoughts or feelings as merely background noise and not attempt to suppress, analyse, or remove them from her mind. The therapist commenced the ATT exercise as per protocol. Gail was asked to focus her attention on three sounds in the room; the therapist's voice, the ticking of a clock, and the hum of a computer. Next, Gail was instructed to attend sequentially to three other sounds or spatial locations outside of the consulting room. This phase was practised for five minutes before the therapist instructed Gail to switch her attention rapidly between the different sounds; and this new phase was again practised for five minutes. The ATT exercise concluded with a divided-attention task, which required Gail to attempt to listen to all of the sounds simultaneously. This was practised for two minutes. After the ATT exercise was completed, Gail re-rated her level of self-focus and found that there had been a three-point shift in the direction of externally focused attention. The therapist reviewed how the ATT was to be implemented for homework and Gail was asked to complete the ATT twice a day; but she was reminded that this should *not* be used as a coping strategy, such as to distract herself from unwanted thoughts and feelings. To assist Gail in practising the ATT for homework, the therapist provided her with a CD version of ATT (www.mct-institute.com).

Session 2

After setting the agenda, the therapist reviewed the MDD-S and noted minimal change in comparison to the previous week, except for a reduction of 15 per cent in her conviction regarding the uncontrollability of rumination. The therapist hypothesized that, during her daily practice of the ATT, Gail had experienced unwanted negative thoughts and had been able to continue with the ATT as prescribed, without engaging in prolonged rumination, thereby obtaining for herself evidence that rumination is controllable. When Gail's ATT homework was reviewed, she reported that she practised the ATT at least once every day and that she had found the task quite difficult but had managed to complete it. In accord with the therapist's hypothesis, Gail reported experiencing negative thoughts during the ATT and started to dwell on them briefly; but she also reported having been able to refocus her attention, as specified in the ATT, and found that rumination ceased.

Modifying uncontrollability beliefs The next step in treatment is modifying beliefs about the uncontrollability of rumination through verbal and behavioural reattribution methods. Gail's account of ATT provided the therapist with a clear entry point for verbal reattribution of her uncontrollability belief by giving him occasion to ask her: 'If rumination is truly uncontrollable, how did it stop during your practice of the ATT?' This question was followed by a broader review of the evidence and counterevidence supporting her uncontrollability beliefs. Gail was able to generate considerable evidence against her uncontrollability belief, which included many examples of times when she had interrupted rumination: these included times when she had to attend to patients at work, or when her daughters needed her help. The therapist also asked Gail a hypothetical question: "Could you choose to ruminate for longer periods of time?" and she replied that it would be an easy thing to do. Hence the therapist highlighted that, if she could increase rumination, then she could also decrease it. Finally, a brief behavioural experiment was used: Gail was simply asked to bring to mind the negative thought that she was a terrible mother and to start and then stop ruminating – which she easily achieved. The therapist then introduced the strategies of *detached mindfulness* and *rumination postponement.*

Detached mindfulness and rumination postponement Detached mindfulness (DM) (Wells & Matthews, 1994) refers to an objective awareness of cognitions and affective sensations, but one that is unaccompanied by any form of conceptual analysis and is non-goal-directed – in other words, it is not a coping response. A theoretical account of DM is provided in chapter 6. In the therapeutic context DM is incompatible with the CAS, and an early goal in MCT is to enable patients to acquire meta-awareness while they reduce conceptual processing. In Gail's case, the therapist began by helping her to differentiate between the occurrence of a spontaneous negative thought (trigger) and her subsequent rumination, and introduced the idea that Gail could decide how to relate and respond to her typical triggering cognitions.

Gail was helped to experience DM by using a free-association task (Wells, 2005). Before the therapist introduced the specific task, a brief discussion on the natural flow and decay of emotionally neutral thoughts over the course of a typical day was conducted. The therapist facilitated the discussion by asking questions such as: 'What happens to the majority of your everyday thoughts? Where do these thoughts go?' Patients quickly come to realize that, for the vast majority of their thoughts, 'detached mindfulness' is the natural processing state; and that negative thoughts do not have to be responded to with sustained conceptual processing.

The free-association task itself was introduced in the following manner:

THERAPIST: In a moment I am going to say a list of common words and I would like you to let your mind roam freely in response to the words. It's important that you do not attempt to control your mind or your response to the words; I would like you just to notice what happens in your mind when I say the words. For some people, not much happens, other people find that pictures or images come into their mind, and some people also report feelings or sensations. I'm now going to say the list of common words: orange, pen, table, tiger, trees, spectacles, breeze, statue. What did you notice when you just watched your mind?

Gail explained that she noticed an image associated with each word and generally each image replaced the previous one, but on occasions the images merged together. She gave the example of seeing the tiger walking behind the trees and then the tiger was wearing spectacles. At this point the therapist checked that the merged images occurred spontaneously and that Gail was not deliberately trying to influence what she experienced or to connect the images in any way. The therapist repeated the task, with the goal of enhancing detachment by asking Gail to be aware that she was a separate observer of her thoughts. The task was repeated a third time, when the therapist interspersed emotionally salient words such as 'useless', 'bad', 'mother' within the set of neutral words. Gail noticed that she began dwell in response to the negative words, but she continued with the task and recognized that each thought/image had a life of its own, and that she could be aware of thoughts and not engage in effortful coping responses. The therapist then introduced rumination postponement by explaining that, rather than responding immediately to negative thoughts with extended thinking, Gail should apply DM each time she noticed typical negative thoughts that acted as a trigger for rumination; in other words she should postpone her ruminative response. The therapist introduced the task in the following manner:

THERAPIST: When you notice thoughts such as 'I'm a bad mother' or 'I can't cope', I'd like you to say to yourself: 'There's a negative thought, I'm not going to do anything with it now, if I want to I'll think about it later.' All I want you to do is to allow the thought to exist without trying to influence it at all, so that means not analysing, not trying to push it out of your mind, not trying to purposely distract yourself. I'd like you to carry on with whatever it was you were doing without engaging with the thought in any way. However, this does not mean you can't ruminate about it later in the day. I'd like you to postpone your rumination until a convenient time later in the day, perhaps 8 p.m.; and then, if you think that you must ruminate about the negative thoughts that have popped into your head during the day, then you can ruminate about them for a maximum of 15 minutes. You do not need to use this rumination time, in fact most people decide not to use the rumination time. However, it would be helpful if you decided to use your rumination time to make a brief note of the reasons why you decided to use it.

DM and rumination postponement were introduced as an experiment, in order to test Gail's belief that rumination was uncontrollable. This phase of treatment requires the therapist to monitor the frequency with which DM and postponement are practised and the proportion of negative thoughts to which they is applied. In the subsequent treatment sessions further experiments and strategies were revised and implemented to systematically weaken Gail's belief that rumination was uncontrollable.

Session 2 finished with further practice of ATT and the practice and goals of the homework tasks reiterated.

Session 3

There were several objectives in this session: (1) to review the scores on the MDD-S, (2) to review the application of DM and rumination postponement, (3) to increase Gail's awareness of triggers for rumination, (4) to supply further practice and refinement of DM, (5) to modify uncontrollability beliefs, and (6) to check the application of the ATT in homework and further in-session practice.

The review of the MDD-S indicated that Gail's belief in the uncontrollability of rumination had dropped from 80 per cent to 40 per cent, being accompanied by a commensurate reported decrease in the severity of her depressive symptoms and frequency of rumination. Gail was still using a range of unhelpful coping behaviours and avoiding particular situations, but the primary target during this session was to further modify her uncontrollability beliefs. The therapist's next step was to assess Gail's application of DM over the course of the previous week.

Assessment of the application of DM and rumination postponement

Successful implementation of MCT requires a careful assessment of the application of DM throughout treatment, but especially in the early sessions. Moreover, a careful assessment of DM offers a rich opportunity to increase meta-awareness and to modify unhelpful metacognitive beliefs and processes. Assessment of DM began with the therapist asking Gail to describe in detail how she had implemented DM in response to triggering thoughts or feelings. Gail had applied DM to approximately 40 per cent of her negative thoughts over the course of the previous week and never used the period set aside for postponed rumination.

The patient–therapist dialogue used in assessing the application of DM and rumination postponement is presented below:

THERAPIST: How frequently did you use detached mindfulness in response to negative thoughts and feelings over the last week?

GAIL: About 40 per cent of the time; mostly for concerns I had at work, although I wasn't able to do it every time.

THERAPIST: Good, it seems like you had quite a lot of success in postponing rumination, what does that tell you about the uncontrollability of rumination?

GAIL: I guess it tells me that I can control it some of the time.

THERAPIST: Let's take a closer look at the thoughts you did engage with. Were they different in any way from the negative thoughts you did not ruminate on?

GAIL: When I had negative thoughts about my family such as how my depression was affecting my daughters and my husband, I found myself ruminating.

THERAPIST: Did you attempt to postpone rumination in response to these thoughts?

GAIL: I guess the honest answer is I didn't really try. I need to know how much my depression is affecting my relationships with my family so that I can do something about it.

At this point in the dialogue, Gail has described a positive belief about rumination, in that it will help her to find ways of improving her relationships with her family. The therapist's primary goal at this stage is to focus on negative metacognitive beliefs about uncontrollability, so that the positive belief may be noted and work may continue on her negative beliefs.

THERAPIST: That's interesting. You've described selecting certain thoughts that you were content not to engage with and others that you felt more compelled to think about. Have you been deciding which thoughts to dwell on and which to let go?

GAIL: I think so.

THERAPIST: What do you think that says about the controllability of rumination?

GAIL: It means I'm deciding to ruminate about some thoughts.

THERAPIST: Ok, so if you are deciding to ruminate, it means you can also decide not to ruminate. The next step is to postpone rumination, or questioning, or any form of analysis to all instances of negative thoughts. Is that something you would be willing to try?

GAIL: I'll give it a go.

At this point Gail described something new: using rumination as a source of self-punishment, because she thought she had adversely affected the lives of her husband and her children, she deserved to 'feel bad'. In response, the therapist reminded her of the disadvantages of using this strategy. In addition, the therapist used her response to further challenge beliefs about uncontrollability by asking Gail: 'If you can decide to ruminate to make yourself feel worse, what does that say about the controllability of rumination?' Gail acknowledged that her rumination was controllable, which appeared to instil a degree of hope, thereby helping her to overcome some of her early hopelessness about the possibility of improvement. It is necessary in MCT to repeatedly demonstrate and highlight to patients the pervasiveness of rumination and at the same time to illustrate how all forms of rumination are under volitional control.

Sessions 4–6

The MCT treatment protocol for depression specifies that modification of positive metacognitive beliefs generally begins when a substantial reduction in negative metacognitive beliefs has been observed. By session 4, Gail was implementing DM in response to a wide array of negative thoughts and affective experiences, which had previously acted as triggers for protracted periods of rumination; and her negative metacognitive beliefs about the uncontrollability of rumination were at 10 per cent. Examination of the MDD-S revealed that there had been substantial reduction in her positive metabeliefs, for example that rumination helped her to understand her depression and would lead her to feel less depressed. These beliefs had reduced from 90 per cent at pre-treatment to 30 per cent by the beginning of session 4. This is a common occurrence in MCT for depression, since patients are exposed to corrective information throughout treatment. For example, as Gail had reduced her level of rumination, she had discovered that it was unnecessary to think through all the possible reasons for her depression in order to feel less depressed, although she still believed that rumination could help her to overcome her depressed mood.

Modifying positive metacognitive beliefs Modification of Gail's positive metacognitive beliefs began by highlighting the extent to which they had reduced since the beginning of therapy. The therapist then asked Gail: 'What do you think the effect is of continuing to hold beliefs about the usefulness of rumination?' Gail recognized that holding these beliefs increased the likelihood of using rumination; but she stated that rumination did sometimes help to solve problems, and she expressed concern about abandoning rumination completely. Rather than immediately questioning the

Table 12.1 Advantages–disadvantages analysis of rumination.

Advantages	*Disadvantages*
1 It lets me work out triggers for my low moods so I can avoid them.	1 It puts a strain on my relationship with my husband.
2 It will help me make amends with my family.	2 It gets in the way of having a good relationship with my daughters.
3 It will help me understand why I get depressed.	3 It makes me more critical of myself and other people.
4 It can help me work out how to cope better.	4 I feel less competent because I can't cope at work.
	5 It makes me feel like life is not worth living.
	6 It takes up too much time.
	7 It produces more questions than answers.
	8 It makes me feels more depressed and out of control.

evidence for the belief, the therapist acknowledged that there might be some advantages to rumination, but that there might be more appropriate ways to solve problems. To develop this idea more fully, the therapist conducted an advantages–disadvantages analysis of rumination. Gail's responses are illustrated in Table 12.1.

It was highlighted that there were more disadvantages than advantages to rumination, and each disadvantage was reinforced. The next step was to critically evaluate and challenge the validity of the advantages generated by Gail by questioning the evidence for each advantage.

In Gail's case, a central positive metacognitive belief was that rumination helped her to solve problems. A range of therapeutic questions were used to modify this belief. Some were direct questions such as these: 'If rumination helps, why haven't you solved the problem yet? What does this tell you about the usefulness of rumination in solving problems?' The therapist also made a paradoxical suggestion: 'You might be right that rumination is helpful, maybe the problem is that you haven't spent enough time ruminating about your problems.' Gail readily acknowledged that rumination did not generally help to solve problems and that engaging in more rumination would adversely affect her mood. Additional verbal reattribution strategies used during this phase of MCT included questioning the mechanism through which rumination works and highlighting that it generates still more problems, exacerbates negative mood, and rarely if ever presents solutions. Continuing on a similar theme, the MCT therapist explores the patient's goals in rumination and questions the effectiveness of this process in achieving the goals in question. The task in this instance is to generate more effective alternatives for achieving goals. Another method involves the therapist's exploring whether patients are setting themselves inappropriate criteria for deciding when to cease rumination – for example, they would stop when they are emotionally stable. An alternative can then be reinforced – for example, the idea that the absence of rumination would more effectively achieve this goal.

RUMINATION EXPERIMENT Although verbal reattribution strategies had reduced Gail's conviction in the belief 'rumination helps to solve problems', her belief level remained at 20 per cent. As positive beliefs are linked to the activation of rumination, it is imperative that these beliefs are challenged effectively, because residual beliefs can limit the degree of therapeutic change and constitute vulnerability to future depressive episodes. Therefore a rumination modulation experiment (Wells, 2009) was used with Gail in which the therapist ascribed the following homework: to ruminate on one day, to follow this by minimal or no rumination on the next day, and to note whether more problems were solved on the rumination day than on the preceding one. Gail came to recognize that, rather than solve problems, rumination generated more questions. Such rumination modulation experiments also modify uncontrollability beliefs, as patients recognize that they can choose to ruminate or not to ruminate.

This phase of treatment also addressed ongoing maladaptive coping strategies – specifically, threat monitoring and avoidant coping in response to mood fluctuations. The therapist also assessed for the presence of other important aspects of perseverative thinking and related clinical issues. Each aspect is illustrated in what follows.

The reduction of threat monitoring The modification of counterproductive attentional strategies is an essential component in MCT for depression. Patients often monitor for signs and symptoms of depression and use the presence or absence of symptoms to determine their own coping response. Gail used several threat-monitoring strategies such as checking her mind for the presence of negative thoughts, because she was driven by the belief that identifying negative thoughts early on would enable her to cope with them more effectively and to prevent relapse. Gail also checked for signs of negative affect, particularly symptoms of tiredness. She believed that, by monitoring for signs of depression, she would be able to have a clear idea of her progress in therapy.

In all these cases the therapist discussed the effect of monitoring on her symptoms and on her level of depression and helped Gail to recognize that these strategies were counterproductive and unnecessary. By highlighting advantages and disadvantages, Gail was able to see that such strategies backfired and she subsequently desisted from using maladaptive attention control activities.

Coping with mood fluctuations Patients with depression tend to respond to fluctuations in mood through counterproductive coping strategies, for example avoidance of previously pleasurable activities, withdrawal from social situations, and self-medication with alcohol. Gail's typical behavioural coping style in response to a decrease in mood was to avoid social interaction by not attending social events, by reducing work hours, and also by withdrawing from conversation with others – for instance her family and her colleagues at meal times. Gail explained that, if she was feeling low, she would avoid activities that involved other people; and she would do this with the explicit metacognitive goal of giving herself more time to work out what was wrong with her. However, Gail explained that, when she felt low, she would become withdrawn in social contexts; this resulted in negative thoughts of inadequacy, which would be a triggering thought for extended rumination. The therapist began by normalizing mood fluctuations and illustrated that most people experience changes in mood. Wells (2009) notes that established behavioural approaches could be adopted to overcome such avoidance and specific activity scheduling could have been utilized. However, in MCT activity scheduling should be used to modify maladaptive metacognitive beliefs – such as the belief that the mind cannot function properly, or the belief that one cannot make choices regardless of how one thinks and feels.

Increasing awareness of the pervasiveness of rumination and worry in depression It is imperative that the therapist fully explores the extent and the nature of perseverative thinking. Patients sometimes only focus on one aspect of rumination and continue to ruminate in response to other intrusive thoughts and memories. For example, Gail described an intrusive memory of being left alone by her friends at college: she would repeatedly examine this event, as she believed it to be integral to the development of her first depressive episode, which set the scene for subsequent depressive episodes. Gail was helped to recognize the counterproductive nature of using rumination in response to this distant memory, and the therapist simply asked her to ban rumination whenever she became aware of the memory.

Additional issues Over the course of therapy, Gail expressed several other concerns, including sleep difficulties. The therapist briefly explored the nature of her sleep difficulties and two main issues emerged: (1) worry about not sleeping occurred at various points during the day and in the lead up to bedtime; and (2) there were protracted periods of worry and rumination when she tried to get to sleep. This type of perseverative thinking was labelled as 'worry', and its similarities with rumination were highlighted. Gail was encouraged to use DM in response to her worries about sleep, and also to implement DM to all forms of worry and rumination when she tried to get sleep. It emerged that she held the belief that she needed to remove the unwanted negative thoughts and worries from her mind before she would be able to sleep. Gail was helped to see that trying to clear her mind of negative thoughts, far from achieving her goal of falling asleep, had the opposite effect.

Sessions 7 and 8

At the start of session 7, Gail reported that during the preceding week she had only engaged in very brief periods of rumination (5–10 minutes a day) and that there were no significant problems with her mood. She also reported that her sleep had improved and that she was more engaged with her family and work colleagues. At pre-treatment, Gail had often avoided talking with her family at meal times, but now she found herself conversing more easily; and the same effect had been observed by her work colleagues. Furthermore, she reported that her husband and daughters had both commented on how much happier she appeared. The final two sessions were devoted to developing new plans for processing and relapse prevention work.

Developing new plans for processing Following the successful amelioration of counterproductive coping strategies (e.g. rumination, worry, threat monitoring, and avoidance) and modification of the underlying positive and negative metacognitive beliefs, the focus of treatment turned to strengthening Gail's alternative metacognitive plans for processing. It is important that patients repeatedly practise new processing plans: this increases the likelihood that they will 'choose' the new plan over the old plan when negative thoughts and feelings assail them in the future. This method therefore functions as a relapse prevention strategy designed to reduce vulnerability to future episodes of prolonged emotional disturbance. Wells (2009) specifies that patients need to maintain awareness of their ruminative thinking and of their maladaptive coping strategies (e.g., avoidance, lowered activity levels, threat monitoring) in order to enable effective development of new processing configurations.

The construction of the new plan begins with a detailed account of the patient's old plan, which consists of a list of triggers that would lead to the activation of the CAS. Providing the patient with a list of triggers increases that patient's awareness of idiosyncratic cognitive events (e.g., negative thoughts, images, memories). Wells (2009) suggests that the plan should be written as a series of summary self-statements; and it is necessary to encourage the patient to implement the new plan in response to triggering thoughts. In Gail's case, the most frequent triggers were negative images, thoughts, and mood fluctuations.

Outlined in Table 12.2 are the old plan and the new plan constructed for Gail.

Practising the new plan is not limited to life outside of therapy sessions but should be implemented in therapy each time the therapist notices an activation of the maladaptive plan – for instance, occurrences of perseverative thinking or inappropriate threat monitoring.

Relapse prevention As a further part of relapse prevention, the therapist worked with Gail towards writing out a 'therapy blueprint'. This process began with his asking Gail to complete her own formulation and to write a list of positive and negative metacognitive beliefs that she held with some degree of conviction at the beginning of therapy. She was asked to generate a statement that focused on each one. For example, the belief 'I cannot stop dwelling on negative thoughts' was answered with 'I've discovered that I can choose not to dwell in response to negative thoughts'.

Gail completed additional questionnaires at the relapse prevention stage in order to ensure that all the essential residual metacognitive beliefs and processes were assessed. The questionnaires used were the Positive Beliefs about Rumination Scale (PBRS) (Papageorgiou & Wells, 2001) and the

Table 12.2 New plan.

Old Plan	*New Plan*
Style of thinking	*Style of thinking*
If I notice a negative thought, I dwell and worry about it.	If I notice a negative thought, I will choose not to engage with it.
I view negative thoughts as accurate depictions of the situation I'm in and then analyse each aspect	I will apply detached mindfulness and view the thought as separate from me and events
In response to feelings of sadness I think about how I got into this situation and try to work out ways of overcoming my low mood.	Tolerate mood fluctuations, do nothing, not even change my goals and behaviour, I am more than these thoughts and feelings.
My behaviours	*My behaviours*
Avoid talking to my family when I feel sad	Continue interacting with family
Reduce levels of activity at home and at work	Maintain activity levels regardless of how I am feeling
Focus of my attention	*Focus of my attention*
Check for the absence and or presence of negative thoughts	Ban all forms of threat monitoring: do not scan for negative thoughts
Scan my body for physical symptoms that I associated with depression, e.g. tiredness, heavy legs,	Do not check body for physical symptoms: If notice physical symptoms, just carry on

Examples of thoughts that triggered rumination: 'I'm incompetent' / 'My husband thinks I'm useless' / 'I'm not a very good mother' / 'I can't cope with life' / 'I'm tired'.
Reframe sentence: *When I notice negative thoughts or feelings, I will simply carry on. I always have choice and control and thoughts or feelings don't take that away.*

Negative Beliefs about Rumination Scale (NBRS: Papageorgiou, Wells, & Meina, 2014). The Metacognitions Questionnaire-30 (MCQ-30) (Wells and Cartwright-Hatton, 2004) was also administered, as it assesses a broader array of metacognitive processes that may be involved in the maintenance of depression, including low levels of cognitive confidence and cognitive self-consciousness. At this stage Gail did not endorse any subscale at a level that required further work. In other words, there were no remaining residual metacognitive beliefs that were of clinical relevance.

A copy of the replacement plan developed in the previous session is included in the relapse prevention summary (see Table 12.2) and represents a synopsis of the strategies to be adopted in response to triggering thoughts and feeling. A copy of the formulation and evidence against the positive and negative metacognitive beliefs held at the start of therapy was also developed and given to Gail.

An integral component of the relapse prevention plan is to help patients deal with the fear of recurrence. The therapist helped Gail to recognize that mood fluctuates and that this is not a sign of depression, but just an indication that mood is variable. It also represents an opportunity to consolidate the skills learnt in therapy. Gail described two counterproductive attentional strategies, guided by maladaptive metacognitive beliefs. She reported monitoring her body for signs and symptoms of depression such as feelings of tiredness and low energy levels. She would also scan her mind for the presence of negative thoughts. Both types of self-monitoring were driven by the belief that being alert for signs and symptoms would help her to deal with them in the future. Interestingly, one of the triggers for this monitoring behaviour was a period of good mood. Gail stated: 'When I have felt happy for a few hours, the thought this won't last pops into my head and sometimes I don't engage with the thought, but sometimes I do.' Identifying these processes in the therapeutic encounter allows the patient to expand his or her metacognitive awareness and flexibility. Vulnerability to relapse is reduced by strengthening these new plans for processing.

Conclusions

This chapter described an eight-session MCT treatment applied to Gail. The treatment presented here is typical of that implemented not only in simple major depressive disorder but also in recurrent and antidepressant resistant cases.

Initial evaluations of MCT for major depressive disorder have produced promising results. In the first evaluation, four patients with recurrent major depressive disorder were treated with four to eight hours of therapy (Wells et al., 2009). All four patients in this case series achieved remission at post-treatment and maintained treatment gains at six-month follow-up. The second study (Wells et al., 2012) that evaluated the efficacy of MCT for major depressive disorder was a small open trial (n = 12). In this study patients received eight one-hour treatment sessions and were assessed at post-treatment and at six-month and one-year follow-up. Overall, there were statistically significant reductions in depressive symptoms and metacognitive beliefs from pre- to post-treatment, and these treatment gains were maintained through to the one-year follow-up. Out of the ten patients who completed the treatment, 80 per cent were recovered at post-treatment and 70 per cent at one-year follow-up on standardized criteria on the BDI. Although the initial investigations of the efficacy of MCT for major depressive disorder are promising, more rigorously controlled evaluations are required before the efficacy of MCT can be determined.

References

Beck, A. T., Steer, R. A., & Brown, G. K. (1996). *Manual for the BDI-II*. San Antonio, TX: Psychological Corporation.

Beck, A. T., Epstein, N., Brown, G., & Steer, R. A. (1988). An inventory for measuring clinical anxiety: Psychometric properties. *Journal of Consulting and Clinical Psychology, 56*, 893–897.

Nolen-Hoeksema, S. (2000). The role of rumination in depressive disorders and mixed anxiety/depressive symptoms. *Journal of Abnormal Psychology, 109*, 504–511.

Papageorgiou, C., & Wells, A. (2001). Positive beliefs about depressive rumination: Development and preliminary validation of a self-report scale. *Behavior Therapy, 32*, 13–26.

Papageorgiou, C., Wells, A., & Meina, L. J. (2014). *Development and preliminary evaluation of the negative beliefs about rumination scale*. Unpublished manuscript.

Wells, A. (1990). Panic disorder in association with relaxation induced anxiety: An attentional training approach to treatment. *Behavior Therapy, 21*, 273–280.

Wells, A. (2005). Detached mindfulness in cognitive therapy: A metacognitive analysis and ten techniques. *Journal of Rational-Emotive and Cognitive Behavior Therapy, 23*, 337–355.

Wells, A. (2009). *Metacognitive therapy for anxiety and depression*. New York: Guilford.

Wells, A., & Cartwright-Hatton, S. (2004). A short form of the Metacognitions Questionnaire: Properties of the MCQ 30. *Behaviour Research and Therapy, 42*, 385–396.

Wells, A., & Matthews, G. (1994). *Attention and emotion: A clinical perspective*. Hove, England: Erlbaum.

Wells, A., & Matthews, G. (1996). Modelling cognition in emotional disorder: The S-REF model. *Behaviour Research and Therapy, 34*, 881–888.

Wells, A., Fisher, P. L., Myers, S., Wheatley, J., Patel, T., & Brewin, C. (2009). Metacognitive therapy in recurrent and persistent depression: A multiple baseline study of a new treatment. *Cognitive Therapy and Research, 33*, 291–300.

Wells, A., Fisher, P. L., Myers, S., Wheatley, J., Patel, T., & Brewin, C. (2012). Metacognitive therapy in treatment-resistant depression: A platform trial. *Behaviour Research and Therapy, 50*, 367–373.

13

Acceptance and Commitment Therapy: Application to the Treatment of Clinical Depression

Kirk D. Strosahl and Patricia J. Robinson

Acceptance and commitment therapy (ACT) is one of several new cognitive and behaviour therapies that are now being referred to as the 'third wave' of behaviour therapy. Although ACT shares many components with other third-wave therapies, it is also distinctive in several important ways. First, the ACT model emphasizes that human suffering arises from the attempt to avoid or eliminate distressing private experiences due to an over-identification with their literal meaning. ACT is scientifically grounded in relational frame theory (RFT), a post-Skinnerian account of human language and of how it functions to regulate human behaviour (Hayes, Barnes-Holmes, & Roche, 2001). A central thesis of RFT and ACT is that culturally instilled rules about what psychological health is and how it is to be achieved are transmitted early in the process of language learning. These rules govern a person's behaviour beyond the boundaries of ordinary awareness; they are also impervious to real-world contingencies. A central cultural rule is that health is defined as the absence of unwanted and distressing private content (which can be thoughts, emotions, memories, or physical sensations). In the presence of such content, the goal is therefore to functionally eliminate or control private experiences that appear to be the antithesis of 'health' as culturally defined. This controlling and eliminating agenda requires the client to engage in more and more behavioural and experiential avoidance strategies over time, which results in constriction of that client's life space. Clinically, this leads to a pattern of avoidance and low life-engagement. Because the processes of experiential avoidance and rule following are endemic to the culture, ACT can be thought of as a transdiagnostic model of how human beings come to suffer.

Treating Depression: MCT, CBT and Third Wave Therapies, First Edition.
Edited by Adrian Wells and Peter L. Fisher.

A second, related feature is that most ACT interventions – particularly those focused on defusion, acceptance, present-moment awareness, and contact with transcendent self – are specifically designed to undermine the hegemony of human language. ACT seeks to destabilize the patient's confidence in his or her 'word machine' by showing how limited the functions of mind really are and how easily they can be programmed. ACT seeks to promote a better discrimination between the functions of the human being and the functions of the mind that accompanies that human being. ACT does not employ mindfulness strategies because they are good in a generic sense; ACT applies these strategies because they have been scientifically shown to destabilize rule-governed behaviours that are otherwise insensitive to direct real-world results. In contrast to some other third-wave therapies, ACT does not rely on any single mindfulness method but rather employs an eclectic mixture of metaphors, experiential exercises, analogies, and classic meditation practices. It is the function of these interventions that is important, not their form. Whereas some depressed patients might be unwilling or unable to complete an intensive multi-session treatment protocol that requires daily meditation practice, the ACT approach is quite flexible and would typically customize mindfulness interventions to fit the preferences and abilities of the patient.

Finally, a third distinctive feature of ACT is its emphasis on value-clarifying processes and value-based actions – which are often referred to as 'committed actions'. As far as we know, no other third-wave treatment explicitly focuses on eliciting values as a fundamental or core process of treatment. In ACT values are seen as verbally derived mental representations that both initiate and reinforce goal-directed behaviours. Often human suffering develops because attempts to control and eliminate unwanted private experience effectively shuts the patient off from valued activities in life. Many valued activities are emotionally complicated and can produce a mixture of pleasant and unpleasant private experience. In order to help the patient reengage in life, ACT tries to help that person to make contact with intrinsically important life directions. In essence, values are the 'fuel' that will motivate the patient to move forward, towards a life worth living, even though s/he will no doubt encounter unwanted and distressing private experiences in doing so. The ACT interventions focusing on acceptance, defusion, present-moment awareness and contact with the transcendent sense of self can all be viewed as ways of preparing the patient to 'make room' for unpleasant private experiences even as s/he moves towards valued life outcomes.

In summary, as its name suggests, ACT seeks to promote acceptance of unwanted private experiences through the application of various mindfulness strategies. These range from observing and witnessing strategies to defusion methods that teach the client to dis-identify with the literal aspects of private experience (for example thoughts, feelings, memories, sensations, images, etc.). As the term 'commitment' in the 'ACT' formula suggests, the larger goal of this form of therapy is to help the client identify and pursue valued life directions that could promote a greater (and ongoing) sense of vitality, purpose, and meaning. Acceptance and mindfulness strategies support this goal, as they enhance the client's ability to experience distressing private experiences, which previously functioned as barriers to vital living.

The ACT approach to depression is quite unique, even counterintuitive at points, and it offers a somewhat refreshing perspective that is distinctively at odds with more traditional, 'syndrome-based', biomedically derived models (see Strosahl & Robinson, 2008 and Zettle, 2007 for a more thorough discussion of this approach). In this chapter we will try to show the application of ACT treatment to the case of Gail, a 48-year-old woman with a long history of repeated episodes of depression. First we will introduce a case conceptualization framework that helps to 'describe' Gail's strengths and weaknesses from an ACT perspective. At that point we will demonstrate various ACT interventions suggested by the case conceptualization process. Since there are numerous entry points in the ACT treatment model, we will also describe how an ACT therapist would adjust course on the basis of Gail's response (or lack of response) to an ACT clinical intervention. All forms of therapy have a dynamic quality that is rooted in assessing and reassessing the client's progress; and ACT is no exception.

Case Conceptualization

Clinicians new to ACT often complain that ACT is a difficult approach to implement because there are so many counterintuitive ideas in the treatment package. To help clinicians new to ACT, we have streamlined the case conceptualization and treatment-planning process by using an assessment system called the 'three pillars of psychological flexibility' (Strosahl, Robinson, & Gustavsson, 2012). The three pillars represent basic response styles that combine to produce psychological flexibility (or rigidity). A response style can be thought of as a 'stance' the person takes towards the job of daily living. To be psychologically flexible means that these response styles complement each other in ways that promote the person's best interests. The three pillars are referred to as being open, being aware and being engaged (or OPEN, AWARE, ENGAGED). The interested reader can access more information about the pillars approach from other sources; here we will demonstrate how this approach can be applied to treatment planning for Gail.

Clinical Application

We can now use this case conceptualization framework to conduct a contextual assessment with Gail. Such assessment might include the following interactions:

THERAPIST Given that you have suffered from depression for so many years, I'm sure you've tried lots of strategies to control your depression. What kinds of things have you tried to get on top of this problem?

GAIL Well, when I get depressed, my energy level gets really bad. I just can't do anything the way I normally do it. I feel tired out all of the time. So, I have to cut back on my activities.

THERAPIST Can you give me some examples of how you do that?

GAIL Well, I cut back on my hours at work by about 50%. When I feel good, I tend to get out of the house and do more social things with my friends and I've pretty much stopped that. I used to take walks to relax on a daily basis and I stopped that because I just feel so worn out. My daughters tend to let me hang out at home and they do more of the housework and cooking.

THERAPIST So, it sounds like one of your major strategies for controlling your mood is to pull back and rest, so to speak. Tell me ... when you do this, how does it affect your mood? Does it help you feel better?

GAIL Well, it helps to take the pressure off because I don't feel I can really perform when I feel depressed, so at least I don't have to worry about making a fool of myself, making a mistake at work or having people notice that I'm not myself. I've been working with a counsellor on this whole issue of my negative thoughts about making mistakes, being humiliated and not feeling worthy but I continue to have those thoughts anyway.

THERAPIST So one result you experience is a feeling a relief from anxiety or fear about not being able to perform in various ways because of your depression. I'm still interested in how, over the long haul, the retreat-and-rest strategy has affected your mood. What does your experience say? Does this strategy make you feel more in control of your depression? Or does it make you feel less in control? Is your depression better now than it was several years ago, or is it worse, or about the same?

GAIL When you put it that way, my depression is probably worse now than before. I have noticed that I'm bored a lot even when I'm not depressed. I hold back on making commitments because I know I won't be able to follow through on them if I get depressed. It seems like the longer this goes on, the more anxious I am about having another depression.

THERAPIST So, how is this affecting your family life?

GAIL Well, I sense that my daughters are unhappy about having to do my chores and the cooking. My husband and I have a lukewarm relationship and I have very little interest in intimacy with him. We haven't really talked about this at all, probably because he is afraid it will cause me to feel even more like a failure.

THERAPIST I'm curious about how your lifestyle changes when you are feeling better. You mentioned that you are more social and outgoing; also that you tend to get out and walk more; and it sounds like you generally work full time when you are not depressed. When you are feeling better, what else is different?

GAIL Well, I am more interested in doing fun things like taking my two daughters shopping, going to movies, or taking weekend getaways with my husband. Yea, I do walk more and I feel just way more motivated to go to work. I have a lot of skills that my boss wants to take advantage of when I'm able to work.

THERAPIST In the past, when you have overcome your depression, did any of these behaviours seem to lead the way out, or do you have a sense of how you bring your mood back to a more resilient state?

GAIL I'm not really sure. I think pulling back and resting helps me weather the storm, so to speak. I usually wait until my energy and motivation return and then I start doing things again. I generally can't get myself to do much of anything as long as I feel depressed and lifeless.

THERAPIST When you were pretty much free from depression for four years in your life, did your lifestyle look more like the one you just described, or was it more the retreat-and-rest approach?

GAIL Oh, definitely it was the first. I was much more involved with my work, my daughters, my husband and friends. I also was a choir member at the church, something I stopped doing because of my fear of not being able to track music and of making a singing mistake that everyone could hear.

On the basis of this exchange, it is relatively straightforward to apply the three pillars to Gail. As can be seen from Table 13.1, we have marked an X to indicate Gail's location on each of the three response-style dimensions, and then we present the historical information and the direct clinical observations that justify the rating we have supplied.

Gail is exhibiting impairments along all three response-style dimensions, the most notable impairment surfacing in the pillar of being aware. Gail is living a life that is devoid of felt purpose and meaning. She is, in ACT terms, 'checked out'. She is heavily fused with her storyline of not only unsuccessfully fighting depression in her past but, more importantly, being fated to suffer from depression in the future. Fusion with this story is responsible for a set of responses that propel her all too rapid flights into inactivity, withdrawal, and isolation at the first signs of depressed mood. It is clear that, even though her behavioural and emotional withdrawal strategies have never worked to control her depression, she continues to use these strategies anyway.

Her story is doubling as a social justification for her continued lack of participation in life. She is citing depression as the 'cause' of her emotional and behavioural withdrawal, when it is in fact the result of these behaviours. This is a good example of *reason giving* – the act of arbitrarily generating cause–effect relationships between private events (depression, low energy, low motivation) and behaviour (withdrawing from family, work, and friends). She has generated a set of 'good' reasons why she is not pulling her weight with her family and is not pursuing any type of meaningful work. Like most natural social units, her various family members have accepted these verbally generated reasons and have modified family roles to accommodate her lack of functioning. Usually this creates secondary relationship issues that typically go unaddressed, as members of Gail's family try to protect her from suffering even more serious and debilitating depression.

The second concern is her pervasive use of behavioural avoidance to solve the issues that she is facing in life. She seems to 'have it down' in terms of producing a steady stream of *depressive behaviours* – that is, *actions that are ostensibly done in the service of reducing depression but in fact increase it*. When her depression worsened, she reduced her work hours, which effectively made work a less meaningful part of her daily context. She coped at home by spending more time in bed, offloading normal parental duties onto her children, and participating less in family relationships. She is actually tuned into the fact that this makes her feel guilty, but she seems

Table 13.1 Case conceptualization: The three pillars of psychological flexibility.

CLOSED OFF X	OPEN
Observations • Seems emotionally numb and doesn't display primary emotions. • Ruminates extensively, probably to distract herself from more painful experiences. • Does not engage in artificial numbing strategies (a positive point). • Views negative moods as disabling. • Stops work and household duties to control mood. • Very preoccupied with controlling her moods.	*Conclusion* Problems with experiential avoidance and fusion with unworkable rules
CHECKED OUT X	**AWARE**
Observations • Complains of boredom. • Uninterested in her job. • Seems disconnected from primary relationships. • Sleeps a lot. • Finds it difficult to get started each day. • Seems to lack direction in life. • Relies excessively on socially prescribed reason giving. • Very fused with her life story of depression.	*Conclusion* Real impairment in ability to stay present
WITHDRAWN X	**ENGAGED**
Observations • Has cut back on work rather than looking for something about which she has some passion. • Uses withdrawal and isolation strategies at home. • Is not addressing the impact of her depression on her marriage even though she knows there is a problem. • Seems willing to be in a passive and dependent role in the family system. • Has engaged in therapy (could be positive, to judge from her agenda).	*Conclusion* Out of contact with personal values and significant behavioural avoidance

oblivious to the relationship between these ongoing feelings of guilt and her depressive affect. This insensitivity to real contingencies functions to help her tolerate her depression. As long as she persists in the pattern of avoidance, she will be fated to experience repeated depressions; so, in this sense, her predictions about her future are exactly correct – for all the wrong reasons.

Assessing the Costs of Avoidance

As the preceding dialogue demonstrates, in order to solve the problem that brought the client into therapy, we normally try to explore all the things that the client has tried so far in order to address the issue. The therapist's demeanour is non-judgemental at this juncture and the therapist settles for an open-ended and 'data collection'-oriented discussion. The therapist also looks for behaviours that led Gail out of her previous depressions. Why did they end at all? Why hasn't she just been chronically depressed since the beginning? When she was functioning 'normally' for four years earlier in life, what was she doing differently in terms of lifestyle, life commitments, self-care behaviours and so forth? Was she engaging in the same kinds of emotional and behavioural avoidance strategies as she is now, or was she doing something different? This type of information would help us evaluate whether she is at all tuned into the fact that specific behaviours got her into depression … and specific behaviours got her out. Very often, clients like Gail are so caught up with their story line of depression dropping in and out of their life (like a pelican bringing a baby) that they are surprised to hear that their behaviour patterns were entirely different when they were doing better. The next step is to assess the cost of behavioural and emotional avoidance strategies, as demonstrated in the following dialogue.

THERAPIST I'm glad you brought up your concerns about the impact of your depression on the family, because another question I had is what has the retreat and rest strategy cost you in your life? It sounds like one cost is that you have at least partly lost your role as mother with your daughters.

GAIL Yes, I feel very guilty about not being there for them as a full-time mother. I can do it when I'm not depressed, but I just don't have the will to stick with it when I'm depressed.

THERAPIST How about your marriage? How has that been impacted?

GAIL We don't have fun together any more and I'm sure my husband resents my dour mood. He is very civil to me, which in a way hurts because it is clear he is struggling to feel close to me. When I get depressed, I just have no interest in sex or intimacy and I just want to be left alone.

THERAPIST So, it sounds like another cost of retreating and resting is that your husband can't depend on you to be available in the relationship. When you are depressed, you are married to your depression rather than to your husband, if that makes sense to you. You become totally absorbed in the process of controlling your mood.

GAIL I know exactly what you are saying. My husband has jokingly said that he sometimes thinks I'm having an affair because of how reclusive and non-communicative I become.

THERAPIST It also sounds like you have a promising career. What impact has the depression had on progress in your career field?

GAIL Because I can't work full time when I'm depressed, my supervisor does not assign me to high profile projects or projects that involve work teams. It is one of the things I regret most about my illness; that I'm passing up a very promising career because I simply cannot be relied on to stay at work.

THERAPIST That has to hurt too, knowing what could have been. You also mentioned that you used to be very involved in your church and were in the choir. What happened there?

GAIL Well, as I told you, I dropped out of the choir and it is very hard for me to get the energy to go to church when I'm depressed. I tend to stay at home and rest in bed instead. That has made it difficult for me to participate in church activities and committees, so I don't go there much any more.

THERAPIST As you describe how your life has been affected, it sounds like you have paid a terrible cost for the strategies you have used to control your depression. The really bitter pill must be that these strategies haven't really worked. Here you are depressed again and telling me that your depression has worsened over the years and that more and more of your daily decision making is being influenced by the prospect of becoming depressed.

In the initial part of the assessment Gail has discovered that her depression management strategies don't really solve the problem of being depressed. She is so fixated on controlling her depression that she is only minimally attentive to the larger pattern of life constriction that she has imposed around her. The issue of 'cost' is therefore of the utmost importance in the ACT approach. Only by getting Gail in touch with the cost of her avoidance strategies is it likely that she will be willing to look at an alternative to the control- and-eliminate agenda she has been pursuing for years. Once again, the therapist's demeanour is non-judgemental, compassionate, and validating. This part of the assessment is usually sobering for the client, so there is no need to take a 'one up' role as the therapist. Gail knows that things are not going well and the therapist is merely helping her create a clear picture of the scope and magnitude of the problem.

Control Is the Problem, Not the Solution

The next phase of the intervention is to reframe the problem and to point to the basic paradox of the control-and-eliminate agenda: the more you attempt to control depression, the more you lose control of your life. Most depressed clients have been socially trained to see the presence of depression as a sign of poor health and as an abnormal state of being. Therefore the goal is to control and eliminate the depression in order to become healthy again. Clients are also socially trained to look for possible causes of depression and either to analyse them out of existence or to reduce exposure to them, if they cannot be eliminated. The paradox of course is that these strategies *are* depression; but they are invariably viewed differently by the client, as demonstrated in the following dialogue.

THERAPIST I'm confused by something that seems to be going on here. On the one hand, you've tried very, very hard to gain control of your depression. You have used a ton of different strategies like not making commitments that you can't keep if you get depressed, reducing your activities and involvements to maintain precious energy when you are depressed, going into therapy to analyse and change thinking that might be leading you into more depression. And you have done this courageously for years, and you've kept at it even in the midst of being discouraged about the results. On the other hand, your depressions are becoming more frequent and they are worsening. You are noticing that this process is really damaging aspects of your life that are really important to you: your relationship with your daughters, your marriage, you career goals, your spiritual connections. You are an intelligent person and I know you are not trying to wreak this kind of havoc in your life. It is almost like there is a trick going on here; where 2 + 2 equals five. You would think that, if these strategies were working for you, the pattern would be exactly the opposite. You would be experiencing fewer depressions and they would be less intense; your relationships with your daughters, husband, and church would be growing, not shrinking. How do you explain this?

GAIL I spend hours thinking about why I can't control my depression and what is wrong with me that this problem just keeps getting worse. I don't know how to answer your question. I can't explain it myself.

THERAPIST Is it possible that the strange loop you are in looks like this: the more you attempt to keep depressions from happening and the more you attempt to control your mood when a depression is present, the less control over your life you get?

GAIL What you are suggesting is that trying to control my depression is actually causing my depression, am I hearing that right?

THERAPIST Exactly. The problem is not that you are incompetent at strategies to control your mood, because you are very competent. The problem might be that it is the strategies themselves that are destined to fail. They not only fail to fulfil their immediate objective, which is to reduce or stop your depression, they also systematically worsen your risk of more depression over time.

This part of the discussion requires a delicate touch, because it is very tempting for the inexperienced therapist to begin lecturing the client in a condescending way about the ineffectiveness of avoidance and control strategies. In this dialogue, the therapist brings the issue up in an almost puzzled way and asks Gail to help make sense of the paradox.

Treatment Flow: What Is Being Avoided?

In ACT, depression is viewed as a state of emotional and behavioural avoidance that protects the patient from primary issues that are far more emotionally loaded. In other words, the ACT therapist is not concerned about the depression per se but rather having the client identify and ultimately approach avoided experiences that have preceded the depression. Put another way, if there is no experiential or behavioural avoidance of the primary issue(s), there is no depression. The next part of the intervention involves broaching this issue.

GAIL So, are you saying that I need to stop my strategies and then I would feel better and be able to return to my life?

THERAPIST What I'm saying is that the tactics you are using so courageously seem to have backfired. I don't know what will happen to you if you stop using these strategies, other than you might keep your depression from worsening over time. There is another issue here as well. If you think of depression as a signal that something is out of balance in your life, then it doesn't make sense to spend all of your energy trying to quiet the signal. That would be like spending precious time and energy getting on a ladder and unplugging the battery on the fire alarm in your smoke-filled house because you are annoyed by the high-pitched sound. That alarm is telling you to get out of the house or to put out a fire that is starting. In your case, if depression was an alarm signal that something is out of balance in your life, do you have a sense of what types of things are out of balance?

GAIL (crying softly) It's my marriage. I find it very hard to be intimate with him or to feel like he is my life partner. It is so obvious when we are together alone that it is hard to even look in his eyes. About ten years ago he had an affair with someone that lasted for about five months, which I found out about quite accidentally. The sad thing is that I was upset, but I was also relieved. We now had a reason to be distant from each other, focus on raising our lovely daughters, and not talk about the problems in our marriage. So are you saying that my depression is caused by this problem in my marriage?

THERAPIST I'm saying that your depression is signalling to you that something is wrong. The other thing your depression does is it keeps your attention focused on managing your mood; then you don't have to deal with the problem that set off the signal in the first place. I'm not saying this is deliberate on your part; just that this seems to be the way depression works. So, here we are today, talking as if your depression is the major problem in your life, when it sounds like the single most important relationship you will ever have in you life is far from what you hoped it would be. I'm wondering ... what types of feelings, thoughts, memories, or sensations show up for you as we talk about your marriage right now?

Gail	I feel sad and lonely. I'm thinking that I've lost my chance to find someone to love. I have this image of being an old lady who is totally cold inside, who has never been warmed from the outside. I feel a lot of fear at the thought of living alone even while I'm with my family.
Therapist	What would happen if you just let these reactions be there, without running from them or trying to numb yourself out by going into depression?
Gail	It hurts too much; it's more than I can bear. You can't expect to be doing this every day and have any hope of being happy in life. This stuff is just going to make me more depressed if I let myself think about it.

There are several clinical objectives to this intervention. First, if we can get Gail to make experiential contact with what she is avoiding, there is generally going to be a reduction in subsequent depressed mood. She is certainly not going to become euphoric by making contact with her dismal marital situation, but she is going to feel what is there to be felt. The alternative that she has been practising is to slip into the numbness of depression. The therapist accentuates this by showing how depression insulates her from far more basic, painful material. Second, by asking Gail to 'sit' with these avoided experiences, the therapist is exposing the evaluations she has about unwanted private experiences and what rules she has been primed to follow in dealing with them. What would it take for Gail to simply allow these experiences to be present? What would happen if that occurred? Third, the therapist is trying to bring Gail into the present moment and simply sit with her experience. When she begins to drift back into avoidance, the therapist brings her back into the moment and asks her to make direct contact with her private experiences.

Another important objective at this point in ACT is to reveal the system of rules that underlies Gail's longstanding pattern of emotional and behavioural avoidance, as exemplified in the following dialogue.

Therapist	When you say it hurts too much to bear, what does it mean for something to hurt too much?
Gail	(hesitating) I guess it means I will be damaged by these reactions; that they are harmful to me.
Therapist	You mean that having your own emotions, memories, images or thoughts, especially the ones that hurt like these do, makes you unhealthy, or that you could be damaged by them somehow?

GAIL No, not if you put it like that, it doesn't. I don't think they mean I'm unhealthy or ill. It does make me unhappy … very unhappy to feel these things.

THERAPIST Do you think that being very unhappy means that you are unhealthy inside?

GAIL Yes, being unhappy the way I am and have been can't possibly be healthy.

THERAPIST Then it seems like the next step is to remove yourself from the unhappiness so that it can't damage you. Is that the basic move you would make here?

GAIL Well, yes. I don't want to feel this unhappiness because it is so painful.

THERAPIST The problem is, since you can't just snap your fingers and eliminate your marital problems, what are you going to do? It sounds like you are in a trap where the only way out is to numb yourself out in a depression.

GAIL Well, at least I have learned to live with being depressed; I'm not sure I could handle living with an active sense of unhappiness about a marriage that I live in every day.

THERAPIST Exactly. That is the trade-off you've been making. Gain control of your unhappiness; lose control of your depression.

In this dialogue Gail is showing that she is *fused* with rules that describe negative private experiences as unhealthy and potentially toxic. She follows these evaluations as if they were primary properties of emotions (i.e., painful feelings are bad for you; positive feelings are good for you). By over-focusing on the control or elimination of unwanted private experiences in the pursuit of getting 'healthy', Gail does not have to deal with the elephant in the living room. She has a failing marriage and it took digging by the therapist to even get her to make contact with that reality. In this case, depression serves a protective function for Gail. It is not much of a life but, as she points out, it sure beats the perceived (and avoided) alternative.

Identifying Barriers

The next step is to help Gail identify the various private experiences that have heretofore functioned as barriers to effective action; these barriers, separately or collectively, are formidable enough to make Gail take the depression option rather than the 'fix the marriage or leave it' option, as the following dialogue demonstrates.

THERAPIST There is another option here that I've noticed you haven't even put on the table for discussion. Approach your husband about your deep sense of alienation from him and either try to involve him in improving the marriage or, if that fails, begin to take steps to end the marriage. Have you ever thought about taking that path?

GAIL I have, and when I do I absolutely freak out. I get scared and panicky; I feel a rush of guilt and then my depression level goes off the charts and then I feel emotionally drained and apathetic for days.

THERAPIST So, let's go into your fear and anxiety. Tell me what shows up for you here and now, as you imagine taking the step of approaching your husband with the intent of fixing this or ending it.

GAIL It might fail. I don't honestly believe that it will get better. I'll end up a divorced middle-aged woman. I don't want to be alone; I've never lived alone and I'm afraid I would fall apart emotionally.

THERAPIST What about the guilt part?

GAIL I would be damaging my daughters; they would be heartbroken if mom and dad separated, and it would be due to me. He is making no waves about this marriage so it will look like I was the negative one. They might take sides and blame me for causing the divorce; that is another source of real anxiety for me.

THERAPIST Any images about life as a single parent?

GAIL What if I get depressed and can't work and support myself? How will I make ends meet even if I don't get depressed? Where would I live? Would my daughters want to come with me, or would they want to stay with their dad? My mind is full of worries like this.

In this dialogue the therapist is just trying to pull out the obstacles that Gail will have to confront if she is to do anything about her marriage other than hide out in her depression. There is also an exposure element to this assessment, as the therapist is having Gail sit with all of her avoided thoughts, emotions, memories, and images and learning to look at them directly.

Restless Mind, Calm Mind

Gail seems to be caught up in a cycle of over-dentification with negative, self-referential thinking that produces a downward spiral of rumination and psychological rigidity. The ACT approach will help her to adopt an observer or witnessing stance when confronted with unwanted private experiences. There is nothing inherently toxic about experiencing unpleasant thoughts, feelings, or memories as long as they are recognized for what they are. As Gail's case demonstrates, negative private experiences become toxic when she fuses with them and turns them into a 'reality' that is viewed as toxic. Gail needs to learn to defuse from her 'reactive mind' and to engage her 'calm mind'.

THERAPIST So, your mind gives you all kinds of negative chatter about what will happen if you try to solve this problem. Let's call this your restless mind. It is the part of your mind that chatters at you 24 hours a day. Right now, it is reacting to our discussion about actually doing something to address what is wrong with your marriage. Like all minds, it is doing its job to warn you of any and all possible dangers that may lie ahead of you. It is going to give you all of the reasons why you should avoid directly addressing this problem in your life. So, you might have to make room for this negative chatter without treating it as truth with a capital T. After all, this is just your mind, and you can witness what is going on in your mind without being drawn into it.

GAIL You are talking about my mind like it is almost another person or a thing that is foreign to my body. I'm not sure what you are trying to say to me.

THERAPIST The fact is that you can hear yourself think if you listen; your mind is literally talking to you. So, in order for you to be able to hear your mind, there must be a you that is listening to all of its' advice. So yes, I'm saying that you are not the same as your mind. You have a mind, but you are not the same as your mind.

GAIL Why does that matter? I can't turn it off, so what am I supposed to do?

THERAPIST One thing you can do is to do nothing when your mind comes at you. The mind is like a tantrum-throwing child. Imagine that you are at the store with your child and she wants a toy but you say no. She starts throwing a tantrum in front of everyone, yelling, screaming, kicking and throwing stuff around. You try to comfort her and that only increases the volume level. She wants you to give her that toy! Eventually, the only way you can respond is to take your child out to the car and put her in the car seat. She needs to cool off and if you continue to pay too close attention to her; the tantrum will continue to get worse. So, while you are driving home, you are certainly aware of the tantrum but you choose to do nothing about it except be aware of it. It is impossible not to hear the tantrum, so your only choice is to be aware of it while choosing to do nothing. The part of your mind that tells you to do nothing is what we will call your calm mind. It is that part of your mind that keeps you calm even in the middle of a tantrum. Sometimes, just taking a deep breath, listening to music, knitting, or drawing will help a person get centred.

GAIL Are you saying that I should combat what my mind is telling me by looking at how my thoughts might be inaccurate and that I should try to come up with a more accurate thought? That is what my previous counsellor had me do, and it works well with some of my negative thoughts but not with others.

THERAPIST Actually, there is another move you can make here. Instead of challenging these provocative thoughts and trying to correct them, you can simply be aware of them as an observer. You don't have to take any action to change the thoughts, emotions, memories, or images you have. They are happening in between your ears; no one else can see them or experience them directly. These are just images about a future that you have not arrived at yet. If you just let them be there without evaluating them or struggling with them, they will assume their rightful position in this process. The main thing that matters for you is what you do with your feet; the steps you take to either address or run from your marital problem.

In this example the therapist elicits from Gail the internal and external barriers that heretofore have blocked her from pursuing a solution to her marital problem. He is using both defusion (it is just your mind talking to you) and acceptance (let it be there without struggle or evaluation) strategies to help Gail sit with this material. Gail had previously been exposed to a more traditional CBT approach of cognitive restructuring and the therapist helped her understand the difference between an acceptance posture and a cognitive disputation approach.

Values as the Fuel

Helping the client identify and follow through with value-based actions is a very distinctive feature of the ACT approach to depression. In Gail's case, part of the cost of being 'checked out' is that she is living in a relationship that is inconsistent with what she wants from life. Staying out of direct contact with this reality is an important part of her depressive response. Her apathy, low energy, and anhedonia make it far less likely that she will 'awaken' to the full extent of her life dilemma and do something about it. She is trading off the immediate pain of dealing with her marriage for the long-term numbness of depression. The only way to awaken her is to help her come into direct contact with her life dreams, their associated values, and the grim reality that she is not living in a way that is consistent with her values. In order to overcome the obstacles she has identified, she will need a strong purpose, which will legitimize the pain that she is likely to experience. Contact with deeply held values functions as a tremendous intrinsic source of motivation; motivation converts into persistence in the face of directly experienced obstacles.

There are several ACT techniques that can help elucidate the client's underlying values. A favourite one is the ACT funeral exercise, which often sets the stage for further dialogue about personal values and vital living.

THERAPIST I want you to imagine that you have died suddenly for some reason and that, through some divine intervention, you are able to attend your funeral in spirit. I want you to imagine that you are listening to the eulogies given in your honor by your husband, your daughters, your friends, co-workers, people you know in church and anyone else who is important to you. I want you to take your time and imagine that you are hearing each of these persons speak about what you meant to them, the mark you left in their lives. Really let yourself get into the situation; you could even imagine that your funeral is being held in your church (15 minutes or so of guided imagery would follow). Tell me, what showed up for you during this exercise?

GAIL I became very sad while I was at my funeral; it struck me that if I had died today, I would not have fulfilled my dreams.

THERAPIST What stood out in that regard?

GAIL My daughters made really beautiful statements about how I had been there for them, had taught them the courage to confront difficult situations in their lives, had been there as a 'rock' of support. I couldn't help but think that I haven't been that kind of person for many years. I've been a part-time mother and the rest of time a person who is way too dependent on them.

THERAPIST So, there is a difference between the person you would like to be for your daughters and the person you are. What about your husband; what did he say about you?

GAIL He basically said I was a wonderful wife and mother but the tone was not heartfelt. He was just saying the words and his face was unmoved. It was spooky and I knew exactly what the real message was.

THERAPIST So, you're saying the eulogy he gave you was as lukewarm as your marriage. What would you have liked to hear him say?

GAIL To see him broken up with grief and not able to control his pain at the loss of me. To say that we shared a passion that never died over our lives together; that I was his best friend, his lover, and his life partner. That one was really hard for me to stick with. I noticed I was trying to skip over him or trying to get him to speed-talk so I could go to the next eulogy.

THERAPIST It sounds like you can see the future getting away from you here. The path you are on now … does it seem like you are heading in the right direction to realize your dreams for your marriage and your daughters?

GAIL No, I'm not heading in that direction at all.

THERAPIST So, sticking with the status quo at home in terms of how you are relating to your daughters and how you are interacting with your husband … Is that consistent with your dreams, or is it taking you away from your dreams?

GAIL It is not what I believe in.

THERAPIST To move yourself in the direction of your dreams, what obstacles will you have to move through to pursue that path?

GAIL I have to face what I'm most afraid of and I can't allow depression to call the shots in my life.

The goal of this very sobering exercise is to get Gail to make contact with personal values that have been suppressed or avoided, and particularly to get Gail to make direct contact with the discrepancy between what she is shooting for in life and what she is getting. The therapist is trying to get Gail to 'wake up' and become mindful that her life is slipping away second by second. There will be no opportunity to rewind her life back to the beginning and to live it right the second time round. This is serious business, and the therapist is helping Gail make contact with the gravity of the choices

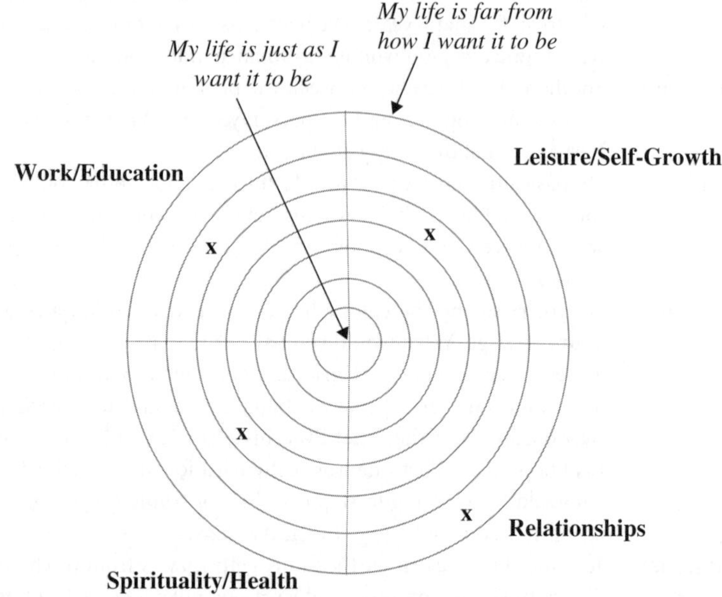

Figure 13.1 Gail's Bull's Eye Values Clarification Results.

life is asking her to make. This approach tends to undermine mindless rule following, so that Gail can begin to focus on strategies that can promote her sense of life direction, life vitality, and meaning.

Value-Based Committed Action

Most clients benefit from activities designed to help them identify concrete behaviours that are value-consistent. We employ a written exercise known as the Bull's Eye Value Clarification Exercise, developed by Tobias Lundgren, a Swedish psychologist (Lundgren, Luoma, Dahl, Strosahl, & Melin, 2012; see Figure 13.1). The Bull's Eye's four quadrants are work/education, relationship, leisure/self-growth, and health/spirituality. First Gail will write out her core values in each of these four areas, with the instruction to think about living a life where anything is possible. This will discourage her from 'disqualifying' life dreams a priori because of imagined internal or external barriers. Then she will place an 'x' on the target, to indicate how consistent her current life trajectory is with her written values.

THERAPIST I notice that you've written out a value for your marriage that says you want to be in a lifelong relationship that is based on love, trust, sharing, and intimacy, in both good times and bad. When you assessed where you are in your marriage right now, where did you put your mark on the target?

GAIL I put it in the outside ring of the target.

THERAPIST So you are saying that you are way off the mark in terms of how you are living in your current marriage?

GAIL Yes.

THERAPIST Now, correcting a life course is kind of like turning around a large cruise ship. The ship has tremendous momentum and it can't turn on a dime. Just like the ship, you can't turn your marriage on a dime either, and it doesn't do any good to turn the rudder hard about, as that will just cause the ship to flounder. The ship has to be coaxed into taking a different direction. Since you marked the target in the outside ring, we don't need to worry right now about hitting the centre of the target, but rather beginning to move that mark closer towards the target. We can do this one ring at a time on the target. If we were to do that, what action could you take in the near future that would be consistent with your values and would signal to you that you were beginning to turn your marriage in the direction you want it to go in?

GAIL I've never even talked with my husband about the impact that the affair had on me. I've always been afraid of the emotions that would come up for me, and for him too. There is a lot of hurt sitting behind that closed door. To ignore it, though, is the opposite of my value about sharing, trust, and intimacy, even if it is painful to me. I think I will ask him to sit down and talk about the affair with me.

THERAPIST So, what would be the biggest barrier to your just sitting down and having this out with him, so you can clear the air and decide which way the two of you will be headed?

GAIL The biggest obstacle is going to be the deep sense of betrayal I'm afraid I will experience.

THERAPIST Would you be willing to have that deep sense of betrayal if you knew it was part and parcel of the life path towards your values?

GAIL We'll see, but I'm willing to try.

THERAPIST I would like to take this one step further if you are willing to go along with this. What about this? Would you be willing to make a commitment right here, right now to take this action on behalf of your values about marriage, knowing full well that you might directly experience your sense of betrayal, loneliness, fear, anxiety and anything else that shows up as you do this? So, we are moving from 'I'll try as long as the emotional consequences aren't too bad' to 'I'll do this regardless of what the consequences are'. Do you see a difference between these two stances?

GAIL One is tentative and I was even thinking as I said I would try that there were some situations where I would probably decide not to try. The second one seems like a declaration that I'm making about the importance of my beliefs.

THERAPIST Exactly, when you make a commitment, you are doing it as much to be true to yourself as you are trying to solve a problem. There is a way to follow a commitment such that even pain becomes part of your health. You aren't approaching your husband because you are afraid of betrayal and loneliness; you are approaching him to talk about your dreams for the future and what you are looking for in a life partner.

GAIL It strikes me that I'm coming out of hiding by doing this and there is no turning back once I do it.

In this dialogue, the therapist is helping Gail identify value–behaviour discrepancies that she is motivated to deal with. The goal is to work with Gail to convert her bigger life values into tangible behaviours. By getting her to identify a specific action that would be consistent with her values, the therapist is increasing the likelihood that she will choose to take action. The therapist also helps her appreciate that any action like this is going to bring to the surface some pain, so the goal is to establish with her that she is willing to expose herself to this pain in the service of living a valued life.

Unfortunately for Gail, there is no 'silver bullet' that will suddenly lift her out of this messy life situation. She will have to make and keep commitments on a daily basis. She will have to establish a new course in her life through these daily actions. Again, committed actions don't have to be heroic in scope; they merely need to be consistent with her goal of forging a more vital relationship with her husband. At the next session, the therapist would help her assess the impact of following through on her commitments to her sense of vitality. Does she feel that this constitutes a positive step forward in terms of following out her values? Did she notice feeling different in some way before, during, and after engaging in the committed action? The goal is to help Gail begin to associate improved personal health and vitality with engaging in approach-oriented, value-consistent actions, not with the absence of personal pain.

Relapse Prevention: Building an ACT Lifestyle

If Gail experiences some level of success with committed actions, changes in mood are also likely to be observed. Ironically, that really isn't the main purpose in ACT. The main purpose is to get Gail to play the game of life and to persist when persistence is useful and desist when that is called for. Like any personal attribute, psychological flexibility can be cultivated through daily practice, something we refer to as the ACT lifestyle. The skills taught in ACT are not designed to eliminate pathology; they are designed to promote health and well-being. In consequence, it will be relatively easy to convince Gail to cultivate her openness, awareness, and engagement as a matter of lifestyle. Not only should Gail periodically monitor her depressive experiences, the therapist would stress the vitality-producing aspects of daily practices such as getting into the present moment, repeating 'value clarification' exercises on a regular basis, making regular self-assessments of life vitality, and so on. Because Gail has a long history of depression, this type of lifestyle planning will be of the utmost importance.

THERAPIST Gail, now that you are back on track in terms of your life direction, I want us to figure out some strategies that will keep you on the mark. What ideas do you have about making the work we have done part of your lifestyle, not just something to use when you get depressed?

GAIL I could post little messages around my house about being a mind watcher and doing valued acts every day. I've always been a list maker and this would fit my style. I could repeat the values exercise every third month or so.

THERAPIST Anything you can think of to stay on top of your depression level so it doesn't sneak up on you?

GAIL I could take a depression test every month or so; also my family members will be good at letting me know when they see any warning signs.

THERAPIST Try to view these different strategies as experiments and to review how they are working at least once a month. A strategy

> might seem promising at first, but later it may prove to be unworkable, and that's OK. We are trying to come up with a lifestyle plan, so it has to be sustainable for years and years. Let's plan on seeing each other in about three months regardless of how well you are doing – and of course you can come back in at any time if you feel things are going south on you.

The goal between sessions is to run a 'field experiment' to see what types of obstacles (both expected and unexpected) show up, and to assess how Gail applies ACT principles to stay on track in her life. At this point in the treatment the therapist is functioning more like a life coach and cheerleader, while at the same time offering immediate access to clinical services if things are not going well for Gail.

Summary

In this chapter we have briefly introduced the core components of ACT treatment for a depressed patient, including a new method for case conceptualization and treatment planning. In a short chapter such as this one there are obviously many nuances in the application of ACT that cannot be properly addressed. The interested reader is encouraged to seek out more in-depth information on the ACT approach to treating depression (see Strosahl & Robinson, 2008 for a patient self-help workbook and Zettle, 2007 for a therapist manual of ACT with depression).

References

Hayes, S., Barnes-Holmes, D., & Roche, B. (Eds). (2001). *Relational frame theory: A post-Skinnerian account of human language and cognition*. New York: Kluwer Academic/Plenum.

Lundgren, T., Luoma, J., Dahl, J., Strosahl, K., & Melin, L. (2012) The Bulls Eye Values Survey: A psychometric evaluation. *Cognitive and Behavioral Practice*, *19*, 518–526.

Strosahl, K., Robinson, P., & Gustavsson, T. (2012). *Brief interventions for radical change: Princples and practice of focused acceptance and commitment therapy*. Oakland, CA: New Harbinger.

Strosahl, K., & Robinson, P. (2008). *The mindfulness and acceptance workbook for depression: Using acceptance and commitment therapy to move through depression and create a life worth living*. Oakland, CA: New Harbinger.

Zettle, R. (2007). *ACT for depression: A clinician's guide to using acceptance and commitment therapy in treating depression*. Oakland, CA: New Harbinger Publications.

Further Reading

Hayes, S., Strosahl, K., & Wilson, K. (2011). *Acceptance and commitment therapy: The process and practice of mindul change*. New York: Guilford.

Strosahl, K., Robinson, P., & Gustavsson, T. (2015). *Inside this moment: Using acceptance and commitment therapy to promote radical change*. Oakland, CA: New Harbinger Publications.

14

Treating Acute Depression with Mindfulness-Based Cognitive Therapy

Ruth A. Baer and Erin Walsh

The case of Gail provides an opportunity to discuss the treatment of acute depression with mindfulness-based cognitive therapy (MBCT) (Segal, Williams, & Teasdale, 2002), a topic of growing interest among researchers and clinicians. Gail is a 48-year-old woman with recurrent major depressive disorder. She has experienced numerous depressive episodes beginning at the age of 19. Her current episode has persisted for 16 months and presents symptoms of low mood, lack of interest, hopelessness, fatigue, guilt, poor concentration, and disrupted sleep. Her score on the Beck Depression Inventory (BDI-II) (Beck, Steer, & Brown, 1996) is 37 (severe). Gail has tried many forms of antidepressant medication without success and is currently taking Paroxetine, with little observable effect. Her previous experience with psychotherapy includes only non-directive forms of counseling, which she has tried many times without significant benefit.

MBCT was developed for the purpose of preventing relapse and recurrence in individuals who have suffered previous episodes of depression but are currently in remission. In an early paper (Teasdale et al., 2000), the developers of MBCT cautioned that it might not be effective with actively depressed participants, because difficulties in concentrating or the intensity of negative thinking might preclude development of the attention and acceptance skills that are central to the programme. Since then, however, many studies, including several randomized trials, have shown that MBCT is feasible and acceptable for acutely depressed participants and results in

Treating Depression: MCT, CBT and Third Wave Therapies, First Edition.
Edited by Adrian Wells and Peter L. Fisher.

clinically significant improvements (for a review, see Metcalf & Dimidjian, 2014). MBCT has been shown to be superior to usual care (Barnhofer et al., 2009; van Aalderen et al., 2012) and psycho-education (Chiesa, Mandelli, & Serretti, 2012) and equivalent to group cognitive behavioural therapy (Manicavasagar, Perich, & Parker, 2012) and to an eight-week course of antidepressant medication (Eisendrath et al., 2015) in reducing depressive symptoms. With Gail as a focal point, the present chapter explores the use of MBCT for active depression and discusses issues requiring additional research.

Overview of MBCT

MBCT groups typically include up to 12 participants and one or two group leaders who meet for eight weekly two-hour sessions. For reasons to be discussed later, group leaders often describe themselves as instructors rather than therapists. Sessions follow a structured format, which consists of in-session practice of one or more mindfulness exercises, discussion of the exercises, discussion of participants' experiences with homework during the preceding week, presentation and discussion of new material, and assignment of homework for the coming week.

Pre-treatment interview

Individual pre-treatment interviews provide an overview of depression and relapse and allow potential participants to discuss their history of depression. The instructor describes the background of MBCT, the nature of the group, empirical evidence for its efficacy, and how the programme might be of benefit. For an acutely depressed patient such as Gail, it can be useful to discuss the nature of rumination and harsh self-criticism as factors that maintain depressive symptoms, so that the practice of mindfulness would make intellectual sense at the outset. Eventually it should also make sense experientially, but this may take time, and therefore the importance of regular attendance at sessions and completion of daily homework exercises is strongly emphasized. The instructor explains that intensive meditation practice will be challenging and encourages the participant to suspend judgement for the duration of the intervention and to commit to wholehearted engagement in the practices, even if results are not immediately obvious. This is especially important for individuals with significant ongoing symptoms of depression, whose motivation to engage in lengthy homework practices should not be assumed but carefully discussed. Gail has expressed hopelessness and pessimism about the likelihood that therapy will help, and therefore it is essential that the pre-treatment interview provide a sufficient explanation of the potential efficacy of mindfulness meditation for Gail to be be genuinely willing to participate fully. Assessment of suicide risk is also critically important. Although Gail is not currently suicidal, this could change, and the group format of MBCT does not allow for careful individual assessment of suicide risk from week to week. Therefore it may be advisable for any participant at potential risk to have an individual therapist who will monitor the patient's emotional state.

Session 1: Automatic pilot

At the beginning of the first session, the group leader establishes a warm and welcoming atmosphere and expresses appreciation that everyone is willing to make the commitment to participate in the programme. Ground rules about confidentiality are reviewed and the importance of regular attendance and consistent homework practice is reiterated. Group members are given the opportunity to introduce themselves and to describe their reasons for participating and how they hope to benefit from the programme. This process should help group members to feel understood and supported. Gail expressed some uncertainty about how the programme might help her, but stated that she was willing to give it a fair chance, in hopes that it might reduce her current symptoms and lead to fewer relapses in the future.

After introductions, the primary purpose of the first session is to begin recognizing the common and pervasive human tendency to function on automatic pilot (without awareness of one's actions). The remainder of the session is devoted to exercises that cultivate awareness of the present moment. The first mindfulness practice is the raisin exercise, which uses an ordinary activity (eating) as a way to become acquainted with mindfulness. Several raisins are given to each group member with the following instruction: 'I would like you focus on these objects and imagine that you have never seen anything like them before.' Over the course of several minutes, group members are guided in an exploration of the tactile sensations, aromas, and visual features of a single raisin as well as of the tastes, movements, and bodily sensations involved in eating it. The process may be repeated with a second or third raisin. The instructor then initiates discussion of this exercise by expressing genuine curiosity and interest in participants' reactions, using statements and open-ended questions such as 'I'm interested in what people experienced during this exercise,' and 'Would anyone like to share what they noticed?' Thoughts, feelings, or images that are volunteered are explored in detail. A wide range of associations may be expressed, including memories or images of distant times and places. The instructor is likely to comment on how interesting it is to see that our minds can travel a long way in a short time. The fact that we have the ability to watch our minds do this will also be noted and will be important throughout the intervention. For example:

INSTRUCTOR Would anyone like to comment on their experiences during this exercise?

GAIL It was different. I noticed I had a lot of thoughts racing through my mind as I handled the raisin. I suppose I was never aware of how many thoughts could arise from such a simple act.

INSTRUCTOR So you seemed to notice that this act of eating was different from how you normally eat. What was unique about this particular experience?

GAIL Well, I guess I usually eat at a much faster pace and don't pay much attention to food. When I took the time to slow down, I was able to become aware of the differing textures and tastes as I chewed.

INSTRUCTOR What did you notice?

GAIL With each bite, the raisin transformed from a bitter and rubbery texture to something much sweeter and softer. I was aware how it changed from bite to bite. I also had several thoughts appear as I chewed.

INSTRUCTOR Can you give an example of one or two thoughts that materialized during the exercise?

GAIL I suppose I remembered the days in grade school when I used to eat raisins for lunch. Then, my mind eventually ended up on my daughters and I wondered what they were having for lunch these days.

INSTRUCTOR Right. So, you noticed that your mind has the tendency to jump around quite a bit despite your intention to focus on particular aspects of the experience only. This is incredibly common, and an important point to raise! You also observed that, when you altered your style of eating, it changed your experience. This is another important observation. By intentionally

> bringing awareness to any experience, you have the ability to enhance it, to notice details you never were attentive to before.

Participants' comments are used to illustrate several key points: (1) minds have a tendency to wander and this is completely normal; (2) we often function on automatic pilot, unaware of what we are doing; and (3) paying attention to things normally done on automatic pilot can change the nature of the experience. The raisin exercise can be summarized as an example of what participants will be doing throughout the course of treatment: training awareness to be more focused on what is actually happening in the present moment. It is helpful to ask if participants can see how this exercise relates to depression. Even at this early stage, participants are likely to grasp the potential utility of paying attention to present-moment experience, and will note that mindful awareness may be more adaptive than behaving on automatic pilot when problems arise.

Next the instructor leads the group in the practice and discussion of the body scan, a 40–45 minute exercise that cultivates concentration, flexibility of attention, and the non-judgemental acceptance of present-moment experience. Participants are asked to lie on the floor with their eyes closed or to sit in chairs if lying down is painful or difficult. The instructor guides the group through each portion of the body, beginning with the left foot and working up to the head. Participants are encouraged to observe sensations (or lack of sensations) in each area, with curiosity and without judgement, and without trying to alter or eliminate them. They are encouraged to notice that the mind is likely to wander, and they are also encouraged to return attention gently to the body when this happens.

Several issues are likely to arise in the discussion of this initial body scan, many related to the general theme of not having done it right or well. Participants may feel that they have failed if their minds wandered or if they felt bored, sleepy, restless, tense, or upset. The central point in responding to these concerns is that there is no such thing as success or failure when practising the body scan. Becoming relaxed or attaining a special state of mind or body is not the goal. Participants are encouraged to adopt a stance of friendly curiosity towards all experiences that arise, even if these are unpleasant or unwanted. Analogies and metaphors are often used. The instructor might suggest that members imagine themselves as mapmakers exploring new territory and therefore interested in everything they encounter ('Ah, here is boredom!'). The goal is to acknowledge whatever arises with interest, openness, and acceptance and without self-blame or criticism.

Plenty of time is allowed for discussing homework for the coming week, which includes practising the body scan on six of the next seven days and performing a routine activity (e.g. brushing teeth) mindfully each day. A 45-minute recording to guide the body scan is provided, along with written summaries of the session and the assigned homework and sheets for recording homework practice. Practical matters that will increase the likelihood of homework completion are discussed, such as where in the house and at what time of day participants will practice and what steps will make this more feasible (such as asking someone to watch the children, putting the dog in or out, or turning off the phone or TV). The session ends with a two- or three-minute sitting meditation that focuses on the breath.

Session 2: Living in our heads

Participants have just spent a week engaged in a new and unfamiliar practice and may be eager to discuss their experiences. However, before discussing the homework, the instructor leads the group in the body scan. Starting each session with a formal practice cultivates the ability to shift out of automatic pilot mode. The subsequent discussion focuses first on the in-session body scan just completed and then shifts to participants' homework experiences. Common themes in these discussions include mind wandering, physical pain or discomfort, boredom or irritation, negative thoughts about the practice (such as 'what is the point of this?' and 'this will never help me'), frustrating external conditions (such as noise in the environment) and difficulty scheduling practice into the daily routine.

Participants are reminded that mind wandering is inevitable and that the point of practice is not to prevent this, but rather to notice when it occurs and to return attention gently to the breath or body, without self-criticism. If pain arises, participants are encouraged to observe the sensations carefully, rather than getting caught up in thoughts about them. If they choose to move the body to relieve the pain, they are encouraged to do so with awareness, bringing an attitude of interest to the sensations involved in moving and to the consequences of having moved. Uncontrollable noise in the environment, such as barking dogs and traffic, provides an excellent opportunity to dispel the common misconception that the practice of meditation requires peace and quiet. Unpleasant noises, along with frustration, anger, disappointment, and other reactions to the noise, can be observed mindfully as part of the practice. Boredom and irritation with the exercise itself and doubts about whether it will help are especially important to address because they are likely to undermine the motivation to practice. Again, the goal is to observe these phenomena as events in the mind, with curiosity, openness, and interest.

Although these perceived obstacles to meditation practice are common in most participants, those who are acutely depressed are likely to experience more intense self-criticism about them. Their self-critical thoughts are likely to be consistent with the feelings of inadequacy that are typical of depression (e.g., 'I can't do this, I fail at everything'). Frequent comments by the instructor about the universality of these experiences and encouragement to respond to them with compassion, acceptance, and non-judging will be helpful. For example:

GAIL	I tried doing the body scan every day but I wasn't very successful.
INSTRUCTOR	How do you mean?
GAIL	Well, my mind wandered all over the place, and a lot of times I couldn't feel any sensations where I was supposed to be feeling them, and just kept thinking that I'm useless at this just like at everything else.
INSTRUCTOR	Thank you for sharing, I am very happy you raised this issue. A lot of times we have an idea of how things are supposed to be. Unfortunately, if our experience does not match this ideal, we believe we are unsuccessful, that we failed. First, I would like to normalize the mind wandering. This is a very common experience. If your mind wanders during the practice, try noticing, 'Oh, there it goes again!' and, as best you can, gently redirecting attention to the current instruction, without giving yourself a hard time.
GAIL	So, if my mind is allowed to wander, what is the point of this exercise?
INSTRUCTOR	I think the most important point is to observe your experience carefully and to accept it for what it is, regardless of what comes along, even mind wandering, or unpleasant thoughts. Remember, there is no right way to practice. During the next exercise, try letting go of expectations and see what it is like to foster a curious, gentle attitude in your moment-to-moment experience.

This approach to experience may seem quite novel to participants and requires persistent practice. For the instructor, compassionate understanding and non-judgemental interest in the entire range of the participants' experiences and reactions is critically important, because it models the stance towards experience that participants are learning to adopt for themselves. The same attitude is directed towards reported difficulties in scheduling time to practice. The instructor will express compassionate concern (but not criticism), will encourage the participant to bring an enquiring mind to this issue during the next week, and will reiterate the importance of doing the exercises in order to benefit from the programme.

Session 2 includes an exercise from cognitive therapy designed to illustrate the impact of thoughts on emotional states. Participants are asked to close their eyes and envision themselves walking down a street and seeing an acquaintance on the other side. They smile and wave but the person fails to notice and walks by. The thoughts, feelings, and sensations experienced while imagining this scene are used to illustrate the ABC model of emotion, in which a situation (A) leads to a thought or interpretation (B), which leads to an emotion (C). The wide variety of thoughts that can occur in response to the same situation illustrates the essential idea that thoughts are not facts. For example, thinking 'I wonder if she's having a bad day' might lead to feelings of care and concern, whereas 'She doesn't like me – nobody likes me' may elicit feelings of sadness and loneliness. 'Why is she being so rude?' might lead to anger, whereas 'People will think I'm an idiot, waving at nobody' could trigger embarrassment. The discussion will also reveal that the more negative thoughts are more common during depressed moods. Recognition of thoughts as they occur, as well as the emotions they tend to evoke, is greatly enhanced through the practice of mindfulness.

Next, the pleasant events calendar is introduced as a homework exercise. Participants are asked to notice at least one pleasant event each day and to note their thoughts, emotions, and sensations on a form provided. This exercise cultivates increased awareness and appreciation of pleasant events when they occur and recognition of the sensations associated with pleasantness. It also encourages catching the thoughts that can turn a pleasant experience into an unpleasant one, such as 'Why doesn't this happen more often?' or 'I don't deserve this'. Additional assigned homework for the following week includes the body scan and mindfulness of breath for 10–15 minutes (each one for six or seven days) and mindful observation of a routine activity each day. The session ends with a brief sitting meditation, which focuses on the sensations associated with breathing.

Session 3: Gathering the scattered mind

Session 3 focuses on mindfulness of breath as a readily available anchor to the present moment. Because many thoughts, emotions, and sensations are likely to arise during this exercise, mindfulness of breath encourages openness to the ongoing experience (regardless of how pleasant or unpleasant it is) and facilitates recognition of habitual, automatic, maladaptive patterns of responding to pleasantness or unpleasantness. Within a 30-minute sitting meditation, participants first practise focusing their attention on the sensations associated with breathing, and then on the body as a whole. For individuals with a history of depression, the discussion following this exercise is likely to include judgemental, self-critical thoughts and rumination about not being able to control the wandering mind, how this inability relates to their other perceived inadequacies, and what this means about their competence or worth. Strong emotions may arise. Rather than trying to control thoughts and emotions, participants are encouraged to observe and label them ('These are judgements', 'Here is anger') with an attitude of friendly interest. A useful metaphor is that these phenomena are like unpleasant acquaintances we meet on the street. Although we might prefer not to see them, we can respond politely.

GAIL — I was trying to do the exercise and I kept thinking about how my daughters are spending so much time on household chores because I don't have the energy, and I was thinking to myself: 'What's wrong with me? Why can't I do these things? I'm such a bad mother.'

INSTRUCTOR — A lot of judgemental and self-critical thoughts were in your mind. As best you can, see if you can just notice and label them as judgements. Sometimes it's useful to think of them as people you don't like who are passing by. When you see them, you can smile politely and say something brief, like 'Hello Mr. Self-Criticism, have a good day!' Then you go on your way, bringing your attention back to where you wanted it to be.

Several points are important in reviewing the pleasant events calendar. Some participants will report that small moments of pleasantness are more frequent than they had realized and that paying close attention to ordinary moments of the day reveals them. Some participants will find that distinguishing between thoughts, emotions, and bodily sensations is a new experience. Identifying these elements of a pleasant experience builds valuable skills for recognizing the elements of more troubling experiences that may signal potential relapses of depression. Finally, some participants are unaccustomed to noticing subtle bodily sensations and may find this difficult. Gentle persistence in practising this type of awareness is helpful in learning to recognize the early signs of those emotional changes that can lead to depression. Because of their persistently low mood and lack of interest and pleasure in things, acutely depressed participants may have more trouble than those in remission in identifying pleasant events. Rather than looking for major events, it can be helpful to emphasize the importance of noticing smaller, momentary experiences such as the feel of a breeze, the sounds of birds chirping, or the smile of a friend. In highly self-critical depressed persons, increased awareness of pleasantness can paradoxically lead to shame and self-criticism about not noticing it previously and about being too negative much of the time (e.g., 'I'm such a mess – I can't even notice these things that are all around me'). Sensitivity is required in helping participants to bring mindful awareness to these thoughts and feelings with an attitude of interest and compassion.

Several other mindfulness practices are taught during this session. The three-minute breathing space is designed to facilitate the generalization of mindfulness skills from formal practices into daily life. It includes three steps, each lasting approximately one minute. The first is to bring non-judgemental awareness to thoughts, emotions, and sensations that are occurring in the present moment, without trying to alter or avoid them, but instead accepting them as they are. The second step is to focus attention on the sensations of breathing in the abdomen and to observe these for about a minute. The third step is to expand awareness to the whole body, including the breath, and to notice sensations throughout the body, including areas of tension or tightness.

Mindful stretching and walking also are introduced in this session. A 10-minute series of slow, gentle stretches is practised. These are based on yoga but are not strenuous and are practised with a non-judging and non-striving attitude. Mindful walking involves walking very slowly, without any destination, and with full attention to the sensations and movements of each step. These practices provide alternative ways to cultivate present-moment, non-judgemental awareness of the body. Some participants report that practising mindful awareness is easier when the body is moving than when it is still, especially if they are feeling agitated or restless.

Homework for the following week consists of gentle yoga for three days, alternating with a combination of gentle stretches (10 minutes) and sitting meditation (20 minutes) for the other three days. The three-minute breathing space is practised three times daily at pre-set times, and participants are asked to complete the unpleasant events calendar – which is identical to the pleasant events calendar, except that in it participants are now recording unpleasant experiences.

Session 4: Recognizing aversion

The purpose of this session is further exploration of the natural human tendencies to categorize experience as pleasant or unpleasant and to cling to pleasant experiences while trying to get rid of unpleasant ones. Skills for recognizing these tendencies and for staying present with the immediate experience are practised, beginning with a 40-minute sitting meditation in which attention is directed first to the breath, then to the body, then to sounds in the environment, and finally to thoughts. Participants are encouraged to observe reactions of attachment and aversion that arise during the exercise, noticing the tendency to be pulled into habitual thought patterns and returning attention to the present moment as best they can.

Attachment and aversion can also be explored during discussion of the unpleasant events calendar and of the homework practices. Participants with ongoing depression may have found it easier to notice unpleasant events than pleasant ones and may have experienced strong feelings of aversion to them. Participants may also be feeling aversion to the meditation practices, which can lead to judgemental, ruminative thoughts and to avoidance of homework. On the other hand, participants who are enjoying the practices may find that they are becoming attached to particular outcomes, such as feeling relaxed or serene. Although this is nice when it happens, the purpose of the practices is not to feel relaxed or serene, but rather to observe whatever is present. Attachment to a particular outcome can lead to frustration, judgement, and rumination if the outcome is not attained. The importance of practising with non-judgemental acceptance and openness to whatever arises is reiterated.

This session also includes a focused discussion of the types of thoughts that are typical in depression. This is aided by passing out copies of the Automatic Thoughts Questionnaire (Hollon & Kendall, 1980), which lists 30 thoughts common in depression – such as 'I'm no good,' 'My life is a mess,' and 'My future is bleak.' Most participants will recognize these as thoughts they often have and may contribute their own specific examples. Gail's most common thoughts included 'I'm useless,' 'I'm a burden to my family,' 'I'm a bad mother,' and 'I'll never feel any better.' An important goal of this exercise is the recognition that such thoughts seem entirely convincing during depressive episodes, but much less so when depression has lifted. This realization contributes to the understanding that thoughts are not facts, that particular thoughts are symptoms of depression, and that thoughts can be seen as mental events to be observed, rather than as absolute truths. This understanding is much more difficult for acutely depressed participants, who are less likely to recognize that their level of belief in these thoughts varies with their mood. Other group members, especially if they are in remission or experiencing milder symptoms, may point out that they felt the same way when they were last depressed.

Gail	To me these things just sound like the truth. Why bother with saying they're just thoughts when they're true?
Other group member	I felt exactly the same way when I was in a heavy depression. Now I look back and I realize that I was sucked in to those thoughts. But you don't have to get sucked in.
Instructor	Yes, that's just it. We're learning to recognize these thoughts as part of the territory of depression. Observing when they come along and saying, 'Ah, here are those thoughts again. I don't need to get sucked into those thoughts right now.'

Although this discussion may be useful for acutely depressed participants, their depressive thoughts tend to be frequent and to seem believable and convincing. Therefore the suggestion that they are 'just thoughts' can induce shame, self-blame, and worsening of mood in individuals accustomed to taking depressive thoughts seriously. At this point in the programme it may be helpful for the instructor to note that these reactions are very common and to encourage the participant to persist in practising, to keep coming to sessions, and in the meantime to breathe with the painful feelings and allow the judgements to come and go.

Recognition of the territory of depression is further strengthened in this session by a review of the criteria for major depressive disorder listed in the DSM-V (APA, 2013). Experiences that participants had interpreted as personal failings can be reconceptualized as symptoms of depression. This encourages a new perspective, which is especially helpful when combined with the increased awareness of bodily sensations that participants have been practising for several weeks. While staying present with the body it is easier to observe depressive thoughts and moods as transient and shifting and as part of a recognized syndrome.

The session ends with a brief review of the central idea in MBCT: that being mindfully present to our experience, even if it is unpleasant, allows us to respond more skilfully to difficulties when they arise. Homework for the coming week consists of guided sitting meditation, the three-minute breathing space three times daily at pre-set times, and additional breathing spaces whenever unpleasant feelings arise.

Session 5: Allowing/letting be

The theme of this session is the cultivation of a new relationship to unwanted experiences – a relationship in which such experiences are accepted just as they are and efforts to avoid or suppress them are discontinued. It can be difficult to understand what this means. Acceptance is not the same as passivity or resignation, in which nothing is done about difficulties. Rather, acceptance involves closely observing unwanted experiences, with an attitude of friendly curiosity, before deciding how to respond to them. Although this may be an uncommon way of meeting adversity in western culture (Santorelli, 1999), it is important for people with a history of depression, because efforts to get rid of unpleasant emotions or thoughts often involve self-critical, ruminative thinking, which starts a cycle that can lead to or prolong a depressive episode (see chapter 8 in this volume).

The session opens with a 40-minute sitting meditation that involves attention to breath, bodily sensations, sounds, and thoughts. In addition, a new element is introduced into the sitting meditation. Participants are asked to call to mind, deliberately, a troubling thought, situation, or problem that has been worrying or upsetting them and to notice the sensations that arise in the body. Attention is focused closely on these sensations, and tendencies to resist them, tense up, or brace against them are observed. Participants are then encouraged to allow themselves to feel these feelings without resistance, by opening up to them willingly; to maintain awareness of the breath along with these sensations; and to imagine directing the breath to the area of the body where the unpleasant sensations are occurring.

Deliberately calling difficult experiences to mind is a very useful exercise. It provides an opportunity to cultivate the skills for approaching rather than avoiding unpleasant thoughts and feelings. Focusing on the body provides an alternative to ruminative thinking. Breathing with the sensations cultivates the ability to let go of resistance and to allow the sensations to come and go in their own time. This exercise can help participants to realize that their typical attitude towards unpleasant experiences is harshly judgemental rather than kind and compassionate and that, by facing and naming difficulties as they arise, they can cultivate greater ease towards negative internal experiences and an improved ability to act constructively while having them. On the other hand, this exercise tends to be difficult for most participants, and can be especially so for those who are acutely depressed. Those whose moods have improved somewhat by session 5 may be unwilling to bring to mind an issue that, they fear, will bring them down again. Those whose mood is still low may be even more reluctant. Although participants can be encouraged to practise this exercise with only mildly troubling issues to begin with, networks of associations can quickly bring powerfully distressing topics to mind, and this leads to strong feelings of aversion and a desire to avoid this practice. Careful explanation of the rationale for this exercise, frequent validation of participants' fear and aversion, clear discussion of adaptive ways to respond to the distress that arises, and reminders to adopt an attitude of gentle and compassionate persistence over time are very important.

GAIL I don't think I can handle this exercise. It's too upsetting. I'm afraid it will just make me worse. Could I do something else instead?

INSTRUCTOR There are several options. It's important to remember that practising mindfulness is a way of taking care of yourself with kindness. It's not boot camp. It's not about forcing things or tormenting yourself. At the same time, taking care of ourselves with kindness sometimes means that we have to be persistent with things that are difficult. Avoidance of the difficult tends to make matters worse over time. So I'm hoping we can find a way for you to work with this practice, rather than giving up on it. Let's think about ways of doing it gently and gradually – perhaps by practising just a few minutes at a time and, if it feels like too much, then shifting attention to the breath or to sounds in the environment, and then trying again later in the day or even another day. What do you think?

Session 5 also includes an expansion of the instructions for the three-minute breathing space that is consistent with the focus on acceptance and allowing of difficulties. When unpleasant feelings arise during daily life, participants are encouraged to observe the sensations of discomfort as these are manifested in the body, to breathe into them, to remind themselves that it is okay to feel this way, and to soften any tension or resistance to the sensations. Homework for the coming week includes sitting meditation on six days and the three-minute breathing space at predetermined times and when stressful situations arise.

Session 6: Thoughts are not facts

This session cultivates the ability to observe the thinking process while decentring from the content of thoughts, a skill that is critically important in reducing vulnerability to depression. The session begins with a 40-minute sitting meditation with focus on breath, body, sounds, and thoughts, and with deliberate introduction of a difficulty, as in session 5. Observation of thoughts is emphasized during this practice. Analogies and metaphors are used in order to encourage an understanding of decentring. For example, participants might imagine themselves seated in a movie theatre and watching their thoughts come and go on the screen. Similarly, they might see the mind as a stage and thoughts as actors who enter, move around, and exit. Some of them speak mundane lines, whereas others are more dramatic. Either way, they are observed with friendly interest until they exit. The mind can be compared to the sky, with thoughts in the form of clouds that pass by. Some clouds are large and threatening, while others are interesting, beautiful, or nondescript. Some move quickly, others slowly. All, however, will pass with time, while the sky will remain. When thoughts are numerous and intensely unpleasant, it can be helpful to focus attention on sensations in the body, or to label the associated emotional states (anxious, tense, frustrated, angry) while allowing the thoughts to flow by, rather like a cascade or waterfall. Standing behind the waterfall may be a helpful image. Repetitive thoughts about particular topics can be labelled *tapes*, thus: 'Ah, here is my "no one understands me" tape.' The difficulty of relating to thoughts in this way, particularly for individuals with a history of depression, is emphasized along with the need for gentle, persistent, non-judgemental practice. Gail was especially struck by the idea of tapes in her head. She was able to identify when her 'I'm a burden to my family' tape was playing, although she continued to have concerns about whether the statements on the tape were true.

This session also includes the moods, thoughts, and alternative viewpoints exercise, which is helpful in demonstrating how ongoing emotions can influence the interpretation of an event. This exercise requires imagining two slightly different scenarios. First, participants imagine that they are feeling down because they've just had an argument with a colleague at work. Shortly afterwards they see another colleague, who rushes off quickly, saying that he or she doesn't have time to talk. Participants write down what they would think in this situation. Next, participants are asked to imagine that they are feeling pleased because their work has just been praised, and then they see a colleague who hurries away, saying that he or she doesn't have time to stop. Again, participants write down what they would think. The first scenario often evokes thoughts of being rejected or angry after the colleague rushes away, whereas the second may lead to thoughts of concern for the colleague or to the idea that he or she was resentful of their achievements. The variety of thoughts elicited by the same set of circumstances, depending on the prevailing emotional state, illustrates again that thoughts cannot be regarded as facts. Homework for the following week includes 40 minutes of meditation every day – for which participants may choose from a variety of recorded meditations – and three-minute breathing spaces, at pre-set times and at times of stress.

Session 7: How can I best take care of myself?

Session 7 focuses on specific actions to take when depression threatens. After the opening sitting meditation and discussion of homework, attention turns to several activities designed to encourage constructive self-care that helps to prevent the recurrence of depression. For example, an exercise illustrating the links between activities and moods is conducted. Participants are asked to create lists of the things they do in a typical day, to note which ones lift the mood and which ones lower it, and to discuss how they could increase positive activities and decrease negative ones in daily life. Positive activities are further categorized into activities that give pleasure (such as seeing a good movie or talking with a friend) and activities that give a sense of mastery (paying the bills, or weeding the garden). Although acutely depressed persons may initially claim that nothing gives them feelings of pleasure or mastery, group discussion is likely to provide examples that will remind them of their own relevant activities. Gail was able to identify reading and talking with friends and family members as activities that give her pleasure when she is not depressed, and cooking and exercise as activities providing a sense of mastery.

A critical element of this session is the discussion of *relapse signatures*: the collection of changes in mind, body, and behaviour unique to each person that signal a potential return of depression. Common examples are irritability, social withdrawal, changes in eating or sleeping, increased fatigue, and reduced motivation for daily tasks. Gail identified anxiety about work, feeling tired, and reduced interest in conversation with co-workers as important indicators of worsening mood. Participants then discuss plans for responding to these changes when they occur. The first step of the plan is always to take a breathing space. After that, participants may choose to observe thoughts mindfully (as discussed in the previous session), to engage in another mindfulness practice, or to take action by doing something from their lists of pleasure and mastery activities. The importance of following the plan even if they don't feel like it, which is quite likely when they are faced with intense negative emotions or thoughts of hopelessness and futility, is emphasized, along with the need to recognize ruminative thinking without being drawn into it.

In preparation for the end of treatment, participants are asked to develop a daily practice that they would like to maintain over the following weeks; and in doing so they may use any combination of formal or informal practices. Daily three-minute breathing spaces are continued. In addition, participants are asked to write down their early warning signs of impending relapse and their action plans for preventing it, including (when appropriate) ways of involving family members or others in helping with these plans.

Session 8: Maintaining and extending new learning

The theme of this session is that regular mindfulness practice maintains the ability to respond skilfully when relapse-related thought patterns are triggered. The session begins with a guided body scan. Participants' relationship to the body scan may have changed in interesting ways since the beginning of the course. Those who previously found it boring may still feel this way, but they often report increased ability to be calmly accepting of boredom. Homework reviews include a final discussion of early warning signs and relapse prevention plans. Looking back and reflecting on what has been learned during the programme occupies the next part of the session. Participants are asked to discuss their reasons for participating, why they chose to stay, what they learned from the experience, and what the biggest obstacles were. Gail noted that decentring from harshly self-critical thoughts had been very difficult and would require ongoing practice, but that she was much better able to label these thoughts when they arose, to view them as tapes playing in her mind, and not to allow them to dictate how she should feel or behave.

Discussion then turns to the future, as participants are asked to describe their plans for maintaining mindfulness practice. These plans will be highly variable. For example, some might wish to sit for 30 minutes a day, while others prefer to alternate yoga with body scans. Breathing spaces and informal practices should also be incorporated. The importance of consistent daily practice, even if only for a brief period of time each day, is emphasized. Participants are encouraged to articulate positive reasons for maintaining a regular practice – for example, being more attentive to family members. Gail reported that she found the yoga practice rewarding. She had noticed that it reminded her of her school days, when she had been active in several sports and had taken great pleasure in her body's capabilities. She intended to alternate yoga practice with sitting mediation and to explore yoga classes in the community. She also revealed her intention to continue practising the three-minute breathing space every day and following it up with a pleasure or mastery activity whenever possible.

The session ends with the group leader passing out a small memento to each participant – a stone, a marble, or a bead. This object is meant to serve as a reminder of the dedication and hard work put in over the past eight weeks and of the experiences shared with the group. Most of all, it is a reminder for participants to continue the work they have started in the course.

Distinctive features of MBCT

MBCT differs from the other treatment approaches described in this volume in several important ways. Perhaps the most obvious one is that, although other interventions teach acceptance, decentring, and mindfulness skills in some form, only MBCT places the intensive practice of formal meditation at its core. This has interesting implications for the role of the therapist and for the balancing of acceptance and change-based strategies that are used. As noted earlier, MBCT group leaders are more likely to describe themselves as mindfulness instructors than as therapists. They are expected to be engaged in their own regular mindfulness practice, to teach from a basis in their own experience of the practice, and to embody a mindful stance in their interactions with group members. That is, they remain aware of their own present-moment experiences and bring an attitude of non-judgemental interest in and curiosity about group members' experiences (rather than efforts to fix or change things). In line with the centrality of non-judgemental acceptance of experience as it occurs, relatively little emphasis is placed on change-based methods. MBCT does not teach participants to make judgements about whether particular thoughts are rational or distorted, to examine the evidence for and against thoughts, to dispute thoughts, or to generate more rational thoughts. Nor does MBCT explicitly train participants to engage in structured problem-solving strategies, improve their interpersonal skills, modify their diet, exercise, or sleep-related behaviours, or manage their time. Instead, MBCT emphasizes the mobilization of clients' internal resources for addressing problems and assumes that individuals who bring mindful awareness to present-moment experience will find skilful ways to manage the specific difficulties that life inevitably presents. As Segal et al. (2002, p. 190) suggest, 'staying present with what is unpleasant in our experience ... allows the process to unfold, lets the "inherent wisdom" of the mind deal with the difficulty, and allows more effective solutions to present themselves.'

Another interesting characteristic of MBCT is the unusual degree of body-focused attention that it cultivates. The rationale for this cultivation is that strong emotions often are manifested as sensations (heaviness, tightness, aching), movements (slowness or agitation), postures (slumping, stooping), or facial expressions (frowning). These bodily conditions can elicit cognitions and overt behaviours, many of which may occur automatically, without much awareness, and may be maladaptive. Awareness of the body cultivates clearer recognition of emotions when they arise and allows a more adaptive way of responding to them. In addition, people with a history of depressive episodes often try to manage painful emotions by thinking about why they have them, what they mean, and how to get rid of them – a process that can become ruminative and increase the risk of relapse. Explicit training in mindful awareness of the body when strong emotions arise provides a helpful alternative to ruminative thinking and cultivates decentering skills. Mindfully attending to the body may also function as an exposure procedure, reducing fear and avoidance of unpleasant bodily sensations (Hayes & Shenk, 2004; Kabat-Zinn, 1982).

Breathing is a useful element of bodily experience on which to focus attention, and for several reasons. Because breathing goes on continuously, something detectable by a shift in attention is always happening in the present moment (inhaling, exhaling, or pausing). One's breath tends to vary (in pace, depth, or smoothness) with emotional and physical states, providing an ever-changing focus of attention that has potentially observable relationships with other aspects of experience. Effort is required to focus attention on one's breath, which reduces the cognitive capacity available for ruminative thinking. However, breathing itself requires no effort and will continue whether it is attended to or not. Breath therefore provides an excellent opportunity to practise observation of an ongoing process without trying to change it. Finally, it must be noted that mindfulness of the body during times of intense emotion is not a strategy for avoiding emotion by turning attention elsewhere. Instead it cultivates awareness of emotional elements, together with the ability and willingness to allow emotional responses to follow their natural course, without engaging in ruminative thinking or in maladaptive escape and avoidance behaviours.

Questions for Future Research

Several important questions about the use of MBCT for acute depression require further study.

Should MBCT be a first-line treatment for acute depression?

As noted earlier, MBCT was originally designed to prevent relapse in people with a history of depression who were currently in remission. Since then, empirical work with patients experiencing acute depression suggests that MBCT is more effective than usual care and psycho-education and equivalent to eight weeks of group CBT or antidepressant medication. A recent meta-analysis of randomized trials of MBCT for patients with a confirmed diagnosis of major depressive disorder (Strauss, Cavanagh, Oliver, & Pettman, 2014) concluded that the effects were consistently strong enough to suggest that MBCT could be offered to such patients alongside other evidence-based treatments, to increase the range of available treatment options. However, direct comparisons between MBCT and the evidence-based treatments with the strongest empirical support for major depressive disorder still have not been conducted. For example, Manicavasagar et al. (2012) compared MBCT to an eight-week group CBT programme and showed significant and equivalent improvements in both groups.

However, cognitive therapy for depression, which has a very strong evidence base, is more commonly administered in 15–25 individual sessions (Young, Rygh, Weinberger, & Beck, 2014). It is not clear whether MBCT would be as effective as cognitive therapy if the latter were provided in its standard form. Similarly, behavioral activation (BA) and interpersonal psychotherapy (IPT) are well supported treatments for acute depression that may include 12–16 or more weekly individual sessions (Dimidjian et al., 2006; Dimidjian, Martell, Herman-Dunn, & Hubley, 2014; Bleiberg & Markowitz, 2014). MBCT has not been directly compared to BA or IPT. Thus it is not yet known whether MBCT is as effective in treating acute depression as any of the best-established first-line treatments.

Is MBCT more effective for some participants than for others?

Studies of MBCT for the prevention of depressive relapse have shown significant benefits for patients with three or more previous episodes, but not for those with fewer previous episodes. Recent data also suggest that MBCT is especially helpful for preventing depressive relapse in people with a history of childhood trauma in addition to depression (Williams et al., 2014). Furthermore, a meta-analysis and systematic review of mindfulness-based interventions, including MBCT, identified several transdiagnostic psychological processes (e.g., rumination) targeted by treatment that mediate symptom reduction (Gu, Strauss, Bond, & Cavanagh, 2015). These findings suggest that individual differences, such as a history of early-life trauma or the tendency to ruminate or self-criticize, may be important in predicting outcomes. Additional factors that may be important include the willingness to participate in a group programme, to engage in meditation exercises, and to make time for home practice – as well as the ability to concentrate sufficiently to benefit from the practices.

How much meditation practice is necessary?

In its standard form, MBCT assigns home practice of approximately one hour per day for six days each week. Formal practices such as the body scan and sitting meditation are usually 45 minutes in duration; additional formal or informal practices may requires another 15 minutes each day. In an early study of MBCT for participants with active depression, Finucane and Mercer (2006) reduced the duration of the formal practices to

25–30 minutes, because of concerns that the concentration problems that are common in acute depression might make the longer practices too difficult. Similarly, Eisendrath et al. (2015) decreased the duration of sitting meditation to 25 minutes, while increasing the duration of the mindful movement practice, because of the increased agitation and decreased attention span typical in acute depression. Most other studies have used the standard 45-minutes practices. Kenny and Williams (2006) reported that the acutely depressed participants in their study were able to complete the 45-minute homework practices if they brought an attitude of kindness and non-judging to these activities. Such an attitude was emphasized strongly by group leaders. Barnhofer et al. (2009) reported that their chronically depressed participants completed about an hour of home practice on five of the six days per week that had been assigned, which suggests that, although they missed one day per week, on average the duration of daily practice was manageable for them. Most studies of MBCT for acute depression do not provide data on the completion of home practice, nor do they report relationships between amount of home practice and extent of improvement. Thus the amount of practice required for clinically significant benefits in this population is unknown (Metcalf & Dimidjian, 2014).

Conclusions

The evidence that MBCT can be helpful for acute depressive episodes continues to grow. It is not yet clear whether MBCT should be considered a first-line treatment for major depressive disorder. If its efficacy can be shown to be comparable to that of the best-established treatments, then MBCT may have practical advantages. As a group intervention requiring only eight weeks, MBCT is potentially cost-effective – an important consideration in dealing with a highly prevalent disorder. In addition, MBCT emphasizes experiential skills training and is often described as a series of classes comprising a course, rather than as a form of psychotherapy. In consequence it may seem less stigmatizing to some participants (Finucane & Mercer, 2006).

For a patient like Gail, who has experienced numerous depressive episodes for which medication and non-directive counselling have been ineffective and who engages in ruminative and self-critical thinking, it seems likely that MBCT will be beneficial, especially if she attends the sessions and does the homework consistently. At this point, it is impossible to say whether MBCT would be as effective as behavioural activation, cognitive therapy, interpersonal psychotherapy, or other approaches. Answering this question requires additional research. Given the promising findings in the current literature, it seems likely that MBCT will be increasingly acknowledged as an effective treatment both for acute depression and for the prevention of relapse.

Acknowledgements

We are grateful to Thorsten Barnhofer, Sandra Coffman, Sona Dimidjian, Stuart Eisendrath and Maura Kenny for clinical insights on the use of MBCT with acutely depressed persons, and to Melanie Fennell, Zindel Segal, and Mark Williams for other helpful comments.

References

APA. (2013). *Diagnostic and statistical manual of mental disorders: DSM-V*. Washington, DC: American Psychiatric Association.

Barnhofer, T., Crane, C., Hargus, E., Amarasinghe, M., Winder, R. & Williams, J. M. G. (2009). Mindfulness-based cognitive therapy as a treatment for chronic depression: A preliminary study. *Behaviour Research and Therapy*, *47*, 366–373.

Beck, A. T., Steer, R. A., & Brown, G. K. (1996). *Manual for the BDI-II*. San Antonio, TX: Psychological Corporation.

Bleiberg, K. L. & Markowitz, J. C. (2014). Interpersonal psychotherapy for depression. In D. H. Barlow (Ed.), *Clinical handbook of psychological disorders: A step-by-step treatment manual* (5th edn, pp. 332–352). New York: Guilford.

Chiesa, A., Mandelli, L., & Serretti, A. (2012). Mindfulness-based cognitive therapy versus psycho-education for patients with major depression who did not achieve remission following antidepressant treatment: A preliminary analysis. *The Journal of Alternative and Complementary Medicine*, *18*, 756–760.

Dimidjian, S., Hollon, S., Dobson, K., Schmaling, K., Kohlenberg, R., Addis, M. … Jacobson, N. (2006). Randomized trial of behavioral activation, cognitive therapy, and antidepressant medication in the acute treatment of adults with major depression. *Journal of Consulting and Clinical Psychology*, *74*, 658–670.

Dimidjian, S., Martell, C. R., Herman-Dunn, R., & Hubley, S. (2014). Behavioral activation for depression. In D. H. Barlow (Ed.), *Clinical handbook of psychological disorders: A step-by-step treatment manual* (5th edn, pp. 353–393). New York: Guilford.

Eisendrath, S. J., Gillung, E., Delucchi, K., Mathalon, D., Yang, T., Satre, D. … & Wolkowitz, O. (2015). A preliminary study: Efficacy of mindfulness-based cognitive therapy versus sertraline as first-line treatments for major depressive disorder. *Mindfulness*, 6, 475–482.

Finucane, A., & Mercer, S. W. (2006). An exploratory mixed methods study of the acceptability and effectiveness of mindfulness-based cognitive therapy for patients with active depression and anxiety in primary care. *BMC Psychiatry*, 6, 14.

Gu, J., Strauss, C., Bond, R., & Cavanagh, K. (2015). How do mindfulness-based cognitive therapy and mindfulness-based stress reduction improve mental health and wellbeing? A systematic review and meta-analysis of mediation studies. *Clinical Psychology Review*, *37*, 1–12.

Hayes, S. C., & Shenk, C. (2004). Operationalizing mindfulness without unnecessary attachments. *Clinical Psychology: Science and Practice*, *11*, 249–254.

Hollon, S. D., & Kendall, P. (1980). Cognitive self-statements in depression: Development of an automatic thoughts questionnaire. *Cognitive Therapy and Research*, *4*, 383–395.

Kabat-Zinn, J. (1982). An outpatient program in behavioral medicine for chronic pain patients based on the practice of mindfulness meditation: Theoretical considerations and preliminary results. *General Hospital Psychiatry*, *4*, 33–47.

Kenny, M. A. & Williams, J. M. G. (2006). Treatment-resistant depressed patients show a good response to mindfulness-based cognitive therapy. *Behaviour Research and Therapy*, *45*, 617–625.

Ma, S. H., & Teasdale, J. D. (2004). Mindfulness-based cognitive therapy for depression: Replication and exploration of differential relapse prevention effects. *Journal of Consulting and Clinical Psychology*, *72*, 31–40.

Manicavasagar, V., Perich, T., & Parker, G. (2012). Cognitive predictors of change in cognitive behaviour therapy and mindfulness-based cognitive therapy for depression. *Behavioural and Cognitive Psychotherapy*, *40*, 227–232.

Metcalf, C. A., & Dimidjian, S. (2014). Extensions and mechanisms of mindfulness-based cognitive therapy: A review of the evidence. *Australian Psychologist*, *49*, 271–279.

Santorelli, S. (1999). *Heal thyself: Lessons on mindfulness in medicine*. New York: Bell Tower.

Segal, Z. V., Williams, J. M. G., & Teasdale, J. D. (2002). *Mindfulness-based cognitive therapy for depression: A new approach to preventing relapse*. New York: Guilford.

Strauss, C., Cavanagh, K., Oliver, A., & Pettman, D. (2014). Mindfulness-based interventions for people diagnosed with a current episode of an anxiety or depressive disorder: A meta-analysis of randomized controlled trials. *PLOS ONE*, *9*(4), e96110.

Teasdale, J. D., Segal, Z. V., Williams, J. M. G., Ridgeway, V. A., Soulsby, J. M., & Lau, M. A. (2000). Prevention of relapse/recurrence in major depression by mindfulness-based cognitive therapy. *Journal of Consulting and Clinical Psychology*, *68*, 615–623.

van Aalderen, J. R., Donders, A., Giommi, F., Spinhoven, P., Barendregt, H., & Speckens, A. (2012). The efficacy of mindfulness-based cognitive therapy in recurrent depressed patients with and without a current depressive episode: A randomized controlled trial. *Psychological Medicine*, *42*, 989–1001.

Williams, J. M. G., Crane, C., Barnhofer, T., Brennan, K., Duggan, D. Fennell, M., … & Russell, I. T. (2014) Mindfulness-based cognitive therapy for preventing relapse in recurrent depression: A randomized dismantling trial. *Journal of Consulting and Clinical Psychology*, *82*, 275–286.

Williams, J. M. G., Teasdale, J. D., Segal, Z. V., & Kabat-Zinn, J. (2007). *The mindful way through depression: Freeing yourself from chronic unhappiness*. New York: Guilford.

Young, J. E., Rygh, J. L., Weinberger, A. D., & Beck, A. T. (2014). Cognitive therapy for depression. In D. H. Barlow (Ed.), *Clinical handbook of psychological disorders: A step-by-step treatment manual* (5th edn, pp. 275–331). New York: Guilford.

15

Behavioural Activation Treatment for Depression

Samuel Hubley, Roselinde Kaiser, and Sona Dimidjian

The behavioural activation (BA) approach to treating depression and preventing relapse includes straightforward treatment strategies that aim to activate clients in order to enhance contact with naturally occurring sources of positive reward and to improve life context. The clinical application of such strategies is based on the assumption that limited experiences of positive reward and increased life problems contribute to depression. The BA model stresses the role of life events and circumstances as well as that of behavioural responses to such challenges in the conceptualization of depression. Treatment focuses directly on modifying such responses in order to improve mood and enrich environment. This chapter highlights the key principles and procedures of the BA approach to depression and discusses their application in the context of the hypothetical treatment of Gail.

Overview

BA is a structured approach that is applied clinically in an idiographic manner. The basic principles and procedures are theoretically defined and comprise a core structure of the intervention; however, the specific application of these strategies can vary considerably from client to client, and it is recommended that therapists tailor the treatment strategies to individual clients. A typical course of treatment involves orienting the client to treatment, assessing treatment goals and functional domains, activating the client, troubleshooting, and preparing a plan to prevent relapse. These core

---

Treating Depression: MCT, CBT and Third Wave Therapies, First Edition.
Edited by Adrian Wells and Peter L. Fisher.

elements are reviewed here as they would be applied in BA therapy with Gail.

Orienting to treatment

Orienting the client to BA is the primary aim of initial treatment sessions. Successful orientation involves presenting the BA model of depression, explaining treatment structure, and clarifying both the client's and the therapist's roles. The overall goal is to provide the client with a clear rationale for the treatment strategies, thereby enhancing the client's motivation and establishing a collaborative framework between therapist and client.

Presenting the treatment model Presenting the treatment model begins with a description of the behavioural approach to depression. Therapists emphasize that BA is based on the proposition that life events and behavioural responses to such events influence the way people feel. It is suggested that depression develops when a person's life provides too few rewards and too many problems. Therapists can point out that a natural and understandable response to a stressful and minimally rewarding life is to pull away from one's world. Unfortunately, this tendency towards avoidance can make depression worse and often interferes with effective problem solving.

Gail's depression was conceptualized as ingrained patterns of behavioural and interpersonal avoidance, which were in turn maintained (via negative reinforcement) by reductions in physical fatigue, social anxiety, and a general sense of feeling overwhelmed. Gail was sleeping more than usual, worked only two days per week and worried that she constantly made mistakes, felt that her relationships with her family had deteriorated, and no longer engaged in activities she used to enjoy. She felt constricted by the narrow range of her behaviours and typically waited for her family to initiate an activity. Gail and her therapist examined how this pattern of avoidance increased her feelings of sadness and guilt and exacerbated her tendency to ruminate about not doing other activities. Through discussion of the BA model, they highlighted together the vicious cycle (see Figure 15.1) in which Gail's pulling away from the world around her ultimately limited rewarding experiences in her life and kept her stuck in depression. The BA model was presented to Gail as an approach that could help her reconnect with previous pastimes and help her gradually return to work and recover a greater sense of intimacy with her family.

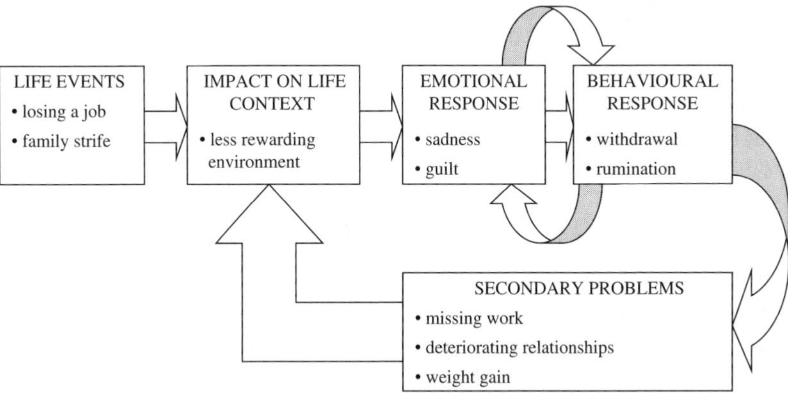

Figure 15.1 Cycle of depression.

Initially Gail perceived the BA model as an oversimplified explanation of her depression and thought that the therapist was simply suggesting that she needed to 'just do more'. Gail's therapist stressed that, if overcoming depression were that simple, Gail would have already figured it out. The therapist told Gail that she would rather learn a new set of skills for coping with challenges and that they would work together systematically to help her reconnect to her life. The therapist explained that she would be a consultant or coach in this process, as someone with expertise in identifying which activities were likely to be most helpful and how she could get started on such activities in manageable ways. Given the chronicity of Gail's depression and her scepticism about treatment (psychotherapy and antidepressant medication had been unsuccessful in the past), it was important for her therapist to maintain optimism with Gail, while simultaneously avoiding oversimplifying the challenge that they faced. Her therapist returned repeatedly to the possible value of systematic and sustained efforts towards activation and to the link between such activation and the alleviation of her current symptoms and the prevention of future episodes.

Thus, in presenting the BA model, the therapist is also encouraged to discuss ways in which this model does and does not apply to the client and elicit questions and feedback throughout the discussion. The therapist encouraged Gail to discuss her concerns about prior treatments' failure to help her feel better or stay better for long. The therapist maintained hope in the face of such concerns but did not 'whitewash' them. She emphasized instead the importance of adopting an experimental approach and of continually evaluating the effects of the treatment strategies as they began to work together. Such direct and open discussions helped the therapist obtain 'buy in' from Gail before moving to assessment and intervention. These discussions were augmented by a written description of the BA approach that Gail took home to read for her first homework assignment (see Martell, Addis, & Jacobson, 2001).

Discussing treatment structure As discussed previously, the actual course of treatment may look very different for different clients; however, structural elements of BA remain consistent across clients. It is helpful to orient clients to the following core elements: within-session structure, between-session practice, and collaboration.

In the first few sessions, Gail's therapist explained the structured nature of BA, including the fact that each session would follow a predictable format. That is, each session would generally begin with a collaborative agenda setting in which she and the therapist mutually decide on which topics to cover and how to organize time. Then the bulk of the session would be spent reviewing previous homework assignments and developing new assignments for the coming week. Typically, Gail's therapist explained that she would take notes during the session and she encouraged Gail to do so too, which encouraged Gail's in-session activation and allowed them both to review the weekly assignment(s) prior to ending the session.

Between-session practice is essential to successful treatment, and Gail's therapist highlighted this in their first session. BA is an action-oriented approach that requires clients to work on treatment goals outside of therapy sessions. From the first session onward, it is important for clients to understand that every week they will be asked to apply to their daily routines principles learned in the session. Although clients and therapists conjointly design homework assignments and develop treatment goals, it is the therapist's responsibility to track weekly assignments, to follow up on progress, and to make therapeutic use of what has been learned. Future sessions focus on the degree to which clients implemented homework assignments, what the client learned, effects on mood, and assessing and troubleshooting barriers. Information gathered from reviewing clients' between-session practice is then used in the formulation of future assignments.

In addition to stressing the importance of between-session practice, it is helpful for therapists to highlight early in therapy the collaborative nature of BA. Gail's therapist emphasized that they would work together collaboratively to identify the topics for discussion for each session and to develop homework assignments. As the overall goal of treatment is to activate clients, therapists encourage clients to actively participate in treatment planning by working with the therapist towards devising promising homework assignments and developing treatment goals. At the beginning of therapy, Gail seemed unsure about the value of what she would offer to this process:

GAIL I doubt I can add much to figuring this out. I've made a mess of most things so far. I'm probably better off just being told what to do by an expert.

THERAPIST I am the expert on treating depression, but you are the expert on Gail. I think if we put our heads together on this we'll be much more likely to identify activities that will have the best chance of helping you feel better.

Not only is enlisting Gail in this way consistent with the collaborative nature of BA, but, as her therapist explained, it maximizes the likelihood that homework assignments will be appropriately individualized.

Clarifying therapists' and clients' roles Apart from providing an orientation to the three structural elements of BA, the first two sessions also include a discussion of therapist and client roles. As noted above, BA therapists are active coaches, providing expertise in behavioural assessment and behaviour change as well as encouragement and support throughout the process of overcoming depression. Clients in BA are also active participants in treatment planning and are asked to work between sessions to implement plans devised in the session. As indicated above, Gail was daunted by the prospect of being a co-leader in her own treatment and tended to defer to her therapist. Gail's therapist empathized with her disquietude and reiterated both the importance of collaborative treatment planning and her confidence in Gail's ability to make relevant changes.

On a final note, as the therapist oriented Gail to treatment, it was helpful to convey a sense of optimism and confidence. Such a stance required both an appreciation for the challenge of depression and a sense of competence in guiding Gail in making changes in her life. If the therapist had failed to show an understanding and appreciation for Gail's distress and for her difficulty in overcoming depression, Gail may have walked away feeling misunderstood, and thus pessimistic about her chances. But the therapist's optimism about improvement and enthusiasm for collaboration were easily recognizable. For the first two sessions, Gail walked out of the door thinking: 'This is a person who understands what having depression is like and can help me overcome it.'

Assessment

The clinical research conducted to date on BA has used structured diagnostic assessments prior to initiating treatment, such as the Structured Clinical Interview for the DSM-IV (SCID) (First, Spitzer, Gibbon, & Williams, 1997), the Hamilton Rating Scale for Depression (HRSD) (Hamilton, 1960), and the Beck Depression Inventory-II (BDI-II) (Beck, Steer, & Brown, 1996). Although formal assessments are not required in routine clinical practice, some diagnostic assessment is recommended at the outset of treatment. For instance, at the pre-treatment screening interview, Gail met the diagnostic criteria for recurrent major depressive disorder (as defined by the DSM-IV: APA, 1994). In addition to this clinical interview, Gail also completed a self-report measure of depressive severity. She scored 37 on the BDI-II (Beck et al., 1996), which indicated a severe level of depressive severity.

Conducting functional analyses is a crucial part of BA and is used to inform many, if not all, treatment decisions. Haynes and O'Brien (1990, p. 654) define functional analysis as 'the identification of important, controllable, causal functional relationships applicable to a specified set of target behaviours for an individual client'. Similarly, we view the process of conducting functional analyses as one of identifying variables that maintain depression and that may become targets for intervention. The results of functional analyses form the foundation of the case conceptualization, supplying the therapist with knowledge about the factors that maintain the depression, about the obstacles to experiences of positive reward, and about behaviours and problem areas suitable for change. Thus assessment is not simply a task of early treatment sessions; therapists continually assess clients' response or lack of response to treatment strategies and clients' between-session experience with homework assignments. In this section we discuss both the 'whats' and the 'hows' of assessment in BA.

What to assess BA therapists often begin with some assessment of *treatment goals*. Long-term goals may not be achieved fully during the course of therapy. However, such goals are likely to have a large antidepressant potential and can help to inform the targets of therapy; in consequence, it is wise to vitalize any and all efforts towards their realization. Goal setting is also important for establishing specific, time-bound objectives that will be targeted by BA interventions. Generally, the overall aim of BA is to help clients to maximize their contact with naturally occurring sources of positive reward and to approach and solve life problems. Typically, short-term and problem-specific goals target avoidance behaviours and disruptions to daily routines. We discuss the application of goal setting in this context below.

When assessing treatment goals, BA therapists commonly ask their clients: 'What would you be doing if you were not depressed?' When asked this question, Gail answered by pointing to a multitude of activities: going to work, doing household chores, spending time with family and friends, gardening, and exercising. Upon further assessment, Gail indicated that, when she was not depressed, she often played tennis with some friend and went jogging with her daughters. Following this discussion, establishing a regular exercise routine and playing tennis once a week became long-term goals for Gail.

In addition to identifying personal treatment goals, it is important to highlight the general goal of replacing *mood-dependent behaviour* with *goal-dependent behaviour*. For instance, oftentimes Gail's decision to engage or not to engage in a behaviour was dictated by her mood. She often remained inactive until she *felt* like doing something. The therapist encouraged Gail to engage in activities that were consistent with her personal goals, regardless of how she was feeling. The therapist found it helpful to explain this shift in motivation in terms of acting 'from the outside in' versus acting 'from the inside out'. This distinction is predicated on the basic assumption that progress towards personal goals is in itself antidepressive.

THERAPIST One thing I've noticed, Gail, is that your activities – whether playing tennis or lying in bed all afternoon – seem to be largely governed by how you feel.

GAIL Well, yes. If I feel good I am much more likely to do something, but if I do not feel good, well, all I want to do is curl up in bed.

THERAPIST That makes perfect sense. It is very easy to act in accordance with how we feel. I like to call that 'mood-dependent behaviour' because it is almost as if your behaviour becomes entirely dependent on your mood. One of our goals together is to replace this 'mood-dependent behaviour' with 'goal-dependent behaviour'

GAIL I am not sure I understand.

THERAPIST Well, it is like you feel a particular way – say depressed – and act accordingly – stay in bed. This kind of mood-dependent behaviour can keep people stuck in depression because you constantly behave in ways that are consistent with feeling depressed. We want to get you behaving in ways that are NOT consistent with depression. Do you follow?

GAIL I am getting there.

THERAPIST Great. Once you start to recognize how actions are related to how you feel, it becomes easier to replace 'mood-dependent behaviour' with 'goal-dependent behaviour'. Now what do you think I mean by 'goal-dependent behaviour'?

GAIL Um I don't know, maybe actions that depend on my goals?

THERAPIST Exactly! Another way to think about this, Gail, is 'inside out' versus 'outside in'. That is, rather than looking 'inside' yourself for motivation, you look 'outside' yourself and decide to do something that is consistent with your goals. Does that make sense?

GAIL So I should do things on the basis of goals we set, not on the basis of how I feel?

THERAPIST Exactly right! And one reason for doing this is that I believe once you see yourself making progress towards your goals, no matter how small the steps, you will start to feel a little better.

Once the therapist has assessed client goals, the primary focus of 'what' to assess in BA turns to *behavioural contingencies*. This concept refers to the antecedents and consequences of client behaviour. For instance, Gail reported that she felt embarrassed when she tried to converse with co-workers and had nothing to say. Identifying such contingencies helped to guide her treatment. Gail and her therapist agreed that this contingency contributed to her missing from work. Moreover, in BA, increasing clients' awareness of such contingent relationships may itself be a key element of positive change.

The first step in conducting a functional analysis involves defining the behaviour that is the focus of assessment. This can be challenging, because the term 'behaviour' represents a broad construct that defies simple definition. In view of this complexity, it is important to begin by defining the behaviour at hand in concrete and objective terms (e.g., frequency, duration, intensity, topography). Such behavioural specificity facilitates narrowing the focus until the essence of the problem is determined. For instance, one problem Gail frequently reported was that she didn't feel like she was a good enough mother. The therapist worked with Gail to operationalize what was meant by 'a not good enough mother'. The therapist elicited specific behaviours that constituted Gail's conception of adequate parenting. Together, they determined that a good mother cooks for her family on a regular basis, keeps the house clean, contributes to the household income, and is interested and involved in her daughters' and her husband's lives. Casting the problem in concrete behavioural terms reduced ambiguity about the nature of the problem and facilitated the identification of specific treatment goals.

Once the client and the therapist agree on the definition of a given behaviour, they start to examine the contingencies that control that behaviour. Contingent relationships that control behaviour take on many forms; they can be (among other possibilities) negative and positive reinforcement contingencies, and context-cued, behaviour-cued, and mood-cued contingencies. The former category is rooted in basic principles of operant conditioning; the latter category is rooted in in classical conditioning. These kinds or categories are discussed below.

Negative and positive reinforcement contingencies pervade all our lives and may serve both adaptive and maladaptive functions. Negative reinforcement occurs when the likelihood of a behaviour increases as a result of the *removal* of a stimulus. Avoidance or escape behaviours are often maintained through negative reinforcement. On the one hand, negative reinforcement contingencies serve us well when they protect us from harm (e.g., as when we put in ear plugs at a noisy concert). On the other hand, they can be detrimental when they become pervasive enough to dominate our response sets and to constrict our behavioural repertoires. For example, Gail used alcohol to temper feelings of hopelessness and anxiety. These aversive feelings were the stimulus and alcohol use was the behaviour that helped remove the noxious stimuli: drinking removed them and was thereby maintained over time through negative reinforcement. However, Gail's drinking also hindered progress towards her personal goal of being physically healthy and gave rise to new problems as well, such as fatigue and worsening physical health. Such negative reinforcement contingencies are often predominant in maintaining and perpetuating depression, and disrupting these patterns can catalyse improvements to mood and life context.

Positive reinforcement occurs when the likelihood of a behaviour increases as a result of the *occurrence* of a stimulus immediately after a response. Like negative reinforcement contingencies, positive reinforcement contingencies, too, can keep people stuck in depression for a long time. For example, by taking on cooking and cleaning responsibilities, Gail's daughters unintentionally reinforced positively Gail's withdrawal and lack of initiative. In addition, Gail acknowledged that she had a tendency to comfort eat when she was feeling especially down, because she liked feeling full. Despite the pleasurable effects associated with her comfort eating, the therapist gently pointed out that this behaviour was inconsistent with her goal of being physically healthy and actually contributed to her depression, because she often felt guilty afterwards.

The other type of contingencies discussed above – context-cued, behaviour-cued and mood-cued – is rooted in classical conditioning, which emphasizes the notion that a given behaviour is more likely to occur in the presence of particular antecedents. The concept of context-cued contingencies refers to the ways in which a particular context elicits a particular behavioural response. Gail's therapist noted that Gail locked herself in her room and cried for hours whenever she saw on the television people who conjured memories of her deceased parents. Behaviour-cued contingencies are ways in which a particular behaviour sets the stage for a particular mood or another behaviour; and mood-cued contingencies are particular mood states that elicit a particular behaviour. For example, if Gail made an error at work, even something as small as a typo, this often set off a chain of behaviours – such as going to the bathroom to cry, feeling embarrassed about her inability to cope with small mistakes, and ultimately going home for the rest of the day. Identifying the antecedents to and the consequences of changes in mood and behaviour was critical to Gail's treatment and cued Gail and her therapist to target these variables for intervention.

How to assess The most common method for gathering the information required for functional analyses is *activity monitoring*. In its most basic form, activity monitoring involves recording daily activities and assigning a mood rating for each activity (see Table 15.1 in the appendix for a sample activity chart). Measuring the degree to which an activity was pleasurable or resulted in a sense of accomplishment (mastery) is an appropriate alternative. Thorough activity monitoring also allows clients and therapists to keep a running track record of their clients' progress with homework assignments, so that adjustments can be made to future assignments. Given the central role of activity monitoring in the assessment process, it is important that clients clearly understand how to do it early in treatment. Through encouragement and conscientious reviews of monitoring assignments, therapists can reinforce clients in all the latter's efforts to monitor their own activities.

Although there are different approaches to activity monitoring, a common method consists of using an activity record in which activities and moods are recorded each hour. Gail's therapist explained the activity record in the second session, asking Gail to complete three days of monitoring prior to their next session.

THERAPIST Gail, I want to show you an activity chart. I use this with all my clients, to get a sense of how people's mood can impact their behaviour and vice-versa. See here, there is a box for each hour of the day. You track in each box what you did and how you felt during that activity.

GAIL Okay, that seems straightforward. But how do I track how I felt? Do I write something in there?

THERAPIST Good question. You certainly can write in descriptions of how you felt. As we get started with the monitoring, you can record a rating for your mood more globally. For instance, I often encourage people to rate their mood on a scale from 0 to 10, where 0 means your best mood ever and 10 means your worst mood ever. As you get more practice, you may start to identify more specific emotions.

GAIL That makes sense, but do I really have to fill this out for every hour of every day? That seems like a lot of work.

THERAPIST Well, the more information we have the better, but to begin with I would like you to start tracking just some of your week – maybe two days during the week and one during the weekend. Does that sound manageable?

Gail appeared overwhelmed by this assignment, expressing her concern that she wouldn't successfully complete the task. It was important for Gail's therapist to remain flexible in response to her concerns and to offer Gail more than one option for monitoring. Such flexibility and responsiveness is a hallmark of competent BA therapists. For example, Gail's therapist proposed that she complete a time sampling procedure, a common alternative to the full-scale activity record. The time sampling procedure requires clients to select specific time frames (a limited number of hours per day or a limited number of days per week) to monitor activities. As was optimal, they selected a range of time periods that represented most of Gail's experiences, and Gail agreed to try to complete the activity record on two weekdays, respectively for the morning period and for the afternoon, and on Saturday, for the evening/night. Clients who have difficulty with the activity record method can also be invited to develop a format that is more suitable to their lifestyle – for instance using scheduling books, personal digital assistants, or diaries.

Skilfully reviewing monitoring assignments is a prerequisite to a successful BA. It is important to review each and every attempt at activity monitoring made by the client. Genuine attention to activity not only promotes more comprehensive case conceptualizations but also positively reinforces clients' attempts to try new behaviours and to complete homework assignments. Failure to review monitoring assignments can undermine the completion of future homework and is generally antithetical to the BA approach.

A competent review of activity monitoring often requires additional discussion and clarification with the client regarding the specifics of each activity recorded and, when done successfully, yields critical information pertaining to the goals of functional analysis listed above. After a well-executed review, therapists should be able to answer the following questions:

- What are the relationships between mood and activity?
- What are the relationships between life context and mood?
- What are some of the factors maintaining the depression?
- What is preventing the client from being active and engaging in life?
- What would the client be doing if he/she were not depressed?
- Which behaviours are most amenable to change?

Even the most skilful BA therapists can run into obstacles when reviewing monitoring assignments. For example, we have noticed that many clients often report that their mood is always depressed, or that they do nothing all day. Such reporting is likely to be due to inaccurate recall, limited range of behaviours, or an underdeveloped ability to differentiate minor fluctuations in mood or behaviour (or both). The third possibility is often the culprit; and teaching clients how to recognize subtle changes in mood – especially to the extent that they are connected to changes in behaviour – is a key task in BA. Teaching clients to notice subtleties begins with the assertion that variability is everywhere and is not random. For instance, even though Gail reported feeling 'down' all day every day, her therapist insisted on finding out whether she felt slightly more 'down' or slightly less 'down' at specific times during the day, or following certain activities. When persuaded to pay closer attention, Gail was able to notice subtle shifts in her mood. Often, when clients experience difficulty with monitoring assignments, it can be helpful to record in the session some portion of the past few days' monitoring.

To summarize, thorough assessment is ongoing throughout the treatment and is critical to successful treatment with BA. Identifying treatment goals, the functional relationship between behaviour and mood, and mood–behaviour contingencies is the primary objective of assessment. Comprehensive assessment in these domains is a prerequisite to the implementation of activation strategies.

Activation strategies

BA does not simply encourage clients to become more active in arbitrary and random ways. Rather BA is an idiographic treatment that respects the heterogeneity of depression and the fact that the course of treatment can vary substantially from client to client. Nonetheless, the following activation strategies are trademarks of BA and likely will be useful in any course of treatment:

- activity scheduling;
- activity structuring;
- modifying avoidance and solving problems;
- targeting routine regulation and rumination;
- troubleshooting.

Activity scheduling Since most work in BA occurs outside the therapist's office, clients rarely leave a session without at least one specific homework assignment. Homework assignments vary across clients and times, and the BA approach does not make a priori assumptions about the type of activities therapists should schedule. However, we recommend scheduling activities in a structured way, regardless of the assignment. It is often helpful for therapists to attend to the following factors when they schedule activities: the client's involvement in developing assignments; a narrow time frame – that is, the scheduling of activities at specific times; and the incorporation of mood ratings for each activity. It is also helpful to ask clients to summarize their homework assignments at the end of each session. As part of this end-of-session summary, Gail's therapist frequently found it helpful to give Gail an activity record that was partially filled out with her homework assignments and with dates of when they should be completed.

Activity structuring Whereas activity scheduling refers to the 'what' and 'when' of an activity, activity structuring refers to the 'how to' of an activity. Attending in detail to the 'how to' of activities reflects therapists' appreciation of the challenge of initiating behaviour change when depressed. It was important for Gail's therapist to structure Gail's activities in a way that maximized the likelihood of success by giving assignments that were within her behavioural repertoire and were consistent with her treatment goals. This process, also referred to as *graded task assignment*, involves identifying the core components of an activity, breaking those components into smaller steps, sequencing these steps, and embedding the contingencies.

Activity structuring may appear easy, but often requires considerable skill. Not only do therapists have to accurately identify the core components of the activity, but they are also required to specify steps that are within the behavioural repertoire of their clients. For instance, a simple assignment such as 'paying bills this week' may suffice for one client, but not for another. In a course of BA with Gail, such an activity needed to be broken down still further. Each of the following steps comprised an activation assignment: going to the post office to buy stamps; clearing off a suitable workspace; organizing the paperwork; counting all the bills; scheduling to pay a specific proportion of them; writing out the cheques and addressing the envelopes at the designated time; and then delivering the bills to the mailbox. In this way the therapist was able to break down the tasks as much as was necessary to *guarantee* success, especially early in therapy. Success with even the smallest of assignments (e.g., buying stamps) improved Gail's mood and positively reinforced future attempts at progressively more complex assignments (e.g., organizing paperwork and writing out the checks).

Establishing assignment contingencies can be a powerful strategy for increasing the likelihood that clients will engage in homework. For example, public commitment helped Gail to follow through with activation assignments. Whenever possible, Gail and her therapist explored the possibility of including the client's friends, family members, and significant others when scheduling activities. When agreeing to work on the bill-paying activities, Gail discussed this plan first with her husband and showed him the activity schedule with the specific times allocated for bill-paying activities. Making use of other contingencies can be helpful as well. For example, at times, Gail treated herself to a small gift when completing an assignment (reward) or called her therapist when electing not to complete an assignment (punishment) – because, for Gail, such contingencies supported the efforts to initiate behaviour change. Finally, clients can also experiment with cuing themselves to engage in an activity by structuring their environment in particular ways. Gail, who was working towards doing more exercise, started putting her gym clothes out the night before, so as to increase the likelihood that she would exercise the following day. The common theme in these examples was to enhance achievement of treatment goals by manipulating the consequences of a given behaviour or by manipulating the context in which it occurred.

Although structuring activities can improve the chances of a client's engaging in a homework assignment, it is also important for therapists to emphasize the role of initiating activities – and not focus exclusively on completing them. Often encouragement or praise from the therapist can serve as a powerful reinforcer for the client. Gail's therapist had established a strong working alliance with her, and both she and Gail recognized that their relationship was an important contingency. Thus Gail's therapist sought to provide encouragement and praise for Gail's initiation of an activity even when Gail did not achieve all of her between-session assignments. Her therapist, for example, praised her for washing two windows of her house, even though Gail had planned to wash all the windows. The aim was to reinforce, in whatever ways possible, any evidence of activation, shaping more sustained activation over time.

We conclude this discussion of activity scheduling and structuring by highlighting the importance of reviewing a client's experience with homework assignments. As mentioned earlier, reviewing homework reinforces the client to engage in future assignments and gives the therapist opportunity to assess what the client has learned, highlight improvements, and address barriers. When working with a depressed client on initial activation assignments, one can be assured that not all clients will complete all the components of every assignment. Thus it is essential for therapists to address incomplete assignments with a non-judgemental, matter-of-fact attitude and to feel comfortable doing this. Many therapists will find that much of BA involves troubleshooting problems with homework assignments and that this process often sheds light on a client's patterns of avoidance. It is our hunch that the sustained and repeated attention, over time, to a narrow set of treatment targets is critical to BA. The therapist's task is continually to assign activities, review activities, troubleshoot activities, and reassign activities. It is important for therapists to maintain their own hope and optimism about change during this process. For instance, it was important for Gail's therapist to consult with colleagues during Gail's treatment in order to maintain hope when Gail experienced repeated problems with activation assignments that targeted her return to work. Through such consultation, the therapist was aided in identifying specific barriers that could be targeted and in developing ways to grade the tasks more effectively. Adopting this problem-solving stance helped to counteract hopelessness about change, avoidance of reviewing homework, or a critical attitude towards Gail's difficulties in completing assignments.

Modifying avoidance and solving problems Given BA's emphasis on promoting activation, treatment strategies are also designed to explicitly target processes that inhibit activation – for instance avoidance behaviours and ruminative thinking. In BA, consequences of depression such as avoidance are seen as natural responses to life's problems that serve specific functions. For example, Gail's therapist explored with Gail the degree to which pulling back from her schedule at work was a form of avoidance. They discussed how much staying home from work reduced Gail's fears about making a mistake and the possibility that Gail's reduced work schedule was being maintained in this way through negative reinforcement (i.e., because it reduced her anxiety in the short run). Gail clearly recognized, however, how reducing her time at work was exacerbating her depression. She reported that, since she reduced her schedule, she increased her sleeping during the day (although she rarely felt rested), felt more tired, and had less energy for household chores as well. Gail also recognized that this behaviour hindered progress towards her long-term goal of getting a promotion at her job. Gail's therapist emphasized the way in which patterns of avoidance kept Gail stuck in depression, precluded other, positive experiences (e.g., a sense of accomplishment after a hard day's work), and exacerbated existing problems (e.g., guilt about not contributing to family income). In this way avoidance behaviours were understood as natural and understandable responses to feeling down, but the vicious cycle of avoidance and continued depression was emphasized. Avoidance behaviours were adaptive in the short term – in that they reduced immediate discomfort – but often were maladaptive when viewed in a larger context.

Given the central role accorded to avoidance in the BA model, therapists can expect to spend a good deal of time addressing such behaviour. Different clients exhibit avoidant behaviour for different reasons, and such variety naturally requires that interventions be individually tailored. However, targeting avoidance generally requires the following approach: assume a collaborative and empathic stance; maintain a problem-solving mindset in generating and evaluating solutions; and use mnemonic devices whenever appropriate.

Significant discomfort was often the reason why Gail tended to avoid situations or experiences. Before attempting any avoidance modification, her therapist conveyed a clear understanding and appreciation of Gail's discomfort. Otherwise the therapist's efforts, no matter how well intentioned, would probably have been premature, ineffective, and even experienced as patronizing. On a foundation of empathy and validation, the therapist began to highlight the ways in which Gail's avoidant behaviour was helpful in the short term, but hindered long-term progress.

THERAPIST Gail, I want to spend some time talking about your work schedule and about how you came to be working less than you would like. Tell me, when did you start cutting back your hours?

GAIL It was about six months ago, I guess. I started coming in late in order to miss the morning rush, so I would not have to run into people as much. Soon I was missing whole days and telling my supervisors that I felt ill. They were very supportive and, since we have had a lot of help from our interns, I was offered the opportunity to cut back my hours to part time. Now I only go in once or twice a week.

THERAPIST Interesting. Can you tell me more about coming late and what you mean by 'missing the morning rush'?

GAIL Well, you know how it is in the morning. Everyone arrives around the same time and you cannot help but bump into people in the hallways or the common areas. I hate all that small talk – 'So Gail, how are you today? How are your daughters?' I just have nothing to say, and then I get all embarrassed and end up mumbling something stupid. I really dread those moments, so I just put myself in a position where I would not have to deal with it.

THERAPIST It makes sense that you would start going in late if you felt uncomfortable every morning.

GAIL And then I would just start skipping whole days. Mary, one of my supervisors, is always so nice when it comes to asking for time off. She never makes me feel guilty and always tells me how valuable I am, so it does not matter if I miss a day here or a couple of days there. When I told her that I just felt tired all the time and that work was really draining me, she actually suggested I do part time.

THERAPIST She makes it very easy for you to miss work and, in a way, almost rewards you by telling you how valuable you are.

GAIL And you know it feels good when she says it right then, but then I think how much work I miss. How valuable can I really be if I am not there?

THERAPIST Good point. I think that is another reason why we have to figure out how to get you working again. But before we start brainstorming I am wondering whether you can tell me more about why going to work is so aversive? What do you dread when you know you have to go in?

GAIL Definitely the small talk. I mean I like my job – it is not the work itself that bothers me but all that small talk and putting on like I am all friendly and interested. More often than not, I just clam up and cannot think of anything to say.

THERAPIST Okay. So it seems that having to converse with people in this way really contributes to your wanting to stay home. Now, do you find your co-workers aversive themselves? Or is it more just these particular situations where you feel socially obligated to interact with them but have nothing to say?

GAIL No, I like them fine. It is just that, when it is my turn to speak, I go blank and nothing comes out. My face gets all red. My palms sweat. Wow, I am starting to feel flushed just talking about it.

THERAPIST That is ok. I think a lot of people would feel embarrassed if they were in a similar situation. I wonder, Gail, whether there is anything you could do before you go to work that would make these conversations easier? Maybe thinking about something interesting your daughters are doing that you could share with your co-workers? Or maybe you could prepare a couple of questions to ask other people so the spotlight is turned on them?

GAIL Hmmm, I never thought of anything like that.

In addressing Gail's patterns of avoidance, it was extremely helpful to approach such patterns as solvable problems. Understanding avoidance patterns typically involved repeatedly reviewing activity monitoring so as to identify the contingencies that maintained the avoidant behaviour. Once Gail and her therapist conceptualized avoidant behaviour in terms of contingencies, they worked together to generate and evaluate a range of alternate solutions. Treatment sessions then focused directly on solving key problems, often by using strategies of activity structuring and scheduling. For example, since Gail avoided making requests to her boss, whom she experienced as intimidating, she and her therapist practised assertive communication in role play: the goal was was to help Gail feel more comfortable and more confident when talking with her boss. They also identified specific steps she could take in order to prepare to return to work – such as getting up in the morning and engaging in a morning routine as though she were going to work.

The use of acronyms can also facilitate the formulation and resolution of avoidance. For instance, the TRAP/TRAC acronym suggests that clients get out of the TRAP and get back on TRAC. Clients and therapists then work together to replace the 'avoidance pattern' with some form of 'alternative coping':

- trigger: avoidance is usually triggered by something (e.g., socializing at work)
- response: people usually respond to the trigger with some emotional experience (e.g., fear of looking stupid)
- avoidance pattern: people usually cope with the emotional response by resorting to some form of avoidance (e.g., reduce hours at work; stay home)
- alternative coping: replace the avoidant behaviour with an approach behaviour (e.g., preparatory work designed to make socializing easier)

A proposed mechanism of change of BA is increasing the client's awareness of avoidance behaviours and replacing them with more adaptive behaviours. For example, as Gail's depression worsened, she started lying in bed for several hours. Upon closer examination, Gail and her therapist determined that part of this behaviour was related to the embarrassment Gail felt when watching her family go through their morning routines while she remained in pyjamas and stayed home from work. Thus a short-term goal for Gail was to get out of bed in no more than 15 minutes after waking up, even if she planned on missing work. In short, Gail's therapist was on the lookout for everyday behaviours that functioned as avoidance and worked with Gail to design alternative coping behaviours.

Targeting rumination Nolen-Hoeksema, Wisco, and Lyubomirsky (2008, p. 400) define rumination as 'a mode of responding to distress that involves repetitively and passively focusing on symptoms of distress and on the possible causes and consequences of these symptoms'. The BA model views rumination as private behaviour that can interfere with the direct experience of activity and can prevent full engagement with one's context.

BA therapists are more concerned with the function – that is, the context and consequences – than with the form – that is, the content – of rumination. Rumination can sabotage activation plans, and clients sometimes report no positive changes in mood after completing an activation assignment when they have been ruminating frequently during the assignment. In such cases, it is important for therapists to assess rumination. For instance, one of Gail's assignments was to cook a weekend meal with her daughters. When she returned the next week, she reported that she took little pleasure, experienced little mastery, and felt 'out of it' all evening. Her therapist learned that, although Gail did indeed spend several hours in the kitchen with her daughters, she spent most of the time thinking about her job, about why she wasn't working full time, about how she had always been would always be depressed, and about the fact that she gave so little to her family. The therapist and Gail explicitly highlighted such behaviours as rumination that had the effect of diminishing Gail's direct contact with a potentially reinforcing activity. Encouraged to retry the assignment with an emphasis on paying special attention to specific details (e.g., the sound of her daughters' laughter, the smell of the meal they were cooking), Gail reported a substantial improvement in her mood. In BA this deliberate focus of attention is defined as 'attention to experience' and bears clear similarities with mindfulness-based strategies used with clients with recurrent depression (Segal, Williams, & Teasdale, 2001). Such strategies are also consonant with 'opposite action all the way' strategies in dialectical behaviour therapy, in which clients are asked to engage *fully and completely* in behaviour that is the opposite of their urge of the moment (Linehan, 1993). Therapists can also guide clients to practise turning their attention to the tasks they are engaged in, as opposed to paying attention to the content of their ruminations; and, at times, they may guide clients to use distraction strategies as well.

Troubleshooting As many clients experience difficulty in completing activation assignments, troubleshooting on a regular basis is a core part of BA. Once again, the therapist must remain empathic and must adopt a problem-solving stance in order to identify the barriers that are interfering with homework assignments and treatment goals. Therapists help clients to figure out how to overcome barriers, keep commitments, and generate and apply solutions. They also help clients to learn to anticipate future events, and they teach them how to cope with problems that may arise. For example, when Gail resumed working on a regular basis, she and her therapist role-played conversations with co-workers, so that Gail could practise coping with the kind of embarrassment she felt when she was at a loss for words. In Gail's treatment, troubleshooting also involved attending to the potential barrier raised by mood to doing homework and to working towards treatment goals. In such cases, the therapist sought to increase Gail's commitment to acting towards a goal rather than acting according to her mood. This attempt involved making statements such as 'You may not feel like doing this when the time comes, even though it seems like a really valuable plan now,' or reminding her of the importance of goal-directed, rather than mood dependent, behaviour. Many therapists will find that troubleshooting requires a repeated and persistent focus on reviewing homework and occupies much of BA treatment.

Relapse prevention

Depression is a highly recurrent disorder (Kessler et. al., 2003). As termination approaches, the remaining sessions should focus on reviewing and consolidating treatment gains in order to prevent future episodes of depression. Specifically, Gail and her therapist discussed what triggered depression in the past, anticipated the situations that may elicit depressive symptoms in the future, and drafted a coping plan that used the key BA principles and strategies that have been helpful. As Gail was susceptible to patterns of withdrawal, avoidance, and rumination when she experienced dysphoria, she and her therapist developed a plan in which, whenever Gail experienced even a small degree of sadness, she would review her list of 'antidepressant activities' (e.g., exercise, call her friend, make a meal, complete a 'do-able' task at work). If Gail felt like staying home from work, she would pause to reevaluate her reasons for wanting to stay home and only call in if she was truly ill. Towards this end, it was important to ensure that Gail had a solid grasp on basic treatment strategies and on how to apply them in the future.

Distinctive Elements of Behavioural Activation

Like a nesting doll, BA emerged from cognitive behaviour therapy and retains many structural elements of its progenitor. These concern the general course of treatment and include the importance accorded to agenda setting, homework, and collaboration. Nevertheless, there are clear theoretical and practical differences between BA and cognitive behaviour therapy. Perhaps most importantly, BA does not target the *content* of cognition and does not aim to alleviate depression by helping clients change maladaptive cognitive processing. Whether BA indirectly influences cognition awaits future research; however, the focus in BA is clearly on promoting behaviour change, not cognitive change.

BA is eminently compatible with many of the other treatments described in this volume, such as metacognitive therapy (MCT), acceptance and commitment therapy (ACT), and mindfulness-based cognitive therapy (MBCT). In many ways, the approach of BA to cognition parallels that of these treatments; however, the BA therapist attends to cognition not as a primary target, but rather when cognition is a barrier to activation. Thus, although the BA therapist may guide a client to use strategies that are functionally similar to meditation practices, the use of meditation is not an explicit and structured target of the treatment as a whole, as it is in MBCT, for example. In addition, implicit in BA is a stance of acceptance; for example, patients are guided repeatedly to act even in the presence of negative emotion. Unlike in treatments such as ACT, however, in BA specific strategies to cultivate acceptance are not employed in an explicit manner.

Finally, BA is often distinguished by its emphasis on simple and straightforward treatment strategies. Unlike other treatments described in this volume, which require substantial supervision, professional experience, and, in some cases, extensive personal practice, BA is possibly easier to learn and provide.

Conclusion

BA helps clients with depression to understand the relationship between their behaviours and their moods and encourages such clients to change the way they feel by changing what they do. This chapter describes basic treatment strategies used in BA and showcases their use in Gail's treatment. In this vignette, BA helped Gail to reconnect with aspects of her life context from which she had withdrawn. Such steps alleviated her depression by allowing her to have rewarding experiences, to approach rather than avoiding problematic areas of her life, and thereby to work towards personal goals. Through systematic and sustained efforts at behaviour change, Gail resumed her normal work schedule, began exercising regularly, and reported satisfaction with the improvements she achieved in her relationship with her daughters and husband by the end of treatment. As a parsimonious therapy that employs a narrow set of strategies, BA may offer promise for the treatment of depression across a broad array of clients and settings.

Appendix

Activity chart

Table 15.1 Instructions.
Record your activity for each hour of the day (what were you doing, with whom, where, etc.). Record a mood rating associated with each activity. Mood is rated between 0 and 10, 0 indicating 'best mood ever' and 10 indicating 'worst mood ever'. Aim to record entries on your activity chart at least every 3–4 hours each day.

	Monday	*Tuesday*	*Wednesday*	*Thursday*	*Friday*	*Saturday*	*Sunday*
7am							
8am							
9am							
10am							
11am							
12pm							
1pm							
2pm							
3pm							
4pm							
5pm							
6pm							
7pm							
8pm							
9pm							
10pm							
11pm							
12am							
1am–7am							

References

APA. (1994). *Diagnostic and statistical manual of mental disorders: DSM-IV*. Washington, DC: American Psychiatric Association.

Beck, A. T., Steer, R. A., & Brown, G. K. (1996). *Manual for the BDI-II*. San Antonio, TX: Psychological Corporation.

First, M. B., Spitzer, R. L., Gibbon, M., & Williams, J. B. W. (1997). *User's guide for the Structured Clinical Interview for DSM-IV Axis I Disorders*. Washington, DC: American Psychiatric Press.

Hamilton, M. A. (1960). A rating scale for depression. *Journal of Neurology, Neurosurgery, and Psychiatry*, *23*, 56–61.

Haynes, S. N., & O'Brien, W. H. (1990). Functional analysis in behaviour therapy. *Clinical Psychology Review*, *10*, 649–668.

Kessler, R. C., Berglund, P., Demler, O., Jin, R., Koretz, D., Merikangas, K. R. … Wang, P. S. (2003). The epidemiology of major depressive disorder: Results from the National Comorbidity Survey Replication (NCS-R). *Journal of the American Medical Assocation*, *289*(23), 3095–3105.

Linehan, M. M. (1993). *Cognitive–behavioural treatment of borderline personality disorder*. New York: Guilford.

Martell, C. R., Addis, M. E., & Jacobson, N. S. (2001). *Depression in context: Strategies for guided action*. New York: Norton.

Nolen-Hoeksema, S., Wisco, B. E., & Lyubomirsky, S. (2008). Rethinking rumination. *Perspectives on Psychological Science*, *3*(5), 400–424.

Segal, Z. V., Williams, J. M. G., & Teasedale, J. T. (2001). *Mindfulness-based cognitive therapy for depression: A new approach to preventing relapse*. New York: Guilford.

Further Reading

Dimidjian, S., Hollon, S. D., Dobson, K. S., Schmaling, K. B., Kohlenberg, R. J., Addis, M. E. … Jacobson, N. S. (2006). Randomized trial of behavioral activation, cognitive therapy, and antidepressant medication in the acute treatment of adults with major depression. *Journal of Consulting and Clinical Psychology*, *74*, 658–670.

16

A Critique of Therapeutic Approaches to Depression: Commonalties and Distinctive Features

Robert L. Leahy

The clinician working with patients with major depressive disorder or dysthymic disorder has the responsibility of helping people cope with a life-threatening problem. People die from depression – and, if they do not die, they certainly suffer. The economic burden of depression is substantial (Stewart, Ricci, Chee, Hahn, & Morganstein, 2003). But the good news is that, if we were able to implement the approaches outlined in this book, fewer people would suffer, fewer would die, and – to add what I consider an anticlimactic observation – we would also save money. Like many readers of these excellent chapters, I am also a practising clinician and I currently draw on all five approaches. Each has merit, but each is different. In this chapter I will share my observations on commonalities, differences, and new directions.

Proponents of different models often emphasize the distinctive and innovative features of their approach, often implicitly assuming what may actually be some of the more powerful common elements. If you read these chapters carefully – and then think, 'How is this different from a psychoanalytic model?' – you will immediately recognize that each of these approaches shares features common to all of them – features that are missing in other clinical models widely practised. Each approach is, of course, a cognitive behavioural therapy (CBT) approach. What does this mean? Quite simply,

Treating Depression: MCT, CBT and Third Wave Therapies, First Edition.
Edited by Adrian Wells and Peter L. Fisher.

each approach proposes that we stay in the present moment as much as possible, socialize the patient to a conceptualization of the model, focus on an agenda or goal for the session, actively structure what is covered, examine how behaviour and thinking are linked together, measure improvement by evaluating symptoms, behaviour, and quality of life, elicit feedback, prepare for setbacks, and emphasize self-help skills or homework assignments.

The behavioural activation (BA) model is clearly one of activity, engagement, and self-help. The patient is immediately asked to change what he or she is doing so as to see what follows from new behavioural patterns. The BA model proposes that depression is a consequence of passivity, avoidance, non-rewarded behaviour, non-contingency, and heightened adversity; and it attempts to enhance self-efficacy and rewarding experiences by increasing rewarding behaviours, decreasing negative or unrewarding behaviours, encouraging the patient to take action rather than ruminate, and setting daily goals that focus on action rather than on passivity. BA is also part of the traditional cognitive therapy model (e.g., 'activity scheduling' and 'graded task assignments'), but in the cognitive model behavioural assignments are used to test out cognitions – for example, 'I will have a terrible time at the party'. The acceptance and commitment therapy (ACT) model links the patient to values – and therefore to goals – and directs the patient towards willingness to tolerate frustration in the service of productive action. Like the BA model, the ACT approach utilizes behavioural assignments; but these assignments are used so as to encourage the patient to pursue valued goals and a life worth living and to practise psychological flexibility while overcoming the desire to avoid unpleasant experiences. The cognitive model begins with the use of activity scheduling and graded task assignments that help challenge the belief that one is helpless and that life is hopeless.

Although the mindfulness-based cognitive therapy (MBCT) approach, the metacognitive therapy (MCT) approach, and the ACT approach are similar to the cognitive therapy approach in helping the patient recognize that thoughts are different from reality, only in the cognitive approach is there an attempt to test out the veridicality of these thoughts by examining the evidence, by setting up behavioural experiments, or by employing other forms of rational disputation or dialogue. On the other hand, while the cognitive approach employs 'decentring' – standing back and recognizing that a thought may differ from a fact – the 'process' or 'experience' of decentring is not a key feature in the cognitive model as it is in the MBCT and MCT models – or, to some degree, in the ACT model. The MBCT model recognizes that thoughts may be associated with the risk for depression, but it is the degree to which the individual gets excessively focused on thoughts, rather than the content of those thoughts, that results in problems. While the MCBT approach does include monitoring negative thoughts and recognizing how these thoughts are associated with depressed mood, there is no attempt there to dispute or test these thoughts, as one would do in following the cognitive therapy model. MBCT recognizes that rumination is a central risk for depression and utilizes exercises in acknowledging the present-moment experience of a thought, while letting it go. The emphasis is on practising awareness without entanglement (chapter 14). The MCT model assists the patient in recognizing that *thinking differently about thinking* can immediately modify the confusing entanglement with ruminative thoughts. This model explores the patient's *beliefs about the function of thoughts* – and the attentional syndrome, for example the process of focusing on negative thoughts – while it encourages the patient to step back, with detachment, into an observer role and to let thoughts 'be'. Thus the metacognitive therapist may be similar to the mindfulness-based cognitive therapist in recognizing the role of rumination as a risk factor in depression; but in MCT it is the patient's 'theory of mind' – or the function of thoughts – that is the distinctive feature.

Let's take a brief, but close look at how these common elements are expressed in each approach. Behavioural change is paramount in all of them. This is, of course, a truism in BA, but it is also true for ACT, which emphasizes behaving in accordance with valued action and tolerating frustration and difficulty in order to accomplish meaningful goals. Behaviour is a central component of cognitive therapy, since there one carries out behavioural experiments in order to test out dysfunctional thinking. And behaviour is also a component of MCT, where patients are encouraged to act productively regardless of the content of their negative thinking. (The MBCT approach places minimal emphasis on behaviour itself, but helps the patient realize that one can act towards goals even in the presence of unwanted, intrusive thoughts.) Each approach socializes the patient into the model, providing him or her with a rationale for its techniques and plan of treatment. The BA therapist illustrates how passivity and avoidance deprive the patient of the opportunity for rewarding experiences, which maintains the depression. The acceptance and commitment therapist demonstrates the hopelessness of past attempts at adaptation and links the patient to valued goals and a meaningful life, while illustrating that one can observe thoughts rather than obey them. The mindfulness-based cognitive therapist often employs a structured group format in which the patient is socialized into the model through a series of mindfulness exercises – beginning with simple awareness of the present moment (the 'raisin' exercise), mindful body scan, and mindful walking designed to assist the patient in practising mindful awareness – while also noticing how the mind drifts off to other sounds, thoughts, sensations, memories and judgements.

The cognitive therapist helps the patient distinguish between thoughts, feelings, and reality and suggests that habitual biases in thinking may account for the feelings of helplessness that plague the patient (chapter 11). In the cognitive model, case conceptualization involves several levels of cognitive assessment: negative automatic thoughts, conditional rules or assumptions, and core beliefs or schemas about self and others. For example, the negative automatic thought 'She thinks I am boring', which reflects mind-reading, becomes problematic because it is related to the conditional rule 'I must get the approval of others to be worthwhile', which is then related to a core belief about self, of the form 'I am defective', and to a core belief about others, of the form 'They are judgemental of me'. This detailed analysis of the content of thoughts and of the relationship among levels of thought can also be integrated into a more complex case conceptualization, which identifies earlier life experiences that give rise to these 'cognitive vulnerabilities' and the problematic strategies of coping – such as avoidance and compensation – that have served to maintain core schemas. The cognitive therapist is particularly focused on categorizing cognitive distortions and on assisting the patient in employing techniques (e.g., cost–benefit analysis, evidence for and against, arguing back at the thought) to recognize how one's mood changes not simply because one has a thought, but because one believes it.

Each of these approaches asks the patient to consider *a new relationship* to the *occurrence* of negative thoughts, whether this relationship consists in taking action, becoming more flexible in the presence of thoughts, examining thoughts as incorrect appraisals, practising mindfulness in the present moment, or using mindful detachment from thoughts. The differences among these approaches will, of course, be important to recognize, but we can still recognize that each calls for a different response to negative thinking. The BA therapist is similar to the acceptance and commitment therapist in proposing that acting towards valued goals or rewarding outcomes will be more valuable than getting 'stuck' on the negative thoughts that occur. To paraphrase a behavioural mantra, 'In the face of adversity, act'. Hence focusing on future goals and values, taking action, being flexible enough to stand apart from the thought and act anyway – these are the prescriptions for behavioural therapists and for acceptance and commitment therapists. But the acceptance and commitment therapist also encourages a new 'observational' stance towards negative thoughts and feelings. Mindfulness allows the patient to acknowledge without struggling and to accept without suppressing. Standing back, observing, and then acting towards goals – these are the adaptive steps in ACT. MBCT places emphasis on acknowledging, in the present moment, the existence of thoughts, sensations, and emotions without attempting to control or judge these experiences, but by approaching the process with curiosity, openness and acceptance.

The metacognitive therapist utilizes 'detached mindfulness' – which asks the patient to observe that a thought occurs (a mental event) and that one has a choice of answering, suppressing, struggling – or allowing it to come and go. The occurrence of a thought, then, is, simply, an 'occurrence' – not a reflection of reality, not a requirement for engagement. Unlike the MBCT's emphasis on attentional deployment towards the present experience (e.g., towards breath or thought), the metacognitive use of detached mindfulness emphasizes awareness of thoughts (meta-awareness) while the subject is simply observing them rather than 'doing' anything about them. Thus, detached mindfulness is less 'complicated' than MBCT's mindfulness as a response to a thought – it is simply awareness while 'doing nothing'. Moreover, the use of detached mindfulness in MCT is directly related to modifying the beliefs that one has about the function of thinking and responding to thoughts. For example, the belief 'I must do something if I have an intrusive thought', is addressed by the 'experiment' of doing 'nothing' other than detached mindful awareness. Unlike MBCT, the metacognitive model attempts to address the patient's 'theory of mind' – in this case, the theory that the individual maintains about how his/her mind functions or must function. The metaphors used in MCT illustrate the observational role of passing, ephemeral thought phenomena – the trains that pass through the station, the clouds that pass in the sky, the telephone call that goes unanswered. Thoughts can exist in parallel with living your life. They do not have to control your life.

The cognitive therapist also asks the patient to stand back and observe a thought ('decentring'). Although few cognitive therapists would describe this as 'mindfulness', it is a 'kind' of mindfulness, if it is diluted. It is a mindful, observing form of recognizing that a thought is a mental event that makes claims about reality or even about obligations, but that a thought can be recognized as 'only a thought'. The cognitive therapist's model differs from these other models of 'dealing' with a thought in that the cognitive therapist takes the thought 'seriously' as an impediment. Thus a wide range of techniques is recruited to test and modify these thoughts – certainly not the strategy of someone taking a mindful stance. Thoughts are not suppressed, they are elicited, examined, tested, and modified. Indeed, evaluating and testing thoughts appears to give them paramount importance – and to suggest that addressing the content of a thought, rather than the process of observing the thought, will be the most valuable strategy.

Each model emphasizes self-help skills – that is, it teaches the patient useful techniques, strategies, or engaging in 'practices' and 'behaviour' in between sessions. This is very different from catharsis models, which emphasize the expression and anticipated relief of psychic energy, or historical models, which suggest that knowing the source changes the impact of past behaviour. Self-help models also differ from models that emphasize the therapeutic relationship as the major source of change. These are not transferential models; they are models of personal empowerment. The assumption in each CBT model is that learning and practising new self-help skills will change the way you function and will help you maintain your gains. Thus each CBT model is collaborative, with a direct exchange between therapist and patient, while the therapist assists the patient in practising new skills – that is, in becoming his/her own therapist. The BA model emphasizes productive and rewarding behaviour, while decreasing no-win behavioural habits. These are behaviours that need to be done. The ACT model proposes commitment to change – and change often implies behaviour and a new way of relating to thoughts. Metaphors, experiences, exposure, identifying and living in accordance with a valued life are all part of the daily self-help regimen. The cognitive model teaches the self-help of identifying and modifying dysfunctional thinking, with homework as a required part of the treatment. And the metacognitive therapist encourages the patient to test out the new metaphors and techniques that are learned in session and to report back how effective these are. Each approach engages the patient as a collaborator – in a sense, as a fellow 'scientist' who will discover the utility (or lack of utility) of the techniques that are learned and practised in session. This is very different from catharsis models, insight therapy, or transference-based approaches. The goal in each of these CBT approaches is for the patient to become his or her own therapist. You might call it 'a game changer'.

Distinctive Features

While recognizing that each of these approaches may share some commonality, there are different emphases, different processes, and different models of change. I will examine several 'features' of these models and will evaluate the degree to which these are distinctive. In particular, I will discuss distancing from thoughts, content of thinking, mental control, avoidance, activation of behaviour, and values and goals.

Distancing and content

By 'distancing' I refer to the ability to stand back from a thought or a situation and observe it as independent from the self or the observer. Distancing is similar to 'decentring' and is the opposite of 'fusion'. Each of these CBT models addresses the issue of distancing, but in different ways.

The ACT model is derived from functional contextualism, an epistemological model that focuses on the function or consequence of thoughts (and other experiences) rather than on a universal truth function. ACT attempts to argue for a pragmatic approach to thinking, drawing on a Skinnerian model of the function of language. ACT rejects what it describes as the 'mechanistic' model of reality that underlies other psychological theories, claiming that these other theories adhere to a correspondence view of truth. The ACT model argues that the content of thoughts is less important for the individual than the function of thoughts. It is essential, according to ACT, to recognize both the context and the function of thoughts. According to this model, the depressed individual 'fuses' words with meanings and reality rather than focusing on the consequences or actual experiences of behaviour. As in the familiar concept of thought–action fusion, ACT suggests that words and meaning are equated in the mind of the individual, as if the word 'chair' becomes equivalent to the actual object of a chair. ACT proponents have criticized cognitive therapy for encouraging patients to become entangled with their thoughts, in the attempt to struggle with these thoughts and suppress them. ACT utilizes mindfulness as a technique to facilitate detachment, flexibility, and independence from thoughts, sensations, and emotions. As Zettle (chapter 7, p. 183) indicates, being 'mindfully aware' in the present moment yields greater psychological flexibility by 'framing private events in the here and now (e.g., "There's a thought")', making the individual disengage from 'temporal' and 'evaluative' relational framing, and allowing him/her the ability to acknowledge a thought without 'struggling' or 'engaging'.

According to ACT, the depressed individual has a rigid and overly demanding conception of the self, which constrains more adaptive and flexible responses, given the situations that may arise. ACT places emphasis on the current experience, current behaviours, and current contexts, whereas the depressed individual may be anchored to reflections and regrets about the past or concerns about the future. ACT attempts to refocus the individual on the current experience, using mindfulness as a technique for enhancing the ability to stay in the present moment in a non-judgemental way.

The metacognitive model is derived from the self-regulatory executive function model (Wells & Matthews, 1994), and treatment focuses on rumination and metacognitive beliefs. The self-regulatory executive function (S-REF) model specifies that emotional disorders are the consequence of a particular style of thinking, which consists of perseverative processes (worry/rumination), counterproductive attentional strategies, and maladaptive coping responses in response to the occurrence of negative thoughts or emotional states. Collectively, these processes constitute the cognitive attentional syndrome (CAS), which is guided by biased metacognition (Wells & Matthews, 1994, 1996). In their description of the metacognitive model, Wells and Matthews indicate the following treatment plan: development of an 'idiosyncratic' conceptualization based on MCT; the patient's socialization into the model – here the authors stress unhelpful self-focused processes such as rumination and excessive attention to one's own sensations and feelings, or the role of passivity and avoidance; increased flexibility of attention, achieved with the help of the attention-training technique (ATT) and designed to reduce self-focus; reattribution strategies; experiential techniques; and metaphors.

The metacognitive model shares with the ACT model the recognition that depressed individuals may become overly focused on the content of their thoughts. Metacognitive therapy utilizes 'detached mindfulness' in order to facilitate greater flexibility and detachment from the content or even the occurrence of a thought. Fisher and Wells' description of detached mindfulness (chapter 12) illustrates how it differs from the mindfulness exercises derived from Buddhist thinking and used in ACT and MBCT. Specifically, the function of detached mindfulness is to test out beliefs about the uncontrollability of thoughts; the patient is encouraged to observe how thinking can be flexibly redirected towards other stimuli. Attention training – which involves attending to a sound, shifting one's attention, and bringing it back – is used to illustrate how attention can be brought under control and, more specifically, how the control of cognition is independent of internal or external events. MCT uses several experiential tasks to illustrate that one can observe how the content of thoughts shifts when not under conscious control. For example, the free association task instructs the patient to listen to a few words repeated by the therapist and then to allow the mind to wander to other thoughts and images. The tiger task involves asking the patient to imagine a tiger and to see what happens in the image. This illustrates that the content of thoughts has a life of its own – that is, content changes without volitional control. The train metaphor asks the patient to consider thoughts to be like a busy station with trains coming and going. The patient can observe the train without getting on it. Finally, the cloud metaphor reflects that idea that thoughts can pass by just like clouds do. In each case, the patient can function as an observer, watching 'mental content' come and go without trying to engage in it or control it. The purpose of these exercises in MCT is to illustrate the nature of the cognitive attentional syndrome and to provide an incompatible and new response to thoughts: namely a response that demonstrates that flexibility and choice are possible, that one can observe thoughts without engaging in their analysis, and that worry and rumination are controllable.

As Clark and Guyitt indicate, the cognitive model recognizes that thoughts and reality are different (chapter 5). The cognitive model describes the process as a 'decentring' – that is, a way of standing back from a thought and examining its content and validity. In cognitive therapy, the therapist helps patients differentiate between thoughts, feelings, behaviours, and reality. Thoughts are distinguished from reality – they are individual 'constructions' of it, not reality itself. It is difficult to understand how the cognitive therapist could be viewed as encouraging fusion with thoughts, when the emphasis is on distinguishing between thoughts and reality by collecting evidence and disputing or testing thoughts as propositions. Moreover, it is difficult to understand how cognitive therapy would encourage suppression of thoughts, when the therapist encourages the patient to identify, record, categorize, rate believability, test, and modify thoughts. In fact cognitive therapy does the opposite of encouraging fusion with thoughts or suppression of thoughts. The cognitive therapist views the content and the credibility of negative thoughts as an essential component of depression. Most of the techniques that are employed are directly related to modifying the content of the thoughts. In cognitive therapy even behavioural activation is subsumed under the process of modifying the content of thoughts. Behavioural experiments are utilized in order to change the belief that 'nothing will work out'. The credibility of thoughts is further examined in terms of identifying and changing the patient's biased information processing – especially confirmation bias and habitual automatic thoughts (e.g., mind reading, personalizing, overgeneralizing, discounting the positives, etc.). In the cognitive model, decentring is used as a means by which one can identify and observe thoughts in order to evaluate their consequences and their validity. Unlike ACT and MCT, which stress the detached and observing stance towards thoughts, cognitive therapy views detachment as a step towards engagement with the content of these thoughts. It would be out of character for a Beckian cognitive therapist to utilize mindfulness meditation as a technique.

The behavioural model places little emphasis on the content or truth value of thoughts and great emphasis on specific goals, action, and rewarding behaviour (chapter 9). Thoughts, in the BA model, are stimuli to which the patient can either respond or not respond. It is behaviour and its consequences that are emphasized, not mindful awareness or detachment from thoughts. In BA, the individual who becomes overly concerned about thoughts may find that excessive rumination is simply another way of remaining passive and avoidant and of thereby missing the opportunities for rewarding behaviour (Martell, Dimidjian, & Herman-Dunn, 2010). Thus the patient who focuses on his or her thoughts might be viewed as remaining passive and avoidant. The content is largely irrelevant – it is the patient's response to the thoughts that matters. In this respect, BA is similar to ACT.

Avoidance

ACT stresses the role of experiential avoidance – that is, the unwillingness of the depressed individual to tolerate unpleasant experiences, which then leads to less flexibility and effectiveness. According to Zettle (chapter 7), experiential avoidance means not only avoiding unpleasant experiences of an external reality, but also avoiding unpleasant thoughts through attempts at thought suppression. Rumination is also viewed as a form of experiential avoidance, since it is directed inwards and leads to avoidance of contact with the external world. ACT proposes that the avoidance of emotions such as sadness and dysphoria leads to depressive responses such as thought suppression and avoidant behaviour. Thus depression is viewed as a response to 'negative mood states'. In a nutshell, since experiential avoidance impedes the ability and flexibility to pursue valued goals, it can cause and maintain depression.

The BA model places considerable emphasis on avoidance and passivity as problematic responses to negative mood. According to this model, individuals respond to their sad feelings by remaining passive and avoiding 'risky' activities, such as proactive behaviour. This passivity and avoidance results in fewer positive rewards and generates further negative mood, which in turn causes further passivity and avoidance. Avoidance in BA is understood in terms of reducing the individual's effectiveness to produce rewarding consequences. An initial and continuing feature of BA is a 'functional analysis' of the patient's response to negative mood states or life events. Behaviour is defined in terms of its frequency, duration, intensity, and topography (chapter 9), which provide ongoing targets for evaluation and behavioural change. This functional analysis examines how problematic responses such as withdrawal, isolation, or passivity are reinforced by their effect – an immediate reduction of anxiety ('I feel relieved, I am not going to the party') – but they undermine the opportunities for more rewarding behaviours. Avoidance works – but only in the short term.

There is less emphasis on the reasons for avoidance in the BA model and more emphasis on the dysfunction that ensues from avoidance. ACT and BA are similar in stressing the role of avoidance in the maintenance of depression; but ACT emphasizes the internal experience, whereas BA stresses active behaviours.

The cognitive model views avoidance in terms of confirmation bias for depressive thoughts. Avoidance prevents the individual from learning that his or her negative beliefs are incorrect, thereby maintaining the depression. For example, the individual who believes that people will reject her if she goes to a party will avoid that party, thereby not allowing herself to disconfirm her negative thoughts. Avoidance is linked to beliefs that confirm the rationality of avoidance. Accordingly, the cognitive therapist will focus on the reasons or the rationale for avoidance – that is, the content of the thoughts that justify avoidance in the patient's view. The cognitive model differs from the ACT model in that it emphasizes avoidance of unpleasant experiences; that is, ACT is an experiential model, whereas the cognitive model stresses the role that avoidance serves in maintaining negative thoughts.

The cognitive model contains a number of techniques aimed at directly addressing the patient's rationale for avoidance. For example, the 'vertical arrow' technique asks the patient to consider the string of implications of confronting the situation: 'If that happened, what would happen next? Then what would happen after that?' Another technique of addressing avoidance is to consider the worst-case scenario and imagine how one would cope. Moreover, cognitive therapists, utilizing ideas derived from Ellis, also ask patients to practise their fear – for example, in 'shame exercises' – or, in the case of panic disorder, to utilize panic induction techniques in order to experience the feared symptoms (D. M. Clark, 1986). For example, in the case of Gail as presented in chapter 7, the patient avoided co-workers and interacting with her daughters because she believed that she was not liked by co-workers and that her daughters would not want to play with her. These thoughts were tested out through behavioural experiments that resulted in reducing the credibility of the thoughts. It is important to realize that cognitive therapy focuses on thoughts in order to reduce their credibility and therefore their power, not in order to suppress them.

The metacognitive model views avoidance as a response to the occurrence of thoughts with a negative content: more precisely, one responds to a thought as if that required avoidance. Thus an individual may believe that negative thoughts must be suppressed because they will go out of control and engulf that individual (chapters 6 and 12). Avoidance is part of a thought suppression strategy that further engages the individual in rumination. In contrast to this entanglement with content, the metacognitive model emphasizes the independence of thinking about thinking. Detached mindfulness exercises train the patient to allow thoughts without controlling them, thus demonstrating that thoughts need not be avoided (Wells, 2009). Moreover, by recognizing that thoughts are simply events that may not be relevant to goals, the individual can treat negative thoughts as background noise, while pursuing real-life experiences that are rewarding and enhance efficacy. Absorption with thought examination and thought control (i.e., the key ingredients of rumination) is viewed as interfering with other real-life goals.

Mental control

The ACT model proposes that individuals may attempt to suppress, avoid, or control negative thoughts or experiences because they believe that all these are problematic, require action, need to be addressed, or are important in some significant way (chapter 7). Implicit in the ACT model is the idea that depression is often the result of overinvolvement in thinking and underinvolvement in valued action. Attempts to control thinking lead to the rebound of these negative and unwanted thoughts, further spiralling into more failed attempts at control. While attempting to control thoughts and feelings, the individual becomes less flexible and further removed from reality (Hayes, Strosahl, & Wilson, 2003).

ACT emphasizes mindfulness by assisting the patient to stand back, defuse a thought, stay in the here and now, and take a non-judgemental attitude to the thought. Mindfulness is understood in terms of relational frame theory, as changing the individual's relationship to the thought. The acceptance and commitment therapist encourages the patient to point to the thought – 'There's a thought' – and to recognize it as an event rather than as something fused with reality or with the patient.

The metacognitive model asserts that attempts to suppress or control negative thoughts maintain problematic coping (thought suppression, thought avoidance, overengagement with the content of thought) and thereby lead to perseveration in ruminating or worrying. The depressed individual holds two sets of beliefs about rumination: positive beliefs that rumination helps solve problems, motivates, and avoids surprise; and negative beliefs that rumination is uncontrollable or will damage one's mind. Thus the depressed ruminator is locked in a catch 22: 'I need to ruminate and I need to stop ruminating'. In the metacognitive model mental control is desirable, but it consists specifically of the patient's discovery that s/he has control over worry and rumination; it is a change in metacognitive beliefs.

The BA model views attempts at mental control as needless, self-directed, and avoidant behavioural patterns. According to this model, mental control is in conflict with adaptive, active, rewarding behaviour in the 'real world'. Mental control further reinforces passivity and isolation, limiting the opportunities for reinforcement. Rather than controlling mental content, the behaviour therapist focuses on controlling reinforcing outcomes. Effectiveness is in the external world.

The cognitive model has sometimes been criticized as emphasizing mental control – that is, suppression of, struggle, or entanglement with thinking. One can view this criticism in two ways. First, it would be hard to imagine how control or suppression of thinking is reflected in the typical techniques employed by cognitive therapists – namely monitoring, rating, labelling, and categorizing thoughts. Second, the evaluation of thoughts – through cost–benefit analysis, semantic techniques, examination of the evidence, and rational role play – is not an attempt to suppress thoughts. Rather this evaluation is an attempt to deprive thoughts of credibility and impact. Consider the following metaphor: rather than putting the brakes on the car, the cognitive therapist will take the air out of the tires. The tires are still there, but the car is not going anywhere.

Rules and valued life

ACT suggests that depressed individuals rigidly follow 'rules' rather than rely on their empirical observation of consequences and experiences; this leads them to repeatedly engage in self-defeating or unrewarding behaviours. Further, ACT places considerable emphasis on valued action, encouraging patients to clarify the dreams, values, and goals that comprise a meaningful life. Once these more encompassing values and goals are in focus, the individual can be encouraged to tolerate difficult experiences and engage in greater flexibility as a means to valued ends.

Zettle claims that self-reference language adds to and maintains the depression: 'Not surprisingly, discomfort in and believability of self-relevant negative thoughts appear to be closely linked and to covary as a function of the level of associated attachment or fusion with them' (chapter 7, p. 180). It is unclear to me, however, how this differs from the cognitive model, which asserts that depressed patients *believe* their negative thoughts about themselves. Depression is not reducible to 'having a negative thought' – it is related, in the cognitive model, *to believing the thought*. The credibility of thoughts is key. It is unclear what is meant by 'associated attachment or fusion', unless this is simply another way of saying that self-critical depressed people believe that their thoughts reflect reality. But this distinction between thoughts and reality is a hallmark of cognitive therapy, not in contradiction to it. Moreover, the ACT model suggests that one is fused with a thought and that ACT helps the individual defuse the thought or distance him-/herself from it. But this is the goal of cognitive therapy as well. Indeed the cognitive therapist encourages the patient to stand back, observe his/her thoughts, record them, evaluate the costs and benefits of the thought, and evaluate the evidence.

ACT places considerable emphasis on a 'valued life', encouraging the patient to identify the values and meanings that are important to him or her. This emphasis on values is an important motivational component of ACT and is not a key part of any of the other CBT approaches discussed here. Linehan (1993) has incorporated values in her modifications of dialectical behaviour therapy.

Although the behaviour therapist and the cognitive therapist might encourage patients to identify short-term and long-term goals, these are not the same as 'values'. According to ACT, behaviours may be reframed in terms of the overall values towards which they are aimed. For example, changing diapers could be a burden or could be reframed as an expression of being a good parent. The cognitive therapist does not typically address the issue of values, but certainly reframing is a key technique in cognitive therapy. For example, losses or 'failures' may be reframed as 'learning experiences'.

The cognitive therapist focuses on 'maladaptive assumptions' or 'conditional rules' – such as 'I must be perfect to be loved', or 'If I fail at something then I am a failure'. These assumptions or rules are related to core beliefs or personal schemas of the form 'I am unlovable' or 'I am incompetent'. The goal of therapy is to identify these assumptions or rules and modify them so that they become more flexible, realistic, and empowering. For example, the conditional rule 'I am a failure if I fail at a task' might be changed to 'Everyone fails at something. I can learn from failure'. Similarly, the cognitive therapist examines the patient's value system to determine whether that system creates more problems for the patient. Values such as 'I must be perfect' or 'I must always please everyone' are examined in terms of pragmatic outcomes. The goal in therapy is to replace inflexible and rigid values and rules with more flexible, realistic, and self-accepting thoughts. However, the cognitive therapist generally does not identify the specific valued action that the acceptance and commitment therapist might identify.

MCT does not include the idea of valued action or clarification of values as a major component of therapy. The emphasis in treatment is to modify the cognitive attentional syndrome so that it does not interfere with living a life that is more rewarding and less encumbered. Values, of course, could become a focus of MCT – there is nothing in the model to preclude it. However, values are not a main concern. The MCT does address the idea of rigid rules in terms of the CAS. Specifically, individuals who are captured by the CAS follow rules such as the following:

'If an intrusive thought occurs, I must attend to it.'
'I must immediately find an answer.'
'I cannot allow a thought to persist. I must stop it.'
'My worry protects me and keeps me from being surprised.'
'My worry is dangerous.'

These metacognitive rules comprise the positive and negative views of rumination and worry and they are targets for change. New, more flexible relationships with intrusive thoughts are encouraged: 'These are only mental events. I can watch them and let them go. I can postpone attending to them. I can get on with life.'

Causal mechanisms and targets for treatment

How does change come about? Implicit in this question is the issue of what we are measuring as a change. The cognitive model measures change in terms of symptoms and content of thinking; the behavioural model stresses changes in rewarding behaviour; the ACT model emphasizes flexibility and effectiveness in pursuing valued goals; and the metacognitive model stresses not only changes in symptoms, but also changes in independence from one's thoughts. Let's take a closer look at each approach.

Behavioural approaches place greater emphasis on actual behaviour and on quality of life. Is the patient actually doing things differently? Is the patient pursuing valued goals? The behavioural approach to depression views the causal mechanism of change as increasing behaviours that lead to reward, decreasing behaviours that lead to negative consequences, decreasing maladaptive avoidance, increasing skills that lead to desired outcomes, and changing the patient's habitual response of passivity and avoidance. Change is focused on acting rather than thinking, or even feeling. The assumption is that acting differently will lead to feeling differently – but one does not wait to feel motivated or feel better to act better. This is a revolutionary concept for many patients who believe that they have to be motivated to change their behaviour. It is behaviour that is activated, not motivation. Indeed motivation may often occur after the behaviour has been reinforced many times.

The ACT model proposes that flexibility, acceptance, and committed action are the processes that underlie change in behaviour and in the quality of life. The ACT model assists the patient in identifying values and goals that 'pull' behaviour forward – it is almost teleological in the sense that the emphasis is on the purpose one has rather than on the reasons, feelings, or thoughts that one might entertain. There is little emphasis on content of thoughts. The ACT model proposes that the content of thought is less important than the individual's relationship with a thought – or the person's relationship with his or her values. Thus one can have a negative thought many times, but treat the thought as a parallel event that does not control or determine feelings or behaviour. Flexibility presupposes an ability to modify behaviour depending on the demands of the situation and in accordance with valued goals. Moreover, flexibility allows one to let go, observe, or accept thoughts and experiences rather than struggle against them. The

ACT model stresses the importance of 'experience' and the willingness to tolerate it rather than demand that it be of a certain way. Thus in ACT the patient can learn to tolerate the sensations of anxiety, but still pursue valued goals. Anxiety becomes disentangled from goal-oriented behaviour.

CBT stresses changes in symptoms such as self-criticism, hopelessness, sadness, indecisiveness, loss of interest, and hopelessness. These symptoms, often assessed with the Beck Depression Inventory (BDI), are subjective reports of experience. One can adapt cognitive therapy to focus on certain symptoms rather than others. For example, the clinician can focus on the cognitive content of self-critical thinking, using a wide variety of cognitive techniques (e.g., defining the terms, examining the costs and benefits, evaluating the evidence). The cognitive model maintains that change occurs because of modifications in the *content* and believability of thoughts – for example, the self-critical patient comes to have more balanced, less negative views of him-/herself. Changes in behaviour, in this model, are subsumed under cognitive processes; hence behaviour is important in behavioural experiments that modify the content of thoughts. An important point to keep in mind is that the credibility of the thought is the essential issue. The cognitive therapist will ask the patient, 'How much do you believe that thought?' and 'How would you rate your feelings when you now have that thought?' Thus the goal is to take away the impact of negative thoughts, not to suppress them.

The metacognitive therapist views the process of change as one of helping the patient to recognize the dual nature of thinking about thinking. Thus the therapist helps the patient to identify positive (e.g., 'My worry prepares me for the worst') and negative ('If I allow myself to worry I will go out of control and become insane') beliefs about rumination or worry. The paradox is resolved when the patient recognizes that intrusive thoughts do not require attention or obedience and that one can observe thoughts as mental events. The mechanism modifies the patient's beliefs about the power and importance of thinking. Outcomes can be evaluated not only in terms of changes in symptoms of depression, but also in the degree to which rumination, worry, and the metacognitive beliefs beneath them persist.

Strengths and Weaknesses

Clinicians may have difficulty deciding which of these four approaches to depression to use. The advantages of the cognitive therapy approach are that there is considerable empirical support for its effectiveness and for its longer-term success in preventing relapse and suicide risk. Also, cognitive therapy is a comprehensive model of psychopathology, providing specific interventions for a wide range of diagnostic categories. It has a comprehensive model of aetiology and personality differences. Cognitive therapy addresses many of the specific symptoms of depression – for example, self-criticism, regrets, helplessness, indecision, hopelessness – with a range of specific techniques. Cognitive therapy uses behavioural techniques (such as graded task assignment, reward menus, activity schedules), and the question has been raised whether these behavioural techniques are sufficient in the absence of cognitive techniques. Nonetheless, the research on cognitive therapy overwhelming supports its effectiveness (chapter 5).

The advantages of BA are that the interventions can be implemented immediately, the model is easily understood by patients, and clinicians do not require extensive training. These are significant advantages in the real world of clinical work, since the dissemination of clinical treatment may depend considerably on the ease of delivery. BA has immense ecological validity – it makes practical sense. For this reason, many people may find it more acceptable. The disadvantages are that it is not a comprehensive model of psychopathology: it lacks any description of aetiology, individual differences, or personality disorders. Of course, one can argue that aetiology is based on learning history and identifying the non-contingency of behaviour in one's socialization history – and that in this way one can account for individual differences. Thus an experience of loss (e.g., of mother) during childhood can be viewed as a loss of reinforcements that predisposes the individual towards depression. The cognitive model would interpret this loss as the basis for persistent negative schemas, which direct attention and memory in a biased way and undermine the sense of personal effectiveness or personal desirability. The behavioural model does not appear to provide a clear explanation of the self-critical content of depression: Why would the absence of reward lead to self-critical thinking? Moreover, one can argue that there is no clear description of the 'meaning' of rewarding experiences: Why are some consequences rewarding while others are not?

The ACT model has the advantage of incorporating behavioural activation, exposure, and decision making, while also linking them to higher values. The emphasis on values is an important part of contemporary ACT and allows the therapist to enrich the meaning of therapy. ACT also has an advantage in that it emphasizes flexibility and tolerance to emotional experience – two important components of adaptation. Disadvantages of this approach include the absence of a model of aetiology, individual differences, and personality disorder. Furthermore, there is no clear description of the values one should pursue – only reliance on the pragmatic criterion of 'whatever works'. But pragmatism is a poor substitute for moral judgement.

ACT has made considerable progress in advancing an innovative and intriguing model of psychopathology. However, some processes identified in the model are consistent with processes in other approaches – especially the approaches described in this volume. For example, fusion with content makes the ACT model not dissimilar to the cognitive model, which distinguishes thoughts from reality, or to the metacognitive model, which stresses the processes or architecture of thinking (e.g., thinking about thinking) rather than the specific content of thoughts. The role of experiential avoidance in ACT is similar to the role of avoidance in behavioural activation theory, although ACT places greater emphasis on the 'experience' of engagement (or avoidance) than on behavioural avoidance. Indeed, it is the strong emphasis on internal experience that characterizes ACT as considerably different from other CBT approaches. It is ironic that a behavioural approach should emphasize internal experience.

Finally, MCT has the advantage of providing a sophisticated model of a theory of mind, focusing on the cognitive attentional syndrome as a factor of vulnerability in relation to rumination and worry. MCT is able to relate experiential exercises and metaphors to modifying the patient's belief about how his or her mind works. Techniques are directed at the patient's maladaptive responses, giving rise to a more adaptive model of mind. Currently MCT does not appear to have a model of aetiology, development, or personality disorders, although the model of mental functioning might be a good template for these investigations.

Future Developments

Each of these CBT approaches provides powerful and effective techniques for change. They all appear to be helpful in the treatment of depression. But a comprehensive theory of depression based on any of these models would require further development. First, of these four theories, the cognitive model is the only one that appears to have a developmental model underpinning it. Thus Beck proposed that early personal schemas about self, other, and the world are established during childhood, as a result of socialization experiences that lead to the emergence of schemas or specific contents (e.g., 'unlovable', 'defective', 'helpless') and of maladaptive rules or conditional assumptions (e.g., 'I must be perfect to be loved'). The behavioural model has an implicit etiological theory of non-contingency of reinforcement of skill deficits; but the model appears to lack a clear etiological approach. Similarly, both ACT and MCT lack aetiological approaches. Now, one can have an excellent theory of change without positing aetiology, but it would be intriguing to see how these theories could expand.

Secondly, each of these theories places very little emphasis on the nature of the therapeutic relationship, although there is significant research to demonstrate that this relationship can have substantial effects on the outcome of therapy. Indeed the relationship may often seem didactic in each of these approaches, although skilled and experienced therapists will often modify their agenda to address the interactions that invariably become part of therapy.

General Conclusions

Psychological therapies have come a long way in the last three decades, with significant contributions from all five of these approaches. There is no definitive evidence to date that one approach is better than any other and no evidence that any one technique or experience is a necessary condition for change. This is because definitive comparative studies of these newer treatments have yet to be conducted. From a practical point of view, psychologists often seek to engage in a form of construct reductionism – for example, 'it all comes down to exposure' or 'it all comes down to changing thoughts'. However, such a process denies closer scrutiny of specific underlying psychological mechanisms that connect exposure or thinking with emotional outcomes such as recovery from depression. The approaches reviewed in this book go beyond reductionism by implicating different mechanisms and processes in treating depression.

References

Clark, D. M. (1986). A cognitive approach to panic. *Behaviour Research & Therapy*, *24*(4), 461–470.

Hayes, S. C., Strosahl, K. D., & Wilson, K. G. (2003). *Acceptance and commitment therapy: An experiential approach to behavior change*. New York: Guilford.

Linehan, M. M. (1993). *Skills training manual for treating borderline personality disorder*. New York: Guilford.

Martell, C. R., Dimidjian, S., & Herman-Dunn, R. (2010). *Behavioral activation for depression: A clinician's guide*. New York: Guilford.

Stewart, W. F., Ricci, J. A., Chee, E., Hahn, S. R., & Morganstein, D. (2003). Cost of lost productive work time among US workers with depression. *Journal of the American Medical Association*, *289*, 3135–3144.

Wells, A. (2009). *Metacognitive therapy for anxiety and depression*. New York: Guilford.

Wells, A., & Matthews, G. (1994). *Attention and emotion: A clinical perspective*. Hove, England: Lawrence Erlbaum.

Wells, A., & Matthews, G. (1996). Modelling cognition in emotional disorder: The S-REF model. *Behaviour Research and Therapy*, *34*, 881–888.

Young, J. E. (1990). *Cognitive therapy for personality disorders: A schema-focused approach*. Sarasota, FL: Professional Resource Exchange.

Further Reading

Beck, A. T. (1967). *Depression: Clinical, experimental and theoretical aspects*. New York: Harper & Row.

Beck, A. T., & Steer, R. A. (1987). *Manual for the Revised Beck Depression Inventory*. San Antonio, TX: Psychological Corporation.

Beck, A. T., Freeman, A., Davis, D. D., Pretzer, J., Fleming, B., Artz, A. … Renton, J. (2004). *Cognitive therapy of personality disorders* (2nd edn). New York: Guilford Press.

Ellis, A., & Harper, R. A. (1975). *A new guide to rational living*. Englewood Cliffs, NJ: Prentice Hall.

Leahy, R. L. (2003). *Cognitive therapy techniques: A practitioner's guide*. New York: Guilford.

Epilogue

In this volume we have brought together theory and practice at the leading edge of depression treatment. We have seen that there are different types of explanation leading to different treatment approaches for the same problem. While cognitive behaviour therapy (CBT) has traditionally focussed on identifying and challenging the content of thoughts and beliefs about the self and the world, other approaches such as metacognitive therapy (MCT) have focused on beliefs about cognition and its regulation (control of worry and rumination). In contrast, the third-wave approaches draw on meditation and acceptance techniques in order to reduce the struggle with suffering. Inevitably conceptual drift occurs in clinical practice, where clinicians draw on several perspectives simultaneously. However, a driving force in producing *Treating Depression* was the view that we must discriminate between approaches, both in order to understand them fully as we set the stage for investigating relative efficacy and in order to integrate and develop techniques in a way that is complementary. These challenges can only be met if therapists and researchers understand at a conceptual *and* practical level what the distinctive features of existing and emerging approaches are really about. We must resist the tendency to lump ideas and principles together as *same as*, for the sake of cognitive economy, without first looking for fundamental differences.

The clinical accounts of the treatments presented in this book will serve to guide clinicians in the real-world application of these therapies. But we must not be complacent in assuming that treatment manuals are sufficient for the acquisition of therapy skills. The most effective application of each of

Treating Depression: MCT, CBT and Third Wave Therapies, First Edition.
Edited by Adrian Wells and Peter L. Fisher.

the treatments described in this volume is crucially dependent on training, supervision, and practice. We believe that this is especially true in the case of clinicians wishing to use a variety of approaches effectively, because they depend on distinct mental models of the therapy process and its goals. For instance, what the therapist does in CBT is to engage the client in a dialogue and in behaviours that put ideas about the self and world to the test of reality. Conversely, the metacognitive therapist must refrain from this type of discourse about 'things' and must instead encourage the patient to reduce the amount of analysis that is linked to negative ideas – in other words to regulate cognition in new ways. However, some analysis of the validity of metacognitive beliefs is expected. In mindfulness and acceptance-based approaches, this struggle with one's inner experience is managed by reducing conceptual activity; but this is accomplished in different and less specific ways, by increasing openness and acceptance and a non-judgemental stance. The therapist must choose not only what to do on the basis of a particular model, but also the best way of doing it within the constraints set by that model. These matters depend on the clinician's acquired knowledge and beliefs about the unique, conflicting, and shared features of therapies. When clinicians are in possession of this knowledge, they can maintain theoretical and practical rigour in what they do and can deliver well-grounded choices and options that make a difference to their patients' lives.

Adrian Wells, PhD
Peter L. Fisher, PhD

Index

AAQ (Acceptance and Action Questionnaire) 179
abandonment 121, 129, 133, 254
  shy children less able to cope with 131
Abela, J. R. Z. 127
Abramson, L. Y. 118, 119, 126, 127, 197
acceptance 320, 321, 335, 344, 349, 350, 356, 361, 414
  breathing space consistent with focus on 357
  increasing 415
  measures of 42
  mindful 250
  non-judgemental 348, 354, 362
  quality characterized by 201
  skilful first step towards preventing relapse 203
  specific strategies to cultivate 390
  widespread 91
  withdrawal of 124
  see also ACT; self-acceptance
accounts of language
  comprehensive and systematic 175
  contextualistic-behavioural 169
  post-Skinnerian 319
acedia 3
acetylcholine 85–86
ACT (acceptance and commitment therapy) 52, 53, 169–193, 242–244, 247, 249–250, 256–258, 390, 395, 397–400, 402–412, 414, 415
  behavioural assignments utilized by 394
  experiential avoidance and 180–181
  fusion in 177–180
  rule following and 183–185
  treating depression with 319–343
  see also AAQ
ACTH (adrenocorticotropic hormone) 87
activity monitoring 229, 234, 378–380, 386
acute depression
  life interference due to 53
  treatment of 196, 207, 234, 344–368
acute-phase CBT 69
  depressive symptoms and 56–61
  patients well at exit from 61–64
  relapse or recurrence 64–68
acute stress disorder 156

Treating Depression: MCT, CBT and Third Wave Therapies, First Edition.
Edited by Adrian Wells and Peter L. Fisher.

Addis, M. E. 178, 179, 237, 372
adjunct therapies 290–291
adrenal glands 87
  see also HPA
aetiology 117, 119, 121, 411, 412
  comprehensive model of 410
  developmental 257
  negative schematic content and 125
affect 135, 148, 151
  depressed/depressive 34, 326
  positive 34
  see also negative affect
affective disorders *see* SADS
affective disturbance 122
affective schemas 124, 125
  see also cognitive-affective schemas
affective sensations/experiences 305, 309
affective states
  severe 200
  unwanted 181
affective symptoms 32, 41
agitation 5, 32, 38, 362, 365
  irritability and 41
  psychomotor retardation vs 27
  restlessness and 353
agoraphobia 158
Akiskal, H. S. 62
Alba, J. W. 134, 135
alcohol 86, 147, 149, 299
  self-medication through 312, 377
alcohol abuse 9, 157
Allen, K. B. 211
Allen, N. B. 195
Allott, R. 157
allowing/letting be 356–358
Alloy, L. B. 118, 126, 127
alprazolam 86
Alvarez, J. 246
Amenson, C. S. 226, 227–278
American College of Neuropsychopharmacology 55
American Psychiatric Institute for Research and Education 43
American Psychiatric Press 31
American Psychological Association Task Force 269
amino acid 92, 92
amitriptyline 93, 231
AMPA receptors 86
amygdala 71, 89, 90, 98, 161
anhedonia 34, 39, 40, 85, 336
antidepressants 38, 57, 90, 98, 150, 230, 235, 267, 345, 363, 374
  chronic treatment 85
  clear need for alternatives to 195
  cognitive and physical side effects 36
  decision to cease taking 293
  failure to respond to 161
  first-generation 92–93
  longer term therapy 96–97
  resistance to 316
  second-generation 93–95
  some individuals cannot take 195
  strong effects on core symptoms 86
  unsuccessful 344, 371
  withdrawal of/from 97, 205
  see also M-ADM; monoamine systems; SGA; TCAs
antiepileptics 86
antihypertensive treatment 82
antipsychotic medication 81, 95, 150
anxiety 147, 150, 160, 163, 236, 250, 273, 333, 340, 360
  alcohol used to temper feelings of 377
  emotional component of 154
  generalized 93, 144
  learning to tolerate sensations of 409
  mild 265, 267, 292, 297
  moderate 292
  prominent 94
  proneness to 155
  psychic 28

reduction of 161, 384, 403
relief from 323
social 93, 154, 228, 370
somatic 28
symptoms of 10, 157
see also anxiety disorders; BAI; HADS
anxiety disorders 30, 157, 161, 252
comorbidity between depression and 10, 182
criteria for 273
social 292
SSRI class have established efficacy for 93
traumatic childhood experiences and 87
see also GAD
APA (American Psychiatric Association) 91–93, 96, 171
see also DSM
apathy 3, 333, 336
Arieti, S. 118
aripiprazole 95
Armento, M. E. A. 226, 227
Artin, K. 35
Asmundson, G. J. G. 186
assessment 4, 15, 24–51, 67, 70, 151, 267, 274, 372, 374–381
behavioural 229, 373
benefits and risks of ongoing treatment 97
cognitive 396
contextual 322
daily mood-monitoring 226
detached mindfulness (DM) and rumination postponement 307
exposure element to 333
follow-up 231, 232
initial 297, 327–328
intake for depression in CT 272–273
metacognitive 298, 299
negative 258
omitting 55
pattern of 270
physiological 228
pre-treatment CR 208, 209
psychosocial functioning 68, 72–73
questionnaire-based 273
readiness for termination 280
reality-based 242
suicide 36, 42, 44, 277, 346
symptom 92, 245
three pillars of psychological flexibility 321–322
ATT (attention-training technique) 152, 160–161, 162, 163, 296, 303–304, 307, 400
attachment 129, 354
abandonment from significant figures 131
associated 181, 406
conceptualized self 176, 177, 181–182
dysfunctional 118
maladaptive 243
attentional-processing style 248
auto-reinforcement 258
Automatic Thoughts Questionnaire 354
autonomous relapse processes 212
autonomy 62, 124, 127, 131, 132, 277
avoidance 132, 146, 212, 249, 270, 296, 312–314, 354, 357, 362, 363, 375, 396, 399
addressing 404
assessing the costs of 326–328
decreased 237
downward spiral of 225
emotional 326, 329, 331
formulation and resolution of 387
increased 224–225, 275–276
ineffectiveness of 329
interpersonal 370

avoidance (*contd.*)
maintained through negative reinforcement 377
maladaptive 408
model that proposes depression is consequence of 394
modifying 381, 384–385
passivity and 394, 395, 400, 403, 408
patterns of 319, 326, 331, 370, 383, 386, 387, 389
reasons or rationale for 403
tendency towards 370
thought 405
triggered 387
see also behavioural avoidance; experiential avoidance
avoidant response 135, 236

BA (behavioural activation) approach 364, 369–392
activity scheduling and 229, 381–384, 391
early models 221–275
empirical status 225–228, 230–233
integration with CBT 233–234
reinforcement schedules and 228–229
rumination and 387–388
severe cases 235
treating depression with 369–392
Baer, L. 36, 37
Baer, Ruth A. 211, 212
Bagby, R. M. 26–27
BAI (Beck Anxiety Inventory) 273, 280, 292
Bains, J. 36
Ball, S. A. 133–134
Baranoff, J. 132, 133
Barber, J. P. 199, 246
Barnard, P. J. 119, 134, 135, 198
Barnes-Holmes, D. 169, 183, 184, 185, 319
Barnhofer, T. 345, 365
barriers 321, 339, 383, 390
assessing and troubleshooting 372
dealing with 349–351
identifying 332–333, 384, 388
internal and external 335, 338
language 35
potential 389
basal ganglia 89, 91
BATD (brief behavioural activation treatment for depression) 235–6
BDI (Beck Depression Inventory) 9, 31–32, 34, 36, 56, 58–63, 92, 98, 160, 205, 231, 267, 317, 409
BDI-FS (Beck Depression Inventory-Fast Screen) 33
BDI-II (Beck Depression Inventory-II) 32, 33, 42, 235, 267, 273, 277, 280, 297, 344, 374
BDI-PC (Beck Depression Inventory for Primary Care) 32–33, 36
BDNF (brain-derived neurotrophic factor) 83, 88, 89
Beach, S. R. 62
Beck, A. T. 52, 53, 71, 118–132, 134–136, 185, 196, 197, 200, 208, 233, 242, 244–247, 253–254, 269–270, 364
see also BAI; BDI
Beck, J. 273, 274, 275, 277, 283
Beevers, C. G. 127
behaviour and its causes 170, 171–172
behaviour-cued contingencies 377, 378, 381
behaviour therapy 231, 319, 405
dialectical 201, 388, 406
rationale for 230
see also CBT
behavioural activation
strategies 233–234, 236, 381–389
theory 221–241, 250–253, 255, 411
see also BA approach

behavioural avoidance 326, 329–330, 331, 411
ingrained patterns of 370
pervasive use of 325
behavioural schemas 125
behavioural symptoms 4, 32
Belaise, C. 62
Bemporad, J. R. 118
benzodiazepines 86
Berg, K. 183
Berns, S. B. 59
Berv, D. A. N. 39
between-session practice 234, 303, 342, 372–373, 383, 398
reinforced 230
see also homework
bidirectionality 122, 177, 180, 182
common type of 173–174
Bieling, P. J. 211
biopsychosocial developmental processes 256
bipolar disorder 29, 38, 71, 86, 207
distinguishing unipolar from 31
identifying and diagnosing 39
see also SAD-P
Bishop, S. 196
Bjelland, I. 37
Blackburn, I. M. 56, 63, 67, 126, 196
Blatt, S. J. 119
blood pressure 92, 94
Bockting, C. 68
Boland, R. J. 4, 12
Bondolfi, G. 204, 205
borderline personality disorder 254
boredom 323, 325, 348, 349, 350, 360
Bourassa, M. G. 9
Bower, G. H. 135
Bowlby, John 118
brain *see* amygdala; basal ganglia; BDNF; Brodman areas; cortex; DBS; ECT; hippocampus; neurotransmitters; TMS; VNS
breath
attention to 349, 354, 356, 357
deep 335, 363, 397
maintaining awareness of 356
mindfulness of 202, 203, 351–354
sitting meditation that focuses on 349, 354, 356, 358
breathing spaces 203, 353, 354, 356, 357–358, 359, 360, 361
Brenner, C. 118
Breslau, N. 88
Brodman areas 90, 91, 99
Brosse, A. L. 56
Brown, K. W. 201, 211, 243
Brownstein, A. J. 170, 171, 172
Bruce, M. L. 127
Buddhist traditions 202, 244
Buis, T. 126
Bulls' Eye Value Clarification Exercise 338
bupropion 94, 95
Butler, A. C. 56, 58
Butler, G. 154

Caldwell, N. D. 183
Campbell, E. A. 181
Campbell, S. E. 154
Canadian Community & Health Survey 9
Cantu, M. S. 226
Cardaciotto, L. 252
Cardiac Depression Scale 31, 33–34, 35
cardiac mortality risk 9
cardiovascular disease 29
Carter, K. 156, 157
Cartwright-Hatton, S. 157, 315
CAS (cognitive-attentional syndrome) 145–149, 152–156, 158, 296, 298, 400, 401, 411
causal role of 159
central feature of 162

CAS (*contd.*)
  DM incompatible with 305
  modifying 407
  triggers that would lead to activation of 314
case conceptualization 273–277, 298–302, 321–326
Cassian, John 3
CBASP (Cognitive Behavioral Analysis System of Psychotherapy) 62, 69
CBT (cognitive behaviour therapy) 145, 244, 246, 269–294, 335, 389–390, 393, 395, 406, 411
  behavioural activation and 233–234
  change after exposure to 68–70
  changes in symptoms stressed in 409
  core technique of 250
  distancing addressed by 399
  each model is collaborative 398
  efficacy for depression 52–80, 250
  group 363, 364
  randomized trials on 71–72
  responses to 127, 161
  second wave in 186
  traditional focus of 414
  treating depression with 269–294
  what the therapist does in 415
  see also acute-phase CBT; MBCT
C-CT (continuation-phase CT) treatment 54, 55, 62, 67–68, 70
CDS (NIMH Collaborative Program on the Psycho-biology of Depression Study) 9, 11–12, 31
  see also Cardiac Depression Scale
cerebral cortex *see* cortex
CES-D (Center for Epidemiological Studies Depression Scale) 34–35
Chambers, L. L. 226
Chambless, D. L. 213, 269
Champion, L. A. 134
Chapman, J. E. 56
Chelminski, I. 61
child-parent experiences 118
Chiu, A. W. 246
Chomsky, Noam 175
Chung, H. 40
CIDI (WHO Composite International Diagnostic Interview) 6
circadian rhythm 88
citalopram 93
Clark, D. A. 123, 124, 125, 132, 244, 401
Clark, D. M. 404
Clark, L. A. 56, 62, 64, 69, 70, 127, 244
classical conditioning 174, 221, 222, 377, 378
clinical depression 158, 231, 253, 365
  ACT application to treatment of 319–343
  chronic 179
  development of 125
  escalation into 181
  onset of 258n(2)
clinical trials 26, 71, 98, 210, 230
  major 62
  multicentre 29
  see also RCTs
clinician ratings 26–31, 38, 42, 273
clomipramine 92, 93
cocaine 82
Coelho, H. F. 204, 205, 206
Coffman, S. J. 235
cognition 34, 98, 121, 170, 250, 251, 284
  behavioural assignments used to test out 394
  beliefs about 146, 148–150, 157–159, 414
  bodily conditions can elicit 362
  comprehensive and systematic account of 175
  content of 390

contextualistic-behavioural account of 169
control of 145, 156, 163, 401
dysfunctional 233
implicit 245
monitored 145
negative 122, 127, 249, 283
objective awareness of 305
patterns of 135
possible to alter 221
power of 281
regulation of 162, 414, 415
rumination has negative effect on 149
techniques to challenge 278
theories of 176
therapies which deemphasize the role of 271
triggering 305
cognitive-affective processing 209
cognitive-affective schemas 125, 253
cognitive-attentional syndrome *see* CAS
cognitive-conceptual schemas 125
cognitive diathesis-stress 118, 126, 253
cognitive-interpersonal conceptualization 119
cognitive personality orientations/constructs *see* autonomy; sociotropy
cognitive reactivity 71, 126, 207–209
reducing the threat of 247
Cognitive Style Questionnaire 126
cognitive symptoms 32, 41
cognitive therapy *see* CBT; MCT
cognitive vulnerability 71, 124–125, 128, 211, 396
high/low 126
mindfulness-based 194, 197–199, 207
preexisting and dormant 118
refinement of 132
collaboration 70–71, 73–74, 97, 196, 272, 286, 372, 384, 389, 398
active 277
enthusiasm for 373–374
establishing 370
international 43
see also CSPP; NIMH
combinatorial entailment 173, 174, 177
compassion 328, 350, 351, 353, 357
concentration 38, 146, 266, 301, 348, 364
difficulty with 4, 25, 32, 297
poor 5, 344
problems common in acute depression 365
reduced 34
conditioning 228
see also classical conditioning; operant conditioning
consciousness, stance towards 247–250
Connolly Gibbons, M. B. 246
content of thoughts 395, 399, 402, 403, 408, 411
decentring from 358
depressed individuals may become overly focused on 400
detailed analysis of 396
differences in 198
identifying and challenging 414
modifying 401, 409
overengagement with 405
content specificity 130, 131
context-cued contingencies 377, 378
control-and-eliminate agenda 320, 328–329
controlled trials 98, 161
placebo 235
randomized 99, 204–207, 210–213, 244, 254, 317
see also clinical trials
Cooper, Z. 117

coping 146, 183, 233, 275, 371, 389
  adaptive 154
  alternative 387
  avoidant 311
  counterproductive methods 312
  helpful 247
  maladaptive 150, 154
  rigid modes of 254
  unhelpful 145, 149–150, 151–152, 153, 307
  with mood fluctuations 312
  see also coping responses; coping strategies; MACAM
coping responses 302, 305, 311
  effortful 306
  maladaptive 130, 132, 296, 400
coping strategies 147, 155, 156, 303
  changes in 246
  counterproductive 296, 297, 313
  less capable use of 84
  maladaptive 298, 311, 314
  metacognitive 145, 159
  problematic 396
  useful 158
  verbal 145
Corruble, E. 27
cortex 99
  medial orbital 90
  medial temporal 90–91
  mesotemporal 98
  see also prefrontal cortex
corticosteroids 89
cortisol 86, 87
Coryell, W. 9
Cottraux, J. 56
CPE (cognitive psychological education) 206
Craighead, W. E. 56, 62, 245, 252
Craigie, M. A. 204, 207
CRH (corticotrophin-releasing hormone) 83, 87
Cronbach's alpha 37, 38, 40
crying 32, 301, 330, 378
CSF (cerebrospinal fluid) 82, 85, 87
CSPP (WHO Collaborative Study on Psychological Problems in General Health Care) 14–15
Cucherat, M. 56
cued contingencies 377, 378, 381
Cuijpers, P. 56, 57
curiosity 196, 211, 347, 350, 362, 397
  friendly 348, 356
  quality characterized by 201

Dagnan, D. 178
Dahl, A. A. 37
Dahl, J. 338
Dalgleish, T. 134, 136
Daly, R. W. 3
DAS (Dysfunctional Attitudes Scale) 125–128, 197, 208, 245
Davies, M. 156
Davis, C. R. 33, 34
Davis, R. N. 183
DBS (deep brain stimulation) 97, 99–100
De Houwer, J. 128
De Raedt, R. 128
death 245
  family member 177
  semantic significance equivalent to 256
  thoughts of 5, 39, 152, 153, 267
decentring 200, 209, 401–402
  see also DM (detached mindfulness)
defusion 320–321, 335
deictic framing 175, 182
Delucchi, K. L. 40
delusions 3, 31
depressed mood 4–5, 28, 39, 40, 41, 282, 356, 380
  alleviation of 150

elevated DAS scores a consequence of 126
information-processing patterns activated in 208
intensified 199
intransient nature of 163
isolation at the first signs of 324
maintenance of 198, 209, 275
negative thoughts and 198, 270, 276, 351, 395
reduction in 331
rumination and 154–155, 178–179, 309
see also anhedonia
depression scales *see* CDS; CES-D; DMI; DRSST; HADS; HAMD; MDD-S; PHQ; SDS
depressive symptoms 9, 13, 42, 62, 63, 123, 150, 245
antidepressant effects on 86
causes of 85, 144
change in 69, 127, 252
comorbid 100
decrease in 295
factors that maintain 345
frequency of 39
identified 24
improvement in 100
intensity of 231–232
interaction that predicts increase in 126–127
measuring 33, 38, 231
metacognitive beliefs and 157
mild 292
minimal or no 70
moderate 70
predicting 126–127, 133
psycho-education about the nature of 203
relatively consistent constellations of 5
residual 12, 36, 70, 205, 207
resolution of 244
self-reported 133
severity of 26, 32, 307
situations that may elicit in the future 389
treatment for 14, 162, 213, 231, 252, 292
underlying cognitive processes and 122
see also acute depression; bipolar disorder; clinical depression; IDS; MDD; QIDS; reduction of depressive symptoms; severe depression; unipolar depression
DeRubeis, R. J. 57, 61, 62, 199, 246
despair 3, 266
desvenlafaxine 94
detached mindfulness *see* DM
Dewick, H. 154
Dexter-Mazza, E. T. 42
diagnosis of MDD 29, 36, 42, 62, 68, 363
criteria for 4–5, 37, 38, 160, 277, 297, 354, 374
differential 31
lifetime 30
physicians sometimes unwilling 15
Dimidjian, S. 57, 61, 62, 63, 235, 237, 251, 255–256, 345, 364, 365, 402
DISH (Depression Interview and Structured Hamilton) 28–29
distress 12, 126, 147, 273, 279
adaptive ways to respond to 357
attempt to avoid or eliminate 319
first major depressive episode often follows 11
powerful topics brought to mind 357
private experiences 319, 320, 321
rumination as mode of responding to 387
strategies used to control 156

distress (*contd.*)
therapist fails to show understanding and appreciation for 373
see also emotional distress
DLPFC (dorsolateral prefrontal cortex) 90, 91
DM (detached mindfulness) 200, 248, 257, 315, 404
metacognitive use of 397, 400
responding to 152–153, 163, 313
rumination postponement and 304–9
DMI-10/DMI-18 (Depression in the Medically Ill) Scales 35–36
Dobson, D. J. G. 270, 271, 272, 273, 286
Dobson, K. S. 10, 57–58, 68, 127, 128, 234, 251, 269–274, 277, 286
dopamine 81, 82, 85, 92
mesolimbic pathway 89
see also NDRIs
Doyle, K. 127, 244
Dozois, D. J. A. 125, 128
Drevets, W. C. 83, 86, 89, 90
DRSST (Depression Rating Scale Standardization Team) 28
DSM *(Diagnostic and Statistical Manual of Mental Disorders)* 4–8, 10, 11, 13, 15, 32, 33, 35–39, 43, 61, 158, 266, 277, 355
see also SCID
duloxetine 94
Dunn, T. W. 64
Dutch patients 41
see also NEMESIS
Dyck, M. J. 125
dysfunctional attitudes 84, 199
see also DAS
dysfunctional schemas 129, 197, 270
core 234
domination of 120
dysphoric mood 178, 180, 181, 198, 202, 207, 209
mild 212
dysthymia 29
comorbid 9, 11
dysthymic disorder 61, 70, 393

Eardley, D. A. 197
early maladaptive schemas 129–133, 246, 253–254
ECT (electro-convulsive therapy) 97, 99
Eifert, G. H. 227
Eisendrath, S. J. 207, 211, 212, 345, 365
Emery, G. 52, 121, 185, 196, 269
emotional distress 145
cognitive-attentional processes that predispose to 119
habitual patterns of reactivity increase 202
information-processing modes that heighten 201
somatic symptoms may be related to 34
emotional regulation 8
EMS (early maladaptive schemas) 129–133, 246, 254
Endicott, J. 11, 29
endogenous depression 91, 100
energy 322, 323, 327, 328, 330, 352, 384
elevated 39
lack of 5
loss of 32, 146
low 316, 324, 336
monitoring for increase in 146
psychic 398
ENRICHD (Enhancing Recovery in Coronary Heart Disease) 29
enzymes 82, 83, 85, 93
EQ (Experiences Questionnaire) 210, 211
Ernst, D. 125

escitalopram 93
ESEMeD (European Study of the Epidemiology of Mental Disorders) 6–7, 8, 13
Eunson, K. M. 196
experiential avoidance 176, 180–181, 182, 185, 186, 319
  ability and flexibility impeded by 402–403
  ACT and 402, 411
  problems with 325
experiential therapies 271
  see also process-experiential therapy
extinction 222, 223, 227, 255

factor analysis 33–34, 37, 39, 41, 133
failure 119, 122, 124, 221, 254, 280, 349, 380
  actual or potential appraisal of 276
  analysing the reasons underlying 145
  control 147
  past/previous 32, 33, 277, 288
  patient doomed to 248
  perceived 123
  personal 145, 147, 300, 323, 407
  prevention of 149, 248
  reframed 407
  treatment 272, 371
fatigue 5, 25, 34, 37, 38, 149, 223, 344, 377, 397
  focus on 150, 151
  increased 360
  perceived 125
  reduction in 370
  repeated catastrophizing about symptoms of 146
Fava, G. A. 36, 39, 62, 67, 94
FDA (US Food and Drug Administration) 56–57, 95–96, 97, 98
Feldman, G. 201, 252
Fennell, M. J. V. 181
Ferster, C. B. 52, 223, 224–225, 235, 236
Finnish adults 41
Finucane, A. 207, 365
First, M. B. 27, 374
Fisher, J. E. 269
Fisher, Peter 243, 249, 400
fluoxetine 92, 93, 95
FMI (Freiburg Mindfulness Inventory) 211
Forman, E. M. 56, 250
Fraley, R. C., 127
Franck, E. 128
Frankl, V. E. 177
Frasure-Smith, N. 9, 13, 34
free-association task 153, 305, 401
Freedland, K. E. 28, 29
Fresco, D. M. 126, 210, 211
Freud, Sigmund 117, 118
Friedman, E. S. 61
Frodl, T. 89, 90
Fuchs, C. Z. 225, 231
functional analysis 52, 230, 237, 378, 403
  critical information pertaining to goals of 380
  defined 374
  first step in conducting 376
functional contextualism 176, 186–187, 258n(2), 399
  overview of 170–173
functional disability 9
Furey, M. L. 86
fusion 174, 176–183, 185–186, 324, 325, 401, 406, 407
  linguistic 258n(2)
  thought-action 399

GABA-A receptors 86
GAD (generalized anxiety disorder) 10, 156, 161, 162, 182

Gado, M. H. 89
Gallop, R. 235
Garfield, S. L. 197
Garst, M. L. 179
Geddes, J. R. 96, 97
Gemar, M. 126, 198, 208
George, M. S. 98
Germer, C. K. 201, 202
Gershenfeld, H. 61
GFI (goodness-of-fit index) 41
Ghaemi, S. N. 39
Ghinassi, F. 160–161
Gibbon, M. 27, 374
Gibson, K. R. 175
Gird, S. 181
Gladstone G. 36, 118, 124, 131
Gloaguen, V. 56
glutamate 86, 88
goal-dependent behaviour 375, 376, 389
Godfrin, K. A. 204, 213
Golden, R. M. 66
Gollan, J. K. 234
Gonzalez, R. 212
good mothers 267, 274, 275
  those who are not 315, 376–377
Gortner, E. T. 234
Gotlib, I. H. 119, 195, 257
Graf, M. 227
grandiose delusions 31
Grant, D. A. 127
Grencoz, T. 158
GRID-HAMD (GRID-Hamilton Rating Scale for Depression) 28, 42
Gross, J. J. 126
Grosscup, S. J. 229
Grundy, C. T. 62
Grundy, E. M. 62
Guide to Treatments that Work (Nathan & Gorman) 62
guilt 5, 28, 32, 181, 185, 267, 344, 378, 384
  depressive affect and 326
  hypothesized 280
  pervasive 276
  prominent feeling of 297
  rush of 333
  sadness and 178, 180, 370, 371
  techniques used to address 286
Guyitt, B. D. 244, 401

Haaga, D. A. F. 125
Haddid, S. K. 118
HADS (Hospital Anxiety and Depression Scale) 34, 36, 37–8
Hadzi-Pavlovic, D. 36
Haeffel, G. J. 127
Hahn, J. 126
Hakstian, A. R. 231
HAMD (Hamilton Rating Scale for Depression) 26–29, 38
  see also GRID-HAMD; HRSD
Hamilton, E. W. 197
Hamilton, K. E. 10, 127
Hamilton, M. A. 26, 56, 273, 374
  see also DISH; HAMD; HRSD
Hamilton Mood Rating Scale 231
Hammen, C. L. 119, 257
HANDS (Harvard Department of Psychiatry/National Depression Screening Day Scale) 36–37
Hanh, Thich 202, 243
Hankin, B. L. 127
Hansen, N. B. 60
Hardy, P. 27
Hare, D. L. 33, 34
Harley, T. A. 155
Harvey, P. O. 90
Hasher, L. 134, 135
Haug, T. T. 37
Hayes, A. M. 44, 201, 252

Hayes, S. C. 169–181, 183–187, 319, 362, 405
Hayhurst, H. 210
Haynes, S. N. 374
helplessness 124, 275, 278, 279, 394, 409, 410, 412
  habitual biases in thinking may account for 396
  learned 86
  monitoring for 291
  perceived 118
Henley, S. S. 66
Herman-Dunn, R. 364, 402
Herrmann, C. 37
Hersen, M. 31
Hillyard, E. J. 154
Hilton, T. 36
hippocampus 88–89, 90, 98
Hirschfeld, R. M. A. 39, 69
Hofmann, S. G. 186, 252
Hogan, M. E. 126
Holeva, V. 156
Hollon, S. D. 57, 60, 61, 63, 64, 68, 126, 200, 213, 234, 235, 354
homework 152, 230, 284, 311, 351, 353, 356, 358, 365, 394, 398
  appropriate 278, 283
  ATT for 303–304, 307
  avoidance of 354
  barriers interfering with 388, 389
  between-session experience with 374
  check of 277–278
  conjointly designed 372
  consistent practice 346, 366
  daily exercises 345
  discussion of 345, 349, 354, 359, 360
  engaging in 382, 383
  importance of 281
  lengthy practices 346
  progress with 378
  promising assignments 373
  repeated 289
  reviewing 277–278, 282, 304, 360, 372, 383, 384, 389
  self-assigned 280
  skills taught in session and applied in 231
  summarizing 381
  undermining the completion of 380
hopelessness 34, 118, 119, 150, 151, 174, 267, 297, 344, 394, 395, 409, 410
  alcohol used to temper feelings of 377
  contribution to 302
  counteracting 384
  helping to overcome 309
  monitoring for 277, 291
  pessimism and 346
  thoughts of 360
Hopko, D. R. 226, 227
Horan, J. J. 233
HPA (hypothalamic-pituitary adrenal axis) 86–87, 88–89
HRSD (Hamilton Rating Scale for Depression) 55–57, 59, 61–64, 205, 273, 374
Huang, F. Y. 40
Hubley, S. 255–256, 364
Huey, D. 178
Huntington's disease 91
Husky, M. M. 127
hypercortisolemia/hypercortisolism 87, 100
hypersensitivity 71, 84
hypersomnia 87
hypoperfusion 90

Iacoviello, B. M. 126, 127
ICD (WHO International Classification of Diseases) 4, 6, 14–15, 43

ICS (interacting cognitive subsystems) model 135–136
IDS (Inventory of Depressive Symptomatology) 38
  see also QIDS
Ilardi, S. S. 56, 245, 252
imipramine 81–82, 93, 127
inactivity 34, 125, 375
  behavioural 296
  depression tends to be dominated by 132
  rapid flights into 324
  strategy for counteracting 152
inference 251
  arbitrary 122
  errors of 122
  negative 119
inferential style 119
information-processing systems 121, 130, 131, 134, 145, 270
  biased 122, 137, 198, 402
  developing technologies in 72
  faulty 275
  maladaptive cognitive structures dominate 118
  negative 207, 247
  patterns activated in depressed mood 208
  self-referential 198
  self-regulation strategy for disengaging from 201
Ingold, T. 175
Ingram, R. E. 118, 119, 121, 125, 131, 200, 208
insomnia 37, 87, 93
  additional advantages for treatment of 95
  initial 266, 297
  symptoms of 4
  see also hypersomnia
interest(s) 38, 284, 299, 322, 349, 350, 377, 386
  decreased 41
  friendly 352, 358
  lack of 266, 344, 353
  loss of 4–5, 33, 150, 283, 409
  low 162
  non-judgemental 351, 362
  reduced 360
  sexual/intimacy 39, 323, 326
intracellular processes 83, 101
intrapsychic representation 118
iproniazid 81
IPT (interpersonal psychotherapy) 53, 57, 195, 364, 366
irritability 39, 41, 360
Irvine, P. 36
Irwin, M. 35
ISCDD (International Society for CNS Drug Development) 28
isolation 226, 325, 403
  mental control reinforces 405
  rapid flights into 324
  social 129

Jacobs, S. C. 125, 127
Jacobson, N. 59, 63, 178, 179, 234, 235, 237, 251, 252, 372
Japanese students 41
Jarrett, R. B. 38, 56, 61–71, 74, 127, 244
Johnson, E. O. 88
Joiner, T. E. 127
Judd, L. L. 53, 62, 194

Kaiser, R. 255–6
Kambara, M. 41
Karyotaki, E. 56
Kashner, M. T. 66
Katz, R. 127
Keller, M. B. 4, 12, 62, 63, 194, 195
Kendall, P. C. 126, 354
Kennedy, S. 126
Kenny, M. A. 207, 365
Kessler, R. C. 5, 6, 7, 8–9, 10, 11, 13, 14, 15, 53, 195, 255, 389
ketamine 86

Kijima, N. 41
KIMS (Kentucky Inventory of Mindfulness Skills) 211
King, P. 161
Kingston, T. 207, 212
Kivelae, S. 41
Klein, D. N. 61
Klugman, J. 39
Korslund, K. E. 42
Kraft, D. 56
Kroenke, K. 40
Kupfer, D. J. 43, 195, 196
Kuyken, W. 68, 204, 205, 207

Lambert, M. J. 60, 62, 252
language 52, 171
  additional behavioural processes may emerge from 170
  function of 399
  interventions designed to undermine hegemony of 320
  organisms that lack 173
  self-reference 406
  stimulus functions transformed and derived through 177
  systems of 257, 258
  theories of 176
  values can be accessed and contacted via 185
  see also accounts of language
language barriers 35
language development 177
language learning process 319
Larson, J. 155, 183
Lau, M. A. 201, 208, 209, 211
Laurenceau, J.-P. 252
law of effect 222
Leader, J. B. 61
learning theory 223
  experimental 212
  social 52
Lejuez, C. W. 226
Lespérance, F. 9, 13, 34
Lewinsohn, P. M. 127, 195, 198, 208, 223–233, 235, 236
Libet, J. 226, 228, 230
life events 270, 370, 371, 403
  adverse 84
  distressing 11
  major 198–199
  onset of depression and 100, 198–199
  previous 178
  role of 369
  severe 197
  unpleasant 180, 256
  see also life stress; negative life events
life stress 86, 117, 119, 127, 155, 255
  major 202
Likert Scale 303
lithium salts 95
living in the past/future 176, 182–183
Lobitz, W. C. 228
Longmore, R. J. 251, 252
López-León, S. 70
Lumry, A. 126
Lundgren, Tobias 338
Luoma, J. 338
Lyubomirsky, S. 157, 183, 198, 387

Ma, S. H. 195, 204, 212, 213
MAAS (Mindful Attention Awareness Scale) 211
MACAM (Measure of Awareness and Coping in Autobiographical Memory) 210
MacArthur Foundation 55, 196
  Initiative on Depression and Primary Care 40
Maciejewski, P. K. 127
Mackiewicz, K. L. 90
Mackintosh, B. 182
MacPhillamy, D. J. 226, 227
M-ADM (maintenance antidepressant medication) 195, 205

MADRS (Montgomery Asberg Depression Rating Scale) 99
maintenance-phase treatments 67, 96–97, 195
  persistent recovery the goal of 55
major depressive disorder *see* MDD
Mandler, G. 134
Manicavasagar, V. 345, 363–364
Markowitz, J. C. 60, 234
Maroudas, C. 119
Marshall, M. B. 26–27
Martell, C. R. 235, 237, 364, 372, 402
Matthews, G. 119, 154, 155, 200, 296, 305, 400
Mayberg, H. S. 90, 91, 99
Mazure, C. M. 117, 127
MBCT (mindfulness-based cognitive therapy) 52, 53, 211–212, 242, 243–244, 247–249, 390, 394–396
  autonomous processes and 212, 346
  decentring in 200, 209
  distinctive features of 361–363
  empirical status 204–212
  meditation and 202, 203, 352–359, 364–365
  overview of 345–361
  questions for future research 363–365
  staying present and 354–356
  theory underlying 194–220
  treating depression with 344–368
MBSR (mindfulness-based stress reduction) 201, 202
McClure, K. S. 26
McGlinchey, J. B. 59
McIntyre, R. S. 28
McLean, P. D. 231
McNamara, K. 233
MCT (metacognitive therapy) 44, 52, 53, 144–168, 242, 295–318, 390, 394, 398
  case formulation 151
  detached mindfulness in 305–307, 397, 400
  effectiveness of 159–162
  empirical support for model 154–159
  MCT *vs* CBT 161
  metacognitive beliefs 146, 148–150, 157–159
  old plan/new plan 315
  preventing relapse 153, 314
  rumination modulation 311
  rumination postponement experiments 305–309
  telephone metaphor 152
  theory underlying 145–151
  treating depression with 295–318
  see also ATT; metacognition; tiger task
MDD (major depressive disorder) 393
  burden of 12–14, 16, 195
  cardiac problems and 13, 33
  causes of 54
  CBT reduces the symptoms of 73
  chronic 53, 69, 160
  comorbidity 8–10
  cost of 13–14
  course of 10–15
  detection of 40
  development of new episodes of 64
  DSM-IV and DSM-V criteria for 61
  epidemiology of 5–10
  episodic 126
  high incidence of 31
  higher risk for females 8
  identification of 14, 15
  lifetime 8, 14
  MCT for 316–317
  novel approaches to managing 195
  poorer recognition of symptoms in minors 14
  potential to prevent or delay episodes of 67

residual symptoms of 73
simple 316
suicide and 13, 16
treatment-resistant 160
vulnerability to 56
see also bipolar disorder; clinical depression; diagnosis of MDD; MDD-S; MDE; NCS-R; prevalence of MDD; recurrent MDD; severe depression; treatment of MDD; unipolar depression
MDD-S (Major Depressive Disorder Scale) 298–299, 304, 307, 309
MDE (major depressive episode) 4, 11, 66
antecedent symptoms meeting criteria for 13
likelihood of recovery from 9
prevalence of 7
see also RDC
MDQ (Mood Disorder Questionnaire) 39
Meadows, E. A. 26
Meadows, G. N. 204, 205, 206
medication 38, 94, 99, 204
addition to prescription of 92, 231
adjunctive use of 95
alerting 85
antipsychotic 81, 95, 150
cost effectiveness of 95
desire to stop using 290
efficacy of 95
eliminating 282, 291
lack of response to 151, 297
newer 84, 86
nonresponse rate to 95
novel 101
older 95
poorer response to 10
psychotropic 15
relapse prevention 96
safety of 95
sedative-hypnotic 86
uniquely valuable 92
see also antidepressants; self-medication; SGA; side effects; SNRIs; SSRIs; TCAs
meditation practices 390, 414
aversion to 354
Buddhist traditions 202
classic 320
daily 203, 320
formal 203, 351, 365
informal 203, 365
intensive 345
mindfulness 201, 202, 206, 213, 346, 402
perceived obstacles to 350
sitting 349, 351–356, 358, 359, 364, 365
Meina, L. J. 315
melancholia 3, 100, 117, 277
Melin, L. 338
mental control 162, 163, 399, 404–6
Mercer, S. W. 207, 365
metabolites 82, 85
metacognition 145, 146–151
beliefs 146, 148–150, 157–159
control strategies 155–157
model in depression 147–151
perseveration and 147
see also MCT; MDD-S; NBRS; PBRS; uncontrollability beliefs
Metacognitions Questionnaire 157
metacognitive therapy *see* MCT
Metalsky, G. I, 118
Metcalf, C. A. 345, 365
MHPG (3-methoxy-4-hydroxypheylglycol) 82
Miller, C. J. 39
Miller, I. W. 127
Miller, N. 127

milnacipran 94
mindfulness 42, 183, 243–244, 247, 253, 258, 271, 320, 321, 388, 399, 402, 405, 415
  breath 352–354
  lack of 248
  see also DM; FMI; KIMS; MAAS; MBCT; Toronto
Minhajuddin, A. 61
Mintun, M. A. 89
Miranda, J. 71, 119, 126, 208
mirtazapine 95
misery 173, 266
MMPI-II (Minnesota Multiphasic Personality Inventory) 230–231
modafinil 85
monoamine systems 81–83, 88, 92–93, 95, 97, 101
mood 33, 34, 72, 135, 232, 249, 281, 284, 313, 323, 359, 372, 379, 389, 390
  altering 221, 242
  brain regions that ultimately modulate 99
  changes in 153, 172, 203, 226, 227, 228, 280, 282, 312, 341, 378, 388, 396
  controlling 322, 325, 327, 329
  daily monitoring of 226
  depressogenic attitudes and beliefs activated by 197–198
  dour 327
  elevated 39
  future 153, 360–361
  good 316
  improvement in 236, 265, 266, 279, 280, 282, 290, 357, 369, 377, 382, 388
  level of belief in thoughts varies with 355
  low(ering) 147, 149, 198, 199, 266, 297, 302, 310, 312, 315, 344, 353, 357
  managing 330
  mild 199, 200
  negative 126, 210, 224, 247, 311, 325, 402, 403
  neural circuitry of 97
  normal 267
  rating of 226, 378, 381, 391
  reasonable 266
  regulation of 89, 97–98
  rumination and 147–151, 301, 302, 310
  sad 38, 126, 208, 225
  severe disturbance of 3
  therapist's abilities to alleviate problems 277
  transient 199
  worsening 298, 300, 355, 360
  see also depressed mood; dysphoric mood; *also following entries prefixed* 'mood'
mood-cued contingencies 377, 378, 381
mood-dependent behaviour 375, 376, 389
mood disorders 29, 30, 31, 52, 252
  chronic or recurrent 64
  one of the most distressing aspects of 12
  preventing and curing 54, 55, 73, 74
  treatments for 53, 169
  see also bipolar disorder; MDQ
mood fluctuations 229, 316
  coping with 312
  daily 152
  minor 380
  negative 247, 314
  normalizing 312
  threat monitoring and avoidant coping in response to 311
  toleration of 315
mood-priming studies 126, 208
Moore, M. T. 210, 211
Moore, R. G. 67, 210

Morina, N. 161
Morrison, A. P. 157
Morrow, J. 155, 183, 198
mothers 276, 288
  bad 300, 306, 352, 355
  better 298
  dysfunctional attachments 118
  loss of 41, 410
  part-time 337
  partly lost role 326
  separation from 87
  terrible 300, 304
  useless 306
  wonderful 337
  see also good mothers
motivational schemas 125
Moulds, M. 182
Mueller, T. I. 9, 53
Mullane, C. M. 226, 227
Munoz, R. F. 232
Murphy, G. E. 197
mutual entailment 173–174, 258
myocardial infarction 9, 29

National Health Service (UK) 13
National Heart, Lung, and Blood Institute Working Group (US) 29
NBRS (Negative Beliefs about Rumination Scale) 158, 315
NCDEU (New Clinical Drug Evaluation Unit) 28
NCS-R (US National Comorbidity Survey Replication Study) 6–7, 8–9, 11, 13, 14, 15
NDRIs (norepinephrine and dopamine reuptake inhibitors) 94
Neckelmann, D. 37
nefazodone 95
negative affect 54, 146, 227
  future 159
  persistence and strengthening of 162
  signs of 312
negative life events 118, 177
  onset of depression and 195
  precipitating 122
  severe 127
  significant 117, 126
negative thoughts 54, 123, 147, 154, 300, 308, 309, 323, 335, 349, 351, 408
  ability to see as passing mental events 210
  automatic 284, 285, 286, 396
  beliefs about uncontrollability of 304
  checking for the presence of 311, 315, 316
  cognitive therapists identify 270
  content of 145, 196, 401, 403
  control of 404, 405
  credibility of 401
  dealing with 152, 153
  depressed patients believe 406
  disconfirming 403
  dwelling on 302, 314, 315
  engagement with 243, 250
  evidence for or against 286
  focused processing of 248
  frequency or form of 180
  fused 181, 185, 186
  goal to take away the impact of 409
  intense 360
  maintaining 403
  manner in which patient reacts to 145
  monitoring for 316, 395
  new observational stance towards 397
  new relationship to occurrence of 396
  persistent focus on 247
  personal identification with 209
  reactivated 200
  recycled and extended 146, 243

negative thoughts (*contd.*)
  self-referential 175, 181
  self-relevant 406
  sources of 150
  specific situations elicit 274
  spontaneous 303, 305
  suppressed 404, 405
  transient 122
  triggers for rumination 149, 306, 312
  trying to clear the mind of 313
  typical 306
  unwanted 178, 304, 313, 404
  see also responses to negative thoughts
NEMESIS (Netherlands Mental Health Survey and Incidence Study) 10–11
neural network models 89–91
neurogenesis 88–89
neuroimaging methods 88, 90, 97, 99, 101
neuromodulation strategies 82, 91, 97–100
  noninvasive 101
neurons
  cortical 87
  gabaergic 86
neuroplasticity 86, 88–89
neuropsychological changes 161
neuroscience 71, 73, 74, 91
neurotransmitters 85–87
  synaptic 82
  see also dopamine; monoamine; noradrenergic systems; serotonin
New York State Psychiatric Institute 30
Nezu, A. M. 24, 25, 26, 33, 42, 272
Nezu, C. M. 24, 25–26, 33, 272
NIH (US National Institutes of Health) 43
NIMH (US National Institute of Mental Health) 74
  Treatment of Depression Collaborative Research Program 57, 127
  see also CDS
Nitschke, J. B. 90
NMDA receptors 86
Nock, M. K. 245
Nolen-Hoeksema, S. 8, 155, 157, 180, 183, 198, 211, 212, 295, 387
noradrenergic systems 82, 84–85, 94
Nordahl, H. M. 161, 246
norepinephrine uptake 92
  see also NDRIs; SNRIs
Normann, N. 161
Nothard, S. 157
NSPB (UK National Survey of Psychiatric Morbidity) 8

O'Brien, W. H. 374
OCD (obsessive-compulsive disorder) 93, 100, 156
O'Donohue, W. 269
Oei, T. P. S. J. 132, 133
Ogles, B. M. 252
olanzapine 95
O'Leary, K. D. 62
openness 345, 349, 350, 397
  cultivating 341
  increasing 415
  mindfulness of breath encourages 352
  non-judgemental 354
  quality characterized by 201
operant conditioning 173, 221, 223, 377
  theoretical precursor to 222
Oxman, M. N. 35

Pahkala, K. 41
panic 10, 93, 333
  comorbid 9

panic disorder 158, 404
Papageorgiou, C. 121, 154, 157, 158, 160, 161, 182, 314, 315
Papakostas, G. I. 94
Parker, G. 36, 118, 124, 131, 345
Parker, L. E. 183
Parkinson's disease 91, 157
paroxetine 93, 265, 297, 344
passivity 225, 356, 395, 400, 408
 mental control reinforces 405
 model that proposes depression is consequence of 394
 reinforced by its effect 403
pathogenesis 117, 169, 176, 177, 179, 248, 249, 253, 256
 areas implicated in 83, 85, 87, 99
 threat of 257
pathology 54
 proximate or distal causation 253–258
 see also psychopathology
pathophysiology 86, 88, 89, 90–91, 98
pathoplasticity 117
Paykel, E. S. 67, 117, 210
PBRS (Positive Beliefs about Rumination Scale) 158, 314
PCP (phencyclidine) 86
Pepper, S. C. 170, 171
perceptual models 52
Perich, T. 345
persecutory delusions 31
personality disorder 24, 128, 254, 410, 411
Persons, J. B. 126
PES (Pleasant Events Schedule) 226, 227, 229, 230
 see also UPES
pessimism 32, 54, 149, 227, 258, 267, 280, 373
 beliefs about the future 274–275
 diminishing 252
 hopelessness and 346
 mindfulness of 277
 statements that assess 33
PET (positron emission tomography) 83, 90, 98
pharmacological strategies 91
 intervention 37, 194, 297
 treatment 11, 15, 246
pharmacotherapy 53, 56, 58, 58, 60, 126, 199, 205, 211
 acute-phase 57, 65, 67, 91–92
 CBASP and 69
 continuation-phase 68, 96
 differential response to 88
 discontinued 68, 73, 196
 first line of 93
 maintenance-phase 96–7, 195
 partial remission through 210
 recovered patients 208
 significant alternative to 196
 suboptimal 57
phenomenological models 52
phobia 10, 158
PHQ (Patient Health Questionnaire) Depression Scales 39–40, 42, 92
physical disorders 7, 9
physiological experiences 223
 autonomic response to aversive stimuli 228
 deactivation 125
 response and behaviour 135
 stress reactions 185
 symptoms 37
physiological schemas 124, 125
pituitary gland 87
 see also HPA
placebos 56, 58, 59, 60, 61, 95, 96–97, 205, 231, 235
 MBCT vs pharmacotherapy vs 211
 pill 57, 68
pleasure 359–360, 361
 goal of encouraging 284
 lack of 353

pleasure (*contd.*)
less than non-depressed peers 228
little 297, 388
loss of 4–5, 32, 33
lower level of 227
see also PES
polymorphism 86, 87
functional 84
genetic 71
Ponniah, K. 234
positive reinforcement 184, 222, 232, 380, 382
activation targets for increasing 229
disruption of 255
low rates of 225
reduced 224
response-contingent 223, 225, 231, 236, 255
unintentional 378
upregulating the experience of 252
Post, R. M. 198–199
Posternak, M. A. 11, 61
Power, M. J. 134
prefrontal cortex 84–85, 89
dorsolateral 90, 91
lateral 90
ventrolateral 90
prevalence of MDD by age and country 7
gender and 7–8
high 31
lifetime 53, 195
overall 6–7
relatively high 62
PRIME-MD (Primary Care Evaluation of Mental Disorders) 40
problem-solving 25, 54, 182, 232, 299, 381, 384–385, 388
comprehensive and systematic account of 175
impaired 13
interference with 370
rumination and 309, 310, 311
structured strategies 362
various deficits identified 42
process-experiential therapy 180, 249
proteins 83
PSG (polysomnography) 88
psychiatric disorders 52
common 40
conceptualized in terms of primal modes 124
diagnoses of 6, 14–15, 32
major 29
prevalence of 5–6, 7
suicide risk 12–13
see also PRIME-MD
psychiatry 24, 35, 117, 226, 245
inpatients 235
oldest device used in 97
outpatients 36
see also American Psychiatric Institute; American Psychiatric Press; APA; HANDS; New York State; NIH; NSPB; University of Massachusetts
psychobiological processes 81–113
see also CDS
psychodynamic therapies 232, 246, 249, 254, 271
psychological breakdown 147
psychological-cognitive symptoms 32
psychological conditions 132
specific 129
psychological disorder 146, 243
detection of 14
MDD highly comorbid with 8–9
metacognitive approach to 157, 159
pattern of thinking and cognitive processing that occurs in 145
S-REF model of 144, 147, 154, 200
strategies in 155–156
treatment of 14, 213
vulnerability to 156

psychological events/processes 30, 32, 176, 177, 183, 256
  accounts of depression 295
  automatic or unconscious 147
  experimental learning theory 212
  functioning 147
  health 319
  human suffering 170
  key variables 148
  mindful response to 175
  parts of the system 172
  research 117
  rumination has negative consequences 154–155
  specific 295
  symptoms 4
  transdiagnostic 145–146, 364
  worry appears to have range of negative effects 154
psychological flexibility 73, 179, 183, 394, 400
  cultivated through daily practice 341
  support in generally limiting 184
  three pillars of 321–2, 325
psychological inflexibility 169, 176, 178, 179, 186
  contributions to 183–184, 185
psychological intervention 24, 37, 297
  brief 296
  prophylactic 199
psychological mechanisms 72, 197
  key 295
  specific underlying, scrutiny of 412
psychological problems 52, 146, 283
psychological rigidity 170, 176, 180, 322, 334
  behaviour that contributes to 182
psychological structure 172, 258n(2)
psychological theories 118, 120, 399
psychological treatment 15, 210
  despondent attitude towards 297
  effective 265
  efficacious 295
psychologists 14, 15, 338, 412
  clinical 29, 134
  cognitive 134
psychology 144, 243
  applied 71
  clinical 265
  social 71
  world hypotheses applicable to 170
  see also headings above prefixed 'psychological'
psychometric properties 26–28, 30, 33–5, 38, 39, 59, 133–134
  adequate 31
  sound 36, 40, 41
  strong 32
psychopathological states 131, 134, 136
  maladaptive schemas that characterize 129–130
psychopathology 100, 169, 246
  ACT model of 176, 411
  comprehensive model of 410
  contributions to various forms of 175
  depressive 258
  information-processing modes that perpetuate 201
  linking operant conditioning to 223
  MCT model of 144–147
  role of beliefs in generation and maintenance of 148–150, 250
  see also metacognitive beliefs
  syndromally classified forms of 171–172
  theories of 253, 256, 296
psychopharmacology 81
psychosocial factors 124, 149, 195
  adjustment 69
  impairment 69, 70
  interventions 60, 67, 194
  persistent dysfunction 69

psychosocial factors (*contd.*)
treatments 53, 73
variables 52
see also biopsychosocial developmental processes; psychosocial functioning
psychosocial functioning 53, 62
assessment of 68, 72–73
deteriorations in 70
improvement in 61, 69
measuring 54
poor 70
suboptimal 73
very good 70
psychotherapy 15, 44, 52, 68, 196, 201, 208, 230, 245, 246, 269, 344, 371
CBT commonly used in 271
depression-specific 66
differential response to 88
failure to respond to 99
formal features typically seen in 270
interpersonal 53, 57, 195, 364, 366
maintenance version of 195
non-specific 231, 271
other depression-specific 65, 66, 67
outcomes of 10, 53
potential utility of 96
twice a week 280
see also CBASP
psychotropic medication 15
PTSD (post-traumatic stress disorder) 93, 156, 161, 236
punishment 156, 159, 184, 185, 227, 382
delayed 222–223
depressed individuals more sensitive to 228
excessive 223
immediate 222
negative 222
positive 222
see also self-punishment
QIDS (Quick Inventory of Depressive Symptomatology) 38, 42
QIDS-SR (Quick Inventory of Depressive Symptomatology-Self Report) 7, 15
quality of life 6, 42, 394, 408
effect of acute phase CT on 69
factors that affect primary-care patients 36
improved 44–45, 201
lower 53
quetiapine 95

Rachman, S. 154
Rains, J. C. 169
RCTs (randomized clinical trials) 44, 57, 61, 62, 169, 250, 271
dismantling 251
double-blind, placebo-controlled 95–96
head-to-head 94
large 63
major 56
RDC (research diagnostic criteria) 11, 29
reactive mind/wise mind 334–335
reality 209, 242, 243, 332, 334, 336
events that should be evaluated against 162
external 402
individual becomes further removed from 405
mechanistic model of 399
painful 129
reflections of 200, 397, 406
testing 203, 415
thoughts and 394, 396, 397, 401, 406, 411
reason giving 177, 178–179
good example of 324
socially prescribed 325
reciprocal inhibition 221

recreational drugs 86
recurrent MDD 11, 16, 29, 53, 96, 158, 274, 277, 344, 388, 389
  causal risk factor in 207–208
  defined 4
  diagnostic criteria for 266, 273, 297, 374
  fewer episodes 12
  important cognitive vulnerability factor for 211
  MBCT in 205, 213
  midlife 100
  preventing depressive relapse in 206
  randomized patients with history of 205
  repeated stress from 89
  techniques specifically crafted to reduce relapse in 194
  treatment of 160, 316
reduction of depressive symptoms 56–61, 127, 194, 244
  antidepressant medication in 345
  CBT in 55, 68, 161, 232
  MBCT in 207, 211
  MCT in 161
  short-term 54
  VNS in 98
Ree, M. J. 204, 207
Rehm, L. P. 52, 225, 230, 231
reinforcement 54, 147, 185, 226, 230, 275, 290, 310, 311, 320, 403, 408, 412
  ability to elicit 224, 228
  absence of 223, 255
  arbitrary 222
  central assumptions regarding 223
  changes in 227, 253
  delayed 222
  differential 175
  immediate 222
  intermittent 223
  interpersonal 228
  limiting opportunities for 405
  loss of 410
  natural 222
  negative 222, 370, 384
  pathogenic 249
  perceived potential for 227
  powerful 383
  reduced 224
  restricted 227, 228
  schedules of 222, 223, 249, 256, 257
  social 229
  temporal sequence of 222
  see also auto-reinforcement; positive reinforcement; reinforcement deprivation; reinforcement contingencies; self-reinforcement
reinforcement contingencies 222, 225
  control over 229
  negative 377
  positive 377–378
reinforcement deprivation 224, 229
relapse 53, 55, 346
  acute-phase CBT responders 64–68
  decreased activation of threshold pathways over time 198–199
  impending 360
  planning 270
  possibility of 292
  potential 203, 204, 213, 353
  predictors of 62, 69, 70, 125, 126, 246
  pre-treatment interviews 345
  protecting against 244, 245, 246, 247, 341–342, 389
  resistance to 246
  risk of 73, 96–97, 127, 194–195, 197, 199–200, 202, 204, 207–213, 362
  vulnerability to 197, 247, 316
  worry about 150

relapse prevention 67, 70, 153, 221, 234, 244, 245, 247, 257–258, 279, 290, 297, 312–316, 360, 389
  acceptance as skilful first step towards 203
  BA approach in 369
  behavioural therapy in 232
  building an ACT lifestyle 341–342
  cognitive therapy in 409–410
  decentred thoughts and feelings help 209–210
  MBCT in 194–220, 344, 363, 364, 366
  MCT in 153, 314, 315
  medications effective for 96
  planning 272, 297
  research on 64
relapse signatures 360
relational framing *see* RFT
reliability and validity 26–27, 28, 35, 44
  good 34
  problems with 133
REM (rapid eye movement) sleep 88
reserpine 82
responses to negative thoughts 297, 302, 303, 306, 400, 404
  activation and execution of specific style of thinking 144
  alternative 163
  detached mindfulness in 307
  greater flexibility introduced in 152
  how individuals regulate cognition in 162
  maladaptive coping 296
Reynolds, M. 156
RFD (Reasons for Depression) Questionnaire 178, 179
RFT (relational frame theory) 169–170, 180, 182–183, 186, 258n(2), 319, 405
  overview of 173–176
Rimes, K. A. 183
RNA (ribonucleic acid) 87, 101
Roberts, L. J. 59
Robins, C. J. 127
Robins, E. 11, 29
Robinson, O. J. 70–71
Robinson, P. J. 321, 322, 342
Roche, B. 319
Rohde, P. 127
Roleofs, J. 159
Ronan, G. F. 26
Rosenquist, K. J. 39
Roth, T. 88
Roussis, P. 156–157
Roy-Byrne, P. P. 71
Ruggiero, K. J. 227
Ruini, C. 62
rule following 331, 407
  excessive 176, 183–185
  mindless 338
  rigid 405
rules 122, 332
  conditional 396, 407
  culturally instilled 319
  decision-making 32
  exclusion 7
  ground 346
  maladaptive 412
  metacognitive 407–408
  unworkable 325
rumination 121, 144–147, 156, 160–161, 176, 178–180, 182, 201, 209, 213, 243, 249, 250, 299–300, 316, 345, 352, 365, 371, 394, 409
  advantages–disadvantages analysis of 309–310
  awareness of 150, 151, 152, 302
  beliefs about uncontrollability of 148, 149, 158, 163, 296, 300, 302, 304, 307, 309, 405
  compliance with reduction strategies 153
  control over 401, 405, 414

deleterious effects on well-being and performance 154
direct and indirect links between depression and 158, 159
disengagement from 202, 297
downward spiral of 334
excessive 402
experimental increases in 157
extended/extensive 312, 325
failures to disrupt 149
frequency of 298, 307, 388
important for therapists to assess 388
inappropriate criteria for deciding when to cease 311
incompatibility between mindfulness and 183
intense 149
key ingredients of 404
limiting 296
maintained 295, 296
MBCT and 207, 211–212
MCT and 144–153
metacognitive control of 257, 303
model of causes 147–151
modulation experiment 311
negative beliefs about 158, 298, 407
negative psychological consequences of 154–155
perseveration in 154, 296, 313, 405
pervasiveness of 162, 309, 312–313
positive beliefs about 158, 162, 163, 248, 308, 405, 407
problem-solving and 183, 310, 311
prolonged 304
protracted periods of 313
recognizing as risk factor in depression 395
reducing and limiting the extent of 152
self-discrepancies and 159
self-report measure of 212
significant post-treatment reduction in 212
susceptibility to patterns of 389
targeting 381, 387–388
tendency to 8, 364, 370
treatment focused on 295–317, 400
triggers for 306, 307, 309, 315
usefulness of 302, 309, 310, 311
vulnerability in relation to 411
see also NBRS; PBRS; *also under following entries prefixed* 'rumination/ruminative'
rumination postponement 163
detached mindfulness and 304–309
Ruminative Response Scale 212
ruminative response style 197, 198
ruminative thinking 360, 363, 384, 395
alternatives to 356–357, 362
control over 303
judgemental 354
need to maintain awareness of 314
self-critical 356
skills for detecting and stopping 163
Rush, A. J. 4, 5, 7, 8, 9, 15, 38, 52, 55, 61, 63, 66, 121, 185, 196, 269
Ryan, R. M. 201, 211, 243
Ryder, A. G. 26–27
Rygh, J. L. 364

sadness 32, 38, 151, 223, 225, 267, 286, 336, 381, 409
analysing reasons underlying/causes of 145, 147
assessing 33
dealing with 162
dysphoria and 402
emptiness and 266
extreme 3
increasing awareness of 149
induction of 91, 126, 208, 209
loneliness and 331, 351
mild 200

sadness (*contd.*)
normal 91, 101
overwhelming 298
persistent feelings of 266
positive beliefs about 149
problematic 181
response to 315, 403
rumination and 162, 301
sadness guilt and 178, 180, 370, 371
subjective state of 125
temporary lowering of mood in response to 198
uncontrollable 149
SAD-P (Screening Assessment of Depression: Polarity) 31
SADS (Schedule for Affective Disorders and Schizophrenia) 29–30
Sahakian, B. J. 70–71
Sakamoto, S. 41
Sanghavi, M. 89
schema theory 117–143, 242, 244–250, 253–254
see also affective schemas; behavioural schemas; cognitive-affective schemas; dysfunctional schemas; EMS; motivational schemas; physiological schemas; self-schemas; SFT
Schettler, P. J. 62
schizophrenia *see* SADS
Schraufhagel, T. J. 71
Schuller, D. R. 26–27
SCID (Structured Clinical Interview for DSM Disorders) 27, 29, 30–31, 272, 374
scopolamine 86
SDS (Zung Self-Rating Depression Scale) 36, 40–41
Seeley, J. R. 195
Segal, Z. V. 31, 57, 61, 62, 119, 121, 122, 125, 126, 127, 135, 194, 196, 197, 198, 199, 208, 212, 213, 344, 362, 388
Seggar, L. B. 60, 62
self-acceptance 62, 407
self-assessments 341
self-awareness 25, 256
self-blame 131, 349, 355
self-care 326, 359–360
self-concept 120
inferior 174
self-consciousness 315
self-control 131, 225, 230
diminished 147
self-criticism 32, 33, 38, 349, 356, 365, 406, 410
cognitive content of 409
harsh 345, 361
high 352
intense 350
pleasantness can lead to 353
tendency to 364
self-defeating behaviour 406
and cognitive patterns 129
self-deficiencies 148
self-defining personality configurations 119
self-directed behaviour 118, 405
self-discrepancies 162
self-dislike 32, 33
self-efficacy 232, 394
self-esteem
implicit 128
loss of 41
self-evaluation 121, 225
self-focus 155, 160, 303
excessive 296
model designed to reduce 400
self-growth 338
self-harm risk 42
self-help 342, 394
cognitive model teaches 398
self-identification 182
self-judgements 154

self-medication 312
self-monitoring 230, 316
  deficits in 225
self-oriented beliefs 274
self-prediction 246
self-punishment 299
  rumination as source of 308
S-REF model 144–147, 154–155, 200, 296
self-referential information 121, 127, 406
  critical thoughts 181
  negative 120, 122, 123, 126, 131, 175, 196, 198, 243, 334
self-reflection 121
self-regulation 145, 201
  emotional 149
  see also S-REF model
self-reinforcement 225, 230, 287
self-relevant information 155
  negative 154, 406
self-report measures 31–41, 42, 56, 128, 231, 267, 273, 298–299
  commonly used 92
  depressive severity 374
  exclusive reliance on 130
  explicit 245
  mindfulness 211
  paper-and-pencil 34
  predicting depressive symptoms 133
  progress monitored through 280
  retrospective 130, 131
  rumination 212
  schema content 125
  see also QIDS-SR; SDS
self-sacrifice 129
self-schemas
  depressogenic 196, 197
  negative 124, 128, 196, 275
  relational 128
self-statements
  negative 177
  summary 314
self-talk 170
self-worth 124
Sembi, S. 161
sensitivity 31, 35–39, 40, 128, 184, 228, 287, 288, 292, 320, 353
  heightened 123
  high rates of 28
  specificity and 5, 25
serotonin 71, 81, 83–84, 92, 101
  essential amino acid needed for synthesis of 82
  see also SNRIs; SSRIs
sertraline 93
session structure 277–281
  see also between-session practice
severe depression 40, 57, 235, 267
  classical symptoms of 85
  most potent TCAs for 94
sexual dysfunctions 93, 96
SFT (schema-focused therapy) 119–120, 128–134
SGA (second-generation antipsychotic) medications 95
  see also aripiprazole; mirtazapine; nefazodone; olanzapine; quetiapine
Shaw, B. F. 52, 121, 127, 196, 232, 269
Sheets, E. S. 56
Sheline, Y. I. 89
Shenk, C. 362
side effects 81, 82, 195
  additional 94
  biological 60
  cognitive 36, 99
  common 93, 94, 99
  differences in incidence of 96
  metabolic 95
  mild 98
  physical 36
  potential 99
  sexual 95
Siegle, G. J. 160–161
Silverman, J. S. 197

Simons, A. D. 197
Skinner, B. F. 169–170, 222–223, 236, 319, 399
sleep 34, 266, 279, 299, 325, 348, 360, 362, 370
  daytime 384
  disrupted 345
  hygiene interventions 282, 283, 290
  inquiries about 32, 273
  see also insomnia; REM sleep; SWS
sleep difficulties 5, 313
sleep disturbance 35, 38
  and regulation 87–88
Smith, G. T. 211
Smyth, P. 126
SNRIs (serotonin-norepinephrine reuptake inhibitors) 93, 94, 95
  therapeutic limitations of 85
  see also desvenlafaxine; duloxetine; milnacipran; venlafaxine
socialization 296, 298, 302, 387, 394, 395, 396, 400, 410
  personal schemas a result of 411
sociotropy 124, 132
somatic disorders 8, 28
somatic symptoms 32, 34, 41
somatic therapies 91
Spada, M. 157
Spijker, J. 9, 10–11
Spitzer, R. L. 11, 27, 29, 39, 40, 374
S-REF (self-regulatory executive function) model 119, 144, 147, 154, 155, 159, 296, 400
  detached mindfulness emerged from 200
SSRIs (selective serotonin reuptake inhibitors) 84, 91, 93, 94, 95
  therapeutic limitations of 85
standard deviation 56, 58
Steward, M. O. 64
stimulants 82, 283
stimulation *see* DBS; TMS; VNS
stimuli 120, 121, 175, 210, 221, 256, 402
  abstract 174
  activating 126, 130
  aversive 228, 377
  bidirectional 173–174
  emotional or disorder-related 155
  flexibly redirected 400
  internal or external 152
  learned emotional associations with 222
  negative 126, 248–249, 255
  noxious 377
  removal of 222, 377
  sham 98
  threatening 84, 155
  visual 174
stimulus functions 172
  transformation of 173, 174, 177, 180, 182
storytelling 177, 179–180
  unhelpful 250
Strauss, J. L. 252
stress 42, 118, 147, 159, 243
  breathing spaces at times of 358, 359
  chronic mild 85
  emotional 35
  exposure to 154
  habitual patterns of reactivity increase 202
  handling of 274
  heightened sensitivity to 123
  information-processing modes that heighten 201
  laboratory 88
  overreaction to 71
  past 255, 288
  physiological 185
  procedures for dealing with 119
  psychological 185, 198
  relationship 288
  repeated 89

symptoms of 156, 157
vulnerability formulation 276
see also cognitive diathesis-stress; distress; life stress; MBSR; PTSD; stress response
stress response 83, 84
dynamic 87
heightened 100
limbic activation in 101
natural and understandable 370
Stroop effect 155
Strosahl, K. D. 169, 177, 321, 322, 338, 342, 405
Strunk, D. R. 64, 246, 247
suicidal ideation 25, 44, 207, 297
suicidality 92, 180, 291–292
monitoring for 277
treatment-emergent 95–96
suicide 28, 38, 83, 201, 291–292
assessment of 36, 42, 44, 277, 346
attempted 5, 12, 245–246, 267
completed 12, 82, 96
MDD and 13, 16
plans of 5
prediction of 13, 245
prevention strategies 13
risk of 12–13, 33, 42, 95–96, 346, 410
thoughts of 5, 32, 33, 172
Sullivan, J. M. 229
suppression/counter-suppression exercise 153
Swendsen, J. D. 127
SWS (slow-wave sleep) 88

Talajic, M. 9
Talkington, J. 226, 227
Tarrier, N. 156
TAU (treatment as usual) 98, 204–205, 206, 212
TCAs (tricyclic antidepressants) 82, 84, 91, 92
most potent 94
see also amitriptyline; clomipramine; imipramine
TCQ (Thought Control Questionnaire) 156–157
Teasdale, J. D. 119, 134, 135–136, 181, 183, 194, 195, 196, 197, 198, 199, 204, 209, 210, 212, 213, 344, 388
teenagers 265
depressed 95–96
pregnant 13
Temple University 126
Thase, M. E. 60, 61, 69, 70, 87, 88, 93–97, 127, 160–161, 234
theory of mind 395, 411
Thera, Nyanaponika 243
therapeutic approaches 229, 251, 393–413
see also ACT; adjunct therapies; behaviour therapy; CBT; DBS; ECT; experiential therapies; MCT; pharmacotherapy; psychodynamic therapies; psychotherapy; schema-focused therapy; TMS; VNS
therapeutic relationship 277, 398, 412
CBT therapists recognize importance of 271
see also session structure
Thorndike, E. L. 222
thought control absorption with 404
beliefs about usefulness of 146
unhelpful strategies 159
see also TCQ
thoughts 144, 148, 151, 177, 179, 202, 288, 319, 321, 330, 331, 347, 359
acceptant of 250
analysing 298, 299
attempting to control 405
automatic 122, 123, 203, 234, 402
avoided 333
bad 146

thoughts (*contd.*)
believability of 409
categorizing 405
changing 412
claim to challenge 250
credibility of 402, 404, 406
death 5, 39, 267
decentring from 200–201, 209–211, 358
depressing/depressive 180, 199, 200, 275, 299, 355, 356, 403
detached mindfulness emphasizes awareness of 397
difficulty of standing back from 152
directly observing 201
disparaging 181
disputing 204, 362, 401
distancing from 399
distorted 362
distressing 156
dysfunctional 279
emotionally neutral 305
evaluating 398
everyday 305
excessive focus on 395
exposure to 212
flexible 407
function of 395, 399
inaccurate 335
independence from 399, 408
intrusive 305, 395, 407, 409
judgemental 352, 354
labelling 405
letting go of 153
maladaptive attachment to 243
monitoring 281, 282, 289, 405
non-judgemental awareness to 353
not engaging with 153
positive and negative beliefs about 157
problematic 276
provocative 335
rating 405
rational 362
realistic 407
reality and 394, 396, 397, 401, 406, 411
ruminative 354, 395
self-accepting 407
self-critical 350, 352, 361
spontaneous 153
subjective experience of 201
suicidal 5, 32, 33
suppression of 401
testing 398, 401
threatening 146, 147
triggering 298, 307, 314, 316
trying to suppress 156, 180
uncontrollable 248, 400
unhealthy 271
unpleasant 334, 350, 356, 358, 402
unwanted 180, 182, 303, 395, 405
usefulness of 234
validity of 54, 234
writing down on paper 203
see also Automatic Thoughts Questionnaire; content of thoughts; negative thoughts; TCQ
'thoughts are not facts' notion 203, 351, 355, 358–359
threat monitoring 145, 151, 148–149, 151, 153, 155, 297, 313
banning all forms of 315
beliefs about usefulness of 146
enabling abandonment of 296
inappropriate 314
reduction of 311–312
Thwaites, R. 178
thyroid hormone 95
tiger task 153, 305–306, 401
TMS (transcranial magnetic stimulation) 97, 98, 99
Tomoda, A. 41
Toronto Mindfulness Scale 211

transdiagnostic models 162, 320, 364
 see also ACT
TRAP/TRAC acronym 387
treatment of MDD 160
 active episodes 194
 acute-phase 69
 effective 14, 16, 53
 evidence-based 363
 leading, scientifically evaluated 52
 minimal adequacy 15
 pharmacological and psychological 15
 seeking 12, 14–15
Treynor, W. 212
trials *see* clinical trials; controlled trials; uncontrolled trials
Truax, P. 59, 178
truth 334, 355, 402
 correspondence view of 399
 nature of 170–171
truth criteria 171, 187
 conflicting 172
 correspondence-based 170, 172
tryptophan 82, 126
Tucker, K. L. 183

uncertainty 34, 95, 346
uncontrollability beliefs 148, 149, 158, 163, 296, 300, 302, 304, 307, 309, 405
uncontrolled trials 160
unipolar depression 31, 39, 71, 207
 treatment of 99
University of Massachusetts
 Medical Center 201
 Psychiatry Scales 28, 41
University of Wisconsin 126
UPES (Unpleasant Events Schedule) 226, 227, 229, 230

validity 54, 234
 see also reliability and validity
valproate 86
value-based actions 320, 336
 committed 338–341
value clarification exercises 338, 341
valued action 184, 341, 396, 407
 ACT places considerable emphasis on 406
 lack of 176, 185–186
 underinvolvement in 404
valued life 183, 321, 340, 398
 rules and 406–408
values 118, 171, 336–337, 340, 341, 399
 ACT and 185, 320, 394, 406
 clarification of 407
 core 338
 discrepant 186
 emphasis on 406, 410
 future 396
 higher 410
 identifying 408
 inflexible and rigid 407
 personal 184, 325
 pursuit of 411
 reaffirmation and clarification of 185
 written 339
Van Emmerik, A. A. P. 161, 163
Van Hasselt, V. B. 31
Van Heeringen, C. 204, 213
Vella, D. D. 127, 155
Velten, E. 178, 209
venlafaxine 94
Vittengl, J. R. 56, 62, 64, 66, 67, 69, 70, 127, 244
VNS (vagus nerve stimulation) 97–98
vulnerability 56, 211, 276, 411
 psychological 118, 156, 207
 relapse 197, 247, 316
 see also cognitive vulnerability

Wagner, A. W. 71
waitlists 56, 58–61, 161, 230, 232
Walker R. 157
Wang, P. S. 10, 13, 14
Watkins, E. 182, 183, 209
weight
loss of 4, 5
steady 267
weight gain 5, 95, 96, 371
significant 4
Weinberger, A. D. 364
Weissman, M. M. 125, 197, 208
Weitz, E. 57
Wells, Adrian 119, 121, 144, 145, 152–8, 160, 161, 182, 200, 243, 249, 296, 298, 303, 305, 311, 312, 314, 315, 400, 404
Wells, T. T. 127
Wexler, D. J. 36
Whitehouse, W. G. 126
WHO (World Health Organization) 43
see also CIDI; CSPP; ICD
Williams, J. B. W. 27
Williams, J. Mark G. 135, 194, 196, 197, 198, 199, 206, 207, 208, 212, 213, 344, 365, 388
Williams, R. M. 209
Williams, S. 126, 208
Wilson, K. G. 405
Wilson, P. H. 231
Wilson, S. 228
Wisco, B. E. 387
withdrawal 124, 125, 225, 236, 276, 325, 371, 390
behavioural 324
depression tends to be dominated by 132
emotional 324
rapid flights into 324
reinforced by its effect 403
social 149, 172, 312, 360
susceptibility to patterns of 389
unintentionally reinforced 378
WMHS (World Mental Health Survey Initiative) 6
Wolpe, J. 221–222
Worrell, M. 251, 252
worry 149, 151, 158, 162, 182, 267, 284, 289, 292, 315, 322, 333, 339, 356, 370, 400
attention allocated in generalized anxiety 144
beliefs about 146, 409
control over 401, 405, 414
dangerous 407
data that have manipulated 159
deleterious effects on well-being and performance 154
laboratory manipulations of 157
limiting the extent of 152
major 282
negative views of 407
perseveration in 154, 156, 296, 313, 405
pervasiveness of 312–313
positive views of 407
protracted periods of 313
range of negative psychological effects in 154
reducing 152, 161
relapse 150
thinking in the form of 145
usefulness of 146
vulnerability in relation to 411
worrying about 147
wrong 286
worthlessness 5, 32, 177
see also self-worth

Yilmaz, E. A. 158
yoga 353, 361

Young, J. E. 119–120, 128–134, 242, 253–254, 364
YSQ-LF (Young Schema Questionnaire-Long Form) 133
Yu, A. R. 209, 211

Zeiss, A. M. 232
Zettle. R. D. 169, 170, 172, 174, 176, 178–181, 183–186, 243, 256–257, 258n(2), 321, 342, 399–400, 402, 406
Zimmerman, M. 61, 62
Zung *see* SDS

Index compiled by Frank Pert